Sources of the Western Tradition

Sources OF THE WESTERN TRADITION

SECOND EDITION

VOLUME I: FROM ANCIENT TIMES TO THE ENLIGHTENMENT

Marvin Perry
Baruch College, City University of New York

Joseph R. Peden
Baruch College, City University of New York

Theodore H. Von Laue
Clark University

George W. Bock, Editorial Associate

HOUGHTON MIFFLIN COMPANY BOSTON

DALLAS GENEVA, ILLINOIS PALO ALTO PRINCETON, NEW JERSEY

Printed in the U.S.A.
Library of Congress Catalog Card Number:
90-83043
ISBN: 0-395-47304-7

Credits

Cover: Isaac van Nickelen, *Interior of St. Bravo's in Haarlem, view to the west.* Dutch painting, 1690s. Musées royaux des Beaux-Arts de Belgique, Bruxelles. *(Photo: G. Cussac)*

List of Sources
Chapter 1

Section 1 P. 5: From *The Epic of Gilgamesh,* trans. N. K. Sanders (Penguin Classics, Revised edition 1964), pp. 89, 91–97, 101–102, 106–112. Copyright © N.K. Sanders, 1960, 1964. Reproduced by permission of Penguin Books Ltd. ***Section 2*** P. 9: From *Babylonian and Assyrian Laws, Contracts, and Letters,* ed. C. M. W. Johns (New York: Charles Scribner's Sons, 1904), pp. 44–67 passim. ***Section 3*** P. 12 and 13: "To Rameses IV" and

Credits continued on page 443

Contents

Chapter 11: Early Modern Society and Politics 347

Chapter 12: The Scientific Revolution 387

Chapter 13: The Enlightenment 411

Preface

Teachers of the Western Civilization survey have long recognized the pedagogical value of primary sources, which are the raw materials of history. The second edition of *Sources of the Western Tradition* contains a wide assortment of documents — over 300 and virtually all primary sources — that have been carefully selected and edited to fit the needs of the survey and to supplement standard texts.

We have based our choice of documents for the two volumes on several criteria. In order to introduce students to those ideas and values that characterize the Western tradition, *Sources of the Western Tradition* emphasizes primarily the works of the great thinkers. While focusing on the great ideas that have shaped the Western heritage, however, the reader also provides a balanced treatment of political, economic, and social history. We have tried to select documents that capture the characteristic outlook of an age and that provide a sense of the movement and development of Western history. The readings are of sufficient length to convey their essential meaning, and we have carefully extracted those passages that focus on the documents' main ideas.

An important feature of the reader is the grouping of several documents that illuminate a single theme; such a constellation of related readings reinforces understanding of important themes and invites comparison, analysis, and interpretation. In Volume I, Chapter 5, for example, Selection 6, "Third-Century Crisis," contains three readings: "Caracalla's Extortions" (from Dio Cassius), "Petition to Emperor Philip," and "Extortions of Maximinus" (from Herodian). In Volume II, Chapter 11, Selection 7, "The Anguish of the Intellectuals," contains readings by José Ortega y Gasset, Thomas Mann, and Arthur Koestler.

An overriding concern of the editors in preparing this compilation was to make the documents accessible — to enable students to comprehend and to interpret historical documents on their own. We have provided several pedagogical features to facilitate this aim. Introductions of three types explain the historical setting, the authors' intent, and the meaning and significance of the readings. First, introductions to each of the twenty-three chapters provide comprehensive overviews to periods. Second, introductions to each numbered section or grouping treat the historical background for the reading(s) that follow(s). Third, each reading has a brief headnote that provides specific details about that reading.

Within some readings, Interlinear Notes, clearly set off from the text of the document, serve as transitions and suggest the main themes of the passages that follow. Used primarily in longer extracts of the great thinkers, these interlinear notes help to guide students through the readings.

To aid students' comprehension, brief, bracketed editorial definitions or notes that explain unfamiliar or foreign terms are inserted into the running text. When terms or concepts in the documents require fuller explanations, these appear at the bottom of pages as editors' footnotes. Where helpful, we have retained the notes of authors, translators, or editors from whose works the documents were acquired. (The latter have asterisks, daggers, etcetera, to distinguish them from our numbered explanatory notes.) The Review Questions that appear at the end of sections enable students to check their understanding of the documents; sometimes the questions ask for comparisons with other readings, linking or contrasting key concepts.

For ancient sources, we have generally selected recent translations that are both faithful to the text and readable. For some seventeenth- and eighteenth-century English documents, the archaic spelling has been retained, when this does not preclude comprehension, in order to show students how the English language has evolved over time.

The pictures that open each chapter illustrate an important theme covered in the chapter. In addition, in each volume there is a five-page section (between Chapters 5 and 6 in Volume I and between Chapters 8 and 9 in Volume II) devoted to art. In Volume I, "Elements of Classical, Medieval, and Renaissance Art" samples sculptural and architectural styles. Volume II's "Developments in Painting from Impressionism to the Abstract" samples the varied styles of painting in the late nineteenth and early twentieth centuries.

For the second edition, we have reworked all chapters. Documents that we have retained have been re-edited; in many cases we have cut extraneous passages, inserted additional notes to clarify historical events and terms, and defined technical words. Wherever possible we have extended the constellation format; many documents used in the first edition and documents added for this edition have been grouped together to illuminate significant themes.

In virtually every chapter, readings that proved to be less useful have been replaced by new ones. The second edition of Volume I contains around twenty-five new sources. For example, in Chapter 3, "The Greeks," to illustrate the theme of humanism we have provided Pindar's ode affirming the pursuit of excellence and the famous passage from *Antigone* in which Sophocles lauds human talents. An excerpt from *Lysistrata* expands the treatment of women in ancient Greece and illustrates Aristophanes' comic genius. Thucydides' reconstruction of a Spartan king's plea for moderation and caution raises fundamental questions about foreign policy, and the passages from *Politics* treat key themes in Aristotle's political philosophy. In Chapter 6, "Early Christianity," a new section, "Christian Worship and Organization," contains readings on church liturgy and the authority of the clergy by Saint Justin Martyr and Saint Ignatius of Antioch. Chapter 8, "The High and Late Middle Ages," includes a new section called "Medieval Universities," with excerpts from John of Salisbury, Chaucer, and medieval students.

Volume II has been more extensively revised. A major change is the new opening chapter, "The Rise of Modernity," which incorporates key readings from three chapters in Volume I: "The Renaissance," "The Reformation," and "Early Modern Society and Politics." This chapter and a new preceding introduction, "The Middle Ages and the Modern World," provide a good basis for approaching the complex issue of modernity, a natural beginning for the second half of the course.

More than fifty new readings appear in the second edition of Volume II. For example, in Chapter 7, "Politics and Society, 1850–1914," two new constellations have been inserted: "The Capitalist Ethic," which contains excerpts from Samuel Smiles's *Self-Help* and *Thrift*; and "The Lower Classes," which treats the problems of the poor in Germany and Britain at the end of the nineteenth century. Excerpts from Mary Wollstonecraft and Emmeline Pankhurst have been added to the section called "Equal Rights for Women." In that same section, the passage from John Stuart Mill has been lengthened. We have added three readings to the section on anti-Semitism: Edouard Drumont, *Jewish France,* Theodore Herzl, *The Jewish State,* and an account of the Kishinev Pogrom. In Chapter 10, "The Russian Revolution and the Soviet Union," a new section titled "The Revolution Denounced and Defended" includes the Proclamation of the Kronstadt Rebels, a socialist condemnation of the Bolshevik regime by Karl Kautsky, and a response to Kautsky by Leon Trotsky. In the last chapter, "The West in an Age of Globalism," we have introduced documents treating the ferment in the Soviet Union and Eastern Europe, women in third world development, and the environment and development (in excerpts from *Our Common Future* by the World Commission on Environment and Development).

Volume I, *From Ancient Times to the Enlightenment,* contains thirteen chapters that cover the period from the rise of civilizations in the ancient Near East to the philosphes of the eighteenth century. Volume II, *From the Renaissance to the Present,* incorporates the last two chapters of Volume I, "The Scientific Revolution" and "The Enlightenment," and has twelve chapters. Marvin Perry, senior editor of the project, researched both volumes. Joseph R. Peden contributed to Volume I and Theodore H. Von Laue to Volume II.

To accompany the second edition is a new *Instructor's Resource Manual with Test Items* by Professor Diane Moczar of Northern Virginia Community College. In addition to an introduction with suggestions on how to use *Sources of the Western Tradition* in class, there are chapter overviews, summaries of the sections, and, for each chapter, several questions for discussion or essay assignments and ten to twenty multiple-choice questions.

We wish to thank the following instructors for their critical reading of the manuscript and for their many valuable suggestions.

Donald B. Epstein, *Clackamas Community College*
Laura Gellott, *University of Wisconsin, Parkside*
Neil Heyman, *San Diego State University*
Lyle E. Linville, *Prince George's Community College*
Diane Moczar, *Northern Virginia Community College*
Walter Petry, *Fairfield University*
Jeremy D. Popkin, *University of Kentucky*
John Sommerville, *University of Florida*
Ira Spar, *Ramapo College of New Jersey*
Joshua B. Stein, *Roger Williams College*
John Turner, *C. W. Post, Long Island University*
Eric D. Weitz, *St. Olaf College*
Steven Werner, *University of Wisconsin Center–Waukesha*
Barbara Winslow, *Baruch College*
Ann Young, *Kearney State College*

We are also appreciative of the efforts of the Houghton Mifflin staff, who with their usual competent professionalism, guided the project from its inception. Joseph Peden wishes to thank his wife, Diana Peden, for her support. I wish to thank Angela Von Laue, who helped to research several chapters in Volume II and carefully read the galleys for that volume. I am especially grateful to George W. Bock, who worked closely with me in every phase of the reader's development, and to my wife, Phyllis Perry, for her encouragement.

M.P.

Part One

The Ancient World

SOURCES OF THE WESTERN TRADITION

CHAPTER

1

The Near East

The world's first civilizations arose some five thousand years ago in the river valleys of Mesopotamia (later Iraq) and Egypt. In these Near Eastern lands people built cities, organized states with definite boundaries, invented writing, engaged in large-scale trade, practiced specialization of labor, and erected huge monuments: all activities that historians associate with civilization. Scholars emphasize the fact that civilizations emerged in the river valleys — the Tigris and Euphrates in Mesopotamia and the Nile in Egypt. When they overflowed their banks, these rivers deposited fertile soil, which could provide a food surplus required to sustain life in cities. The early inhabitants of these valleys drained swamps and built irrigation works, enabling them to harness the rivers for human advantage. In the process they also strengthened the bonds of cooperation, a necessary ingredient of civilization.

Religion and myth were the central forces in these early civilizations. They pervaded all phases of life, providing people with satisfying explanations for the operations of nature and the mystery of death and justifying traditional rules of morality. Natural objects — the sun, the river, the mountain — were seen either as gods or as the abodes of gods. The political life of the Near East was theocratic: that is, people regarded their rulers as either divine or as representatives of the gods and believed that law originated with the gods. Near Eastern art and literature were dominated by religious themes.

The Sumerians, founders of urban life in Mesopotamia, developed twelve city-states in the region of the lower Euphrates near the Persian Gulf. Each city-state included a city and the farmland around it; each had its own government and was independent of the other city-states. In time the Sumerians were conquered, and their cities were incorporated into kingdoms and empires. However, as Akkadians, Elamites, Babylonians, and other peoples of the region adopted and built upon Sumerian religion, art, and literary forms, the Sumerian achievement became the basis of a coherent Mesopotamian civilization that lasted some three thousand years.

Early in its history Egypt became a centralized state under the rule of a pharaoh, who was viewed as both a man and a god. The pharaoh's authority was all-embracing, and all

NEFERTITI, 1360 B.C., the beautiful wife of Akhenaton, pharaoh of Egypt. Her husband sought to replace the many Egyptian gods with the worship of the sun god, Aton. (*Ägyptisches Museum. Staatliche Museen Preussischer Kulturbesitz, Berlin* [West])

Egyptians were subservient to him. Early in their history, the Egyptians developed cultural patterns that were to endure for three thousand years; the ancient Egyptians looked to the past, seeking to maintain the ways of their ancestors.

Although the cultural patterns of both civilizations were similar — the dominant role of religion and theocratic kingship — there were significant differences between the two. Whereas in Egypt the pharaoh was considered divine, rulers in Mesopotamia were regarded as exceptional human beings whom the gods had selected to act as their agents. Second, the natural environment of the Egyptians fostered a sense of security and an optimistic outlook toward life. Natural barriers — deserts, the Mediterranean Sea, and cataracts in the Nile — protected Egypt from invasion, and the overflowing of the Nile was regular and predictable, ensuring a good harvest. In contrast, Mesopotamia, without natural barriers, suffered from frequent invasions, and the Tigris and Euphrates rivers were unpredictable. Sometimes there was insufficient overflow, and the land was afflicted with drought; at other times, rampaging floods devastated the fields. These conditions promoted a pessimistic outlook, which pervaded Mesopotamian civilization.

After 1500 B.C., the Near East entered a period of empire building. In the late sixth century B.C., the Persians, the greatest of the empire builders, conquered all the lands from the Nile River to the Indus River in India. Persia united Egypt, Mesopotamia, and other Near Eastern lands into a world-state and brought together the regions' various cultural traditions. In the first half of the fifth century B.C., the Persians tried to add the city-states of Greece to their empire; the ensuing conflict was of critical importance for the history of Western civilization (see pages 60–63).

Egyptians, Mesopotamians, and other Near Eastern peoples developed a rich urban culture and made important contributions to later civilizations. They established bureaucracies, demonstrated creativity in art and literature, fashioned effective systems of mathematics, and advanced the knowledge of architecture, metallurgy, and engineering. The wheel, the plow, the phonetic alphabet, and the calendar derive from the Near East. Both the Hebrews and the Greeks, the principal sources of Western civilization, had contact with these older civilizations and adopted many of their cultural forms. But, as we shall see, even more important for the shaping of Western civilization was how the Hebrews and the Greeks broke with the essential style of Near Eastern society and conceived new outlooks, new points of departure for the human mind.

1 ▾ Mesopotamian Protest Against Death

The *Epic of Gilgamesh,* the greatest work of Mesopotamian literature, was written about 2000 B.C. It utilized legends about Gilgamesh, probably a historical figure who ruled the city of Uruk about 2600 B.C. The story deals with a profound theme — the human protest against death. In the end, Gilgamesh learns to accept reality: there is no escape from death. While the *Epic of Gilgamesh* is an expression of the pessimism that pervaded Mesopotamian life, it also reveals the Mesopotamians' struggle to come to terms with reality.

≪ *EPIC OF GILGAMESH* ≫

The *Epic of Gilgamesh* involves the gods in human activities. Because King Gilgamesh, son of a human father and the goddess Ninsun, drives his subjects too hard, they appeal to the gods for help. The gods decide that a man of Gilgamesh's immense vigor and strength requires a rival with similar attributes with whom he would contend. The creation goddess, Aruru, is instructed to create a man worthy of Gilgamesh. From clay she fashions Enkidu in the image of Anu, the god of the heavens and father of all the gods. Enkidu is a powerful man who roams with the animals and destroys traps set by hunters, one of whom appeals to King Gilgamesh. The two of them, accompanied by a harlot, find Enkidu at a watering place frequented by animals. The harlot removes her clothes and seduces Enkidu, who spends a week with her, oblivious to everything else. After this encounter, the bond between Enkidu and the animals is broken. He now enters civilization and is befriended by Gilgamesh, with whom he slays the terrible monster Humbaba.

Returning to Uruk after the encounter with Humbaba, Gilgamesh washes away the grime of battle and dons his royal clothes; thus arrayed he attracts the goddess of love, Ishtar, patroness of Uruk, who proposes marriage, but because of Ishtar's previous marriages and infidelities, Gilgamesh refuses. Ishtar falls into a bitter rage and appeals to her father, the god Anu, to unleash the fearful Bull of Heaven on Gilgamesh. However, Gilgamesh and Enkidu together slay the beast. To avenge the deaths of Humbaba and the Bull of Heaven, the gods decide that Enkidu shall die. In the following passage, Enkidu dreams of his impending death and the House of Darkness, from which no one returns.

When the daylight came Enkidu got up and cried to Gilgamesh, "O my brother, such a dream I had last night. Anu, Enlil, Ea and heavenly Shamash took counsel together, and Anu said to Enlil, 'Because they have killed the Bull of Heaven, and because they have killed Humbaba who guarded the Cedar Mountain one of the two must die.'. . ."

So Enkidu lay stretched out before Gilgamesh: his tears ran down in streams and he said to Gilgamesh, "O my brother, so dear as you are to me, brother, yet they will take me from you." Again he said, "I must sit down on the threshold of the dead and never again will I see my dear brother with my eyes."

. . . In bitterness of spirit he poured out his heart to his friend. "It was I who cut down the cedar, I who levelled the forest, I who slew Humbaba and now see what has become of me. Listen, my friend, this is the dream I dreamed last night. The heavens roared, and earth rumbled back an answer; between them stood I before an awful being, the sombre-faced man-bird; he had directed on me his purpose. His was a vampire face, his foot was a lion's foot, his hand was an eagle's talon. He fell on me and his claws were in my hair, he held me fast and I smothered; then he transformed me so that my arms became wings covered with feathers. He turned his stare towards me, and he led me away to the palace of Irkalla, the Queen of Darkness, to the house from which none who enters ever returns, down the road from which there is no coming back.

"There is the house whose people sit in darkness; dust is their food and clay their meat. They are clothed like birds with wings for covering, they see no light, they sit in darkness. I entered the house of dust and I saw the kings of the earth, their crowns put away for ever; rulers and princes, all those who once wore kingly crowns and ruled the world in the days of old. They who had stood in the place of the gods like Anu and Enlil, stood now like servants to fetch baked meats in the house of dust, to carry cooked meat and cold water from the water-skin. In the house of dust which I entered were high priests and acolytes, priests of the incantation and of ecstasy; there were servers of the temple, and there was Etana, that king of Kish whom the eagle carried to heaven in the days of old. I saw also Samuqan, god of cattle, and there was Ereshkigal the Queen of the Underworld; and Belit-Sheri squatted in front of her, she who is recorder of the gods and keeps the book of death. She held a tablet from which she read. She raised her head, she saw me and spoke: 'Who has brought this one here?' Then I awoke like a man drained of blood who wanders alone in a waste of rushes; like one whom the bailiff has seized and his heart pounds with terror."

Gilgamesh had peeled off his clothes, he listened to his words and wept quick tears, Gilgamesh listened and his tears flowed. . . .

This day on which Enkidu dreamed came to an end and he lay stricken with sickness. One whole day he lay on his bed and his suffering increased. He said to Gilgamesh, the friend on whose account he had left the wilderness, "Once I ran for you, for the water of life, and I now have nothing." A second day he lay on his bed and Gilgamesh watched over him but the sickness increased. A third day he lay on his bed, he called out to Gilgamesh, rousing him up. Now he was weak and his eyes were blind with weeping. Ten days he lay and his suffering increased, eleven and twelve days he lay on his bed of pain. Then he called to Gilgamesh, "My friend, the great goddess cursed me and I must die in shame. I shall not die like a man fallen in battle; I feared to fall, but happy is the man who falls in the battle, for I must die in shame." And Gilgamesh wept over Enkidu. With the first light of dawn he raised his voice and said to the counsellors of Uruk:

"Hear me, great ones of Uruk,
I weep for Enkidu, my friend,
Bitterly moaning like a woman mourning
I weep for my brother.
O Enkidu, my brother,
You were the axe at my side,
My hand's strength, the sword in my belt,
The shield before me,
A glorious robe, my fairest ornament;
An evil Fate has robbed me.

. . .

All the people of Eridu
Weep for you Enkidu.

. . .

What is this sleep which holds you now?
You are lost in the dark and cannot hear
me."

He touched his heart but it did not beat, nor did he lift his eyes again. When Gilgamesh touched his heart it did not beat. So Gilgamesh laid a veil, as one veils the bride, over his friend. He began to rage like a lion, like a lioness robbed of her whelps. This way and that he paced round the bed, he tore out his hair and strewed it around. He dragged off his splendid robes and flung them down as though they were abominations.

In the first light of dawn Gilgamesh cried out, "I made you rest on a royal bed, you reclined on a couch at my left hand, the princes of the earth kissed your feet. I will cause all the people of Uruk to weep over you and raise the dirge of the dead. The joyful people will stoop with sorrow; and when you have gone to the earth I will let my hair grow long for your sake, I will wander through the wilderness in the skin of a lion." The next day also, in the first light, Gilgamesh lamented; seven days and seven nights he wept for Enkidu, until the worm fastened on him. Only then he gave him up to the earth, for the Anunnaki, the judges [of the dead],[1] had seized him. . . .

▷ In his despair, Gilgamesh is confronted with the reality of his own death. Yearning for eternal life, he seeks Utnapishtim, legendary king of the city of Shurrupak, a man to whom the gods had granted everlasting life.

Bitterly Gilgamesh wept for his friend Enkidu; he wandered over the wilderness as a hunter, he roamed over the plains; in his bitterness he cried, "How can I rest, how can I be at peace? Despair is in my heart. What my brother is now, that shall I be when I am dead. Because I am afraid of death I will go as best I can to find Utnapishtim whom they call the Faraway, for he has entered the assembly of the gods." So Gilgamesh travelled over the wilderness, he wandered over the grasslands, a long journey, in search of Utnapishtim, whom the gods took after the deluge; and they set him to live in the land of Dilmun, in the garden of the sun; and to him alone of men they gave everlasting life. . . .

▷ In the garden of the gods, Gilgamesh speaks with Siduri, the divine winemaker, who tells him that his search for eternal life is hopeless.

". . . My friend who was very dear to me and who endured dangers beside me, Enkidu my brother, whom I loved, the end of mortality has overtaken him. I wept for him seven days and nights till the worm fastened on him. Because of my brother I am afraid of death, because of my brother I stray through the wilderness and cannot rest. But now, young woman, maker of wine, since I have seen your face do not let me see the face of death which I dread so much."

She answered, "Gilgamesh, where are you hurrying to? You will never find that life for which you are looking. When the gods created man they allotted to him death, but life they retained in their own keeping. As for you, Gilgamesh, fill your belly with good things; day and night, night and day, dance and be merry, feast and rejoice. Let your clothes be fresh, bathe yourself in water, cherish the little child that holds your hand, and make your wife happy in your embrace; for this too is the lot of man."

But Gilgamesh said to Siduri, the young woman, "How can I be silent, how can I rest, when Enkidu whom I love is dust, and I too shall die and be laid in the earth. You live by the sea-shore and look into the heart of it; young woman, tell me now, which is the way to Utnapishtim, the son of Ubara-Tutu? What directions are there for the passage; give me, oh, give me directions, I will cross the Ocean if it is possible; if it is not I will wander still farther in the wilderness.". . .

---

[1]Throughout the text, words in brackets have been added as glosses by the editors. Brackets around glosses from the original sources have been changed to parentheses to distinguish them.

▷ Siduri instructs Gilgamesh how to reach Utnapishtim. Ferried across the "waters of death" by a boatman, Gilgamesh meets Utnapishtim. But he, too, cannot give Gilgamesh the eternal life for which he yearns.

. . . "Oh father Utnapishtim, you who have entered the assembly of the gods, I wish to question you concerning the living and the dead, how shall I find the life for which I am searching?"

Utnapishtim said, "There is no permanence. Do we build a house to stand for ever, do we seal a contract to hold for all time? Do brothers divide an inheritance to keep for ever, does the flood-time of rivers endure? It is only the nymph of the dragon-fly who sheds her larva and sees the sun in his glory. From the days of old there is no permanence. The sleeping and the dead, how alike they are, they are like a painted death. What is there between the master and the servant when both have fulfilled their doom? When the Anunnaki, the judges, come together, and Mammetun the mother of destinies, together they decree the fates of men. Life and death they allot but the day of death they do not disclose."

▷ The tale concludes with one of several Near Eastern flood stories that preceded the account of Noah in Genesis.

REVIEW QUESTIONS

1. What was the fate of the dead as revealed in Enkidu's dream?
2. Describe the stages of Gilgamesh's reaction to Enkidu's death. Do these seem plausible psychologically? Explain.
3. What practical advice did the goddess Siduri offer the grieving hero?
4. What philosophic consolation did Utnapishtim offer Gilgamesh?
5. Historians often comment on the pessimism of the Mesopotamians. How is this pessimism reflected in the *Epic of Gilgamesh?*

▼▼▼

2 ▾ Mesopotamian Concepts of Justice

A significant source of information about the life of the ancient peoples of Mesopotamia is a code of laws issued about 1750 B.C. by the Babylonian king Hammurabi (1792–1750 B.C.). Discovered by archaeologists in 1901, the code was inscribed on a stone that shows the king accepting the laws from the sun god, Shamash, who was also the Babylonian god of justice.

These laws offer striking insights into the moral values, class structure, gender relationships, and roles of kingship and religion in Babylonian society. The 282 laws cover a range of public and private matters: marriage and family relations, negligence, fraud, commercial contracts, duties of public officials, property and inheritance, crimes and punishments, and techniques of legal procedure. The prologue to the code reveals the Mesopotamian concept of the priest-king — a ruler chosen by a god to administer his will on earth. In it, Hammurabi asserted that he had a divine duty to uphold justice in the land, to punish the wicked, and to further the welfare of the people.

CODE OF HAMMURABI

Two distinct approaches to choice of punishment for crime are found in Hammurabi's code with its numerous laws. In some instances, the guilty party is required to pay a monetary compensation to the victim, a tradition traceable to the earliest known Sumerian laws. Another approach, also found in the later Hebrew codes of law, is the principle of exact retaliation: "an eye for an eye, a tooth for a tooth."

Another feature of Hammurabi's code is that the penalties vary according to the social status of the victim. Three classes are represented: free men and women (called *patricians* in the reading here); commoners (or *plebeians*), not wholly free, but dependents of the state or perhaps serfs on landed estates; and slaves. The patricians are protected by the law of retaliation. People of the lower classes receive only monetary compensation if they are victims of a crime.

196. If a man has knocked out the eye of a patrician, his eye shall be knocked out.

197. If he has broken the limb of a patrician, his limb shall be broken.

198. If he has knocked out the eye of a plebeian or has broken the limb of a plebeian, he shall pay one mina[1] of silver.

199. If he has knocked out the eye of a patrician's servant, or broken the limb of a patrician's servant, he shall pay half his value.

200. If a patrician has knocked out the tooth of a man that is his equal, his tooth shall be knocked out.

201. If he has knocked out the tooth of a plebeian, he shall pay one-third of a mina of silver. . . .

209. If a man has struck a free woman with child, and has caused her to miscarry, he shall pay ten shekels[2] for her miscarriage.

210. If that woman die, his daughter shall be killed.

211. If it be the daughter of a plebeian, that has miscarried through his blows, he shall pay five shekels of silver.

212. If that woman die, he shall pay half a mina of silver.

213. If he has struck a man's maid and caused her to miscarry, he shall pay two shekels of silver.

214. If that woman die, he shall pay one-third of a mina of silver.

▷ Many laws relating to business transactions show the importance of trade in Mesopotamian society and the willingness of the government to intervene in order to regulate the practices of the marketplace.

218. If a surgeon has operated with the bronze lancet on a patrician for a serious injury, and has caused his death, or has removed a cataract for a patrician, with the bronze lancet, and has made him lose his eye, his hands shall be cut off.

219. If the surgeon has treated a serious injury of a plebeian's slave, with the bronze lancet, and has caused his death, he shall render slave for slave.

220. If he has removed a cataract with the bronze lancet, and made the slave lose his eye, he shall pay half his value.

[1]The mina was a weight of silver used to express monetary value. (Throughout the text, the editors' notes carry numbers, whereas notes from the original sources are indicated by asterisks, daggers, etcetera. An exception is made for editorial notes pertaining to Scriptures, which have symbols rather than numbers.)

[2]The shekel, also a weight of monetary value, was worth far less than the mina.

221. If a surgeon has cured the limb of a patrician, or has doctored a diseased bowel, the patient shall pay five shekels of silver to the surgeon.

222. If he be a plebeian, he shall pay three shekels of silver.

223. If he be a man's slave, the owner of the slave shall give two shekels of silver to the doctor. . . .

228. If a builder has built a house for a man, and finished it, he shall pay him a fee of two shekels of silver, for each *SAR*[3] built on.

229. If a builder has built a house for a man, and has not made his work sound, and the house he built has fallen, and caused the death of its owner, that builder shall be put to death.

230. If it is the owner's son that is killed, the builder's son shall be put to death.

231. If it is the slave of the owner that is killed, the builder shall give slave for slave to the owner of the house.

232. If he has caused the loss of goods, he shall render back whatever he has destroyed. Moreover, because he did not make sound the house he built, and it fell, at his own cost he shall rebuild the house that fell. . . .

271. If a man has hired oxen, a wagon, and its driver, he shall pay one hundred and sixty *KA*[4] of corn daily. . . .

275. If a man has hired a boat, its hire is three *ŠE*[5] of silver daily.

▷ The outcome of some procedures depended upon the will of the gods: for example, an accused woman could place her fate in the hands of a god by plunging into a river, canal, or reservoir; if she did not drown, she was declared innocent. In other cases, legal culpability could be removed by invoking a god to bear witness to the truth of one's testimony. The law was particularly harsh on perjurers and those who made grave charges that they could not prove in court.

[3]A *SAR* was a measure of land.
[4]*KA* stood for a bulk measure.
[5]*ŠE* was another monetary weight of silver.

1. If a man has accused another of laying a *nêrtu* (death spell?) upon him, but has not proved it, he shall be put to death.

2. If a man has accused another of laying a *kišpu* (spell) upon him, but has not proved it, the accused shall go to the sacred river, he shall plunge into the sacred river, and if the sacred river shall conquer him, he that accused him shall take possession of his house. If the sacred river shall show his innocence and he is saved, his accuser shall be put to death. He that plunged into the sacred river shall appropriate the house of him that accused him.

3. If a man has borne false witness in a trial, or has not established the statement that he has made, if that case be a capital trial, that man shall be put to death.

4. If he has borne false witness in a civil law case, he shall pay the damages in that suit. . . .

9. If a man has lost property and some of it be detected in the possession of another, and the holder has said, "A man sold it to me, I bought it in the presence of witnesses"; and if the claimant has said, "I can bring witnesses who know it to be property lost by me"; then the alleged buyer on his part shall produce the man who sold it to him and the witnesses before whom he bought it; the claimant shall on his part produce the witnesses who know it to be his lost property. The judge shall examine their pleas. The witnesses to the sale and the witnesses who identify the lost property shall state on oath what they know. Such a seller is the thief and shall be put to death. The owner of the lost property shall recover his lost property. The buyer shall recoup himself from the seller's estate.

▷ The laws concerned with family relationships placed great power in the hands of husbands and fathers, yet the code tried to protect women and children from neglect and mistreatment. Divorce initiated by either husband or wife was permitted under specific circumstances.

141. If a man's wife, living in her husband's house, has persisted in going out, has acted the fool, has wasted her house, has belittled her husband, he shall prosecute her. If her husband has said, "I divorce her," she shall go her way; he shall give her nothing as her price of divorce. If her husband has said, "I will not divorce her," he may take another woman to wife; the wife shall live as a slave in her husband's house.

142. If a woman has hated her husband and has said, "You shall not possess me," her past shall be inquired into, as to what she lacks. If she has been discreet, and has no vice, and her husband has gone out, and has greatly belittled her, that woman has no blame, she shall take her marriage-portion and go off to her father's house.

143. If she has not been discreet, has gone out, ruined her house, belittled her husband, she shall be drowned. . . .

148. If a man has married a wife and a disease has seized her, if he is determined to marry a second wife, he shall marry her. He shall not divorce the wife whom the disease has seized. In the home they made together she shall dwell, and he shall maintain her as long as she lives. . . .

168. If a man has determined to disinherit his son and has declared before the judge, "I cut off my son," the judge shall inquire into the son's past, and, if the son has not committed a grave misdemeanor such as should cut him off from sonship, the father shall (not) disinherit his son.

169. If he has committed a grave crime against his father, which cuts him off from sonship, for the first offence he shall pardon him. If he has committed a grave crime a second time, the father shall cut off his son from sonship. . . .

195. If a son has struck his father, his hands shall be cut off.

▷ One of the most unusual features of the law dealt with the failure of the government officials of a city or a district to prevent banditry. The code held the governor responsible for the breach of the peace and required him to compensate the bandit's victim. Government officials found guilty of extortion, bribery, or use of public employees for private purposes were severely punished.

---

23. If the highwayman has not been caught, the man that has been robbed shall state on oath what he has lost and the city or district governor in whose territory or district the robbery took place shall restore to him what he has lost.

24. If a life (has been lost), the city or district governor shall pay one mina of silver to the deceased's relatives. . . .

34. If either a governor, or a prefect, has appropriated the property of a levymaster,[6] has hired him out, has robbed him by high-handedness at a trial, has taken the salary which the king gave to him, that governor, or prefect, shall be put to death. . . .

[6]A levy-master was a military official.

REVIEW QUESTIONS

1. What does Hammurabi's code reveal about the social structure of Babylonian society?
2. Explain how seeking the intervention of a god was used in the legal procedures of Babylonian society.
3. Describe the probable status of women in Babylonian society as revealed in Hammurabi's code.
4. According to the code, what qualities might a husband expect in his wife?
5. How did Hammurabi attempt to ensure a high degree of competence in professional services?

6. How did the law attempt to control the exchange practices of the marketplace?
7. How did Hammurabi attempt to hold government officials responsible for properly carrying out the duties of their offices?

---

3 ▾ Divine Kingship

Theocratic monarchy, in which the ruler was considered either a god or a representative of the gods, was the basic political institution of ancient Near Eastern civilization. Kings were believed to rule in accordance with divine commands, and law was viewed as god-given. Theocracy as a form of government that subordinates the individual to the gods and their earthly representatives is compatible with mythical thought that sees nature and human destiny controlled by divine beings.

The theocratic mind of the Near East did not conceive the idea of political freedom. Mesopotamians and Egyptians were not free citizens but subjects who obeyed unquestioningly the edicts of their god-kings or priest-kings. Nor did Near Easterners arrive at a rational way of analyzing the nature and purpose of government and the merits or demerits of political institutions. To them the power of their gods and rulers was absolute and not an issue for discussion or reflection.

Divine kingship was the basic political institution of ancient Egyptian civilization. The Egyptians believed their king or pharaoh to be both a god and a man, the earthly embodiment of the god Horus. He was regarded as a benevolent protector who controlled the flood waters of the Nile, kept the irrigation system in working order, maintained justice in the land, and expressed the will of the gods by his words. It was expected that when the pharaoh died and joined his fellow gods, he would still help his living subjects. The Egyptians rejoiced in the rule of their all-powerful god-king.

HYMNS TO THE PHARAOHS

The first reading is a hymn to the new god-king Rameses IV (c. 1166 B.C.). The second reading is a hymn to a deceased pharaoh, perhaps Unnos (c. 2600 B.C.).

TO RAMESES IV

What a happy day! Heaven and earth rejoice, (for) thou art the great lord of Egypt.

They that had fled have come again to their towns, and they that were hidden have again come forth.

They that hungered are satisfied and happy, and they that thirsted are drunken.

They that were naked are clad in fine linen, and they that were dirty have white garments.

They that were in prison are set free, and he that was in bonds is full of joy.

They that were at strife in this land are reconciled. High Niles [beneficial floods] have come from their sources, that they may refresh the hearts of others.

Widows, their houses stand open, and they suffer travellers to enter.

Maidens rejoice and repeat their songs of gladness (?). They are arrayed in ornaments and say (?): "——— he createth generation on generation. Thou ruler, thou wilt endure for ever."

The ships rejoice on the deep ———.
They come to land with wind or oars,
They are satisfied . . . when it is said:
"King Hekmaatrē-Beloved-of-Amūn[1] again weareth the crown.
The son of [the sun-god] Rē, Ramesses, hath received the office of his father."
All lands say unto him:
"Beautiful is Horus on the throne of Amūn who sendeth him forth,
(Amūn) the protector of the Prince, who bringeth every land."

TO A DECEASED PHARAOH

The King has not died the death: he has become one who rises (like the morning sun) from the horizon. He rests from life (like the setting sun) in the West, but he dawns anew in the East. O King, you have not departed dead: you have departed living! Have you said that he would die? — nay, he dies not: this king lives for ever. He has escaped his day of death. O lofty one among the imperishable stars! — you shall not ever perish. Loose the embalming bandages! — they are not bandages (at all): they are the tresses of the goddess Nephthys (as she leans down over you). Men fall, and their name ceases to be: therefore God takes hold of this king by his arm, and leads him to the sky, that he may not die upon earth amongst men. This king flies away from you, you mortals. He is not of the earth, he is of the sky. He flies as a cloud to the sky, he who was like a bird at the masthead. He goes up to heaven like the hawks, and his feathers are like those of the wild geese; he rushes at heaven like a crane, he kisses heaven like the falcon, he leaps to heaven like the locust. He ascends to the sky! He ascends to the sky on the wind, on the wind! The stairs of the sky are let down for him that he may ascend thereon to heaven. O gods, put your arms under the king: raise him, lift him to the sky. To the sky! To the sky! To the great throne amongst the gods!

[1]Hekmaatrē was another name of this pharaoh.

GUIDELINES FOR THE RULER

Generally, pharaohs were mindful of their responsibilities. To prepare his son to rule, a pharaoh or his vizier (a high executive officer) might compile a list of instructions, like the ones that follow. These instructions were most likely composed by a vizier of King Issi (c. 2400 B.C.).

If thou art a leader and givest command to the multitude, strive after every excellence, until there be no fault in thy nature. Truth is good and its worth is lasting, and it hath not been disturbed since the day of its creator,* whereas he that transgresseth its ordinances is punished. It lieth as a (right) path in front of him that knoweth nothing. Wrong-doing (?) hath never yet brought its venture to port. Evil indeed winneth wealth, but the strength of truth is that it endureth, and the (upright) man saith: "It is the property of my father.". . .†

*Rē [the sun god], who brought truth into the world.

†That my father brought me up in the ways of truth is the best thing that he has bequeathed me.

▷ The following excerpts came from the instructions of Amenemhet I (1991–1962 B.C.), who prepared them for his son.

I gave to the poor and nourished the orphan, I caused him that was nothing to reach the goal, even as him that was of account. . . .

None hungered in my years, none thirsted in them. Men dwelt in (peace) through that which I wrought; . . . all that I commanded was as it should be. . . .

▷ These instructions were prepared for King Merikare (c. 2050 B.C.) by his father.

Be not evil, it is good to be kindly. Cause thy monument‡ to endure through the love of thee. . . . Then men thank God on thine account, men praise thy goodness and pray for thine health. . . . But keep thine eyes open, one that is trusting will become one that is afflicted. . . .

Do right so long as thou abidest on the earth. Calm the weeper, oppress no widow, expel no man from the possessions of his father. . . . Take heed lest thou punish wrongfully.

Exalt not the son of one of high degree more than him that is of lowly birth, but take to thyself a man because of his actions.

‡The remembrance of thee.

REVIEW QUESTIONS

1. For whom was the accession of a new king a cause of rejoicing?
2. What concept of kingship was implied in the second hymn?
3. What was the king expected to do for his subjects?
4. Discuss the role of religion in sustaining the authority of rulers over their subjects.

4 ▾ Discovery of a Pharaoh's Tomb

Among the richest mines of information about past civilizations are tombs excavated by archaeologists. Because of an almost universal belief that life continued in some form after death and that human beings continued to have needs in the afterlife, most ancient peoples buried their dead with furnishings or objects that were expected to be useful in the land of the dead. Through magical procedures, the dead could enjoy the use of these items, such as tools, weapons, clothing and jewelry, food and drink, statues of themselves or others, paintings or models of scenes from daily life. The number and richness of the objects buried reflected the wealth and social standing of the deceased. But even the poorest were provided with food and drink to ensure survival in the afterlife.

Most of our knowledge of ancient Egyptian civilization comes from tombs and their contents. Not only did Egypt's dry climate fortunately preserve organic material, such as papyrus, wood, ivory, and bone, but, along with effective methods of embalming, it also kept intact bodies for thousands of years. Archaeologists have gathered a detailed picture of daily life in ancient Egypt from the wall paintings, furnishings, architecture, and mummies found in hundreds of ancient tombs excavated along the Nile and in its vicinity.

Among the most spectacular discoveries was that of the tomb of Tutankha-

men (c. 1352–1344 B.C.) by the English archaeologist Howard Carter in November 1922. Carter was the first modern scholar to see an intact royal burial chamber. Although the antechamber and annex had been broken into soon after the burial, the grave robbers had been interrupted before they could loot the inner tomb itself. The pharaoh's tomb was resealed, buried under mounds of earth until Carter's discovery almost 3,300 years later.

Howard Carter *≪ THE TOMB OF TUTANKHAMEN ≫*

Carter reported that the tomb of Tutankhamen was very small and simple in design compared to those of other kings. It consisted of a sunken entrance staircase, a descending passage, an antechamber with an annex, a burial chamber, and a small storeroom. The antechamber and annex were filled with rich furnishings. These rooms had been plundered in antiquity of whatever jewels or gold objects that had originally been stored there. Within the burial chamber Carter found a succession of four boxlike shrines, one within the other, designed to house the pharaoh's sarcophagus (outer coffin). The sense of awe and emotion of the archaeologist as he approached the innermost shrine is captured in his report.

. . . With suppressed excitement I carefully cut the cord, removed that precious seal, drew back the bolts, and opened the doors, when a fourth shrine was revealed, similar in design and even more brilliant in workmanship than the last. The decisive moment was at hand! An indescribable moment for an archaeologist! What was beneath and what did that fourth shrine contain? With intense excitement I drew back the bolts of the last and unsealed doors; they slowly swung open, and there, filling the entire area within, effectually barring any further progress, stood an immense yellow quartzite sarcophagus stone coffin, intact, with the lid still firmly fixed in its place, just as the pious hands had left it. It was certainly a thrilling moment, as we gazed upon the spectacle enhanced by the striking contrast — the glitter of metal — of the golden shrines shielding it. Especially striking were the outstretched hand and wing of a goddess sculptured on the end of the sarcophagus, as if to ward off an intruder. It symbolized an idea beautiful in conception, and, indeed, seemed an eloquent illustration of the perfect faith and tender solicitude for the well-being of their loved one, that animated the people who dwelt in that land over thirty centuries ago. . . .

▷ Inside the sarcophagus, Carter discovered three coffins, one within the other, which had to be carefully opened and removed before he could reach his ultimate quest, the mummified body of Tutankhamen.

We found between the third and fourth shrines ceremonial bows and arrows, and with them, a pair of the gorgeous flabella [fans] — the insignia of princes, fans so prominent in scenes where kings are depicted, carried by inferior officers behind their chief. Beautiful specimens they were — one lying at the head, the other along the south side of the innermost shrine. The one at the head, wrought in sheet-gold, bears a charming and historical scene of the young King Tut-ankh-Amen in his chariot, followed by his favourite hound, hunting ostrich for feathers for the fan, as the inscription upon the handle says in "the Eastern desert of Heliopolis;" on the reverse side of the fan, also finely embossed and chased [decorated with raised and engraved designs], the young "Lord of Valour" is depicted returning triumphant, his quarry, two ostriches, borne on the shoulders of two attendants who precede him, the plumes under his arm. . . .

. . . Taking apart the sides, ends and doors of this innermost shrine was a much easier undertaking. It enclosed and, as it proved, exactly fitted the sarcophagus. It was the last of those complex problems involved in the dismantling of the four shrines, hallowed as they were by ancient memories. Our task of over eighty days was thus ended. . . .

. . . For ourselves it was the one supreme and culminating moment — a moment looked forward to ever since it became evident that the chambers discovered, in November, 1922, must be the tomb of Tut-ankh-Amen. . . . None of us but felt the solemnity of the occasion, none of us but was affected by the prospect of what we were about to see — the burial custom of a king of ancient Egypt of thirty-three centuries ago. How would the king be found?. . .

The tackle for raising the lid was in position. I gave the word. Amid intense silence the huge slab, broken in two, weighing over a ton and a quarter, rose from its bed. The light shone into the sarcophagus. A sight met our eyes that at first puzzled us. It was a little disappointing. The contents were completely covered by fine linen shrouds. The lid being suspended in mid-air, we rolled back those covering shrouds, one by one, and as the last was removed a gasp of wonderment escaped our lips, so gorgeous was the sight that met our eyes: a golden effigy [image] of the young boy king, of most magnificent workmanship, filled the whole of the interior of the sarcophagus. This was the lid of a wonderful anthropoid [human-like] coffin, some 7 feet in length, resting upon a low bier in the form of a lion, and no doubt the outermost coffin of a series of coffins, nested one within the other, enclosing the mortal remains of the king. Enclasping the body of this magnificent monument are two winged goddesses, Isis and Neith, wrought in rich gold-work upon gesso,[1] as brilliant as the day the coffin was made. To it an additional charm was added, by the fact that, while this decoration was rendered in fine low bas-relief, the head and hands of the king were in the round, in massive gold of the finest sculpture, surpassing anything we could have imagined. The hands, crossed over the breast, held the royal emblems — the Crook and the Flail — encrusted with deep blue faience.[2] The face and features were wonderfully wrought in sheet-gold. The eyes were of aragonite [white crystalline limestone] and obsidian [black volcanic glass], the eyebrows and eyelids inlaid with lapis lazuli glass. There was a touch of realism, for while the rest of this anthropoid coffin, covered with feathered ornament, was of brilliant gold, that of the bare face and hands seemed different, the gold of the flesh being of different alloy, thus conveying an impression of the greyness of death. Upon the forehead of this recumbent figure of the young boy king were two emblems delicately worked in brilliant inlay — the Cobra and the Vulture — symbols of Upper and Lower Egypt, but perhaps the most touching by its human simplicity was the tiny wreath of flowers around these symbols, as it pleased us to think, the last farewell offering of the widowed girl queen to her husband, the youthful representative of the "two Kingdoms."[3]

Among all that regal splendour, that royal magnificence — everywhere the glint of gold — there was nothing so beautiful as those few withered flowers, still retaining their tinge of colour. They told us what a short period three thousand three hundred years really was — but Yesterday and the Morrow. In fact, that little touch of nature made that ancient and our modern civilization kin. . . .

---

[1]Gesso is a kind of gypsum or plaster used over the surface of walls for painting or sculpting raised decorative patterns.

[2]Faience is a glazed earthenware.

[3]Egypt was politically and administratively composed of two separate kingdoms: Lower Egypt, the region of the Nile Delta, and, farther south, Upper Egypt, the valley stretching from the delta to the first cataract of the Nile. Usually the same king ruled both lands, but each had its own capital and government.

We raised the third coffin contained in the shell of the second, which now rested on the top of the sarcophagus, and moved them into the Antechamber where they were more accessible, both for examination and manipulation. It was then that the wonder and magnitude of our last discovery more completely dawned upon us. This unique and wonderful monument — a coffin over 6 feet in length, of the finest art, wrought in solid gold of 23 to 33 millimetres in thickness — represented an enormous mass of pure bullion.

How great must have been the wealth buried with those ancient Pharaohs! What riches that valley must have once concealed! Of the twenty-seven monarchs buried there, Tut-ankh-Amen was probably of the least importance. How great must have been the temptation to the greed and rapacity of the audacious contemporary tomb robbers! What stronger incentive can be imagined than those vast treasures of gold! The plundering of royal tombs, recorded in the reign of Rameses IX, becomes easily intelligible when the incentive to these crimes is measured by this gold coffin of Tut-ankh-Amen. It must have represented fabulous wealth to the stonecutters, artisans, water-carriers and peasants — to contemporary workers generally, such as the men implicated in the tomb robberies. . . .

Before us, occupying the whole of the interior of the golden coffin, was an impressive, neat and carefully made mummy, over which had been poured anointing unguents as in the case of the outside of its coffin — again in great quantity — consolidated and blackened by age. In contradistinction to the general dark and sombre effect, due to these unguents, was a brilliant, one might say magnificent, burnished gold mask or similitude of the king, covering his head and shoulders, which, like the feet, had been intentionally avoided when using the unguents. The mummy was fashioned to symbolize Osiris.[4] The beaten gold mask, a beautiful and unique specimen of ancient portraiture, bears a sad but calm expression suggestive of youth overtaken prematurely by death. Upon its forehead, wrought in massive gold, were the royal insignia — the Nekhebet vulture and Buto serpent[5] — emblems of the Two Kingdoms over which he had reigned. To the chin was attached the conventional Osiride beard, wrought in gold and lapis-lazuli-coloured glass; around the throat was a triple necklace of yellow and red gold and blue faience disk-shaped beads; pendent from the neck by flexible gold inlaid straps was a large black resin scarab[6] that rested between the hands. . . . The burnished gold hands, crossed over the breast, separate from the mask, were sewn to the material of the linen wrappings, and grasped the Flagellum [flail] and Crozier [crook] — the emblems of Osiris. Immediately below these was the simple outermost linen covering, adorned with richly inlaid gold trappings pendent from a large pectoral-like figure of the *Ba* bird or soul, of gold cloisonné[7] work, its full-spread wings stretched over the body. . . .

▷ When the royal mummy was finally removed from its innermost coffin, Carter and his colleagues began their detailed examination of the 3,300-year-old remains of the teenage pharaoh.

The removal of the final wrappings that protected the face of the king needed the utmost care, as owing to the carbonized state of the head there was always the risk of injury to the very fragile features. We realized the peculiar importance and responsibility attached to our

[4]Osiris, one of the principal gods of Egypt, died and was resurrected to life to rule over the underworld, the land of the dead. He was also the god of fertility. He presided over the last judgment of each dead soul and was identified with the dead king.

[5]Nekhebet was a guardian goddess of Upper Egypt, depicted as a vulture, and Buto, in the form of a snake, was a local god of Lower Egypt.

[6]The scarab beetle was considered by the Egyptians to represent the soul, and amulets were often made in the form of scarabs.

[7]Cloisonné is a kind of enamel work in which the surface color is placed within hollows formed by thin strips of welded wire set in patterns.

task. At the touch of a sable brush the last few fragments of decayed fabric fell away, revealing a serene and placid countenance, that of a young man. The face was refined and cultured, the features well formed, especially the clearly marked lips, and I think I may here record . . . the first and most striking impression to all present: namely, the remarkable structural resemblance to his father-in-law, Akh-en-Aten[8] — an affinity that has been visible on the monuments.

There is one point more of great interest: the king's head shows that, through the convention of the period, the finer contemporary representations of the king upon the monuments, beyond all doubt, are accurate portraits of Tut-ankh-Amen.

[8]Akhenaten ruled Egypt from c. 1369 to 1353 B.C. He attempted to suppress all gods of Egypt except himself and Aten (Aton), a sun god, but his religion and policies were reversed by his opponents after his death.

Upon the king's neck there were two kinds of symbolical collars and twenty amulets grouped in six layers, and between each of these layers were numerous linen bandages. . . .

This profusion of amulets and sacred symbols placed on the neck of the King are of extreme significance, suggesting as they do how greatly the dangers of the Underworld were feared for the dead. No doubt they were intended to protect him against injury on his journey through the hereafter. The quality and quantity of these protective symbols would naturally depend on his high rank and wealth, as well as upon the affection of his survivors. The actual meaning of many of them is not clear, nor do we know the exact nomenclature, nor the powers ascribed to them. However, we do know that they were placed there for the help and guidance of the dead, and made as beautiful and costly as possible. . . .

REVIEW QUESTIONS

1. The Egyptians believed that objects could be used by the dead through magic to re-enact the pleasures of life. What kinds of objects were left in the burial chamber for the enjoyment of Pharaoh Tutankhamen? What pleasures were they expected to bring to the dead king?
2. Totemism is the depiction of some force or god in the shape of an animal or other physical emblem. What totems were used by the ancient Egyptians to depict their gods in the tomb of Tutankhamen?
3. What evidence was found of the tremendous wealth produced by the people of Egypt and used for the needs of the king?
4. Why was the mummy of the king dressed with the symbols of Osiris?
5. Why was there a profusion of amulets around the king's neck?
6. Why was the discovery of Tutankhamen's tomb of such special significance?

---

5 ▾ Religious Inspiration of Akhenaten

Pharaoh Amenhotep IV (1369–1353 B.C.) was a religious mystic who conceived of divinity in a manner approaching monotheism. He suppressed the worship of the many gods of Egypt and insisted that only Aton — the sun god — and himself, the king and son of Aton, be worshiped by the Egyptians. Aton was viewed as the creator of the world, a god of love, peace, and justice. To promote the exclusive worship of Aton and himself, Amenhotep changed his name to Akhenaten ("It is well with Aton"), and near modern Tell El-Amarna he built a

new capital city, Akhataten, which became the center of the new religious cult. The new religion perished quickly after Akhenaten's death. Nor is there any evidence that this step toward a monotheistic conception of the divine had any later influence on the Hebrews.

The masses of Egypt were not influenced by Akhenaten's religious inspiration, and he was resisted by the priests, who clung to traditional beliefs. His immediate successors abandoned the new capital and had the monuments to Aton destroyed.

≪ *HYMN TO ATON* ≫

Akhenaten's religious outlook inspired remarkable works of art and literature. In the following hymn, Akhenaten glorifies Aton in words that are reminiscent of Psalm 104 (see pages 37–38).

Thou appearest beautifully on the horizon of heaven,
Thou living Aton, the beginning of life!
When thou art risen on the eastern horizon,
Thou hast filled every land with thy beauty.
Thou art gracious, great, glistening, and high over every land;
Thy rays encompass the lands to the limit of all that thou hast made. . . .

At daybreak, when thou arisest on the horizon,
When thou shinest as the Aton by day,
Thou drivest away the darkness and givest thy rays.
The Two Lands[1] are in festivity *every day,*
Awake and standing upon (their) feet,
For thou hast raised them up.
Washing their bodies, taking (their) clothing,
Their arms are (raised) in praise at thy appearance.
All the world, they do their work.

All beasts are content with their pasturage;
Trees and plants are flourishing.
The birds which fly from their nests,
Their wings are (stretched out) in praise to thy *ka.*[2]
All beasts spring upon (their) feet.
Whatever flies and alights,
They live when thou hast risen (for) them.
The ships are sailing north and south as well,
For every way is open at thy appearance.
The fish in the river dart before thy face;
Thy rays are in the midst of the great green sea.

Creator of seed in women,
Thou who makest fluid into man,
Who maintainest the son in the womb of his mother,
Who soothest him with that which stills his weeping,
Thou nurse (even) in the womb,
Who givest breath to sustain all that he had made!
When he descends from the womb to *breathe*
On the day when he is born,
Thou openest his mouth completely,
Thou suppliest his necessities.
When the chick in the egg speaks within the shell,
Thou givest him breath within it to maintain him.
When thou hast made him his fulfillment within the egg, to break it,
He comes forth from the egg to speak at his completed (time);
He walks upon his legs when he comes forth from it.

---

[1]The Two Lands were the two political divisions of Egypt, Upper and Lower Egypt. They were usually governed by the same king.

[2]The *ka* was a protective and guiding spirit, which each person was thought to have.

How manifold it is, what thou hast made!
They are hidden from the face (of man).
O sole god, like whom there is no other!
Thou didst create the world according to thy desire,
Whilst thou wert alone:
All men, cattle, and wild beasts,
Whatever is on earth, going upon (its) feet,
And what is on high, flying with its wings.

The countries of Syria and Nubia,[3] the *land* of Egypt,
Thou settest every man in his place,
Thou suppliest their necessities:
Everyone has his food, and his time of life is reckoned.
Their tongues are separate in speech,
And their natures as well;
Their skins are distinguished,
As thou distinguishest the foreign peoples.
Thou makest a Nile in the underworld,[4]
Thou bringest it forth as thou desirest
To maintain the people (of Egypt)
According as thou madest them for thyself,
The lord of all of them, wearying (himself) with them,
The lord of every land, rising for them,
The Aton of the day, great of majesty.

[3]Syria was an ancient country, larger than modern Syria, north of modern Israel and Jordan; Nubia was a kingdom located south of the first cataract of the Nile. It is now in Sudan.

[4]The Egyptians believed that the source of their Nile was in a huge body of water, which they called Nun, under the earth.

REVIEW QUESTIONS

1. Why was the sun a likely choice for a god conceived as one and universal?
2. What were some of the gifts of Aton to humanity?
3. What does the poem reveal about Akhenaten's view of the world and its peoples?

---

6 ▾ The Assyrian Empire

The Assyrians, a Semitic people from the region of what is now northern Iraq, went through several stages of empire building. At its height in the seventh century B.C., the Assyrian Empire stretched from Egypt to Persia (modern Iran). The king, representative of the god Ashur, governed absolutely, and nobles, appointed by the crown, kept order in the provinces. Traveling inspectors checked on the performance of these officials. A network of roads and an effective messenger service enabled Assyrian rulers to keep informed about potential unrest and to crush rebellions. Conquered peoples were permitted a substantial amount of independence so long as they paid tribute to their Assyrian overlords, but uprisings were ruthlessly suppressed.

INSCRIPTION OF TIGLATHPILESER I

In the following reading, Tiglathpileser I (1115–1077 B.C.) described his conquests and the subjugation of rebellious subjects.

Tiglath-pileser, the powerful king, king of hosts, who has no rival, king of the four quarters (of the world), king of all rulers, lord of lords, king of kings; the lofty prince. . . . who rules over the nations, . . . the legitimate shepherd whose name is exalted above all rulers; the lofty judge, whose weapons Ashur[1] has sharpened, and whose name, as ruler over the four quarters (of the world), he has proclaimed forever; the conqueror of distant lands, which form the boundaries on north and south; the brilliant day, whose splendour overthrows the world's regions; the terrible, destroying flame, which like the rush of the storm sweeps over the enemy's country; who . . . has no adversary, and overthrows the foes of Ashur.

Ashur and the great gods who have enlarged my kingdom, who have given me strength and power as my portion, commanded me to extend the territory of their (the gods') country, putting into my hand their powerful weapons, the cyclone of battle. I subjugated lands and mountains, cities and their rulers, enemies of Ashur, and conquered their territories. With sixty kings I fought, spreading terror (among them), and achieved a glorious victory over them. A rival in combat, or an adversary in battle, I did not have. To Assyria I added more land, to its people I added more people, enlarging the boundaries of my land and conquering all (neighbouring?) territories.

In the beginning of my government, five kings . . . with an army of twenty thousand men . . . — and whose power no king had ever broken and overcome in battle — trusting to their strength rushed down and conquered the land of Qummuh (Commagene).[2] With the help of Ashur, my lord, I gathered my war chariots and assembled my warriors; I made no delay, but traversed Kashiari,[3] an almost impassable region. I waged battle in Qummuh with these five kings and their twenty thousand soldiers and accomplished their defeat. Like the Thunderer (the storm god Adad) I crushed the corpses of their warriors in the battle that caused their overthrow. I made their blood to flow over all the ravines and high places of mountains. I cut off their heads and piled them up at the walls of their cities like heaps of grain. I carried off their booty, their goods, and their property beyond reckoning. Six thousand, the rest of their troops, who had fled before my weapons and had thrown themselves at my feet, I took away as prisoners and added to the people of my country.

At that time I marched also against the people of Qummuh, who had become unsubmissive, withholding the tax and tribute due to Ashur, my lord. I conquered Qummuh to its whole extent, and carried off their booty, their goods, and their property; I burned their cities with fire, destroyed, and devastated.

[1]Ashur was the patron god of the Assyrians. He is identified with the earlier Babylonian god Marduk.

[2]Commagene was a region along the upper Euphrates River in northern Syria.

[3]Kashiari was a mountainous area in Mesopotamia.

REVIEW QUESTIONS

1. What was the relationship between the king and the god Ashur?
2. What duties were expected of an Assyrian king?
3. What duties did subjects owe to the Assyrian king? What was the price of resistance to the king's commands?
4. What appear to be the character and purpose of warfare in the days of the Assyrian Empire?

7 ▾ The Myth-making Outlook of the Ancient Near East

The civilizations of the ancient Near East were based on a way of thinking that is fundamentally different from the modern scientific outlook. The peoples of Mesopotamia and Egypt interpreted nature and human experience through myths, which narrated the deeds of gods who in some distant past had brought forth the world and human beings. These myths made the universe and life intelligible for Near Eastern people.

The difference between scientific thinking and mythical thinking is profound. The scientific mind views physical nature as an *it* — inanimate, impersonal, and governed by universal law. The myth-making (mythopoeic) mind sees nature as personified — alive, with individual wills, gods, and demons who manipulate things according to their desires. The scientific mind holds that natural objects obey universal rules; hence the location of planets, the speed of objects, and the onset of a hurricane can be predicted. The myth-making mind has no awareness of repetitive laws inherent in nature; rather it attributes all occurrences to the actions of gods, whose behavior is often unpredictable. The scientific mind appeals to reason — it analyzes nature logically and systematically and searches for general principles that govern the phenomena. The myth-making mind explains nature and human experience by narrating stories about the gods and their deeds. Myth is an expression of the poetic imagination; it proclaims a truth that is emotionally satisfying, not one that has been arrived at through intellectual analysis and synthesis. It gives order to human experiences and justifies traditional rules of morality. Mythical explanations of nature and human experience, appealing essentially to the imagination, enrich perception and feeling; they make life seem less overwhelming and death less frightening.

PERSONIFICATION OF NATURAL OBJECTS

The mythopoeic mind accounts for causation by personifying inanimate substances. To explain through personification is to seek the *who* behind events, to attribute these events to the will of a god (or to an object suffused with divine presence). Thus if a river did not rise, it was because it refused to do so; either the river or the gods were angry at the people.

The following excerpts from Mesopotamian literature are examples of personification. While we regard table salt as an ordinary mineral, to the Mesopotamians it was alive, a fellow being. In one passage, a person appeals to salt to end his bewitchment. In the second, an afflicted person who believes himself bewitched calls on fire to destroy his enemies.

O SALT

O Salt, created in a clean place,
For food of gods did *Enlil* [father of the Sumerian gods] destine thee.
Without thee no meal is set out in *Ekur,*
Without thee god, king, lord, and prince do not smell incense.
I am so-and-so, the son of so-and-so,
Held captive by enchantment,
Held in fever by bewitchment.
O Salt, break my enchantment! Loose my spell!
Take from me the bewitchment! — And as My Creator
I shall extol thee.

SCORCHING FIRE

Scorching Fire, warlike son of Heaven,
Thou, the fiercest of thy brethren,
Who like Moon and Sun decidest lawsuits —
Judge thou my case, hand down the verdict.
Burn the man and woman who bewitched me;
Burn, O Fire, the man and woman who bewitched me;
Scorch, O Fire, the man and woman who bewitched me;
Burn them, O Fire;
Scorch them, O Fire;
Take hold of them, O Fire;
Consume them, O Fire;
Destroy them, O Fire.

≪ *ENUMA ELISH* ≫ *THE BABYLONIAN GENESIS*

The Mesopotamian creation epic *Enuma elish* is another example of mythical thinking. Marduk, the chief god of Babylon, slays Tiamat, a primal mother identified with the salt sea, and then proceeds to construct the cosmos from her carcass.

"Stand thou up, that I and thou meet in single combat!"
When Tiamat heard this,
She was like one possessed; she took leave of her senses.
In fury Tiamat cried out aloud.
To the roots her legs shook both together.
She recites a charm, keeps casting her spell,
While the gods of battle sharpen their weapons.
Then joined issue Tiamat and Marduk, wisest of gods.
They strove in single combat, locked in battle.
The lord spread out his net to enfold her,
The Evil Wind, which followed behind, he let loose in her face.
When Tiamat opened her mouth to consume him,
He drove in the Evil Wind that she close not her lips.
As the fierce winds charged her belly,
Her body was distended and her mouth was wide open.
He released the arrow, it tore her belly,
It cut through her insides, splitting the heart.
Having thus subdued her, he extinguished her life.
He cast down her carcass to stand upon it.
After he had slain Tiamat, the leader,
Her band was shattered, her troupe broken up;
And the gods, her helpers who marched at her side,
Trembling with terror, turned their backs about,
In order to save and preserve their lives.
Tightly encircled, they could not escape.
He made them captives and he smashed their weapons.
Thrown into the net, they found themselves ensnared;

Placed in cells, they were filled with wailing;
Bearing his wrath, they were held imprisoned.

. . .

When he had vanquished and subdued his adversaries,

. . .

[Marduk] turned back to Tiamat whom he had bound.
The lord trod on the legs of Tiamat,
With his unsparing mace he crushed her skull.
When the arteries of her blood he had severed,
The North Wind bore (it) to places undisclosed.
On seeing this, his fathers were joyful and jubilant,
They brought gifts of homage, they to him.
Then the lord paused to view her dead body,
That he might divide the monster and do artful works.
He split her like a shellfish into two parts:
Half of her he set up and ceiled it as sky,
Pulled down the bar and posted guards.
He bade them to allow not her waters to escape.
He crossed the heavens and surveyed the regions.

. . .

[There] He constructed stations for the great gods,
Fixing their astral likenesses as constellations.
He determined the year by designating the zones:
He set up three constellations for each of the twelve months.

. . .

In her [Tiamat's] belly he established the zenith.
The Moon he caused to shine, the night (to him) entrusting.
He appointed him a creature of the night to signify the days. . . .
When Marduk hears the words of the gods,
His heart prompts (him) to fashion artful works.
Opening his mouth, he addresses [the god] Ea
To impart the plan he had conceived in his heart:
"Blood I will mass and cause bones to be.
I will establish a savage, 'man' shall be his name.
Verily, savage-man I will create.
He shall be charged with the service of the gods
That they might be at ease!"

≪ LAMENT FOR UR ≫
THE GODS AND HUMAN DESTINY

Mesopotamians and Egyptians believed that their destinies were determined by the gods. Drought, hurricanes, sickness, law, and foreign invasion were all attributed to divine intervention. In the "Lament for Ur," the assembly of the gods decides to punish the Sumerian city-state of Ur.

Enlil called the storm.
The people mourn.
Winds of abundance he took from the land.
The people mourn.
Good winds he took away from Sumer.
The people mourn.
Deputed [assigned] evil winds.
The people mourn.
Entrusted them to Kingaluda, tender of storms.
He called the storm that annihilates the land.
The people mourn.
He called disastrous winds.
The people mourn.
Enlil — choosing Gibil (fire god) as his helper —
called the (great) hurricane of heaven.
The people mourn.
The (blinding) hurricane howling across the skies —

the people mourn —
the storm that annihilates the land roaring
over the earth —
the people mourn —
the tempest unsubduable like breaks through
levees,
beats down upon, devours the city's ships,
(all these) he gathered at the base of heaven.
The people mourn.

(Great) fires he lit that heralded the storm.
The people mourn.
And lit on either flank of furious winds
the searing heat of desert.
Like flaming heat of noon this fire
scorched. . . .
The storm ordered by Enlil in hate,
the storm which wears away the country,
covered Ur like a cloth,
veiled it like a linen sheet. . . .

On that day did the storm leave the city;
that city was a ruin.
O father Nanna (the moon god), that town
was left a ruin.
The people mourn.
On that day did the storm leave the country.
The people mourn.
Its people ('s corpses), not potsherds,
littered the approaches.
The walls were gaping;
the high gates, the roads,
were piled with dead.
In the wide streets,
where feasting crowds (once) gathered,
jumbled they lay.

In all the streets and roadways bodies lay.
In open fields that used to fill with dancers,
the people lay in heaps.

The country's blood now filled its holes.
like metal in a mold;
bodies dissolved — like butter left in the sun.

REVIEW QUESTIONS

1. What is myth? How does mythical thought differ from scientific thought?
2. The world view of ancient Mesopotamia was based on myth and magic. Discuss this statement.
3. On what occasions might the ancient Mesopotamians have turned to the gods for help?
4. According to the Babylonians, how was the human race created?
5. How did the ancient Mesopotamians explain certain natural disasters?
6. It has been said that humans are myth-making animals and that all human societies create and sustain themselves by inventing myths. Discuss.

תקופת טבת
סרטן
תאומים

The Hebrews

Two ancient peoples, the Hebrews (Jews) and the Greeks, are the principal founders of Western civilization. From the Hebrews derives the concept of *ethical monotheism* — the belief in one God who demands righteous behavior from his human creations — which is an essential element of the Western tradition.

The Hebrews originated in Mesopotamia and migrated to Canaan (Palestine). Some Hebrews who journeyed to Egypt to become farmers and herdsmen were forced to labor for the Egyptian state. In the thirteenth century B.C., Moses, who believed that he was doing God's bidding, led the Hebrews from Egypt — the biblical Exodus. While wandering in the Sinai Desert, the Hebrews were uplifted and united by a belief in Yahweh, the One God. In the eleventh century B.C., some two hundred years after they had begun the conquest of Canaan, the Hebrews were unified under the leadership of Saul, their first king. Under Solomon (d. 922 B.C.) the kingdom of Israel reached the height of its power and splendor.

The Hebrews borrowed elements from the older civilizations of the Near East. Thus there are parallels between Babylonian literature and biblical accounts of the Creation, the Flood, and the Tower of Babel. Nevertheless, Israelite religion marks a profound break with the outlook of the surrounding civilizations of the Near East.

There are two fundamental characteristics of ancient Near Eastern religion. First, the Near Eastern mind saw gods everywhere in nature; the moon and stars, rivers and mountains, thunder and wind storms were either gods or the dwelling places of gods. The Near Eastern mind invented myths — stories about the gods' birth, deeds, death, and resurrection. Second, Near Eastern gods were not fully sovereign. The peoples of the Near East believed that the gods issued forth from a realm that existed before they did; that the gods' power and their very existence depended on prior conditions. Near Eastern gods grew old, became ill, required food, and even died — all limitations on their power. The gods were subject to magic and destiny — powers that preceded them in time and surpassed them in power — and if the gods did wrong, destiny, or fate, punished them.

Hebrew religious thought evolved through the history

TEMPLE FLOOR MOSAIC. Images in Hebrew art are extremely rare because of the injunction in the Second Commandment against graven images. This floor mosaic from Beth Alpha synagogue in Israel is a zodiacal calendar. (© *Zev Radovan, Jerusalem*) and experience of the Jewish people. Over the centuries the Hebrew view of God came to differ markedly from Near Eastern ideas about the gods and the world. For the Hebrews, God was not only one, he was also *transcendent* — above nature. This means that natural objects were not divine, holy, or alive, but were merely God's creations. In contrast to the Near Eastern gods, Yahweh was fully sovereign, absolutely free; there were no limitations whatsoever on his power. He was eternal and the source of all in the universe; he did not answer to fate but himself determined the consequences of wrongdoing; he was not subject to any primordial power or to anything outside or above him.

The Hebrew conception of God led to a revolutionary view of the individual. The Hebrews believed that God had given men and women moral autonomy — the capacity to choose between good and evil. Therefore, men and women had to measure their actions by God's laws and were responsible for their own behavior. Such an outlook led people to become aware of themselves — their moral potential and personal worth. From the Hebrews came a fundamental value of the Western tradition — the inviolable worth and dignity of the individual.

---

1 ▾ Old Testament Faith: Ethical Monotheism

The Hebrew Scriptures, which form the Old Testament of the Christian Bible, are a collection of thirty-nine books written over several centuries by several authors. It is a record of more than a thousand years of ancient Jewish history and religious development. Believed by both Jews and Christians to be divinely inspired revelation, the Old Testament is one of the most influential documents in human history.

Lawrence Boadt
READING THE OLD TESTAMENT

Lawrence Boadt, a contemporary Roman Catholic clergyman and Old Testament scholar, analyzes the essential themes of the Hebrew Scriptures.

THE ONLY GOD

Thus the *first and most important* theological theme found in the Old Testament is that *God is one.* This may seem like a small statement, but it governs everything. Israel lived in a world with many competing gods and many debased ideas about divine power. The polytheism of its neighbors was based on an attempt to understand the forces of nature and the mysteries of life that faced humans every day. Why is there drought, sickness and death? How do we find blessing of good crops, children, security and peace? The common answer was to recognize different divine powers everywhere, often with competing aims and attitudes toward human beings. The means of relating to these gods was, in effect, to *manipulate* them into doing what we needed or wanted. Elaborate rituals and rites that *imitated* the force of storms or the generating acts of sex gradually led to an attitude toward divine beings as glorified humans complete with all our envies, pettiness, moods and self-interest. The world and its gods were nearly identical. In contrast, Israel insisted on a single divine being who ordered and controlled everything out of love for the goodness of creation. The creation story in Genesis I makes this clear. . . .

Above all, this God ruled human history and actively guided, protected, cared for and was involved in human affairs — the whole Bible tells this story. It affirms everywhere that God was never to be confused with the created things of the world. The Old Testament returns again and again to the themes that God is *holy,* God is *King.* God is *Shepherd* or *Father,* God is *Creator* — always to emphasize the transcendence of God. God is near the world but never of it. As Jeremiah[1] 23:23 [–24] puts it, "Am I a God nearby, says the Lord, and not a God far away?" "Do I not fill heaven and earth?" Perhaps the highest point in Old Testament theology is reached in the famous prayer of Deuteronomy[2] 6 on this very point: "Hear, O Israel,[3] the Lord our God is one Lord, and you shall love the Lord your God with all your heart and with all your spirit and with all your power."

GOD ACTIVE IN HISTORY

This brings us right to the heart of the *second important theological theme* in the Old Testament. God is an actor in history. Israel is literally created by the action of God. God reveals that history is not neutral, but is a stage for the discovery of the *self-revealing* God. Israel thus proclaims that pagan ideas of circular time, those unending repeating cycles of events in which nothing is ever really new, must be discarded for good. History is *ever new,* it moves ahead, and we can grow better or worse in it, and we can certainly learn from it. This insight flows from the worship and adoration of a transcendent God. If God is not merely part of nature, tied to its ups and downs and its wet seasons and dry, God can act *upon* it. Some years ago, the term "salvation history" for the Old Testament was very popular. It expressed the sense that Israel remembered and learned from those moments when God acted in the events which were most crucial to its past existence. . . . It underscores Israel's breakthrough insight that God not only *cares about* humans but operates in a carefully *ordered* and loving way for the *good* of humans — and always has.

---

[1]Jeremiah was a major Hebrew prophet who lived in the seventh and early sixth century B.C. He urged moral reform, denounced pagan practices among his fellow Hebrews, and accurately prophesied the destruction of Jerusalem by the Babylonians.

[2]Deuteronomy is the fifth book of both Hebrew and Christian Bibles. It summarizes the ancient Hebrew laws and the obligations of the people under the Mosaic covenant. (See Footnote 7.)

[3]The name *Israel* is used to designate both the Hebrews and the land occupied by them after their exodus from Egypt. The Hebrew Scriptures say that the land was originally given by God to the patriarch Jacob.

Above all, this insight into divine activity declares that God was a *Liberator and Savior.* He delivers the patriarchs Abraham, Isaac and Jacob;[4] he saves Moses[5] and the slaves at the Red Sea; he hears the cry of the poor and listens to them in the psalms. . . .

PERSONAL RESPONSE AND PRAYER

The *third important theological theme,* which follows from the second about God as *actor* in *time,* asserts the necessity of *human response* to what God does. . . . God . . . demands. . . . a *personal* response of friendship, loyalty, obedience, and communication. . . . The great prophets . . . not only speak in God's name but watch over and *insist upon* concrete replies by Israel in both deeds and words. The very creation of the Bible as a sacred book stems from the awareness that Israel must express itself fully before God — both in the telling of its story and in the constant praise of the living and present God in its midst, and even in the rather bold and daring questioning by wisdom writers who seek to understand their relationship with God more deeply.

Our *fourth theme* is really a concrete application of this human response — *prayer* — or the *praise of God.* The Bible is history and catechetics,[6] speculative thought and poetry and entertaining tales and much more, but all of it is praise of God. Israel was a community that learned to place its purpose and hopes and self-understanding only in God. . . . *All of the biblical text* tells the glory of God. . . .

COVENANT AND TRADITION

The *fifth theological theme* might be called *community* and *covenant.*[7] The Old Testament came into existence as the remembering by an ongoing community who received what had been the testimony of others and took responsibility for it. Above all, they clung stubbornly to a conviction that God had indeed entered into a special relationship of *covenant* with them — a covenant that established bonds of loyalty and responsibility between God and humanity in the person of Israel. . . . It is our task now to recognize how this formed and preserved the true *inner bond* of Israel as a *community* which maintained a profound respect for the worth and love of the neighbor — as Leviticus[8] 19:18 points out so strongly when it demands *love of neighbor* as much as of oneself.

A *sixth important theme* follows from the last one. Israel is above all a people of *tradition* and *institutions.* It is *torah,* "teaching" or, even better, "way of life." Israel does not shrink from including sacrifice laws and regulations about bodily ailments and sanitary practices right next to moral and ethical demands for justice and humility and caring. The Old Testament is a rather awkward collection of materials because it reflects *all* the different sides of life in community. We should keep in mind that the traditions come from a very long period of time, at least a thousand years, and probably much more. . . .

THE PROPHETS AND JUSTICE

A *significant seventh theme* that follows from an honest wrestling with Israel's sense of concrete

---

[4]Abraham, Isaac, and Jacob were father, son, and grandson, considered together the patriarchs of the Hebrew people. Jacob's sons, according to the Hebrew Scriptures, were the founders of the twelve tribes into which the Hebrews were originally organized.

[5]According to the Hebrew Scriptures, Moses, believing himself to be God's agent, led the Hebrews from slavery among the Egyptians. In a mystical encounter with God on Mount Sinai, he received the basic moral code, the Ten Commandments.

[6]*Catechetics* means instruction.

[7]A covenant is an agreement binding two parties to mutual obligations. In the Hebrew Scriptures, both Abraham and Moses entered into covenants with God, who promised his special concern for the Hebrews in return for their loyalty and obedience to his divine commands.

[8]Leviticus, the third book of the Bible and the Hebrew Scriptures, details the ritual ceremonies for divine worship by the Hebrews.

existence in the world is found in the *tension between God's will and our often sinful and selfish response.* Israel was no pollyanna that thought of human nature as always good and God as always forgiving of any and every fault. The Israelites never failed to proclaim God to be a God of mercy, as Exodus[9] 34 expresses it, "slow to anger and rich in kindness," but they tempered it with a true awareness of *justice.* God does indeed make demands on the community, demands that they be *like* God. If the claim of Genesis[10] 1:26 means anything when it says that humans are made in the image and likeness of God, it means that we too have moral choice and moral responsibility. Leviticus 19 insists over and over that Israel obey God's laws because God is *holy.* If God indeed faithfully treats the world in an ethical and right fashion, acting solely out of love and goodness, then the *proper* human response must be in kind.

This explains the central vitality of *prophecy* to the Old Testament tradition. The prophets[11] are the *ethical watchdogs* par excellence. They should not be seen only as radical innovators or rebels against the laws and traditions. They recalled tradition to the people, showing them how God had acted in the past, and what the covenant had taught, and insisting that Israel not forget the freedom of God to act in new ways or the faithfulness of God that would not overlook repeated violations of the covenant. The prophetic word indeed stands in judgment on Israel's behavior only because Israel *forgets.* Ethics is therefore not divorced from the great sense of tradition but stands within it. There is no picture of God in the Hebrew Scriptures, unlike in many of the pagan myths and prayers, that ever *forgets* that he is a God of *action* who demands *actions* in return. God always acted rightly, and all Israel must act rightly because they remember as their sacred duty what God is. . . .

HOPE AND THE FUTURE

The office of the prophet as watchdog and critic and challenger of Israel's evil ways is balanced by the fact that the prophetic office also brings comfort and hope in times of trouble and loss. This is itself an *eighth theological* theme: *hope* and *optimism* about the future. Biblical theologians often speak about "eschatology"[12] in the Bible and mean by it the dynamic expectation that God will act in the future. This is not just the natural assumption that he will work tomorrow as he did today, but the much greater confidence that God has all of time and human history under a plan and that there will be moments of profound change when he intervenes. This conviction took shape in any number of crisis moments facing Israel in the Old Testament — the rise of the kings in the tenth century, the loss of northern Israel and ten of 12 tribes in the eighth century, and the loss of land, temple, king and independence in the sixth century. Never in any of these crises did Israel come to the conclusion that God would *not act* again. They interpreted disasters as punishment for their own evil for the most part, and the prophets frequently warned the people that God had future punishment in mind if they would not *convert* their ways. But there always remained a conviction, even when the prophets used the most absolute and damning language condemning Israel, that God would *renew* or *restore* because above all God was faithful.

[9]Exodus, the second book of the Bible, contains the account of the Hebrews' plight in Egypt and their flight (exodus) under the divinely inspired leadership of Moses to the Sinai Desert.

[10]Genesis, the first book of the Bible, contains the Hebrew account of the origin of the world and the early history of the human race, up through the three patriarchs Abraham, Isaac, and Jacob.

[11]The biblical prophets were spiritually inspired people who believed that they were commanded by God to carry his message to the Hebrews. They foretold divine punishment for disobedience to God's laws.

[12]Eschatology is that branch of theology that studies death and the afterlife and the last days of the world.

This led to the hope of a *messiah,*[13] a figure sent by God, greater than any king of the past, who would bring about the full flowering of Israel. Such hopes were really quite late in the Old Testament period and are only mildly reflected in the actual books of the Bible — an example is Daniel[14] — but were very common among other writings and in Jewish groups just before the time of Christ. . . .

The sense of hope should be coupled with *another theme — the goodness of the world* and of the creation that God has made. Hope is rooted ultimately in the knowledge of a good God. Israel has many beautiful passages in its Scriptures that express this deep conviction of God's majestic power and blessing on all of creation. . . .

Many scholars wondered why the Bible had so little to say of an *afterlife.* Only in one of the latest books of the Bible, Daniel, does such a belief emerge clearly. Perhaps Israel focused itself so strongly on the covenant with the *now-community* that it had little room for wondering how that bond could be continued after death. But eventually the radical belief that *God was good* without fail — from beginning to ultimate end — led to an equal assertion that God could raise the dead who had suffered unjustly — could preserve the faithful Israelite into the life to come. It remains a minor theme in the Hebrew Scriptures but takes a much more central place in light of the resurrection of Jesus [for Christianity].

THE MYSTERY OF GOD'S WAYS

Finally, we should conclude with a *last theme of importance:* the Bible is *wisdom.* Wisdom books are not just appendages but form a very important layer of tradition that affirms that God made humans *rational and free,* with divine powers of *searching* and *choosing* and behaving ethically. Wisdom writings boost the goodness of being human and seek to explore dimensions of God and the problem of relating to God that troubled everyone. Israel never developed philosophers like the Greeks who exalted human reason as a power that answers to nothing but itself. Israel maintained that the *search* for wisdom *must be done* in awe and fear of the Lord. Greeks were skeptical of how the gods could actually interact with the created world. Israel *never doubted* how active and directly present God was to the world. Israel's wisdom thinkers instead turned the believers' questions and difficult problems of suffering and inequalities among people toward the *mystery of existence.* God's ways were not our ways, and while we can see God at work we cannot understand with our insights the what or why. But covenant love for the one God demanded both proper reverence for divine transcendence and bountiful hope for divine nearness.

---

[13]The Hebrew word *Messiah* (in Greek, *Christos*) means "anointed one." In the Hebrew Scriptures, it refers to a priestly ruler or one who would restore righteousness to the people. In the Christian interpretation, it refers to Jesus.

[14]The Book of Daniel is attributed to a prophet who lived among the Hebrew exiles in Babylonia during the sixth century B.C. Actually written during the second century B.C., it reflects the struggle of the Hebrews to remain faithful to God amid a polytheistic alien culture, and it describes the coming of a messianic savior.

REVIEW QUESTIONS

1. What was the Hebrew conception of the nature of the deity? In what ways did it markedly differ from that of Israel's Near Eastern neighbors?
2. What did the Hebrews believe God demanded of them?
3. How did the concept of covenant contribute to the creation of the Hebrew nation?
4. What was the function of the prophets in Hebrew society? What is the enduring significance of their achievement?

5. Why was the recording of history and adherence to tradition of such importance among the Hebrews?
6. Why did the Hebrews view the world and its future with hope and optimism?
7. How did the knowledge pursued by the Greeks differ from the wisdom sought by the Hebrews?

---

2 ▾ Hebrew Cosmogony and Anthropology

Among the topics treated in Genesis, the first book of the Bible, are God's creation of the universe and human beings, the original human condition in the Garden of Eden, and the origin of evil with Adam and Eve's disobedience of God and their resultant expulsion from Eden.

≪ *GENESIS* ≫

The first three chapters from the book of Genesis follow. The first chapter presents the *cosmogony* and *anthropology* of the Jews. Hebrew cosmogony — that is, their view of the generation of the universe and all that is in it — exemplifies God's majesty and power. Although Genesis is similar to other Near Eastern creation myths, it also sharply breaks with the essential outlook of the time. In Genesis, nature is no longer inhabited by mythical gods, and inanimate objects are not suffused with life. The Hebrews did not worship the moon and stars and mountains and rivers, but they regarded nature as the orderly creation of one supreme and eternal being.

How the Hebrews conceived of the creation of men and women and their position in the universe — the anthropology of the Jews — is dealt with in verses 26–31. The Hebrews' conception of the individual created in God's image and subordinate to nothing except God is as revolutionary as their idea of God, for this conception confers great power and dignity upon human beings.

1 In the beginning God created the heavens and the earth. [2]The earth was without form and void, and darkness was upon the face of the deep; and the Spirit of God was moving over the face of the waters.

3 And God said, "Let there be light"; and there was light. [4]And God saw that the light was good; and God separated the light from the darkness. [5]God called the light Day, and the darkness he called Night. And there was evening and there was morning, one day.

6 And God said, "Let there be a firmanent in the midst of the waters, and let it separate the waters from the waters." [7]And God made the firmament and separated the waters which were under the firmament from the waters which were above the firmament. And it was so. [8]And God called the firmament Heaven. And there was evening and there was morning, a second day.

9 And God said, "Let the waters under the heavens be gathered together into one place, and let the dry land appear." And it was so. [10]God called the dry land Earth, and the waters that were gathered together he called Seas. And God saw that it was good. [11]And God said, "Let the earth put forth vegetation, plants yielding seed, and fruit trees bearing fruit in which is

their seed, each according to its kind, upon the earth." And it was so. [12]The earth brought forth vegetation, plants yielding seed according to their own kinds, and trees bearing fruit in which is their seed, each according to its kind. And God saw that it was good. [13]And there was evening and there was morning, a third day.

14 And God said, "Let there be lights in the firmament of the heavens to separate the day from the night; and let them be for signs and for seasons and for days and years, [15]and let them be lights in the firmament of the heavens to give light upon the earth." And it was so. [16]And God made the two great lights, the greater light to rule the day, and the lesser light to rule the night; he made the stars also. [17]And God set them in the firmament of the heavens to give light upon the earth, [18]to rule over the day and over the night, and to separate the light from the darkness. And God saw that it was good. [19]And there was evening and there was morning, a fourth day.

20 And God said, "Let the waters bring forth swarms of living creatures, and let birds fly above the earth across the firmament of the heavens." [21]So God created the great sea monsters and every living creature that moves, with which the waters swarm, according to their kinds, and every winged bird according to its kind. And God saw that it was good. [22]And God blessed them, saying, "Be fruitful and multiply and fill the waters in the seas, and let birds multiply on the earth." [23]And there was evening and there was morning, a fifth day.

24 And God said, "Let the earth bring forth living creatures according to their kinds: cattle and creeping things and beasts of the earth according to their kinds." And it was so. [25]And God made the beasts of the earth according to their kinds and the cattle according to their kinds, and everything that creeps upon the ground according to its kind. And God saw that it was good.

26 Then God said, "Let us make man in our image, after our likeness; and let them have dominion over the fish of the sea, and over the birds of the air, and over the cattle, and over all the earth, and over every creeping thing that creeps upon the earth." [27]So God created man in his own image, in the image of God he created him; male and female he created them. [28]And God blessed them, and God said to them, "Be fruitful and multiply, and fill the earth and subdue it; and have dominion over the fish of the sea and over the birds of the air and over every living thing that moves upon the earth." [29]And God said, "Behold, I have given you every plant yielding seed which is upon the face of all the earth, and every tree with seed in its fruit; you shall have them for food. [30]And to every beast of the earth, and to every bird of the air, and to everything that creeps on the earth, everything that has the breath of life, I have given every green plant for food." And it was so. [31]And God saw everything that he had made, and behold, it was very good. And there was evening and there was morning, a sixth day.

▷ The second chapter of Genesis contains a retrospective view of the creation of the universe; a second account of man's creation from "the dust of the ground," a description of the Garden of Eden, into which man was placed, with the injunction that he may eat freely of every tree in the garden, except the tree of the knowledge of good and evil, and an account of God's creation of woman from the rib of man as a companion for him. In Genesis, Eden was an idyllic garden, a paradise, in which the first human beings lived. It has been compared to the mythic land of the blessed, Dilmun, described in the Babylonian epic *Gilgamesh.* In Eden, human beings were free of death, illness, pain, and a consciousness of evil, or sin.

---

2 Thus the heavens and the earth were finished, and all the host of them. [2]And on the seventh day God finished his work which he had done, and he rested on the seventh day from all his work which he had done. [3]So God blessed the seventh day and hallowed it, because on it God rested from all his work which he had done in creation.

4 These are the generations of the heavens and the earth when they were created.

In the day that the LORD God made the earth and the heavens, [5]when no plant of the field was yet in the earth and no herb of the field had yet sprung up — for the LORD God had not caused it to rain upon the earth, and there was no man to till the ground; [6]but a mist went up from the earth and watered the whole face of the ground — [7]then the LORD God formed man of dust from the ground, and breathed into his nostrils the breath of life; and man became a living being. [8]And the LORD God planted a garden in Eden, in the east; and there he put the man whom he had formed. [9]And out of the ground the LORD God made to grow every tree that is pleasant to the sight and good for food, the tree of life also in the midst of the garden, and the tree of the knowledge of good and evil. . . .

15 The LORD God took the man and put him in the garden of Eden to till it and keep it. [16]And the LORD God commanded the man, saying, "You may freely eat of every tree of the garden; [17]but of the tree of the knowledge of good and evil you shall not eat, for in the day that you eat of it you shall die."

18 Then the LORD God said, "It is not good that the man should be alone; I will make him a helper fit for him." [19]So out of the ground the LORD God formed every beast of the field and every bird of the air, and brought them to the man to see what he would call them; and whatever the man called every living creature, that was its name. [20]The man gave names to all cattle, and to the birds of the air, and to every beast of the field; but for the man there was not found a helper fit for him. [21]So the LORD God caused a deep sleep to fall upon the man, and while he slept took one of his ribs and closed up its place with flesh; [22]and the rib which the LORD God had taken from the man he made into a woman and brought her to the man. [23]Then the man said,

"This at last is bone of my bones
  and flesh of my flesh;
she shall be called Woman,
  because she was taken out of Man."

[24]Therefore a man leaves his father and his mother and cleaves to his wife, and they become one flesh. [25]And the man and his wife were both naked, and were not ashamed.

▷ The third chapter of Genesis deals with the origin of evil. When Adam and Eve disobeyed God by eating from the tree of knowledge, they were driven from the Garden of Eden. For the Hebrews the expulsion from paradise marks the beginning of human history, suffering, and death. This passage provides one of the fundamental explanations of evil in the Western tradition, the Judaic conception, later to be refashioned by Saint Paul into the Christian notion of original sin. The language of the biblical narrative is naive and framed in mythic imagery, but the ideas present are timeless.

---

3 Now the serpent was more subtle than any other wild creature that the LORD God had made. He said to the woman, "Did God say, 'You shall not eat of any tree of the garden'?" [2]And the woman said to the serpent, "We may eat of the fruit of the trees of the garden; [3]but God said, 'You shall not eat of the fruit of the tree which is in the midst of the garden, neither shall you touch it, lest you die.'" [4]But the serpent said to the woman, "You will not die. [5]For God knows that when you eat of it your eyes will be opened, and you will be like God, knowing good and evil." [6]So when the woman saw that the tree was good for food, and that it was a delight to the eyes, and that the tree was to be desired to make one wise, she took of its fruit and ate; and she also gave some to her husband, and he ate. [7]Then the eyes of both were opened, and they knew that they were naked; and they sewed fig leaves together and made themselves aprons.

8 And they heard the sound of the LORD God walking in the garden in the cool of the day, and the man and his wife hid themselves from the presence of the LORD God among the trees of the garden. [9]But the LORD God called to the man, and said to him, "Where are you?" [10]And he said, "I heard the sound of thee in the garden, and I was afraid, because I was naked; and I hid myself." [11]He said, "Who told you that you were naked? Have you eaten of the tree of

which I commanded you not to eat?" [12]The man
said, "The woman whom thou gavest to be with
me, she gave me fruit of the tree, and I ate."
[13]Then the LORD God said to the woman,
"What is this that you have done?" The woman
said, "The serpent beguiled me, and I ate."
[14]The LORD God said to the serpent,

"Because you have done this,
cursed are you above all cattle,
and above all wild animals;
upon your belly you shall go,
and dust you shall eat
all the days of your life.

[15]I will put enmity between you and the
woman,
and between your seed and her seed;
he shall bruise your head,
and you shall bruise his heel."

[16]To the woman he said,

"I will greatly multiply your pain in
childbearing;
in pain you shall bring forth children,
yet your desire shall be for your husband,
and he shall rule over you."

[17]And to Adam he said,

"Because you have listened to the voice of
your wife,
and have eaten of the tree
of which I commanded you,
'You shall not eat of it,'
cursed is the ground because of you;
in toil you shall eat of it all the days of
your life;

[18]thorns and thistles it shall bring forth to you;
and you shall eat the plants of the field.

[19]In the sweat of your face
you shall eat bread
till you return to the ground,
for out of it you were taken;
you are dust,
and to dust you shall return."

20 The man called his wife's name Eve, because she was the mother of all living. [21]And
the LORD God made for Adam and for his wife
garments of skins, and clothed them.

22 Then the LORD God said, "Behold, the
man has become like one of us, knowing good
and evil; and now, lest he put forth his hand
and take also of the tree of life, and eat, and
live for ever" — [23]therefore the LORD God sent
him forth from the garden of Eden, to till the
ground from which he was taken. [24]He drove
out the man; and at the east of the garden of
Eden he placed the cherubim [winged angels],
and a flaming sword which turned every way,
to guard the way to the tree of life.

REVIEW QUESTIONS

1. What was the Hebrew view of the origin and the worth of the created world?
2. What was the Hebrew view of humanity's role in the world?
3. What was the relationship established between the Creator and the first man and woman?
4. What does the story of Adam and Eve reveal about the Hebrew conception of good and evil?
5. Compare the Mesopotamian account of the origin of the world with that found in the book of Genesis.
6. Compare the Mesopotamian concept of the role of human beings in relation to the gods with that suggested by the Hebrew book of Genesis.

3 ▾ God's Greatness and Human Dignity

The Hebrew view of God produced a concept of human dignity. In God's plan for the universe, the Hebrews believed, human beings are the highest creation,

subordinate only to God. Of all God's creatures, only they have been given the freedom to choose between good and evil. To human beings God granted dominion over the earth and the seas.

The Psalms in the Hebrew Scriptures contain 150 hymns extolling Yahweh, some of them written by King David, who ruled c. 1000–961 B.C. In addition to his great success as a warrior and administrator, David was renowned as a harpist and composer.

≪ *PSALM 8* ≫

In the following song, the psalmist rejoices in the greatness of God and marvels in the Lord's love for human beings, expressed in God's having given them dominion over the earth and its creatures.

O LORD, our Lord,
how majestic is thy name in all the earth!

Thou whose glory above the heavens is chanted
2 by the mouth of babes and infants,
thou hast founded a bulwark because of thy foes,
to still the enemy and the avenger.

3 When I look at thy heavens, the work of thy fingers,
the moon and the stars which thou hast established;
4 what is man that thou art mindful of him,
and the son of man that thou dost care for him?
5 Yet thou hast made him little less than God,
and dost crown him with glory and honor.
6 Thou hast given him dominion over the works of thy hands;
thou hast put all things under his feet,
7 all sheep and oxen,
and also the beasts of the field,
8 the birds of the air, and the fish of the sea,
whatever passes along the paths of the sea.

9 O LORD, our Lord,
how majestic is thy name in all the earth!

≪ *PSALM 104* ≫

Psalm 104 praises God's majesty and lauds him for the wonders of his creation — the earth and all its creatures.

Bless, the LORD, O my soul!
O LORD my God, thou art very great!
Thou art clothed with honor and majesty,
2 who coverest thyself with light as with a garment,
who hast stretched out the heavens like a tent,
3 who hast laid the beams of thy chambers on the waters,
who makest the clouds thy chariot,
who ridest on the wings of the wind,
4 who makest the winds thy messengers,
fire and flame thy ministers.
5 Thou didst set the earth on its foundations,
so that it should never be shaken.
6 Thou didst cover it with the deep as with a garment;
the waters stood above the mountains.
7 At thy rebuke they fled;
at the sound of thy thunder they took to flight.

8 The mountains rose, the valleys sank down
to the place which thou didst appoint for them.
9 Thou didst set a bound which they should not pass,
so that they might not again cover the earth.

10 Thou makest springs gush forth in the valleys;
they flow between the hills,
11 they give drink to every beast of the field;
the wild asses quench their thirst.
12 By them the birds of the air have their habitation;
they sing among the branches.
13 From thy lofty abode thou waterest the mountains;
the earth is satisfied with the fruit of thy work.

14 Thou dost cause the grass to grow for the cattle,
and plants for man to cultivate,
that he may bring forth food from the earth,
15 and wine to gladden the heart of man,
oil to make his face shine,
and bread to strengthen man's heart.
16 The trees of the LORD are watered abundantly,
the cedars of Lebanon which he planted.
17 In them the birds build their nests;
the stork has her home in the fir trees.
18 The high mountains are for the wild goats;
the rocks are a refuge for the badgers.
19 Thou hast made the moon to mark the seasons;
the sun knows its time for setting.
20 Thou makest darkness, and it is night,
when all the beasts of the forest creep forth.
21 The young lions roar for their prey,
seeking their food from God.
22 When the sun rises, they get them away
and lie down in their dens.
23 Man goes forth to his work
and to his labor until the evening.
24 O LORD, how manifold are thy works!
In wisdom hast thou made them all;
the earth is full of thy creatures.
25 Yonder is the sea, great and wide,
which teems with things innumerable,
living things both small and great.
26 There go the ships,
and Leviathan [a sea monster]
which thou didst form to sport in it.

27 These all look to thee,
to give them their food in due season.
28 When thou givest to them, they gather it up;
when thou openest thy hand, they are filled with good things.
29 When thou hidest thy face, they are dismayed;
when thou takest away their breath, they die
and return to their dust.
30 When thou sendest forth thy Spirit, they are created;
and thou renewest the face of the ground.

31 May the glory of the LORD endure for ever,
may the LORD rejoice in his works,
32 who looks on the earth and it trembles,
who touches the mountains and they smoke!
33 I will sing to the LORD as long as I live;
I will sing praise to my God while I have being.
34 May my meditation be pleasing to him,
for I rejoice in the LORD.
35 Let sinners be consumed from the earth,
and let the wicked be no more!
Bless the LORD, O my soul!
Praise the LORD!

REVIEW QUESTIONS

1. What do the psalms reveal about the Hebrew view of God? Of human beings? Of nature?
2. Compare Psalm 104 with Akhenaten's Hymn to Aton (pages 19–20).

4 ▾ The Covenant and the Ten Commandments

Central to Hebrew religious thought was the covenant that the Hebrews believed had been made between God and themselves. The Hebrews believed that God had chosen them to be the first recipients of his law. They did not hold that this honor was bestowed on them because they were better than other nations or that they had done something special to earn it. Rather they viewed the covenant as an awesome responsibility; God had chosen them to set an example of righteous behavior to the other nations.

≪ *EXODUS* ≫
THE COVENANT

As described in Exodus, the Israelite leader Moses received the covenant on Mount Sinai at the time of the Hebrews' flight from Egypt and wanderings in the wilderness of the Sinai Desert.

3 And Moses went up to God, and the LORD
called him out of the mountain, saying, "Thus
you shall say to the house of Jacob, and tell the
people of Israel: 4 You have seen what I did to
the Egyptians, and how I bore you on eagles'
wings and brought you to myself. 5 Now therefore, if you will obey my voice and keep
my covenant, you shall be my own possession among all peoples; for all the earth is
mine, 6 and you shall be to me a kingdom of
priests and a holy nation. These are the words
which you shall speak to the children of Israel."
7 So Moses came and called the elders of the
people, and set before them all these words
which the LORD had commanded him. 8 And all
the people answered together and said, "All
that the LORD has spoken we will do." And
Moses reported the words of the people to the
LORD. 9 And the LORD said to Moses, "Lo, I am
coming to you in a thick cloud, that the people
may hear when I speak with you, and may also
believe you for ever." (Exodus 19)

≪ *EXODUS* ≫
THE TEN COMMANDMENTS

Together with the covenant, Moses received the Ten Commandments, which specified God's moral laws. Chapter 20 sets forth the Ten Commandments.

17 Then Moses brought the people out of the
camp to meet God; and they took their stand
at the foot of the mountain. 18 And Mount Sinai
was wrapped in smoke, because the LORD descended upon it in fire; and the smoke of it
went up like the smoke of a kiln, and the whole
mountain quaked greatly. 19 And as the sound of
the trumpet grew louder and louder, Moses
spoke, and God answered him in thunder.
20 And the LORD came down upon Mount Sinai,

to the top of the mountain; and the LORD called Moses to the top of the mountain, and Moses went up. . . .

20 And God spoke all these words, saying,

2 "I am the LORD your God, who brought you out of the land of Egypt, out of the house of bondage.

3 "You shall have no other gods before me.

4 "You shall not make yourself a graven image, or any likeness of anything that is in heaven above, or that is in the earth beneath, or that is in the water under the earth; [5]you shall not bow down to them or serve them; for I the LORD your God am a jealous God, visiting the iniquity of the fathers upon the children to the third and the fourth generation of those who hate me, [6]but showing steadfast love to thousands of those who love me and keep my commandments.

7 "You shall not take the name of the LORD your God in vain; for the LORD will not hold him guiltless who takes his name in vain.

8 "Remember the sabbath day, to keep it holy. [9]Six days you shall labor, and do all your work; [10]but the seventh day is a sabbath to the LORD your God; in it you shall not do any work, you, or your son, or your daughter, your manservant, or your maidservant, or your cattle, or the sojourner who is within your gates; [11]for in six days the LORD made heaven and earth, the sea, and all that is in them, and rested the seventh day; therefore the LORD blessed the sabbath day and hallowed it.

12 "Honor your father and your mother, that your days may be long in the land which the LORD your God gives you.

13 "You shall not kill.

14 "You shall not commit adultery.

15 "You shall not steal.

16 "You shall not bear false witness against your neighbor.

17 "You shall not covet your neighbor's house; you shall not covet your neighbor's wife, or his manservant, or his maidservant, or his ox, or his ass, or anything that is your neighbor's."

18 Now when all the people perceived the thunderings and the lightnings and the sound of the trumpet and the mountain smoking, the people were afraid and trembled; and they stood afar off, [19]and said to Moses, "You speak to us, and we will hear; but let not God speak to us, lest we die." [20]And Moses said to the people, "Do not fear; for God has come to prove you, and that the fear of him may be before your eyes, that you may not sin."

21 And the people stood afar off, while Moses drew near to the thick cloud where God was.

REVIEW QUESTIONS

1. In Exodus, what did God promise the Hebrews if they entered into a covenant with him?
2. According to Exodus, what specific requirements did God set with respect to the Hebrews' conduct toward him? Toward other human beings?

---

5 ▾ Humaneness of Hebrew Law

The new awareness of the individual that was produced by the Hebrew concept of God found expression in Hebrew law, which was recorded in the Torah, the first five books of the Scriptures. For the Hebrews, the source of law was, of

course, God, and because God is good, his law must be concerned with human welfare. Israelite law incorporated the legal codes and oral traditions of the older civilizations of the Near East. In contrast to the other law codes of the Near East, however, Hebrew laws were more concerned with people than with property; they expressed a humane attitude toward slaves and rejected the idea (so clearly demonstrated in the Code of Hammurabi) of one law for nobles and another for commoners.

≪ LEVITICUS ≫
NEIGHBOR AND COMMUNITY

To the Hebrews, laws governing economic, social, and political relationships gave practical expression to God's universal standards of morality. Leviticus, the third book in the Scriptures, contains laws governing actions dealing with neighbors and the community.

9 "When you reap the harvest of your land, you
shall not reap your field to its very border, neither shall you gather the gleanings after your
harvest. [10]And you shall not strip your vineyard
bare, neither shall you gather the fallen grapes
of your vineyard; you shall leave them for the
poor and for the sojourner: I am the LORD
your God.
11 "You shall not steal, nor deal falsely, nor
lie to one another. [12]And you shall not swear by
my name falsely, and so profane the name of
your God: I am the LORD.
13 "You shall not oppress your neighbor or
rob him. The wages of a hired servant shall not
remain with you all night until the morning.
[14]You shall not curse the deaf or put a stumbling block before the blind, but you shall fear
your God: I am the LORD.
15 "You shall do no injustice in judgment;
you shall not be partial to the poor or defer to
the great, but in righteousness shall you judge
your neighbor. [16]You shall not go up and down
as a slanderer among your people, and you shall
not stand forth against the life of your neighbor: I am the LORD.
17 "You shall not hate your brother in your
heart, but you shall reason with your neighbor,
lest you bear sin because of him. [18]You shall not
take vengeance or bear any grudge against the
sons of your own people, but you shall love your
neighbor as yourself: I am the LORD. . . .
33 "When a stranger sojourns with you in
your land, you shall not do him wrong. [34]The
stranger who sojourns with you shall be to you
as the native among you, and you shall love him
as yourself. . . ." (Leviticus 19)

≪ DEUTERONOMY ≫
JUDGES, WITNESSES, AND JUSTICE

The book of Deuteronomy was composed in the seventh century B.C., some six centuries after the exodus from Egypt. Written as though it were a last speech of Moses advising the people how to govern themselves as they entered the land of Canaan, Deuteronomy reflects the new problems faced by the Hebrews who had already established a kingdom and lived in a settled urban society. In

presenting their reform program, the authors of Deuteronomy linked their message to the authority of Moses. The central theme of these verses is the attainment of justice.

18 "You shall appoint judges and officers in all your towns which the LORD your God gives you, according to your tribes; and they shall judge the people with righteous judgment. [19]You shall not pervert justice; you shall not show partiality; and you shall not take a bribe, for a bribe blinds the eyes of the wise and subverts the cause of the righteous. [20]Justice, and only justice, you shall follow, that you may live and inherit the land which the LORD your God gives you. . . ." (Deuteronomy 16)

15 "A single witness shall not prevail against a man for any crime or for any wrong in connection with any offence that he has committed; only on the evidence of two witnesses, or of three witnesses, shall a charge be sustained. [16]If a malicious witness rises against any man to accuse him of wrongdoing, [17]then both parties to the dispute shall appear before the LORD, before the priests and the judges who are in office in those days; [18]the judges shall inquire diligently, and if the witness is a false witness and has accused his brother falsely, [19]then you shall do to him as he had meant to do to his brother; so you shall purge the evil from the midst of you. . . ." (Deuteronomy 19)

15 "You shall not give up to his master a slave who has escaped from his master to you; [16]he shall dwell with you, in your midst, in the place which he shall choose within one of your towns, where it pleases him best; you shall not oppress him. . . ." (Deuteronomy 23)

14 "You shall not oppress a hired servant who is poor and needy, whether he is one of your brethren or one of the sojourners who are in your land within your towns; [15]you shall give him his hire on the day he earns it, before the sun goes down (for he is poor, and sets his heart upon it); lest he cry against you to the LORD, and it be sin in you.

16 "The fathers shall not be put to death for the children, nor shall the children be put to death for the fathers; every man shall be put to death for his own sin.

17 "You shall not pervert the justice due to the sojourner or to the fatherless, or take a widow's garment in pledge; [18]but you shall remember that you were a slave in Egypt and the LORD your God redeemed you from there; therefore I command you to do this.

19 "When you reap your harvest in your field, and have forgotten a sheaf in the field, you shall not go back to get it; it shall be for the sojourner, the fatherless, and the widow; that the LORD your God may bless you in all the work of your hands. [20]When you beat your olive trees, you shall not go over the boughs again; it shall be for the sojourner, the fatherless, and the widow. [21]When you gather the grapes of your vineyard, you shall not glean it afterward; it shall be for the sojourner, the fatherless, and the widow. [22]You shall remember that you were a slave in the land of Egypt; therefore I command you to do this. . . ." (Deuteronomy 24).

REVIEW QUESTIONS

1. Show how an awareness of justice pervaded Hebrew law.
2. According to the law, how were family members and neighbors to be treated?
3. What judicial procedures were followed to ensure a fair hearing in a court of law?
4. What was the attitude of the Hebrew law toward slaves and foreigners residing among the Hebrews?
5. What did the law require respecting the needs of the poor, widows, and orphans?

6 ▾ The Age of Classical Prophecy

Ancient Jewish history was marked by the rise of prophets — spiritually inspired persons who believed that God had chosen them to remind the Jews of their duties to God and his law. These prophets carried God's message to the leaders and the people and warned of divine punishments for disobedience to God's commandments.

The prophetic movement — the age of classical prophecy — which emerged in the eighth century B.C., creatively expanded Hebrew religious thought. Prophets denounced exploitation of the poor, the greed of the wealthy, and the oppressive behavior of the powerful as a betrayal of Yahweh, a violation of his moral laws. They insisted that the core of Hebrew faith was not ritual but morality. Their concern for the poor and their attack on injustice received reemphasis in the Christian faith and thus became incorporated into the Western ideal of social justice.

≪ *ISAIAH* ≫
SOCIAL JUSTICE

The prophets' insistence that rituals were not the essence of the law and their passion for righteousness are voiced in the Scriptures by Isaiah of Jerusalem, who lived in the mid-eighth century B.C. Scholars agree that Isaiah of Jerusalem did not write all sixty-six chapters that make up the Book of Isaiah. Some material appears to have been written by his disciples and interpreters, and Chapters 40 to 55, composed two centuries later, are attributed to a person given the name Second Isaiah. The following verses come from Isaiah of Jerusalem.

11"What to me is the multitude of your
sacrifices?
says the LORD;
I have had enough of burnt offerings of rams
and the fat of fed beasts;
I do not delight in the blood of bulls,
or of lambs, or of he-goats.

12When you come to appear before me,
who requires of you
this trampling of my courts?*
13Bring no more vain offerings;
incense is an abomination to me.
New moon and sabbath and the calling of
assemblies —
I cannot endure iniquity and solemn
assembly.
14Your new moons and your appointed feasts
my soul hates;
they have become a burden to me,
I am weary of bearing them.
15When you spread forth your hands,
I will hide my eyes from you;
even though you make many prayers,
I will not listen;
your hands are full of blood.
16Wash yourselves; make yourselves clean;
remove the evil of your doings
from before my eyes;
cease to do evil,

*In the New English Bible, this passage appears as follows:
"who asked you for this?
No more shall you trample my courts."

[17] learn to do good;
seek justice,
correct oppression;
defend the fatherless,
plead for the widow.
(Isaiah 1)

▷ Isaiah denounced the rich and the powerful for exploiting the poor.

[13]The LORD has taken his place to contend,
he stands to judge his people.
[14]The LORD enters into judgment
with the elders and princes of his people:
"It is you who have devoured the vineyard,
the spoil of the poor is in your houses.
[15]What do you mean by crushing my people,
by grinding the face of the poor?"
says the Lord GOD of hosts.
(Isaiah 3)

≪ *SECOND ISAIAH* ≫ *THE ATTACK ON IDOLATRY*

Many books in the Hebrew Scriptures contain attacks on idolatry — the making and worship of idols or images — a common practice in the Near East. Condemnations of idolatry often appear in the Scriptures together with statements of God's uniqueness and greatness (see Exodus 20:2–5, page 40). The Scriptures warn the Hebrews that lapsing into idol worship breaches the covenant and defies Yahweh. Psalmists and prophets were appalled that other peoples of the Near East worshiped stone and wood idols and served them. When people worship these human creations, said the prophets, they diminish themselves; they become morally dead like the objects they themselves made. Later Jewish and Christian thinkers have viewed this attack on idol worship as a liberating act; it implies that God decries the deification not only of man-made objects but also of human beings, human institutions, and human aspirations. Second Isaiah ridiculed the belief that idols are divine and described the self-delusion of those who fashion and worship these images.

9 All who make idols are nothing, and the
things they delight in do not profit; their witnesses neither see nor know, that they may be
put to shame. [10]Who fashions a god or casts an
image, that is profitable for nothing? [11]Behold,
all his fellows shall be put to shame, and the
craftsmen are but men; let them all assemble,
let them stand forth, they shall be terrified,
they shall be put to shame together.

12 The ironsmith fashions it and works it
over the coals; he shapes it with hammers, and
forges it with his strong arm; he becomes hungry and his strength fails, he drinks no water
and is faint. [13]The carpenter stretches a line, he
marks it out with a pencil; he fashions it with
planes, and marks it with a compass; he shapes
it into the figure of a man, with the beauty of
a man, to dwell in a house. [14]He cuts down
cedars; or he chooses a holm tree* or an oak and
lets it grow strong among the trees of the forest;
he plants a cedar and the rain nourishes it.
[15]Then it becomes fuel for a man; he takes a part
of it and warms himself, he kindles a fire and
bakes bread; also he makes a god and worships
it, he makes it a graven image and falls down
before it. [16]Half of it he burns in the fire; over
the half he eats flesh, he roasts meat and is satisfied; also he warms himself and says, "Aha, I
am warm, I have seen the fire!" [17]And the rest

*"Holm tree" means a tree that is growing near water, in low land. — Ed.

of it he makes into a god, his idol; and falls down to it and worships it; he prays to it and says, "Deliver me, for thou art my god!"

18 They know not, nor do they discern; for he has shut their eyes, so that they cannot see, and their minds, so that they cannot understand. [19]No one considers, nor is there knowledge or discernment to say, Half of it I burned in the fire, I also baked bread on its coals, I roasted flesh and have eaten; and shall I make the residue of it an abomination? Shall I fall down before a block of wood? [20]He feeds on ashes; a deluded mind has led him astray, and he cannot deliver himself or say, "Is there not a lie in my right hand?" (Isaiah 44)

≪ *ISAIAH* ≫ *PEACE AND HUMANITY*

Isaiah of Jerusalem envisioned the unity of all people under God. This universalism drew out the full implications of Hebrew monotheism. In Isaiah's vision all peoples would live together in peace and harmony. Some of these lines are inscribed on the building that houses the United Nations in New York City.

[2]It shall come to pass in the latter days
that the mountain of the house of the LORD
shall be established as the highest of the mountains,
and shall be raised above the hills;
and all the nations shall flow to it,
[3] and many peoples shall come, and say:
"Come, let us go up to the mountain of the LORD,
to the house of the God of Jacob;
that he may teach us his ways
and that we may walk in his paths."
For out of Zion shall go forth the law,
and the word of the LORD from Jerusalem.
[4]He shall judge between the nations,
and shall decide for many peoples;
and they shall beat their swords into plowshares,
and their spears into pruning hooks;
nation shall not lift up sword against nation,
neither shall they learn war any more.
(Isaiah 2)

REVIEW QUESTIONS

1. What were some of the ritual acts and ceremonies practiced by the Hebrews?
2. What was the prophets' attitude toward rituals?
3. The prophets' ideas transmitted through Christianity formed the basis for the Western conception of social justice. Discuss this statement.
4. How did the Hebrew prophets view idols and those who made them?
5. What did Isaiah say about those who worshiped idols?
6. What does the concept *humanity* mean? The Hebrew prophets are one source of the idea of humanity. Discuss this statement.

The Greeks

Hebrew ethical monotheism, which gave value to the individual, is one source of Western civilization. Another source came from the ancient Greeks, who originated scientific and philosophic thought, created democracy, and developed a humanistic outlook. From about 750 B.C. to 338 B.C. the Greek world consisted of small, independent, and self-governing city-states. Within this political-social context, the Greeks made their outstanding contributions to civilization.

In contrast to the Egyptians and Mesopotamians, the Greeks developed rational-scientific, rather than mythical, interpretations of nature and the human community. In trying to understand nature, Greek philosophers proposed physical explanations: that is, they gradually omitted the gods from their accounts of how nature came to be the way it is. Greek intellectuals also analyzed government, law, and ethics in logical and systematic ways. It was the great achievement of Greek thinkers to rise above magic, miracles, mystery, and custom and to assert that reason was the avenue to knowledge. The emergence of rational attitudes did not, of course, end traditional religion, particularly for the peasants, who remained devoted to their ancient cults, gods, and shrines. But what distinguishes the Greeks is that alongside an older religious-mythical tradition arose a philosophic-scientific view of the natural world and human culture.

The Greeks, who defined human beings by their capacity to use reason, also declared the principle of political liberty. Egyptians and Mesopotamians were subject to the authority of god-kings and priest-kings; the common people did not participate in political life, and there was no awareness of individual liberty. In contrast, many Greek city-states, particularly Athens, developed democratic institutions and attitudes. In the middle of the fifth century B.C., when Athenian democracy was at its height, adult male citizens were eligible to hold public office and were equal before the law; in the assembly, which met some forty times a year, they debated and voted on the key issues of state. Whereas Mesopotamians and Egyptians believed that law had been given to them by the gods, the Greeks came to understand that law was a human creation, a product of human reason. The Athenians abhorred rule by absolute rulers and held

BRONZE HEAD FROM HERCULANEUM, Roman city buried by the eruption of Mount Vesuvius in 79 A.D. The sculpture, a Roman copy of a Greek original, c. 250 B.C., is believed to be the Greek philosopher Democritus of Abdera, propounder of atomic theory. (*Alinari/Art Resource, N.Y.*)

that people can govern themselves. While expressing admiration for the Greek political achievement, modern critics also point out several limitations of Greek democracy, notably slavery and the inability of women to participate in political life.

The Greeks originated the Western humanist tradition. They valued the human personality and sought the full cultivation of human talent. In the Greek view, a man of worth pursued excellence: that is, he sought to mold himself in accordance with the highest standards and ideals. Greek art, for example, made the human form the focal point of attention and exalted the nobility, dignity, self-assurance, and beauty of the human being.

Greek culture has a distinctive style that enables us to see it as an organic whole. To the English classicist H. D. F. Kitto, the common thread that runs through Greek philosophy, literature, and art is "a sense of the wholeness of things" — the conviction that the universe contains an inherent order, that law governs both nature and human affairs, and that this law can be comprehended by human reason.

Although the Greek city-states shared a common culture, they frequently warred with each other. Particularly ruinous was the Peloponnesian War (431–404 B.C.) between Athens and Sparta and their allies. The drawn-out conflict, marked by massacres and civil wars within city-states, shattered the Greek world spiritually. Increasingly, a narrow individualism and worsening factional disputes weakened the bonds of community within the various city-states. Moreover, learning little from the Peloponnesian War, the Greeks continued their internecine conflicts. Finally, by 338 B.C. the weakened city-states were conquered by Philip II of Macedonia, a kingdom to the north of Greece. Although the Greek cities continued to exist, they had lost their political independence; Greek civilization was entering a new phase.

Philip's famous son, Alexander the Great, a romantic adventurer and brilliant commander, inherited the Macedonian kingdom and conquered the vast Persian Empire. After Alexander died in 323 B.C. at the age of thirty-two, his generals could not hold together the empire, which extended from Egypt to the frontiers of India. By 275 B.C. it was broken into three parts, each named for a dynasty: the Ptolemies in Egypt, the Seleucids in Asia, and the Antigonids in Macedonia and Greece. The rulers of these kingdoms were Macedonians, and their generals and high officials were Greek; the style of government, not in the democratic tradition of the Greek city-states, was modeled after the absolute rule by priest-kings and god-kings typical of the Near East.

Alexander's conquest of the Near East marks a second stage in the evolution of Greek civilization (Hellenism). The first stage, the *Hellenic Age,* began about 800 B.C. with the earliest city-states and lasted until Alexander's death; at that time Greek civilization entered the *Hellenistic Age,* which lasted until 30 B.C., when Egypt, the last Hellenistic kingdom, lost its independence to Rome.

The Hellenistic Age inherited many cultural achievements of the earlier Hellenic Age, but crucial differences exist between the two eras. The self-sufficient and independent *polis* (city-state), the center of life in the Hellenic Age, was diminished in power and importance by larger political units, kingdoms headed by absolute monarchs. Although Greek cities continued to exercise considerable control over domestic affairs, they had lost to powerful monarchs their freedom of action in foreign affairs.

A second characteristic of the Hellenistic Age was cosmopolitanism, an intermingling of peoples and cultural traditions. In the Hellenic Age, the Greeks had drawn a sharp distinction between Greek and non-Greek. In the wake of Alexander's conquests, however, thousands of Greek soldiers, merchants, and administrators settled in Near Eastern lands, bringing with them Greek language, customs, and culture. Many upper-class citizens of Near Eastern cities, regardless of their ethnic backgrounds, came under the influence of Greek civilization. At the same time, Mesopotamian, Egyptian, and Persian ways, particularly religious practices and beliefs, spread westward into regions under the sway of Greek civilization.

---

1 ▾ Homer, The Educator of Greece

The poet Homer, who probably lived during the eighth century B.C., helped shape the Greek outlook. His great epics, *The Iliad* and *The Odyssey,* contain the embryo of the Greek humanist tradition: the concern with man and his achievements. "To strive always for excellence and to surpass all others" — in these words lies the essence of the Homeric hero's outlook. In the warrior-aristocratic world of Homer, excellence is primarily interpreted as bravery and skill in battle. The Homeric hero is driven to demonstrate his prowess, to assert himself, to win honor, and to earn a reputation.

The Iliad deals in poetic form with the Trojan War, which probably was waged in the thirteenth century B.C., between the Mycenaean Greeks and the Trojans of Asia Minor. At the outset Homer states his theme: the wrath of

Achilles that brought so much suffering to the Greeks. Agamemnon, their king, has deprived the great warrior Achilles of his rightful prize, the captive girl Briseis. Achilles will not submit to this grave insult to his honor and refuses to join the Greeks in combat against the Trojans. In this way he intends to make Agamemnon pay for his arrogance, for without the Greeks' greatest warrior, Agamemnon will have no easy victories. With Achilles on the sidelines, the Greeks suffer severe losses.

Destiny is at work: the "wicked arrogance" of Agamemnon and the "ruinous wrath" of Achilles have caused suffering and death among the Greek forces. For Homer, human existence has a pattern — a universal plan governs human affairs. People, even the gods, operate within a certain unalterable framework; their deeds are subject to the demands of destiny or necessity. Later Greek thinkers would express this idea of a universal order in philosophic and scientific terms.

Homer
≪ THE ILIAD ≫

The following passages from *The Iliad* demonstrate the Homeric ideal of excellence. In the first, Hector of Troy, son of King Priam, prepares for battle. Hector's wife Andromache pleads with him to stay within the city walls, but Hector, in the tradition of the Homeric hero, feels compelled to engage in combat to show his worth and gain honor.

Hector looked at his son and smiled, but said nothing. Andromache, bursting into tears, went up to him and put her hand in his. "Hector," she said, "you are possessed. This bravery of yours will be your end. You do not think of your little boy or your unhappy wife, whom you will make a widow soon. Some day the Achaeans [Greeks] are bound to kill you in a massed attack. And when I lose you I might as well be dead. There will be no comfort left, when you have met your doom — nothing but grief. I have no father, no mother, now. My father fell to the great Achilles when he sacked our lovely town, Cilician Thebe[1] of the High Gates. . . . I had seven brothers too at home. In one day all of them went down to Hades' House.[2] The great Achilles of the swift feet killed them all. . . .

"So you, Hector, are father and mother and brother to me, as well as my beloved husband. Have pity on me now; stay here on the tower; and do not make your boy an orphan and your wife a widow. . . ."

"All that, my dear," said the great Hector of the glittering helmet, "is surely my concern. But if I hid myself like a coward and refused to fight, I could never face the Trojans and the Trojan ladies in their trailing gowns. Besides, it would go against the grain, for I have trained myself always, like a good soldier, to take my place in the front line and win glory for my father and myself. . . ."

As he finished, glorious Hector held out his arms to take his boy. But the child shrank back with a cry to the bosom of his girdled nurse, alarmed by his father's appearance. He was frightened by the bronze of the helmet and the horsehair plume that he saw nodding grimly down at him. His father and his lady mother had to laugh. But noble Hector quickly took

[1]The Cilicians were a tribe of Asia Minor; Thebe (Thebes) was one of their cities.

[2]Hades refers both to the god of the underworld and to the underworld itself.

his helmet off and put the dazzling thing on the ground. Then he kissed his son, dandled him in his arms, and prayed to Zeus [the chief god] and the other gods: "Zeus, and you other gods, grant that this boy of mine may be, like me, pre-eminent in Troy; as strong and brave as I; a mighty king of Ilium [Troy]. May people say, when he comes back from battle, 'Here is a better man than his father.' Let him bring home the bloodstained armour of the enemy he has killed, and make his mother happy."

Hector handed the boy to his wife, who took him to her fragrant breast. She was smiling through her tears, and when her husband saw this he was moved. He stroked her with his hand and said: "My dear, I beg you not to be too much distressed. No one is going to send me down to Hades before my proper time. But Fate is a thing that no man born of woman, coward or hero, can escape. Go home now, and attend to your own work, the loom and the spindle, and see that the maidservants get on with theirs. War is men's business; and this war is the business of every man in Ilium, myself above all."

▷ Many brave Greek warriors die in battle, including Achilles' best friend Patroclus, slain by the Trojan Hector. Achilles now sets aside his quarrel with Agamemnon (who has appealed to Achilles) and joins the battle. King Priam urges his son not to fight the mighty Achilles, but Hector, despite his fears, faces Achilles and meets his death. In this passage, the grief-stricken Priam goes to Achilles and requests Hector's body. Achilles responds with compassion. This scene shows that although Homer sees the essence of life as the pursuit of glory, he is also sensitive to life's brevity and to the suffering that pervades human existence.

. . . Big though Priam was, he came in unobserved, went up to Achilles, grasped his knees and kissed his hands, the terrible, man-killing hands that had slaughtered many of his sons. Achilles was astounded when he saw King Priam, and so were all his men. . . .

But Priam was already praying to Achilles. "Most worshipful Achilles," he said, "think of your own father, who is the same age as I, and so has nothing but miserable old age ahead of him. No doubt his neighbours are oppressing him and there is nobody to save him from their depredations. Yet he at least has one consolation. While he knows that you are still alive, he can look forward day by day to seeing his beloved son come back from Troy; whereas my fortunes are completely broken. I had the best sons in the whole of this broad realm, and now not one, not one I say, is left. There were fifty when the Achaean expedition came. Nineteen of them were borne by one mother and the rest by other ladies in my palace. Most of them have fallen in action, and Hector, the only one I still could count on, the bulwark of Troy and the Trojans, has now been killed by you, fighting for his native land. It is to get him back from you that I have come to the Achaean ships, bringing this princely ransom with me. Achilles, fear the gods, and be merciful to me, remembering your own father, though I am even more entitled to compassion, since I have brought myself to do a thing that no one else on earth has done — I have raised to my lips the hand of the man who killed my son."

Priam had set Achilles thinking of his own father and brought him to the verge of tears. Taking the old man's hand, he gently put him from him; and overcome by their memories they both broke down. Priam, crouching at Achilles' feet, wept bitterly for man-slaying Hector, and Achilles wept for his father, and then again for Patroclus. The house was filled with the sounds of their lamentation. But presently, when he had had enough of tears and recovered his composure, the excellent Achilles leapt from his chair, and in compassion for the old man's grey head and grey beard, took him by the arm and raised him. Then he spoke to him from his heart: "You are indeed a man of sorrows and have suffered much. How could you dare to come by yourself to the Achaean ships into the presence of a man who has killed so many of your gallant sons? You have a heart of iron. But pray be seated now, here on this chair, and let us leave our sorrows, bitter though they are, locked up in our own hearts, for weeping is cold comfort and does little good. We men are wretched things, and the gods, who have no cares themselves, have woven sorrow into the very pattern of our lives."

REVIEW QUESTIONS

1. What arguments were used by Hector's wife to persuade him to avoid battle with Achilles? Why did he refuse to heed her pleas?
2. As the Greeks read and even memorized *The Iliad* as part of their education for adulthood, what kinds of values did they wish to pass on to their young people?
3. In the last selection, Priam suddenly appeared in Achilles' tent. How was Achilles affected by this encounter, and what lesson did he draw from it?

---

2 ▾ Early Greek Philosophy: The Emancipation of Thought from Myth

In the sixth century B.C., Greeks living in the city of Miletus in Ionia, the coast of Asia Minor, conceived a nonmythical way of viewing nature, a feat that marks the origins of philosophic and scientific thought. Traditionally, natural occurrences like earthquakes and lightning had been attributed to the gods. But early Greek thinkers, called cosmologists because they were interested in the nature and structure of the universe, were the first to see nature as a system governed by laws that the intellect could ascertain. The cosmologists sought physical rather than supernatural explanations for natural events. This new approach made possible a self-conscious and systematic investigation of nature and a critical appraisal of proposed theories; in contrast, the mythical view that the gods regulate nature did not invite discussion and questioning.

Aristotle
THALES OF MILETUS

Thales of Miletus (c. 624–c. 548 B.C.) is considered the founder of Ionian philosophy. He wanted to know how nature came to be the way it is, and he did not turn to traditional legends for an answer. Thales said that water was the basic element of nature and that through a natural process — similar to the formation of ice or steam — water gave rise to everything else in the universe. Thales revolutionized thought because in searching for a first cause in nature he omitted the gods. What we know about Thales' view of nature comes essentially from Aristotle (see page 94). A brief reference to Thales from Aristotle's *Metaphysics* follows.

Most of the philosophers thought that principles in the form of matter were the only principles of all things: for the original source of all existing things, that from which a thing first comes-into-being and into which it is finally destroyed, the substance persisting but changing in its qualities, this they declare is the element and first principle of existing things . . . for there must be some natural substance, either one or more than one, from which the other things come-into-being, while it is preserved. Over the number, however, and the form of this kind of principle they do not all agree; but Thales, the founder of this type of philosophy, says that it is water (and therefore declared that the earth is on water), perhaps taking this supposition from seeing the nurture of all things to be moist, and the warm itself coming-to-be from this and living by this (that from which they come-to-be being the principle of all things) — taking the supposition both from this and from the seeds of all things having a moist nature, water being the natural principle of moist things.

ANAXIMANDER

Anaximander (c. 611–547 B.C.), another Ionian, also held that a single element was the wellspring of nature, but he rejected any specific substance such as water, holding instead that something indefinite, which he called the Boundless or the Infinite, was the source of all things. Anaximander attempted to explain how natural objects and living things had derived from this primary mass. What is remarkable about Anaximander's cosmogony was the omission of the gods or any supernatural agency in the origin of life and the formation of the world. All that we know about Anaximander comes from brief passages in the writings of several ancient scholars.

Of those who say that it is one, moving, and infinite, Anaximander, son of Praxiades, a Milesian, the successor and pupil of Thales, said that the principle and element of existing things was the *apeiron* (indefinite, *or* infinite), being the first to introduce this name of the material principle. He says that it is neither water nor any other of the so-called elements, but some other *apeiron* nature, from which come into being all the heavens and the worlds in them.

For he (Anaximander) thought that things were born not from one substance, as Thales thought from water, but each from its own particular principles. These principles of individual things he believed to be infinite, and to give birth to innumerable worlds and whatsoever arises in them; and those worlds, he thought, are now dissolved, now born again, according to the age to which each is able to survive.

He says that that which is productive from the eternal of hot and cold was separated off at the coming-to-be of this world, and that a kind of sphere of flame from this was formed round the air surrounding the earth, like bark round a tree. When this was broken off and shut off in certain circles, the sun and the moon and the stars were formed. . . .

The heavenly bodies come into being as a circle of fire separated off from the fire in the world, and enclosed by air. There are breathing-holes, certain pipe-like passages, at which the heavenly bodies show themselves; accordingly eclipses occur when the breathing-holes are blocked up. The moon is seen now waxing, now waning according to the blocking or opening of the channels. The circle of the sun is 27 times the size of (the earth, that of) the moon (18 times); the sun is highest, and the circles of the fixed stars are lowest. . . .

———

Winds occur when the finest vapours of the air are separated off and when they are set in motion by congregation; rain occurs from the exhalation that issues upwards from the things beneath the sun, and lightning whenever wind breaks out and cleaves the clouds. . . .

———

(On thunder, lightning, thunderbolts, whirlwinds and typhoons.) Anaximander says that all these things occur as a result of wind: for whenever it is shut up in a thick cloud and then bursts out forcibly, through its fineness and lightness, then the bursting makes the noise, while the rift against the blackness of the cloud makes the flash. . . .

———

Anaximander said that the first living creatures were born in moisture, enclosed in thorny barks; and that as their age increased they came forth on to the drier part and, when the bark had broken off, they lived a different kind of life for a short time.

———

Further he says that in the beginning man was born from creatures of a different kind; because other creatures are soon self-supporting, but man alone needs prolonged nursing. For this reason he would not have survived if this had been his original form.

———

Anaximander of Miletus conceived that there arose from heated water and earth either fish or creatures very like fish; in these man grew, in the form of embryos retained within until puberty; then at last the fish-like creatures burst and men and women who were already able to nourish themselves stepped forth.

Living creatures came into being from moisture evaporated by the sun. Man was originally similar to another creature — that is, to a fish.

———

[H]e declares . . . that originally men came into being inside fishes, and that having been nurtured there — like sharks — and having become adequate to look after themselves, they then came forth and took to the land.

Aristotle
PYTHAGORAS

Pythagoras (c. 580–507 B.C.) was born on the island of Samos, a major Greek cultural and commercial center in the eastern Aegean Sea; as a young man, he migrated to southern Italy, where the Greeks had established colonies. A deep religiosity pervaded the thought of Pythagoras and his followers, who sought to purify the soul and to achieve salvation. Believing that the soul undergoes a reincarnation in animals, Pythagoreans would not eat meat. The Pythagoreans' great contribution to scientific thought was their conviction that nature contains an inherent mathematical order. Thus, continuity exists between the Pythagoreans and Isaac Newton and Albert Einstein, who expressed the laws underlying the cosmos in mathematical terms more than two thousand years later. Aristotle's description of the Pythagoreans follows.

. . . the Pythagoreans, as they are called, devoted themselves to mathematics; they were the first to advance this study, and having been brought up in it they thought its principles were the principles of all things. Since of these principles numbers are by nature the first, and in numbers they seemed to see many resemblances to the things that exist and come into being — more than in fire and earth and water (such and such a modification of numbers being justice, another being soul and reason, another being opportunity — and similarly almost all other things being numerically expressible); since, again, they saw that the attributes and the ratios of the musical scales were expressible in numbers; since, then, all other things seemed in their whole nature to be modelled after numbers, and numbers seemed to be the first things in the whole of nature, they supposed the elements of numbers to be the elements of all things, and the whole heaven to be a musical scale and a number. And all the properties of numbers and scales which they could show to agree with the attributes and parts and the whole arrangement of the heavens, they collected and fitted into their scheme.

REVIEW QUESTIONS

1. In Aristotle's accounts, what did most early Greek philosophers believe to be the basic element or principle of all things?
2. According to Aristotle, on what point did these same philosophers disagree among themselves?
3. What did Thales think was the basic principle of all things? How did Aristotle say that Thales came to this conclusion?
4. What was Anaximander's view about the basic principle of all things?
5. What was Anaximander's theory about the origin of the human species?
6. Compare the Hebrew account of the creation of the world and mankind with that of Anaximander. To what extent do the two accounts differ in purpose and literary genre?
7. Why did the Pythagoreans think the study of mathematics was essential to the understanding of the nature of all things?
8. Early Greek philosophy marks a breaking away from mythical thinking and the emergence of scientific thought. Discuss this statement.

---

3 ▾ The Expansion of Reason

The new method of inquiry initiated by the Ionian natural philosophers found expression in other areas of Greek culture. Thus, in the Greek medical school headed by Hippocrates (c. 460–377 B.C.) on the island of Cos, doctors consciously attacked magical practices and beliefs, seeing them as hindrances to understanding causes and cures of disease. The historian Thucydides (c. 460–400 B.C.) sought logical explanations for human events, and the Sophists applied reason to traditional religion, law, and morality.

Hippocrates
≪ THE SACRED DISEASE ≫
THE SEPARATION OF MEDICINE FROM MYTH

In the following excerpt from "The Sacred Disease," a Hippocratic doctor rejects the belief that epilepsy is a sacred disease. Instead he maintains that epilepsy,

like all other diseases, has a natural explanation and denounces as "charlatans and quacks" those who claim that gods cause the disease.

I. I am about to discuss the disease called "sacred." It is not, in my opinion, any more divine or more sacred than other diseases, but has a natural cause, and its supposed divine origin is due to men's inexperience, and to their wonder at its peculiar character. Now while men continue to believe in its divine origin because they are at a loss to understand it, they really disprove its divinity by the facile method of healing which they adopt, consisting as it does of purifications and incantations. But if it is to be considered divine just because it is wonderful, there will be not one sacred disease but many, for I will show that other diseases are no less wonderful and portentous, and yet nobody considers them sacred. For instance, quotidian fevers, tertians and quartans seem to me to be no less sacred and god-sent than this disease,* but nobody wonders at them. . . .

II. My own view is that those who first attributed a sacred character to this malady were like the magicians, purifiers, charlatans and quacks of our own day, men who claim great piety and superior knowledge. Being at a loss, and having no treatment which would help, they concealed and sheltered themselves behind superstition, and called this illness sacred, in order that their utter ignorance might not be manifest. They added a plausible story, and established a method of treatment that secured their own position. They used purifications and incantations; they forbade the use of baths, and of many foods that are unsuitable for sick folk. . . .

But if to eat or apply these things engenders and increases the disease, while to refrain works a cure, then neither is godhead to blame nor are the purifications beneficial; it is the foods that cure or hurt, and the power of godhead disappears.

III. Accordingly I hold that those who attempt in this manner to cure these diseases cannot consider them either sacred or divine; for when they are removed by such purifications and by such treatment as this, there is nothing to prevent the production of attacks in men by devices that are similar. If so, something human is to blame, and not godhead. He who by purifications and magic can take away such an affliction can also by similar means bring it on, so that by this argument the action of godhead is disproved. By these sayings and devices they claim superior knowledge, and deceive men by prescribing for them purifications and cleansings, most of their talk turning on the intervention of gods and spirits.

*Because of the regularity of the attacks of fever, which occur every day (quotidians), every other day (tertians), or with intermission of two whole days (quartans).

Thucydides
METHOD OF HISTORICAL INQUIRY

Thucydides' history was another expression of the movement from myth to reason that pervaded every aspect of Greek culture. Mesopotamians and Egyptians kept annals purporting to narrate the deeds of gods and their human agents. The Greeks carefully investigated events — the first people to examine the past with a critical eye. Thucydides examined men's actions and their motives, explicitly rejected divine explanations for human occurrences, searched for natural causes, and based his conclusions on evidence. In this approach, he was influenced by the empiricism of the Hippocratic physicians. For Thucydides, a work

of history, as distinguished from poetry, was a creation of the rational mind and not an expression of the poetic imagination. Thus, in Thucydides' *History of the Peloponnesian War* there was no place for legend, for myth, for the fabulous — all hindrances to historical truth. In the following passage, Thucydides describes his method of inquiry.

I began my history at the very outbreak of the war, in the belief that it was going to be a great war and more worth writing about than any of those which had taken place in the past. My belief was based on the fact that the two sides were at the very height of their power and preparedness, and I saw, too, that the rest of the Hellenic [Greek] world was committed to one side or the other; even those who were not immediately engaged were deliberating on the courses which they were to take later. This was the greatest disturbance in the history of the Hellenes, affecting also a large part of the non-Hellenic world, and indeed, I might almost say, the whole of mankind. For though I have found it impossible, because of its remoteness in time, to acquire a really precise knowledge of the distant past or even of the history preceding our own period, yet, after looking back into it as far as I can, all the evidence leads me to conclude that these periods were not great periods either in warfare or in anything else. . . .

In investigating past history, and in forming the conclusions which I have formed, it must be admitted that one cannot rely on every detail which has come down to us by way of tradition. People are inclined to accept all stories of ancient times in an uncritical way — even when these stories concern their own native countries. . . .

. . . Most people, in fact, will not take trouble in finding out the truth, but are much more inclined to accept the first story they hear.

However, I do not think that one will be far wrong in accepting the conclusions I have reached from the evidence which I have put forward. It is better evidence than that of the poets, who exaggerate the importance of their themes, or of the prose chroniclers, who are less interested in telling the truth than in catching the attention of their public, whose authorities cannot be checked, and whose subject-matter, owing to the passage of time, is mostly lost in the unreliable streams of mythology. We may claim instead to have used only the plainest evidence and to have reached conclusions which are reasonably accurate, considering that we have been dealing with ancient history. As for this present war, even though people are apt to think that the war in which they are fighting is the greatest of all wars and, when it is over, to relapse again into their admiration of the past, nevertheless, if one looks at the facts themselves, one will see that this was the greatest war of all.

In this history I have made use of set speeches some of which were delivered just before and others during the war. I have found it difficult to remember the precise words used in the speeches which I listened to myself and my various informants have experienced the same difficulty; so my method has been, while keeping as closely as possible to the general sense of the words that were actually used, to make the speakers say what, in my opinion, was called for by each situation.

And with regard to my factual reporting of the events of the war I have made it a principle not to write down the first story that came my way, and not even to be guided by my own general impressions; either I was present myself at the events which I have described or else I heard of them from eye-witnesses whose reports I have checked with as much thoroughness as possible. Not that even so the truth was easy to discover: different eye-witnesses give different accounts of the same events, speaking out of partiality for one side or the other or else from imperfect memories. And it may well be that my history will seem less easy to read because of the absence in it of a romantic element. It will be enough for me, however, if these words of mine are judged useful by those who want to understand clearly the events which happened in the past and which (human nature being what it is) will, at some time or other and in much the same ways, be repeated in the future. My work is not a piece of writing designed to meet the taste of an immediate public, but was done to last for ever.

Critias
RELIGION AS A HUMAN INVENTION

After the Greek philosophers of Asia Minor began to employ natural, rather than supernatural, explanations for nature, Greek thinkers on the mainland applied reason to human affairs. Exemplifying this trend were the Sophists, who wandered from city to city teaching rhetoric, grammar, poetry, mathematics, music, and gymnastics. The Sophists sought to develop their students' minds, and they created a secular curriculum — for these reasons they enriched the humanist tradition of the West.

The Sophist Critias (c. 480 B.C.–403 B.C.) was a poet, philosopher, orator, and historian; also he was originally an eager follower of Socrates. Later, Critias became the most bloodthirsty of the so-called Thirty Tyrants, oligarchs who seized control of Athens in 404 B.C. and massacred their democratic opponents. The following passage, a surviving fragment of a play by Critias, demonstrates the Sophists' use of critical thought.

There was a time when the life of men was unordered, bestial and the slave of force, when there was no reward for the virtuous and no punishment for the wicked. Then, I think, men devised retributory laws, in order that Justice might be dictator and have arrogance as its slave, and if anyone sinned, he was punished. Then, when the laws forbade them to commit open crimes of violence, and they began to do them in secret, a wise and clever man invented fear (of the gods) for mortals, that there might be some means of frightening the wicked, even if they do anything or say or think it in secret. Hence he introduced the Divine (religion), saying that there is a God flourishing with immortal life, hearing and seeing with his mind, and thinking of everything and caring about these things, and having divine nature, who will hear everything said among mortals, and will be able to see all that is done. And even if you plan anything evil in secret, you will not escape the gods in this; for they have surpassing intelligence. In saying these words, he introduced the pleasantest of teachings, covering up the truth with a false theory; and he said that the gods dwelt there where he could most frighten men by saying it, whence he knew that fears exist for mortals and rewards for the hard life: in the upper periphery, where they saw lightnings and heard the dread rumblings of thunder, and the starry-faced body of heaven, the beautiful embroidery of Time the skilled craftsman, whence come forth the bright mass of the sun, and the wet shower upon the earth. With such fears did he surround mankind, through which he well established the deity with his argument, and in a fitting place, and quenched lawlessness among men. . . . Thus, I think, for the first time did someone persuade mortals to believe in a race of deities.

REVIEW QUESTIONS

1. According to the Hippocratic author, what is the logical flaw in the argument of those who attribute epilepsy, the "sacred disease," to the intervention of the gods?
2. What were some methods that Thucydides said he would use to make his history more accurate and credible?
3. What was revolutionary about Critias' approach to religion?
4. What evidence did Critias offer for his argument?
5. In what sense did Critias' own career illustrate his views on the existence of the gods and their relationship to morality?

---

4 ▾ Humanism

The Greeks conceived the humanist outlook, one of the pillars of Western civilization. They urged human beings to develop their physical, intellectual, and moral capacities to the fullest, to shape themselves according to the highest standards, and to make their lives as harmonious as a flawless work of art. Such an aspiration required intelligence and self-mastery.

Pindar
THE PURSUIT OF EXCELLENCE

The poet Pindar (c. 518–438 B.C.) expressed the Greek view of excellence in his praise for a victorious athlete. Life is essentially tragic — triumphs are short-lived, misfortunes are many, and ultimately death overtakes everyone; still, human beings must demonstrate their worth by striving for excellence.

He who wins of a sudden, some noble prize
In the rich years of youth
Is raised high with hope; his manhood takes wings;
He has in his heart what is better than wealth
But brief is the season of man's delight.
Soon it falls to the ground;
Some dire decision uproots it.
— Thing of a day! such is man: a shadow in a dream.
Yet when god-given splendour visits him
A bright radiance plays over him, and how sweet is life!

Sophocles
THE WONDERS OF MAN

In a famous passage from his play *Antigone,* Sophocles (c. 496–406 B.C.) lauded human talents.

Numberless are the world's wonders, but none
More wonderful than man; the stormgray sea
Yields to his prows, the huge crests bear him
high;
Earth, holy and inexhaustible, is graven
With shining furrows where his plows have
gone
Year after year, the timeless labor of stallions.

The lightboned birds and beasts that cling to
cover,
The lithe fish lighting their reaches of dim
water,
All are taken, tamed in the net of his mind;
The lion on the hill, the wild horse windy-
maned,
Resign to him; and his blunt yoke has broken
The sultry shoulders of the mountain bull.

Words also, and thought as rapid as air,
He fashions to his good use; statecraft is his,
And his the skill that deflects the arrows of
snow,
The spears of winter rain: from every wind
He has made himself secure — from all but
one;
In the late wind of death he cannot stand.

O clear intelligence, force beyond all measure!
O fate of man, working both good and evil!
When the laws are kept, how proudly his city
stands!
When the laws are broken, what of his city
then?
Never may the anárchic man find rest at my
hearth,
Never be it said that my thoughts are his
thoughts.

REVIEW QUESTIONS

1. What human virtues did the Greek poets praise?
2. Why did the Greeks consider the poets as educators?

---

5 ▾ The Persian Wars

In 499 B.C., the Ionian Greeks in Asia Minor revolted against their Persian rulers; Athens sent twenty ships to aid the Ionians. To punish the Athenians, Darius I, king of Persia, sent a force to the peninsula of Attica, where Athens is located. In 490 B.C. on the plains of Marathon, an Athenian army of about 10,000 men defeated the Persians. Ten years later, Xerxes, Darius' son and heir, organized a huge invasion force aimed at making Greece a Persian province. Realizing that their independence and freedom were at stake, many Greek cities put aside their quarrels and united against the common enemy. In 480 B.C. on the Bay of Salamis near Athens, the Athenian navy defeated the Persian armada, and the next year the Spartan army crushed the Persians at Plataea.

Herodotus
≪ THE HISTORIES ≫

Herodotus (c. 484–c. 424 B.C.), often called "the father of history," wrote about the most important events of his lifetime, the Persian Wars. Although the gods

were present in Herodotus' narrative, they played a far less important role than they had in Greek mythology or in Near Eastern annals. Herodotus visited Persian lands and found much to praise there. Nevertheless, he was struck by the contrast between Greek freedom and Persian absolutism, between the free Greek citizen and the Persian subject who knew only obedience to the king's commands.

A second theme prevalent in *The Histories* is punishment for *hubris,* or arrogance. Xerxes, in seeking to rule both Asia and Greece, was seen as exhibiting such arrogance. In the following excerpt, Herodotus discusses Xerxes' ambition.

In this book, the result of my inquiries into history, I hope to do two things: to preserve the memory of the past by putting on record the astonishing achievements both of our own and of the Asiatic peoples; secondly, and more particularly, to show how the two races came into conflict. . . .

. . .

Xerxes began his reign by building up an army for a campaign in Egypt. The invasion of Greece was at first by no means an object of his thoughts; but Mardonius — the son of Gobryas and Darius' sister and thus cousin to the king — who was present in court and had more influence with Xerxes than anyone else in the country, used constantly to talk to him on the subject. "Master," he would say, "the Athenians have done us great injury, and it is only right that they should be punished for their crimes. By all means finish the task you already have in hand; but when you have tamed the arrogance of Egypt, then lead an army against Athens. Do that, and your name will be held in honour all over the world, and people will think twice in future before they invade your country." And to the argument for revenge he would add that Europe was a very beautiful place; it produced every kind of garden tree; the land there was everything that land should be — it was, in short, too good for anyone in the world except the Persian king. Mardonius' motive for urging the campaign was love of mischief and adventure and the hope of becoming governor of Greece himself; and after much persistence he persuaded Xerxes to make the attempt. . . .

After the conquest of Egypt, when he was on the point of taking in hand the expedition against Athens, Xerxes called a conference of the leading men in the country, to find out their attitude towards the war and explain to them his own wishes. When they met, he addressed them as follows: "Do not suppose, gentlemen, that I am departing from precedent in the course of action I intend to undertake. We Persians have a way of living, which I have inherited from my predecessors and propose to follow. . . . Of our past history you need no reminder; for you know well enough the famous deeds of Cyrus,[1] Cambyses,[2] and my father Darius, and their additions to our empire. Now I myself, ever since my accession, have been thinking how not to fall short of the kings who have sat upon this throne before me, and how to add as much power as they did to the Persian empire. And now at last I have found a way to win for Persia not glory only but a country as large and as rich as our own — indeed richer than our own — and at the same time to get satisfaction and revenge. That, then, is the object of this meeting — that I may disclose to you what it is that I intend to do. I will bridge the Hellespont[3] and march an army through Europe into Greece, and punish the Athenians

[1]Cyrus, the founder of the Persian Empire, ruled from 559 to 529 B.C.

[2]Cambyses was king of Persia from 529 to 521 B.C. When he conquered Egypt, it temporarily became a Persian province.

[3]The Hellespont is the narrow strait connecting the Aegean Sea with the Sea of Marmora. At one point it is less than a mile wide.

for the outrage they committed upon my father and upon us. As you saw, Darius himself was making his preparations for war against these men; but death prevented him from carrying out his purpose. I therefore on his behalf, and for the benefit of all my subjects, will not rest until I have taken Athens and burnt it to the ground, in revenge for the injury which the Athenians without provocation once did to me and my father. These men, you remember, came to Sardis with Aristagoras[4] the Milesian — a mere slave of ours — and burnt the temples, and the trees that grew about them; and you know all too well how they served our troops under Datis and Artaphernes,[5] when they landed upon Greek soil. For these reasons I have now prepared to make war upon them, and, when I consider the matter, I find several advantages in the venture: if we crush the Athenians and their neighbours in the Peloponnese,[6] we shall so extend the empire of Persia that its boundaries will be God's own sky. With your help I shall pass through Europe from end to end and make it all one country, so that the sun will not look down upon any land beyond the boundaries of what is ours. For if what I am told is true, there is not a city or nation in the world which will be able to withstand us, once Athens and Sparta are out of the way. Thus the guilty and the innocent alike shall bear the yoke of servitude. . . ."

The first to speak after the king was Mardonius. "Of all Persians who have ever lived," he began, "and of all who are yet to be born, you, my lord, are the greatest. Every word you have spoken is true and excellent, and you will not allow the wretched Ionians in Europe to make fools of us. It would indeed be an odd thing if we who have defeated and enslaved the Sacae, Indians, Ethiopians, Assyrians,[7] and many other great nations for no fault of their own, but merely to extend the boundaries of our empire, should fail now to punish the Greeks who have been guilty of injuring us without provocation. . . . Well then, my lord, who is likely to resist you when you march against them with the millions of Asia at your back, and the whole Persian fleet? Believe me, it is not in the Greek character to take so desperate a risk. But should I be wrong — should the courage born of ignorance and folly drive them to do battle with us, then they will learn that we are the best soldiers in the world. Nevertheless, let us take this business seriously and spare no pains; success is never automatic in this world — nothing is achieved without trying."

Xerxes' proposals were made to sound plausible enough by these words of Mardonius, and when he stopped speaking there was a silence. For a while nobody dared to put forward the opposite view, until Artabanus, taking courage from the fact of his relationship to the king — he was a son of Hystaspes and therefore Xerxes' uncle — rose to speak. . . . "It is my duty to tell you what you have to fear from them: you have said you mean to bridge the Hellespont and march through Europe to Greece. Now suppose — and it is not impossible — that you were to suffer a reverse by sea or land, or even both. These Greeks are said to be great fighters — and indeed one might well guess as much from the fact that the Athenians alone destroyed the great army we sent to attack them under Datis and Artaphernes. Or, if you will, suppose they were to succeed upon one element only — suppose they fell upon our fleet and defeated it, and then sailed to the Hellespont and destroyed the bridge: then, my lord, you would indeed be in peril. . . .

[4]Aristagoras, the ruler of Miletus, encouraged the other cities of Ionia to revolt against the Persians.

[5]Datis and Artaphernes were the commanders of the Persian forces defeated by the Athenians at Marathon.

[6]The Peloponnese (Peloponnesus) is the largest peninsula of southern Greece.

[7]The Sacae lived in Bactria, above the Iranian Plateau; the Indians just west of the Indus River. Ethiopia of that time means a land along the west side of the Red Sea. The Assyrians were a people inhabiting land between the Tigris and Euphrates rivers.

"I urge you, therefore, to abandon this plan; take my advice and do not run any such terrible risk when there is no necessity to do so. . . .

"You know, my lord, that amongst living creatures it is the great ones that God smites with his thunder, out of envy of their pride. The little ones do not vex him. It is always the great buildings and the tall trees which are struck by lightning. It is God's way to bring the lofty low. Often a great army is destroyed by a little one, when God in his envy puts fear into the men's hearts, or sends a thunderstorm, and they are cut to pieces in a way they do not deserve. For God tolerates pride in none but Himself."

REVIEW QUESTIONS

1. What were the motives of the Persians in planning Xerxes' invasion of Greece? What do these motives suggest about the nature of the Persian imperial system?
2. What factors were considered by the Persians in choosing a strategy for the war?
3. Herodotus was not a witness to the debate between Mardonius and Artabanus. What does this indicate about his reliability as a historian?
4. What dangers did Artabanus foresee in the proposed invasion of Greece?

---

6 ▾ Greek Drama

Western drama is an art form that originated in Greece. It had its beginnings in the religious ceremonies of the Greeks and initially served a ritual function linking the Greeks with their gods. In the hands of the great Greek dramatists, drama gradually became less concerned with the activities of the gods, emphasizing instead human personality and universal human themes.

Sophocles
≪ ANTIGONE ≫

In *Antigone,* the dramatist Sophocles expresses the Greeks' high esteem for humanity and its potential. He also deals with a theme that recurs in Western thought over the centuries: the conflict between individual morality and the requirements of the state, between personal conscience and the state's laws. Creon, king of Thebes, forbids the burial of Polyneikes, Antigone's brother, because he rebelled against the state. The body, decrees Creon, shall remain unburied, food for dogs and vultures, despite the fact that Antigone is his niece and betrothed to his son. Antigone believes that a higher law compels her to bury her brother, even though this means certain death for her and for her sister Ismene, if the latter helps Antigone.

SCENE II

CREON *(Slowly, dangerously)*
And you, Antigone,
You with your head hanging — do you confess this thing?

ANTIGONE I do. I deny nothing.

CREON *(To* SENTRY)
You may go.

(Exit SENTRY.)
(To ANTIGONE)

Tell me, tell me briefly:
Had you heard my proclamation touching this matter?

ANTIGONE It was public. Could I help hearing it?

CREON And yet you dared defy the law.

ANTIGONE I dared.
It was not God's proclamation. That final Justice
That rules the world below makes no such laws.

Your edict, King, was strong,
But all your strength is weakness itself against
The immortal unrecorded laws of God.
They are not merely now: they were, and shall be,
Operative for ever, beyond man utterly.

I knew I must die, even without your decree:
I am only mortal. And if I must die
Now, before it is my time to die,
Surely this is no hardship: can anyone
Living, as I live, with evil all about me,
Think Death less than a friend? This death of mine
Is of no importance; but if I had left my brother
Lying in death unburied, I should have suffered.
Now I do not.
You smile at me. Ah Creon,
Think me a fool, if you like; but it may well be
That a fool convicts me of folly.

CHORAGOS[1] Like father [Oedipus], like daughter: both headstrong, deaf to reason!
She has never learned to yield.

CREON She has much to learn.
The inflexible heart breaks first, the toughest iron
Cracks first, and the wildest horses bend their necks
At the pull of the smallest curb.

---

[1]The choragos was a single commentator on the action of the play.

Pride? In a slave?
This girl is guilty of a double insolence.
Breaking the given laws and boasting of it.
Who is the man here,
She or I, if this crime goes unpunished?
Sister's child, or more than sister's child,
Or closer yet in blood — she and her sister [Ismene]
Win bitter death for this!

(*To servants*)

Go, some of you,
Arrest Ismene. I accuse her equally.
Bring her: you will find her sniffling in the house there.

Her mind's a traitor: crimes kept in the dark
Cry for light, and the guardian brain shudders;
But how much worse than this
Is brazen boasting of barefaced anarchy!

ANTIGONE Creon, what more do you want than my death?

CREON Nothing.
That gives me everything.

ANTIGONE Then I beg you: kill me.
This talking is a great weariness: your words
Are distasteful to me, and I am sure that mine
Seem so to you. And yet they should not seem so:
I should have praise and honor for what I have done.
All these men here would praise me.
Were their lips not frozen shut with fear of you.

(*Bitterly*)

Ah the good fortune of kings,
Licensed to say and do whatever they please!

CREON You are alone here in that opinion.

ANTIGONE No, they are with me. But they keep their tongues in leash.

CREON Maybe. But you are guilty, and they are not.

ANTIGONE There is no guilt in reverence for the dead.

CREON But Eteocles — was he not your brother too?

ANTIGONE My brother too.

CREON And you insult his memory?

ANTIGONE (*Softly*)
The dead man would not say that I insult it.

CREON He would: for you honor a traitor as much as him.

ANTIGONE His own brother, traitor or not, and equal in blood.

CREON He made war on his country. Eteocles defended it.

ANTIGONE Nevertheless, there are honors due all the dead.

CREON But not the same for the wicked as for the just.

ANTIGONE Ah Creon, Creon,
Which of us can say what the gods hold wicked?

CREON An enemy is an enemy, even dead.

ANTIGONE It is my nature to join in love, not hate.

(*Finally losing patience*)

CREON
Go join them, then; if you must have your love,
Find it in hell!

CHORAGOS But see, Ismene comes:

(*Enter* ISMENE, *guarded.*)

Those tears are sisterly, the cloud
That shadows her eyes rains down gentle sorrow.

CREON You too, Ismene,
Snake in my ordered house, sucking my blood
Stealthily — and all the time I never knew
That these two sisters were aiming at my throne!
Ismene,
Do you confess your share in this crime, or deny it?
Answer me.

ISMENE Yes, if she will let me say so. I am guilty.

ANTIGONE (*Coldly*)
No, Ismene. You have no right to say so.
You would not help me, and I will not have you help me.

ISMENE But now I know what you meant; and I am here
To join you, to take my share of punishment.

ANTIGONE The dead man and the gods who rule the dead
Know whose act this was. Words are not friends.

ISMENE Do you refuse me, Antigone? I want to die with you:
I too have a duty that I must discharge to the dead.

ANTIGONE You shall not lessen my death by sharing it.

ISMENE What do I care for life when you are dead?

ANTIGONE Ask Creon. You're always hanging on his opinions.

ISMENE You are laughing at me. Why, Antigone?

ANTIGONE It's a joyless laughter, Ismene.

ISMENE But can I do nothing?

ANTIGONE Yes. Save yourself. I shall not envy you. . . .

. . .

SCENE III

CHORAGOS But here is Haimon, King, the last of all your sons.
It is grief for Antigone that brings him here.
And bitterness at being robbed of his bride?

(*Enter* HAIMON.)

CREON We shall soon see, and no need of diviners.
— Son,
You have heard my final judgment on that girl:
Have you come here hating me, or have you come
With deference and with love, whatever I do?

HAIMON I am your son, father. You are my guide.
You make things clear for me, and I obey you.
No marriage means more to me than your continuing wisdom.

CREON Good. That is the way to behave: subordinate
Everything else, my son, to your father's will.
This is what a man prays for, that he may get
Sons attentive and dutiful in his house,
Each one hating his father's enemies,
Honoring his father's friends. But if his sons
Fail him, if they turn out unprofitably,
What has he fathered but trouble for himself
And amusement for the malicious?
So you are right
Not to lose your head over this woman.
Your pleasure with her would soon grow cold, Haimon,
And then you'd have a hellcat in bed and elsewhere.
Let her find her husband in Hell!
Of all the people in this city, only she
Has had contempt for my law and broken it.

Do you want me to show myself weak before the people?
Or to break my sworn word? No, and I will not.
The woman dies.

I suppose she'll plead "family ties." Well, let her.
If I permit my own family to rebel,
How shall I earn the world's obedience?
Show me the man who keeps his house in hand,
He's fit for public authority.

I'll have no dealings
With law-breakers, critics of the government:
Whoever is chosen to govern should be obeyed —
Must be obeyed, in all things, great and small,
Just and unjust! O Haimon,
The man who knows how to obey, and that man only,
Knows how to give commands when the time comes.
You can depend on him, no matter how fast
The spears come: he's a good soldier, he'll stick it out.

Anarchy, anarchy! Show me a greater evil!
This is why cities tumble and the great houses rain down,
This is what scatters armies!

No, no: good lives are made so by discipline.
We keep the laws then, and the lawmakers,
And no woman shall seduce us. If we must lose,
Let's lose to a man, at least! Is a woman stronger than we?

CHORAGOS Unless time has rusted my wits,
What you say, King, is said with point and dignity.

HAIMON (*Boyishly earnest*)
Father:
Reason is God's crowning gift to man, and you are right
To warn me against losing mine. I cannot say —
I hope that I shall never want to say! — that you
Have reasoned badly. Yet there are other men
Who can reason, too; and their opinions might be helpful.
You are not in a position to know everything
That people say or do, or what they feel:
Your temper terrifies them — everyone
Will tell you only what you like to hear.
But I, at any rate, can listen; and I have heard them
Muttering and whispering in the dark about this girl.
They say no woman has ever, so unreasonably,
Died so shameful a death for a generous act:
"She covered her brother's body. Is this indecent?
She kept him from dogs and vultures. Is this a crime?
Death? — She should have all the honor that we can give her!"

This is the way they talk out there in the city.

. . .

Forget you are angry! Let yourself be moved!
I know I am young; but please let me say this:
The ideal condition
Would be, I admit, that men should be right by instinct;
But since we are all too likely to go astray,
The reasonable thing is to learn from those who can teach.

CHORAGOS You will do well to listen to him, King,
If what he says is sensible. And you, Haimon,
Must listen to your father. — Both speak well.

CREON You consider it right for a man of my years and experience
To go to school to a boy?

HAIMON It is not right
If I am wrong. But if I am young, and right,
What does my age matter?

CREON You think it right to stand up for an anarchist?

HAIMON Not at all. I pay no respect to criminals.

CREON Then she is not a criminal?

HAIMON The City [Thebes] would deny it, to a man.

CREON And the City proposes to teach me how to rule?

HAIMON Ah. Who is it that's talking like a boy now?

CREON My voice is the one voice giving orders in this City!

HAIMON It is no City if it takes orders from one voice.

CREON The State is the King!

REVIEW QUESTIONS

1. What was Antigone's justification for disobeying the command of the king?
2. What was Antigone's reaction to the threat of capital punishment for her act?
3. What practical reasons made Creon determined to put Antigone to death?
4. What practical reasons did Haimon use to argue against Antigone's execution?
5. What was Creon's view of his rights as a king?
6. Greek dramatists addressed a mass audience in democratic Athens. What public issues are reflected in Sophocles' *Antigone?*

---

7 ▾ Athenian Greatness

The fifty years following the Persian Wars marked Athens' golden age. The central figure in Athenian political life for much of this period was Pericles (c. 495–429 B.C.), a gifted statesman and military commander. In the opening stage of the Peloponnesian War between Athens and Sparta (431–404 B.C.), Pericles delivered an oration in honor of the Athenian war dead. Throughout the speech, as reconstructed by the historian Thucydides (see pages 56–58), Pericles brilliantly described Athenian greatness.

Thucydides
THE FUNERAL ORATION OF PERICLES

Pericles contrasted Sparta's narrow conception of excellence with the Athenian ideal of the self-sufficiency of the human spirit. The Spartans subordinated all personal goals and interests to the demands of the Spartan state. As such, Sparta — a totally militarized society — was as close as the ancient Greeks came to a modern totalitarian society. The Athenians, said Pericles, did not require grinding military discipline in order to fight bravely for their city. Their cultivation of the mind and love of beauty did not make them less courageous.

To be sure, Pericles' "Funeral Oration," intended to bolster the morale of a people locked in a brutal war, idealized Athenian society. Athenians did not always behave in accordance with Pericles' high principles. Nevertheless, as both Pericles and Thucydides knew, Athenian democracy was an extraordinary achievement.

"Let me say that our system of government does not copy the institutions of our neighbours. It is more the case of our being a model to others, than of our imitating anyone else. Our constitution is called a democracy because power is in the hands not of a minority but of the whole people. When it is a question of settling private disputes, everyone is equal before the law; when it is a question of putting one person before another in positions of public responsibility, what counts is not membership of a particular class, but the actual ability which the man possesses. No one, so long as he has it in him to be of service to the state, is kept in political obscurity because of poverty. And, just as our political life is free and open, so is our day-to-day life in our relations with each other. We do not get into a state with our next-door neighbour if he enjoys himself in his own way, nor do we give him the kind of black looks which, though they do no real harm, still do hurt people's feelings. We are free and tolerant in our private lives; but in public affairs we keep to the law. This is because it commands our deep respect.

"We give our obedience to those whom we put in positions of authority, and we obey the laws themselves, especially those which are for the protection of the oppressed, and those unwritten laws which it is an acknowledged shame to break.

"And here is another point. When our work is over, we are in a position to enjoy all kinds of recreation for our spirits. There are various kinds of contests [in poetry, drama, music, and athletics] and sacrifices regularly throughout the year; in our own homes we find a beauty and a good taste which delight us every day and which drive away our cares. Then the greatness of our city brings it about that all the good things from all over the world flow in to us, so that to us it seems just as natural to enjoy foreign goods as our own local products.

"Then there is a great difference between us and our opponents, in our attitude towards military security. Here are some examples: Our city is open to the world, and we have no periodical deportations in order to prevent people observing or finding out secrets which might be of military advantage to the enemy. This is because we rely, not on secret weapons, but on our own real courage and loyalty. There is a difference, too, in our educational systems. The Spartans, from their earliest boyhood, are submitted to the most laborious training in courage; we pass our lives without all these restrictions, and yet are just as ready to face the same dangers as they are. Here is a proof of this: When the Spartans invade our land, they do not come by themselves, but bring all their allies with them; whereas we, when we launch an attack abroad, do the job by ourselves, and, though fighting on foreign soil, do not often fail to defeat opponents who are fighting for their own hearths and homes. As a matter of fact none of our enemies has ever yet been confronted with our total strength, because we have to divide our attention between our navy and the many missions on which our troops are sent on land. Yet, if our enemies engage a detachment of our forces and defeat it, they give themselves credit for having thrown back our entire army; or, if they lose, they claim that they were beaten by us in full strength. There are certain advantages, I think, in our way of meeting danger voluntarily, with an easy mind, instead of with a laborious training, with natural rather than with state-induced courage. We do not have to spend our time practising to meet sufferings which are still in the future; and when they are actually upon us we show ourselves just as brave as these others who are always in strict training. This is one point in which, I think, our city deserves to be admired. There are also others:

"Our love of what is beautiful does not lead to extravagance; our love of the things of the mind does not make us soft. We regard wealth as something to be properly used, rather than as something to boast about. As for poverty, no one need be ashamed to admit it: the real shame is in not taking practical measures to escape from it. Here each individual is interested not only in his own affairs but in the affairs of the state as well: even those who are mostly occupied with their own business are extremely well-informed on general politics — this is a peculiarity of ours: we do not say that a man who takes no interest in politics is a man who minds his own business; we say that he has no business here at all. We Athenians, in our own persons, take our decisions on policy or submit them to proper discussions: for we do not think that there is an incompatibility between words and deeds; the worst thing is to rush into action before the consequences have been properly debated. And this is another point where we differ from other people. We are capable at the same time of taking risks and of estimating them beforehand. Others are brave out of ignorance; and, when they stop to think, they begin to fear. But the man who can most truly be accounted brave is he who best knows the meaning of what is sweet in life and of what is terrible, and then goes out undeterred to meet what is to come.

"Again, in questions of general good feeling there is a great contrast between us and most other people. We make friends by doing good to others, not by receiving good from them. This makes our friendship all the more reliable, since we want to keep alive the gratitude of those who are in our debt by showing continued goodwill to them: whereas the feelings of one who owes us something lack the same enthusiasm, since he knows that, when he repays our kindness, it will be more like paying back a debt than giving something spontaneously. We are unique in this. When we do kindness to others, we do not do them out of any calculations of profit or loss: we do them without afterthought, relying on our free liberality. Taking everything together then, I declare that our city is an education to Greece, and I declare that in my opinion each single one of our citizens, in all the manifold aspects of life, is able to show himself the rightful lord and owner of his own person, and do this, moreover, with exceptional grace and exceptional versatility. And to show that this is no empty boasting for the present occasion, but real tangible fact, you have only to consider the power which our city possesses and which has been won by those very qualities which I have mentioned. Athens, alone of the states we know, comes to her testing time in a greatness that surpasses what was imagined of her. In her case, and in her case alone, no invading enemy is ashamed at being defeated, and no subject can complain of being governed by people unfit for their responsibilities. Mighty indeed are the marks and monuments of our empire which we have left. Future ages will wonder at us, as the present age wonders at us now."

REVIEW QUESTIONS

1. What did Pericles consider the chief characteristics of a democratic form of government?
2. How did certain economic factors affect the quality of life in Athens?
3. According to Pericles, how did the Athenians differ from the Spartans in their views on education and military training?
4. What were the attitudes of the Athenians to such things as wealth, learning, and public affairs?
5. What did Pericles see as the positive values of democratic methods of decision making?
6. How did the Athenians react to the needs of their neighbors?

---

8 ▾ The Status of Women in Classical Greek Society

Women occupied a subordinate position in Greek society. A woman's chief functions were to bear male heirs for her husband and to manage his household. In Athens, respectable women were secluded in their homes; they did not go into the marketplace or eat at the same table as their husbands and guests. Nor did women have political rights; they could not vote or hold office. In order to exercise her property rights, a woman was advised by a male guardian — usually a father, husband, brother, or son.

Parents usually arranged the marriage of their daughters. A father who discovered that his daughter had been unchaste could sell her into slavery. Adultery was a crime. A husband was compelled by law to divorce his adulterous wife and could have her lover executed.

Xenophon
≪ OECONOMICUS ≫

A philosopher's notion of a woman's place in society appears in the following passage from *Oeconomicus* (Estate Management) by Xenophon (c. 428–354 B.C.). An Athenian soldier, historian, and friend of the philosopher Socrates (see page 83), Xenophon uses a conversation between Socrates and his friend Ischomachus as a way to discuss a wife's role in the Greek household.

" 'Ah, Ischomachus,' said I, 'that is just what I want to hear from you. Did you yourself train your wife to be of the right sort, or did she know her household duties when you received her from her parents?'

" 'Why, what knowledge could she have had, Socrates, when I took her for my wife? She was not yet fifteen years old when she came to me, and up to that time she had lived in leading-strings [cords by which children were supported when beginning to walk], seeing, hearing and saying as little as possible. . . .

" 'Well, Socrates, as soon as I found her docile and sufficiently domesticated to carry on conversation, I questioned her to this effect.

" ' "Tell me, dear, have you realised for what

reason I took you and your parents gave you to me? For it is obvious to you, I am sure, that we should have had no difficulty in finding someone else to share our beds. But I for myself and your parents for you considered who was the best partner of home and children that we could get. My choice fell on you, and your parents, it appears, chose me as the best they could find. Now if God grants us children, we will then think out how we shall best train them. For one of the blessings in which we shall share is the acquisition of the very best of allies and the very best of support in old age; but at present we share in this our home. For I am paying into the common stock all that I have, and you have put in all that you brought with you. And we are not to reckon up which of us has actually contributed the greater amount, but we should know of a surety that the one who proves the better partner makes the more valuable contribution."

" 'My wife's answer was as follows, Socrates: "How can I possibly help you? What power have I? Nay, all depends on you. My duty, as my mother told me, is to be discreet."

" ' "And since both the indoor and the outdoor tasks demand labour and attention, God from the first adapted the woman's nature, I think, to the indoor and man's to the outdoor tasks and cares.

" ' "For he made the man's body and mind more capable of enduring cold and heat, and journeys and campaigns; and therefore imposed on him the outdoor tasks. To the woman, since he has made her body less capable of such endurance, I take it that God has assigned the indoor tasks. And knowing that he had created in the woman and had imposed on her the nourishment of the infants, he meted out to her a larger portion of affection for new-born babes than to the man. And since he imposed on the woman the protection of the stores also, knowing that for protection a fearful disposition is no disadvantage, God meted out a larger share of fear to the woman than to the man; and knowing that he who deals with the outdoor tasks will have to be their defender against any wrong-doer, he meted out to him again a larger share of courage. But because both must give and take, he granted to both impartially memory and attention; and so you could not distinguish whether the male or the female sex has the larger share of these. And God also gave to both impartially the power to practise due self-control, and gave authority to whichever is the better — whether it be the man or the woman — to win a larger portion of the good that comes from it. And just because both have not the same aptitudes, they have the more need of each other, and each member of the pair is the more useful to the other, the one being competent where the other is deficient.

" ' "Now since we know, dear, what duties have been assigned to each of us by God, we must endeavour, each of us, to do the duties allotted to us as well as possible. The law, moreover, approves of them, for it joins together man and woman. And as God has made them partners in their children, so the law appoints them partners in the home. And besides, the law declares those tasks to be honourable for each of them wherein God has made the one to excel the other. Thus, to the woman it is more honourable to stay indoors than to abide in the fields, but to the man it is unseemly rather to stay indoors than to attend to the work outside." ' "

Aristophanes
≪ LYSISTRATA ≫

Aristophanes (c. 448–c. 380 B.C.), greatest Athenian comic playwright, wrote *Lysistrata* in 412 B.C. to convy his revulsion for the Peloponnesian War that was destroying Greece. In the play, the women of Athens, led by Lysistrata, resolve

to refrain from intercourse with their husbands and lovers until the men make peace. When the women seize the Acropolis — the rocky hill in the center of Athens — the men resort to force but are doused with water. At this point a commissioner, accompanied by four constables, enters and complains about the disturbance; Koryphaios, one of the doused men, vents his anger. The ensuing dialogue between the commissioner and Lysistrata reflects some attitudes of Greek men and women toward each other.

KORYPHAIOS Sir, you haven't heard the half of it. They laughed at us!
Insulted us! They took pitchers of water
and nearly drowned us! We're still wringing out our clothes,
for all the world like unhousebroken brats.

COMMISSIONER Serves you right, by Poseidon [an oath]!
Whose fault is it if these women-folk of ours
get out of hand? We coddle them,
we teach them to be wasteful and loose. . . .

. . .

Well, what do you expect?
Look at me, for example. I'm a Public Officer,
and it's one of my duties to pay off the sailors.
And where's the money? Up there in the Akropolis!
And those blasted women slam the door in my face!
But what are we waiting for?
— Look here, constable,
stop sniffing around for a tavern, and get us
some crowbars. We'll force their gates! As a matter of fact,
I'll do a little forcing myself.

(*Enter* LYSISTRATA, *above, with* MYRRHINE, KALONIKE, *and the* BOIOTIAN)

LYSISTRATA No need of forcing.
Here I am, of my own accord. And all this talk
about locked doors — ! We don't need locked doors,
but just the least bit of common sense.

COMMISSIONER Is that so, ma'am!
— Where's my constable?
— Constable,
arrest that woman, and tie her hands behind her.

LYSISTRATA If he touches me, I swear by Artemis [Greek goddess of the moon]
there'll be one scamp dropped from the public pay-roll tomorrow!

. . .

COMMISSIONER Lord, what a mess! And my constables seem ineffective.
But — women get the best of us? By God, no!
— Skythians!
Close ranks and forward march!

LYSISTRATA "Forward," indeed!
By the Two Goddesses [oath], what's the sense in *that*?
They're up against four companies of women
armed from top to bottom.

COMMISSIONER Forward, my Skythians!

. . .

(General mêlée; the Skythians yield)

. . .

CHORUS
Of all the beasts that God hath wrought (STROPHE 1)
What monster's worse than woman?
Who shall encompass with his thought
Their guile unending? No man.

They've seized the Heights, the Rock, the Shrine —
But to what end? I wot [know] not.
Sure there's some clue to their design!
Have you the key? I thought not.

KORYPHAIOS We might question them, I suppose. But I warn you, sir,
don't believe anything you hear! It would be un-Athenian
not to get to the bottom of this plot.

COMMISSIONER Very well.
My first question is this: Why, so help you God,
did you bar the gates of the Akropolis?

LYSISTRATA Why?
To keep the money, of course. No money, no war.

COMMISSIONER You think that money's the cause of war?

LYSISTRATA I do.

. . .

COMMISSIONER And what will you do?

LYSISTRATA What a question! From now on, we intend
to control the Treasury.

COMMISSIONER Control the Treasury!

LYSISTRATA Why not? Does that seem strange? After all,
we control our household budgets.

COMMISSIONER But that's different!

LYSISTRATA "Different"? What do you mean?

COMMISSIONER I mean simply this:
it's the Treasury that pays for National Defense.

LYSISTRATA Unnecessary. We propose to abolish war.

COMMISSIONER Good God. — And National Security?

LYSISTRATA Leave that to us.

COMMISSIONER You?

LYSISTRATA Us.

COMMISSIONER We're done for, then!

LYSISTRATA Never mind.
We women will save you in spite of yourselves.

COMMISSIONER What nonsense!

LYSISTRATA If you like. But you must accept it, like it or not.

COMMISSIONER Why, this is downright subversion!

LYSISTRATA Maybe it is.
But we're going to save you, Judge. . . .

COMMISSIONER But the idea
of women bothering themselves about peace and war!

LYSISTRATA Will you listen to me?

COMMISSIONER Yes. But be brief, or I'll —

LYSISTRATA This is no time for stupid threats.

COMMISSIONER By the gods,
I can't stand any more!

AN OLD WOMAN Can't stand? Well, well.

COMMISSIONER That's enough out of you, you old buzzard!
Now, Lysistrata: tell me what you're thinking.

LYSISTRATA Glad to.
Ever since this war began
We women have been watching you men, agreeing with you,
keeping our thoughts to ourselves. That doesn't mean
we were happy: we weren't for we saw how things were going;
but we'd listen to you at dinner
arguing this way and that.
— Oh you, and your big
Top Secrets! —
And then we'd grin like little patriots
(though goodness knows we didn't feel like grinning) and ask you:
"Dear, did the Armistice come up in Assembly today?"
And you'd say, "None of your business! Pipe down," you'd say.
And so we would.

AN OLD WOMAN *I* wouldn't have, by God!

COMMISSIONER You'd have taken a beating, then!
— Go on.

LYSISTRATA Well, we'd be quiet. But then, you know, all at once
you men would think up something worse than ever.
Even *I* could see it was fatal. And, "Darling," I'd say,
"have you gone completely mad?" And my husband would look at me
and say, "Wife, you've got your weaving to attend to.
"Mind your tongue, if you don't want a slap. 'War's
" 'a man's affair'!"

COMMISSIONER Good words, and well pronounced.

LYSISTRATA You're a fool if you think so.
It was hard enough
to put up with all this banquet-hall strategy.
But then we'd hear you out in the public square:
"Nobody left for the draft-quota here in Athens?"
you'd say; and, "No," someone else would say, "not a man!"
And so we women decided to rescue Greece.
You might as well listen to us now: you'll have to, later.

COMMISSIONER *You* rescue Greece? Absurd.

LYSISTRATA You're the absurd one.

COMMISSIONER You expect me to take orders from a woman?
I'd die first!

LYSISTRATA Heavens, if that's what's bothering you, take my veil,
here, and wrap it around your poor head.

KALONIKE Yes,
and you can have my market-basket, too.
Go home, tighten your girdle, do the washing, mind
your beans! "War's
a woman's affair!"

. . .

COMMISSIONER All this is beside the point.
Will you be so kind
as to tell me how you mean to save Greece?

LYSISTRATA Of course.
Nothing could be simpler.

COMMISSIONER I assure you, I'm all ears.

LYSISTRATA Do you know anything about weaving?
Say the yarn gets tangled: we thread it
this way and that through the skein, up and down,
until it's free. And it's like that with war.
We'll send our envoys
up and down, this way and that, all over Greece,
until it's finished.

COMMISSIONER Yarn? Thread? Skein?
Are you out of your mind? I tell you,
war is a serious business.

LYSISTRATA So serious
that I'd like to go on talking about weaving.

COMMISSIONER All right. Go ahead.

LYSISTRATA The first thing we have to do
is to wash our yarn, get the dirt out of it.
You see? Isn't there too much dirt here in Athens?
You must wash those men away.
Then our spoiled wool —
that's like your job-hunters, out for a life
of no work and big pay. Back to the basket,
citizens or not, allies or not,
or friendly immigrants.
And your colonies?
Hanks [looped bundles] of wool lost in various places. Pull them
together, weave them into one great whole,
and our voters are clothed for ever.

COMMISSIONER It would take a woman
to reduce state questions to a matter of carding and weaving.

LYSISTRATA You fool! Who were the mothers whose sons sailed off
to fight for Athens in Sicily?

COMMISSIONER Enough!
I beg you, do not call back those memories.

LYSISTRATA And then,
instead of the love that every woman needs,
we have only our single beds, where we can dream
of our husbands off with the Army.
Bad enough for wives!
But what about our girls, getting older every day,
and older, and no kisses?

COMMISSIONER Men get older, too.

LYSISTRATA Not in the same sense.
A soldier's discharged,
and he may be bald and toothless, yet he'll find
a pretty young thing to go to bed with.
But a woman!
Her beauty is gone with the first grey hair.
She can spend her time
consulting the oracles and the fortune-tellers,
but they'll never send her a husband.

(*The women then pour water on the* COMMISSIONER.)

REVIEW QUESTIONS

1. What qualifications did Ischomachus require in a wife?
2. What appears to have been the purpose of marriage among the Greeks?
3. What did Ischomachus consider the special responsibilities of a good wife? What were the obligations of a good husband?
4. Throughout *Lysistrata* Aristophanes alluded to the grievances of Greek women. List as many of these grievances as you can.
5. What attitudes of ancient Greek males toward females are reflected in our own modern society?

---

9 ▾ The Peloponnesian War

After the defeat of the Persian invaders in 479 B.C., the Athenians organized a mutual defense pact, called the Delian League, among the smaller Greek states. With the largest population and greatest wealth and naval forces, Athens became the dominant power within the league. In the course of time, Athens converted the alliance from an organization of equal sovereign states to an empire under Athenian control. This outcome aroused suspicion among the other Greek states in the Peloponnese, particularly Sparta, that an imperialistic Athens was a threat to their own independence and freedom. That fear precipitated the Peloponnesian War (431–404 B.C.), which devastated the Greek world during the late fifth century B.C.

Elected general during the war, Thucydides (see page 56) was banished from Athens for failing to rescue Amphipolis, a town under attack by Sparta. During his twenty-year exile, Thucydides gathered information about the war, which he correctly viewed as an event of world-historical importance. He was also right to regard his account as a unique documentary achievement that would serve as a model for future historians.

Above all, Thucydides studied politics, the lifeblood of Athenian society. For him, history was essentially the study of political behavior. Consistent with the Greek character, Thucydides sought underlying patterns and general truths pertaining to statesmanship and political power. His chronicle contains rich insights into human nature, the techniques of demagogues, the ruinous consequences of mob behavior, and the spiritual deterioration of men under the stress of war.

Thucydides
A SPARTAN KING'S PLEA FOR A PRUDENT FOREIGN POLICY, AND THE MELIAN DIALOGUE

Thucydides reconstructed speeches between Athenian envoys and Spartan leaders prior to the declaration of war. This device allowed him to summarize the

views of both sides. Hoping to deter Sparta from declaring war, the Athenians described their past services to the Greeks in the Persian Wars and defended their imperialism, arguing that it was only proper that the weak, in this instance Athens' allies, submit to superior strength.

Thucydides next describes the reaction of the Spartans to the speech of the Athenian envoys. Though the majority are prepared to declare war immediately, the Spartan king urges caution, carefully considering the factors that make Athens a formidable enemy and the disadvantages that Sparta will face in such a conflict. Because the Spartans are brave and wise, he says, they can afford to be slow and cautious in undertaking so hazardous a task as war with such a powerful enemy. He advises continuing negotiations for peace while preparing for the possibility of war. But his plea for moderation is rejected by the Spartans.

A SPARTAN KING'S PLEA

. . . [T]he Spartan King Archidamus, a man who had a reputation for both intelligence and moderation, came forward and made the following speech:

"Spartans, in the course of my life I have taken part in many wars, and I see among you people of the same age as I am. They and I have had experience, and so are not likely to share in what may be a general enthusiasm for war, nor to think that war is a good thing or a safe thing. And you will find, if you look carefully into the matter, that this present war which you are now discussing is not likely to be anything on a small scale. When we are engaged with Peloponnesians and neighbours, the forces on both sides are of the same type, and we can strike rapidly where we wish to strike. With Athens it is different. Here we shall be engaged with people who live far off, people also who have the widest experience of the sea and who are extremely well equipped in all other directions, very wealthy both as individuals and as a state, with ships and cavalry and hoplites [foot soldiers], with a population bigger than that of any other place in Hellas, and then, too, with numbers of allies who pay tribute to them. How, then, can we irresponsibly start a war with such a people? What have we to rely upon if we rush into it unprepared? Our navy? It is inferior to theirs, and if we are to give proper attention to it and build it up to their strength, that will take time. Or are we relying on our wealth? Here we are at an even greater disadvantage: we have no public funds, and it is no easy matter to secure contributions from private sources. Perhaps there is ground for confidence in the superiority which we have in heavy infantry and in actual numbers, assets which will enable us to invade and devastate their land. Athens, however, controls plenty of land outside Attica and can import what she wants by sea. And if we try to make her allies revolt from her, we shall have to support them with a fleet, since most of them are on the islands. What sort of war, then, are we going to fight? If we can neither defeat them at sea nor take away from them the resources on which their navy depends, we shall do ourselves more harm than good. We shall then find that we can no longer even make an honourable peace, especially if it is thought that it was we who began the quarrel. For we must not bolster ourselves up with the false hope that if we devastate their land, the war will soon be over. I fear that it is more likely that we shall be leaving it to our children after us. So convinced am I that the Athenians have too much pride to become the slaves of their own land, or to shrink back from warfare as though they were inexperienced in it.

"Not that I am suggesting that we should calmly allow them to injure our allies and should turn a blind eye to their machinations. What I do suggest is that we should not take up arms at the present moment; instead we should send to them and put our grievances before them; we should not threaten war too openly, though at the same time we should make it clear that we are not going to let them have their own way. In the meantime we should be making our own preparations by winning over new allies both among Hellenes and among foreigners — from any quarter, in fact, where we can increase our naval and financial resources. No one can blame us for securing our own safety by taking foreigners as well as Greeks into our alliance when we are, as is the fact, having our position undermined by the Athenians. At the same time we must put our own affairs in order. If they pay attention to our diplomatic protests, so much the better. If they do not, then, after two or three years have passed, we shall be in a much sounder position and can attack them, if we decide to do so. And perhaps when they see that our actual strength is keeping pace with the language that we use, they will be more inclined to give way. . . .

"As for being slow and cautious — which is the usual criticism made against us — there is nothing to be ashamed of in that. . . . 'Slow' and 'cautious' can equally well be 'wise' and 'sensible.'. . .

"Let us never give up this discipline which our fathers have handed down to us and which we still preserve and which has always done us good. Let us not be hurried, and in one short day's space come to a decision which will so profoundly affect the lives of men and their fortunes, the fates of cities and their national honour. We ought to take time over such a decision. And we, more than others, can afford to take time, because we are strong. As for the Athenians, I advise sending a mission to them about Potidaea [a northern Greek city subject to Athens] and also about the other cases where our allies claim to have been ill treated. Especially is this the right thing to do since the Athenians themselves are prepared to submit to arbitration, and when one party offers this it is quite illegal to attack him first, as though he was definitely in the wrong. And at the same time carry on your preparations for war. This decision is the best one you can make for yourselves, and is also the one most likely to inspire fear in your enemies."

▷ The Athenians, who saw no conflict between imperialism and democracy, considered it natural for strong states to dominate weaker ones. This view coincided with the position of those Sophists (see page 58) who argued that might makes right. The classic expression of this view is found in Thucydides' history.

During the war, Athens decided to invade the island of Melos, which resisted this unprovoked act of aggression. Thucydides reconstructed a dialogue on the matter between Athenian envoys and Melian officials. Subsequently, Athens attacked. After capturing the town, the Athenians slaughtered the men, enslaved the women and children, and colonized the territory. Following is the famous Melian Dialogue.

THE MELIAN DIALOGUE

MELIANS No one can object to each of us putting forward our own views in a calm atmosphere. That is perfectly reasonable. What is scarcely consistent with such a proposal is the present threat, indeed the certainty, of your making war on us. We see that you have come prepared to judge the argument yourselves, and that the likely end of it all will be either war, if we prove that we are in the right, and so refuse to surrender, or else slavery.

ATHENIANS If you are going to spend the time in enumerating your suspicions about the future, or if you have met here for any other reason except to look the facts in the face and on the basis of these facts to consider how you can save your city from destruction, there is no point in our going on with this discussion. If, however, you will do as we suggest, then we will speak on.

MELIANS It is natural and understandable that people who are placed as we are should have recourse to all kinds of arguments and different points of view. However, you are right in saying that we are met together here to discuss the safety of our country and, if you will have it so, the discussion shall proceed on the lines that you have laid down.

ATHENIANS Then we on our side will use no fine phrases saying, for example, that we have a right to our empire because we defeated the Persians, or that we have come against you now because of the injuries you have done us — a great mass of words that nobody would believe. And we ask you on your side not to imagine that you will influence us by saying that you, though a colony of Sparta, have not joined Sparta in the war, or that you have never done us any harm. Instead we recommend that you should try to get what it is possible for you to get, taking into consideration what we both really do think; since you know as well as we do that when these matters are discussed by practical people, the standard of justice depends on the equality of power to compel and that in fact the strong do what they have the power to do and the weak accept what they have to accept.

MELIANS Then in our view (since you force us to leave justice out of account and to confine ourselves to self-interest) — in our view it is at any rate useful that you should not destroy a principle that is to the general good of all men — namely, that in the case of all who fall into danger there should be such a thing as fair play and just dealing, and that such people should be allowed to use and to profit by arguments that fall short of a mathematical accuracy. And this is a principle which affects you as much as anybody, since your own fall would be visited by the most terrible vengeance and would be an example to the world.

ATHENIANS . . . What we shall do now is to show you that it is for the good of our own empire that we are here and that it is for the preservation of your city that we shall say what we are going to say. We do not want any trouble in bringing you into our empire, and we want you to be spared for the good both of yourselves and of ourselves.

MELIANS And how could it be just as good for us to be the slaves as for you to be the masters?

ATHENIANS You, by giving in, would save yourselves from disaster; we, by not destroying you, would be able to profit from you.

MELIANS So you would not agree to our being neutral, friends instead of enemies, but allies of neither side?

ATHENIANS No, because it is not so much your hostility that injures us; it is rather the case that, if we were on friendly terms with you, our subjects would regard that as a sign of weakness in us, whereas your hatred is evidence of our power. . . .[Our subjects think] that those who still preserve their independence do so because they are strong, and that if we fail to attack them it is because we are afraid. So that by conquering you we shall increase not only the size but the security of our empire. We rule the sea and you are islanders, and weaker islanders too than the others; it is therefore particularly important that you should not escape. . . .

MELIANS Then surely, if such hazards are taken by you to keep your empire . . . we who are still free would show ourselves great cowards and weaklings if we failed to face everything that comes rather than submit to slavery.

ATHENIANS No, not if you are sensible. This is no fair fight, with honour on one side and shame on the other. It is rather a question of saving your lives and not resisting those who are far too strong for you.

MELIANS Yet we know that in war fortune sometimes makes the odds more level than could be expected from the difference in numbers of the two sides. And if we surrender, then all our hope is lost at once, whereas, so long as we remain in action, there is still a hope that we may yet stand upright.

ATHENIANS Hope, that comforter in danger! If one already has solid advantages to fall back upon, one can indulge in hope. . . . [D]o not be like those people who, as so commonly happens, miss the chance of saving themselves in a human and practical way, and, when every clear and distinct hope has left them in their adversity, turn to what is blind and vague, to prophecies and oracles and such things which by encouraging hope lead men to ruin.

MELIANS It is difficult, and you may be sure that we know it, for us to oppose your power. . . . Nevertheless we trust that the gods will give us fortune as good as yours, because we are standing for what is right against what is wrong; and as for what we lack in power, we trust that it will be made up for by our alliance with the Spartans, who are bound, if for no other reason, then for honour's sake, and because we are their kinsmen, to come to our help. Our confidence, therefore, is not so entirely irrational as you think.

ATHENIANS . . . Our opinion of the gods and our knowledge of men lead us to conclude that it is a general and necessary law of nature to rule wherever one can. . . . [W]ith regard to your views about Sparta and your confidence that she, out of a sense of honour, will come to your aid, we must say that we congratulate you on your simplicity but do not envy you your folly. . . .

. . . You, if you take the right view . . . will see that there is nothing disgraceful in giving way to the greatest city in Hellas when she is offering you such reasonable terms — alliance on a tribute-paying basis and liberty to enjoy your own property. And, when you are allowed to choose between war and safety, you will not be so insensitively arrogant as to make the wrong choice. This is the safe rule — to stand up to one's equals, to behave with deference towards one's superiors, and to treat one's inferiors with moderation. Think it over again, then, when we have withdrawn from the meeting, and let this be a point that constantly recurs to your minds — that you are discussing the fate of your country, that you have only one country, and that its future for good or ill depends on this one single decision which you are going to make.

The Athenians then withdrew from the discussion. The Melians, left to themselves, reached a conclusion which was much the same as they had indicated in their previous replies. Their answer was as follows:

MELIANS Our decision, Athenians, is just the same as it was at first. We are not prepared to give up in a short moment the liberty which our city has enjoyed from its foundation for 700 years. We put our trust in the fortune that the gods will send and which has saved us up to now, and in the help of men — that is, of the Spartans; and so we shall try to save ourselves. But we invite you to allow us to be friends of yours and enemies to neither side, to make a treaty which shall be agreeable to both you and us, and so to leave our country.

REVIEW QUESTIONS

1. What arguments were advanced by the Spartan king in support of his foreign policy views?
2. What practical political factors, according to the Athenians, justified their refusal to respect the Melians' neutrality?
3. What political reasons influenced the Melian rejection of the Athenian demands?
4. What was the ethical basis of the Athenian policy?
5. In what sense did the foreign policy debate between the Melians and the Athenians reflect the new rationalist spirit in Greek society?

---

10 ▾ Socrates: The Rational Individual

Socrates (469–399 B.C.) marked a decisive turning point in Greek philosophy and in the history of Western thought. The Socratic conception of the rational

individual became an essential component of the tradition of classical humanism. Socrates agreed with the Sophists that the study of physical nature was less important than the study of man. But whereas the Sophists concentrated on teaching specific skills — how to excel in debates, for example — Socrates was concerned with comprehending and improving human character. Although ethical concerns lay at the center of Socrates' thought, he never provided a list of ethical commands; in Socratic philosophy, there is nothing comparable to the Ten Commandments. What he did provide was a method of arriving at knowledge: dialectic, or the dialogue.

For Socrates, the dialogue (the asking and answering of questions between two or more individuals) was the sole avenue to moral insights and self-knowledge. The interchange implied that one human mind was not a passive vessel into which a teacher, another human being, poured knowledge. Participants in a dialogue were obliged to play an active role and to think critically about human values. The use of the dialogue implied further that relations between people should involve rational discussion through which people learn from each other and improve themselves.

When Socrates was seventy, he was accused of corrupting the youth of Athens and of not believing in the city's gods but in other, new divinities, and he went on trial for his life.

Plato
≪ THE APOLOGY ≫

Knowledge of Socrates' trial comes principally from *The Apology* written by Plato (see page 88), Socrates' most illustrious student. (The original meaning of *apology* was a defense or explanation.) In the first passage from *The Apology,* presented below, Socrates tells the court that the Delphic Oracle, the prophetess of Apollo at Delphi, had said that there was no one wiser than Socrates. Not considering himself wise, Socrates resolved to discover what the oracle meant, by conversing with people reputed to be wise.

I want to a man who seemed wise: thinking that there, if anywhere, I should prove the answer wrong, and be able to say to the oracle, "You said that I am the wisest of men; but this man is wiser than I am." So I examined him — I need not tell you his name, he was a public man, but this was the result, Athenians. When I conversed with him, I came to see that, though many persons, and chiefly he himself, thought that he was wise, yet he was not wise. And then I tried to show him that he was not wise, though he fancied that he was; and by that I gained his hatred, and the hatred of many of the bystanders. So when I went away, I thought to myself, "I am wiser than this man: neither of us probably knows anything that is really good, but he thinks that he has knowledge, when he has it not, while I, seeing that I have no knowledge, do not think that I have." In this point, at least, I seem to be a little wiser than he is; I do not think that I know what I do not know. Next I went to another man, who seemed to be still wiser, with just the same result. And there again I gained his hatred. . . .

After the public men I went to the poets, tragic, dithyrambic [frenzied], and others, thinking there to find myself manifestly more ignorant than they. So I took up the poems on which I thought that they had spent most pains, and asked them what they meant wishing also for instruction. I am ashamed to tell you the truth, my friends, but I must say it. In short, almost any of the bystanders would have spoken better about the works of these poets than the poets themselves. So I soon found that it is not by wisdom that the poets create their works, but by a certain natural power, and by inspiration, like soothsayers and prophets: for though such persons say many fine things, they know nothing of what they say. And the poets seemed to me to be in a like case. And at the same time I perceived that, because of their poetry, they thought that they were the wisest of men in other matters too, which they were not. So I went away again, thinking that I had the same advantage over them as over the public men.

Finally I went to the artisans: for I was conscious, in a word, that I had no knowledge at all, and I was sure that I should find that they knew many fine things. And in that I was not mistaken. They knew what I did not know, and so far they were wiser than I. But, Athenians, it seemed to me that the skilled craftsmen made the same mistake as the poets. Each of them claimed to have great wisdom in the highest matters because he was skilful in his own art; and this fault of theirs threw their real wisdom into the shade. So I asked myself on behalf of the oracle whether I would choose to remain as I was, neither wise in their wisdom nor ignorant in their ignorance, or to have both, as they had them. And I made answer to myself and to the oracle that it were better for me to remain as I was.

This search, Athenians, has gained me much hatred of a very fierce and bitter kind, which has caused many false accusations against me; and I am called by the name of wise. For the bystanders always think that I am wise myself in any matter wherein I convict another man of ignorance. But in truth, my friends, perhaps it is God who is wise: and by this oracle he may have meant that man's wisdom is worth little or nothing. He did not mean, I think, that Socrates is wise: he only took me as an example, and made use of my name, as though he would say to men: "He among you is wisest, who, like Socrates, is convinced that for wisdom he is verily worthless." And therefore I still go about searching and testing every man whom I think wise, whether he be a citizen or a stranger, according to the word of the God [Apollo]; and whenever I find that he is not wise, I point that out to him in the service of the God. And I am so busy in this pursuit that I have never had leisure to take any part worth mentioning in public matters, or to look after my private affairs. I am in very great poverty by my service to the God.

And besides this, the young men who follow me about, who are the sons of wealthy persons and with much leisure, by nature delight in hearing men cross-questioned: and they often imitate me among themselves: then they try their hand at cross-questioning other people. And, I imagine, they find a great abundance of men who think that they know a great deal, when in truth they know little or nothing. And then the persons who are cross-questioned are angry with me instead of with themselves: and say that Socrates is an abominable fellow who corrupts the young. And when they are asked, Why, what does he do? what does he teach? they have nothing to say; but, not to seem at a loss, they repeat the stock charges against all philosophers, and say that he investigates things in the air and under the earth, and that he teaches people to disbelieve in the gods, and "to make the worst appear the better reason." For I fancy they would not like to confess the truth, that they are shown up as mere ignorant pretenders to knowledge. And so they have filled your ears with their fierce slanders for a long time, for they are zealous and fierce, and numerous: they are well-disciplined too, and plausible in speech. . . .

▷ Had Socrates been willing to compromise and to stop teaching his philosophy, it is likely that he would not have received the death penalty. However, for Socrates the pursuit of truth was the highest human activity; it involved the person's whole being. It transformed the individual, enabling him to live in accordance with moral values that had been arrived at through thought and that could be defended rationally.

. . . But I know well that it is evil and base to do wrong and to disobey my better, whether he be man or god. And I will never choose what I know to be evil, and fear and fly from what may possibly be a good. And so, even if you acquit me now, and do not listen to Anytus' [his prosecutor's] argument that I ought never to have been brought to trial, if I was to be acquitted; and that as it is, you are bound to put me to death, because if I were to escape, all your children would forthwith be utterly corrupted by practising what Socrates teaches: if you were therefore to say to me, "Socrates, this time we will not listen to Anytus: we will let you go: but on this condition, that you cease from carrying on this search, and from philosophy: if you are found doing that again, you shall die:" I say, if you offered to let me go on these terms, I should reply: — "Athenians, I hold you in the highest regard and love; but I will obey the God rather than you: and as long as I have breath and power I will not cease from philosophy, and from exhorting you and setting forth the truth to any of you whom I meet, saying as I am wont, 'My excellent friend, you are a citizen of Athens, a city very great and very famous for wisdom and power of mind: are you not ashamed of caring so much for the making of money, and for reputation and honour? Will you not spend thought or care on wisdom and truth and the perfecting of your soul?'" And if he dispute my words, and say that he does care for these things, I shall not forthwith release him and go away: I shall question him and cross-examine him: and if I think that he has not virtue, though he says that he has, I shall reproach him for setting the least value on the most important things; and the greater value on the more worthless. This shall I do to every one whom I meet, old or young, citizen or stranger; but especially to the citizens, for they are more nearly akin to me. For know well, the God commands me so to do. And I think that nothing better has ever happened to you in your city than my service to the God. For I spend my whole life in going about persuading you all, both young and old, to give your first and chiefest care to the perfection of your souls: and not till you have done that to care for your bodies or your wealth. I tell you, that virtue does not come from wealth, but that wealth and every other good, whether public or private, which men have, come from virtue. If then I corrupt the youth by this teaching, the mischief is great; but if any man says that I teach anything else, he speaks falsely. And therefore, Athenians, I say, either listen to Anytus, or do not listen to him: either acquit me, or do not acquit me: but be sure that I shall not alter my life; no, not if I have to die for it many times.

Do not interrupt me, Athenians. Remember the request which I made to you, and listen to my words. I think that it will do you good to hear them. I have something more to say to you, at which perhaps you will cry out: but do not do that. Be sure that if you kill me, a man such as I say I am, you will harm yourselves more than you will harm me. Meletus [another enemy prosecutor] and Anytus can do me no harm; that is impossible, for I do not think that God will allow a good man to be harmed by a bad one. They may indeed kill me, or drive me into exile, or deprive me of my civil rights; and perhaps Meletus and others think these things great evils. But I do not think so: I think that to do as he is doing, and to try to kill a man unjustly, is a much greater evil. And now, Athenians, I am not going to argue for my own sake at all, as you might think, but for yours, that you may not sin against the God and reject his gift to you, by condemning me. If you put me to death, you will hardly find another man to fill my place. The God has sent me to attack the city, if I may use a ludicrous simile, just as if it were a great and noble horse, which was rather sluggish from its size and needed a gadfly to rouse it: and I think that I am the gadfly that the God has set upon the city: for I never cease settling on you as it were at every point, and rousing, and exhorting, and reproaching each man of you all day long. You will hardly find any one else, my friends, to fill my place: and, if you take my advice, you will spare my life. You are indignant, as drowsy persons are when they are awakened, and, of course, if you are persuaded by Anytus, you could easily kill me with a single blow, and then sleep on undisturbed for the rest of your lives. . . .

Perhaps someone will say, "Why cannot you withdraw from Athens, Socrates, and hold your peace?" It is the most difficult thing in the world to make you understand why I cannot do that. If I say that I cannot hold my peace because that would be to disobey the God, you will think that I am not in earnest and will not believe me. And if I tell you that no greater good can happen to a man than to discuss human excellence every day and the other matters about which you have heard me arguing and examining myself and others, and that an unexamined life is not worth living, then you will believe me still less. But that is so, my friends, though it is not easy to persuade you. . . .

▷ Socrates is convicted and sentenced to death.

. . . Perhaps, my friends, you think that I have been convicted because I was wanting in the arguments by which I could have persuaded you to acquit me, if I had thought it right to do or to say anything to escape punishment. It is not so. I have been convicted because I was wanting, not in arguments, but in impudence and shamelessness — because I would not plead before you as you would have liked to hear me plead, or appeal to you with weeping and wailing, or say and do many other things which I maintain are unworthy of me, but which you have been accustomed to from other men. But when I was defending myself, I thought that I ought not to do anything unworthy of a free man because of the danger which I ran, and I have not changed my mind now. I would very much rather defend myself as I did, and die, than as you would have had me do, and live. . . .

And now I wish to prophesy to you, Athenians, who have condemned me. For I am going to die, and that is the time when men have most prophetic power. And I prophesy to you who have sentenced me to death that a far more severe punishment than you have inflicted on me will surely overtake you as soon as I am dead. You have done this thing, thinking that you will be relieved from having to give an account of your lives. But I say that the result will be very different. There will be more men who will call you to account, whom I have held back, though you did not recognize it. And they will be harsher toward you than I have been, for they will be younger, and you will be more indignant with them. For if you think that you will restrain men from reproaching you for not living as you should, by putting them to death, you are very much mistaken. That way of escape is neither possible nor honorable. It is much more honorable and much easier not to suppress others, but to make yourselves as good as you can. This is my parting prophecy to you who have condemned me.

REVIEW QUESTIONS

1. In Socrates' dialogue with the "wise" men, what was the wisdom that Socrates alone seemed to possess?
2. What is the "Socratic method" of seeking knowledge? Why is it effective?
3. What was the popular image of philosophers among Athenians?

4. According to Socrates, what is the true vocation of a philosopher? What price may the philosopher pay for his effort?
5. Why did some Athenians believe that Socrates corrupted the young?
6. What did Socrates say would be his reaction if he were offered an acquittal on the condition that he give up teaching his philosophy? What were his reasons?
7. Compare Socrates' view of his vocation with that of the Hebrew prophets.

---

11 ▾ Plato: The Philosopher-King

Plato (c. 429–347 B.C.), an Athenian aristocrat and disciple of Socrates, based his philosophy on Socrates' teachings. Plato was greatly affected by the deterioration of Athenian politics during and immediately after the Peloponnesian War. The rise of demagogues, the violent conflicts between oligarchs and democrats, and the execution of Socrates convinced Plato that Athenian democracy was a failure. His hostility toward democracy also stemmed from his upper-class background and temperament.

Socratic philosophy held promise of reforming the individual through the critical use of reason. Plato felt that the individual could not undergo a moral transformation while living in a wicked and corrupt society. If the individual were to achieve virtue, the state must be reformed.

Plato
≪ THE REPUBLIC ≫

In *The Republic,* Plato proposed organizing government in harmony with the needs of human nature. Those people who are driven by a desire for food, possessions, and sexual gratification, Plato said, should be farmers, tradesmen, or artisans. Those who are naturally courageous and assertive should be soldiers. And the few who have the capacity for wisdom — the philosophers — should be entrusted with political power.

In the ideal state, Plato asserted, the many would be ruled by the few who have a natural endowment for leadership. These philosopher-kings, the finest product of the state's carefully designed educational program, would wield absolute power: the people would lose their right to participate in political affairs, and the state would manufacture propaganda and strictly control education in order to keep the masses obedient. In exchange, the citizens would gain leaders distinguished by their rationality, wisdom, and virtue. In the form of a dialogue between Socrates and a man called Glaucon, Plato in the following reading presented his views on the character of the philosopher.

[SOCRATES] Unless either philosophers become kings in their countries or those who are now called kings and rulers come to be sufficiently inspired with a genuine desire for wisdom; unless that is to say, political power and philosophy meet together . . . there can be no rest from troubles, my dear Glaucon, for states, nor yet, as I believe, for all mankind. . . . There is no other way of happiness either for the state or for the individual. . . .

Now . . . we must, I think, define . . . whom we mean by these lovers of wisdom who, we have dared to assert, ought to be our rulers. Once we have a clear view of their character, we shall be able to defend our position by pointing to some who are naturally fitted to combine philosophic study with political leadership, while the rest of the world should accept their guidance and let philosophy alone.

[GLAUCON] Yes, this is the moment for a definition. . . .

[S] . . . One trait of the philosophic nature we may take as already granted: a constant passion for any knowledge that will reveal to them something of that reality which endures for ever and is not always passing into and out of existence. And, we may add, their desire is to know the whole of that reality; they will not willingly renounce any part of it as relatively small and insignificant, as we said before when we compared them to the lover and to the man who covets honour.

[G] True.

[S] Is there not another trait which the nature we are seeking cannot fail to possess — truthfulness, a love of truth and a hatred for falsehood that will not tolerate untruth in any form?

[G] Yes, it is natural to expect that.

[S] It is not merely natural, but entirely necessary that an instinctive passion for any object should extend to all that is closely akin to it; and there is nothing more closely akin to wisdom than truth. So the same nature cannot love wisdom and falsehood; the genuine lover of knowledge cannot fail, from his youth up, to strive after the whole of truth.

[G] I perfectly agree.

[S] Now we surely know that when a man's desires set strongly in one direction, in every other channel they flow more feebly, like a stream diverted into another bed. So when the current has set towards knowledge and all that goes with it, desire will abandon those pleasures of which the body is the instrument and be concerned only with the pleasure which the soul enjoys independently — if, that is to say, the love of wisdom is more than a mere pretence. Accordingly, such a one will be temperate and no lover of money; for he will be the last person to care about the things for the sake of which money is eagerly sought and lavishly spent.

[G] That is true.

[S] Again, in seeking to distinguish the philosophic nature, you must not overlook the least touch of meanness. Nothing could be more contrary than pettiness to a mind constantly bent on grasping the whole of things, both divine and human.

[G] Quite true.

[S] And do you suppose that one who is so high-minded and whose thought can contemplate all time and all existence will count this life of man a matter of much concern?

[G] No, he could not.

[S] So for such a man death will have no terrors.

[G] None.

[S] A mean and cowardly nature, then, can have no part in the genuine pursuit of wisdom.

[G] I think not.

[S] And if a man is temperate and free from the love of money, meanness, pretentiousness, and cowardice, he will not be hard to deal with or dishonest. So, as another indication of the philosophic temper, you will observe whether, from youth up, he is fair-minded, gentle, and sociable.

[G] Certainly.

[S] Also you will not fail to notice whether he is quick or slow to learn. No one can be expected to take a reasonable delight in a task in which much painful effort makes little headway. And if he cannot retain what he learns, his forgetfulness will leave no room in his head for knowledge; and so, having all his toil for nothing, he can only end by hating himself as well as his fruitless occupation. We must not, then, count a forgetful mind as competent to pursue wisdom; we must require a good memory.

[G] By all means.

[S] Further, there is in some natures a crudity and awkwardness that can only tend to a lack of measure and proportion; and there is a close affinity between proportion and truth. Hence, besides our other requirements, we shall look for a mind endowed with measure and grace, which will be instinctively drawn to see every reality in its true light.

[G] Yes.

[S] Well then, now that we have enumerated the qualities of a mind destined to take its full part in the apprehension of reality, have you any doubt about their being indispensable and all necessarily going together?

[G] None whatever.

[S] Then have you any fault to find with a pursuit which none can worthily follow who is not by nature quick to learn and to remember, magnanimous and gracious, the friend and kinsman of truth, justice, courage, temperance?

▷ Plato said that genuine philosophers are "those whose passion it is to see the truth." For Plato, unlike the Sophists, standards of beauty, justice, and goodness exist that are universally valid — that apply to all peoples at all times. Plato held that these standards are in a higher world, the realm of Forms or Ideas. This world of Forms is known only through the mind, not the senses. For example, a sculptor observes many bodies but they all possess flaws; in his mind's eye he perceives the world of Ideas and tries to reproduce with his art the perfect human form. Plato says that the ordinary person, basing opinion on everyday experience, has an imperfect understanding of beauty, goodness, and justice, whereas the philosopher, through reason, reaches beyond sense perception to the realm of Forms and discovers truth. Such people are the natural rulers of the state; only they are capable of a correct understanding of justice; only they have the wisdom to reform the state in the best interests of all its citizens.

The distinction between a higher world of truth and a lower world of imperfection, deception, and illusion is illustrated in Plato's famous Allegory of the Cave. Plato, through the dialogue of Socrates and Glaucon, compares those persons without a knowledge of the Forms to prisoners in a dark cave.

[S] Next, said I, here is a parable to illustrate the degrees in which our nature may be enlightened or unenlightened. Imagine the condition of men living in a sort of cavernous chamber underground, with an entrance open to the light and a long passage all down the cave. Here they have been from childhood, chained by the leg and also by the neck, so that they cannot move and can see only what is in front of them, because the chains will not let them turn their heads. At some distance higher up is the light of a fire burning behind them; and between the prisoners and the fire is a track with a parapet built along it, like the screen at a puppet-show, which hides the performers while they show their puppets over the top.

[G] I see, said he.

[S] Now behind this parapet imagine persons carrying along various artificial objects, including figures of men and animals in wood or stone or other materials, which project above the parapet. Naturally, some of these persons will be talking, others silent.

[G] It is a strange picture, he said, and a strange sort of prisoners.

[S] Like ourselves, I replied; for in the first place prisoners so confined would have seen nothing of themselves or of one another, except the shadows thrown by the fire-light on the wall of the Cave facing them, would they?

[G] Not if all their lives they had been prevented from moving their heads.

[S] And they would have seen as little of the objects carried past.

[G] Of course.

[S] Now, if they could talk to one another, would they not suppose that their words referred only to those passing shadows which they saw?

[G] Necessarily.

[S] And suppose their prison had an echo from the wall facing them? When one of the people crossing behind them spoke, they could only suppose that the sound came from the shadow passing before their eyes.

[G] No doubt.

[S] In every way, then, such prisoners would recognize as reality nothing but the shadows of those artificial objects.

[G] Inevitably. . . .

▷ To the prisoners chained in the cave, the shadows of the artificial objects constitute reality. When a freed prisoners ascends from the cave to the sunlight, he sees a totally different world. Returning to the cave, he tries to tell the prisoners that the shadows are only poor imitations of reality, but they laugh at him, for their opinions have been shaped by the only world they know. The meaning of the parable is clear: the philosophers who ascend to the higher world of Forms possess true knowledge; everyone else possesses mere opinions, deceptive beliefs, and illusions. The philosophers have a duty to guide the ignorant.

[S] Now consider what would happen if their release from the chains and the healing of their unwisdom should come about in this way. Suppose one of them were set free and forced suddenly to stand up, turn his head, and walk with eyes lifted to the light; all these movements would be painful, and he would be too dazzled to make out the objects whose shadows he had been used to see. What do you think he would say, if someone told him that what he had formerly seen was meaningless illusion, but now, being somewhat nearer to reality and turned towards more real objects, he was getting a truer view? Suppose further that he were shown the various objects being carried by and were made to say, in reply to questions, what each of them was. Would he not be perplexed and believe the objects now shown him to be not so real as what he formerly saw?

[G] Yes, not nearly so real.

[S] And if he were forced to look at the firelight itself, would not his eyes ache, so that he would try to escape and turn back to the things which he could see distinctly, convinced that they really were clearer than these other objects now being shown to him?

[G] Yes.

[S] And suppose someone were to drag him away forcibly up the steep and rugged ascent and not let him go until he had hauled him out into the sunlight, would he not suffer pain and vexation at such treatment, and, when he had come out into the light, find his eyes so full of its radiance that he could not see a single one of the things that he was now told were real?

[G] Certainly he would not see them all at once.

[S] He would need, then, to grow accustomed before he could see things in that upper world. At first it would be easiest to make out shadows, and then the images of men and things reflected in water, and later on the things themselves. After that, it would be easier to watch the heavenly bodies and the sky itself by night, looking at the light of the moon and stars rather than the Sun and the Sun's light in the day-time.

[G] Yes, surely.

[S] Last of all, he would be able to look at the Sun and contemplate its nature, not as it appears when reflected in water or any alien medium, but as it is in itself in its own domain.

[G] No doubt.

[S] And now he would begin to draw the conclusion that it is the Sun that produces the seasons and the course of the year and controls everything in the visible world, and moreover is in a way the cause of all that he and his companions used to see.

[G] Clearly he would come at last to that conclusion.

[S] Then if he called to mind his fellow prisoners and what passed for wisdom in his former dwelling place, he would surely think himself happy in the change and be sorry for them. They may have had a practice of honouring and commending one another, with prizes for the man who had the keenest eye for the passing shadows and the best memory for the order in which they followed or accompanied one another, so that he could make a good guess as to which was going to come next. Would our released prisoner be likely to covet those prizes or to envy the men exalted to honour and power in the Cave? Would he not feel like Homer's Achilles, that he would far sooner "be on earth as a hired servant in the house of a landless man" or endure anything rather than go back to his old beliefs and live in the old way?

[G] Yes, he would prefer any fate to such a life.

[S] Now imagine what would happen if he went down again to take his former seat in the Cave. Coming suddenly out of the sunlight, his eyes would be filled with darkness. He might be required once more to deliver his opinion on those shadows, in competition with the prisoners who had never been released, while his eyesight was still dim and unsteady; and it might take some time to become used to the darkness. They would laugh at him and say that he had gone up only to come back with his sight ruined; it was worth no one's while even to attempt the ascent. If they could lay hands on the man who was trying to set them free and lead them up, they would kill him.

[G] Yes, they would.

[S] Every feature in this parable, my dear Glaucon, is meant to fit our earlier analysis. The prison dwelling corresponds to the region revealed to us through the sense of sight, and the firelight within it to the power of the Sun. The ascent to see the things in the upper world you may take as standing for the upward journey of the soul into the region of the intelligible; then you will be in possession of what I surmise, since that is what you wish to be told. Heaven knows whether it is true; but this, at any rate, is how it appears to me. In the world of knowledge, the last thing to be perceived and only with great difficulty is the essential Form of Goodness. Once it is perceived, the conclusion must follow that, for all things, this is the cause of whatever is right and good; in the visible world it gives birth to light and to the lord of light, while it is itself sovereign in the intelligible world and the parent of intelligence and truth. Without having had a vision of this Form no one can act with wisdom, either in his own life or in matters of state. . . .

▷ For Plato, the perfect state, like the well-formed soul, is one governed by reason. By contrast, in the imperfect state, as in the imperfect soul, greed, selfishness, desire, and disorder predominate. Democracy is flawed, said Plato, because most people lack the ability to deal intelligently with matters of state. In the end, said Plato, the democratic state degenerates into anarchy, and the way is prepared for a tyrant. Plato viewed the tyrant as the most despicable of persons. A slave to his own passions, said Plato, the tyrant is like a lunatic who "dreams that he can lord it over all mankind and heaven besides." The character of the philosopher is the very opposite of the sick soul of the tyrant. In the following passage, Plato discusses what he regards as democracy's weaknesses.

[S] And when the poor win, the result is a democracy. They kill some of the opposite party, banish others, and grant the rest an equal share in civil rights and government, officials being usually appointed by lot.

[G] Yes, that is how a democracy comes to be established, whether by force of arms or because the other party is terrorized into giving way.

[S] Now what is the character of this new régime? Obviously the way they govern themselves will throw light on the democratic type of man.

[G] No doubt.

[S] First of all, they are free. Liberty and free speech are rife everywhere; anyone is allowed to do what he likes.

[G] Yes, so we are told.

[S] That being so, every man will arrange his own manner of life to suit his pleasure. The result will be a greater variety of individuals than under any other constitution. So it may be the finest of all, with its variegated pattern of all sorts of characters. Many people may think it the best, just as women and children might admire a mixture of colours of every shade in the pattern of a dress. At any rate if we are in search of a constitution, here is a good place to look for one. A democracy is so free that it contains a sample of every kind; and perhaps anyone who intends to found a state, as we have been doing, ought first to visit this emporium of constitutions and choose the model he likes best.

[G] He will find plenty to choose from.

[S] Here, too, you are not obliged to be in authority, however competent you may be, or to submit to authority, if you do not like it; you need not fight when your fellow citizens are at war, nor remain at peace when they do, unless you want peace; and though you may have no legal right to hold office or sit on juries, you will do so all the same if the fancy takes you. . . .

. . . When he [the democrat] is told that some pleasures should be sought and valued as arising from desires of a higher order, others chastised and enslaved because the desires are base, he will shut the gates of the citadel against the messengers of truth, shaking his head and declaring that one appetite is as good as another and all must have their equal rights. So he spends his days indulging the pleasure of the moment, now intoxicated with wine and music, and then taking to a spare diet and drinking nothing but water; one day in hard training, the next doing nothing at all, the third apparently immersed in study. Every now and then he takes a part in politics, leaping to his feet to say or do whatever comes into his head. . . . His life is subject to no order or restraint, and he has no wish to change an existence which he calls pleasant, free, and happy.

That well describes the life of one whose motto is liberty and equality. . . .

In a democratic country you will be told that liberty is its noblest possession, which makes it the only fit place for a free spirit to live in.

[G] True; that is often said.

[S] Well then, as I was saying, perhaps the insatiable desire for this good to the neglect of everything else may transform a democracy and lead to a demand for despotism. A democratic state may fall under the influence of unprincipled leaders, ready to minister to its thirst for liberty with too deep draughts of this heady wine; and then, if its rulers are not complaisant enough to give it unstinted freedom, they will be arraigned as accursed oligarchs and punished. Law-abiding citizens will be insulted as nonentities who hug their chains; and all praise and honour will be bestowed, both publicly and in private, on rulers who behave like subjects and subjects who behave like rulers. In such a state the spirit of liberty is bound to go to all lengths. . . .

. . . The parent falls into the habit of behaving like the child, and the child like the parent: the father is afraid of his sons, and they show no fear or respect for their parents, in order to assert their freedom. . . . To descend to smaller matters, the schoolmaster timidly flatters his pupils, and the pupils make light of their masters as well as of their attendants. Generally speaking, the young copy their elders, argue with them, and will not do as they are told; while the old, anxious not to be thought disagreeable tyrants, imitate the young and condescend to enter into their jokes and amusements. . . .

Putting all these items together, you can see the result: the citizens become so sensitive that they resent the slightest application of control as intolerable tyranny, and in their resolve to have no master they end by disregarding even the law, written or unwritten.

[G] Yes, I know that only too well.

[S] Such then, I should say, is the seed, so full of fair promise, from which springs despotism.

REVIEW QUESTIONS

1. According to Plato, what character traits did a philosopher possess? What traits were incompatible with the vocation of a philosopher?

2. According to the Allegory of the Cave, what is reality and what is mere illusion?
3. In the cave parable, what was the likely fate of the person who, having seen reality more perfectly than his fellows, tried to convince them of their blind ignorance?
4. What was the means by which a person could come to know the essential Forms of reality?
5. Why did Plato believe that philosophers would be the best rulers of the commonwealth?
6. Why did Plato believe that liberty could open the door to despotism?
7. What did Plato find so objectionable in a democracy?
8. What did Plato seem to mean by the term *liberty*?
9. Explain why you agree or disagree with Plato's characterization of democratic societies.

---

12 ▾ Aristotle: Science and Politics

Aristotle (384–322 B.C.) was born at Stagira, a Greek city-state on the Macedonian coast. About 367, he came to Athens to study with Plato and remained a member of Plato's Academy for twenty years. In 342 B.C., Philip II, king of Macedonia, invited Aristotle to tutor his son Alexander, who was then fourteen years old. When Alexander succeeded Philip and set out to conquer the Persian Empire, Aristotle left Macedonia for Athens, where he opened a school of philosophy called the Lyceum, named for a nearby temple to Apollo Lyceus. Aristotle synthesized the thought of earlier philosophers, including his teacher Plato, and was the leading authority of his day in virtually every field of knowledge.

Aristotle *≪ HISTORY OF ANIMALS ≫ AND ≪ POLITICS ≫*

Scientific thinking encompasses both rationalism and empiricism. Rationalism — pursuit of truth through thought alone, independent of experience with the natural world — was advocated by Plato. This approach points in the direction of theoretical mathematics. Like Plato, Aristotle valued reason, but unlike his teacher he also had great respect for the concrete details of nature obtained through sense experience. In *History of Animals,* Aristotle demonstrated his empirical approach: observing nature and collecting, classifying, and analyzing data. Aristotle's empiricism is the foundation of such sciences as geology, botany, and biology. The first excerpt illustrates his careful observation of the development of a chick embryo.

When he turned to the study of politics, Aristotle also followed an empirical methodology. He undertook a series of historical studies of the constitutions of 158 Greek states. The most significant and complete study that has survived

describes the constitution of Athens. On the basis of these extensive surveys, Aristotle proceeded to write *Politics,* his masterwork of political philosophy, excerpted in the second reading.

HISTORY OF ANIMALS

. . . With the common hen after three days and three nights there is the first indication of the embryo; with larger birds the interval being longer, with smaller birds shorter. Meanwhile the yolk comes into being, rising towards the sharp end, where the primal element of the egg is situated, and where the egg gets hatched; and the heart appears, like a speck of blood, in the white of the egg. This point beats and moves as though endowed with life, . . . and a membrane carrying bloody fibres now envelops the yolk. . . . A little afterwards the body is differentiated, at first very small and white. The head is clearly distinguished, and in it the eyes, swollen out to a great extent. This condition of the eyes lasts on for a good while, as it is only by degrees that they diminish in size and collapse. At the outset the under portion of the body appears insignificant in comparison with the upper portion. . . . The life-element of the chick is in the white of the egg, and the nutriment comes through the navel-string out of the yolk.

When the egg is now ten days old the chick and all its parts are distinctly visible. The head is still larger than the rest of its body, and the eyes larger than the head, but still devoid of vision. The eyes, if removed about this time, are found to be larger than beans, and black; if the cuticle be peeled off them there is a white and cold liquid inside, quite glittering in the sunlight, but there is no hard substance whatsoever. Such is the condition of the head and eyes. At this time also the larger internal organs are visible. . . .

About the twentieth day, if you open the egg and touch the chick, it moves inside and chirps; and it is already coming to be covered with down, when, after the twentieth day is past, the chick begins to break the shell. The head is situated over the right leg close to the flank, and the wing is placed over the head. . . .

▷ In the following selection from *Politics,* Aristotle begins by defining the nature of a state and its purpose.

POLITICS

It is clear therefore that the state cannot be defined merely as a community dwelling in the same place and preventing its members from wrong-doing and promoting the exchange of goods and services. Certainly all these must be present if there is to be a state, but even the presence of every one of them does not *ipso facto* [by that fact] make a state. The state is intended to enable all, in their households and their kinships, to live *well,* meaning by that a full and satisfying life. . . .

. . . [W]e must lay it down that the political association which we call a state exists not simply for the purpose of living together but for the sake of noble actions. Those who do noble deeds are therefore contributing to the quality of the political association, and those who contribute most are entitled to a larger share [of political power] than those who, though they may be equal or even superior in free birth and family, are inferior in noble deeds and so in the essential goodness that belongs to the *polis.* Similarly, they are entitled to a larger share than those who are superior in riches but inferior in goodness.

▷ He then addresses the problem of where the sovereign power of the state ought to reside.

. . . "Where ought the sovereign power of the state to reside?" With the people? With the propertied classes? With the good? With one man, the best of all the good? With one man, the tyrant? There are objections to all these. Thus suppose we say the people is the supreme authority, then if they use their numerical superiority to make a distribution of the property of the rich, is not that unjust? It has been done by a valid decision of the sovereign power, yet what can we call it save the very height of injustice? Again, if the majority, having laid their hands on everything, distribute the possessions of the few, they are obviously destroying the state. But that cannot be goodness which destroys its possessor and justice cannot be destructive of the state. So it is clear that this process, though it may be the law, cannot be just. Or, if that is just, the actions taken by a tyrant must be just; his superior power enables him to use force, just as the masses force their will on the rich. Thirdly, if it is just for the few and wealthy to rule, and if they too rob and plunder and help themselves to the goods of the many, is that just? If it is, then it is just in the former case also. The answer clearly is that all these three are bad and unjust. The fourth alternative, that the good should rule and have the supreme authority, is also not free from objection; it means that all the rest must be without official standing, debarred from holding office under the constitution. The fifth alternative, that one man, the best, should rule, is no better; by making the number of rulers fewer we leave still larger numbers without official standing. It might be objected too that it is a bad thing for any human being, subject to all possible disorders and affections of the human mind, to be the sovereign authority, which ought to be reserved for the law itself. But that will not make any difference to the cases we have been discussing; the law itself may have a bias towards oligarchy or democracy, so that exactly the same results will ensue. . . .

. . . [A]t the moment it would seem that the most defensible, perhaps even the truest, answer to the question would be to say that the majority ought to be sovereign, rather than the best, where the best are few. For it is possible that the many, no one of whom taken singly is a good man, may yet taken all together be better than the few, not individually but collectively, in the same way that a feast to which all contribute is better than one given at one man's expense. For where there are many people, each has some share of goodness and intelligence, and when these are brought together, they become as it were one multiple man with many pairs of feet and hands and many minds. So too in regard to character and powers of perception. That is why the general public is a better judge of works of music and poetry; some judge some parts, some others, but their joint pronouncement is a verdict upon the whole. And it is this assembling in one what was before separate that gives the good man his superiority over any individual man from the masses.

▷ Aristotle seeks to determine what is the best constitution. His conclusion reflects the premise developed in his *Ethics* that moderation, or the middle way, is the path to virtue in all things. So, Aristotle says that in forming a constitution for the state, power should reside in the hands of the middle class rather than the aristocracy or the poor.

If we were right when in our *Ethics* we stated that Virtue is a Mean and that the happy life is life free and unhindered and according to virtue, then the best life must be the middle way, [or the mean] . . . between two extremes which it is open to those at either end to attain. And the same principle must be applicable to the goodness or badness of cities and states. For the constitution of a city is really the way it lives.

In all states there are three sections of the community — the very well-off, the very badly-off, and those in between. Seeing therefore that it is agreed that moderation and a middle position are best, it is clear that in the matter of possessions to own a middling amount is best of all. This condition is most obedient to reason, and following reason is just what is difficult both for the exceedingly rich, handsome, strong, and well-born, and for the opposite, the extremely poor, the weak, and the downtrodden. The former commit deeds of violence on a large scale, the latter are delinquent and wicked in petty ways. The misdeeds of the one class are due to *hubris* [overweening pride, arrogance], the misdeeds of the other to rascality. Add the fact that it is among the members of the middle section that you find least reluctance to hold office as well as least eagerness to do so; and both these are detrimental to states. There are other drawbacks about the two extremes. Those who have a super-abundance of all that makes for success, strength, riches, friends, and so forth, neither wish to hold office nor understand the work; and this is ingrained in them from childhood on; even at school they are so full of their superiority that they have never learned to do what they are told. Those on the other hand who are greatly deficient in these qualities are too subservient. So they cannot command and can only obey in a servile régime, while the others cannot obey in any régime and can command only in a master-slave relationship. The result is a state not of free men but of slaves and masters, the one full of envy, the other of contempt. Nothing could be farther removed from friendship or from the whole idea of a shared partnership in a state. Sharing is a token of friendship; one does not share even a journey with people one does not like. The state aims to consist as far as possible of those who are like and equal, a condition found chiefly among the middle section. And so the best government is certain to be found in this kind of city, whose composition is, we maintain, a natural one. The middle class is also the steadiest element, the least eager for change. They neither covet, like the poor, the possessions of others, nor do others covet theirs, as the poor covet those of the rich. So they live less risky lives, not scheming and not being schemed against. Phocylides's [sixth-century B.C. poet] wish was therefore justified when he wrote "Those in the middle have many advantages; that is where I wish to be in society."

It is clear then both that the political partnership which operates through the middle class is best, and also that those cities have every chance of being well-governed in which the middle class is large, stronger if possible than the other two together, or at any rate stronger than one of them. For the addition of its weight to either side will turn the balance and prevent the extravagances of the opposition. For this reason it is a happy state of affairs when those who take part in the life of the state have a moderate but adequate amount of property; for where one set of people possesses a great deal and the other nothing, the result is either extreme democracy or unmixed oligarchy or a tyranny due to the excesses of the other two. Tyranny often emerges from an over-enthusiastic democracy or from an oligarchy, but much more rarely from middle-class constitutions or from those very near to them.

The superiority of the middle type of constitution is clear also from the fact that it alone is free from fighting among factions. Where the middle element is large, there least of all arise faction and counter-faction among citizens. And for the same reason the larger states are free from danger of splitting; they are strong in the middle. In small states it is easy for the whole body of citizens to become divided into two, leaving no middle at all, and they are nearly all either rich or poor. Democracies too are safer than oligarchies in this respect and longer lasting thanks to their middle class, which is always more numerous and more politically important in democracies than in oligarchies. For when the unpropertied class without the support of a middle class gets on top by weight of numbers, things go badly and they soon come to grief.

REVIEW QUESTIONS

1. In *History of Animals,* what details show Aristotle's empiricism?
2. According to Aristotle, what are the characteristic features of a true political community?
3. Aristotle urged moderation as a guiding principle for human life. In what way did he apply it to the life of the political community?
4. What problems did Aristotle find when sovereign power resided with the people? With the propertied classes? With the good? With the tyrant? Why did he conclude that government by the majority was preferable to the other forms?
5. Why did he believe that state power should rest with the middle class rather than with the aristocracy or the poor?
6. Explain what Aristotle might have feared from the "tyranny of overenthusiastic democracy"?
7. How did the writers of the U.S. Constitution try to avoid government by the "tyranny" of democratic majority rule?

---

13 ▾ Alexander the Great and the Hellenistic World

Alexander the Great (356–323 B.C.) was just twenty when his father, Philip II of Macedonia, conqueror of the Greek city-states, was assassinated. Possessing boundless ambition and irrepressible energy, Alexander led his forces into Asia Minor in 334 B.C. with the objective of conquering the huge Persian Empire. In the ensuing campaigns, he demonstrated superb skill as a military planner and leader, and his army marched all the way to India, winning every battle. Although Alexander left a son, Alexander IV, by his wife Roxane, political chaos followed Alexander's premature death in 323 B.C. By 275 B.C., his empire was broken into three regions, ruled by the Ptolemies, Seleucids, and Antigonids — royal dynasties founded by Alexander's generals.

Alexandria, capital of the Ptolemaic kingdom of Egypt, was founded by Alexander and was the leading city of the Hellenistic world. Its state-supported museum and library attracted the outstanding scholars of the age. In contrast to the inhabitants of the polis of classical Greece, Alexandria's inhabitants were multi-ethnic; among others, they included Greeks, Macedonians, Egyptians, Jews, and Syrians.

Plutarch
THE FORTUNE OF ALEXANDER

The Greek biographer Plutarch (c. A.D. 46–120) provides a glowing account of Alexander in the following passage from *Moralia.* Plutarch saw Alexander as a

philosopher in action and an apostle of universalism and human brotherhood. Many modern historians reject this assessment of Alexander's intentions; however, they recognize the significance of Alexander's conquests in reducing the distinctions between Near Easterners and Greeks.

In such poverty and in circumstances fraught with such uncertainty, a stripling, scarcely older than a boy, had the daring to hope for Babylon and Susa [the Persian capital]; nay more, to conceive the project of dominion over all the world, relying only on the thirty thousand foot and four thousand cavalry. . . .

Was, then, Alexander ill-advised and precipitate in setting forth with such humble resources to acquire so vast an empire? By no means. For who has ever put forth with greater or fairer equipment than he: greatness of soul, keen intelligence, self-restraint, and manly courage, with which Philosophy herself provided him for his campaign? Yes, the equipment that he had from Aristotle his teacher when he crossed over into Asia [Minor] was more than what he had from his father Philip. . . . [H]is true equipment was philosophic teaching, and treatises on Fearlessness and Courage, and Self-restraint also, and Greatness of Soul. . . . For from his words, from his deeds, and from the instruction which he imparted, it will be seen that he was indeed a philosopher. . . .

. . . [It was the] wondrous power of [Alexander's] Philosophic Instruction, that brought the Indians[1] to worship Greek gods, and the Scythians[2] to bury their dead, not to devour them! . . . [W]hen Alexander was civilizing Asia, Homer was commonly read, and the children of the Persians, of the Susianians, and of the Gedrosians[3] learned to chant the tragedies of Sophocles and Euripides. . . . Plato wrote a book on the One Ideal Constitution, but because of its forbidding character he could not persuade anyone to adopt it; but Alexander established more than seventy cities among savage tribes, and sowed all Asia[4] with Grecian [forms of government] and thus overcame its uncivilized and brutish manner of living. Although few of us read Plato's *Laws,* yet hundreds of thousands have made use of Alexander's laws, and continue to use them. Those who were vanquished by Alexander are happier than those who escaped his hand; for these had no one to put an end to the wretchedness of their existence, while the victor compelled those others to lead a happy life. . . . Thus Alexander's new subjects would not have been civilized, had they not been vanquished; Egypt would not have its Alexandria, nor Mesopotamia its Seleuceia, nor Sogdiana its Prophthasia, nor India its Bucephalia,[5] nor the Caucasus a Greek city hard by; for by the founding of cities in these places savagery was extinguished and the worse element, gaining familiarity with the better, changed under its influence. If, then,

---

[1]Alexander's empire extended into the present-day Punjab, in northwestern India, at its farthest eastern boundaries.

[2]The Scythians, nomads roaming an area north of the Black Sea, were a wild and barbaric people known from very ancient times, but still mysterious to historians.

[3]The Susianians lived in and near the city of Susa, the capital of the Persian Empire; the Gedrosians lived just north of the Arabian Sea, in what is now southeastern Iran and western Pakistan.

[4]"All Asia" referred to western Asia Minor at first, then, as Alexander's conquests spread further, the term was broadened to include the other territory to the east, extending to India and Soviet Central Asia of today.

[5]Seleuceia (named for one of Alexander's generals) was near modern Baghdad. Prophthasia, a city founded by Alexander, was in Sogdiana, now Soviet Central Asia, located north of Afghanistan. Bucephalia, on a northern branch of the Indus River, was named for Alexander's horse Bucephalus.

philosophers take the greatest pride in civilizing and rendering adaptable the intractable and untutored elements in human character, and if Alexander has been shown to have changed the savage natures of countless tribes, it is with good reason that he should be regarded as a very great philosopher.

▷ Plutarch asserts that Alexander was inspired by high ideals — the oneness of humanity and human equality — that became the core principle of Stoicism, the leading philosophy of the Hellenistic world (see Chapter 5, Section 3).

Moreover, the much-admired *Republic* of Zeno, the founder of the Stoic sect, may be summed up in this one main principle: that all the inhabitants of this world of ours should not live differentiated by their respective rules of justice into separate cities and communities, but that we should consider all men to be of one community and one polity, and that we should have a common life and an order common to us all, even as a herd that feeds together and shares the pasturage of a common field. This Zeno wrote, giving shape to a dream or, as it were, shadowy picture of a well-ordered and philosophic commonwealth; but it was Alexander who gave effect to the idea. For Alexander did not follow Aristotle's advice to treat the Greeks as if he were their leader, and other peoples as if he were their master; to have regard for the Greeks as for friends and kindred, but to conduct himself toward other peoples as though they were plants or animals; for to do so would have been to cumber his leadership with numerous battles and banishments and festering seditions. But, as he believed that he came as a heaven-sent governor to all, and as a mediator for the whole world, those whom he could not persuade to unite with him, he conquered by force of arms, and he brought together into one body all men everywhere, uniting and mixing in one great loving-cup, as it were, men's lives, their characters, their marriages, their very habits of life. He bade them all consider as their fatherland the whole inhabited earth, as their stronghold and protection his camp, as akin to them all good men, and as foreigners only the wicked; they should not distinguish between Grecian and foreigner by Grecian cloak and targe [shield], or scimitar [curved sword] and jacket; but the distinguishing mark of the Grecian should be seen in virtue, and that of the foreigner in iniquity; clothing and food, marriage and manner of life they should regard as common to all, being blended into one by ties of blood and children. . . .

. . . For he did not overrun Asia like a robber nor was he minded to tear and rend it, as if it were booty and plunder bestowed by unexpected good fortune, after the manner in which Hannibal later descended upon Italy. . . . But Alexander desired to render all upon earth subject to one law of reason and one form of government and to reveal all men as one people, and to this purpose he made himself conform. But if the deity that sent down Alexander's soul into this world of ours had not recalled him quickly, one law would govern all mankind, and they all would look toward one rule of justice as though toward a common source of light. But as it is, that part of the world which has not looked upon Alexander has remained without sunlight.

REVIEW QUESTIONS

1. According to Plutarch, what were Alexander's greatest advantages as he set out to conquer the Persian Empire?
2. What proof did Plutarch offer that Alexander was truly a philosopher?
3. What were the political ideals of the Stoic philosopher Zeno?

4. According to Plutarch, how did Alexander's policies reflect Stoic philosophic ideals?

---

14 ▾ Hellenistic Philosophy: Epicureanism

Hellenistic philosophy marks a second stage in the evolution of Greek thought. In the Hellenic Age, philosophers dealt primarily with the individual's relationship to the city-state. In the Hellenistic Age, philosophers were concerned with defining the individual's relationship to a wider, often competitive and hostile community that consisted of a plurality of peoples and a variety of cultures. In particular, the later philosophers sought to help people become ethically self-sufficient so that they could attain peace of mind in such an environment. Among the most significant schools of philosophy that emerged during the Hellenistic Age were Stoicism (see Chapter 5, Section 3) and Epicureanism.

Epicureanism was named for its founder, Epicurus (341–270 B.C.). He established a school at Athens in 307 or 306 B.C. To achieve peace of mind, taught Epicurus, one should refrain from worrying about death or pleasing the gods, avoid intense involvements in public affairs, cultivate friendships, and pursue pleasure prudently.

Epicurus
THE PRUDENT PURSUIT OF PLEASURE

The following excerpts from Epicurus' works reveal his prescription for achieving emotional well-being. The passages have been grouped according to particular subjects.

THE GODS

. . . We must grasp this point, that the principal disturbance in the minds of men arises because they think that these celestial bodies are blessed and immortal, and yet have wills and actions and motives inconsistent with these attributes; and because they are always expecting or imagining some everlasting misery [inflicted on them by the gods], such as is depicted in legends, or even fear the loss of feeling in death . . . and, again, because they are brought to this pass not by reasoned opinion, but rather by some irrational presentiment . . . and, by learning the true causes of celestial phenomena and all other occurrences that come to pass from time to time, we shall free ourselves from all which produces the utmost fear in other men.

It is vain to ask of the gods what a man is capable of supplying for himself.

DEATH

. . . So death, the most terrifying of ills, is nothing to us, since so long as we exist, death is not with us; but when death comes, then we do not exist. It does not then concern either the living or the dead, since for the former it is not, and the latter are no more.

But the many at one moment shun death as the greatest of evils, at another yearn for it as a respite from the evils in life. But the wise man neither seeks to escape life nor fears the cessation of life, for neither does life offend him nor does the absence of life seem to be any evil. And just as with food he does not seek simply the larger share and nothing else, but rather the most pleasant, so he seeks to enjoy not the longest period of time, but the most pleasant.

REASON AND PHILOSOPHY

Let no one when young delay to study philosophy, nor when he is old grow weary of his study. For no one can come too early or too late to secure the health of his soul. And the man who says that the age for philosophy has either not yet come or has gone by is like the man who says that the age for happiness is not yet come to him, or has passed away. Wherefore both when young and old a man must study philosophy, that as he grows old he may be young in blessings through the grateful recollection of what has been and that in youth he may be old as well, since he will know no fear of what is to come. We must then meditate on the things that make our happiness, seeing that when that is with us we have all, but when it is absent we do all to win it.

A man cannot dispel his fear about the most important matters if he does not know what is the nature of the universe but suspects the truth of some mythical story. So that without natural science it is not possible to attain our pleasures unalloyed.

We must not pretend to study philosophy, but study it in reality: for it is not the appearance of health that we need, but real health.

LIVING WELL

When, therefore, we maintain that pleasure is the end, we do not mean the pleasures of profligates and those that consist in sensuality, as is supposed by some who are either ignorant or disagree with us or do not understand, but freedom from pain in the body and from trouble in the mind. For it is not continuous drinkings and revellings, nor the satisfaction of lusts, nor the enjoyment of fish and other luxuries of the wealthy table, which produce a pleasant life, but sober reasoning, searching out the motives for all choice and avoidance, and banishing mere opinions, to which are due the greatest disturbance of the spirit.

Of all this the beginning and the greatest good is prudence. Wherefore prudence is a more precious thing even than philosophy; for from prudence are sprung all the other virtues, and it teaches us that it is not possible to live pleasantly without living prudently and honourably and justly. . . .

Of all the things which wisdom acquires to produce the blessedness of the complete life, far the greatest is the possession of friendship.

We must release ourselves from the prison of affairs and politics.

A free life cannot acquire many possessions, because this is not easy to do without servility to mobs or monarchs. . . .

The noble soul occupies itself with wisdom and friendship. . . .

The first measure of security is to watch over one's youth and to guard against what makes havoc of all by means of pestering desires.

REVIEW QUESTIONS

1. What did Epicurus regard as the causes of people's fears and anxieties? Why? How did he propose to free people from emotional distress?
2. According to Epicurus, how should the wise man regard death?
3. Why did Epicurus insist on the importance of constant study of philosophy?
4. What kinds of things did Epicurus urge people to avoid? What kinds of things did he urge them to cherish?

The Roman Republic

The city-state was the foundation of Greek society in the Hellenic Age; in the Hellenistic Age, Greek cities became subordinate to larger political units, ruled by autocratic monarchs. Hellenistic philosophers conceived of a still broader political arrangement: a world-state in which people of different nationalities were bound together by the ties of common citizenship and law that applied to all. It was Rome's great achievement to construct such a world-state.

Roman history falls into two broad periods — the Republic and the Empire. The Roman Republic began in 509 B.C., with the overthrow of the Etruscan monarchy and lasted until 27 B.C., when Octavian (Augustus) became in effect the first Roman emperor, ending almost five hundred years of republican self-government. For the next five hundred years, Rome would be governed by emperors.

In 264 B.C., when the Roman Republic had established dominion over the Italian peninsula, there were four other great powers in the Mediterranean world. Carthage controlled North Africa, Corsica, Sardinia, and parts of Spain and Sicily. The other powers — Macedonia, Egypt, and Syria — were the three Hellenistic kingdoms carved out of the empire of Alexander the Great. By 146 B.C., Rome had emerged victorious over the other powers, and by 30 B.C. they were all Roman provinces.

The Roman Republic, which had conquered a vast empire, was not destroyed by foreign armies but by internal weaknesses. In the century after 133 B.C., the senate, which had governed Rome well during its march to empire, degenerated into a self-seeking oligarchy; it failed to resolve critical domestic problems and fought to preserve its own power and prestige. When Rome had been threatened by foreign enemies, all classes united in a spirit of patriotism. This social harmony broke down when the threat from outside diminished, and the Republic was torn by internal dissension and civil war.

A ROMAN WARSHIP WITH LEGIONNAIRES, on a relief from the Temple of Fortuna Primigenia, first century B.C. Roman soldiers fought on sea as well as on land, conquering nations throughout the Mediterranean area during the eras of the Republic and the Empire. (*Alinari/Art Resource, N.Y.*)

I ▾ Rome's March to World Empire

The Hellenistic Age was characterized by a movement away from the parochial outlook of the city-state to a world-view. Rome's expansion from a city-state to a world empire that embraced many different nationalities exemplified the universalism of the Hellenistic Age. Polybius (c. 204–c. 122 B.C.), the greatest historian of the era, sought to explain Rome's accomplishment. His world history is a concrete illustration of this cosmopolitanism.

In the tradition of Thucydides, Polybius, also Greek, believed that the duty of the historian was to teach moral lessons, to enlighten and not to entertain. Like Thucydides, too, he analyzed events with clinical objectivity and looked for laws that might govern the course of history. He wrote: "For as a living creature is rendered wholly useless if deprived of its eyes, so if you take truth from History what is left is but an idle unprofitable tale." But whereas Thucydides wrote about the Peloponnesian War that convulsed the Greek city-states, Polybius took the entire Mediterranean world as his subject. The historian, said Polybius, was required to do more than describe this or that episode; he must assemble the parts in order to obtain a clearer picture of the whole.

Polybius
FROM CITY-STATE TO WORLD-STATE

In the following reading, Polybius explains the reasons for his study of history. He says that the rise of Rome to a world power compels the historian to seek an accurate understanding of an event for which the past affords no precedent. Another reading from his *Histories* describes discipline in the Roman army.

[A UNIVERSAL HISTORY]

There can surely be nobody so petty or so apathetic in his outlook that he has no desire to discover by what means and under what system of government the Romans succeeded in less than fifty-three years* in bringing under their rule almost the whole of the inhabited world, an achievement which is without parallel in human history. Or from the opposite point of view, can there be anyone so completely absorbed in other subjects of contemplation or study that he could find any task more important than to acquire this knowledge?

The arresting character of my subject and the grand spectacle which it presents can best be illustrated if we consider the most celebrated empires of the past which have provided historians with their principal themes, and set them beside the dominion of Rome. Those which qualify for such a comparison are the following. The Persians for a certain period exercised their rule and supremacy over a vast territory, but every time that they ventured to pass beyond the limits of Asia† they endangered the security

*From 220 B.C. — the start of the Second Punic War — to 167 B.C.

†Both Aeschylus and Herodotus associate this overstepping of the frontier with *hubris* (human arrogance), which attracts *nemesis* (retribution). The events in question were Darius' Scythian expedition and his and Xerxes' invasions of Greece.

not only of their empire but of their own existence. The Lacedaemonians [Spartans] after contending for many years for the leadership of Greece at last achieved it, but were only able to hold it unchallenged for a bare twelve years.‡ The rule of the Macedonians in Europe extended only from the lands bordering the Adriatic to the Danube, which would appear to be no more than a small fraction of the continent. Later, by overthrowing the Persian Empire, they also became the rulers of Asia;§ but although they were then regarded as having become the masters of a larger number of states and territories than any other people before them, they still left the greater part of the inhabited world in the hands of others. They did not even once attempt to dispute the possession of Sicily, Sardinia or Africa, and the most warlike tribes of western Europe were, to speak the plain truth, unknown to them. The Romans, on the other hand, have brought not just mere portions but almost the whole of the world under their rule, and have left an empire which far surpasses any that exists today or is likely to succeed it. In the course of this work I shall explain more clearly how this supremacy was acquired, and it will also become apparent what great advantages those who are fond of learning can enjoy from the study of serious history. . . .

. . . Now in earlier times the world's history had consisted, so to speak, of a series of unrelated episodes, the origins and results of each being as widely separated as their localities, but from this point onwards history becomes an organic whole: the affairs of Italy and of Africa are connected with those of Asia and of Greece, and all events bear a relationship and contribute to a single end. This, then, is the reason why I have chosen that specific date as the starting-point for my work. For it was after their victory over the Carthaginians in the Hannibalic [Second Punic] War that the Romans came to believe that the principal and most important step in their efforts to achieve universal dominion had been taken, and were thereby encouraged to stretch out their hands for the first time to grasp the rest, and to cross with an army into Greece and the lands of Asia. . . .

Now my history possesses a certain distinctive quality which is related to the extraordinary spirit of the times in which we live, and it is this. . . . It is the task of the historian to present to his readers under one synoptical [comprehensive] view the process by which she [Rome] has accomplished this general design. It was this phenomenon above all which originally attracted my attention and encouraged me to undertake my task. The second reason was that nobody else among our contemporaries has set out to write a general history; certainly if they had done so I should have had far less incentive to make the attempt myself. But as it is I notice that while various historians deal with isolated wars and certain of the subjects connected with them, nobody, so far as I am aware, has made any effort to examine the general and comprehensive scheme of events, when it began, whence it originated, and how it produced the final result. I therefore thought it imperative not to overlook or allow to pass into oblivion this phenomenon. . . .

‡Polybius, who was not favourably disposed to Athens, makes no mention of the preeminence of the Athenians in the fifth century B.C. The Spartan hegemony is reckoned from 405 B.C. (Lysander's defeat of the Athenians at Aegospotami) to 394 B.C. (the defeat of the Spartans by Conon the Athenian at Cnidos with the help of a Persian fleet).

§After Darius' death in 330 B.C. Alexander became the Great King and ruler over Egypt, Syria, Asia Minor, and the eastern provinces of the Persian Empire.

▷ The discipline and dedication of its citizen-soldiers help explain Rome's success in conquering a world empire. The following account tells how the commanders enforced obedience and fostered heroism.

[THE ROMAN ARMY]

A court-martial composed of the tribunes immediately sits to try him [a soldier], and if he is found guilty, he is punished by beating *(fustuarium).* This is carried out as follows. The tribune takes a cudgel and lightly touches the condemned man with it, whereupon all the soldiers fall upon him with clubs and stones, and usually kill him in the camp itself. But even those who contrive to escape are no better off. How indeed could they be? They are not allowed to return to their homes, and none of their family would dare to receive such a man into the house. Those who have once fallen into this misfortune are completely and finally ruined. The *optio* [lieutenant] and the *decurio* [sergeant] of the squadron are liable to the same punishment if they fail to pass on the proper orders at the proper moment to the patrols and the *decurio* of the next squadron. The consequence of the extreme severity of this penalty and of the absolute impossibility of avoiding it is that the night watches of the Roman army are faultlessly kept.

The ordinary soldiers are answerable to the tribunes [elected military administrators] and the tribunes to the consuls [commanders]. A tribune, and in the case of the allies a prefect [commander of a large unit], has power to inflict fines, distrain on [confiscate] goods, and to order a flogging. The punishment of beating to death is also inflicted upon those who steal from the camp, those who give false evidence, those who in full manhood commit homosexual offences, and finally upon anyone who has been punished three times for the same offence. The above are the offences which are punished as crimes. The following actions are regarded as unmanly and dishonourable in a soldier: to make a false report to the tribune of your courage in the field in order to earn distinction; to leave the post to which you have been assigned in a covering force because of fear; and similarly to throw away out of fear any of your weapons on the field of battle. For this reason the men who have been posted to a covering force are often doomed to certain death. This is because they will remain at their posts even when they are overwhelmingly outnumbered on account of their dread of the punishment that awaits them. Again, those who have lost a shield or a sword or any other weapon on the battlefield often hurl themselves upon the enemy hoping that they will either recover the weapon they have lost, or else escape by death from the inevitable disgrace and the humiliations they would suffer at home.

If it ever happens that a large body of men break and run in this way and whole maniples [units of 120 to 300 men] desert their posts under extreme pressure, the officers reject the idea of beating to death or executing all who are guilty, but the solution they adopt is as effective as it is terrifying. The tribune calls the legion [large military unit] on parade and brings to the front those who are guilty of having left the ranks. He then reprimands them sharply, and finally chooses by lot some five or eight or twenty of the offenders, the number being calculated so that it represents about a tenth[1] of those who have shown themselves guilty of cowardice. Those on whom the lot has fallen are mercilessly clubbed to death in the manner I have already described. The rest are put on rations of barley instead of wheat, and are ordered to quarter themselves outside the camp in a place which has no defences. The danger and the fear of drawing the fatal lot threatens every man equally, and since there is no certainty on whom it may fall, and the public disgrace of receiving rations of barley is shared by all alike, the Romans have adopted the best possible practice both to inspire terror and to repair the harm done by any weakening of their warlike spirit.

The Romans also have an excellent method of encouraging young soldiers to face danger. Whenever any have especially distinguished themselves in a battle, the general assembles the troops and calls forward those he considers to have shown exceptional courage. He praises them first for their gallantry in action and for anything in their previous conduct which is particularly worthy of mention, and then he distributes gifts such as the following: to a man

---

[1]This custom is the origin of the word *decimate,* from the Latin *decem,* ten.

who has wounded one of the enemy, a spear; to one who has killed and stripped an enemy, a cup if he is in the infantry, or horse-trappings if in the cavalry — originally the gift was simply a lance. These presentations are not made to men who have wounded or stripped an enemy in the course of a pitched battle, or at the storming of a city, but to those who during a skirmish or some similar situation in which there is no necessity to engage in single combat, have voluntarily and deliberately exposed themselves to danger.

At the storming of a city the first man to scale the wall is awarded a crown of gold. In the same way those who have shielded and saved one of their fellow-citizens or of the allies are honoured with gifts from the consul, and the men whose lives they have preserved present them of their own free will with a crown; if not, they are compelled to do so by the tribunes who judge the case. Moreover, a man who has been saved in this way reveres his rescuer as a father for the rest of his life and must treat him as if he were a parent. And so by means of such incentives even those who stay at home feel the impulse to emulate such achievements in the field no less than those who are present and see and hear what takes place. For the men who receive these trophies not only enjoy great prestige in the army and soon afterwards in their homes, but they are also singled out for precedence in religious processions when they return. On these occasions nobody is allowed to wear decorations save those who have been honoured for their bravery by the consuls, and it is the custom to hang up the trophies they have won in the most conspicuous places in their houses, and to regard them as proofs and visible symbols of their valour. So when we consider this people's almost obsessive concern with military rewards and punishments, and the immense importance which they attach to both, it is not surprising that they emerge with brilliant success from every war in which they engage.

REVIEW QUESTIONS

1. Why did Polybius see the need for a universal history?
2. In what ways did Polybius see the empires of the Persians, Spartans, and Macedonians as inferior to that of the Romans?
3. What did Polybius think was the point at which the Romans decided to seek a world empire?
4. Why did Polybius believe the study of history to be important?
5. What inducements to bravery were offered by Roman commanders to their troops?
6. How did the Romans ensure strict discipline among their troops?
7. What offenses constituted a breach of military discipline?
8. What significance did Polybius attribute to the Roman system of military discipline?

---

2 ▾ Exploitation of the Provinces

The Greeks expressed their genius in philosophy and the arts, the Romans in government and law. Rome generally allowed its subjects a large measure of self-government, respected local religions and customs, and reduced the constant warfare that had plagued the Mediterranean world. But there was also a negative side to Roman rule. The conquest of a great number of lands and

peoples gave the Roman ruling class innumerable opportunities to enhance their wealth by exploiting the empire's subjects. Senators appointed to govern provinces frequently amassed large fortunes through bribery, extortion, the confiscation of properties, and the enslavement and sale of the captured populace.

Efforts by provincial victims to seek justice by prosecuting the malefactors before the extortion court in Rome were often thwarted by collusion between the senators accused and the senators who served as judges and jurors. One such case was the trial of Gaius Verres, ex-governor of Sicily, who was prosecuted for his crimes by the great orator Marcus Tullius Cicero (106–43 B.C.).

Cicero
ORATION AGAINST VERRES

Cicero, acting on behalf of the Sicilians, portrays Verres' crimes while the defendant was governor of Sicily. He links them to the greater problem of the disastrous decline in the moral reputation and authority of the whole senatorial order. After Cicero's devastating revelations, Verres, recognizing the futility of a defense, fled into exile.

. . . Nothing, [Verres] declares, is too sacred to be corrupted by money; nothing too strong to resist its attack. If the secrecy with which his projects are put into effect were comparable to the criminality which inspires their design, he might, to some extent or at some stage, have kept them from my notice. But so far, conveniently enough, his unbelievable unscrupulousness has been matched by a peculiar degree of folly. He has grabbed his wealth without any attempt at concealment; and he has let everyone see the schemes and intrigues by which he hopes to corrupt his judges. . . .

But the most conspicuous and numerous instances and demonstrations of his criminality come from his governorship in Sicily. For three long years he so thoroughly despoiled and pillaged the province that its restoration to its previous state is out of the question. A succession of honest governors, over a period of many years, could scarcely achieve even a partial rehabilitation. While Verres was governor the Sicilians enjoyed the benefit neither of their own laws, nor of the Roman Senate's decrees, nor even of the rights to which everyone in the world is entitled. All the property that anyone in Sicily still has for his own today is merely what happened to escape the attention of this avaricious lecher, or survived his glutted appetites.

In Sicily, during those three years, not a single lawsuit was decided without his connivance. Inheritances from a father or grandfather, however authentic, were cancelled — if Verres said the word. Under a new and immoral ruling, the properties of farmers were robbed of countless sums. Allies of unassailable loyalty were treated as enemies; Roman citizens were tortured and put to death like slaves. Criminals of the deepest dye would bribe their way to acquittal, while men of impeccable honesty were prosecuted in their absence, and convicted and banished unheard. Powerfully fortified harbours, great and well-protected cities, were left open for pirates and robbers to attack. Sicilian soldiers and sailors, allies and friends of ours, were starved to death. Splendid, beautifully equipped fleets were squandered and thrown away. It was an appalling disgrace for our country.

Then again, ancient monuments given by wealthy monarchs to adorn the cities of Sicily, or presented or restored to them by victorious Roman generals, were ravaged and stripped bare, one and all, by this same governor. Nor was it only statues and public monuments that he treated in this manner. Among the most sacred and revered Sicilian sanctuaries, there was not a single one which he failed to plunder; not one single god, if only Verres detected a good work of art or a valuable antique, did he leave in the possession of the Sicilians.

When I turn to his adulteries and similar outrages, considerations of decency deter me from giving details of these loathsome manifestations of his lusts. Besides, I do not want, by describing them, to worsen the calamities of the people who have not been permitted to save their children and their wives from Verres' sexual passions. It is, however, incontestable that he himself did not take the slightest precaution to prevent these abominations from becoming universally known. On the contrary, I believe that every man alive who has heard the name of Verres would be able to recount the atrocities which he has committed. . . .

▷ Since the Senate took control of the extortion court ten years earlier, says Cicero, worsening corruption has sullied the reputation of the entire senatorial order. Such behavior has grave political consequences.

For I am going to disclose to you, with full corroborating evidence, the whole story of all the abominable crimes which have been perpetrated in the courts during these ten years since they were first transferred to the Senate. Gentlemen, here are the facts which I am going to reveal to the people of Rome. While the Order of Knights[1] controlled the courts, for nearly fifty years not one single knight who was a judge incurred the slightest suspicion of allowing his verdict to be influenced by a bribe. Yet after the courts had been transferred to the Senate — after you had escaped, every one of you, from the Roman people's control — Quintus Calidius,[2] on being found guilty, was able to remark that no ex-praetor could honourably be convicted for less than three million sesterces![3]

Again, then the Senator Publius Septimius Scaevola[4] was condemned by an extortion court presided over by Quintus Hortensius[5] — then praetor — his fine had to be expressly adjusted because, while a member of a court, he had accepted a bribe. The successful prosecutions of other Senators . . . for stealing public funds, and . . . for high treason, likewise clearly established that they had been bribed while serving as judges. . . .

You can imagine, then, how I shall feel if I discover that the same kind of criminal irregularity has occurred in the present case! In this connexion I must record a fact which many witnesses can corroborate. When Gaius Verres was in Sicily, a number of people heard him saying this sort of thing on various occasions: "I have a powerful friend! Whatever I steal from the province, I am sure he will protect me. My intention is not just to make money for myself: I have mapped out the three years of my Sicilian governorship like this. I shall consider myself to be doing nicely if I can earmark one year's profits for my own use, the second year's for my protectors and counsel, and the whole of the third year's — the richest and most lucrative — for the judges who try me!"

This reminds me of a remark I made . . . recently, when the judges for this case were being challenged . . . that, one of these days, communities from the provinces would send deputations to the people of Rome requesting that the extortion law and its court should be

---

[1]The Order of Knights (the Equestrian Order) originated as cavalry members in the Roman army, but during the years of the late Republic, they constituted a special legal caste and were selected on the basis of their assessed wealth.

[2]Quintus Calidius, a senator who had been governor of Spain, had been condemned for extortion in 77 B.C.

[3]Sesterces were Roman coins. Originally of silver, they were later made of bronze. One sestertius was worth a quarter of a silver denarius, the basic coin of the Roman monetary system.

[4]Publius Septimius Scaevola had been a senator; he was punished in 72 B.C. for extortion.

[5]Quintus Hortensius (114–50 B.C.), a famous Roman orator, often worked with Cicero on legal cases.

abolished. For if no such court existed, they suppose that each governor would only take away with him enough for himself and his children. At present, on the other hand, with the courts as they are, a governor takes enough for himself, and his protectors, and his counsel, and the president of the court, and the judges! In other words there is no end to it. A greedy man's lust for gain they could satisfy, but they cannot afford a guilty man's acquittal. How peculiarly glorious our courts have become, how scintillating is our Order's prestige, when Rome's allies pray that the courts which our ancestors created for their benefit should be struck out of existence!

Besides, would Verres ever have been so optimistic unless he, too, had absorbed this same deplorable opinion concerning yourselves? His evident agreement with this view ought — if possible — to make you hate him even more than other Romans do: seeing that in greed, criminality, and perjury he regards you as his equals.

In God's name, gentlemen, I pray you to devote all your care and all your foresight to facing this situation. It is evident to me, and I give you solemn warning, that heaven itself has vouchsafed you this opportunity of rescuing our entire Order from its present unpopularity, disgrace, ill-fame, and scandal. People believe that strictness and good faith are not to be found in our courts — indeed, that the courts themselves no longer have any reality. So we Senators are scorned and despised by the people of Rome: long have we laboured under this painful burden of disrepute.

REVIEW QUESTIONS

1. Why did Cicero want to prosecute Verres?
2. What did Cicero say was Verres' view of public morality in the late years of the Roman Republic?
3. What crimes were attributed to Verres?
4. What crimes did Cicero say were committed within the extortion courts in Rome?
5. If the corruption in the courts and in the governance of the provinces existed as Cicero described, why did the Roman senate not reform the courts and the provincial governments?
6. How would such conditions contribute to the fall of the Republican government, according to Cicero?

---

3 ▾ Roman Slavery

Slavery was practiced in ancient times, in many lands and among most peoples. Although conditions might vary in detail from place to place, essentially a slave was a human being who was considered legally to be a piece of property, not a person with normal citizen's rights. Age, sex, skills, ethnic origin, demeanor, appearance, and personal character determined a slave's value in the marketplace. The status of slave was usually hereditary, but a person might be enslaved for debt or as a penalty for crime. Pirates would kidnap and sell their captives as slaves. But the most common source of slaves was defeated people captured during wars. They were assigned to all kinds of work, and their labors were vital in sustaining the luxury and leisure of the Roman upper classes. Even fam-

ilies of modest fortunes could usually afford a slave to do domestic chores, to help farm, or to assist in the family's business or craft.

Diodorus Siculus
SLAVES: TORMENT AND REVOLT

The Roman war machine created hundreds of thousands of slaves during the last centuries of the Republic and the early centuries of the imperial age. Under the Republic, the Romans were notably harsh toward slaves; until the full influence of Greek Stoic philosophy penetrated the governing class, little was done to protect them from the absolute power of their Roman masters. Diodorus Siculus (of Sicily) (c. 80–c. 29 B.C.), a Greek historian, describes the condition of Roman slaves toiling in silver and gold mines in Iberia (present-day Spain) and then tells of an uprising of slaves that lasted from 135 to 132 B.C.

[THE ORDEAL OF SLAVES IN THE MINES]

. . . After the Romans had made themselves masters of Iberia, a multitude of Italians have swarmed to the mines and taken great wealth away with them, such was their greed. For they purchase a multitude of slaves whom they turn over to the overseers of the working of the mines; and these men, opening shafts in a number of places and digging deep into the ground, seek out the seams of earth which are rich in silver and gold; and not only do they go into the ground a great distance, but they also push their diggings many stades [measure equalling about 607 feet] in depth and run galleries off at every angle, turning this way and that, in this manner bringing up from the depths the ore which gives them the profit they are seeking. . . .

But to continue with the mines, the slaves who are engaged in the working of them produce for their masters revenues in sums defying belief, but they themselves wear out their bodies both by day and by night in the diggings under the earth, dying in large numbers because of the exceptional hardships they endure. For no respite or pause is granted them in their labours, but compelled beneath blows of the overseers to endure the severity of their plight, they throw away their lives in this wretched manner, although certain of them who can endure it, by virtue of their bodily strength and their persevering souls, suffer such hardships over a long period; indeed death in their eyes is more to be desired than life, because of the magnitude of the hardships they must bear.

[A SLAVE REVOLT IN SICILY]

There was never a sedition of slaves so great as that which occurred in Sicily, whereby many cities met with grave calamities, innumerable men and women, together with their children, experienced the greatest misfortunes, and all the island was in danger of falling into the power of fugitive slaves. . . .

. . . The Servile [slave] War broke out for the following reason. The Sicilians, having shot up in prosperity and acquired great wealth, began to purchase a vast number of slaves, to whose bodies, as they were brought in droves from the slave markets, they at once applied marks and brands. The young men they used as cowherds, the others in such ways as they happened to be useful. But they treated them with a heavy hand in their service, and granted them the most meagre care, the bare minimum for food and clothing. . . .

The slaves, distressed by their hardships, and frequently outraged and beaten beyond all reason, could not endure their treatment. Getting together as opportunity offered, they discussed the possibility of revolt, until at last they put their plans into action. . . . The beginning of the whole revolt took place as follows.

There was a certain Damophilus of Enna [a city in central Sicily], a man of great wealth but insolent of manner; he had abused his slaves to excess, and his wife Megallis vied even with her husband in punishing the slaves and in her general inhumanity towards them. The slaves, reduced by this degrading treatment to the level of brutes, conspired to revolt and to murder their masters. Going to Eunus [a Syrian slave believed to be a seer and magician] they asked him whether their resolve had the favour of the gods. He, resorting to his usual mummery, promised them the favour of the gods, and soon persuaded them to act at once. Immediately, therefore, they brought together four hundred of their fellow slaves and, having armed themselves in such ways as opportunity permitted, they fell upon the city of Enna, with Eunus at their head and working his miracle of the flames of fire for their benefit. When they found their way into the houses they shed much blood, sparing not even suckling babes. Rather they tore them from the breast and dashed them to the ground, while as for the women — and under their husbands' very eyes — but words cannot tell the extent of their outrages and acts of lewdness! By now a great multitude of slaves from the city had joined them, who, after first demonstrating against their own masters their utter ruthlessness, then turned to the slaughter of others. When Eunus and his men learned that Damophilus and his wife were in the garden that lay near the city, they sent some of their band and dragged them off, both the man and his wife, fettered and with hands bound behind their backs, subjecting them to many outrages along the way. Only in the case of the couple's daughter were the slaves seen to show consideration throughout, and this was because of her kindly nature, in that to the extent of her power she was always compassionate and ready to succour the slaves. Thereby it was demonstrated that the others were treated as they were, not because of some "natural savagery of slaves," but rather in revenge for wrongs previously received. The men appointed to the task, having dragged Damophilus and Megallis into the city, as we said, brought them to the theatre, where the crowd of rebels had assembled. But when Damophilus attempted to devise a plea to get them off safe and was winning over many of the crowd with his words, Hermeias and Zeuxis, men bitterly disposed towards him, denounced him as a cheat, and without waiting for a formal trial by the assembly the one ran him through the chest with a sword, the other chopped off his head with an axe. Thereupon Eunus was chosen king, not for his manly courage or his ability as a military leader, but solely for his marvels and his setting of the revolt in motion. . . .

Established as the rebels' supreme commander, he called an assembly and put to death all the citizenry of Enna except for those who were skilled in the manufacture of arms: these he put in chains and assigned them to this task. He gave Megallis to the maidservants to deal with as they might wish; they subjected her to torture and threw her over a precipice. He himself murdered his own masters, Antigenes and Pytho. Having set a diadem upon his head, and arrayed himself in full royal style, he proclaimed his wife queen (she was a fellow Syrian and of the same city), and appointed to the royal council such men as seemed to be gifted with superior intelligence. . . .

. . . In three days Eunus had armed, as best he could, more than six thousand men, besides others in his train who had only axes and hatchets, or slings, or sickles, or fire-hardened stakes, or even kitchen spits; and he went about ravaging the countryside. Then, since he kept recruiting untold numbers of slaves, he ventured even to do battle with Roman generals, and on joining combat repeatedly overcame them with his superior numbers, for he now had more than ten thousand soldiers.

Soon after, engaging in battle with a general arrived from Rome, Lucius Hypsaeus [the Roman governor], who had eight thousand Sicilian troops, the rebels were victorious, since they now numbered twenty thousand. Before long their band reached a total of two hundred thousand,[1] and in numerous battles with the Romans they acquitted themselves well, and failed but seldom. As word of this was bruited about, a revolt of one hundred and fifty slaves, banded together, flared up in Rome, of more than a thousand in Attica, and of yet others in Delos [an island off the southeastern Greek coast] and many other places. But thanks to the speed with which forces were brought up and to the severity of their punitive measures, the magistrates of these communities at once disposed of the rebels and brought to their senses any who were wavering on the verge of revolt. In Sicily, however, the trouble grew. Cities were captured with all their inhabitants, and many armies were cut to pieces by the rebels, until Rupilius, the Roman commander, recovered Tauromenium [Taormina] for the Romans by placing it under strict siege and confining the rebels under conditions of unspeakable duress and famine: conditions such that, beginning by eating the children, they progressed to the women, and did not altogether abstain even from eating one another. . . .

Finally, after Sarapion, a Syrian, had betrayed the citadel, the general laid hands on all the runaway slaves in the city, whom, after torture, he threw over a cliff. From there he advanced to Enna, which he put under siege in much the same manner, bringing the rebels into extreme straits and frustrating their hopes. . . . Rupilius captured this city also by betrayal, since its strength was impregnable to force of arms. Eunus, taking with him his bodyguards, a thousand strong, fled in unmanly fashion. . . .

. . . He met such an end as befitted his knavery, and died at Morgantina [in central Sicily]. Thereupon Rupilius, traversing the whole of Sicily with a few picked troops, sooner than had been expected rid it of every nest of robbers.

[1]The ancients often exaggerated numbers; the slaves probably raised an army of some 70,000.

REVIEW QUESTIONS

1. How did Roman masters view the slaves who toiled in the Iberian mines?
2. According to Diodorus Siculus, what were the causes of the slave revolt in Sicily?
3. What were the consequences of the early success of the Sicilian slaves' uprising?
4. What motives prompted the many atrocities committed by both sides in the Servile War?
5. Which qualities of leadership were demonstrated by Eunus?

4 ▾ Women in Republican Society

The status of women in late republican Roman society was considerably better than that of Greek women during the classical age. Like the Greek, Roman law had originally placed each female under the jurisdiction of a male, the *paterfamilias* (literally, "family father"), but Roman women obtained some freedom from male control during the times of the late Republic and the early Empire. Although women never achieved full civil equality and they could not formally participate in the political institutions of Rome, they did eventually exercise

much practical control over their own property and indirectly exercised political influence through their husbands, sons, and fathers.

Livy
CATO PROTESTS AGAINST THE DEMANDS OF ROMAN WOMEN

A remarkable example of the political power and public participation of women in Roman society was recorded by the Roman historian Livy (Titus Livius, 59 B.C.–A.D. 17). The incident centered on a demand in 195 B.C. by Roman women that the senate repeal a law passed in 215 B.C. during the Second Punic War. In the following reading from his *History of Rome,* Livy presents the demands of the women and then reports the speech of Consul Marcus Porcius Cato the Elder (234–149 B.C.), a strong defender of traditional Roman morals and manners.

Amid the anxieties of great wars, either scarce finished or soon to come, an incident occurred, trivial to relate, but which, by reason of the passions it aroused, developed into a violent contention. Marcus Fundanius and Lucius Valerius, tribunes of the people, proposed to the assembly the abrogation of the Oppian law. The tribune Gaius Oppius had carried this law in the heat of the Punic War, in the consulship of Quintus Fabius and Tiberius Sempronius,* that no woman should possess more than half an ounce of gold or wear a parti-coloured garment or ride in a carriage in the City or in a town within a mile thereof, except on the occasion of a religious festival. The tribunes Marcus and Publius Iunius Brutus were supporting the Oppian law, and averred that they would not permit its repeal; many distinguished men came forward to speak for and against it; the Capitoline[1] was filled with crowds of supporters and opponents of the bill. The matrons could not be kept at home by advice or modesty or their husbands' orders, but blocked all the streets and approaches to the Forum,[2] begging the men as they came down to the Forum that, in the prosperous condition of the state, when the private fortunes of all men were daily increasing, they should allow the women too to have their former distinctions restored. The crowd of women grew larger day by day; for they were now coming in from the towns and rural districts. Soon they dared even to approach and appeal to the consuls, the praetors, and the other officials, but one consul, at least, they found adamant, Marcus Porcius Cato, who spoke thus in favour of the law whose repeal was being urged.

"If each of us, citizens, had determined to assert his rights and dignity as a husband with respect to his own spouse, we should have less trouble with the sex as a whole; as it is, our liberty, destroyed at home by female violence, even here in the Forum is crushed and trodden underfoot, and because we have not kept them individually under control, we dread them collectively. . . . But from no class is there not the greatest danger if you permit them meetings and gatherings and secret consultations. . . .

". . . For myself, I could not conceal my blushes a while ago, when I had to make my way to the Forum through a crowd of women. Had not respect for the dignity and modesty of some individuals among them rather than of the sex as a whole kept me silent, lest they should seem to have been rebuked by a consul,

---

*215 B.C.

[1]"Capitoline," the name of a prominent citadel in Rome, refers here to a public space on that hill where popular assemblies were frequently held to hear political debates or to conduct elections.

[2]The Forum was the main square in ancient Rome. It lay at the foot of the Capitoline Hill.

I should have said, 'What sort of practice is this, of running out into the streets and blocking the roads and speaking to other women's husbands? Could you not have made the same requests, each of your own husband, at home? Or are you more attractive outside and to other women's husbands than to your own? And yet, not even at home, if modesty would keep matrons within the limits of their proper rights, did it become you to concern yourselves with the question of what laws should be adopted in this place or repealed.' Our ancestors permitted no woman to conduct even personal business without a guardian to intervene in her behalf; they wished them to be under the control of fathers, brothers, husbands; we (Heaven help us!) allow them now even to interfere in public affairs, yes, and to visit the Forum and our informal and formal sessions. What else are they doing now on the streets and at the corners except urging the bill of the tribunes and voting for the repeal of the law? Give loose rein to their uncontrollable nature and to this untamed creature and expect that they will themselves set bounds to their licence; unless you act, this is the least of the things enjoined upon women by custom or law and to which they submit with a feeling of injustice. It is complete liberty or, rather, if we wish to speak the truth, complete licence that they desire.

"If they win in this, what will they not attempt? Review all the laws with which your forefathers restrained their licence and made them subject to their husbands; even with all these bonds you can scarcely control them. What of this? If you suffer them to seize these bonds one by one and wrench themselves free and finally to be placed on a parity with their husbands, do you think that you will be able to endure them? The moment they begin to be your equals, they will be your superiors. . . .

". . . No law is entirely convenient for everyone; this alone is asked, whether it is good for the majority and on the whole. . . . I should like to know what it is which has caused the panic-stricken matrons to rush out into the streets and barely refrain from entering the Forum and a public meeting. . . .

". . . What pretext, respectable even to mention, is now given for this insurrection of the women? 'That we may glitter with gold and purple,' says one, 'that we may ride in carriages on holidays and ordinary days, that we may be borne through the city as if in triumph over the conquered and vanquished law and over the votes which we have captured and wrested from you; that there may be no limits to our spending and our luxury.'

"You have often heard me complaining of the extravagance of the women and often of the men, both private citizens and magistrates even, and lamenting that the state is suffering from those two opposing evils, avarice and luxury, which have been the destruction of every great empire. The better and the happier becomes the fortune of our commonwealth day by day and the greater the empire grows — and already we have crossed into Greece and Asia, places filled with all the allurements of vice, and we are handling the treasures of kings — the more I fear that these things will capture us rather than we them. . . .

". . . Do you wish, citizens, to start a race like this among your wives, so that the rich shall want to own what no other woman can have and the poor, lest they be despised for their poverty, shall spend beyond their means? Once let these women begin to be ashamed of what they should not be ashamed, and they will not be ashamed of what they ought. She who can buy from her own purse will buy; she who cannot will beg her husband. Poor wretch that husband, both he who yields and he who yields not, since what he will not himself give he will see given by another man. . . ."

. . . When these speeches against and for the bill had been delivered, the next day an even greater crowd of women appeared in public, and all of them in a body beset the doors of those tribunes, who were vetoing their colleagues' proposal, and they did not desist until the threat of veto was withdrawn by the tribunes. After that there was no question that all the tribes would vote to repeal the law. The law was repealed twenty years after it was passed.

Quintus Lucretius Vespillo
A FUNERAL EULOGY FOR A ROMAN WIFE

Documenting intimate relationships between Roman men and women is difficult because ordinary people were unlikely to write about such things. Although personal records are scant or now lost, glimpses have survived in the writings of historians and poets or as inscriptions on tombstones.

In the late Republic, it became more common for distinguished men to pronounce funeral eulogies for distinguished female as well as male members of their families. One such eulogy was composed by the ex-Consul Quintus Lucretius Vespillo for his wife Turia, who died about 8 B.C. Though marriages among persons of the higher social ranks were usually undertaken for political and economic considerations, clearly this couple had gone beyond such a formal alliance to achieve a most touching love.

Before the day fixed for our marriage, you were suddenly left an orphan, by the murder of your parents in the solitude of the country. . . .

Through your efforts chiefly, their death did not remain unavenged. . . .

In our day, marriages of such long duration, not dissolved by divorce, but terminated by death alone, are indeed rare. For our union was prolonged in unclouded happiness for forty-one years. Would that it had been my lot to put an end to this our good fortune and that I as the older — which was more just — had yielded to fate.

Why recall your inestimable qualities, your modesty, deference, affability, your amiable disposition, your faithful attendance to the household duties, your enlightened religion, your unassuming elegance, the modest simplicity and refinement of your manners? Need I speak of your attachment to your kindred, your affection for your family — when you respected my mother as you did your own parents and cared for her tomb as you did for that of your own mother and father, — you who share countless other virtues with Roman ladies most jealous of their fair name? These qualities which I claim for you are your own, equalled or excelled by but few; for the experience of men teaches us how rare they are.

With common prudence we have preserved all the patrimony which you received from your parents. Intrusting it all to me, you were not troubled with the care of increasing it; thus did we share the task of administering it, that I undertook to protect your fortune, and you to guard mine. . . .

You gave proof of your generosity not only towards several of your kin, but especially in your filial devotion. . . . You brought up in your own home, in the enjoyment of mutual benefits, some young girls of your kinship. And that these might attain to a station in life worthy of our family, you provided them with dowries. . . .

I owe you no less a debt than Cæsar Augustus [27 B.C.–A.D. 14, emperor of Rome] himself, for this my return from exile to my native land. For unless you had prepared the way for my safety, even Cæsar's promises of assistance had been of no avail. So I owe no less a debt to your loyal devotion than to the clemency of Cæsar.

Why shall I now conjure up the memory of our domestic counsels and plans stored away in the hidden recesses of the heart? — That, aroused by the sudden arrival of messages from you to a realization of the present and imminent perils, I was saved by your counsel? That you suffered me not to be recklessly carried away by a foolish rashness, or that, when bent on more temperate plans, you provided for me a safe retreat, having as sharers in your plans for my safety, when an exile, — fraught with danger as they were for you all, — your sister and her husband. . . .

▷ Vespillo then relates what happened to his wife when she begged his enemy M. Lepidus to honor her husband's writ of pardon from Octavian Caesar.

. . . Then prostrating yourself at his feet, he not only did not raise you up, — but, dragged along and abused as though a common slave, your body all covered with bruises, yet with unflinching steadfastness of purpose, you recalled to him Cæsar's edict (of pardon) and the letter of felicitation on my return, that accompanied it. Braving his taunts and suffering the most brutal treatment, you denounced these cruelties publicly so that he (Lepidus) was branded as the author of all my perils and misfortunes. And his punishment was not long delayed.

Could such courage remain without effect? Your unexampled patience furnished the occasion for Cæsar's clemency, and, by guarding my life, he branded the infamous and savage cruelty (of the tyrant Lepidus). . . .

When all the world was again at peace and the Republic reestablished, peaceful and happy days followed. We longed for children, which an envious fate denied us. Had Fortune smiled on us in this, what had been lacking to complete our happiness? But an adverse destiny put an end to our hopes. . . . Disconsolate to see me without children . . . you wished to put an end to my chagrin by proposing to me a divorce, offering to yield the place to another spouse more fertile, with the only intention of searching for and providing for me a spouse worthy of our mutual affection, whose children you assured me you would have treated as your own. . . .

I will admit that I was so irritated and shocked by such a proposition that I had difficulty in restraining my anger and remaining master of myself. You spoke of divorce before the decree of fate [death] had forced us to separate, and I could not comprehend how you could conceive of any reason why you, still living, should not be my wife, you who during my exile had always remained most faithful and loyal. . . .

Would that our time of life had permitted our union to have endured until I, the older, had passed away — which was more just — and that you might perform for me the last sad rites and that I might have departed, leaving you behind, with a daughter to replace me at your side.

By fate's decree your course was run before mine. You left me the grief, the heart-ache, the longing for you, the sad fate to live alone. . . .

The conclusion of this discourse will be that you have deserved all, and that I remain with the chagrin of not being able to give you all. Your wishes have always been my supreme law; and whatever it will be permitted me to accord them still, in this I shall not fail.

May the gods, the Manes [spirits of dead ancestors, considered godlike], assure and protect your repose!

REVIEW QUESTIONS

1. Why was Cato so shocked by and angry at the sight of women demanding repeal of a law concerning them?
2. Although Roman women legally had no political rights, what methods did they use to influence the political decisions of Roman men?
3. What did Cato's remarks reveal about the attitudes held toward women by the more old-fashioned Roman males?

4. What virtues did a Roman husband expect in his wife? What did he consider her duties to be?
5. What specific actions of Turia indicate that Roman women were capable of a wider range of liberties than they usually enjoyed?

---

5 ▾ Tiberius Gracchus and the Crisis in Agriculture

The wars of expansion had a disastrous effect on Roman agriculture. Hannibal's ravaging of Italian farmlands and the obligatory military service that kept peasants away from their fields for long periods left many small farms in near ruins. The importation of thousands of prisoners of war to work as slaves on large plantations also squeezed small farmers out of business. Sinking ever deeper into debt and poverty, many lost their lands and went to Rome, where lack of jobs condemned them to permanent poverty. The once sturdy and independent Roman farmer, who had done all that his country had asked of him, became part of a vast urban underclass — poor, embittered, and alienated.

Plutarch
TIBERIUS GRACCHUS

Tiberius Gracchus (163–133 B.C.), a scion of one of Rome's most honored families, was distressed by this injustice. Moreover, he realized that small landowners were the backbone of the Roman army. Elected tribune (an office created in 493 B.C. to protect plebeian rights), Tiberius Gracchus in 133 B.C. proposed land reforms that the senatorial nobility regarded as a potential menace to their property. They also viewed Tiberius Gracchus as a threat to their political authority. The Roman nobility feared that this popular reformer was building a following among the commoners in order to undermine senatorial rule and that his real ambition was to subvert republican institutions and to become a tyrant, a one-man ruler. This fear was strengthened when Tiberius, in violation of constitutional custom, announced that he would seek reelection as tribune. Senatorial extremists killed Tiberius Gracchus and some three hundred of his followers. The Republic had entered an age of political violence that would eventually destroy it. (Tiberius' younger brother, Gaius, became tribune in 123 B.C. and suffered a fate similar to his brother's.) The following account of Tiberius Gracchus is by Plutarch, the second-century Greek biographer.

Of the territory which the Romans won in war from their neighbours, a part they sold, and a part they made common land, and assigned it for occupation to the poor and indigent among the citizens, on payment of a small rent into the public treasury. And when the rich began to offer larger rents and drove out the poor, a law was enacted forbidding the holding by one person of more than five hundred acres of land. For a short time this enactment gave a check to the rapacity of the rich, and was of assistance to the poor, who remained in their places on the land which they had rented and occupied the allotment which each had held from the outset. But later on the neighbouring rich men, by means of fictitious personages, transferred these rentals to themselves, and finally held most of the land openly in their own names. Then the poor, who had been ejected from their land, no longer showed themselves eager for military service, and neglected the bringing up of children, so that soon all Italy was conscious of a dearth of freemen, and was filled with gangs of foreign slaves, by whose aid the rich cultivated their estates, from which they had driven away the free citizens. An attempt was therefore made to rectify this evil, and by Caius Laelius[1] the comrade of Scipio; but the men of influence opposed his measures, and he, fearing the disturbance which might ensue, desisted, and received the surname of *Wise* or *Prudent* [for the Latin word "sapiens" would seem to have either meaning]. Tiberius, however, on being elected tribune of the people, took the matter directly in hand. . . .

He did not, however, draw up his law by himself, but took counsel with the citizens who were foremost in virtue and reputation. . . .

. . . And it is thought that a law dealing with injustice and rapacity so great was never drawn up in milder and gentler terms. For men who ought to have been punished for their disobedience and to have surrendered with payment of a fine the land which they were illegally enjoying, these men it merely ordered to abandon their injust acquisitions upon being paid their value, and to admit into ownership of them such citizens as needed assistance. But although the rectification of the wrong was so considerate, the people were satisfied to let bygones be bygones if they could be secure from such wrong in the future; the men of wealth and substance, however, were led by their greed to hate the law, and by their wrath and contentiousness to hate the law-giver, and tried to dissuade the people by alleging that Tiberius was introducing a re-distribution of land for the confusion of the body politic, and was stirring up a general revolution.

But they accomplished nothing; for Tiberius, striving to support a measure which was honourable and just with an eloquence that would have adorned even a meaner cause, was formidable and invincible, whenever, with the people crowding around the rostra [speaker's platforms], he took his stand there and pleaded for the poor. "The wild beasts that roam over Italy," he would say, "have every one of them a cave or lair to lurk in; but the men who fight and die for Italy enjoy the common air and light, indeed, but nothing else; houseless and homeless they wander about with their wives and children. And it is with lying lips that their imperators[2] exhort the soldiers in their battles to defend sepulchres and shrines from the enemy; for not a man of them has an hereditary altar, not one of all these many Romans an ancestral tomb, but they fight and die to support others in wealth and luxury, and though they are styled masters of the world, they have not a single clod of earth that is their own."

Such words as these, the product of a lofty spirit and genuine feeling, and falling upon the ears of a people profoundly moved and fully aroused to the speaker's support, no adversary of Tiberius could successfully withstand.

---

[1]Caius Laelius Sapiens, a leading military hero in the Third Punic War and a close friend of Scipio Aemilianus, the conqueror of Carthage, attempted unsuccessfully to resettle the poor on public land.

[2]First, a commander, general, or captain in the army, later *imperator* meant "emperor."

REVIEW QUESTIONS

1. Why did Tiberius Gracchus feel it necessary to redistribute state-owned public lands?
2. How were earlier efforts to keep land widely distributed among the people thwarted?
3. According to Plutarch, what was the reaction of the senatorial class to the reform proposed by Tiberius Gracchus?

---

6 ▾ The Decline of the Republic

In 133 B.C. the Romans effectively controlled all the lands that touched the Mediterranean Sea. The old enemies of Rome, Carthage and Macedonia, had become Roman provinces; the Hellenistic kingdoms of Syria and Egypt were clients of Rome without effective power to challenge Roman hegemony. The Mediterranean Sea had become a "Roman lake."

Yet, at the very moment of its imperial supremacy, the internal order and institutions of the Roman Republic began to break down. The senatorial leaders, who had served Rome responsibly in its march to empire, no longer governed effectively. The ruling class engaged in shameless corruption in administering the provinces, resorted to bribery and force to maintain control over public offices, and failed to solve the deeply rooted problems that afflicted the state. In the century following the assassination of Tiberius Gracchus in 133 B.C., the Republic was torn by conspiracies to seize the state, civil wars, assassinations, mob violence, and confiscations of property by political opponents.

Sallust
THE CONSPIRACY OF CATILINE AND THE JUGURTHINE WAR

In the dark days of the Republic after the assassination of Julius Caesar in 44 B.C., the Roman politician and historian Sallust (Gaius Sallustius Crispus, 86–35 B.C.) reflected on the causes of the Republic's collapse. In his account of a failed coup d'état that occurred in 63 B.C., Sallust contrasted the virtues of the early Republic with the moral decline that set in after the destruction of Carthage. Having failed to be elected consul in 63 B.C., Catiline, a Roman noble, organized a conspiracy to seize the state. The coup d'état was thwarted by the vigorous action of the consul Cicero, who arrested the known conspirators and had them executed. Catiline, who led an army against the forces loyal to the government, was defeated and killed. A second reading discusses the effects of the misuse of power.

[MORAL DETERIORATION]

In peace and war [in the early Republic], as I have said, virtue was held in high esteem. The closest unity prevailed, and avarice was a thing almost unknown. Justice and righteousness were upheld not so much by law as by natural instinct. They quarrelled and fought with their country's foes; between themselves the citizens contended only for honour. In making offerings to the gods they spared no expense; at home they lived frugally and never betrayed a friend. By combining boldness in war with fair dealing when peace was restored, they protected themselves and the state. There are convincing proofs of this. In time of war, soldiers were often punished for attacking against orders or for being slow to obey a signal of recall from battle, whereas few ever ventured to desert their standards or to give ground when hard pressed. In peace, they governed by conferring benefits on their subjects, not by intimidation; and when wronged they would rather pardon than seek vengeance.

Thus by hard work and just dealing the power of the state increased. Mighty kings were vanquished, savage tribes and huge nations were brought to their knees; and when Carthage, Rome's rival in her quest for empire, had been annihilated [in 146 B.C.], every land and sea lay open to her. It was then that fortune turned unkind and confounded all her enterprises. To the men who had so easily endured toil and peril, anxiety and adversity, the leisure and riches which are generally regarded as so desirable proved a burden and a curse. Growing love of money, and the lust for power which followed it, engendered every kind of evil. Avarice destroyed honour, integrity, and every other virtue, and instead taught men to be proud and cruel, to neglect religion, and to hold nothing too sacred to sell. Ambition tempted many to be false, to have one thought hidden in their hearts, another ready on their tongues, to become a man's friend or enemy not because they judged him worthy or unworthy but because they thought it would pay them, and to put on the semblance of virtues that they had not. At first these vices grew slowly and sometimes met with punishment; later on, when the disease had spread like a plague, Rome changed: her government, once so just and admirable, became harsh and unendurable.

▷ Reflecting on the last stages of the Republic's decline, Sallust believed that men had learned a most dangerous lesson: that they could gain power and wealth through violence and corruption rather than through virtue and self-restraint.

Never in its history — it seems to me — had the empire of Rome been in such a miserable plight. From east to west all the world had been vanquished by her armies and obeyed her will; at home there was profound peace and abundance of wealth, which mortal men esteem the chiefest of blessings. Yet there were Roman citizens obstinately determined to destroy both themselves and their country. In spite of two senatorial decrees, not one man among all the conspirators was induced by the promise of reward to betray their plans, and not one deserted from Catiline's camp. A deadly moral contagion had infected all their minds. And this madness was not confined to those actually implicated in the plot. The whole of the lower orders, impatient for a new régime, looked with favour on Catiline's enterprise.* In this they only did what might have been expected of them. In every country paupers envy respectable citizens and make heroes of unprincipled characters, hating the established order of things and hankering after innovation; discontented with their own lot, they are bent on general upheaval. Turmoil and rebellion bring them carefree profit, since poverty has nothing to lose.

The city populace were especially eager to

---

*This surely cannot have been true. Sallust must be exaggerating the popular support for the conspiracy.

fling themselves into a revolutionary adventure. There were several reasons for this. To begin with, those who had made themselves conspicuous anywhere by vice and shameless audacity, those who had wasted their substance by disgraceful excesses, and those whom scandalous or criminal conduct had exiled from their homes — all these had poured into Rome till it was like a sewer. Many, remembering Sulla's victory,[1] and seeing men who had served under him as common soldiers now risen to be senators, or so rich that they lived as luxuriously as kings, began to hope that they too, if they took up arms, might find victory a source of profit. Young men from the country, whose labour on the farms had barely kept them from starvation, had been attracted by the private and public doles available at Rome, and preferred an idle city life to such thankless toil. These, like all the rest, stood to gain by public calamities. It is no wonder, therefore, that these paupers, devoid of moral scruple and incited by ambitious hopes, should have held their country as cheap as they held themselves. Those also to whom Sulla's victory had brought disaster by the proscription of their parents, the confiscation of their property, and the curtailment of their civil rights, looked forward with no less sanguine expectations to what might result from the coming struggle. Moreover, all the factions opposed to the Senate would rather see the state embroiled than accept their own exclusion from political power.

Such was the evil condition by which, after an interval of some years, Rome was once more afflicted. After the restoration of the power of the tribunes in the consulship of Pompey and Crassus,†[2] this very important office was obtained by certain men whose youth intensified their natural aggressiveness. These tribunes began to rouse the mob by inveighing against the Senate, and then inflamed popular passion still further by handing out bribes and promises, whereby they won renown and influence for themselves. They were strenuously opposed by most of the nobility, who posed as defenders of the Senate but were really concerned to maintain their own privileged position. The whole truth — to put it in a word — is that although all disturbers of the peace in this period put forward specious pretexts, claiming either to be protecting the rights of the people or to be strengthening the authority of the Senate, this was mere pretence: in reality, every one of them was fighting for his personal aggrandizement. Lacking all self-restraint, they [stopped] at nothing to gain their ends, and both sides made ruthless use of any successes they won.

▷ In another work, *The Jugurthine War,* Sallust broke off his narrative about war with an African kingdom following the overturning of its government by a man named Jugurtha and described the decay of the Republic. Sallust's digression points out the impact of moral decline on Republican politics.

[THE DANGERS OF POLITICAL EXTREMISM]

The division of the Roman state into warring factions, with all its attendant vices, had originated some years before, as a result of peace and of that material prosperity which men regard as the greatest blessing. Down to the de-

---

[1]Lucius Cornelius Sulla (c. 138–78 B.C.) was a successful politician and general, whose rivalry with another politician and general, Gaius Marius (c. 155–86 B.C.), led to civil war. After seizing Rome and massacring his opponents, Sulla made himself dictator and increased the power of the aristocratic senate, suppressing the office of tribune of the people. The latter had been used by Tiberius and Gaius Gracchus, among others (see pages 121–122), to better the condition of the poorer classes.

†In 70 B.C.

[2]Pompey (Gnaeus Pompeius, 106–48 B.C.) and Crassus (Marcus Licinius Crassus, c. 115–53 B.C.) held the office of consul in 55 B.C. In 59 B.C., together with Julius Caesar, they had formed a political alliance called a triumvirate (meaning "group of three men"), which dominated Roman government for the next decade.

struction of Carthage, the people and Senate shared the government peaceably and with due restraint, and the citizens did not compete for glory or power; fear of its enemies preserved the good morals of the state. But when the people were relieved of this fear, the favourite vices of prosperity — licence and pride — appeared as a natural consequence. Thus the peace and quiet which they had longed for in time of adversity proved, when they obtained it, to be even more grievous and bitter than the adversity. For the nobles started to use their position, and the people their liberty, to gratify their selfish passions, every man snatching and seizing what he could for himself. So the whole community was split into parties, and the Republic, which hitherto had been the common interest of all, was torn asunder. The nobility had the advantage of being a close-knit body, whereas the democratic party was weakened by its loose organization, its supporters being dispersed among a huge multitude. One small group of oligarchs had everything in its control alike in peace and war — the treasury, the provinces, public offices, all distinctions and triumphs. The people were burdened with military service and poverty, while the spoils of war were snatched by the generals and shared with a handful of friends. Meantime, the soldiers' parents or young children, if they happened to have a powerful neighbour, might well be driven from their homes. Thus the possession of power gave unlimited scope to ruthless greed, which violated and plundered everything, respecting nothing and holding nothing sacred, till finally it brought about its own downfall. For the day came when noblemen rose to power who preferred true glory to unjust dominion: then the state was shaken to its foundations by civil strife, as by an earthquake.

So when Tiberius and Gaius Gracchus, men whose ancestors had done much in the Punic and other wars to increase the powers of Rome, sought to establish the liberty of the common people and expose the crimes of the oligarchs, the guilty nobles took fright and opposed their proceedings by every means at their disposal. . . . First Tiberius was butchered when he was actually a tribune; a few years later — because he tried to follow in his brother's footsteps — Gaius suffered the same fate when he was a member of the board of three appointed for founding citizen colonies, and also Marcus Fulvius Flaccus.[3] Admittedly the Gracchi, in their eagerness for victory, went too far. But good men should be prepared to submit even to injustice rather than do wrong in order to defeat it. As it was, the nobles took advantage of their victory to indulge their desire for revenge: they killed or banished numbers of people — conduct which did little to increase their power, but rather caused them to live the rest of their lives in fear. This is what generally ruins great states — when each party will [stop] at nothing to overcome its opponents, and having done so, takes vengeance on them without mercy.

[3]Marcus Fulvius Flaccus, a supporter of the Gracchian reforms, was tribune in 122 B.C. He was killed by members of the opposition.

REVIEW QUESTIONS

1. To what qualities and virtues did Sallust attribute the greatness of Rome?
2. How did the personal vices of the Romans contribute to a breakdown of peaceable civil government?
3. What vices did Sallust believe would ruin even the greatest states?
4. Why are democracies or republics particularly endangered by greed and corruption among public officials?

7 ▾ Reflections on Patriotism and Tyranny

After 59 B.C., Rome was controlled by Julius Caesar, Pompey, and Crassus. This triumvirate, with its supporters, held most of the offices of state and carried out its policies without scruple in a period of increasing violence among political factions. By 50 B.C., Crassus was dead, and the alliance between Pompey and Caesar turned into rivalry. Caesar gained prestige by military conquests: the Gauls in France; the Germans across the Rhine; and the Britons, to open Britannia (England) to Roman trade and influence. Caesar's enemies, who belonged to an ultra-aristocratic faction headed by Cato the Younger, persuaded Pompey to join in recalling Caesar to Rome. The senate ordered Caesar to disband his army and return to the capital city.

In January of 49 B.C., Caesar responded to this challenge by leading his army across the Rubicon River, the northeastern border of Italy proper. This act opened the civil war. The senate turned over to Pompey the command of the government and army and fled Rome as Caesar openly made war on the legitimate authorities of the Roman state.

Cicero
A LETTER TO ATTICUS AT ROME

Cicero, a statesman who had worked to heal the breach between the rival parties and had urged peace and compromise, now faced a hard decision about his role as a patriot. In a letter written from his country house at Formiae (now Formia) to his closest political friend, Atticus, Cicero pondered his moral dilemma. In the end, Cicero chose to join the Republicans, and after their defeat he was pardoned by Caesar and returned to public life.

Formiae, 12 March 49 B.C.

Though I do not relax nowadays except while I am writing to you or reading your letters, still I feel the lack of subject-matter for a letter and I believe you feel the same. The easy, intimate exchanges we are accustomed to are out of the question in these critical times; and every topic relating to the crisis we have already exhausted. However, so as not to succumb completely to morbid reflections, I have put down certain questions of principle — relating to political behaviour — which apply to the present crisis. As well as distracting me from my miserable thoughts, this has given me practice in judging the problems at issue. Here is the sort of thing:

Should one stay in one's country even if it is under totalitarian rule?

Is it justifiable to use any means to get rid of such rule, even if they endanger the whole fabric of the state? Secondly, do precautions have to be taken to prevent the liberator from becoming an autocrat himself?

If one's country is being tyrannized, what are the arguments in favour of helping it by verbal means and when occasion arises, rather than by war?

Is it statesmanlike, when one's country is under a tyranny, to retire to some other place and remain inactive there, or ought one to brave any danger in order to liberate it?

If one's country is under a tyranny, is it right to proceed to its invasion and blockade?

Ought one, even if not approving of war as a means of abolishing tyranny, to join up with the right-minded party in the struggle against it?

Ought one in matters of patriotic concern to share the dangers of one's benefactors and friends, even if their general policy seems to be unwise?

If one has done great services to one's country, and because of them has received shameful and jealous treatment, should one nevertheless voluntarily endanger oneself for one's country's sake, or is it legitimate, eventually, to take some thought for oneself and one's family, and to refrain from fighting against the people in power?

Occupying myself with such questions, and marshalling the argument on either side in Greek and Latin, I take my mind off my troubles for a little; though the problems I am here posing are far from irrelevant to them. But I am afraid I am being a trouble to you: for if the man carrying this letter makes good speed he will bring it to you on the day when you are due for your [recurring] fever.

REVIEW QUESTIONS

1. Describe Cicero's analytic method as he tried to make a political decision in a period of great crisis and confusion.
2. From the questions he raised, what options did Cicero consider for his own possible role in the civil war?
3. Cicero pondered the possibility that the "liberator" might himself become an "autocrat." Why was that likely to happen?
4. What was Cicero's attitude toward the use of violence to resolve political disputes?

---

8 ▾ The Meaning of Caesar's Assassination

Caesar's dictatorship left the future of the Republic uncertain. He seemed undecided about how to recast the government of Rome. Caesar's pardoning of many political enemies and restoring them to political office seemed to signal that eventually he would reinstitute the old Republican constitution, with some minor reforms, as the dictator Sulla had done a generation earlier. Some senators came increasingly to believe, however, that Caesar did not intend to follow Sulla's example. They saw many signs that Caesar sought to establish a typical Hellenistic monarchy over Rome with himself as absolute king. The very word *king* was abhorrent to patriotic Romans, who gloried in their status as free citizens of a five-centuries-old republic. Finally, on the Ides (the fifteenth) of March, 44 B.C., Julius Caesar was slain by some sixty senators, who acted, they said, to restore the liberty of the Roman people. Their leaders were Marcus Junius Brutus (82–42 B.C.) and Gaius Cassius (d. 42 B.C.), both of whom Caesar had previously pardoned.

Cicero
JUSTIFYING THE ASSASSINATION

In the following reading from *On Duties,* Cicero, who was not one of the assassins, justifies the killing of Caesar.

Our tyrant deserved his death for having made an exception of the one thing that was the blackest crime of all. Why do we gather instances of petty crime — legacies criminally obtained and fraudulent buying and selling? Behold, here you have a man who was ambitious to be king of the Roman People and master of the whole world; and he achieved it! The man who maintains that such an ambition is morally right is a madman; for he justifies the destruction of law and liberty and thinks their hideous and detestable suppression glorious. But if anyone agrees that it is not morally right to be king in a state that once was free and that ought to be free now, and yet imagines that it is advantageous for him who can reach that position, with what remonstrance or rather with what appeal should I try to tear him away from so strange a delusion? For, oh ye immortal gods! can the most horrible and hideous of all murders — that of fatherland — bring advantage to anybody, even though he who has committed such a crime receives from his enslaved fellow-citizens the title of "Father of his Country"?

Dio Cassius
IN DEFENSE OF CAESAR AND MONARCHY

The reputation of Julius Caesar changed over the centuries. Some 250 years after Caesar's assassination, the Roman historian and politician Dio Cassius (c. A.D. 150–235), writing in Greek, acknowledged that Caesar was not blameless in bringing about the tragedy that led to his death and renewal of civil war between Caesar's friends and enemies. Yet, examining events since Caesar's time, he argued that monarchy is superior to republicanism and condemned the assassination.

. . . [A] baleful frenzy . . . fell upon certain men through jealousy of [Caesar's] advancement and hatred of his preferment to themselves caused his death unlawfully, while it added a new name to the annals of infamy; it scattered [Caesar's] decrees to the winds and brought upon the Romans seditions and civil wars once more after a state of harmony. His slayers, to be sure, declared that they had shown themselves at once destroyers of Caesar and liberators of the people: but in reality they impiously plotted against him, and they threw the city into disorder when at last it possessed a stable government. Democracy, indeed, has a fair-appearing name and conveys the impression of bringing equal rights to all through equal laws, but its results are seen not to agree at all with its title. Monarchy, on the contrary, has an unpleasant sound, but is a most practical form of government to live under. For it is easier to find a single excellent man than many of them, and if even this seems to some a difficult feat, it is quite inevitable that the other alternative should be acknowledged to be impossible; for it does not belong to the majority of men to acquire virtue. And again, even though a base man should obtain supreme power, yet he is preferable to the masses of like character, as the history of the Greeks and barbarians and of the Romans themselves proves. For successes have always been greater and more frequent in the case both of cities and of individuals under kings than under popular rule, and disasters do [not] happen [so frequently] under monarchies as under mob-rule. Indeed, if ever there has been a prosperous democracy, it has in any case been at its best for only a brief period, so long, that is, as the people had neither the numbers nor the strength sufficient to cause insolence to spring up among them as the result of good fortune or jealousy as the result of ambition. But for a city, not only so large in itself, but also ruling the finest and the greatest part of the known world, holding sway over men of many and diverse natures, possessing many men of great wealth, occupied with every imaginable pursuit, enjoying every imaginable fortune, both individually and collectively, — for such a city, I say, to practise moderation under a democracy is impossible, and still more is it impossible for the people, unless moderation prevails, to be harmonious. Therefore, if Marcus Brutus and Gaius Cassius had only reflected upon these things, they would never have killed the city's head and protector nor have made themselves the cause of countless ills both to themselves and to all the rest of mankind then living.

It happened as follows, and his death was due to the cause now to be given. He had aroused dislike that was not altogether unjustified, except in so far as it was the senators themselves who had by their novel and excessive honours encouraged him and puffed him up, only to find fault with him on this very account and to spread slanderous reports how glad he was to accept them and how he behaved more haughtily as a result of them. It is true that Caesar did now and then err by accepting some of the honours voted him and believing that he really deserved them; yet those were most blameworthy who, after beginning to honour him as he deserved, led him on and brought blame upon him for the measures they had passed. He neither dared, of course, to thrust them all aside, for fear of being thought contemptuous, nor, again, could he be safe in accepting them; for excessive honour and praise render even the most modest men conceited, especially if they seem to be bestowed with sincerity.

REVIEW QUESTIONS

1. What did Cicero consider "the blackest crime of all"?
2. What did Dio Cassius consider the chief crime of Caesar's assassins?
3. What were some of the advantages of a monarchial form of government as listed by Dio Cassius? Would Cicero agree? Why or why not?
4. What were Dio Cassius' criticisms of "democracy"?

The Roman Empire

In the chaotic years following Julius Caesar's assassination in 44 B.C., Octavian (Augustus) emerged victorious over his rivals, becoming the unchallenged ruler of Rome. Although eager for personal power, Augustus was by no means a self-seeking tyrant; he was a creative statesman who prevented the renewal of civil war that had plagued the Republic and introduced needed reforms in Italy and the provinces. His long reign, from 27 B.C. to A.D. 14, marks the beginning of the *Pax Romana,* the Roman Peace, which endured until A.D. 180.

The period of the Pax Romana was one of the finest in the ancient world. Revolts against Roman rule were few, and Roman legions ably defended the Empire's borders. The Mediterranean world had never enjoyed so many years of peace, effective government, and economic well-being. Stretching from Britain to the Arabian Desert and from the Danube River to the sands of the Sahara, the Roman Empire united some seventy million people. In many ways the Roman Empire was the fulfillment of the universalism and cosmopolitanism of the Hellenistic Age. The same law bound together Italians, Spaniards, North Africans, Greeks, Syrians, and other peoples. Although dissatisfaction was sometimes violently expressed and separatist tendencies persisted, notably in Judea and Gaul, people from diverse backgrounds viewed themselves as Romans even though they had never set foot in the capital city.

In the seventy years following Augustus' reign, political life was sometimes marred by conspiracies and assassinations, particularly after an emperor's death left the throne vacant. Marcus Cocceius Nerva, who reigned from A.D. 96 to 98, introduced a practice that led to orderly succession and gave Rome four exceptionally competent emperors. He adopted as his son and designated as his heir Trajan (Marcus Ulpius Traianus), a man of proven ability. From the accession of Nerva to the death of Marcus Aurelius Antoninus in A.D. 180, the Roman Empire was ruled by the "Five Good Emperors." Marcus Aurelius abandoned the use of adoption and allowed his son Commodus (Marcus Aurelius Commodus Antoninus, A.D. 180–192) to succeed to the throne. An extravagant despot, Commodus was murdered in A.D. 192.

MARCUS AURELIUS, Roman emperor (161–180). In this relief, Marcus rides through the Roman Forum, having been accorded a triumph after defending the empire against barbarian incursions. (*Alinari/Art Resource, N.Y.*)

During the third century the Roman Empire suffered

hard times, and the ordered civilization of the Pax Romana was destroyed. The Empire was plunged into anarchy as generals vied for the throne. Taking advantage of the weakened border defenses, the barbarians (Germanic tribesmen) crossed the Danube frontier and pillaged Roman cities. Both civil war and barbarian attacks greatly disrupted the Roman economy, which even during good times suffered from basic weaknesses.

Two later emperors — Diocletian (G. Aurelius Valerius Diocletianus, A.D. 285–305) and Constantine (Flavius Valerius Constantinus, A.D. 306–337) — tried to keep the Empire from dissolution by tightening control over the citizenry. Although heavy taxes, requisitioning of goods, and forced labor provided some stability, these measures also turned many citizens against the oppressive state. At the end of the fourth and the opening of the fifth century, several barbarian tribes poured into the Empire in great numbers. In succeeding decades Germanic tribes overran Roman provinces and set up kingdoms on lands that had been Roman. The Roman Empire in the west fell; the eastern provinces, however, survived as the Byzantine Empire.

The history of the Roman Empire influenced Western civilization in many ways. From Latin, the language of Rome, came the Romance languages: French, Italian, Spanish, Portuguese, and Rumanian. Roman law became the basis of the legal codes of most modern European states. Rome preserved Greek culture, the foundation of Western learning and aesthetics, and spread it to other lands. And Christianity, the religion of the West, was born in the Roman Empire.

1 ▾ The Imperial Office

The greatest achievement of Caesar Augustus (Octavian), grand-nephew and adopted son of Julius Caesar, was undoubtedly the step-by-step building of a new constitutional structure for the Roman Empire. This political system, called by modern historians the Principate, has been described as a monarchy disguised as an oligarchical republic. The Roman antimonarchial tradition, nurtured for five centuries under the Republican regime, had contributed directly to Julius Caesar's assassination. Augustus was wise enough, as he created a stable central executive office for the Empire, to camouflage the monarchial reality of his regime by maintaining the outer forms of the old Republic's constitution.

Augustus' chief innovation was creating the office of ***Princeps*** (First Citizen), which combined a number of Republican offices and powers and placed them

at the disposal of one man. Desiring to maintain the appearance of traditional republican government, he refused to be called king. The Senate gave him the semi-religious and revered name Augustus (venerable). In effect, however, he was the first Roman emperor. He cultivated the support of the traditional constituents of the Roman state — the senatorial nobility, knights, and public contractors, residents of the capital, soldiers and veterans, and the wealthy and politically useful provincial subjects of Rome. At the time of his death in A.D. 14, Augustus successfully passed on his imperial office to his chosen heir, his adopted son Tiberius.

Augustus
≪ THE ACHIEVEMENTS OF THE DIVINE AUGUSTUS ≫

In *Res gestae divi Augusti (The Achievements of the Divine Augustus),* a document composed shortly before his death and left to be published with his will, Augustus gave an account of those achievements for which he wanted to be remembered. A careful reading reveals the image Augustus chose to promote to justify his emperorship. It also describes the many responsibilities of holders of that office.

I drove into exile the murderers of my father [Julius Caesar], avenging their crime through tribunals established by law; and afterwards, when they made war on the republic, I twice defeated them in battle.

I undertook many civil and foreign wars by land and sea throughout the world, and as victor I spared the lives of all citizens who asked for mercy. When foreign peoples could safely be pardoned I preferred to preserve rather than to exterminate them. The Roman citizens who took the soldier's oath of obedience to me numbered about 500,000. I settled rather more than 300,000 of these in colonies or sent them back to their home towns after their period of service; to all these I assigned lands or gave money as rewards for their military service. . . .

The dictatorship was offered to me by both senate and people in my absence and when I was at Rome in the consulship of Marcus Marcellus and Lucius Arruntius, but I refused it. I did not decline in the great dearth of corn to undertake the charge of the corn-supply, which I so administered that within a few days I delivered the whole city from apprehension and immediate danger at my own cost and by my own efforts. . . . The senate and people of Rome agreed that I should be appointed supervisor of laws and morals without a colleague and with supreme power, but I would not accept any office inconsistent with the custom of our ancestors. The measures that the senate then desired me to take I carried out in virtue of my tribunician power. . . .

To each member of the Roman plebs [common populace] I paid under my father's will 300 sesterces,[1] and in my own name I gave them 400 each from the booty of war in my fifth consulship, and once again in my tenth

---

[1]Sesterces, during the reign of Augustus, were small coins of bronze, each worth one hundredth of a gold *aureus,* or a quarter of a silver denarius, the basic coin of the Roman monetary system. Brunt (editor of source) notes that a Roman legionary soldier of this period earned 900 sesterces a year, out of which the cost of uniform, food, and arms was deducted. A Roman whose assessed wealth came to at least 400,000 sesterces qualified to enter the order of knights; to be a senator required one million sesterces.

consulship I paid out 400 sesterces as a largesse to each man from my own patrimony, and in my eleventh consulship I bought grain with my own money and distributed twelve rations apiece, and in the twelfth year of my tribunician power I gave every man 400 sesterces for the third time. These largesses of mine never reached fewer than 250,000 persons. . . .

. . . I paid monetary rewards to soldiers whom I settled in their home towns after completion of their service, and on this account I expended about 400,000,000 sesterces.

Four times I assisted the treasury with my own money, so that I transferred to the administrators of the treasury 150,000,000 sesterces. . . .

I restored the Capitol[2] and the theatre of Pompey, both works at great expense without inscribing my own name on either. I restored the channels of the aqueducts, which in several places were falling into disrepair through age, and I brought water from a new spring into the aqueduct called Marcia, doubling the supply. I completed the Forum Julium[3] and the basilica between the temples of Castor and Saturn,[4] works begun and almost finished by my father. . . .

I gave three gladiatorial games in my own name and five in that of my sons or grandsons; at these games some 10,000 men took part in combat. Twice in my own name and a third time in that of my grandson I presented to the people displays by athletes summoned from all parts. I produced shows in my own name four times and in place of other magistrates twenty-three times. . . . I gave beast-hunts of African beasts in my own name or in that of my sons and grandsons in the circus or forum or amphitheatre on twenty-six occasions, on which about 3,500 beasts were destroyed.

I made the sea peaceful and freed it of pirates. In that war I captured about 30,000 slaves who had escaped from their masters and taken up arms against the republic, and I handed them over to their masters for punishment.

I extended the territory of all those provinces of the Roman people on whose borders lay peoples not subject to our government. I brought peace to the Gallic and Spanish provinces as well as to Germany, throughout the area bordering on the [Atlantic] Ocean from Cadiz [in Spain] to the mouth of the Elbe [in northwestern Germany]. I secured the pacification of the Alps. . . . The Pannonian peoples [in western Hungary] . . . were conquered through the agency of Tiberius Nero[5] who was then my stepson and legate; I brought them into the empire of the Roman people, and extended the frontier of Illyricum[6] to the banks of the Danube. . . .

In my sixth and seventh consulships, after I had extinguished civil wars, and at a time when with universal consent I was in complete control of affairs, I transferred the republic from my power to the dominion of the senate and people of Rome. For this service of mine I was named Augustus by decree of the senate, and the door-posts of my house were publicly wreathed with bay leaves and a civic crown was fixed over my door and a golden shield was set in the Curia Julia,[7] which, as attested by the inscription thereon, was given me by the senate and people of Rome on account of my courage, clemency, justice and piety. After this time I excelled all in influence, although I possessed no more official power than others who were my colleagues in the several magistracies.

In my thirteenth consulship the senate, the equestrian order and the whole people of Rome gave me the title of Father of my Country. . . .

---

[2]Here "Capitol" refers to the temple of Jupiter, patron of Rome, on the Capitoline Hill.

[3]The Forum (Square) Julium was surrounded by a covered portico. Begun by Julius Caesar, it was finished by Augustus.

[4]Saturn was a Roman agricultural god associated with the Greek god Cronus. Castor, brother of Pollux and Helen of Troy, was the son of Jupiter by a mortal. The twins Castor and Pollux were deified in Rome for having helped the Romans in a battle.

[5]Tiberius Nero, Augustus' adopted son and designated heir, reigned as emperor from A.D. 14 to 37.

[6]Illyricum was a Roman province on the Adriatic Sea; it is now part of Yugoslavia.

[7]The Curia Julia, also begun by Julius Caesar and completed by Augustus, was a courthouse.

Tacitus
THE IMPOSITION OF ONE-MAN RULE

Not all Romans accepted Augustus' own evaluation of his achievements. In this reading, the Roman historian Cornelius Tacitus (c. A.D. 55–c. 117) described how Augustus seduced the Roman people into accepting monarchial rule.

[Augustus] seduced the army with bonuses, and his cheap food policy was successful bait for civilians. Indeed, he attracted everybody's goodwill by the enjoyable gift of peace. Then he gradually pushed ahead and absorbed the functions of the senate, the officials, and even the law. Opposition did not exist. War or judicial murder had disposed of all men of spirit. Upper-class survivors found that slavish obedience was the way to succeed, both politically and financially. They had profited from the revolution, and so now they liked the security of the existing arrangement better than the dangerous uncertainties of the old régime. Besides, the new order was popular in the provinces. There, government by Senate and People was looked upon sceptically as a matter of sparring dignitaries and extortionate officials. The legal system had provided no remedy against these, since it was wholly incapacitated by violence, favouritism, and — most of all — bribery.

To safeguard his domination Augustus made his sister's son Marcellus a priest and an aedile[1] — in spite of his extreme youth — and singled out Marcus Agrippa,[2] a commoner but a first-rate soldier who had helped to win his victories, by the award of two consecutive consulships; after the death of Marcellus, Agrippa was chosen by Augustus as his son-in-law. Next the emperor had his stepsons Tiberius and Nero Drusus[3] hailed publicly as victorious generals. . . .

At this time there was no longer any fighting — except a war against the Germans. . . . In the capital the situation was calm. The titles of officials remained the same. Actium[4] had been won before the younger men were born. Even most of the older generation had come into a world of civil wars. Practically no one had ever seen truly Republican government. The country had been transformed, and there was nothing left of the fine old Roman character. Political equality was a thing of the past; all eyes watched for imperial commands.

[1]An aedile was a minor municipal magistrate, responsible for petty criminal cases, and for the supervision of markets and public games — gladiator combats and chariot races.

[2]Marcus Agrippa (c. 63–12 B.C.), Augustus' son-in-law, was his closest associate and virtually co-emperor; he predeceased Augustus.

[3]Nero Drusus (38–9 B.C.), one of Augustus' stepsons, was the father of Emperor Claudius (ruled A.D. 41–54).

[4]The Battle of Actium, fought in the sea off west-central Greece, pitted forces of Antony and Cleopatra against those of Augustus. Augustus' victory gave him sole control of the Roman Empire.

REVIEW QUESTIONS

1. How did Augustus try to win the favor of the soldiers, his former enemies, and the poor of Rome?
2. How did Augustus attempt to disguise the real character of his political power?
3. What military role was an emperor expected to play?
4. Describe the functions of an emperor of Rome as suggested by the career of Augustus.

5. Why, according to Tacitus, was the Augustan principate so successful?
6. How did Augustus plan to perpetuate his regime?

---

2 ▾ Imperial Culture

The reign of Augustus marks the golden age of Latin literature. This outpouring of literary works stemmed in part from the patronage of authors by Augustus and other prominent Romans. Roman poets and dramatists used Greek models, just as Roman philosophers, mathematicians, scientists, doctors, and geographers did. Not surprisingly, writers of the Augustan Age often expressed strong patriotic sentiments and were extravagant in their praise of Augustus.

Virgil
≪ THE AENEID ≫

The poet Virgil (Publius Vergilius Maro, 70–19 B.C.) admired Augustus, who was his patron, for ending the civil wars and bringing order to the Roman world. Augustus urged Virgil to compose a grand opus that would glorify Rome's imperial achievement — the emperor knew that he would find an honored place in such a work. It took Virgil ten years to produce the *Aeneid,* which was not fully completed when he died. Augustus disobeyed Virgil's deathbed request that the manuscript be destroyed, and the patriotic poem became Rome's national epic.

The *Aeneid* was greatly influenced by Homer's *Iliad* and *Odyssey* (see Chapter 3). In *The Iliad,* Homer dealt with the conflict between the early Greeks and the Trojans. Roman legend held that a Trojan remnant led by Prince Aeneas, son of Venus (the goddess of love) and a mortal father, Anchises, escaped the sacking of Troy. (Caesar Augustus claimed descent from the goddess Venus through Aeneas.) In book six, Aeneas, escorted by the Sybil, prophetess and priestess of Apollo, descends to the underworld in order to reach his father. There his father's soul describes the illustrious future that will be Rome's.

. . . Turn your two eyes
This way and see this people, your own Romans.
Here is Caesar, and all the line of Iulus [founder of the Julian family],
All who shall one day pass under the dome
Of the great sky: this is the man, this one,
Of whom so often you have heard the promise,
Caesar Augustus, son of the deified [Julius Caesar],
Who shall bring once again an Age of Gold
To Latium,[1] to the land where Saturn [Roman god] reigned
In early times. He will extend his power
Beyond the Garamants[2] and Indians,
Over far territories north and south

. . .

---

[1]Latium was the ancient country in which stood the towns of Lavinium and Alba Longa; Rome was established in that region and became its most significant city.
[2]The Garamants (Garamantes) were a warlike nomadic people living in the northwestern Sahara.

Others will cast more tenderly in bronze
Their breathing figures, I can well believe,
And bring more lifelike portraits out of marble;
Argue more eloquently, use the pointer
To trace the paths of heaven accurately
And accurately foretell the rising stars.
Roman, remember by your strength to rule
Earth's peoples — for your arts are to be these:
To pacify, to impose the rule of law,
To spare the conquered, battle down the proud.

Quintilian
≪ *THE EDUCATION OF AN ORATOR* ≫

Quintilian (Marcus Fabius Quintilianus, c. A.D. 35–c. 90), the leading Roman rhetorician of his day, was born in Spain and educated in Rome. After many years of teaching the children of the Roman elite, Quintilian wrote a systematic treatise on education, *The Education of the Orator,* which provided shrewd insights into the learning process and emphasized the making of well-rounded, cultured orators and good citizens as important goals for the instructor. Excerpts from this work are given below.

My aim, then, is the education of the perfect orator. The first essential for such an one is that he should be a good man, and consequently we demand of him not merely the possession of exceptional gifts of speech, but of all the excellences of character as well. For I will not admit that the principles of upright and honourable living should, as some have held, be regarded as the peculiar concern of philosophy. The man who can really play his part as a citizen and is capable of meeting the demands both of public and private business, the man who can guide a state by his counsels, give it a firm basis by his legislation and purge its vices by his decisions as a judge, is assuredly no other than the orator of our quest. . . .

I prefer that a boy should begin with Greek, because Latin, being in general use, will be picked up by him whether we will or no; while the fact that Latin learning is derived from Greek is a further reason for his being first instructed in the latter. . . . The study of Latin ought therefore to follow at no great distance and in a short time proceed side by side with Greek. The result will be that, as soon as we begin to give equal attention to both languages, neither will prove a hindrance to the other.

Some hold that boys should not be taught to read till they are seven years old, that being the earliest age at which they can derive profit from instruction and endure the strain of learning. . . . Those however who hold that a child's mind should not be allowed to lie fallow for a moment are wiser. Why, again, since children are capable of moral training, should they not be capable of literary education? I am well aware that during the whole period of which I am speaking we can expect scarcely the same amount of progress that one year will effect afterwards. . . .

I am not however so blind to differences of age as to think that the very young should be forced on prematurely or given real work to do. Above all things we must take care that the child, who is not yet old enough to love his studies, does not come to hate them and dread the bitterness which he has once tasted, even when the years of infancy are left behind. His studies must be made an amusement: he must be questioned and praised and taught to rejoice when he has done well; sometimes, too, when he refuses instruction, it should be given to some other to excite his envy, at times also he must be engaged in competition and should be allowed to believe himself successful more often than not, while he should be encouraged to do his best by such rewards as may appeal to his tender years. . . .

. . . It is the master's duty as well, if he is engaged on the task of training unformed minds and prefers practical utility to a more ambitious programme, not to burden his pupils at once with tasks to which their strength is unequal, but to curb his energies and refrain from talking over the heads of his audience. Vessels with narrow mouths will not receive liquids if too much be poured into them at a time, but are easily filled if the liquid is admitted in a gentle stream or, it may be, drop by drop; similarly you must consider how much a child's mind is capable of receiving: the things which are beyond their grasp will not enter their minds, which have not opened out sufficiently to take them in. . . .

Still, all our pupils will require some relaxation, not merely because there is nothing in this world that can stand continued strain . . . but because study depends on the good will of the student, a quality that cannot be secured by compulsion. Consequently if restored and refreshed by a holiday they will bring greater energy to their learning and approach their work with greater spirit of a kind that will not submit to be driven. I approve of play in the young; it is a sign of a lively disposition; nor will you ever lead me to believe that a boy who is gloomy and in a continual state of depression is ever likely to show alertness of mind in his work, lacking as he does the impulse most natural to boys of his age. Such relaxation must not however be unlimited: otherwise the refusal to give a holiday will make boys hate their work, while excessive indulgence will accustom them to idleness. There are moreover certain games which have an education value for boys. . . . Games too reveal character in the most natural way, at least that is so if the teacher will bear in mind that there is no child so young as to be unable to learn to distinguish between right and wrong, and that the character is best moulded, when it is still guiltless of deceit and most susceptible to instruction: for once a bad habit has become engrained, it is easier to break than bend. There must be no delay, then, in warning a boy that his actions must be unselfish, honest, self-controlled, and we must never forget the words of Virgil, "So strong is custom formed in early years."

I disapprove of flogging, although it is the regular custom and meets with the acquiescence of Chrysippus,[1] because . . . it is a disgraceful form of punishment and fit only for slaves, and is in any case an insult, as you will realise if you imagine its infliction at a later age. . . . And though you may compel a child with blows, what are you to do with him when he is a young man no longer amenable to such threats and confronted with tasks of far greater difficulty? Moreover when children are beaten, pain or fear frequently have results of which it is not pleasant to speak and which are likely subsequently to be a source of shame, a shame which unnerves and depresses the mind and leads the child to shun and loathe the light. . . . I will content myself with saying that children are helpless and easily victimised, and that therefore no one should be given unlimited power over them. I will now proceed to describe the subjects in which the boy must be trained, if he is to become an orator, and to indicate the age at which each should be commenced.

As soon as the boy has learned to read and write without difficulty, it is the turn for the teacher of literature. My words apply equally to Greek and Latin masters, though I prefer that a start should be made with a Greek: in either case the method is the same. This profession may be most briefly considered under two heads, the art of speaking correctly and the interpretation of the poets; but there is more beneath the surface than meets the eye. For the art of writing is combined with that of speaking, and correct reading precedes interpretation, while in each of these cases criticism has its work to perform. . . . Nor is it sufficient to have read the poets only; every kind of writer

---

[1]Chrysippus (280–207 B.C.) was considered second only to Zeno among the Stoic philosophers.

must be carefully studied, not merely for the subject matter, but for the vocabulary; for words often acquire authority from their use by a particular author. Nor can such training be regarded as complete if it stop short of music, for the teacher of literature has to speak of metre and rhythm: nor again if he be ignorant of astronomy, can he understand the poets; for they, to mention no further points, frequently give their indications of time by reference to the rising and setting of the stars. Ignorance of philosophy is an equal drawback, since there are numerous passages in almost every poem based on the most intricate questions of natural philosophy. . . . No small powers of eloquence also are required to enable the teacher to speak appropriately and fluently on the various points which have just been mentioned. For this reason those who criticise the art of teaching literature as trivial and lacking in substance put themselves out of court. Unless the foundations of oratory are well and truly laid by the teaching of literature, the superstructure will collapse. The study of literature is a necessity for boys and the delight of old age, the sweet companion of our privacy and the sole branch of study which has more solid substance than display.

Juvenal
≪ THE SATIRES ≫

Juvenal (Decimus Junius Juvenalis, c. A.D. 60–c. 131), Rome's greatest satirical poet, found much fault with the Rome of his day. The streets were crowded, noisy, and unsafe; bullies itched to fight; criminals stole and murdered; the poor suffered even more than other Romans. The following excerpt from *The Satires* is Juvenal's account of the underside of life in Rome.

. . . A man's word
Is believed just to the extent of the wealth in his coffers stored.
Though he swear on all the altars from here to Samothrace,[1]
A poor man isn't believed. . . .

Anyway, a poor man's the butt of jokes if his cloak has a rip
Or is dirty, if his toga is slightly soiled, if a strip
Of leather is split in his shoes and gapes, if coarse thread shows
New stitches patching not one but many holes. Of the woes
Of unhappy poverty, none is more difficult to bear
Than that it heaps men with ridicule. Says an usher, "How dare
You sit there? Get out of the rows reserved for knights to share. . . ."

. . . What poor man ever inherits
A fortune or gets appointed as clerk to a magistrate?
Long ago the penniless Romans ought to have staged a great
Mass walkout. It's no easy job for a man to advance
When his talents are balked by his impoverished circumstance,
But in Rome it's harder than elsewhere. . . .

Here most of the sick die off because they get no sleep
(But the sickness is brought on by the undigested heap
Of sour food in their burning stomachs), for what rented flat

[1]Samothrace, an island in the northern Aegean Sea, is best known today as the place where the famous statue of the Winged Victory (Nike) was found.

Allows you to sleep? Only rich men in
this city have that.
There lies the root of the illness — carts
rumbling in narrow streets
And cursing drivers stalled in a traffic
jam — it defeats
All hope of rest. . . .

. . . Though we hurry, we merely crawl;
We're blocked by a surging mass ahead,
a pushing wall
Of people behind. A man jabs me,
elbowing through, one socks
A chair pole against me, one cracks my
skull with a beam, one knocks
A wine cask against my ear. My legs are
caked with splashing
Mud, from all sides the weight of
enormous feet comes smashing
On mine, and a soldier stamps his
hobnails through to my sole. . . .

. . . a piece of a pot
Falls down on my head, how often a
broken vessel is shot
From the upper windows, with what a
force it strikes and dints
The cobblestones! . . .

The besotted bully, denied his chance in
the shabby bars
Of killing somebody, suffers torments,
itching to fight.
Like Achilles[2] bemoaning his friend, he
tosses about all night,
Now flat on his face, now on his back —
there's no way at all
He can rest, for some men can't sleep till
after a bloody brawl.
But however rash and hot with youth
and flushed with wine,
He avoids the noble whose crimson cloak
and long double line
Of guards with brass lamps and torches
show they're too much to handle.
But for me, whom the moon escorts, or
the feeble light of a candle
Whose wick I husband and trim — he
has no respect for me.
Now hear how the pitiful fight begins —
if a fight it be,

When he delivers the punches and I am
beaten to pulp.
He blocks my way and tells me to stop. I
stop, with a gulp —
What else can you do when a madman
stronger than you attacks?. . .

This is the poor man's freedom: having
been soundly mauled
And cut to pieces by fists, he begs and
prays, half dead,
To be allowed to go home with a few
teeth still in his head.

But these aren't your only terrors. For
you can never restrain
The criminal element. Lock up your
house, put bolt and chain
On your shop, but when all's quiet,
someone will rob you or he'll
Be a cutthroat perhaps and do you in
quickly with cold steel. . . .

[2]Achilles, leader of the Greeks in Homer's *Iliad,* let his best friend Patroclus wear his (Achilles') armor into battle; Patroclus was killed and Achilles was torn by grief.

REVIEW QUESTIONS

1. According to Virgil, what was Rome's destiny and the basis of its greatness?
2. Why did Virgil find such favor with Caesar Augustus?
3. What role do poets play in shaping the values of a culture?
4. What were Quintilian's aims as a teacher of Roman youth?
5. What were some of the educational methods Quintilian favored?
6. What argument did Quintilian make against flogging students?

7. According to Juvenal, what were some of the hazards facing a resident of the imperial capital city?
8. What did Juvenal see as the fate of the poor man in the imperial capital?

3 ▾ Roman Stoicism

Stoicism, the leading school of thought in the Hellenistic world, appealed to Roman thinkers. Founded by Zeno of Citium (335–267 B.C.), who established an academy in Athens, Stoicism taught that universal principles, or natural law, underlay the universe. Natural laws applied to all people and were grasped through reason, which was common to all human beings. Stoicism gave expression to the universalism of the Hellenistic Age; it held that all people — Greek and barbarian, free and slave, rich and poor — were essentially equal, for they all had the capacity to reason and were all governed by the same universal laws. Living according to the law of reason that pervades the cosmos provides the individual with the inner fortitude to deal with life's misfortunes, said the Stoics; it is the path to virtue. In the tradition of Socrates, the Stoics regarded people as morally self-sufficient, capable of regulating their own lives. The Romans valued the Stoic emphasis on self-discipline and the molding of character according to worthy standards. The Stoic doctrine of natural law that applied to all peoples harmonized with the requirements of Rome's multinational Empire.

Seneca
≪ THE EPISTLES ≫

Lucius Annaeus Seneca (4 B.C.–A.D. 65) was born at Corduba (Cordova), Spain, into a highly educated family: his father, for example, was a distinguished rhetorician, politician, and historian. Sent to school in Rome, Seneca studied rhetoric and philosophy, particularly Stoicism. From A.D. 54 to 62, he was a key advisor to the emperor Nero (A.D. 54–68). Later the notoriously unstable emperor accused Seneca of participating in a conspiracy against him and compelled him to commit suicide.

In traditional Stoic fashion, Seneca held that individuals belong to two commonwealths, the city where they are born and the kingdom of humanity, which is worldwide. In serving this superior commonwealth, individuals become aware of their moral potential. The virtuous tone of Seneca's writings (they had a great appeal to Christians) contrasted with the realities of his life, for Seneca used his political influence for self-enrichment and condoned murder to enhance his political power. Despite this discrepancy between Seneca's words and deeds, he was one of the few Romans to denounce the gladiatorial events as barbaric, and he urged humane treatment of slaves. The sentiments expressed in the following letters (epistles) to his friend Lucilius, a prominent Roman civil servant, reveal Seneca's Stoic humanitarianism.

EPISTLE 7

But nothing is more harmful to a good disposition than to while the time away at some public show. I return from such entertainments more greedy, more dissipated, nay, even more cruel and inhuman. By chance I fell in with a public show at midday, expecting some sport, buffoonery [clownish amusement], or other relaxation, now that the spectators had seen their fill of human gore. All the bloody deeds of the morning were mere mercy: for now, all trifling apart, they commit downright murder. The combatants have nothing with which to shield the body; they are exposed to every stroke of their antagonist; and every stroke is a wound. And this some prefer to their fighting well armored! There is no helmet or shield to repel the blow; no defense, no art — for these are but so many balks and delays of death. In the morning men are exposed to lions and bears; at noon gladiators who fight to the death are ordered out against one another, and the conqueror is detained for another slaughter. Death alone puts an end to this business. "Kill, burn, scourge," is all they cry. "Why is he so afraid of the sword's point? Why is he so timorous to kill? Why does he not die more manfully?" They are urged on with floggings if they refuse to fight and are obliged to give and take wounds with an open breast. They are called upon to cut one another's throats.

EPISTLE 47

It by no means displeases me, Lucilius, to hear from those who confer with you, that you live on friendly terms with your slaves. This attests to your good sense and education. Are they slaves? No, they are men; they are comrades; they are humble friends. Nay, rather fellow-servants, if you reflect on the equal power of Fortune over both you and them. I therefore laugh at those who think it scandalous for a gentleman to permit, at times, his servant to sit down with him at supper. Why should he not? It is only proud custom that has ordained that a master dine surrounded by at least a dozen slaves and stuff himself, while the poor servants are not allowed to open their lips, even to speak. The slightest murmur is restrained by a rod; nor are mere accidents excused, such as a cough, a sneeze, or a hiccup. Silence interrupted by a word is sure to be punished severely. Thus the slaves must stand, perhaps the whole night, without taking a bit of food or drink or speaking a word. Whence it often happens that such as are not allowed to speak before their masters will speak disrespectfully of them behind their backs. In contrast, those slaves who have been allowed not only to speak before their masters, but sometimes with them, whose mouths were not sewed up, have been ready to incur the most imminent danger, even to the sacrificing of their lives, for their master's safety. Slaves are not naturally our enemies, but we make them such.

I pass by the more cruel and inhuman actions, wherein we treat slaves not as men but as beasts of burden. . . .

Were you to consider, that he whom you call your slave, is sprung from the same origin, enjoys the same climate, breathes the same air, and is subject to the same condition of life and death as yourself, you will think it possible to see him as a free-born person, as he is free to see you as a slave. After the fall of Marius,[1] how many people born of the most splendid parentage and not unjustly expecting a senatorial office for their exploits in war, did fortune cut down? She made one a shepherd, another a caretaker of a country cottage. Can you now despise the man whose fortune is such, into which, while you despise it, you may fall?

I will not discuss at length the treatment of slaves towards whom we behave cruelly and arrogantly. But this is the essence of what I would prescribe: treat your inferiors as you would have a superior treat you. As often as you think of the power that you have over a slave, reflect on

---

[1]Gaius Marius (c. 155–86 B.C.) was a famous Roman general.

the power that your master has over you. But you say, "I have no master." Be it so. The world goes well with you at present; it may not do so always. You may one day be a slave yourself. Do you know at what time Hecuba[2] became a slave, or Croesus,[3] or the mother of Darius,[4] or Plato, or Diogenes?[5] Live therefore courteously with your slave; talk with him, dine with him.

[2]Hecuba, the wife of Priam, king of Troy, was enslaved by the Greeks after their conquest of Troy.

[3]Croesus, king of Lydia in Asia Minor from 560 to 546 B.C., was famous for his wealth, but died in slavery after losing his kingdom in battle.

[4]Darius III of Persia (336–330 B.C.) was defeated by Alexander the Great, who also captured Darius' mother, wives, and children.

[5]Diogenes (c. 412–323 B.C.), a famous Greek philosopher of the Cynic school, was captured by pirates and put up for sale in Crete. He is reported to have said, "Sell me to that man; he needs a master." He was bought by a wealthy Greek, who restored his freedom.

Marcus Aurelius
≪ MEDITATIONS ≫

Emperor Marcus Aurelius Antoninus (A.D. 161–180) was the last of the great Roman Stoics and the last of the so-called Five Good Emperors. His death brought an end to the Pax Romana. A gentle and peace-loving man, Marcus Aurelius was not spared violence and personal misfortune during his reign. Troops returning from Syria brought back a plague, which spread throughout the Empire. Marcus hurried to the east to quell an uprising by the commander of the forces in Asia, who declared himself emperor. Although the mutiny quickly died out, Marcus Aurelius' wife perished on the journey. Four of his five sons died young, and his fifth son, Commodus, who succeeded to the throne, was a tyrant.

For the last fourteen years of his life, Marcus Aurelius had to deal with tribesmen from north of the Danube who broke through the defenses and plundered what is now the Balkan peninsula. Marcus took personal command of the hard-pressed legions on the frontier. During this period he wrote the *Meditations,* twelve books containing his reflections on duty, human dignity, the self-sufficiency of reason, and other themes traditionally discussed by Stoic thinkers. Written in Greek, this deeply personal expression of Stoic philosophy has been called "the highest ethical product of the ancient mind." Excerpts from the *Meditations* follow.

BOOK TWO

Begin each day by telling yourself: Today I shall be meeting with interference, ingratitude, insolence, disloyalty, ill-will, and selfishness — all of them due to the offenders' ignorance of what is good or evil. But for my part I have long perceived the nature of good and its nobility, the nature of evil and its meanness, and also the nature of the [evildoer] himself, who is my brother (not in the physical sense, but as a fellow-creature similarly endowed with reason and a share of the divine); therefore none of those things can injure me, for nobody can implicate me in what is degrading. Neither can I be angry with my brother or fall foul of him; for he and I were born to work together, like a man's two hands, feet, or eyelids, or like the upper and lower rows of his teeth. To obstruct each other is against Nature's law — and what is irritation or aversion but a form of obstruction?

A little flesh, a little breath, and a Reason to rule all — that is myself. . . . As one already on the threshold of death, think nothing of the first — of its viscid [thick] blood, its bones, its web of nerves and veins and arteries. The breath, too; what is that? A whiff of wind; and not even the same wind, but every moment puffed out and drawn in anew. But the third, the Reason, the master — on this you must concentrate. Now that your hairs are grey, let it play the part of a slave no more, twitching puppetwise at every pull of self-interest; and cease to fume at destiny by ever grumbling at today or lamenting over tomorrow. . . .

Hour by hour resolve firmly, like a Roman and a man, to do what comes to hand with correct and natural dignity, and with humanity, independence, and justice. Allow your mind freedom from all other considerations. This you can do, if you will approach each action as though it were your last, dismissing the wayward thought, the emotional recoil from the commands of reason, the desire to create an impression, the admiration of self, the discontent with your lot. See how little a man needs to master, for his days to flow on in quietness and piety: he has but to observe these few counsels, and the gods will ask nothing more.

BOOK THREE

If mortal life can offer you anything better than justice and truth, self-control and courage — that is, peace of mind in the evident conformity of your actions to the laws of reason, and peace of mind under the visitations of a destiny you cannot control — if, I say, you can discern any higher ideal, why, turn to it with your whole soul, and rejoice in the prize you have found. . . .

Never value the advantages derived from anything involving breach of faith, loss of self-respect, hatred, suspicion, or execration of others, insincerity, or the desire for something which has to be veiled and curtained. One whose chief regard is for his own mind, and for the divinity within him and the service of its goodness, will strike no poses, utter no complaints, and crave neither for solitude nor yet for a crowd. . . . No other care has he in life but to keep his mind from straying into paths incompatible with those of an intelligent and social being. . . .

BOOK FOUR

Men seek for seclusion in the wilderness, by the seashore, or in the mountains — a dream you have cherished only too fondly yourself. But such fancies are wholly unworthy of a philosopher, since at any moment you choose you can retire within yourself. Nowhere can man find a quieter or more untroubled retreat than in his own soul; above all, he who possesses resources in himself, which he need only contemplate to secure immediate ease of mind — the ease that is but another word for a well-ordered spirit. Avail yourself often, then, of this retirement, and so continually renew yourself. Make your rules of life brief, yet so as to embrace the fundamentals; recurrence to them will then suffice to remove all vexation, and send you back without fretting to the duties to which you must return. . . .

If the power of thought is universal among mankind, so likewise is the possession of reason, making us rational creatures. It follows, therefore, that this reason speaks no less universally to us all with its "thou shalt" or "thou shalt not." So then there is a world-law; which in turn means that we are all fellow-citizens and share a common citizenship, and that the world is a single city. Is there any other common citizenship that can be claimed by all humanity? And it is from this world-polity that mind, reason, and law themselves derive. If not, whence else? As the earthy portion of me has its origin from earth, the watery from a different element, my breath from one source and my hot and fiery parts from another of their own elsewhere (for nothing comes from nothing, or can return to nothing), so too there must be an origin for the mind. . . .

BOOK FIVE

At day's first light have in readiness, against disinclination to leave your bed, the thought that "I am rising for the work of man." Must I grumble at setting out to do what I was born for, and for the sake of which I have been brought into the world? Is this the purpose of my creation, to lie here under the blankets and keep myself warm? "Ah, but it is a great deal more pleasant!" Was it for pleasure, then, that you were born, and not for work, not for effort? Look at the plants, the sparrows, ants, spiders, bees, all busy at their own tasks, each doing his part towards a coherent world-order; and will you refuse man's share of the work, instead of being prompt to carry out Nature's bidding? "Yes, but one must have some repose as well." Granted; but repose has its limits set by nature, in the same way as food and drink have; and you overstep these limits, you go beyond the point of sufficiency; while on the other hand, when action is in question, you stop short of what you could well achieve.

REVIEW QUESTIONS

1. Why did Seneca urge that slaves be treated with kindness and respect?
2. What was the common treatment of slaves among the Romans, according to Seneca?
3. What Stoic philosophic principle influenced Seneca's view of the proper relationship between the free man and the slave?
4. Why was Marcus Aurelius prepared to meet the business of the day in a spirit of calm and patience and cooperation?
5. What virtues did Marcus Aurelius believe should guide human actions?
6. How did a Stoic philosopher seek tranquility of mind and spirit?
7. According to the Stoic Marcus Aurelius, what was the purpose of human life?

4 ▾ Provincial Administration

During the Pax Romana, Roman officials governed territories that extended from Britain, Spain, and present-day Morocco in the west to Mesopotamia and Armenia in the east; from the Rhine and Danube rivers in western and central Europe to the Sahara in northern Africa. The Empire reached its greatest geographic extent under Emperor Trajan (A.D. 98–117), who conquered Dacia (heartland of modern Rumania). The basic unit of political administration, the city, met most of the daily political and social needs of the population. Above the level of the city governments were the Roman provincial authorities, led by governors usually appointed by and responsible directly to the emperor. The senate's role in governing the provinces gradually declined, and the burdens of ruling the vast territory fell largely on the emperor. This enormous task proved daunting for all but the most energetic and conscientious emperors.

CORRESPONDENCE BETWEEN PLINY THE YOUNGER AND EMPEROR TRAJAN

A series of letters exchanged between Emperor Trajan and Gaius Plinius Caecilius (Pliny the Younger, c. A.D. 61–c. 112), governor of the Roman province of Bithynia, located in the northwestern corner of Asia Minor, reveal the many problems Roman provincial officials faced. Given the highly personal character of the imperial office, provincial officials like Pliny, even when urged not to do so, tended to refer most problems directly to the emperor for policy guidance.

XXXIII

Pliny to the Emperor Trajan

While I was visiting another part of the province, a widespread fire broke out in Nicomedia[1] which destroyed many private houses and also two public buildings (the Elder Citizens' Club and the Temple of Isis)[2] although a road runs between them. It was fanned by the strong breeze in the early stages, but it would not have spread so far but for the apathy of the populace; for it is generally agreed that people stood watching the disaster without bestirring themselves to do anything to stop it. Apart from this, there is not a single fire engine anywhere in the town, not a bucket nor any apparatus for fighting a fire. These will now be provided on my instructions.

Will you, Sir, consider whether you think a company of firemen might be formed, limited to 150 members? I will see that no one shall be admitted who is not genuinely a fireman, and that the privileges granted shall not be abused: it will not be difficult to keep such small numbers under observation.

XXXIV

Trajan to Pliny

You may very well have had the idea that it should be possible to form a company of firemen at Nicomedia on the model of those existing elsewhere, but we must remember that it is societies like these which have been responsible for the political disturbances in your province, particularly in its towns. If people assemble for a common purpose, whatever name we give them and for whatever reason, they soon turn into a political club. It is a better policy then to provide the equipment necessary for dealing with fires, and to instruct property owners to make use of it, calling on the help of the crowds which collect if they find it necessary.

XXXIX

Pliny to the Emperor Trajan

The theatre at Nicaea,[3] Sir, is more than half built but is still unfinished, and has already cost more than ten million sesterces,[4] or so I am told — I have not yet examined the relevant accounts. I am afraid it may be money wasted. The building is sinking and showing immense cracks, either because the soil is damp and soft or the stone used was poor and friable [crumbly]. We shall certainly have to consider whether it is to be finished or abandoned, or even demolished, as the foundations and sub-

---

[1]Nicomedia was the capital city of the province of Bithynia.

[2]Isis, the chief Egyptian goddess and consort of Osiris, was widely worshipped throughout the Roman Empire.

[3]Nicaea was another city in Bithynia. The Roman theater was an open-air structure, consisting of the flat stage used by the performers, the orchestra (close to the stage, a place where senators and nobles sat), and the auditorium, a sloped stand or rows of stone benches on which the rest of the audience sat. Dramas and declamations of poetry were given in the theaters.

[4]One sestertius (plural, sesterces) equals one quarter of a silver denarius.

structure intended to hold up the building may have cost a lot but look none too solid to me. There are many additions to the theatre promised by private individuals, such as a colonnade on either side and a gallery above the auditorium,[5] but all these are now held up by the stoppage of work on the main building which must be finished first.

The citizens of Nicaea have also begun to rebuild their gymnasium[6] (which was destroyed by fire before my arrival) on a much larger and more extensive scale than before. They have already spent a large sum, which may be to little purpose, for the buildings are badly planned and too scattered. Moreover, an architect — admittedly a rival of the one who drew up the designs — has given the opinion that the walls cannot support the superstructure in spite of being twenty-two feet thick, as the rubble core has no facing of brick.

The people of Claudiopolis[7] are also building, or rather excavating, an enormous public bath in a hollow at the foot of a mountain. The money for this is coming either from the admission fees already paid by the new members of the town council elected by your gracious favour, or from what they will pay at my demand. So I am afraid there is misapplication of public funds at Nicaea. . . .

. . . I am therefore compelled to ask you to send out an architect to inspect both theatre and bath and decide whether it will be more practicable, in view of what has already been spent, to keep to the original plans and finish both buildings as best we can, or to make any necessary alterations and changes of site so that we do not throw away more money in an attempt to make some use of the original outlay.

[5]The word *auditorium* was also used in the modern sense, a lecture room or courtroom; the word means "listening place."

[6]As now, a gymnasium was a place where Greek and Roman wrestlers competed, and other small-scale athletic feats were performed. It was also a hall where citizens heard lectures or debates and socialized.

[7]Claudiopolis was another city in the Roman province of Bithynia.

XL
Trajan to Pliny

The future of the unfinished theatre at Nicaea can best be settled by you on the spot. It will be sufficient for me if you let me know your decision. But, once the main building is finished, you will have to see that private individuals carry out their promises of adding to the theatre.

These poor Greeks all love a gymnasium; so it may be that they were too ambitious in their plans at Nicaea. They will have to be content with one which suits their real needs.

As for the bath at Claudiopolis, which you say has been started in an unsuitable site, you must decide yourself what advice to give. You cannot lack architects: every province has skilled men trained for this work. It is a mistake to think they can be sent out more quickly from Rome when they usually come to us from Greece.

XXXI
Pliny to the Emperor Trajan

You may stoop when necessary, Sir, to give ear to my problems, without prejudice to your eminent position, seeing that I have your authority to refer to you when in doubt.

In several cities, notably Nicomedia and Nicaea, there are people who were sentenced to service in the mines or the arena, or to other similar punishments, but are now performing the duties of public slaves and receiving an annual salary for their work. Since this was told me I have long been debating what to do. I felt it was too hard on the men to send them back to work out their sentences after a lapse of many years, when most of them are old by now, and by all accounts are quietly leading honest lives, but I did not think it quite right to retain criminals in public service; and though I realized there was nothing to be gained by supporting these men at public expense if they did no work, they might be a potential danger if they were left to starve. I was therefore obliged to leave the whole question in suspense until I could consult you.

You may perhaps want to know how they came to be released from the sentences passed on them. I asked this question myself, but received no satisfactory answer to give you, and although the records of their sentences were produced, there were no documents to prove their release. But people have stated on their behalf that they had been released by order of the previous governors or their deputies, and this is confirmed by the unlikelihood that any unauthorized person would take this responsibility.

XXXII

Trajan to Pliny

Let us not forget that the chief reason for sending you to your province was the evident need for many reforms. Nothing in fact stands more in need of correction than the situation described in your letter, where criminals under sentence have not only been released without authority but are actually restored to the status of honest officials. Those among them who were sentenced within the last ten years and were released by no proper authority must therefore be sent back to work out their sentences. But if the men are elderly and have sentences dating back farther than ten years, they can be employed in work not far removed from penal labour, cleaning public baths and sewers, or repairing streets and highways, the usual employment for men of this type.

XXVI

Pliny to the Emperor Trajan

As a result of your generosity to me, Sir, Rosianus Geminus became one of my closest friends; for when I was consul he was my quaestor [financial officer]. I always found him devoted to my interests, and ever since then he has treated me with the greatest deference and increased the warmth of our public relations by many personal services. I therefore pray you to give your personal attention to my request for his advancement; if you place any confidence in my advice you will bestow on him your favour. He will not fail to earn further promotion in whatever post you place him. I am sparing in my praises because I trust that his sincerity, integrity and application are well known to you already from the high offices he has held in Rome beneath your own eyes, as well as from his service in the army under your command.

I still feel that I have not given adequate expression to the warmth of my affection, and so once more I pray you, Sir, most urgently, to permit me to rejoice as soon as possible in the due promotion of my quaestor — that is to say, in my own advancement in his person.

REVIEW QUESTIONS

1. Why was Trajan opposed to the formation of a fire company?
2. What kinds of public works did the Greek inhabitants of Roman Bithynia seem to favor?
3. What administrative problems did Roman officials face in managing public works projects?
4. What ethical problems did Pliny confront in his province?
5. On what issues did Trajan choose to assert his authority?
6. What kinds of problems in the administration of the Roman Empire are implicit in these letters between Pliny and Trajan?

5 ▾ The Roman Peace

The two-hundred-year period from Augustus' assumption of sole power in 27 B.C. to the death of Emperor Marcus Aurelius in A.D. 180 marks the Pax Romana, the Roman Peace. Roman poets and officials extolled the Roman achievement — the creation of a well-run world-state that brought order and stability to the different nations of the Mediterranean world.

Aelius Aristides
≪ THE ROMAN ORATION ≫: THE BLESSINGS OF THE PAX ROMANA

In the following reading, Aelius Aristides, a second-century Greek intellectual, glowingly praises the Pax Romana in an oration that was probably delivered in Rome. In the tradition of Roman orators, Aelius used hyperbole and exaggeration. Nevertheless, the oration does capture the universalism and cosmopolitanism that characterized the Roman Empire.

"If one considers the vast extent of your empire he must be amazed that so small a fraction of it rules the world, but when he beholds the city and its spaciousness it is not astonishing that all the habitable world is ruled by such a capital. . . . Your possessions equal the sun's course. . . . You do not rule within fixed boundaries, nor can anyone dictate the limits of your sway. . . . Whatever any people produces can be found here, at all times and in abundance. . . . Egypt, Sicily, and the civilized part of Africa are your farms; ships are continually coming and going. . . .

"Vast as it is, your empire is more remarkable for its thoroughness than its scope: there are no dissident or rebellious enclaves. . . . The whole world prays in unison that your empire may endure forever.

"Governors sent out to cities and peoples each rule their charges, but in their relations to each other they are equally subjects. The principal difference between governors and their charges is this — they demonstrate the proper way to be a subject. So great is their reverence for the great Ruler [the emperor], who administers all things. Him they believe to know their business better than they themselves do, and hence they respect and heed him more than one would a master overseeing a task and giving orders. No one is so self-assured that he can remain unmoved upon hearing the emperor's name; he rises in prayer and adoration and utters a twofold prayer — to the gods for the Ruler, and to the Ruler for himself. And if the governors are in the least doubt concerning the justice of claims or suits of the governed, public or private, they send to the Ruler for instructions at once and await his reply, as a chorus awaits its trainer's directions. Hence the Ruler need not exhaust himself by traveling to various parts to settle matters in person. It is easy for him to abide in his place and manage the world through letters; these arrive almost as soon as written, as if borne on wings.

"But the most marvelous and admirable achievement of all, and the one deserving our fullest gratitude, is this. . . . You alone of the imperial powers of history rule over men who are free. You have not assigned this or that region to this nabob or that mogul; no people has been turned over as a domestic and bound holding — to a man not himself free. But just as citizens in an individual city might designate magistrates, so you, whose city is the whole world, appoint governors to protect and provide for the governed, as if they were elective, not to lord it over their charges. As a result, so far from disputing the office as if it were their own, governors make way for their successors readily when their term is up, and may not even await their coming. Appeals to a higher jurisdiction are as easy as appeals from parish to county. . . .

"But the most notable and praiseworthy feature of all, a thing unparalleled, is your magnanimous conception of citizenship. All of your subjects (and this implies the whole world) you have divided into two parts: the better endowed and more virile, wherever they may be, you have granted citizenship and even kinship; the rest you govern as obedient subjects. Neither the seas nor expanse of land bars citizenship; Asia and Europe are not differentiated. Careers are open to talent. . . . Rich and poor find contentment and profit in your system; there is no other way of life. Your polity is a single and all-embracing harmony. . . .

"You have not put walls around your city, as if you were hiding it or avoiding your subjects; to do so you considered ignoble and inconsistent with your principles, as if a master should show fear of his slaves. You did not overlook walls, however, but placed them round the empire, not the city. The splendid and distant walls you erected are worthy of you; to men within their circuit they are visible, but it requires a journey of months and years from the city to see them. Beyond the outermost ring of the civilized world you drew a second circle, larger in radius and easier to defend, like the outer fortifications of a city. Here you built walls and established cities in diverse parts. The cities you filled with colonists; you introduced arts and crafts and established an orderly culture. . . . Your military organization makes all others childish. Your soldiers and officers you train to prevail not only over the enemy but over themselves. The soldier lives under discipline daily, and none ever deserts the post assigned him.

"You alone are, so to speak, natural rulers. Your predecessors were masters and slaves in turn; as rulers they were counterfeits, and reversed their positions like players in a ball game. . . . You have measured out the world, bridged rivers, cut roads through mountains, filled the wastes with posting stations, introduced orderly and refined modes of life. . . .

"Be all gods and their offspring invoked to grant that this empire and this city flourish forever and never cease until stones float upon the sea and trees forbear to sprout in the springtide. May the great Ruler and his sons be preserved to administer all things well."

Tacitus
THE OTHER SIDE OF THE PAX ROMANA

Not all peoples in the Roman Empire welcomed Roman rule. Some nations, particularly Jews, Gauls, Britons, and Egyptians, saw themselves as victims of brutal domination and rose in revolt against their Roman governors. Our knowledge of their motives and grievances is usually secondhand, being found in the records of their enemies — the Romans and their collaborators.

Cornelius Tacitus, Roman historian and orator (see also page 135), wrote a biography of his father-in-law, Agricola, a general who completed the conquest

of northern Britain. In this work, Tacitus describes the character and motives of Roman imperialism from a Briton's viewpoint. The speech that follows is uttered by Calgacus, a leader of the northern, or Caledonian, tribes during the Roman campaign in the years A.D. 77–83. The ideas expressed, however, are those that Tacitus, a well-informed Roman of high social rank, believed the victims of Roman military conquest held about their situation.

"Whenever I consider why we are fighting and how we have reached this crisis, I have a strong sense that this day of your splendid rally may mean the dawn of liberty for the whole of Britain. You have mustered to a man, and to a man you are free. There are no lands behind us, and even the sea is menaced by the Roman fleet. The clash of battle — the hero's glory — has become the safest refuge for the coward. Battles against Rome have been lost and won before — but never without hope; we were always there in reserve. We, the choice flower of Britain, were treasured in her most secret places. Out of sight of subject shores, we kept even our eyes free from the defilement of tyranny. We, the last men on earth, the last of the free, have been shielded till to-day by the very remoteness and the seclusion for which we are famed. We have enjoyed the impressiveness of the unknown. But to-day the boundary of Britain is exposed; beyond us lies no nation, nothing but waves and rocks and the Romans, more deadly still than they, for you find in them an arrogance which no reasonable submission can elude. Brigands of the world, they have exhausted the land by their indiscriminate plunder, and now they ransack the sea. The wealth of an enemy excites their [greed], his poverty their lust of power. East and West have failed to glut their maw [stomach]. They are unique in being as violently tempted to attack the poor as the wealthy. Robbery, butchery, rapine, the liars call Empire; they create a desolation and call it peace.

"We instinctively love our children and our kinsmen above all else. These are torn from us by conscription to slave in other lands. Our wives and sisters, even if they are not raped by Roman enemies, are seduced by them in the guise of guests and friends. Our goods and fortunes are ground down to pay tribute, our land and its harvest to supply corn, our bodies and hands to build roads through woods and swamps — all under blows and insults. Slaves, born into slavery, once sold, get their keep from their masters. But as for Britain, never a day passes but she pays and feeds her enslavers. In a private household it is the latest arrival who is always the butt of his fellow-slaves; so, in this establishment, where all the world have long been slaves, it is we, the cheap new acquisitions, who are picked out for extirpation. You see, we have no fertile lands, no mines, no harbours, which we might be spared to work. Courage and martial spirit we have, but the master does not relish them in the subject. Even our remoteness and seclusion, while they protect, expose us to suspicion. Abandon, then, all hope of mercy and at last take courage, whether it is life or honour that you hold most dear. . . . Let us, then, uncorrupted, unconquered as we are, ready to fight for freedom but never to repent failure, prove at the first clash of arms what heroes Caledonia[1] has been holding in reserve. . . . Or can you seriously think that those Gauls or Germans[2] — and, to our bitter shame, many Britons too! — are bound to Rome by genuine loyalty or love? They may be lending their life-blood to foreign tyrants, but they were enemies of Rome much longer than they have been her slaves. Apprehension and terror are weak bonds of affection; once

---

[1]Caledonia was the name given by the Romans to the section of Scotland north of what is now the Firth of Forth.

[2]The Gauls consisted of several groups of tribes in modern Belgium, the Netherlands, France, and Switzerland. The Germans (Germani) who had been conquered by Rome lived north of the Gauls, just south of the Rhine; the rest of the Germani occupied a large territory north and east of the Rhine.

break them, and, where fear ends, hatred will begin. All that can goad men to victory is on our side. . . . In the ranks of our very enemies we shall find hands to help us. . . . They [the Romans] have nothing in reserve that need alarm us — only forts without garrisons, colonies of grey-beards, towns sick and distracted between rebel subjects and tyrant masters. Here before us is their general, here his army; behind are the tribute, the mines and all the other whips to scourge slaves. Whether you are to endure these for ever or take summary vengeance, this field must decide. On, then, into action and, as you go, think of those that went before you and of those that shall come after."

Josephus
RESISTANCE TO ROMAN RULE IN JUDEA

The Jews of Judea were a particularly thorny problem for Rome. Tolerant of the diverse religions of the empire and aware of the Jews' commitment to strict monotheism, the Romans did not interfere with Jewish beliefs and exempted Jews from emperor worship. However, at times the Romans offended Jewish sensibilities; Emperor Caligula (A.D. 37–41), for example, ordered a golden statue of himself to be placed in Jerusalem's holy temple. Refusing to accept loss of political independence and subjection to hated idolators, Jewish militants launched a full-scale war of liberation in A.D. 66. After a terrible struggle, the Jews finally were crushed by superior Roman might.

Emperor Vespasian (Titus Flavius Sabinus Vespasianus), who reigned A.D. 69–79, and his son Titus (A.D. 79–81), who was commander of the victorious Roman forces and heir-apparent to the throne — staged a triumphal procession in Rome. Behind their chariot, Jewish captives were paraded in chains, and Roman soldiers carried Jewish sacred objects taken from the temple. To commemorate the event, the Romans erected the Arch of Titus, which still stands.

The Jewish revolt was described by Flavius Josephus (originally Joseph ben Mathias, c. A.D. 37–c. 100), a Jewish commander who surrendered to Rome and became an active collaborator. In the following reading, Josephus gives his report of a speech by Herod Agrippa II, the Jewish king of Chalcis, to the north of Palestine. According to Josephus, Herod Agrippa felt that a revolt against the overwhelming power of Rome was doomed. Jewish militants did not heed pleas for caution.

". . . I grant that the ministers of Rome are unbearably harsh; does it follow that all the Romans are persecuting you, including Caesar? Yet it is on them that you are going to make war! It is not by their wish that an unscrupulous governor comes from Rome, nor can western eyes see the goings-on in the east; it is not easy in Rome even to get up-to-date news of what happens here. It would be absurd because of the trifling misdemeanours of one man to go to war with a whole nation, and such a nation — a nation that does not even know what it is all about! Our grievances can be quickly put right; the same procurator [Roman governor] will not be here for ever, and his successors are almost sure to be more reasonable. But once set on foot, war cannot easily be either broken off or fought to a conclusion without disaster. . . .

"Where are the men, where are the weapons

you count on? Where is the fleet that is to sweep the Roman seas? Where are the funds to pay for your expeditions? Do you think you are going to war with Egyptians and Arabs? Look at the far-flung empire of Rome and contrast your own impotence. Why, our forces have been worsted even by our neighbours again and again, while their arms have triumphed over the whole world! And even the world is not big enough to satisfy them; Euphrates is not far enough to the east, or Danube to the north, or Libya and the desert beyond to the south, or Cadiz to the west; but beyond the Ocean they have sought a new world, carrying their arms as far as Britain, that land of mystery. Why not face facts? Are you richer than the Gauls, stronger than the Germans, cleverer than the Greeks, more numerous than all the nations of the world? What gives you confidence to defy the power of Rome?

"It is terrible to be enslaved, it will be said. How much worse for Greeks, who surpass every nation under the sun in nobility and fill such a wide domain, and yet bow before the fasces[1] of a Roman governor, as do the Macedonians, who have a better right than you to demand their liberty! And what of the five hundred cities of Asia [a large province in Asia Minor]? Do they not without a garrison bow before one governor and the consular fasces? Need I mention the Heniochi, the Colchians, and the Tauric race,[2] the peoples near the Bosporus,[3] the Black Sea, and the Sea of Azov?[4] At one time they recognized not even a native ruler, and now they submit to 3,000 legionaries, while forty warships keep the peace on the sea where before none but pirates sailed. How justly Bithynia, Cappadocia, Pamphylia, Lycia, and Cilicia[5] might demand liberty! Yet without armed pressure they pay their dues.

"Then there are the Thracians [in modern Bulgaria], spread over a country five days' march in width and seven in length, more rugged and much more defensible than yours, a country whose icy blasts are enough to halt an invader. Yet 2,000 Roman guards suffice to maintain order. Their neighbours the Illyrians, whose land extends from Dalmatia [modern Yugoslavia] to the Danube frontier, need only two legions to keep them quiet; in fact Illyrians unite with Romans to halt Dacian [tribes from the area of Rumania] raids. The Dalmatians again, who have so often tried to shake off the yoke and have always been driven by defeat to rally their forces and revolt again, now live peaceably under one Roman legion!

"But if any people might reasonably be tempted to rebel by its peculiar advantages, that people is the Gauls, provided as they are with such marvellous natural defences, on the east the Alps, on the north the Rhine, on the south the Pyrenees, on the west the [Atlantic] Ocean. Yet in spite of these immense obstacles, in spite of the huge total of 305 nations [tribes], in spite of the prosperity that wells up from their soil and enables them to flood the whole world with their goods, they submit to being the milch cow of Rome and receiving from her hands what they themselves have produced! And this they tolerate, not from effeminacy or racial inferiority — they fought for eighty years to save their liberty — but because they are overawed by the might of Rome and still more by her destiny, which wins her more victories than do her arms. So Gaul is kept in order by 1,200 soldiers — hardly more men than she has cities!

"Then Spain — in the fight for independence

---

[1]Fasces, a bundle of birch rods with an ax tied into the center and protruding above them, were carried in the presence of a Roman consul as a symbol of his magisterial powers of punishment over the people.

[2]The Heniochi, Colchians, and Taurians (Tauri) were tribes that lived along the northeastern borders of the Black Sea, the Sea of Azov, and in the Crimea.

[3]The Bosporus, in this context, was the Crimean peninsula and land to the east of it. Today, the term is used for a narrow passage of water between the part of Turkey in Asia Minor and the part in Europe.

[4]Called in Roman times the Palus Maeotis, the Sea of Azov is a body of water bordered by the Soviet Ukraine and opens through a narrow strait into the Black Sea.

[5]Bithynia, Cappadocia, Pamphylia, Lycia, and Cilicia, former independent kingdoms conquered by the Romans, made up almost all of Asia Minor.

the gold from her soil could not save her, nor could the vast stretch of land and sea that separates her from Rome, nor the tribes of Lusitania [modern Portugal] and Cantabria [north coastal Spain] with their passion for fighting, nor the neighbouring Ocean that terrifies even the natives with its tides. Crossing the cloud-capped Pyrenees and advancing their arms beyond the Pillars of Hercules[6] the Romans enslaved Spain too. Yet to guard this remote and almost invincible nation requires but one legion![7]

"Which of you has not heard of the Germans,[8] with their inexhaustible manpower? You have, I am sure, seen their magnificent physique on many occasions, for on every side Roman masters have German slaves; yet this people occupies an immense area, their physique is surpassed by their pride, from the bottom of their hearts they despise death, and when enraged they are more dangerous than the fiercest of wild beasts. Yet the Rhine is the limit of their aggression and the Romans with eight legions have tamed them, enslaving the prisoners and driving the entire nation to seek refuge in flight.

"Consider the defences of the Britons, you who feel so sure of the defences of Jerusalem. They are surrounded by the Ocean and inhabit an island as big as this continent; yet the Romans crossed the sea and enslaved them, and four legions keep that huge island quiet. But why should I say more about that, when even the Parthians [of western Iran], the most warlike race of all, rulers of so many nations and protected by such vast forces, send hostages to Rome, and on Italian soil may be seen, humbly submitting for the sake of peace, the aristocrats of the east.

"Almost every nation under the sun bows down before the might of Rome. . . .

"Possibly some of you suppose that you are making war in accordance with agreed rules, and that when the Romans have won they will be kind to you, and will not think of making you an example to other nations by burning down your Holy City [Jerusalem] and destroying your entire race. I tell you, not even if you survive will you find a place of refuge, since every people recognizes the lordship of Rome or fears that it will have to do so. Again, the danger threatens not only ourselves here but also those who live in other cities; for there is not a region in the world without its Jewish colony. All these, if you go to war, will be massacred by your opponents, and through the folly of a few men every city will run with Jewish blood. . . ."

[6]The peaks on either side of the Strait of Gibraltar, which connects the Mediterranean Sea and the Atlantic Ocean, were called the Pillars of Hercules.

[7]The Roman legion was a military unit, subdivided into smaller groups as in a modern army brigade, and comprised about six thousand men.

[8]For the Germans, see note 2 on page 151.

REVIEW QUESTIONS

1. What characteristics of Roman imperial government most impressed the author of the oration?
2. In what sense did Aelius Aristides consider the inhabitants of the Roman Empire to be free?
3. What kinds of people were invited to collaborate with the Romans in managing the Empire?
4. What factors contributed to making the Mediterranean world a "single city"?
5. According to Tacitus, speaking for Calgacus, what factors motivated the British resistance to Rome?
6. What factors motivated the Roman invaders?
7. What potential weaknesses in the Roman imperial system did Tacitus have Calgacus mention?
8. What faults in the Romans' administration of their subject peoples were readily admitted by Herod Agrippa in his speech to the Jews, as reported by Josephus?

9. What facts made it unlikely that a Jewish rebellion could succeed, according to Herod Agrippa?
10. What fate did Herod Agrippa foresee for the Jews living outside Judea, elsewhere in the Roman Empire, if the Judeans revolted?

---

6 ▾ Third-Century Crisis

An extravagant tyrant, Marcus Aurelius' son Commodus (Lucius Aelius Aurelius, A.D. 180–192) was an unworthy successor, and his reign marks the close of the Pax Romana. For the next hundred years the Empire was burdened by economic, political, and military crises. For much of the third century, barbarian tribesmen broke through the northern frontier defenses and plundered the Balkans, Greece, Asia Minor, northern Italy, Gaul, and Spain; the Persians invaded the Empire from the east. The legions, consisting predominantly of the least Romanized provincials, used their weapons to place their own commanders on the throne. During the ensuing civil wars, the soldiers looted the towns as if they were an invading army. Rome was drifting into anarchy.

The devastations by barbarians and the soldiers wrecked the economy, which was further damaged by crushing taxes and requisitions of goods and by inflation caused by debased coinage. Everywhere, people were fleeing from plundering barbarians or soldiers, from warring armies, and from government officials who extorted taxes and goods and services from an already overburdened population.

Dio Cassius
CARACALLA'S EXTORTIONS

The reign (A.D. 211–217) of Caracalla provides an early example of the crushing demands imposed by the state on its citizenry. The following account comes from the *Roman History* of Dio Cassius.

[Caracalla] was fond of spending money upon the soldiers, great numbers of whom he kept in attendance upon him, alleging one excuse after another and one war after another; but he made it his business to strip, despoil, and grind down all the rest of mankind, and the senators by no means least. In the first place, there were the gold crowns that he was repeatedly demanding, on the constant pretext that he had conquered some enemy or other; and I am not referring, either, to the actual manufacture of the crowns — for what does that amount to? — but to the vast amount of money constantly being given under that name by the cities for the customary "crowning," as it is called, of the emperors. Then there were the provisions that we were required to furnish in great quantities on all occasions, and this without receiving any remuneration and sometimes actually at additional cost to ourselves — all of which supplies he either bestowed upon the soldiers or else peddled out; and there were the gifts which he demanded from the wealthy citizens and from the various communities; and the taxes, both the new ones which he promulgated and the ten per cent. tax that he instituted in place of the five per cent. tax applying to the emancipation of slaves, to bequests, and to all legacies. . . . But apart from all these burdens, we were also compelled to build at our own expense all sorts of houses for him whenever he set out from Rome, and costly lodgings in the middle of even the very shortest journeys; yet he not only never lived in them, but in some cases was not destined even to see them. Moreover, we constructed amphitheatres and race-courses wherever he spent the winter or expected to spend it, all without receiving any contribution from him; and they were all promptly demolished, the sole reason for their being built in the first place being, apparently, that we might become impoverished.

The emperor himself kept spending the money upon the soldiers, as we have said, and upon wild beasts and horses; for he was for ever killing vast numbers of animals, both wild and domesticated, forcing us to furnish most of them, though he did buy a few. One day he slew a hundred boars at one time with his own hands. . . . In everything he was very hot-headed and very fickle, and he furthermore possessed the craftiness of his mother and the Syrians, to which race she belonged. He would appoint some freedman or other wealthy person to be director of the games in order that the man might spend money in this way also; and he would salute the spectators with his whip from the arena below and beg for gold pieces like a performer of the lowest class. . . . To such an extent was the entire world, so far as it owned his sway, devastated throughout his whole reign, that on one occasion the Romans at a horse-race shouted in unison this, among other things: "We shall do the living to death,* that we may bury the dead." Indeed, he often used to say: "Nobody in the world should have money but me; and I want it to bestow upon the soldiers." Once when Julia [Domna, his mother] chided him for spending vast sums upon them and said, "There is no longer any source of revenue, either just or unjust, left to us," he replied, exhibiting his sword, "Be of good cheer, mother: for as long as we have this, we shall not run short of money."

Moreover to those who flattered him he distributed both money and goods.

*Or . . . "We are stripping the living."

PETITION TO EMPEROR PHILIP

A petition presented about A.D. 245 to Emperor Philip (M. Julius Philippus, 244–249) reveals the desperation of the peasants.

We who flee as suppliants to the refuge of your divinity are the entire population of your most sacred estate. We are suffering extortion and illegal exactions beyond all reason at the hands of those who ought to preserve the public welfare. . . . Military commanders, soldiers, and powerful and influential men in the city and your officials . . . swoop down upon us, take us away from our work, requisition our plow oxen, and illegally exact what is not due them. As a result we are suffering extraordinary injustice by this extortion. We wrote about all this to your majesty, Augustus,[1] when you held the prefecture of the Praetorian Guard[2] . . . and how your divinity was moved the rescript [emperor's official answer] quoted herewith makes clear: "We have transmitted the content of your petition to the governor, who will see to it that

[1]The title Augustus was originally given by the senate to Octavian, the first emperor. It later became the title of all his successors. (See page 132).

[2]The Praetorian Guard, commanded by a prefect *(praefectus)*, was the official troop of imperial bodyguards.

there is no further cause for complaint." But inasmuch as this rescript has brought us no aid, it has resulted that we are still suffering throughout the countryside illegal exactions of what is not owing, as certain parties assault us and trample upon us unjustly, and we are still suffering extraordinary extortion at the hands of the officials, and our resources have been exhausted and the estates deserted.

Herodian
EXTORTIONS OF MAXIMINUS

Raised to imperial office by his own rebellious troops, Maximinus (A.D. 235–238) was desperate for money to pay the soldiers and to run the state. He therefore robbed the urban middle class. This account of Maximinus comes from Herodian of Antioch (c. A.D. 165–c. 255), a Syrian Greek who served in the imperial bureaucracy. He wrote a history of the Roman Empire that covered the time from the death of Marcus Aurelius (A.D. 180) to the accession of Gordian III (A.D. 238).

. . . Other battles took place in which Maximinus won praise for his personal participation, for fighting with his own hands, and for being in every conflict the best man on the field. . . . He threatened (and was determined) to defeat and subjugate the German nations as far as the ocean.

This is the kind of military man the emperor was, and his actions would have added to his reputation if he had not been much too ruthless and severe toward his associates and subjects. What profit was there in killing barbarians when greater slaughter occurred in Rome and the provinces? Or in carrying off booty captured from the enemy when he robbed his fellow countrymen of all their property? . . . Anyone who was merely summoned into court by an informer was immediately judged guilty, and left with all his property confiscated. It was thus possible every day to see men who yesterday had been rich, today reduced to paupers, so great was the avarice of the tyrant, who pretended to be insuring a continuous supply of money for the soldiers. The emperor's ears were always open to slanderous charges, and he spared neither age nor position. He arrested on slight and trivial charges many men who had governed provinces and commanded armies, who had won the honor of a consulship, or had gained fame by military victories. . . . After insulting and torturing these prisoners, he condemned them to exile or death.

As long as his actions affected only individuals and the calamities suffered were wholly private, the people of the cities and provinces were not particularly concerned with what the emperor was doing. Unpleasant things which happen to those who seem to be fortunate or wealthy are not only a matter of indifference to the mob, but they often bring pleasure to mean and malicious men, who envy the powerful and the prosperous. After Maximinus had impoverished most of the distinguished men and confiscated their estates, which he considered small and insignificant and not sufficient for his purposes, he turned to the public treasuries; all the funds which had been collected for the citizens' welfare or for gifts, all the funds being held in reserve for shows or festivals, he transferred to his own personal fortune. The offerings which belonged to the temples, the statues of the gods, the tokens of honor of the heroes, the decorations on public buildings, the adornments of the city, in short, any material suitable for making coins, he handed over to the mints. But what especially irked the people and aroused public indignation was the fact that, although no fighting was going on and no enemy was under arms anywhere, Rome appeared to be a city under siege. Some citizens, with angry shaking of fists, set guards around the temples, preferring to die before the altars than to stand by and see their country ravaged. From that time on, particularly in the cities and the provinces, the hearts of the people were filled with rage. The soldiers too were disgusted with his activities, for their relatives and fellow citizens complained that Maximinus was acting solely for the benefit of the military.

For these reasons, and justifiably, the people were aroused to hatred and thoughts of revolt.

REVIEW QUESTIONS

1. What were Dio Cassius' principal criticisms of Caracalla's administration of the state?
2. What personal vices of Caracalla aroused Dio Cassius' contempt?
3. What is revealed by the peasants' petition to the Emperor Philip about the character of the Roman government in the third century?
4. Who seems to have suffered most under the rule of Maximinus?
5. What were the principal problems facing the emperors in the third century?

---

7 ▾ The Demise of Rome

The conquest of the western provinces of the Roman Empire by various Germanic tribes in the fifth century A.D. was made easier by the apathy and frequent collaboration of Roman citizens themselves. Many Romans had grown to hate the bureaucratic oppressors who crushed them with constant demands for excessive and unfair taxes, forced labor on government projects, extortion, and all the evils of a police state. In some areas of Gaul and Spain, peasants had revolted and successfully defended their homes and farms against the Roman authorities. When such barbarians as the Visigoths, Vandals, and Ostrogoths entered the region, many Romans welcomed them as liberators and cooperated with them in establishing their new kingdoms.

Salvian
POLITICAL AND SOCIAL INJUSTICE

The conditions that made such dramatic conquests possible are well delineated in a book called *The Governance of God,* by Salvian (Salvianus) of Marseilles (c. A.D. 400–470). A Christian priest, Salvian was an eyewitness to the end of Roman rule in Gaul. He describes the political and moral causes of the collapse of the Roman state in the west in the following reading.

What towns, as well as what municipalities and villages are there in which there are not as many tyrants as *curiales.*[1] Perhaps they glory in this name of tyrant because it seems to be considered powerful and honored. For, almost all robbers rejoice and boast, if they are said to be more fierce than they really are. What place is there, as I have said, where the bowels of widows and orphans are not devoured by the leading men of the cities, and with them those of almost all holy men? . . . Not one of them [widows and orphans], therefore, is safe. In a manner, except for the very powerful, neither is anyone safe from the devastation of general brigandage, unless they are like the robbers themselves. To this state of affairs, indeed, to this crime has the world come that, unless one is bad, he cannot be safe. . . .

All the while, the poor are despoiled, the widows groan, the orphans are tread underfoot, so much so that many of them, and they are not of obscure birth and have received a liberal education, flee to the enemy lest they die from the pain of public persecution. They seek among the barbarians the dignity of the Roman because they cannot bear barbarous indignity among the Romans. Although these Romans differ in religion and language from the barbarians to whom they flee, and differ from them in respect to filthiness of body and clothing, nevertheless, as I have said, they prefer to bear among the barbarians a worship unlike their own rather than rampant injustice among the Romans.

▷ Salvian tells how Roman citizens are deserting Rome to live under the rule of the Goths and other barbarian invaders. Moreover, in many parts of Spain and Gaul (France), peasants called *Bagaudae* have rebelled and established zones free from Roman authority.

Thus, far and wide, they migrate either to the Goths[2] or to the Bagaudae, or to other barbarians everywhere in power; yet they do not repent having migrated. They prefer to live as freemen under an outward form of captivity than as captives under an appearance of liberty. Therefore, the name of Roman citizens, at one time not only greatly valued but dearly bought, is now repudiated and fled from, and it is almost considered not only base but even deserving of abhorrence.

And what can be a greater testimony of Roman wickedness than that many men, upright and noble and to whom the position of being a Roman citizen should be considered as of the highest splendor and dignity, have been driven by the cruelty of Roman wickedness to such a state of mind that they do not wish to be Romans? . . .

I am now about to speak of the Bagaudae who were despoiled, oppressed and murdered by evil and cruel judges. After they had lost the right of Roman citizenship, they also lost the honor of bearing the Roman name. We blame their misfortunes on themselves. We ascribe to them a name which signifies their downfall. We give to them a name of which we ourselves are the cause. We call them rebels. We call those outlaws whom we compelled to be criminal.

For, by what other ways did they become Bagaudae, except by our wickedness, except by the wicked ways of judges, except by the proscription and pillage of those who have turned the assessments of public taxes into the benefit of their own gain and have made the tax levies their own booty? Like wild beasts, they did not rule but devoured their subjects, and feasted not only on the spoils of men, as most robbers are wont to do, but even on their torn flesh and, as I may say, on their blood.

[1]In the late years of the Roman Empire, the *curiales* were the members of the municipal councils. They were forced to act as tax collectors for the central government and to pay from their own pockets whatever sums they could not collect from the overtaxed inhabitants.

[2]The Goths were Germanic tribes that invaded Rome. The Visigoths invaded Italy in the early fifth century and seized Rome for a few days. This was the first time in eight centuries that a foreign enemy had entered the capital. Later the Visigoths occupied large areas of Spain and Gaul. In the late fifth century, the Ostrogoths invaded and conquered Italy, establishing a kingdom there.

Thus it happened that men, strangled and killed by the robberies of judges, began to live as barbarians because they were not permitted to be Romans. They became satisfied to be what they were not, because they were not permitted to be what they were. They were compelled to defend their lives at least, because they saw that they had already completely lost their liberty. . . .

But what else can these wretched people wish for, they who suffer the incessant and even continuous destruction of public tax levies. To them there is always imminent a heavy and relentless proscription. They desert their homes, lest they be tortured in their very homes. They seek exile, lest they suffer torture. The enemy is more lenient to them than the tax collectors. This is proved by this very fact, that they flee to the enemy in order to avoid the full force of the heavy tax levy. This very tax levying, although hard and inhuman, would nevertheless be less heavy and harsh if all would bear it equally and in common. Taxation is made more shameful and burdensome because all do not bear the burden of all. They extort tribute from the poor man for the taxes of the rich, and the weaker carry the load for the stronger. There is no other reason that they cannot bear all the taxation except that the burden imposed on the wretched is greater than their resources. . . .

Therefore, in the districts taken over by the barbarians, there is one desire among all the Romans, that they should never again find it necessary to pass under Roman jurisdiction. In those regions, it is the one and general prayer of the Roman people that they be allowed to carry on the life they lead with the barbarians. And we wonder why the Goths are not conquered by our portion of the population, when the Romans prefer to live among them rather than with us. Our brothers, therefore, are not only altogether unwilling to flee to us from them, but they even cast us aside in order to flee to them.

Jerome
THE FATE OF ROME

Saint Jerome (Hieronymus, c. A.D. 340–420) was one of the major theologians and scriptural scholars of the late Roman period. He left Rome itself to join a monastery in Bethlehem in Judea, where he studied Hebrew and began work on a monumental new translation of the Hebrew and Christian Scriptures into Latin. This new edition, called the Vulgate (written in the Latin of the common people), became the standard text of the Bible in the Western church for more than a thousand years. In the following letter to Agenuchia, a highborn lady of Gaul, Saint Jerome bemoans the fate of Rome, once so proud and powerful. The letter, dated A.D. 409, was written at a critical moment: the Visigoths had accepted a huge ransom to end their siege of Rome.

Nations innumerable and most savage have invaded all Gaul. The whole region between the Alps and the Pyrenees, the ocean and the Rhine, has been devastated by the Quadi, the Vandals, the Sarmati, the Alani, the Gepidae, the hostile Heruli, the Saxons, the Burgundians, the Alemanni, and the Pannonians [barbarian tribes]. O wretched Empire! Mayence [Mainz], formerly so noble a city, has been taken and ruined, and in the church many thousands of men have been massacred. Worms has been destroyed after a long siege. Rheims, that powerful city, Amiens, Arras, Speyer, Strasburg,* — all have seen their citizens led

*The names of modern cities here used are not in all cases exact equivalents for the names of the regions mentioned by Jerome.

away captive into Germany. Aquitaine and the provinces of Lyons and Narbonne, all save a few towns, have been depopulated; and these the sword threatens without, while hunger ravages within. I cannot speak without tears of Toulouse, which the merits of the holy Bishop Exuperius have prevailed so far to save from destruction. Spain, even, is in daily terror lest it perish, remembering the invasion of the Cimbri;[1] and whatsoever the other provinces have suffered once, they continue to suffer in their fear.

I will keep silence concerning the rest, lest I seem to despair of the mercy of God. For a long time, from the Black Sea to the Julian Alps,[2] those things which are ours have not been ours; and for thirty years, since the Danube boundary was broken, war has been waged in the very midst of the Roman Empire. Our tears are dried by old age. Except a few old men, all were born in captivity and siege, and do not desire the liberty they never knew. . . .

▷ When the Visigoths led by Alaric sacked Rome in 410, Jerome lamented in another passage.

Who could believe that Rome, built upon the conquest of the whole world, would fall to the ground? that the mother herself would become the tomb of her peoples?

[1]The Cimbri, originally from what is now Denmark, spread southward to invade Spain, Gaul, and Italy in the late part of the second century B.C. They were defeated by the Roman general Marius (c. 157–86 B.C.).

[2]The mountains called the Julian Alps are in what is now Yugoslavia.

Pope Gregory I
THE END OF ROMAN GLORY

In the late sixth century, the Lombards, the last Germanic tribe to invade those lands that had once been Roman, swept down the Tiber valley and in 593 were at the gates of Rome. At that time, Pope Gregory I, the Great (590–604), descendant of a prominent and wealthy Roman senatorial family, reflected on Rome, once the mistress of the world.

We see on all sides sorrows; we hear on all sides groans. Cities are destroyed, fortifications razed to the ground, fields devastated, the land reduced to solitude. No husbandman is left in the field, few inhabitants remain in the cities, and yet these scanty remnants of the human race are still each day smitten without ceasing. . . . Some men are led away captive, others are mutilated, others slain before our eyes. What is there, then, my brethren to please us in this world?

What Rome herself, once deemed the Mistress of the World, has now become, we see — wasted away with afflictions, grievous and many, with the loss of citizens, the assaults of enemies, the frequent fall of ruined buildings. . . . For where is the Senate? Where is the People [the State]? The bones are dissolved, the flesh is consumed, all the pomp of the dignities of this world is gone. . . .

Yet even we who remain few as we are, still are daily smitten with the sword, still are daily crushed by innumerable afflictions. . . . For the Senate is no more, and the People has perished, yet sorrow and sighing are multiplied daily among the few that are left. Rome is, as it were, already empty and burning. . . . But where are they who once rejoiced in her glory? Where is their pomp? Where their pride? Where their constant and immediate joy? . . .

. . . The Sons of men of the world, when they wished for worldly advancement came together from all parts of the earth to this city. But now behold! she is desolate. Behold! she is wasted away. No one hastens to her for worldly advancement.

REVIEW QUESTIONS

1. What conditions did Salvian report as prevailing among the poorer inhabitants of the western Roman empire in the fifth century A.D.?
2. Whom did Salvian blame for the rebellion of the Bagaudae?
3. According to Salvian, what misdeeds alienated the Roman people from their rulers?
4. What were the consequences of the Germanic invasions as depicted by Saint Jerome and Pope Gregory?

---

8 ▾ Rome's Legacy of Law

One of the most significant legacies of Rome to Western civilization is the system of law developed by the Romans over many centuries. Roman law evolved into three distinct types: the civil law *(ius civile),* which was peculiar to the Roman state and applicable only to its citizens; the law of nature *(ius naturale),* an unchanging, everlasting, universal law that was binding on all persons by reason of their common humanity; the law of nations *(ius gentium),* an international law governing the relationship between Romans and other peoples. The law of nations was fashioned by Roman jurists as Rome came into contact with and conquered other cultures; it incorporated elements from Roman civil law and the legal traditions of the other peoples, particularly the Greeks. Roman jurists held that the law of nations accorded with natural law: that is, it rested upon principles of reason that were common to all humans.

Roman law eventually became the basis for the legal systems of all modern European states except England and Ireland. As Europeans established colonial empires in Asia, Africa, and the Americas, they carried with them the principles inherited from Roman law.

Justinian
≪ CORPUS IURIS CIVILIS ≫

The principles of Roman law are drawn from many sources, from the statutes of emperors, edicts of magistrates, and commentaries of learned jurists, such as Ulpian (Domitius Ulpianus, d. A.D. 228), Gaius (c. A.D. 130–180), and Julius Paulus (second–third century A.D.). These past laws and judicial commentaries were culled and selectively incorporated in the *Corpus Iuris Civilis,* the imperial code drawn up by order of Emperor Justinian (A.D. 527–565) and promulgated in A.D. 534. It has been said that next to the Bible, no book has had a deeper impact on Western civilization than Justinian's code. It became the official body

of laws of the eastern Roman (or Byzantine) Empire through the Middle Ages and was gradually reintroduced into western Europe in the twelfth century. Roman law continued in the postmedieval world and formed the basis of common law in all Western lands except England and its dependencies, where its influence was less marked. Some principles of Roman law are readily recognizable in today's legal systems, as the following excerpts indicate.

• The Divine Trajan stated in a Rescript addressed to Julius Frontonus that anyone who is absent should not be convicted of crime. Likewise, no one should be convicted on suspicion; for the Divine Trajan stated in a Rescript to Assiduus Severus: "It is better to permit the crime of a guilty person to go unpunished than to condemn one who is innocent."

• No one suffers a penalty for merely thinking.

• Proof is incumbent upon the party who affirms a fact, not upon him who denies it.

• In inflicting penalties, the age and inexperience of the guilty party must always be taken into account.

• Nothing is so opposed to consent, which is the basis of *bona fide* contracts, as force and fear; and to approve anything of this kind is contrary to good morals.

• The crime or the punishment of a father can place no stigma upon his son; for each one is subjected to fate in accordance with his conduct, and no one is appointed the successor of the crime of another.

• Women are excluded from all civil or public employments; therefore they cannot be judges, or perform the duties of magistrates, or bring suits in court, or become sureties for others, or act as attorneys.

A minor, also, must abstain from all civil employments.

• Every person should support his own offspring, and anyone who thinks that he can abandon his child shall be subjected to the penalty prescribed by law. We do not give any right to masters or to patrons to recover children who have been abandoned, when children exposed by them, as it were, to death, have been rescued through motives of pity, for no one can say that a child whom he has left to perish belongs to him.

• The authority and observance of long-established custom should not be treated with contempt, but it should not prevail to the extent of overcoming either reason or law.

▷ Not all principles of Roman law have been incorporated into the legal codes of modern societies. One example is the use of torture to test the testimony of witnesses, particularly those of low social status. In those lands where Roman law remained in effect, torture was legal until the eighteenth century, when it was purged from European judicial systems.

• Torture is employed in the detection of crime, but a beginning should not be made with its application; and, therefore, in the first place, evidence should be resorted to, and if the party is liable to suspicion, he shall be compelled by torture to reveal his accomplices and crimes.

• Where several culprits are implicated in the same offence, they should be examined in such a way as to begin with the one who appears to be more timid than the others, and of tender age.

• Torture is not applied in pecuniary matters, unless when an investigation is made with reference to property belonging to an estate; other things, however, are established by oath, or by the evidence of witnesses.

• Torture should not be inflicted upon a minor under fourteen years of age, as the Divine Pius stated in a Rescript addressed to Caecilius Jubentinus.

• All persons, however, without exception, shall be tortured in a case of high treason which has reference to princes, if their testimony is necessary, and circumstances demand it.

• Torture should not be applied to the extent that the accuser demands, but as reason and moderation may dictate.

• In questions where freedom is involved it is not necessary to seek for the truth by the torture of those whose status is in dispute.

• It was declared by the Imperial Constitutions that while confidence should not always be reposed in torture, it ought not to be rejected as absolutely unworthy of it, as the evidence obtained is weak and dangerous, and inimical to the truth; for most persons, either through their power of endurance, or through the severity of the torment, so despise suffering that the truth can in no way be extorted from them. Others are so little able to suffer that they prefer to lie rather than to endure the question, and hence it happens that they make confessions of different kinds, and they not only implicate themselves, but others as well.

• The Edict of the Divine Augustus, which he published during the Consulate of Vivius Avitus and Lucius Apronianus, is as follows: "I do not think that torture should be inflicted in every instance, and upon every person; but when capital and atrocious crimes cannot be detected and proved except by means of the torture of slaves, I hold that it is most effective for ascertaining the truth, and should be employed."

REVIEW QUESTIONS

1. What were some of the restrictions suffered by women under Roman law?
2. What role did custom play in Roman law?
3. On whom did the burden of proof lie in a Roman trial?
4. What liberties did Roman laws protect?
5. What conditions invalidated any contract?
6. How were minor children treated under Roman law, as suggested by the selections here?
7. In what ways did the Roman emperors limit the use of torture?
8. Under what circumstances did the emperors clearly approve the use of torture?

ELEMENTS OF CLASSICAL, MEDIEVAL, AND RENAISSANCE ART

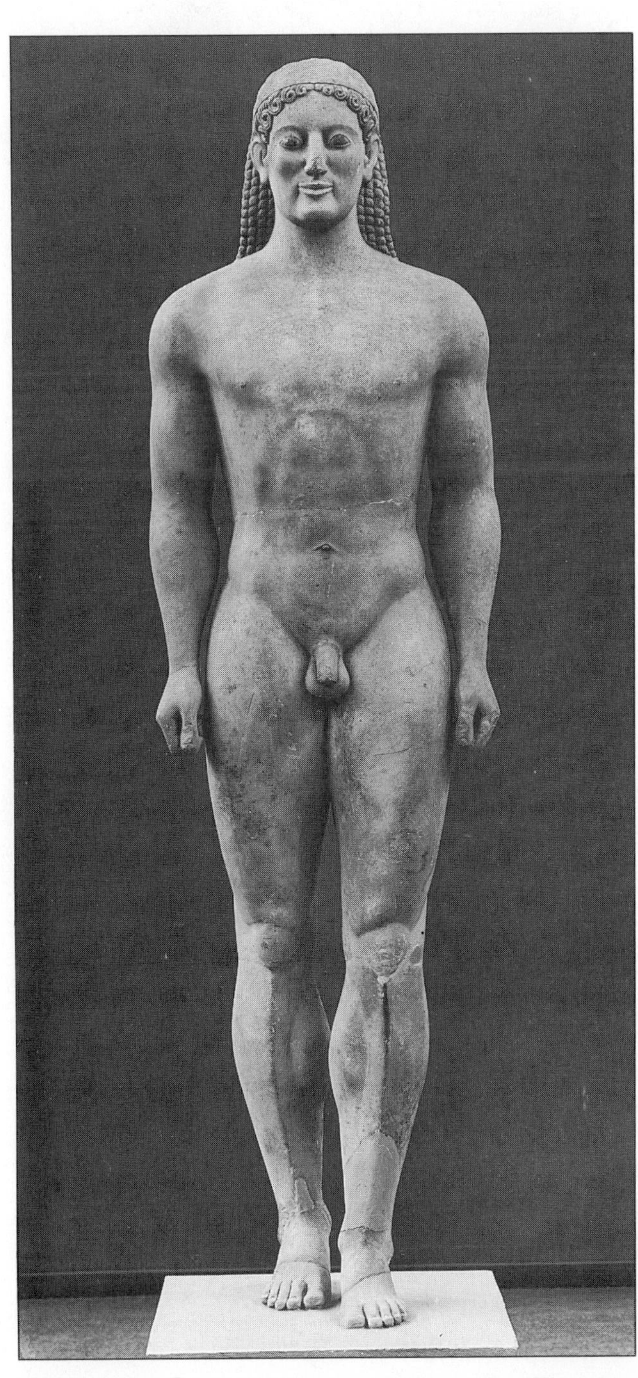

Kroisos (Kouros from Anavyos), c. 525 B.C., marble, height 6′ 4″. This Greek sculpture is representative of the funerary statues erected for military heroes who died in battle. Typical of early Greek sculptures, which borrowed this formal pose from the Egyptians, the kouros (young man) appears stiff and awkward, but the artist shows an awareness of volume, elasticity, and anatomical detail. (*Hirmer Verlag München*)

Zeus or Poseidon, c. 450 B.C., bronze, height 6′ 10″. The large, free-standing figure — whether it depicts Zeus, chief of the Olympian gods, or Poseidon, god of the waters, is uncertain — demonstrates the heightened naturalism and idealized beauty, along with the technical innovations in bronze casting, that the classical Greeks developed. In addition, the pose expresses a balance of forces — the god's weight is on his forward striding left foot with his left arm also stretched out, while his right leg and arm counterbalance the other limbs. The fingers of the right hand are curved to grasp the missing weapon. (*Hirmer Verlag München*)

Family in Imperial Procession, 13–9 B.C., marble, height 63". The imperial procession shown here is just a portion of the large frieze from the Ara Pacis, the altar of peace honoring the Emperor Augustus, in Rome. The frieze records an actual historical event, while also capturing the more naturalistic characteristics of the participants, combining fact with art. Roman artists continued the Greeks' interest in realism and detail. (*Marburg/Art Resource, N.Y.*)

Portrait of a Roman, c. 80 B.C., marble, lifesize. Roman artists excelled at creating the ever-popular portrait busts. While the busts were as naturalistic and detailed as classical Greek sculpture, the Romans strove for realism rather than idealism in their art. This portrait of a Roman citizen reveals the subject's dynamic personality, authority, and character through precise sculptural detail. (*Alinari/Art Resources, N.Y.*)

Interior of Reims Cathedral, after 1251. The Gothic cathedral became a monumental symbol of human spiritual aspirations and a physical manifestation of a hierarchical universe bridging Heaven and earth. The soaring cruciform buildings were achieved in stone by the use of slender colonnettes, perforated walls, pointed arches, and flying buttresses, all technical innovations of the Gothic master builders. In addition to evoking religious fervor, these cathedrals became the showpieces of the local rulers, displaying their wealth and power through sheer size and opulence. (*Photo © Jean Roubier*)

Reims Cathedral Statues, after 1251. The warrior is shown receiving the Sacrament of Communion from a priest before departing on a crusade. These two sculptures represent the two distinct realms of medieval life: the religious and the secular. Sculptural forms, as well as the colorful stained-glass windows, not only served as decorations for Gothic cathedrals, but also depicted characters and scenes, both biblical and secular, from which the mainly illiterate congregations could learn and draw inspiration. While High Gothic sculpture was not as naturalistic as classical Greek works, there was definitely a move away from the archaic stylings of earlier Christian art. (*Photo © Jean Roubier*)

Michelangelo Buonarroti (1475–1564): *David,* 1501–1504, marble, height 13′ 5″. When Michelangelo's sculpture of the biblical David was first installed in front of the Palazzo Vecchio in Renaissance Florence, it instantly became a symbol of the Florentine Republic, a source of civic pride in this era of humanism. *David* also embodies the Renaissance motto, "Man is the measure of all things." Michelangelo's masterpiece embodies the new ideas of the Renaissance, glorifying not only the human spirit, but the human body and mind as well. (*Alinari/ Art Resource, N.Y.*)

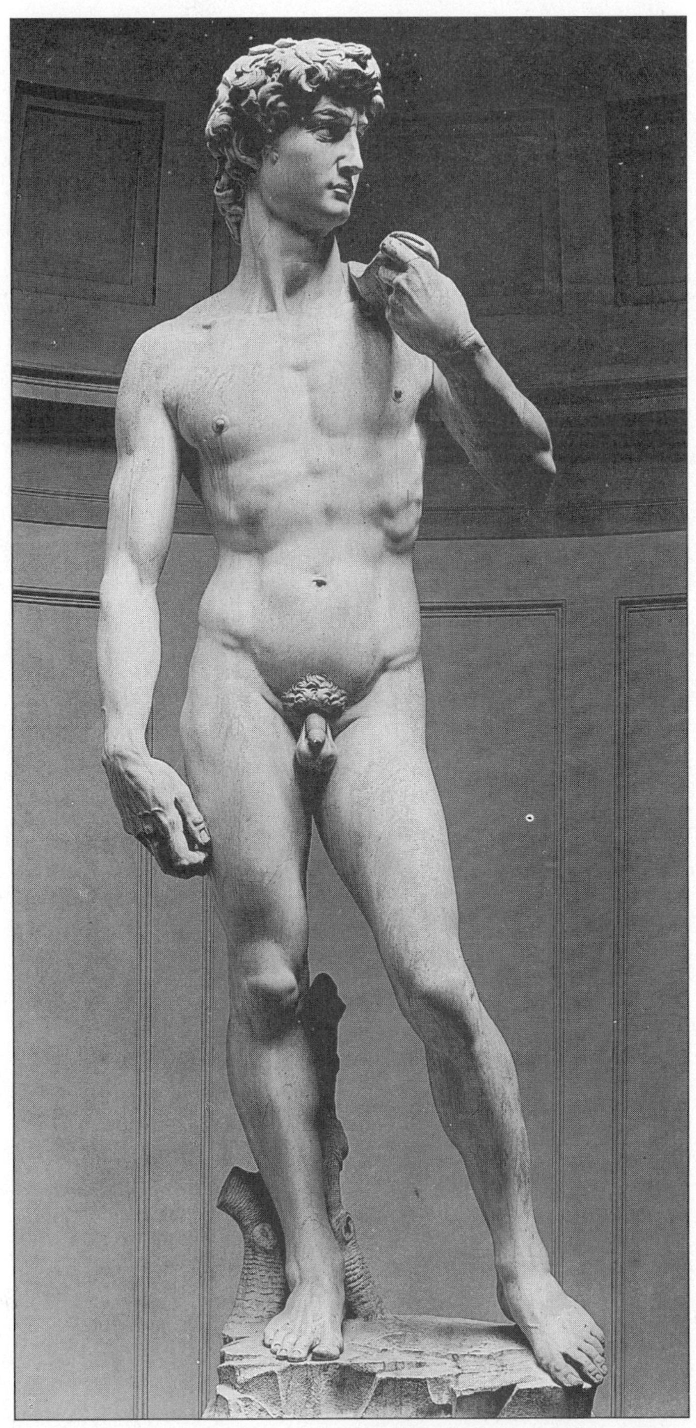

SANCTVS·
BLASIVS

SOURCES OF THE WESTERN TRADITION

CHAPTER 6

Early Christianity

Christianity, the core religion of Western civilization, emerged during the first century of the Roman Empire. The first Christians were followers of Jesus Christ, a Jew, who, in the tradition of the Hebrew prophets, called for a moral reformation of the individual. Jesus' life, teachings, crucifixion, and the belief that he had risen from the dead convinced his followers that Jesus had shown humanity the way to salvation. Dedicated disciples spread this message throughout the Mediterranean world.

Surviving persecution and gaining in numbers, Christians influenced all classes from slave to aristocrat, and Christianity had become the state religion of Rome by the end of the fourth century. The reasons for the spread and triumph of Christianity are diverse. The poor and oppressed of the Roman world were drawn to Jesus' message of love and compassion, his concern for humanity; the promise of eternal life had an immense attraction to people who were burdened with misfortune and fearful of death. Jesus' call for a moral transformation of the individual addressed itself to the inner conscience of men and women of all social classes.

The Judeo-Christian and Greco-Roman (classical humanist) traditions constitute the foundations of Western civilization. Nevertheless, they represent two contrasting views of the world. For classical humanists, the ultimate aim of life was the achievement of excellence in this world, the maximum cultivation of human talent; Christians subordinated this world to a higher reality. For Christians, the principal purpose of life was the attainment of salvation — entrance into a heavenly kingdom after death.

In the Greco-Roman tradition, reason was autonomous: that is, the intellect depended on its own powers and neither required nor accepted guidance from a supernatural authority. For example, Socrates held that ethical standards were arrived at through rational thought alone; they were not divine commandments revealed to human beings by a heavenly lawmaker. Conservative Christian churchmen, believing that Greek intellectualism posed a threat to Christian teachings, wanted nothing to do with Greek philosophy. But other Christians, recognizing the value of Greek philosophy, sought to integrate Greek learning into the Christian framework. Greek philosophy, they said, could help Christians clarify, organize, and explain their teachings. Those who advocated studying and utilizing Greek

SAINT BASIL THE GREAT (c. 330–379), central figure in a twelfth-century mosaic in the Capella Palatina in Palermo, Italy. Basil, one of the great Cappadocian Fathers, became bishop of Caesarea and established the rules that became the standards for monasteries in the east. (*Alinari/Art Resource, N.Y.*)

philosophy prevailed; thus Christianity preserved rational thought, the priceless achievement of the Greek mind. In the process, however, philosophy lost its autonomy, for early Christian thinkers insisted that to reason properly one must first believe in God and his revelation, with the Bible as the ultimate authority. Without these prior conditions, the Christians argued, reason would lead to error. Thus, for early Christian thinkers, unlike their Greek predecessors, reason was not autonomous: it was subject to divine authority as interpreted by the church.

In the late Roman Empire, when Roman institutions were breaking down and classical values were being discarded, Christianity was a dynamic movement. Surviving the barbarian invasions, the Christian church gave form and direction to the European culture that emerged in the Middle Ages.

---

1 ▾ The Teachings of Jesus

During the reign (A.D. 14–37) of the Emperor Tiberius, the Roman governor in Judea, Pontius Pilate, executed on charges of sedition an obscure Jewish religious teacher, Jesus of Nazareth. While performing healings and exorcisms, Jesus expounded a message of hope and salvation for sinners who repented. To the Jews who were attracted to Jesus' person and teachings, Jesus appeared to be a new prophet or even the long-awaited Messiah, the divinely promised leader who would restore Israel to freedom and usher in a new age.

Jesus made enemies among those powerful Jewish leaders who believed that the popular preacher was undermining their authority and weakening respect for their teachings on the requirements of Jewish law. The Romans viewed Jesus as a political agitator who might lead the Jews in a revolt against Roman rule. Some Jewish leaders denounced Jesus to the Roman authorities, who executed him.

After the death of Jesus, his loyal followers, who believed in his resurrection, continued to preach his teachings, forming small congregations of those faithful to his mission and words. They soon spread out as missionaries to Jewish and Gentile communities throughout the Roman Empire. These followers of Jesus, the Messiah, or in Greek, *Christos* (the Anointed One), were the founders of the Christian church.

Like Socrates, Jesus himself never wrote a book; all we know of his life and teachings come from writings attributed to his disciples and passed down orally through them until put in written form some thirty to seventy years after his death. These primary sources include the gospels ("good news") attributed to the Saints Mark, Matthew, Luke, and John; the letters of Saint Paul and others; the Acts of the Apostles, a historical account of their missionary work; and the book of Revelation, a prophetic portrayal of the coming messianic kingdom of Jesus and God's destruction of the powers of evil. These works, written several

decades after Jesus' death and collected together definitively in the fourth century, comprise the New Testament, the Christian sacred scriptures. They reflect the ways in which the early Christians remembered Jesus' teachings and the meaning of his life and ministry.

≪ *THE GOSPEL ACCORDING TO SAINT MARK* ≫

In this reading from Saint Mark's Gospel, Jesus stated in a few words the core of his ethical teaching.

28 And one of the scribes* came up and heard
them disputing with one another, and seeing
that he answered them well, asked him,
"Which commandment is the first of all?"
[29]Jesus answered, "The first is, 'Hear, O Israel:
The Lord our God, the Lord is one;† [30]and you
shall love the Lord your God with all your
heart, and with all your soul, and with all your
mind, and with all your strength.' [31]The second
is this, 'You shall love your neighbor as yourself.' There is no other commandment greater
than these." [32]And the scribe said to him, "You
are right, Teacher; you have truly said that he
is one, and there is no other but he; [33]and to
love him with all the heart, and with all the
understanding, and with all the strength, and
to love one's neighbor as oneself, is much more
than all whole burnt offerings and sacrifices."
[34]And when Jesus saw that he answered wisely,
he said to him, "You are not far from the kingdom of God." And after that no one dared to
ask him any question. (Mark 12)

*Scribes were not only copyists of the scrolls that contained Jewish law, but they were also students of that law.

Editors' footnotes for Bible readings in this chapter are not numbered, to eliminate confusion with verse numbers. — Eds.

†"Hear, O Israel" occurs in the Judaic Book of Deuteronomy as the "first law," that of monotheism (one God). Here, as a Jew, Jesus was reminding his followers of this fact. — Eds.

≪ *THE GOSPEL ACCORDING TO SAINT MATTHEW* ≫

In the gospel of Saint Matthew, Jesus outlined to his disciples the attitudes pleasing to God.

5 Seeing the crowds, he went up on the
mountain, and when he sat down his disciples came to him. [2]And he opened his mouth
and taught them, saying:
3 "Blessed are the poor in spirit, for theirs is
the kingdom of heaven.
4 "Blessed are those who mourn, for they
shall be comforted.
5 "Blessed are the meek, for they shall inherit the earth.
6 "Blessed are those who hunger and thirst
for righteousness, for they shall be satisfied.
7 "Blessed are the merciful, for they shall obtain mercy.
8 "Blessed are the pure in heart, for they
shall see God.
9 "Blessed are the peacemakers, for they shall
be called sons of God.
10 "Blessed are those who are persecuted for
righteousness' sake, for theirs is the kingdom
of heaven.
11 "Blessed are you when men revile you and

persecute you and utter all kinds of evil against you falsely on my account. [12]Rejoice and be glad, for your reward is great in heaven, for so men persecuted the prophets who were before you. . . ." (Matthew 5)

▷ A characteristic feature of Jesus' teaching — one that angered the Jewish leaders — was a demand that his followers go beyond the letter of the Jewish law. In the tradition of the Hebrew prophets, Jesus stressed the ethical demands that underlie this law and urged a moral transformation of human character, based on a love of God and neighbor. In the next reading from Saint Matthew, Jesus reinterpreted the Hebrew commandments on killing, adultery, divorce, vengeance, the definition of a neighbor, and almsgiving.

---

17 "Think not that I have come to abolish the law and the prophets; I have come not to abolish them but to fulfil them. [18]For truly, I say to you, till heaven and earth pass away, not an iota, not a dot, will pass from the law until all is accomplished. [19]Whoever then relaxes one of the least of these commandments and teaches men so, shall be called least in the kingdom of heaven; but he who does them and teaches them shall be called great in the kingdom of heaven. [20]For I tell you, unless your righteousness exceeds that of the scribes and Pharisees,* you will never enter the kingdom of heaven.

21 "You have heard that it was said to the men of old, 'You shall not kill; and whoever kills shall be liable to judgment.' [22]But I say to you that every one who is angry with his brother shall be liable to judgment; whoever insults his brother shall be liable to the council, and whoever says, 'You fool!' shall be liable to the hell of fire. [23]So if you are offering your gift at the altar, and there remember that your brother has something against you, [24]leave your gift there before the altar and go; first be reconciled to your brother, and then come and offer your gift. [25]Make friends quickly with your accuser, while you are going with him to court, lest your accuser hand you over to the judge, and the judge to the guard, and you be put in prison; [26]truly, I say to you, you will never get out till you have paid the last penny.

27 "You have heard that it was said, 'You shall not commit adultery.' [28]But I say to you that every one who looks at a woman lustfully has already committed adultery with her in his heart. [29]If your right eye causes you to sin, pluck it out and throw it away; it is better that you lose one of your members than that your whole body be thrown into hell. [30]And if your right hand causes you to sin, cut it off and throw it away; it is better that you lose one of your members than that your whole body go into hell.

31 "It was also said, 'Whoever divorces his wife, let him give her a certificate of divorce.' [32]But I say to you that every one who divorces his wife, except on the ground of unchastity, makes her an adulteress; and whoever marries a divorced woman commits adultery.

33 "Again you have heard that it was said to the men of old, 'You shall not swear falsely, but shall perform to the Lord what you have sworn.' [34]But I say to you, Do not swear at all, either by heaven, for it is the throne of God, [35]or by the earth, for it is his footstool, or by Jerusalem, for it is the city of the great King. [36]And do not swear by your head, for you cannot make one hair white or black. [37]Let what you say be simply 'Yes' or 'No'; anything more than this comes from evil.

38 "You have heard that it was said, 'An eye for an eye and a tooth for a tooth.' [39]But I say to you, Do not resist one who is evil. But if any one strikes you on the right cheek, turn to him the other also; [40]and if any one would sue you and take your coat, let him have your cloak as well; [41]and if any one forces you to go one mile,

*The Pharisees were a sect within Judaism; they adopted a flexible attitude toward Mosaic Law, allowing for various interpretations and granting authority to oral tradition as well as to written Scripture. Unlike the aristocratic Sadducees, the Pharisees were concerned with social injustice and had the support of the common people — Eds.

go with him two miles. [42]Give to him who begs
from you, and do not refuse him who would
borrow from you.

43 "You have heard that it was said, 'You
shall love your neighbor and hate your enemy.'
[44]But I say to you, Love your enemies and pray
for those who persecute you,[45] so that you may
be sons of your Father who is in heaven; for he
makes his sun rise on the evil and on the good,
and sends rain on the just and on the unjust.
[46]For if you love those who love you, what reward have you? Do not even the tax collectors
do the same? [47]And if you salute only your
brethren, what more are you doing than others?
Do not even the Gentiles† do the same? [48]You,
therefore, must be perfect, as your heavenly Father is perfect.

6 "Beware of practicing your piety before
men in order to be seen by them; for then
you will have no reward from your Father who
is in heaven.

[2]"Thus, when you give alms, sound no trumpet before you, as the hypocrites do in the syn-
agogues‡ and in the streets, that they may be
praised by men. Truly, I say to you, they have
their reward. [3]But when you give alms, do not
let your left hand know what your right hand
is doing, [4]so that your alms may be in secret;
and your Father who sees in secret will reward
you. . . ." (Matthew 5–6)

†Gentiles meant non-Jews; many religions were represented in the cosmopolitan Roman Empire of that period. — Eds.

‡Synagogues, originally a name given to substitutes outside Judea for the Temple in Jerusalem, coexisted with the Temple; they were places for public prayer and study of the Hebrew Scriptures. — Eds.

REVIEW QUESTIONS

1. What did Jesus believe to be the basic tenets of religion?
2. What virtues and types of behavior did Jesus praise?
3. From the readings, quote ways in which Jesus said that his teachings went beyond the strict letter of the Hebrew law.

---

2 ▾ Saint Paul's View of Jesus, His Mission, and His Teaching

After the execution of Jesus by the Roman authorities in Judea around A.D. 30, his disciples, believing that he had risen from the dead, sought a clearer understanding of his life and teachings. They became convinced that Jesus' mission, calling people to repent their sins and receive God's forgiveness and to conduct their lives according to a high code of ethics, must be carried on. They proceeded to spread the "good news" to their fellow Jews and eventually to other peoples throughout the Roman world.

The disciples of Jesus were soon joined in this great mission by a man known to us as Saint Paul, the first great theologian of the new Christian church. Saint Paul started life as a pious Jew named Saul. He was born in Tarsus, a Greek city in Asia Minor. A Roman citizen as well as a Pharisee, Paul studied the Hebrew Scriptures in Judea and joined in the early persecution of Jesus' followers. But, through a visionary experience, Paul was converted to the belief that Jesus was the Messiah. He traveled widely throughout Syria, Asia Minor, and Greece,

converting both Jews and non-Jews. He kept in touch with the new Christian communities by visits and letters. Several of the latter are included in the New Testament. He died around A.D. 65.

≪ *THE LETTER OF PAUL TO THE EPHESIANS* ≫

In the following letter addressed to the Christian community in Ephesus, a major Greek city in western Asia Minor, Paul explains the meaning of Jesus as the Messiah, and tells how that meaning should be reflected in a Christian's daily life. The Letter to the Ephesians has been attributed to Paul, but now many scholars, on the basis of linguistic analysis, believe that the author was not Paul himself, but a close adherent of Pauline theology.

17 Now this I affirm and testify in the Lord,
that you must no longer live as the Gentiles do,
in the futility of their minds; [18]they are darkened in their understanding, alienated from the
life of God because of the ignorance that is in
them, due to their hardness of heart; [19]they have
become callous and have given themselves up
to licentiousness, greedy to practice every kind
of uncleanness. [20]You did not so learn Christ! —
[21]assuming that you have heard about him and
were taught in him, as the truth is in Jesus.
[22]Put off your old nature which belongs to your
former manner of life and is corrupt through
deceitful lusts, [23]and be renewed in the spirit of
your minds, [24]and put on the new nature, created after the likeness of God in true righteousness and holiness.
25 Therefore, putting away falsehood, let
every one speak the truth with his neighbor, for
we are members one of another. [26]Be angry but
do not sin; do not let the sun go down on your
anger, [27]and give no opportunity to the devil.
[28]Let the thief no longer steal, but rather let
him labor, doing honest work with his hands,
so that he may be able to give to those in need.
[29]Let no evil talk come out of your mouths, but
only such as is good for edifying, as fits the
occasion, that it may impart grace to those who
hear. [30]And do not grieve the Holy Spirit of
God, in whom you were sealed for the day of
redemption. [31]Let all bitterness and wrath and
anger and clamor and slander be put away from
you, with all malice, [32]and be kind to one another, tenderhearted, forgiving one another, as
God in Christ forgave you. (Ephesians 4)

≪ *THE FIRST LETTER OF PAUL TO THE CORINTHIANS* ≫

In a letter to the Christians of Corinth, the great commercial center of Roman Greece, Paul defined love and declared it to be the essential foundation of a Christian life.

[31]But earnestly desire the higher gifts.
And I will show you a still more excellent way.
13 If I speak in the tongues of men and of
angels, but have not love, I am a noisy
gong or a clanging cymbal. [2]And if I have prophetic powers, and understand all mysteries
and all knowledge, and if I have all faith, so as
to remove mountains, but have not love, I am
nothing. [3]If I give away all I have, and if I deliver my body to be burned, but have not love,
I gain nothing.
4 Love is patient and kind; love is not jealous

or boastful; [5]it is not arrogant or rude. Love does not insist on its own way; it is not irritable or resentful; [6]it does not rejoice at wrong, but rejoices in the right. [7]Love bears all things, believes all things, hopes all things, endures all things.

8 Love never ends; as for prophecy, it will pass away; as for tongues, they will cease; as for knowledge, it will pass away. [9]For our knowledge is imperfect and our prophecy is imperfect; [10]but when the perfect comes, the imperfect will pass away. [11]When I was a child, I spoke like a child, I thought like a child, I reasoned like a child; when I became a man, I gave up childish ways. [12]For now we see in a mirror* dimly, but then face to face. Now I know in part; then I shall understand fully, even as I have been fully understood. [13]So faith, hope, love abide, these three; but the greatest of these is love. (1 Corinthians 12–13)

*The mirror of the ancients was made of a highly polished metal; it would not reflect, however, as clearly as a modern one. — Eds.

REVIEW QUESTIONS

1. According to Paul, how did the lives of non-Jews (Gentiles) differ from those of followers of Christ?
2. How did Paul expand the meaning of the word *love,* which Jesus said was the summation of all other commandments of God?
3. How did Paul encourage Christians to mature in their knowledge of God?

3 ▾ Christianity and Society

Although the principal concern of Jesus' followers was the attainment of salvation, Christians still had to deal with the world and its ways. In the process of doing so, they developed attitudes and customs that have had an enduring influence on Western culture.

Athenagoras
SEXUALITY AND FAMILY LIFE

Christians, Paul taught, expected each other to uphold high standards of personal chastity, avoiding all occasions of sexual impurity by thought or deed. Even within marriage, sexual intercourse was linked to procreation, not pleasure. Many even condemned a second marriage, challenging widows and widowers to remain chaste. Abortion was condemned, as was divorce. Athenagoras, a contemporary of Emperor Marcus Aurelius, was an Athenian philosopher who became a Christian. Writing in the late second century, Athenagoras described what he saw as Christian attitudes toward sex and family morals.

. . . But we are so far from practising promiscuous intercourse, that it is not lawful among us to indulge even a lustful look. "For," saith He, "he that looketh on a woman to lust after her, hath committed adultery already in his heart." [Matthew 5:28] Those, then, who are forbidden to look at anything more than that for which God formed the eyes, which were intended to be a light to us, and to whom a wanton look is adultery, the eyes being made for other purposes, and who are to be called to account for their very thoughts, how can any one doubt that such persons practise self-control? For our account lies not with human laws, which a bad man can evade, . . . but we have a law which makes the measure of rectitude to consist in dealing with our neighbour as ourselves. On this account, too, according to age, we recognise some as sons and daughters, others we regard as brothers and sisters, and to the more advanced in life we give the honour due to fathers and mothers. On behalf of those, then, to whom we apply the names of brothers and sisters, and other designations of relationship, we exercise the greatest care that their bodies should remain undefiled and uncorrupted; for the Logos[1] again says to us, "If any one kiss a second time because it has given him pleasure, (he sins);" adding, "Therefore the kiss, or rather the salutation, should be given with the greatest care, since, if there be mixed with it the least defilement of thought, it excludes us from eternal life." (Probably from an Apocryphal gospel not included by the church in the New Testament)

CHAPTER XXXIII
Chastity of the Christians with Respect to Marriage

Therefore, having the hope of eternal life, we despise the things of this life, even to the pleasures of the soul, each of us reckoning her his wife whom he has married according to the laws laid down by us, and that only for the purpose of having children. For as the husbandman throwing the seed into the ground awaits the harvest, not sowing more upon it, so to us the procreation of children is the measure of our indulgence in appetite. Nay, you would find many among us, both men and women, growing old unmarried, in the hope of living in closer communion with God. But if the remaining in virginity and in the state of an eunuch brings nearer to God, while the indulgence of carnal thought and desire leads away from Him, in those cases in which we shun the thoughts, much more do we reject the deeds. For we bestow our attention, not on the study of words, but on the exhibition and teaching of actions, — that a person should either remain as he was born, or be content with one marriage; for a second marriage is only a specious adultery. "For whosoever puts away his wife," says He, "and marries another, commits adultery;" [Matthew 19:9] not permitting a man to send her away whose virginity he has brought to an end, nor to marry again. For he who deprives himself of his first wife, even though she be dead, is a cloaked adulterer, resisting the hand of God — because in the beginning God made one man and one woman — and dissolving the strictest union of flesh with flesh, formed for the intercourse of the race. . . .

[1]*Logos*, Greek for *word*, is used in the New Testament in the Gospel of John to designate both God and Jesus, as a divinity. The Stoics used *logos* to mean Divine Reason.

▷ Early Christians, who were repelled by all forms of violence, were particularly incensed by the malicious accusation that they engaged in cannibalism. Athenagoras responds to this charge.

CHAPTER XXXV
The Christians Condemn and Detest All Cruelty

What man of sound mind, therefore, will affirm, while such is our character, that we are murderers? For we cannot eat human flesh till we have killed some one. The former charge, therefore, being false, if any one should ask them in regard to the second, whether they have seen what they assert, not one of them would be so barefaced as to say that he had. And yet we have slaves, some more and some fewer, by whom we could not help being seen; but even of these, not one has been found to invent even such things against us. For when they know that we cannot endure even to see a man put to death, though justly, who of them can accuse us of murder or cannibalism? Who does not reckon among the things of greatest interest the contests of gladiators and wild beasts, especially those which are given by you? But we, deeming that to see a man put to death is much the same as killing him, have abjured such spectacles. How, then, when we do not even look on, lest we should contract guilt and pollution, can we put people to death? And when we say that those women who use drugs to bring on abortion commit murder, and will have to give an account to God for the abortion, on what principle should we commit murder?

REVIEW QUESTIONS

1. What was Athenagoras' view on sexual relations within and outside marriage?
2. According to Athenagoras, what was the purpose of Christian marriage?
3. What evidence did Athenagoras offer to dispel rumors that Christians were secret cannibals and murderers?
4. Do the moral viewpoints of Athenagoras find any echo in modern society?

---

4 ▾ The Persecutions

Under Roman law, all cults had to be approved by the authorities, and religious associations were licensed by the state. At first, the Christians were assumed to be members of a Jewish sect, and as Judaism was a legal religion, the authorities did not intervene in the work of the Christian missionaries except as they were involved in disputes within the Jewish community. By the reign of Emperor Nero (A.D. 54–68), Roman officials had become aware that the new Christian churches were composed of many Gentiles as well as Jews, and could no longer reasonably be considered a legitimate part of the privileged Jewish religious community. The first major persecution broke out in the city of Rome when Nero, to put down a rumor that he had set afire a large section of the city, decided to focus blame for the disaster on the small Christian community. When the unpopular Christians were arrested, they pleaded guilty not to arson, but to the crime of being Christians: that is, to belonging to an illegal sect or association. The penalty for such unlicensed association was death. Those who denied they were Christians and agreed to offer sacrifice to the gods of Rome were released.

PERSECUTIONS AT LYONS AND VIENNE

During the second century, Christians were at times victims of mob actions, usually stimulated by some disaster like an outbreak of disease, an earthquake, a drought, or other communal catastrophe attributed to the anger of the gods. Christians' pacifism and their refusal to participate in the worship of the state deities, in processions and festivals, and in theatrical performances and gladiatorial games made them increasingly unpopular.

The next reading is a letter sent in A.D. 177 by the Christians of the cities of Lyons and Vienne in Gaul (France) to fellow Christians in Asia and Phrygia (both in modern Turkey). The letter describes a group of Christians arrested and reviled by enraged mobs.

First, indeed, they [the Christians] endured nobly the sufferings heaped upon them by the general populace, clamors, blows, being dragged along, robberies, stonings, imprisonments, and all that an enraged mob loves to inflict on opponents and enemies. Then they were taken to the forum by . . . the ordained authorities of the city and were examined in the presence of the whole multitude. Having confessed, they were imprisoned until the arrival of the governor. When they were afterwards brought before him and he treated us with all manner of cruelty. . . .

. . . [Some refused to renounce their faith in Christ, but others] appeared unprepared and untrained and still weak, unable to endure the strain of a great contest. Of these about ten became apostates [renounced their religion], who caused us great pain and excessive sorrow, and weakened the zeal of the others who had not yet been seized, and who, although suffering all kinds of evil, were constantly with the martyrs and did not abandon them. . . . And some of our servants who were heathens were seized because the governor had ordered that we should all be examined in public.

These by the wiles of Satan, fearing the tortures which they saw the saints suffering and urged by the soldiers to do this, accused us falsely of Thyestean banquets[1] and Oedipodean incests[2] and of deeds which it is not lawful for us to speak of, or think of, and which we do not believe men ever committed. When these accusations were reported all raged like wild beasts against us. . . . Then finally the holy martyrs endured sufferings beyond all description and Satan strove earnestly that some blasphemies might be uttered by them also.

But the whole rage of the people, governor and soldiers was aroused exceedingly against Sanctus, deacon from Vienne, and against Maturus, a recent convert but a noble combatant, and against Attalus, a native of Pergamus [a city in Asia Minor], who had always been a pillar and a foundation in that place, and against Blandina [a slave] through whom Christ showed that what appears mean, deformed and contemptible to men is of great glory with God through love for Him, shown in power and not boasting in appearance. For while we all, together with her mistress on earth, who was herself also one of the combatants among the martyrs, feared lest in the strife she should be unable to make her confession on account of her bodily weakness, Blandina was filled with such power that she was delivered and raised above those who took turns in torturing her in every manner from dawn till evening; and they confessed that they were defeated and had nothing more which they could do to her. They marvelled at her endurance, for her whole body was mangled and broken; and they testified that one form of torture was sufficient to destroy life, to say nothing of so many and so great tortures. But the blessed one, like a noble athlete, renewed her strength . . ., and her comfort, refreshment and relief from suffering was in saying, "I am a Christian" and "Nothing vile is done by us."

. . . Maturus, Sanctus, Blandina and Attalus were therefore led to the wild beasts in the amphitheatre, and in order to give to the heathen public a spectacle of cruelty, a day was especially appointed for our people to fight with the wild beasts. Accordingly Maturus and Sanctus again passed through the whole torture

[1]Thyestes, in Greek myth, was forced to eat his own sons at a banquet; the reference is to cannibalism.

[2]Oedipus, the protagonist of several Greek dramas, unwittingly committed incest with his mother.

in the amphitheatre, not as if they had suffered nothing at all before, but rather as if having overcome the adversary already in many kinds of contests they were now striving for the crown itself. They endured again the running the gauntlet customary in that place and the attacks from the wild beasts and everything that the raging multitude, who cried out from one place or another, desired, and at last the iron chair in which their bodies were roasted and tormented them with the fumes. Not even with this did the tortures cease, but they raged still more, desiring to overcome their patience, and they did not hear a word from Sanctus except the confession [that he was a Christian] which he had made from the beginning. These accordingly, after their life had continued for a very long time through the great conflict, died at last, after having furnished a spectacle to the world throughout that day instead of all the varieties of gladiatorial combats.

But Blandina suspended on a stake was exposed as food for the wild beasts which should fall upon her. Because she seemed to be suspended in the manner of a cross and because of her earnest prayers, she encouraged the contestants greatly. They looking upon her in her conflict, beheld with their eyes, through their sister, Him who had suffered for them in order to persuade those who trust in Him that everyone who suffers for the glory of Christ has eternal fellowship with the living God. And as none of the beasts touched her at that time, she was taken down from the stake and led away again to the prison, to be preserved for another contest. . . .

▷ The Roman authorities frequently set free anyone who denied his Christian faith and was willing to worship a Roman god, usually the divine emperor.

. . . For Caesar had written that these [Christians] should be put to death, but if any should deny they should be dismissed. At the beginning of the festival held there, which is attended by throngs of people from all nations, the governor had the blessed ones brought to the judgment-seat to be a show and spectacle for the multitude. Therefore he examined them again, and as many as seemed to be Roman citizens he had beheaded, the others he sent to the wild beasts.

Christ was glorified greatly in those who had previously denied him, for contrary to the expectation of the heathen, they confessed. For these were examined separately as about to be set free, and when they confessed, they were added to the number of the martyrs. But those who never had a particle of faith . . . or any thought of the fear of God . . . blasphemed the way through their apostacy. . . .

. . . The bodies of the martyrs after having been exposed and exhibited in every manner for six days, were afterwards burned and reduced to ashes by the lawless men and thrown in the river Rhone which flows close by, so that no remnants of them might still be seen on the earth. And they did this as if they were able to overcome God and prevent their coming to life again, in order, as some said, "that they may have no hope of a resurrection, trusting in which they bring to us a certain foreign and strange religion, and despise awful punishments and are ready with joy to suffer death. Now let us see whether they will rise again, and if their God is able to aid them and rescue them from our hands."

REVIEW QUESTIONS

1. For what crimes were the Christians arrested, tried, and executed?
2. Why were the Christians tortured?
3. What did the Christians especially fear when some of them were arrested?

4. What do the stories of the martyrs suggest about the moral character of Roman society?

---

5 ▾ Christianity and Greco-Roman Learning

Should the cultural inheritance of the Greco-Roman world be retained or discarded? This posed a formidable problem for early Christian thinkers. Those who urged abandoning Greco-Roman learning argued that such knowledge would corrupt the morality of the young and would lead Christians to doubt Scripture. On the other hand, several Christian intellectuals, particularly those educated in the Greco-Roman classics, defended the study of pagan works. Their view ultimately prevailed.

Christians preserved the intellectual tradition of Greece. However, philosophy underwent a crucial change: philosophic thought among Christians had to be directed in accordance with the requirements of their faith. The intellect was not fully autonomous; it could not question or challenge Christian teachings but had to accept the church's dictums regarding God's existence, the creation of the universe, the mission of Jesus, and the purpose of life and death.

Tertullian
WHAT HAS JERUSALEM TO DO WITH ATHENS?

A native of Carthage, Tertullian (Quintus Septimus Florens Tertullianus, c. A.D. 160–c. 240) became a Christian about A.D. 190 and thereafter was a defender of Christian morals against both pagans and less rigorous Christians. He emphasized the sacredness of life and the Christian abhorrence of violence. His ***Prescriptions Against Heretics*** reveals hostility toward Greco-Roman learning, an attitude shared by some other early Christian thinkers.

. . . Worldly wisdom culminates in philosophy with its rash interpretation of God's nature and purpose. It is philosophy that supplies the heresies[1] with their equipment. . . . The idea of a mortal soul was picked up from the Epicureans,[2] and the denial of the restitution of the flesh was taken from the common tradition of the philosophical schools. . . . Heretics and philosophers [ponder] the same themes and are caught up in the same discussions. What is the origin of evil and why? The origin of man, and how? . . . A plague on Aristotle, who taught them dialectic [logical argumentation], the art which destroys as much as it builds, which changes its opinions like a coat, forces its conjectures, is stubborn in argument, works hard at being contentious and is a burden even to itself. For it reconsiders every point to make sure it never finishes a discussion.

From philosophy come those fables and . . . fruitless questionings, those "words that creep

---

[1]A heresy is any belief that differs from the official or standard views on a doctrine.

[2]Chapter 3, Section 14.

like as doth a canker." To hold us back from such things, the Apostle [Paul] testifies expressly in his letter to the Colossians [Colossians 2:8] that we should beware of philosophy. "Take heed lest any man [beguile] you through philosophy or vain deceit, after the tradition of men," against the providence of the Holy Ghost. He had been at Athens where he had come to grips with the human wisdom which attacks and perverts truth, being itself divided up into its own swarm of heresies by the variety of its mutually antagonistic sects. What has Jerusalem to do with Athens, the Church with [Plato's] Academy, the Christian with the heretic? Our principles come from the Porch of Solomon,[3] who had himself taught that the Lord is to be sought in simplicity of heart. I have no use for a Stoic or a Platonic or a dialectic Christianity. After Jesus Christ we have no need of speculation, after the Gospel no need of research. When we come to believe, we have no desire to believe anything else; for we begin by believing that there is nothing else which we have to believe.

[3]The Stoic philosophers took their name from the Greek word *stoa,* porch, the place where Zeno, their founder, used to teach. *Porch of Solomon* is used to designate the teachings of King Solomon, who built the great Temple in Jerusalem. Tertullian makes it clear he follows Solomon's wisdom.

Clement of Alexandria
IN DEFENSE OF GREEK LEARNING

In the following passage, Clement of Alexandria (c. A.D. 150–c. 220) expresses his admiration for Greek learning. A Greek Christian theologian, Clement combined Christianity with Platonism.

The Greeks should not be condemned by those who have merely glanced at their writings, for comprehension of these works requires careful investigation. Philosophy is not the originator of false practices and base deeds as some have calumniated it; nor does it beguile us and lead us away from faith.

Rather philosophy is a clear image of truth, a divine gift to the Greeks. Before the advent of the Lord, philosophy helped the Greeks to attain righteousness, and it is now conducive to piety; it supplies a preparatory teaching for those who will later embrace the faith. God is the cause of all good things: some given primarily in the form of the Old and the New Testament; others are the consequence of philosophy. Perchance too philosophy was given to the Greeks primarily till the Lord should call the Greeks to serve him. Thus philosophy acted as a schoolmaster to the Greeks, preparing them for Christ, as the laws of the Jews prepared them for Christ.

The way of truth is one. But into it, as into a perennial river, streams flow from all sides. We assert that philosophy, which is characterized by investigation into the form and nature of things, is the truth of which the Lord Himself said, "I am the truth." Thus Greek preparatory culture, including philosophy itself, is shown to have come down from God to men.

Some do not wish to touch either philosophy or logic or to learn natural science. They demand bare faith alone, as if they wished, without bestowing any care on the vine, straightway to gather clusters from the first. I call him truly learned who brings everything to bear on the truth; so that from geometry, music, grammar, and philosophy itself, he culls what is useful and guards the faith against assault. And he who brings everything to bear on a right life, learning from Greeks and non-Greeks, this man is an experienced searcher after truth. And how necessary it is for him who desires to be partaker of the power of God to treat of intellectual subjects by philosophising.

According to some, Greek philosophy apprehended the truth accidentally, dimly, partially. Others will have it that Greek philosophy was instituted by the devil. Several hold that certain powers descending from heaven inspired the whole of philosophy. But if Greek philosophy does not comprehend the whole of truth and does not encompass God's commandments, yet it prepares the way for God's teachings; training in some way or other, molding character, and fitting him who believes in Providence for the reception of truth.

REVIEW QUESTIONS

1. Why did Tertullian oppose the study of pagan literature on the part of Christians?
2. Why did Clement of Alexandria favor the study of pagan learning?

---

6 ▾ Christian Worship and Organization

The organizational structure of the Christian church had taken its basic historical form early in the second century. The presiding officer or bishop of the local Christian community was elected to serve all as teacher, spiritual father, ruler, and leader in the liturgical services. Assisted by presbyters (elders or priests) and deacons, the bishop normally presided at baptisms and the weekly liturgy, or worship service. The congregation usually met in private homes where they prayed, sang, and heard readings from the Holy Scriptures. The high point of the gathering was the Eucharistic celebration (Communion), followed by thanksgiving and a sharing of gifts.

Saint Justin Martyr
ON THE LITURGY OF THE CHURCH

The fundamental acts of liturgical worship of the early Christian church were substantially fashioned from the religious practices of first-century Judaism. The first part of the service, consisting of readings from the Scriptures, the singing of psalms, and the sermon, was taken from the morning Sabbath service at the synagogue. The second part — consisting of the commemoration of the Last Supper of Jesus and the distribution of the Eucharist — also resembles certain religious practices among the Essenes, a Jewish sect existing at the time of Christ. The following description of a baptismal liturgy and the normal Sunday liturgy — written by Saint Justin Martyr (c. A.D. 110–c. 165), a Christian philosopher — comes from his letter to Emperor Marcus Aurelius defending the reputation of Christians.

How we dedicated ourselves to God when we were made new through Christ I will explain. . . . Those who are persuaded and believe that the things we teach and say are true, and promise that they can live accordingly, are instructed to pray and beseech God with fasting for the remission of their past sins, while we pray and fast along with them. Then they are brought by us where there is water, and are reborn by the same manner of rebirth by which we ourselves were reborn; for they are then washed in the water in the name of God the Father and Master of all, and of our Saviour Jesus Christ, and of the Holy Spirit. For Christ said, "Unless you are born again you will not enter into the Kingdom of heaven.". . .

We, . . . after thus washing the one who has been convinced and signified his assent, lead him to those who are called brethren, where they are assembled. They then earnestly offer common prayers for themselves and the one who has been illuminated and all others everywhere, that we may be made worthy, having learned the truth, to be found in deed good citizens and keepers of what is commanded, so that we may be saved with eternal salvation. On finishing the prayers we greet each other with a kiss. Then bread and a cup of water and mixed wine are brought to the president of the brethren [the bishop] and he, taking them, sends up praise and glory to the Father of the universe through the name of the Son and of the Holy Spirit, and offers thanksgiving at some length that we have been deemed worthy to receive these things from him. When he has finished the prayers and the thanksgiving, the whole congregation present assents, saying, "Amen." "Amen" in the Hebrew language means, "So be it." When the president has given thanks and the whole congregation has assented, those whom we call deacons give to each of those present a portion of the consecrated bread and wine and water, and they take it to the absent.

This food we call Eucharist, of which no one is allowed to partake except one who believes that the things we teach are true, and has received the washing for forgiveness of sins and for rebirth, and who lives as Christ handed down to us. For we do not receive these things as common bread or common drink; but as Jesus Christ our Saviour being incarnate by God's word took flesh and blood for our salvation, so also we have been taught that the food consecrated by the word of prayer which comes from him, from which our flesh and blood are nourished by transformation, is the flesh and blood of that incarnate Jesus. For the apostles in the memoirs composed by them, which are called Gospels, thus handed down what was commanded them: that Jesus, taking bread and having given thanks, said, "Do this for my memorial, this is my body"; and likewise taking the cup and giving thanks he said, "This is my blood"; and gave it to them alone. This also the wicked demons in imitation handed down as something to be done in the mysteries of Mithra [a Persian deity, especially popular with Roman soldiers]; for bread and a cup of water are brought out in their secret rites of initiation, with certain invocations which you either know or can learn.

After these (services) we constantly remind each other of these things. Those who have more come to the aid of those who lack, and we are constantly together. Over all that we receive we bless the Maker of all things through his Son Jesus Christ and through the Holy Spirit. And on the day called Sunday there is a meeting in one place of those who live in cities or the country, and the memoirs of the apostles or the writings of the prophets are read as long as time permits. When the reader has finished, the president in a discourse urges and invites (us) to the imitation of these noble things. Then we all stand up together and offer prayers. And, as said before, when we have finished the prayer, bread is brought, and wine and water, and the president similarly sends up prayers and thanksgivings to the best of his ability, and the congregation assents, saying the Amen; the distribution, and reception of the consecrated (elements) by each one, takes place and they are sent to the absent by the deacons. Those who prosper, and who so wish, contribute, each one as much as he chooses to. What is collected is deposited with the president, and he takes care of orphans and widows, and those who are in want on account of sickness or any other cause, and those who are in bonds, and the strangers who are sojourners among (us), and, briefly, he is the protector of all those in need. We all hold this common gathering on Sunday, since it is the first day, on which God transforming darkness and matter made the universe, and Jesus Christ our Saviour rose from the dead on the same day.

Saint Ignatius of Antioch
ON THE AUTHORITY OF THE CLERGY

The role of the clergy and its relationship to the faithful laity were outlined in a letter sent c. A.D. 107 by Saint Ignatius, bishop of Antioch (capital of Roman Syria), to the Christians of Tralles, a small city in western Asia Minor. Ignatius wrote this while under arrest and en route to Rome for trial for being a Christian; he was ultimately martyred under Emperor Trajan (A.D. 98–117). The letter reflects the tensions caused within the church by outbreaks of heresy and other disputes and by Ignatius' insistence on loyalty to the authority of the official clergy.

Well do I realize what a character you have — above reproach and steady under strain. It is not just affected, but it comes naturally to you, as I gathered from Polybius, your bishop. By God's will and that of Jesus Christ, he came to me in Smyrna [a city in Asia Minor], and so heartily congratulated me on being a prisoner for Jesus Christ that in him I saw your whole congregation. I welcomed, then, your godly good will, which reached me by him, and I gave thanks that I found you, as I heard, to be following God.

For when you obey the bishop as if he were Jesus Christ, you are (as I see it) living not in a merely human fashion but in Jesus Christ's way, who for our sakes suffered death that you might believe in his death and so escape dying yourselves. It is essential, therefore, to act in no way without the bishop, just as you are doing. Rather submit even to the presbytery as to the apostles of Jesus Christ. He is our Hope, and if we live in union with him now, we shall gain eternal life. Those too who are deacons of Jesus Christ's "mysteries"[1] must give complete satisfaction to everyone. For they do not serve mere food and drink, but minister to God's Church. They must therefore avoid leaving themselves open to criticism, as they would shun fire.

Correspondingly, everyone must show the deacons respect. They represent Jesus Christ, just as the bishop has the role of the Father, and the presbyters are like God's council and an apostolic band. You cannot have a church without these. I am sure that you agree with me in this. . . .

I urge you, therefore — not I, but Jesus Christ's love — use only Christian food. Keep off foreign fare, by which I mean heresy. For those people [i.e., heretics] mingle Jesus Christ with their teachings just to gain your confidence under false pretenses. It is as if they were giving a deadly poison mixed with honey and wine, with the result that the unsuspecting victim gladly accepts it and drinks down death with fatal pleasure.

Be on your guard, then, against such people. This you will do by not being puffed up and by keeping very close to (our) God, Jesus Christ, and the bishop and the apostles' precepts. Inside the sanctuary a man is pure; outside he is impure. That means: whoever does anything without bishop, presbytery, and deacons does not have a clear conscience. . . .

[1]The word *mysteries* refers to the central act of Christian liturgical worship, the communal mystical union with Jesus Christ achieved by eating consecrated bread and wine (the Eucharist, or Holy Communion).

The Smyrnaeans and Ephesians send their greetings with love. Remember the church of Syria in your prayers. I am not worthy to be a member of it: I am the least of their number Farewell in Jesus Christ. Submit to the bishop as to (God's) law, and to the presbytery too. All of you, love one another with an undivided heart. My life is given for you, not only now but especially when I shall get to God.

REVIEW QUESTIONS

1. What practices of the early church contributed to the sense of community fellowship?
2. What gave the Eucharist its special place in the worship of early Christians?
3. What was the role of a bishop in the early Christian church?
4. What were the special duties of the deacons?
5. Why did Saint Ignatius fear heresy and quarrels within the churches? How did he hope to minimize their consequences?
6. In what ways do modern Christian churches reflect the organization and character of early Christian churches? How do they differ?

---

7 ▾ Monastic Life

In the late third century A.D., inspired by Jesus' example of self-denial and seeking to escape from the distractions of worldly concerns, some zealous Christians withdrew to the deserts of Roman Egypt in search of peace and isolation. They turned their minds wholly to prayer, contemplation, and ascetic practices. These hermits were the earliest Christian monks. In time, some hermits banded together to form monastic communities, living under written rules that established a form of monastic government and way of life.

The hermit or monk "took up the Cross" — that is, emulated the way of Christ through a life of prayer, introspective self-examination, hard work, and ascetic practices like fasting, sexual abstinence, physical deprivation, and poverty. The hermitage and the monastery were schools for sanctity; thus the hermits and monks have been the spiritual models for many male and female Christians from late Roman times down to the present age.

Saint Benedict of Nursia
THE BENEDICTINE RULE

The monastic way of life soon spread from Egypt to Palestine and Syria and eventually throughout the Christian Roman Empire. In Italy, Benedict of Nursia (c. 480–547), scion of a wealthy Roman family, founded twelve monasteries, the best known being at Monte Cassino in the mountains of southern Italy. Benedict wrote a set of rules for the governance of his monks; the Benedictine Rule became the model for many monasteries throughout Latin Christendom. In the first extract, Benedict summarizes the purpose and principles of monastic life.

. . . Therefore we are constrained to found a school for the service of the Lord. In its organization we hope we shall ordain nothing severe, nothing burdensome; but if there should result anything a little irksome by the demands of justice for the correction of vices and the persevering of charity, do not therefore, through fear, avoid the way of salvation, which cannot be entered upon save through a narrow entrance, but in which, as life progresses and the heart becomes filled with faith, one walks in the unspeakable sweetness of love; but never departing from His control, and persevering in His doctrine in the monastery until death, let us with patience share in the sufferings of Christ, that we may be worthy to be partakers in His kingdom. . . .

WHAT THE ABBOT SHOULD BE LIKE

The abbot who is worthy to rule a monastery ought to remember by what name they are called, and to justify by their deeds the name of a superior. For he is believed to take the place of Christ in the monastery, since he is called by his name, as the apostle says: "Ye have received the spirit of adoption of sons, whereby we call, Abba, Father."

And so the abbot ought not (God forbid) to teach or decree or order anything apart from the precept of the Lord; but his rules and his teaching ought always to be leavened with the leaven of divine justice in the minds of his disciples; and let the abbot be always mindful that in the great judgment of God, both his teaching and the obedience of his disciples will be weighed in the balance. And let the abbot know that whatever the master finds lacking in the sheep will be charged to the fault of the shepherd. Only in case the pastor has shown the greatest diligence in his management of an unruly and disobedient flock, and has given his whole care to the correction of their evil doings, will that pastor be cleared at the judgment of God and be able to say with the prophet, "I have not hid thy righteousness within my heart, I have declared thy faithfulness and thy salvation, but they despising have scorned me"; then let the punishment of eternal death itself fall upon the disobedent sheep of his care.

Therefore when anyone takes on himself the name of abbot, he should govern his disciples by a twofold teaching, that is, let him show forth all the good and holy things by his deeds rather than by his words; to ready disciples he ought to set forth the commands of God in words, but to the hard of heart, and to the simple-minded he ought to illustrate the divine precepts in his deeds. And all things which he has taught his disciples to be wrong, let him demonstrate in his action that they should not be done, lest sometime God should say to him, a sinner: "Why dost thou declare my statutes or take my testimony in thy mouth? Thou hast hated instruction and cast My word behind thee"; and again: "Thou who hast seen the mote in thy brother's eyes, hast not seen the beam in thine own eye."

Let him not be a respecter of persons in the monastery. Let not one be loved more than another, unless he shall have found someone to be better than another in good deeds and in obedience; let not a freeman be preferred to one coming from servitude, unless there be some good and reasonable cause; but if according to the dictates of justice it shall have seemed best to the abbot, let him do this with anyone of any rank whatsoever; otherwise let each keep his own place, since, whether bond or free, we are all one in Christ, and under one God we bear the same burden of service, for there is no respect of persons with God; only in this regard are we distinguished with him if we are found better and more humble than others in our good deeds. Therefore let his love for all be the same, and let one discipline be put upon all according to merit. . . .

ABOUT CALLING THE BROTHERS TO COUNCIL

Whenever anything especial is to be done in the monastery, the abbot shall convoke the whole body and himself set forth the matter at issue. And after listening to the advice of the brothers, he shall consider it by himself, and shall do what he shall have judged most useful. Now we say all should be called to the council, because the Lord often reveals to the younger brother what is best to be done.

But let the brothers give advice with all subjection of humility and not presume to defend boldly what seemed good to them, but rather rely on the judgment of the abbot, and all obey him in what he has judged to be for their welfare. But just as it is fitting that the disciples obey the master, so is it incumbent on him to dispose everything wisely and justly.

Therefore, let all follow the rule of the master in all things, and let no one depart from it rashly; let no one in the monastery follow the desire of his own heart. And let no one strive with his abbot shamelessly either within or without the monastery; and if he shall have presumed to do so, let him be subjected to the regular discipline. And let the abbot himself do all things in the fear of God and in the observance of the rule, knowing that he must without doubt render account unto God, the most just judge, for all his judgments.

If there are any matters of minor importance to be done for the welfare of the monastery, let the abbot take the advice only of the elders, as it is written: "Do all things with counsel, and after it is done thou wilt not repent."

CONCERNING THOSE WHO, BEING OFTEN REBUKED, DO NOT AMEND

If any brother, having frequently been rebuked for any fault, do not amend even after he has been excommunicated, a more severe rebuke shall fall upon him; — that is, the punishment of the lash shall be inflicted upon him. But if he do not even then amend; or, if perchance — which God forbid, — swelled with pride he try even to defend his works: then the abbot shall act as a wise physician. If he have applied the fomentations, the ointments of exhortation, the medicaments of the Divine Scriptures; if he have proceeded to the last blasting of excommunication, or to blows with rods, and if he sees that his efforts avail nothing: let him also — what is greater — call in the prayer of himself and all the brothers for him: that God who can do all things may work a cure upon an infirm brother. But if he be not healed even in this way, then at last the abbot may use the pruning knife, as the apostle says: "Remove evil from you," etc.: lest one diseased sheep contaminate the whole flock.

WHETHER BROTHERS WHO LEAVE THE MONASTERY OUGHT AGAIN TO BE RECEIVED

A brother who goes out, or is cast out, of the monastery for his own fault, if he wish to return, shall first promise every amends for the fault on account of which he departed; and thus he shall be received into the lowest degree — so that thereby his humility may be proved. But if he again depart, up to the third time he shall be received. Knowing that after this every opportunity of return is denied to him.

CONCERNING BOYS UNDER AGE, HOW THEY SHALL BE CORRECTED

Every age or intelligence ought to have its proper bounds. Therefore as often as boys or youths, or those who are less able to understand how great is the punishment of excommunication: as often as such persons offend, they shall either be afflicted with excessive fasts, or coerced with severe blows, that they may be healed.

CONCERNING THE RECEPTION OF GUESTS

All guests who come shall be received as though they were Christ; for He Himself said: "I was a stranger and ye took Me in." And to all, fitting honour shall be shown; but, most of all, to servants of the faith and to pilgrims. When, therefore, a guest is announced, the prior or the brothers shall run to meet him, with every office of love. And first they shall pray together; and thus they shall be joined together in peace. Which kiss of peace shall not first be offered, unless a prayer have preceded; on account of the wiles of the devil. In the salutation itself, moreover, all humility shall be exhibited. In the case of all guests humility shall be exhibited. In the case of all guests arriving or departing: with inclined head, or with prostrating of the whole body upon the ground, Christ, who is also received in them, shall be adored.

▷ The monks gathered together for prayer seven times in the course of the day. Prayers were chanted from set texts.

CONCERNING THE ART OF SINGING

Whereas we believe that there is a divine presence, and that the eyes of the Lord look down everywhere upon the good and the evil: chiefly then, without any doubt, we may believe that this is the case when we are assisting at divine service. Therefore let us always be mindful of what the prophets says: "Serve the Lord in all fear"; and before the face of the Divinity and His angels; and let us so stand and again, "Sing wisely"; and "in the sight of the angels I will sing unto thee." Therefore let us consider how we ought to conduct ourselves and sing that our voice may accord with our intention.

CONCERNING REVERENCE FOR PRAYER

If when to powerful men we wish to suggest anything, we do not presume to do it unless with reverence and humility: how much more should we supplicate with all humility, and devotion of purity, God who is the Lord of all. And let us know that we are heard, not for much speaking, but for purity of heart and compunction of tears. And, therefore, prayer ought to be brief and pure; unless perchance it be prolonged by the influence of the inspiration of the divine grace. When assembled together, then, let the prayer be altogether brief; and, the sign being given by the prior, let us rise together.

CONCERNING THE DAILY MANUAL LABOR

Idleness is the enemy of the soul. And therefore, at fixed times, the brothers ought to be occupied in manual labour; and again, at fixed times, in sacred reading.

CONCERNING HUMILITY

. . . If we wish to attain to the height of the greatest humility, and to that divine exaltation which is attained by the humility of this present life, we must mount by our own acts that ladder which appeared in a dream to Jacob,[1] upon which angels appeared unto him ascending and descending. For that ascent and descent can only be understood by us to be this: to ascend by humility, to descend through pride. . . .

Now the first grade of humility is this: keeping the fear of God before his eyes, let him avoid forgetfulness and ever remember all the precepts of the Lord; and continually consider in his heart that eternal life which is prepared for those who fear God, just as the mockers of God fall into hell. . . .

The fifth grade of humility is this, if one reveals to the abbot in humble confession all the vain imaginings that come into his heart, and all the evil he has done in secret. . . .

This is the eighth grade of humility; if a monk do nothing except what the common rule

[1]Jacob, a patriarch of ancient Israel, had a dream about angels ascending and descending a ladder between heaven and earth; the dream is recounted in the Old Testament.

of the monastery or the examples of his superior urges him to do.

The ninth grade of humility is this: if a monk keep his tongue from speaking and keeping silence speaks only in answer to questions, since the Scripture says that "sin is not escaped by much speaking," and "a talkative man is not established in the earth."

The tenth grade of humility is this, that he be not easily moved nor prompt to laughter, since it is written: "The fool raiseth his voice in laughter."

The eleventh grade of humility is this: if, when the monk speaks, he says few words and those to the point, slowly and without laughter, humbly and gravely; and be not loud of voice, as it is written: "A wise man is known by his few words."

The twelfth grade of humility is this: that a monk conduct himself with humility not only in his heart but also in his bearing, in the sight of all; that is, in the service of God, in the oratory [chapel], in the monastery, in the garden, on the road, in the field; and everywhere, sitting or walking or standing, let him always have his head bowed, and his eyes fixed on the ground. Always mindful of his sins, let him think of himself as being already tried in the great judgment, saying in his heart what that publican, spoken of in the gospel, said with his eyes fixed on the earth: "Lord, I a sinner am not worthy to lift mine eyes to the heavens;" and again with the prophet: "I am bowed down and humbled wheresoever I go." . . .

REVIEW QUESTIONS

1. Describe the governing principles of a Benedictine monastery.
2. Describe the principal daily duties of the monk.
3. Why was humility considered so vital to the vocation of a monk?
4. How did Benedictine monasticism help to form Western cultural values?

---

8 ▾ The Christian World-View

Building on the life and teachings of Jesus as reported in the Gospels and apostolic letters collected in the New Testament, the early Christian thinkers formulated a comprehensive world-view. The Christian view stressed the sinful nature of human beings — their almost unlimited capacity for evildoing. The church taught that only through the gift of God's grace could individuals overcome the consequences of sin and obtain salvation. Christian leaders drew a sharp distinction between a spiritual realm (called the City of God by Saint Augustine) and the secular world (the City of Man), where Christians had to live out their earthly, material existence. Christians were urged to live in the world, but not to live by its values. Rather, they must imitate the ways of Jesus in thought, word, and deed, as interpreted by the authorities of the church.

The task of living a Christian life in a secular world was not easy. Not the least of the problems was how Christians could relate to the political power structure of earthly societies. The task of finding a Christian basis for relations between church and state has been a continuous process since early Christian times. It has had wide repercussions in creating a distinctive Christian view of the legitimate powers of the state.

Saint Augustine
≪ *THE CITY OF GOD* ≫

Augustine (Aurelius Augustinus, A.D. 354–430), bishop of Hippo (now Souk-Ahras in modern Algeria), was one of the great theologians of the early Christian church. He formulated a view of life and of the individual that became definitive for Western Christians until it was partially superseded by the writings of Thomas Aquinas in the thirteenth century. Although Augustine admired the achievements of Socrates and Plato, he could not accept their central premise: that in the search for truth the individual relied on reason alone.

The sacking of Rome by the Visigoths in A.D. 410 shocked the entire Roman world. Pagans blamed the catastrophe on the Christians; by abandoning the old gods, said pagans, Christians had brought down the wrath of heaven on Rome. In reply to these charges, Saint Augustine wrote the *City of God,* setting forth the Christian view of the world and humanity.

The theme of the first group of passages from Augustine's *City of God* is a crucial element in the Christian outlook: that when human beings turn away from God to follow their own desires as Adam and Eve did, they fall into evil and become afflicted with many miseries, which can only be relieved through God's grace.

I have already said, in previous Books, that God had two purposes in deriving all men from one man. His first purpose was to give unity to the human race by the likeness of nature. His second purpose was to bind mankind by the bond of peace, through blood relationship, into one harmonious whole. I have said further that no member of this race would ever have died had not the first two [Adam and Eve] — one created from nothing and the second from the first — merited this death by disobedience. The sin which they committed was so great that it impaired all human nature — in this sense, that the nature has been transmitted to posterity with a propensity to sin and a necessity to die. . . .

When a man lives "according to man" and not "according to God" he is like the Devil. . . .

When man lives according to himself, that is to say, according to human ways and not according to God's will, then surely he lives according to falsehood. Man himself, of course, is not a lie, since God who is his Author and Creator could not be the Author and Creator of a lie. Rather, man has been so constituted in truth that he was meant to live not according to himself but to Him who made him — that is, he was meant to do the will of God rather than his own. It is a lie not to live as a man was created to live.

Man indeed desires happiness even when he does so live as to make happiness impossible. . . . The happiness of man can come not from himself but only from God, and that to live according to oneself is to sin, and to sin is to lose God. . . .

Moreover, our first parents [Adam and Eve] only fell openly into the sin of disobedience because, secretly, they had begun to be guilty. Actually, their bad deed could not have been done had not bad will preceded it; what is more, the root of their bad will was nothing else than pride. For, "pride is the beginning of all sin." And what is pride but an appetite for inordinate exaltation? Now, exaltation is inordinate when the soul cuts itself off from the very Source [God] to which it should keep close and somehow makes itself and becomes an end to itself. This takes place when the soul becomes inordinately pleased with itself, and such self-pleasing occurs when the soul falls away from the unchangeable Good which ought to please the soul far more than the soul can please itself. Now, this falling away is the soul's own doing, for, if the will had merely remained firm in the love of that higher immutable Good which lighted its mind into knowledge and warmed its will into love, it would not have turned away in search of satisfaction in itself and, by so doing, have lost that light and warmth. And thus Eve would not have believed that the serpent's lie was true, nor would Adam have preferred the will of his wife to the will of God. . . .

This life of ours — if a life so full of such great ills can properly be called a life — bears witness to the fact that, from its very start, the race of mortal men has been a race condemned. Think, first, of that dreadful abyss of ignorance from which all error flows and so engulfs the sons of Adam in a darksome pool that no one can escape without the toll of toils and tears and fears. Then, take our very love for all those things that prove so vain and poisonous and breed so many heartaches, troubles, griefs, and fears; such insane joys in discord, strife, and war; such wrath and plots of enemies, deceivers, sycophants; such fraud and theft and robbery; such perfidy and pride, envy and ambition, homicide and murder, cruelty and savagery, lawlessness and lust; all the shameless passions of the impure — fornication and adultery, incest and unnatural sins, rape and countless other uncleannesses too nasty to be mentioned; the sins against religion — sacrilege and heresy, blasphemy and perjury; the iniquities against our neighbors — calumnies and cheating, lies and false witness, violence to persons and property; the injustices of the courts and the innumerable other miseries and maladies that fill the world, yet escape attention.

It is true that it is wicked men who do such things, but the source of all such sins is that radical canker [sinfulness] in the mind and will that is innate in every son of Adam. . . .

Yet, for all this blight of ignorance and folly, fallen man has not been left without some ministries of Providence, nor has God, in His anger, shut up His mercies. There are still within the reach of man himself, if only he will pay the price of toil and trouble, the twin resources of law and education. With the one, he can make war on human passion; with the other, he can keep the light of learning lit even in the darkness of our native ignorance. . . .

From this all but hell of unhappiness here on earth, nothing can save us but the grace of Jesus Christ, who is our Saviour, Lord and God. In fact, the very meaning of the name, Jesus, is Saviour, and when we say "save" we mean, especially, that He saves us from passing from the misery of this mortal life to a still more miserable condition, which is not so much a life as death. . . .

▷ Augustine saw a conflict between the earthly city, visible, temporal, and corrupt, and the City of God, invisible, eternal, and perfect. Those Christians favored with God's grace lived in this earthly city as strangers and pilgrims passing through on their journey to their true homeland, the heavenly kingdom. The fate of the earthly city was of no ultimate concern to these Christians. For Augustine, this earthly world represented the forces of evil that would finally be destroyed at the end of time, when Christ would come again.

What we see, then, is that two societies have issued from two kinds of love. Worldly society has flowered from a selfish love which dared to despise even God, whereas the communion of saints is rooted in a love of God that is ready to trample on self. In a word, this latter relies on the Lord, whereas the other boasts that it can get along by itself. The city of man seeks the praise of men, whereas the height of glory for the other is to hear God in the witness of conscience. The one lifts up its head in its own boasting; the other says to God: "Thou art my glory, thou liftest up my head."

In the city of the world both the rulers themselves and the people they dominate are dominated by the lust for domination; whereas in the

City of God all citizens serve one another in charity, whether they serve by the responsibilities of office or by the duties of obedience. The one city loves its leaders as symbols of its own strength; the other says to its God: "I love thee, O Lord, my strength." Hence, even the wise men in the city of man live according to man, and their only goal has been the goods of their bodies or of the mind or of both; though some of them have reached a knowledge of God, "they did not glorify him as God or give thanks but became vain in their reasonings, and their senseless minds have been darkened. For while professing to be wise" (that is to say, while glorying in their own wisdom, under the domination of pride), "they have become fools, and they have changed the glory of the incorruptible God for an image made like to corruptible man and to birds and four-footed beasts and creeping things" (meaning that they either led their people, or imitated them, in adoring idols shaped like these things), "and they worshipped and served the creature rather than the Creator who is blessed forever." In the City of God, on the contrary, there is no merely human wisdom, but there is a piety which worships the true God as He should be worshiped and has as its goal that reward of all holiness whether in the society of saints on earth or in that of angels of heaven, which is "that God may be all in all." . . .

▷ Augustine says that history reveals the intermingling of the City of God and the City of Man in time and space, and the incessant combat between the partisans of these two cities. This struggle will continue until time itself is annulled by God when Christ returns — and the saints are separated from sinners at the Last Judgment. Then the saints will join Jesus and be with him for eternity, and the sinners will be separated from God and confined to hell, also for eternity.

. . . In the eternal City of God, each and all of the citizens are personally immortal with an immortality which the holy angels never lost and which even human beings can come to share. This is to be achieved by the supreme omnipotence of the Creator, the Founder of the City. . . .

Who can measure the happiness of heaven, where no evil at all can touch us, no good will be out of reach; where life is to be one long laud extolling God, who will be all in all; where there will be no weariness to call for rest, no need to call for toil, no place for any energy but praise. . . .

. . . There will be such poise, such grace, such beauty as become a place where nothing unbecoming can be found. Wherever the spirit wills, there, in a flash, will the body be. Nor will the spirit ever will anything unbecoming either to itself or to the body.

In heaven, all glory will be true glory, since no one could ever err in praising too little or too much. True honor will never be denied where due, never be given where undeserved, and, since none but the worthy are permitted there, no one will unworthily ambition glory. Perfect peace will reign, since nothing in ourselves or in any others could disturb this peace.

Saint Benedict of Nursia
THE CHRISTIAN WAY OF LIFE

In the following selection from his monastic book of rules, Saint Benedict of Nursia advises his monks on the attitudes and conduct necessary to live a virtuous Christian life.

WHAT ARE THE INSTRUMENTS OF GOOD WORKS

In the first place, to love the Lord God with the whole heart, whole soul, whole strength, then his neighbor as himself.

Then not to kill, not to commit adultery, not to steal, not to covet, not to bear false witness, to honor all men, and what anyone would not have done to him, let him not do to another. To deny himself, that he may follow Christ, to chasten the body, to renounce luxuries, to love fasting. To relieve the poor, to clothe the naked, to visit the sick, to bury the dead, to help in tribulation, to console the afflicted.

To make himself a stranger to the affairs of the world, to prefer nothing before the love of Christ, not to give way to anger, not to bear any grudge, not to harbour deceit in the heart, not to forsake charity. Not to swear, lest haply he perjure himself, to utter truth from his heart and his mouth. Not to return evil for evil, not to do injuries, but rather to bear them patiently, to love his enemies, not to curse again those who curse him, but rather to bless them, to endure persecution for righteousness' sake. Not to be proud, not given to wine, not gluttonous, not addicted to sleep, not slothful, not given to murmur, not a slanderer. To commit his hope to God; when he sees anything good in himself to attribute it to God, and not to himself, but let him always know that which is evil is his own doing, and impute it to himself. To fear the day of judgment, to dread hell, to desire eternal life with all spiritual longing, to have the expectation of death every day before his eyes. To watch over his actions at all times, to know certainly that in all places the eye of God is upon him; those evil thoughts which come into his heart to dash to pieces on Christ, and to make them known to his spiritual senior. To keep his lips from evil and wicked discourse, not to be fond of much talking, not to speak vain words or such as provoke laughter, not to love much or violent laughter. To give willing attention to the sacred readings, to pray frequently every day, to confess his past sins to God, in prayer, with tears and groanings; from thence forward to reform as to those sins.

Not to fulfill the desires of the flesh, to hate his own will, in all things to obey the commands of the abbot, even though he himself (which God forbid) should do otherwise, remembering our Lord's commands: "What they say, do; but what they do, do ye not." Not to desire to be called a saint before he is one, but first to be one that he may be truly called one; every day to fulfill the commands of God in his deeds, to love chastity, to hate no one, not to have jealousy or envy, not to love contention, to avoid self-conceit; to reverence seniors, to love juniors, to pray for enemies in the love of Christ, to be reconciled with his adversary, before the going down of the sun, and never to despair of the mercy of God. . . .

Pope Gelasius I
CHURCH AND STATE

Emperor Constantine's conversion to Christianity in the early fourth century dramatically changed the Christian church's relationship to the Roman state. After nearly three centuries of periodic persecution, the church now enjoyed imperial patronage, and Christianity was an accepted religion. Though still not a majority of the population, the Christian community grew rapidly through the fourth century and gained new power.

Finally, about 392, Emperor Theodosius I (A.D. 379–395) outlawed the tradi-

tional pagan cults and established Christianity as the official religion of the Roman state. Though welcome, this new status created problems for the church, which was treated more and more as if it were a department of the imperial government. Interference in matters of doctrine and discipline by imperial rulers were resisted by a clergy used to internal freedom of action, who recognized no spiritual authority but Christ and the Scriptures.

In the late fifth century, Pope Gelasius I (492–496), the bishop of Rome, tried to establish clear boundaries between the legitimate sphere of authority of the state and that of the church. In the following letter to the Emperor Anastasius (491–518), written in 494, Pope Gelasius I established the church's theoretical ground rules for future church-state relations.

. . . Two there are, august emperor, by which this world is chiefly ruled, the sacred authority *(auctoritas)* of the priesthood and the royal power *(potestas)*. Of these the responsibility of the priests is more weighty in so far as they will answer for the kings of men themselves at the divine judgement. You know, most clement son, that, although you take precedence over all mankind in dignity, nevertheless you piously bow the neck to those who have charge of divine affairs and seek from them the means of your salvation, and hence you realize that, in the order of religion, in matters concerning the reception and right administration of the heavenly sacraments, you ought to submit yourself rather than rule, and that in these matters you should depend on their judgment rather than seek to bend them to your will. For if the bishops themselves, recognizing that the imperial office was conferred on you by divine disposition, obey your laws so far as the sphere of public order is concerned lest they seem to obstruct your decrees in mundane matters, with what zeal, I ask you, ought you to obey those who have been charged with administering the sacred mysteries? Moreover, just as no light risk attends pontiffs[1] who keep silent in matters concerning the service of God, so too no little danger threatens those who show scorn — which God forbid — when they ought to obey. And if the hearts of the faithful should be submitted to all priests in general who rightly administer divine things, how much more should assent be given to the bishop of that see[2] which the Most High [God] wished to be pre-eminent over all priests, and which the devotion of the whole church has honored ever since. As Your Piety is certainly well aware, no one can ever raise himself by purely human means to the privilege and place of him whom the voice of Christ has set before all, whom the church has always venerated and held in devotion as its primate.[3] The things which are established by divine judgement can be assailed by human presumption; they cannot be overthrown by anyone's power.

[1]Originally designating a Roman magistrate, the Latin word *pontifex* became applied to any priest. Here it refers to bishops.

[2]A see is a bishop's center of authority or community, over which he has power of decision in religious matters.

[3]The primate (originally from a Latin word for first) is the "first" bishop: that is, the bishop of Rome, who, as the successor of Saint Peter, was here recognized as the presiding bishop over the entire Christian church.

REVIEW QUESTIONS

1. According to Saint Augustine, why did God choose to have the human race descend from a common ancestor, Adam?

2. What did Augustine believe the consequences of Adam's sin to be?
3. What did Augustine say that the true focus of a person's life should be?
4. For Augustine, what happened when a soul cut itself off from God?
5. What kind of world did Augustine see resulting from human sinfulness?
6. Where was the true hope of human happiness, according to Augustine?
7. Describe the "earthly city" as Augustine outlined it.
8. Describe the "heavenly city" as described by Augustine.
9. What were the sources used by Saint Benedict in listing the "instruments of good works"?
10. Were Benedict's counsels directed only to his monks, or did they have more general validity?
11. What was Pope Gelasius' view of the governance of the world?
12. Why did Gelasius think that priests had greater responsibilities than secular rulers?
13. Upon what did the pope believe his authority ultimately depended?
14. What argument did the pope make to persuade the emperor that divine affairs were not the business of an emperor?
15. What principle did Gelasius propose for church-state relations?

Part Two

The Middle Ages

The Early Middle Ages

The establishment of Germanic kingdoms in the fifth and sixth centuries on Roman lands marked the end of the ancient world and the start of the Middle Ages, a period that spanned a thousand years. During the Middle Ages the center of Western civilization shifted northward from the lands bordering the Mediterranean Sea to parts of Europe that Greco-Roman civilization had barely penetrated.

The Early Middle Ages (500–1050) marked an age of transition. The humanist culture that characterized the Greco-Roman past had disintegrated, and a new civilization was emerging in Latin Christendom, which covered western and central Europe. Medieval civilization consisted of a blending of the remnants of Greco-Roman culture with Germanic customs and Christian principles. The central element was Christianity; the Christian view of a transcendent God and the quest for salvation pervaded the medieval outlook, and the church was the dominant institution.

During the Early Middle Ages, Latin Christendom was a pioneer society struggling to overcome invasions, a breakdown of central authority, a decline in trade and town life, and a deterioration of highly refined culture. The Latin Christian church, centered in Rome and headed by the pope, progressively gave form and unity to the new civilization. Christian clergy preserved some of the learning of the ancient world, which they incorporated into the Christian outlook. Dedicated missionaries converted various Germanic, Celtic, and Slavic peoples to Latin Christianity. From Italy to the North Sea and from Ireland to Poland, an emerging Christian tradition was providing unity to people with differing cultural traditions.

The center of emerging medieval civilization was the kingdom of the Franks, located in Gaul (France) and western Germany. Migrating westward from their homeland in the valley of the Rhine River, the Germanic Franks conquered Roman Gaul in the fifth and sixth centuries. Charlemagne (768–814), the greatest of the Frankish rulers, added large areas of Germany and Italy to his kingdom. On Christmas Day in the year 800, Pope Leo III crowned Charlemagne emperor of the Romans, a sign that the memory of Imperial Rome still persisted. Without Roman law, a professional civil service, and great cities serving as centers of trade, however, Charlemagne's empire was only a pale

CHARLEMAGNE (768–814), being crowned Holy Roman emperor by Pope Leo III at St. Peter's Basilica in Rome on Christmas Day, 800 B.C. This fifteenth-century illustration shows Charles, humbly kneeling before the pope, in a medieval interpretation of the event. (*Giraudon/Art Resource, N.Y.*)

shadow of the Roman Empire. Rather, the crowning of a German king as emperor of the Romans by the pope signified something new: the intermingling of Germanic, Christian, and Roman elements that came to characterize medieval Latin Christendom.

Charlemagne's empire rested more on the strength of the emperor's personality than it did on viable institutions. Charlemagne's heirs were unable to hold the empire together; power passed gradually into the hands of large landholders, who exercised governmental authority in their own regions. Also contributing to this decline in centralized authority were devastating raids by Muslims from Spain, North Africa, and Mediterranean islands; Northmen from Scandinavia; and Magyars from western Asia. Europe had entered an age of feudalism, in which public authority was dispersed among lords and held as if it were private inheritable property.

Feudalism rested on an economic base known as manorialism. Although family farms owned by free peasants still existed, the essential agricultural arrangement in medieval society was the village community (manor), headed by a lord or his steward and farmed by serfs, who were bound to the land. A lord controlled at least one manorial village; great lords might possess hundreds. Much land was held by various clerical institutions; the church's manors were similar to those run by nonclerics.

Feudalism was an improvised response to the challenge posed by ineffectual central authority, and it provided some order and law during a period of breakdown. Medieval feudal practices were not uniform but differed from region to region. In later centuries, when kings reasserted their authority and fashioned strong central governments, the power of lords declined.

The medieval civilization of Latin Christendom arose on the ruins of the western provinces of the Roman Empire. The eastern provinces, however, wealthier, more populous, and less burdened by invaders, survived the fall of the Roman Empire in the West. From their capital at Constantinople, Roman emperors continued to rule the eastern Roman Empire, called the Byzantine Empire, until the middle of the fifteenth century. While Germanic peoples and western Slavs were embracing Latin Christianity, Byzantine missionaries were converting southern and eastern Slavs, including Russians, to Greek (or Orthodox) Christianity.

During the Early Middle Ages, Byzantine civilization was far more advanced than Latin Christendom. At a time when urban life had dwindled in the West, Constantinople was a great metropolis and center of high culture. And yet it was Latin Christendom, not Byzantium, that eventually produced the modern world.

I ▾ Converting the Germanic Peoples to Christianity

From its beginnings, Christianity sought to carry to all peoples its offer of salvation through faith in Jesus. After Christianity had become the religion of the Roman state, pagan cults were suppressed. When the western Roman provinces fell under the power of invading Germanic tribes, Christian Romans faced the task of converting their new rulers to their religion.

The ability of the Christian religion to penetrate and absorb alien cultures while preserving its own core beliefs was continually to be tested in the Early Middle Ages. Roman Britain had been invaded in the fifth century by various tribes from northwestern Germany, Denmark, and the Netherlands. Among these tribes were the Angles (from which the word ***English*** is derived), the Saxons, and the Jutes. The Romano-Britons, who were Christians, were forced to retreat westward to occupy what became the Celtic-speaking Christian principalities of Cornwall, Wales, and Cumberland. Pagan Germans ruled the rest of England.

Bede
≪ HISTORY OF THE ENGLISH CHURCH AND PEOPLE ≫

The English monk called the Venerable Bede (673–735), in his ***History of the English Church and People,*** cites a letter from Pope Gregory I (the Great) written in 601. In the letter, the pope forwarded instructions for Augustine of Canterbury, whom he had appointed leader of a mission to convert the English to Christianity. He wrote his emissary to tell Augustine to win the favor of the pagan English by accommodating the requirements of Christian beliefs to the existing non-Christian cultural practices, as the first excerpt shows.

Conducting missionary work among the Germanic peoples was almost impossible without the permission of their rulers. Since Germanic kings were responsible for fostering the goodwill of the tribal gods toward their people, any change in religion held a political as well as a religious connotation, as the second passage reveals.

When these [missionaries] had left, the holy father Gregory sent after them letters worthy of our notice, which show most clearly his unwearying interest in the salvation of our nation. The letter runs as follows:

"To our well loved son Abbot[1] Mellitus: Gregory, servant of the servants of God.

"Since the departure of yourself and your companions, we have been somewhat anxious, because we have received no news of the success of your journey. Therefore, when by God's help you reach our most reverend brother, Bishop Augustine,[2] we wish you to inform him that we have been giving careful thought to the affairs of the English, and have come to the conclusion that the temples of the idols in that country should on no account be destroyed. He is to destroy the idols, but the temples themselves are to be aspersed [sprinkled] with holy water, altars set up, and relics enclosed in them. For if these temples are well built, they are to be purified from devil-worship,[3] and dedicated to the service of the true God. In this way, we hope that the people, seeing that its temples are not destroyed, may abandon idolatry and resort to these places as before, and may come to know and adore the true God. And since they have a custom of sacrificing many oxen to devils, let some other solemnity be substituted in its place, such as a day of Dedication[4] or the Festivals of the holy martyrs [saints' days] whose relics are enshrined there. On such occasions they might well construct shelters of boughs for themselves around the churches that were once temples, and celebrate the solemnity with devout feasting. They are no longer to sacrifice beasts to the Devil, but they may kill them for food to the praise of God, and give thanks to the Giver of all gifts for His bounty. If the people are allowed some worldly pleasures in this way, they will more readily come to desire the joys of the spirit. For it is certainly impossible to eradicate all errors from obstinate minds at one stroke, and whoever wishes to climb to a mountain top climbs gradually step by step, and not in one leap. It was in this way that God revealed Himself to the Israelite people in Egypt, permitting the sacrifices formerly offered to the Devil to be offered thenceforward to Himself instead. So He bade them sacrifice beasts to Him, so that, once they became enlightened, they might abandon a wrong conception of sacrifice, and adopt the right. For, while they were to continue to offer beasts as before, they were to offer them to God instead of to idols, thus transforming the idea of sacrifice. Of your kindness, you are to inform our brother Augustine of this policy, so that he may consider how he may best implement it on the spot. God keep you safe, my very dear son." . . .

▷ In this passage from Bede's history, King Edwin (585–633) of Northumbria, one of seven kingdoms of Britain, seeks his leading councillors' approval before converting to Christianity. Some motives for accepting Christianity are revealed in the royal council's discussion.

When Paulinus[5] had spoken, the king answered that he was both willing and obliged to accept the Faith which he taught, but said that he must discuss the matter with his principal advisers and friends, so that if they were in agreement, they might all be cleansed [baptized] together in Christ the Fount of Life. Paulinus agreed, and the king kept his promise. He

[1]The elected head of a monastic community, the abbot was supposed to rule justly and paternally following the constitution (rule) of the community.

[2]Augustine (not to be confused with Augustine of Hippo) was an Italian monk who was sent in 597 to convert the English to Christianity. He established his see (bishopric) at Canterbury and founded others at Rochester and London, successfully directing missionary activity in the southern part of what is now England.

[3]As Christianity was monotheistic, it denied the validity of any other gods. Therefore, Christians customarily designated the pagan deities as "devils," or evil spirits.

[4]The anniversary of the dedication or consecration of a church was celebrated as a holiday.

[5]Puulinus was a Roman monk sent in 601 by Pope Gregory I to aid Augustine of Canterbury. In 627 he was consecrated bishop of York, where he baptized King Edwin of Northumbria.

summoned a council of the wise men, and asked each in turn his opinion of this new faith and new God being proclaimed.

Coifi, the High Priest, replied without hesitation: "Your Majesty, let us give careful consideration to this new teaching, for I frankly admit that, in my experience, the religion that we have hitherto professed seems valueless and powerless. None of your subjects has been more devoted to the service of the gods than myself, yet there are many to whom you show greater favour, who receive greater honours, and who are more successful in all their undertakings. Now, if the gods had any power, they would surely have favoured myself, who have been more zealous in their service. Therefore, if on examination these new teachings are found to be better and more effectual, let us not hesitate to accept them."

Another of the king's chief men signified his agreement with this prudent argument, and went on to say: "Your Majesty, when we compare the present life of man with that time of which we have no knowledge, it seems to me like the swift flight of a lone sparrow through the banqueting-hall where you sit in the winter months to dine with your thanes[6] and counsellors. Inside there is a comforting fire to warm the room; outside, the wintry storms of snow and rain are raging. This sparrow flies swiftly in through one door of the hall, and out through another. While he is inside, he is safe from the winter storms; but after a few moments of comfort, he vanishes from sight into the darkness whence he came. Similarly, man appears on earth for a little while, but we know nothing of what went before this life, and what follows. Therefore if this new teaching can reveal any more certain knowledge, it seems only right that we should follow it." The other elders and counsellors of the king, under God's guidance, gave the same advice.

Coifi then added that he wished to hear Paulinus' teaching about God in greater detail; and when, at the king's bidding, this had been given, the High Priest said: "I have long realized that there is nothing in what we worshipped, for the more diligently I sought after truth in our religion, the less I found. I now publicly confess that this teaching clearly reveals truths that will afford us the blessings of life, salvation, and eternal happiness. Therefore, your Majesty, I submit that the temples and altars that we have dedicated to no advantage be immediately desecrated and burned." In short, the king granted blessed Paulinus full permission to preach, renounced idolatry, and professed his acceptance of the Faith of Christ. And when he asked the High Priest who should be the first to profane the altars and shrines of the idols, together with the enclosures that surrounded them, Coifi replied: "I will do this myself, for now that the true God has granted me knowledge, who more suitably than I can set a public example, and destroy the idols that I worshipped in ignorance?" So he formally renounced his empty superstitions, and asked the king to give him arms and a stallion — for hitherto it had not been lawful for the High Priest to carry arms, or to ride anything but a mare — and, thus equipped, he set out to destroy the idols. Girded with a sword and with a spear in his hand, he mounted the king's stallion and rode up to the idols. When the crowd saw him, they thought he had gone mad, but without hesitation, as soon as he reached the temple, he cast a spear into it and profaned it. Then, full of joy at his knowledge of the worship of the true God, he told his companions to set fire to the temple and its enclosures and destroy them. The site where these idols once stood is still shown, not far east of York,[7] beyond the river Derwent, and is known as Goodmanham. Here it was that the High Priest, inspired by the true God, desecrated and destroyed the altars that he had himself dedicated.

So King Edwin, with all the nobility and a

---

[6]A thane ranked just below a nobleman.

[7]York (founded by the Romans as Eboracum) was the principal town of northern Britain during the Middle Ages. It became an archbishopric (major see) in the early eighth century, and later a major political center during the period of Viking rule.

large number of humbler folk, accepted the Faith and were washed in the cleansing waters of Baptism in the eleventh year of his reign, which was the year 627, and about one hundred and eighty years after the first arrival of the English in Britain.

Einhard
FORCIBLE CONVERSION UNDER CHARLEMAGNE

Although most conversions were based on peaceful persuasion or a voluntary act of consent, occasionally Christianity was imposed by force. Thus, after his long wars against the pagan Saxons, Charlemagne required the Saxons to adopt Christianity and be assimilated into the Frankish kingdom. In his biography of Charlemagne, the Frankish historian Einhard (770–840) described this event.

No war ever undertaken by the Frank nation was carried on with such persistence and bitterness, or cost so much labor, because the Saxons,[1] like almost all the tribes of Germany, were a fierce people, given to the worship of devils, and hostile to our religion, and did not consider it dishonorable to transgress and violate all law, human and divine. Then there were peculiar circumstances that tended to cause a breach of peace every day. Except in a few places, where large forests or mountain ridges intervened and made the bounds certain, the line between ourselves and the Saxons passed almost in its whole extent through an open country, so that there was no end to the murders, thefts, and arsons on both sides. In this way the Franks became so embittered that they at last resolved to make reprisals no longer, but to come to open war with the Saxons [in 772]. Accordingly war was begun against them, and was waged for thirty-three successive years with great fury; more, however, to the disadvantage of the Saxons than of the Franks. It could doubtless have been brought to an end sooner, had it not been for the faithlessness of the Saxons. It is hard to say how often they were conquered, and humbly submitting to the King, promised to do what was enjoined upon them, gave without hesitation the required hostages, and received the officers sent them from the King. They were sometimes so much weakened and reduced that they promised to renounce the worship of devils, and to adopt Christianity, but they were no less ready to violate these terms than prompt to accept them, so that it is impossible to tell which came easier to them to do; scarcely a year passed from the beginning of the war without such changes on their part. But the King did not suffer his high purpose and steadfastness — firm alike in good and evil fortune — to be wearied by any fickleness on their part, or to be turned from the task that he had undertaken; on the contrary, he never allowed their faithless behavior to go unpunished, but either took the field against them in person, or sent his counts[2] with an army to wreak vengeance and exact righteous satisfaction. At last, after conquering and subduing all who had offered resistance, he took ten thousand of those that lived on the banks of the Elbe,[3] and settled them, with their wives and children, in many different bodies here and there in Gaul and Germany. The war that had lasted so many years was at length ended by their acceding to the

---

[1]The Saxons were members of a Germanic tribe living between the Rhine and Elbe rivers.

[2]Counts were royal officials exercising the king's authority in districts called counties.

[3]The Elbe River, in central Germany, flows northwestward into the North Sea.

terms offered by the King; which were renunciation of their national religious customs and the worship of devils, acceptance of the sacraments of the Christian faith and religion, and union with the Franks to form one people.

REVIEW QUESTIONS

1. How did Pope Gregory hope to ease the transition of the English from paganism to Christian belief and practice?
2. What pagan practices did Pope Gregory forbid?
3. Why did the pagan priest Ciofi recommend that conversion to Christianity ought to be considered seriously by the king and his council?
4. What other considerations motivated the royal councilors to favor adopting Christianity?
5. What was the significance of Ciofi's act of desecration of the Northumbrian gods' temple?
6. What factors contributed to the hostility between Saxons and Franks?
7. What measures did Charlemagne undertake to eliminate the threat of the Saxons?
8. What role did politics play in the conversion of the Germanic peoples to Christianity?

---

2 ▾ The Transmission of Learning

Learning, which had been in retreat in the Late Roman Empire, continued its decline in the unsettled conditions following Rome's demise. The old Roman schools closed, and many scientific and literary works of the ancient world were either lost or neglected. Knowledge of the Greek language in western Europe virtually disappeared, and except for clerics, few people could read or write Latin. The few learned people generally did not engage in original thought but preserved and transmitted surviving elements of the Greco-Roman past.

One such scholar was Cassiodorus (c. 490–575), who served three Ostrogothic kings in Italy. Cassiodorus wrote theological treatises and the twelve-volume *History of the Goths,* but his principal achievement was collecting Greek and Latin manuscripts. Like other Christian scholars before and after him, Cassiodorus maintained that the study of secular literature was an aid to understanding sacred writings. He retired to a monastery where he fostered the monastic practice of copying Christian and pagan manuscripts. Without this effort of monks, many important secular and Christian writings might have perished.

Cassiodorus
THE MONK AS SCRIBE

In the following reading from his Introduction to *Divine and Human Readings,* Cassiodorus gave his views on the importance of the monastic scribe's vocation. Cassiodorus believed that through his pen the scribe preaches the word of God and is inspired by his text to know God more fully.

ON SCRIBES AND THE REMEMBERING OF CORRECT SPELLING

1. I admit that among those of your tasks which require physical effort that of the scribe,[1] if he writes correctly, appeals most to me; and it appeals, perhaps not without reason, for by reading the Divine Scriptures he wholesomely instructs his own mind and by copying the precepts of the Lord he spreads them far and wide. Happy his design, praiseworthy his zeal, to preach to men with the hand alone, to unleash tongues with the fingers, to give salvation silently to mortals, and to fight against the illicit temptations of the devil with pen and ink. Every word of the Lord written by the scribe is a wound inflicted on Satan. And so, though seated in one spot, with the dissemination of his work he travels through different provinces. The product of his toil is read in holy places; people hear the means by which they may turn themselves away from base desire and serve the Lord with heart undefiled. Though absent, he labors at his task. I cannot deny that he may receive a renovation of life from these many blessings, if only he accomplishes things of this sort, not with a vain show of ambition, but with upright zeal. Man multiplies the heavenly words, and in a certain metaphorical sense, if one may so express himself, that which the virtue of the Holy Trinity utters is written by a trinity of fingers. O sight glorious to those who contemplate it carefully! With gliding pen the heavenly words are copied so that the devil's craft, by means of which he caused the head of the Lord to be struck during His passion, may be destroyed. They deserve praise too for seeming in some way to imitate the action of the Lord, who, though it was expressed figuratively, wrote His law with the use of His all-powerful finger. Much indeed is there to be said about such a distinguished art, but it is enough to mention the fact that those men are called scribes *(librarii)* who serve zealously the just scales *(libra)* of the Lord.

2. But lest in performing this great service copyists introduce faulty words with letters changed or lest an untutored corrector fail to know how to correct mistakes, let them read the works of ancient authors on orthography [spelling]. . . .

. . . I have collected as many of these works as possible with eager curiosity. . . . [If you] read [them] with unremitting zeal, they will completely free you from the fog of ignorance, so that what was previously unknown may become for the most part very well known.

3. In addition to these things we have provided workers skilled in bookbinding, in order that a handsome external form may clothe the beauty of sacred letters; in some measure, perhaps, we imitate the example in the parable of the Lord,* who amid the glory of the heavenly banquet has clothed in wedding garments those whom He judges worthy of being invited to the table. And for the binders, in fitting manner, unless I err, we have represented various styles of binding in a single codex,[2] that he who so desires may choose for himself the type of cover he prefers.

4. We have also prepared cleverly constructed lamps which preserve their illuminating flames and feed their own fire and without human attendance abundantly maintain a very full clearness of most copious light; and the fat oil in them does not fail, although it is burned continually with a bright flame.

5. Nor have we by any means allowed you to be unacquainted with the hour meters which have been discovered to be very useful to the human race. I have provided a sundial for you for bright days and a water clock which points

---

[1]Scribes were persons trained to copy by hand the texts of books, or to take dictation.

*Matthew 22:11.

[2]A codex consists of the rectangular sheets on which scribes have written, bound together on one side, like a modern book. Invented in the late first century A.D., the codex gradually replaced scrolls as the predominant way to store written texts.

out the hour continually both day and night, since on some days the bright sun is frequently absent, and rain water passes in marvellous fashion into the ground, because the fiery force of the sun, regulated from above, fails. And so the art of man has brought into harmony elements which are naturally separated; the hour meters are so reliable that you consider an act of either as having been arranged by messengers. These instruments, then, have been provided in order that the soldiers of Christ,[3] warned by most definite signs, may be summoned to the carrying out of their divine task as if by sounding trumpets.

[3]"Soldiers of Christ" is a metaphor to describe the monks in their vocation.

REVIEW QUESTIONS

1. Why was it necessary for a monk to be literate?
2. Why did Cassiodorus consider the vocation of a monastic scribe both holy and praiseworthy?
3. What were some of the work conditions under which a monastic scribe copied and produced a book?
4. Why were books decorated with both paintings and handsome bindings?
5. What contribution did the monasteries make to the development of medieval culture?

---

3 ▾ The Carolingian Renaissance

The Early Middle Ages witnessed a marked decline in learning and the arts. Patronage of both the liberal and the visual arts by the old Roman aristocracy was not widely copied by the Germanic ruling class that replaced the Romans. Support for learning and the arts shifted from secular to ecclesiastical patrons. Monasteries became the new centers for intellectual and artistic activities, and Christian themes and values almost entirely displaced the worldly values of Greco-Roman culture.

Under the patronage of Charlemagne (742–814), the great Frankish emperor, a conscious revival of classical Greek and Roman learning and the visual arts occurred. Charlemagne realized that his great empire could not be effectively governed without a cadre of highly literate and widely knowledgeable administrators. To educate the leaders of the Frankish empire, Charlemagne sponsored a number of reforms designed to improve the educational institutions and the quality of literacy and learning in his realm. At court, he completely reformed the school conducted for the children of his family and his courtiers and recruited the best scholars in western Europe to staff it. Among these scholars was the English deacon Alcuin of York (735–804), who became his chief advisor on educational and religious affairs. They aimed at restoring classical learning to serve the needs of the new Christian culture.

Einhard
CHARLEMAGNE'S APPRECIATION OF LEARNING

The revival of classical learning and the visual arts under Charlemagne is called the Carolingian Renaissance, a cultural awakening that helped shape medieval civilization. One of Charlemagne's most significant decisions was ordering the making of copies of old manuscripts dating back to Roman times. Much of today's knowledge of Roman learning and literature comes from surviving Carolingian copies of older Latin texts that no longer exist. In the first reading, Charlemagne's biographer Einhard describes western Europe's greatest royal patron since the fall of the western Roman Empire.

Charles [Charlemagne] had the gift of ready and fluent speech, and could express whatever he had to say with the utmost clearness. He was not satisfied with command of his native language merely, but gave attention to the study of foreign ones, and in particular was such a master of Latin that he could speak it as well as his native tongue; but he could understand Greek better than he could speak it. He was so eloquent, indeed, that he might have passed for a teacher of eloquence. He most zealously cultivated the liberal arts, held those who taught them in great esteem, and conferred great honors upon them. He took lessons in grammar of the deacon Peter of Pisa,[1] at that time an aged man. Another deacon, Albin of Britain, surnamed Alcuin, a man of Saxon extraction, who was the greatest scholar of the day, was his teacher in other branches of learning. The King spent much time and labor with him studying rhetoric, dialectics, and especially astronomy; he learned to reckon, and used to investigate the motions of the heavenly bodies most curiously, with an intelligent scrutiny. He also tried to write, and used to keep tablets and blanks in bed under his pillow, that at leisure hours he might accustom his hand to form the letters; however, as he did not begin his efforts in due season, but late in life, they met with ill success.

He cherished with the greatest fervor and devotion the principles of the Christian religion, which had been instilled into him from infancy. Hence it was that he built the beautiful basilica[2] at Aix-la-Chapelle,[3] which he adorned with gold and silver and lamps, and with rails and doors of solid brass. He had the columns and marbles for this structure brought from Rome and Ravenna,[4] for he could not find such as were suitable elsewhere. He was a constant worshipper at this church as long as his health permitted, going morning and evening, even after nightfall, besides attending mass; and he took care that all the services there conducted should be administered with the utmost possible propriety, very often warning the sextons not to let any improper or unclean thing be brought into the building or remain in it. He provided it with a great number of sacred vessels of gold and silver and with such a quantity of clerical robes that not even the doorkeepers

---

[1]Peter of Pisa, a famous grammarian (in Latin, the international language of the Middle Ages), was brought from Italy to teach at the school in Charlemagne's palace. He encouraged interest in pre-Christian classical writing, which influenced the court poets of that era.

[2]A basilica is a rectangular-shaped church, whose main chamber is divided by columns into a central nave and side aisles. There was usually a semi-circular apse at the narrow end facing the east, which was the visual focal point and the location of the main altar.

[3]Aix-la-Chapelle, now Aachen, was Charlemagne's capital. It was located in what is now western Germany, near the Netherlands-Belgium frontier.

[4]Ravenna, in northeastern Italy, was the final capital of the western Roman Empire, in the fifth century; in the sixth and seventh centuries it was the capital of the Byzantine governors of Italy. Ravenna is famous for its magnificent sixth-century churches and mosaic art.

who fill the humblest office in the church were obliged to wear their everyday clothes when in the exercise of their duties. He was at great pains to improve the church reading and psalmody [singing], for he was well skilled in both, although he neither read in public nor sang, except in a low tone and with others.

He was very forward in succoring the poor, and in that gratuitous generosity which the Greeks call alms, so much so that he not only made a point of giving in his own country and his own kingdom, but when he discovered that there were Christians living in poverty in Syria, Egypt, and Africa, at Jerusalem, Alexandria, and Carthage, he had compassion on their wants, and used to send money over the seas to them. . . .

Charlemagne
AN INJUNCTION TO MONASTERIES TO CULTIVATE LETTERS

In a letter to the Abbot Baugulf of Fulda (in Germany), Charlemagne announced his decision to use monasteries as schools for training future clergymen in grammar, writing, and rhetoric.

Charles, by the grace of God, King of the Franks and Lombards and Patrician of the Romans, to Abbot Baugulf and to all the congregation, also to the faithful committed to you, we have directed a loving greeting by our ambassadors in the name of omnipotent God.

Be it known, therefore, to your devotion pleasing to God, that we, together with our faithful, have considered it to be useful that the bishoprics and monasteries entrusted by the favor of Christ to our control, in addition to the [rule] of monastic life and the intercourse of holy religion, . . . also ought to be zealous in [the cultivation of letters], teaching those who by the gift of God are able to learn, according to the capacity of each individual, so that just as the observance of the rule imparts order and grace to honesty of morals, so also zeal in teaching and learning may do the same for sentences, so that those who desire to please God by living rightly should not neglect to please him also by speaking correctly. For it is written: "Either from thy words thou shalt be justified or from thy words thou shalt be condemned."*

For although correct conduct may be better than knowledge, nevertheless knowledge precedes conduct. Therefore, each one ought to study what he desires to accomplish, so that . . . the mind may know more fully what ought to be done, as the tongue hastens in the praises of omnipotent God without the hindrances of errors. For since errors should be shunned by all men, . . . the more they ought to be avoided as far as possible by those who are chosen for this very purpose alone, so that they ought to be the especial servants of truth. For when in the years . . . [past], letters were often written to us from several monasteries in which it was stated that the brethren who dwelt there offered up in our behalf sacred and pious prayers, we have recognized in most of these letters both correct thoughts and uncouth expressions; because what pious devotion dictated faithfully to the mind, the tongue, uneducated on account of the neglect of study, was not able to express in the letter without error. . . . We began to fear lest perchance, as the skill in writing was less, so also the wisdom for understanding the Holy Scriptures might be much less than it rightly ought to be. And we all know well that, although errors of speech are

---

*Matthew, xii. 37.

dangerous, far more dangerous are errors of the understanding. Therefore, we exhort you not only not to neglect the study of letters, but also with most humble mind, pleasing to God, to study earnestly in order that you may be able more easily and more correctly to penetrate the mysteries of the divine Scriptures. Since, moreover, images . . . and similar figures are found in the sacred pages, no one doubts that each one in reading these will understand the spiritual sense more quickly if previously he shall have been fully instructed in the mastery of letters. Such men truly are to be chosen for this work as have both the will and the ability to learn and a desire to instruct others. And may this be done with a zeal as great as the earnestness with which we command it.

REVIEW QUESTIONS

1. Charlemagne was intelligent but ill educated. From your reading, give evidence to support this statement.
2. Why was Charlemagne so anxious to raise the educational standards of all the members of the clergy in his empire?
3. What steps did Charlemagne take to improve the quality of the liturgical services of the Frankish church?
4. In what ways did Einhard convey an image of Charlemagne as a pious and virtuous Christian king? Was Einhard unbiased in his evaluation?
5. Why did Charlemagne conduct extensive diplomatic contact with the Moslem rulers of Syria, Egypt, and Africa?
6. Why has Charlemagne been regarded as one of the greatest kings of the early medieval period?

---

4 ▾ Vassalage

In societies in which the state's role in regulating human relationships is minimal, law and order are maintained through custom and contract. This condition prevailed in the Early Middle Ages, particularly among the Germanic peoples. Laws were based on the community's assumptions about what was right and wrong, enforced by public opinion and community-approved use of force. To enforce law and to protect oneself and one's family, a person formed contractual ties with others and sought security and justice in mutual aid. A principal form of such a contract was called vassalage. By its terms, two free men of different means bound themselves to assistance and loyal support. The socially and economically superior man was called the lord; the man of inferior social status was called the vassal. The vassal pledged to be loyal and fight on behalf of his lord when called upon, in return for the lord's loyalty and protection when they were needed. The contract was lifelong and had deep emotional meaning in addition to the obvious self-interest of both parties.

Vassalage was a dynamic relationship, ever changing in content and meaning

according to time, place, and circumstances. In the Carolingian Empire, vassalage was practiced by all members of the free class wealthy enough to afford weapons. Charlemagne and his successors tried to use vassalage as a means of controlling their warlike subjects and organizing them to serve more effectively for the defense of their realms. Eventually, the kings' vassals used their military skills, their own landed wealth, and political power to diminish royal power. The royal vassals then became the true center of authority within medieval society.

An important part of the lord–vassal relationship was the lord's grant of a fief to his vassal. The fief might be any object of value that reflected the vassal's social status and the lord's respect for his services. A fief could be a war horse, sword, and suit of armor, a public office, a right to collect a tax or toll or authority to hold a court of justice in a specified district. The most sought-after fief was a land grant — one or more manors from which to draw income. Fiefs were held for the duration of the bond of vassalage. If the bond was broken by death or disloyalty, the fief was forfeited to its grantor. By the late ninth century, however, fiefs had become hereditary, as had the right to be a vassal to a specific lord.

Galbert of Bruges
COMMENDATION AND THE OATH OF FEALTY

This reading contains an eyewitness account of the ceremony of commendation (investiture) in which vassals swore an oath of fealty (loyalty) to their new lord, William Clito, the count of Flanders, in 1127, and were then invested with their fiefs. The account comes from an early twelfth-century chronicle written by a Flemish notary, Galbert of Bruges (a major medieval commercial city in Flanders, now part of Belgium).

Through the whole remaining part of the day those who had been previously enfeoffed [given fiefs] by the most pious count Charles,[1] did homage to the count, taking up now again their fiefs and offices and whatever they had before rightfully and legitimately obtained. On Thursday the seventh of April, homages were again made to the count being completed in the following order of faith and security.

First they did their homage thus. The count asked if he was willing to become completely his man, and the other replied, "I am willing;" and with clasped hands, surrounded by the hands of the count, they were bound together by a kiss. Secondly, he who had done homage gave his fealty to the representative of the count in these words, "I promise on my faith that I will in future be faithful to count William, and will observe my homage to him completely against all persons in good faith and without deceit," and thirdly, he took his oath to this upon the relics of the saints. Afterward, with a little rod which the count held in his hand, he gave investitures to all who by this agreement had given their security and homage and accompanying oath.

[1]Charles, count of Flanders, was murdered on March 2, 1127.

Fulbert, Bishop of Chartres
OBLIGATIONS OF LORDS AND VASSALS

In a letter written in 1020 to William, Duke of Aquitaine, Bishop Fulbert (c. 920–1028) of Chartres summarizes the obligations of the lord and the vassal.

To William most glorious duke of the Aquitanians,[1] bishop Fulbert [asks] the favor of his prayers.

Asked to write something concerning the form of fealty, I have noted briefly for you on the authority of the books the things which follow. He who swears fealty to his lord ought always to have these six things in memory; what is harmless, safe, honorable, useful, easy, practicable. Harmless, that is to say that he should not be injurious to his lord in his body; safe, that he should not be injurious to him in his secrets or in the defences through which he is able to be secure; honorable, that he should not be injurious to him in his justice or in other matters that pertain to his honor; useful, that he should not be injurious to him in his possessions; easy or practicable, that that good which his lord is able to do easily, he make not difficult, nor that which is practicable he make impossible to him.

However, that the faithful vassal should avoid these injuries is proper, but not for this does he deserve his holding; for it is not sufficient to abstain from evil, unless what is good is done also. It remains, therefore, that in the same six things mentioned above he should faithfully counsel and aid his lord, if he wishes to be looked upon as worthy of his benefice and to be safe concerning the fealty which he has sworn.

The lord also ought to act toward his faithful vassal reciprocally in all these things. And if he does not do this he will be justly considered guilty of bad faith, just as the former, if he should be detected in the avoidance of or the doing of or the consenting to them, would be perfidious and perjured.

[1]The Aquitanians inhabited the kingdom of Aquitaine in southwestern France — later a province of France.

Dhouda of Septimania
THE IDEAL RELATIONSHIP BETWEEN LORD AND VASSAL

Dhouda, the wife of Bernard, Marquis of Septimania (an ancient territory in southern France), composed a handbook in 843 for her eldest son. This *Manual* was intended to instruct him on his duties to his new lord, King Charles the Bald (840–877), son of King Louis the Pious (814–840), whose chamberlain Dhouda's husband had been.

An admonition relating to your lord.

Since God, as I believe, and your father Bernard have chosen you, in the flower of your youth, to serve Charles [the King],[1] as your lord, I urge you ever to remember the record of your family, illustrious on both sides, and not

[1]Charles the Bald, one of Charlemagne's grandsons, was at first king of Aquitaine, then king of France (843–877), and then Holy Roman Emperor (875–877) crowned by the pope.

to serve your master simply to satisfy him outwardly, but to maintain towards him and his service in all things a devoted and certain fealty both of body and soul. . . . That is why, my son, I exhort you to maintain faithfully all that is in your charge, with all your strength of body and soul, as long as your life shall last. . . . May the madness of infidelity be ever far from you; may evil never find such a place in your heart as to render you unfaithful to your lord in any matter whatsoever. . . . But I do not fear this on your part or on the part of those who serve with you. . . . Therefore, my son William, you who are of our blood, show yourself towards your lord, as I have already urged, true, vigilant, useful and most prompt to his service. In every matter which concerns the power and welfare of the king, both within the kingdom and without, show that wisdom with which God has plentifully endowed you. Read the lives and words of the holy men of former times, and you will find there how to serve your lord and be faithful to him in all things. And when you receive his commands, apply yourself faithfully to execute them. Observe also and regard carefully those who show the greatest fidelity and assiduity in his service, and learn of them the way in which to act.

REVIEW QUESTIONS

1. Describe the three-part ceremony by which a man commended himself as a vassal to a lord.
2. In the Middle Ages, contracts were symbolized and publicly noted by the use of various gestures or ritual acts. What were some of the gestures and acts used by vassals and lords?
3. From the readings, what indication did you find that vassalage was not merely a legal contract, but that it involved ethical and emotional dimensions?
4. What were the obligations required of a vassal under an oath of fealty?
5. What obligations did a lord owe to his vassal?

---

5 ▾ The Feudal Lord as Warrior

Feudal lords did not engage in productive labor as did serfs, merchants, and craftsmen. Manual labor and commerce were considered degrading for men of their rank and skills. Lords were professional warriors; combat was what they relished, trained for, and eagerly sought. They used their wealth to obtain armor and weapons, and even their sports, hunting and tournaments, prepared them for battle.

Bertran de Born
IN PRAISE OF COMBAT

The spirit of the feudal warrior is captured in the following poem by Bertran de Born (c. 1140–c. 1215), a French nobleman from the bishopric of Périgord in southern France. He is acknowledged to have been a superior poet of his day, a good warrior, and a clever intriguer who stirred up troubles between the kings

of France and England. His poetry captures the excitement and pageantry of medieval warfare.

I love the springtide of the year
When leaves and blossoms do abound,
And well it pleases me to hear
The birds that make the woods resound
With their exulting voices.
And very well it pleases me
Tents and pavilions pitched to see,
And oh, my heart rejoices
To see armed knights in panoply [full armor]
Of war on meadow and on lea [pasture].

I like to see men put to flight
By scouts throughout the countryside,
I like to see, armed for the fight,
A host of men together ride;
And my delight's unbounded
When castles strong I see assailed,
And outworks smashed, whose strength has
  failed,
And near the walls, surrounded
By moats, and by strong stakes enrailed,
The host that has the ramparts scaled.

And well I like a noble lord
When boldly the attack he leads,
For he, whene'er he wields his sword,
Inspires his men by his brave deeds,
Their hearts with courage filling.
When tide of battle's at the flood,
Each soldier then, in fighting mood,
To follow should be willing,
For no man is accounted good
Till blows he's given and withstood.

Axes and swords and spears and darts,
Shields battered in with many a blow,
We'll see when first the battle starts,
And clash of arms as foe meets foe;
The steeds of dead and dying
Wildly will rush throughout the field,
And all who wish to be revealed
As brave will e'er be trying
How best their axes they may wield,
For they would rather die than yield.

Not so much joy in sleep have I,
Eating and drinking please me less
Than hearing on all sides the cry
"At them!" and horses riderless
Among the woodlands neighing.
And well I like to hear the call
Of "Help!" and see the wounded fall,
Loudly for mercy praying,
And see the dead, both great and small,
Pierced by sharp spearheads one and all.

Barons, without delaying,
Pawn every city, castle, hall,
And never cease to fight and brawl.

REVIEW QUESTIONS

1. What qualities were expected from a medieval leader in combat?
2. What purpose did this ballad ascribe to war?
3. Why did the poet urge the barons to pawn their properties?
4. What challenge did the warrior spirit present to Christianity?

---

6 ▾ The Burdens of Serfdom

The feudal lord's way of life was made possible by the toil of the serfs who worked on the manors. Serfs, who were not free persons, had some rights but many burdensome obligations. Unlike slaves, they could not be sold off the land or dispossessed from their landholdings. Their tenure on their farms was hered-

itary, but they owed heavy rent to the landlord in the form of labor and a share of their crops and livestock. There were many restrictions on their personal freedom: they needed the landlord's permission to leave the estate, to marry, or to pass on personal property to their heirs. In return, they received security; they were defended by the landlords against outside aggressors or fellow serfs.

The labor services usually took up half the work week of the serf. He was required to plant, plow, and harvest the lord's fields, repair roads, fix fences, clear ditches, and cart goods to barns and markets. Although specific obligations varied from time to time and manor to manor, they were sufficiently onerous to encourage the serfs to seek freedom; in later centuries, when the opportunity presented itself, a serf might flee to a nearby town or to newly developed lands, or might purchase certain freedoms from the manorial lord. The serfs' struggle to rid themselves of the burdens of serfdom took centuries. It was largely successful in western Europe by the fifteenth century. But in eastern Europe, serfdom was imposed on the formerly free peasantry in the sixteenth and seventeenth centuries. Remnants of serfdom in western Europe survived until the French Revolution. Serfdom was abolished in central and eastern Europe in the mid-nineteenth century.

THE CUSTOMS OF THE MANOR OF DARNHALL

The first reading from the customs of the manor of Darnhall (variously spelled in the original manuscripts) in Cheshire, a rural county in northwestern England, details the general burdens of serfs. The manor of Darnhall belonged to an order of monks. In the year 1326, the abbot of the monastery drew up this custumal, a document reaffirming his rights over the serfs.

Here begin the customs of the bond-tenants[1] of the manor of Dernale [Darnhall].

One is that they ought to [appear in] court at the will of the lord, or of his bailiff,[2] upon being summoned only, even during the night, and they ought all to come the next day.

And whereas some of them have been accustomed to give part of their land to their sons, so that it came about that after their death their sons have by the carelessness of the bailiffs of the place been received as holding those same lands without doing to the lord anything for their seisin[3] in their father's time; those sons who hold land ought to do suit of court [to sue], or obtain the lord's grace to redeem the suit at the will of the lord, on account of the great loss which has by this means been suffered by the lord.

Also they all [must use] the mill under pain of forfeiture of their grain, if they at any time withdraw suit; and every year they owe pannage[4] for their pigs.

Also they ought to make redemption of their daughters, if they wish to marry out of the manor, at the will of the lord.

They will also give *leyrwithe*[5] for their daughters, if they fall into carnal sin.

Also, when any one of them dieth, the lord shall have all the pigs of the deceased, all his

[1]Bond-tenants was another name for serfs; they were also known as bondmen.

[2]The bailiff was an agent appointed by the landlord (that is, the lord of the manor) to manage the manor, collect rents, and levy fines for breaches of the lord's rules (custom).

[3]*Seisin* is a legal term meaning possession of property.

[4]Pannage was the right to pasture swine in the lord's forest.

[5]*Leyrwithe* (also *leyrwite*) was the name given to the fine levied by the lord on a female serf found guilty of fornication.

goats, all his mares at grass, and his horse also, if he had one for his personal use, all his bees, all his bacon-pigs, all his cloth of wool and flax, and whatsoever can be found of gold and silver. The lord also shall have all his brass pots or pot, if he have one (but who of these bond-tenants will have a brass pot for cooking his food in?), because at their death the lord ought to have all things of metal. . . .

Also the lord shall have the best ox for a "hereghett,"[6] and holy Church another. After this the rest of the animals ought to be divided thus, if the deceased has children, to wit, into three parts — one for the lord, one for the wife, one for the children; and if he leaves no children, they shall be divided into two parts — one for the lord and one for the wife of the deceased, equally. Also if they have corn, in grange [barn] or in field, then the wife of the deceased ought to choose her part, to wit, half the corn in the grange or the field, as she chooses. And if she choose her part in the field, then all the corn in the grange shall remain wholly to the lord; and if she choose her part in the grange, then all the corn in the fields shall remain wholly to the lord, together with his moiety [half] and share in the granges; always provided that, wheresoever the wife shall choose her part, whether in grange or in field, the lord shall have his moiety and part, with her and against her; and all the other corn, in the place where the woman does not choose, shall remain to the lord; and if he has children, or a child, the division shall be made in the same way into three parts, to wit, among the lord, the wife of the deceased and his children; also if there are many children [their share shall be divided] among them.

Also it is not lawful for the bond-tenant to make a will, or bequeath anything, without licence of the lord of the manor.

And as to the sheep, let them be divided like all the other goods of the deceased which ought to be divided. But this is inserted in this place by itself, because, when the convent first came to Darnhale, the bond-tenants said that no division ought to be made of the sheep, but that all the sheep ought to remain wholly to the wife of the deceased. Which is quite false, because they always used to divide them without gainsaying it at all, until Warin le Grantuenour was bailiff of Darnhale; and while he was bailiff he was corrupted with presents, and did not exact the lord's share of all things in his time; and afterwards the bond tenants endeavoured to make this a precedent and custom, which they by no means ought to do, because they have been accustomed so to do according to the customs of this manor in the times of former lords.

Moreover, the whole land of the deceased shall be in the hands of the lord, until he who is next, that is to say, he who ought to succeed the deceased — whom, according to the custom of the neighbourhood, they call the heir — shall make such a fine with the lord as shall correspond with the value of the land and the will of the lord. . . .

. . . Also, if the lord wishes to buy corn or oats, or anything else, and they have such things to sell, it shall not be lawful to them to sell anything elsewhere, except with the lord's licence [permission], if the lord is willing to pay them a reasonable price.

Also it is to be known that it is the custom of the manor to pay assize[7] rents equally at the four terms of the year, to wit, at Christmas, the Annunciation of the Blessed Mary [March 25], at the feasts of St. John the Baptist [June 24] and St. Michael [September 29].

Amercements [fines] of courts ought always to be levied within a fortnight after the holding of the court, or sooner, if the lord will; . . . and the lord's mercy [fine] is according to his will or the will of his bailiff, so that they can take according to the amount of the trespass and measure of the offence.

---

[6]*Hereghett,* usually spelled *heriot* or *heregeld,* was any property that had been lent by a lord to a now-deceased serf, plus a fine levied on his property and paid to the lord after his death. It often consisted of the lord's choice of the serf's best livestock.

[7]The rent of assize was a fixed rent paid by the freeholder to the lord. "Assize" refers to fixing any measure.

MANORIAL COURTS

Serfs were subject to the judicial power of their landlords for any infraction of manorial rules of management. The next reading, from the records of a thirteenth-century English manorial court, lists cases heard by the court, the jurors' decisions, and the penalties fixed.

John Sperling complains that Richard of Newmere on the Sunday next before S. Bartholomew's day [August 24] last past with his cattle, horses, and pigs wrongfully destroyed the corn on his (John's) land to his damage to the extent of one thrave [a measure] of wheat, and to his dishonour to the extent of two shillings; and of this he produces suit. And Richard comes and defends all of it. Therefore let him go to the law six handed.* His pledges,[1] Simon Combe and Hugh Frith.

Hugh Free in mercy [fined] for his beast caught in the lord's garden. Pledges, Walter Hill and William Slipper. Fine 6d [sixpence].

(The) twelve jurors say that Hugh Cross has right in the bank and hedge about which there was a dispute between him and William White. Therefore let him hold in peace and let William be distrained[2] for his many trespasses. (Afterwards he made fine for 12d.) . . .

From the whole township of Little Ogbourne, except seven, for not coming to wash the lord's sheep, 6s. [shillings] 8d.

Gilbert Richard's son gives 5s. for licence to marry a wife. Pledge, Seaman. Term (for payment,) the Purification [February 2].

*I.e., he must appear with six companions who will swear to his innocence.

[1]Pledges were persons, like today's bail bondsmen, who stood surety for someone who was ordered to appear later in court or who must pay a fine.

[2]To distrain means to force a person to comply with a court order by seizing and holding his movable property.

William Jordan in mercy for bad ploughing on the lord's land. Pledge, Arthur. Fine, 6d.

The parson of the Church is in mercy for his cow caught in the lord's meadow. Pledges, Thomas Ymer and William Coke.

From Martin Shepherd 6d. for the wound that he gave Pekin.

Ragenhilda of Bec gives 2s. for having married without licence. Pledge, William of Primer.

The Court presented that William Noah's son is the born bondman of the lord and a fugitive and dwells at Dodford. Therefore he must be sought. They say also that William Askil, John Parsons and Godfrey Green have furtively carried off four geese from the vill of Horepoll.

It was presented that Robert Carter's son by night invaded the house of Peter Burgess and in felony threw stones at his door so that the said Peter raised the hue [alarm]. Therefore let the said Robert be committed to prison. Afterwards he made fine with 2s.

All the ploughmen of Great Ogbourne are convicted by the oath of twelve men . . . because by reason of their default (the land) of the lord was ill-ploughed whereby the lord is damaged to the amount of 9s. . . . And Walter Reaper is in mercy for concealing (i.e. not giving information as to) the said bad ploughing. Afterwards he made fine with the lord with 1 mark [13 shillings, fourpence].

REVIEW QUESTIONS

1. How did a lord profit from the marital and sexual practices of the serfs?
2. What happened to the serf's property upon his death?

3. In the manor of Darnhall, what complication regarding the customs of the manor had arisen because of the corrupt practices of a former bailiff?
4. Describe the judicial procedures of the manorial court as found in the second reading.
5. What restrictions were placed upon the serfs' right to buy or sell goods and services where they pleased?
6. Why was trespass a common problem on a manor?

---

7 ▾ Germanic Kingship and Law

The Germanic peoples' traditions of government and law differed from those of the Romans. The Germans gave loyalty to a tribal chief, whereas the Romans belonged to an impersonal state that ruled citizens of many nationalities. Roman law was written and applied to all citizens throughout the Empire, regardless of nationality. At the time of the invasions, Germanic law consisted of unwritten tribal customs that applied only to people of a particular tribe and permitted blood feuds and trial by ordeal.

The duties of the Germanic kings varied from nation to nation; all were expected to be effective warriors, but few seem to have been law-givers like the Roman emperors. The powers of Germanic kings were limited by tribal custom and by their need to win the consent of the assembled leaders of the people for any new policy affecting people's lives or property. The kings were subject to the customary law, and their role in law enforcement was quite limited compared to the police powers exercised by Roman emperors. The right of people to settle disputes among themselves by blood feud was generally recognized.

Germanic ideas of kingship and law underwent slow modification under the influence of the Christian church and Roman imperial traditions. The church promoted a new model of kingship, that of the biblical Hebrew King David. In the eighth century, to Christianize the traditional religious character of Germanic kingship, the church began to anoint and inaugurate the Germanic kings in liturgical ceremonies similar to those used to consecrate bishops and priests. In time, the secular Germanic practice of selecting kings was combined with new liturgical ceremonies, through which the chosen king was given sacral dignity. According to church theory, the king was chosen for royal office by God; he was called upon to uphold divine law, to defend Christianity, to protect the weak, and to rule justly.

Widukind of Corvey
THE CORONATION OF OTTO I

In this passage from the chronicle ***Rerum Gestarum Saxonicarum (On the Deeds of the Saxons),*** a German historian, Widukind of Corvey (d. c. 1004), describes the coronation of the Saxon Otto I (the Great, 936–973), as monarch of the Germans. (The last of the Carolingian kings had died in 911.) The account shows

the mingling of the traditional Germanic practice of designation of a chosen heir by the previous king, the successor's subsequent election by the leading nobles and acclamation by the people, and the church ceremony of anointing and crowning the new king.

After the death of Henry (936), the father of his country and greatest and best of all kings, the Franks and Saxons[1] chose as their prince his son Otto, who had already been designated king by his father. They ordered the coronation to be held at the palace in Aachen, the place of universal election. . . .

And when they had arrived, the dukes and the great lords with a force of the chief vassals gathered in the portico of the basilica of Charlemagne. They placed the new ruler on the throne that had been constructed there, giving him their hands and offering fealty; promising their help against all his enemies, they made him king according to their custom.

While this part of the ceremony was being carried out by the dukes and other magistrates, Archbishop Hildibert of Mainz awaited the procession of the new king with all the priestly order and the commoners in the basilica. The archbishop awaited the procession of the king, holding the crozier[2] in his right hand and wearing the alb, the pallium, and the chasuble.[3] When the king came forward, he advanced to meet him, touching the king's right hand with his left. Then he led the king to the middle of the sanctuary and turned to the people standing about them (ambulatories[4] had been constructed above and below in that round basilica so that all the people might have a good view).

"Lo," Hildibert said, "I bring before you Lord Otto elected by God, formerly designated by Henry, now made king by all the princes. If this election pleases you, signify by raising your right hand to heaven." To this all the people raising their right hands on high loudly called down prosperity on the new ruler.

The king, dressed in a close-fitting tunic according to the Frankish custom, was escorted behind the altar, on which lay the royal insignia — sword with sword-belt, cloak with bracelets, staff with sceptre and diadem. . . .

When the question of who should crown the king arose, two bishops besides Hildibert were considered eligible: the bishop of Trier because his city was the most ancient and had been founded by St Peter, and the bishop of Cologne because the place of coronation — Aachen — was in his diocese. But both of these men who would have enjoyed the honour deferred to the pre-eminence of Archbishop Hildibert.

Going to the altar and taking from it the sword with sword-belt and turning to the king, he said: "Accept this sword, with which you may chase out all the adversaries of Christ, barbarians, and bad Christians, by the divine authority handed down to you and by the power of all the empire of the Franks for the most lasting peace of all Christians."

Then taking the bracelets and cloak, he clothed him saying, "These points (of the cloak) falling to the ground will remind you with what zeal of faith you should burn and how you ought to endure in preserving peace to the end."

Then taking the sceptre and staff, he said: "With these symbols you may be reminded that you should reproach your subjects with paternal castigation, but first of all you should extend the hand of mercy to ministers of God, widows, and orphans. And never let the oil of compassion be absent from your head in order that you

---

[1]The Saxons were members of a Germanic tribe that lived in northwestern Germany between the Elbe and Rhine rivers.

[2]A crozier is a staff shaped like a shepherd's crook. It is carried during liturgical services by bishops and abbots as a symbol of their pastoral office.

[3]The alb, pallium, and chasuble are liturgical vestments worn by Christian clergy.

[4]An ambulatory consists of aisled spaces around the sides and the east end of the central chamber of a church, usually separated from the central portion by columns.

may be crowned with eternal reward in the present and in the future."

After having been sprinkled with holy oil and crowned with a golden diadem by the bishops Hildibert and Wikfried (of Cologne) and all legal consecration having been completed, the king was led to the throne, to which he ascended by means of a spiral staircase. The throne of marvellous beauty had been constructed between two marble pillars, and from there the king could see and be seen by all.

Wipo
TRIAL BY ORDEAL

The unwritten customs of the people constituted early Germanic law. As the Germanic peoples settled down and were converted to Christianity, their kings began to have these common laws committed to writing. In the process, Christian influences made their impact. A traditional Germanic judicial procedure involved the use of ordeals, during which the gods were invoked to establish innocence. Sometimes the ordeal consisted of the defendant's carrying a hot iron bar by hand for some distance; in another ordeal the defendant plunged an arm into a pot of boiling water to retrieve a hot stone. The judges then waited to see how well the hand or arm healed before deciding whether or not the party was innocent. Other methods included trial by combat and by immersion in cold water to test whether the accused would sink or float. At first, the church substituted its own rituals to sustain the divine efficacy of such ordeals, but in 1215 at the Fourth Lateran Council, it withdrew its support for trial by ordeal, and the practice ceased. The growth of royal power and the influence of Roman legal traditions in medieval universities made the old German ordeal procedure no longer tolerable.

In the following passage, an eleventh-century chronicler, Wipo, described an ordeal by combat. This took place in 1033 when Emperor Conrad II (1027–1039) was settling a dispute between some Saxon subjects and their Slavic neighbors, the Luitzes (who lived east of the Elbe River in northern Germany); he chose combat between warriors selected to champion each side's claims as a means to determine the outcome.

The emperor having levied a force in Saxony marched upon the Luitzes, a people who were formerly half Christians but who have wickedly apostatized and are now become thorough pagans. In their district he put an end to an implacable strife in a wonderful manner. Between the Saxons and the pagans at that time fighting and raids were being carried on incessantly, and when the emperor came he began to inquire which side had first broken the peace that had long been observed inviolate between them. The pagans said that the peace had been disturbed first by the Saxons, and they would prove this by the duel if the emperor would so direct. On the other side the Saxons pledged themselves to refute the pagans in like manner by single combat, though as a matter of fact their contention was untrue. The emperor after consulting his princes permitted the matter to be settled between them by a duel, though this was not a very wise act. Two champions, each selected by his own side, immediately engaged. The Christian, trusting in his faith alone, though faith without the works of justice is dead, began the attack fiercely without diligently considering that God, who is the Truth, who maketh His sun to shine upon the evil and the good, and the rain to fall upon the just and the unjust, decides all things by a true judgment. The pagan on the other hand resisted stoutly, having before his eyes only the consciousness of the truth for which he was fighting. Finally the Christian fell wounded by the pagan. Thereupon his party were seized with such elation and presumption that, had the emperor not been present, they would forthwith have rushed upon the Christians; but the emperor constructed the fortress Werben in which he placed a garrison of soldiers to check their incursions and bound the Saxon princes by an oath and by the imperial commands to a unanimous resistance against the pagans. Then he returned to Franconia [a province in central Germany].

Alfred the Great
BLOOD FEUDS

In Germanic law, there was usually no public prosecution for crimes. Victims or their surviving kinsmen were expected to prosecute the alleged criminal. They might arrange to get help from others in the community, and they had the right of conducting a vendetta, or blood feud, against the alleged criminal and possibly his kinsmen. The effort to bring the blood feud under control for the good of the community was encouraged by the church and frequently by the kings.

In this reading, Anglo-Saxon (English) King Alfred the Great (871–900) established with his councilors' consent a law whereby the pursuit of blood feud was permitted only if certain procedures were followed that would offer time and occasion for peaceful mediation and adjudication of the dispute. Because blood feuds made life insecure, Alfred sought to limit their legality.

Also we enjoin, that a man who knows his adversary to be residing at home, shall not have recourse to violence before demanding justice of him.

1. If he has power enough to surround his adversary and besiege him in his house, he shall keep him therein seven days, but he shall not fight against him if he (his adversary) will consent to remain inside (his residence). And if, after seven days, he will submit and hand over his weapons, he shall keep him unscathed for thirty days, and send formal notice of his position to his kinsmen and friends.

2. If, however, he flees to a church, the privileges of the church shall be respected, as we have declared above.

3. If, however, he has not power enough to besiege him in his house, he shall ride to the *ealdorman*[1] and ask him for help. If he will not help him, he shall ride to the king before having recourse to violence.

4. And further, if anyone chances on his enemy, not having known him to be at home, and if he will give up his weapons, he shall be detained for thirty days, and his friends shall be informed (of his position). If he is not willing to give up his weapons, then violence may be used against him. If he is willing to surrender and hand over his weapons, and anyone after

[1]The ealdorman (from which the modern term *alderman* derives) was the chief royal officer of an English shire or county.

that uses violence against him (the pursued), he shall pay any sum which he incurs, whether wergeld[2] or compensation for wounds, as well as a fine, and his kinsman shall forfeit his claim to protection as a result of his action.

5. We further declare that a man may fight on behalf of his lord, if his lord is attacked, without becoming liable to vendetta [family vengeance, feuds]. Under similar conditions a lord may fight on behalf of his man.

6. In the same way a man may fight on behalf of one who is related to him by blood, if he is attacked unjustly, except it be against his lord. This we do not permit.

7. A man may fight, without becoming liable to vendetta, if he finds another (man) with his wedded wife, within closed doors or under the same blanket; or (if he finds another man) with his legitimate daughter (or sister); or with his mother, if she has been given in lawful wedlock to his father.

[2]Wergeld was money paid in recompense for an injury or death; it was paid to the victim or his surviving relatives. The amount varied according to the victim's legal status or political office.

REVIEW QUESTIONS

1. What were the steps by which the German king was formally installed in his office?
2. What part did the people play in the choosing of the king?
3. What obligations did the bishops impose upon the new king before he was anointed and crowned?
4. Why did the historian Wipo believe Emperor Conrad II's acceptance of the trial by ordeal was "not very wise"?
5. Why were both pagans and Christians willing to rely on the ordeal by combat?
6. Under what conditions could a man legally fight a blood feud or vendetta?

The High and Late Middle Ages

The High Middle Ages (1050–1300) were an era of growth and vitality in Latin Christendom. Improvements in technology and cultivation of new lands led to an increase in agricultural production; the growing food supply, in turn, reduced the number of deaths from starvation and malnutrition, and better cultivation methods freed more people to engage in nonagricultural pursuits, particularly commerce.

During the Early Middle Ages, Italian towns had maintained a weak link with the Byzantine lands in the eastern Mediterranean. In the eleventh century, the Italians gained ascendancy over Muslim fleets in the Mediterranean and rapidly expanded their trade with the Byzantine Empire and North Africa. The growing population provided a market for silk, sugar, spices, dyes, and other Eastern goods. Other mercantile avenues opened up between Scandinavia and the Atlantic coast; between northern France, Flanders, and England; and along the rivers between the Baltic Sea in the north and the Black Sea and Constantinople in the southeast.

The revival of trade and the improved production of food led to the rebirth of towns in the eleventh century. During the Early Middle Ages, urban life had largely disappeared in Latin Christendom except in Italy, and even Italian towns had declined since Roman times both in population and as centers of trade and culture. During the twelfth century, towns throughout Latin Christendom became active centers of commerce and intellectual life. The rebirth of town life made possible the rise of a new social class: the middle class, consisting of merchants and artisans. These townspeople differed significantly from the clergy, the nobles, and the serfs — the other social strata in medieval society. The world of the townspeople was the marketplace rather than the church, the castle, or the manorial village. These merchants and artisans resisted efforts by lords to impose obligations upon them, as their livelihood required freedom from such constraints. The middle class became a dynamic force for change.

The High Middle Ages were also characterized by political and religious vitality. Strong kings extended their authority over more and more territory, often at the expense

THE MEDIEVAL SCHOLAR on this illuminated page is shown surrounded by bound manuscripts. In the Middle Ages, the first universities were established. There is continuity between these medieval universities and universities today. (*Osterreichische Nationalbibliothek*)

of feudal lords; in the process, they laid the foundation of the modern European state system. By the eleventh century the autonomy of the church — its freedom to select its own leaders and to fulfill its moral responsibilities — was threatened by kings and lords who appointed bishops and abbots to ecclesiastical offices. In effect, the churches and monasteries were at the mercy of temporal rulers, who distributed church positions as patronage, awarding them to their families, vassals, and loyal servants. These political appointees often lacked the spiritual character to maintain high standards of discipline among the clergy or monks they supervised. Many clergy resented the subordination of the church to the economic and political interests of kings and lords. They held that for the church to fulfill its spiritual mission, it must be free from lay control.

The crisis within the church was dramatically addressed by a small band of clergy, mostly monks, who managed to elect to the papacy a series of committed reformers. These popes condemned clerical marriages, deeming them uncanonical, because they risked subordinating the church's interests to those of the clergymen's wives and children. Priests were required to be celibate like bishops and monks. The reformers also pressed for the systematic exclusion of the laity from participation in the governing of the church. In calling for the abolition of lay investiture, that is, the formal installation of clergy to their office by temporal lords, the papacy encountered bitter opposition. As head of the church, charged with the mission of saving souls, popes refused to accept a subordinate position to temporal rulers.

Economic, political, and religious vitality was complemented by a cultural and intellectual awakening. The twelfth and thirteenth centuries marked the high point of medieval civilization. The Christian outlook, with its otherworldly emphasis, shaped and inspired this awakening. Christian scholars rediscovered the writings of ancient Greek thinkers, which they tried to harmonize with Christian teachings. In the process, they constructed an impressive philosophical system that integrated Greek rationalism into the Christian world-view. The study of Roman law was revived, and some of its elements were incorporated into church law. A varied literature expressed both secular and religious themes, and a distinctive form of architecture, the Gothic, conveyed the overriding Christian concern with things spiritual.

During the Late Middle Ages, roughly the fourteenth and early fifteenth centuries, medieval civilization declined. In contrast to the vigor of the twelfth and thirteenth centuries, the fourteenth century was burdened by crop failures, famine, plagues, and reduced population. The church also came under attack from reformers who challenged clerical authority and questioned church teachings, from powerful kings who resisted papal interference in the political life of their kingdoms, and from political theorists who asserted that the pope had no authority to intervene in matters of state. In the city-states of Italy, a growing secularism signified a break with medieval other-worldliness and heralded the emergence of the modern outlook.

I ▾ The Revival of Trade and the Growth of Towns

Several factors contributed to economic vitality in the High Middle Ages: the end of the Viking raids in northwestern Europe, greater political stability provided by kings and powerful lords, and increased agricultural productivity, which freed some people to work at other pursuits and facilitated a population increase. The prime movers in trade were the merchant adventurers, a new class of entrepreneurs. Neither bound to the soil nor obligated to lifelong military service, merchants traveled the sea lanes and land roads to distant places in search of goods that could profitably be traded in other markets.

HOW TO SUCCEED IN BUSINESS

In the following reading from *The King's Mirror,* an anonymous thirteenth-century Norseman outlined the characteristics and skills a merchant needed and described the hazards of the job. In typical medieval fashion, he emphasized the moral dimensions of commercial transactions.

The man who is to be a trader will have to brave many perils, sometimes at sea and sometimes in heathen lands, but nearly always among alien peoples; and it must be his constant purpose to act discreetly wherever he happens to be. On the sea he must be alert and fearless.

When you are in a market town, or wherever you are, be polite and agreeable; then you will secure the friendship of all good men. Make it a habit to rise early in the morning, and go first and immediately to church. . . .

. . . When the services are over, go out to look after your business affairs. If you are unacquainted with the traffic of the town, observe carefully how those who are reputed the best and most prominent merchants conduct their business. You must also be careful to examine the wares that you buy before the purchase is finally made to make sure that they are sound and flawless. And whenever you make a purchase, call in a few trusty men to serve as witnesses as to how the bargain was made.

You should keep occupied with your business till breakfast or, if necessity demands it, till midday; after that you should eat your meal. Keep your table well provided and set with a white cloth, clean victuals, and good drinks. Serve enjoyable meals, if you can afford it. After the meal you may either take a nap or stroll about a little while for pastime and to see what other good merchants are employed with, or whether any new wares have come to the borough which you ought to buy. On returning to your lodgings examine your wares, lest they suffer damage after coming into your hands. If they are found to be injured and you are about to dispose of them, do not conceal the flaws from the purchaser: show him what the defects are and make such a bargain as you can; then you cannot be called a deceiver. Also put a good price on your wares, though not too high, and yet very near what you see can be obtained; then you cannot be called a foister [trickster].

Finally, remember this, that whenever you have an hour to spare you should give thought to your studies, especially to the law books; for it is clear that those who gain knowledge from books have keener wits than others, since those who are the most learned have the best proofs for their knowledge. Make a study of all the laws. . . . If you are acquainted with the law, you will not be annoyed by quibbles when you have suits to bring against men of your own class, but will be able to plead according to law in every case.

But although I have most to say about laws, I regard no man perfect in knowledge unless he has thoroughly learned and mastered the customs of the place where he is sojourning. And if you wish to become perfect in knowledge, you must learn all the languages, first of all Latin and French, for these idioms are most widely used; and yet, do not neglect your native tongue or speech.

. . . Train yourself to be as active as possible, though not so as to injure your health. Strive never to be downcast, for a downcast mind is always morbid; try rather to be friendly and genial at all times, of an even temper and never moody. Be upright and teach the right to every man who wishes to learn from you; and always associate with the best men. Guard your tongue carefully; this is good counsel, for your tongue may honor you, but it may also condemn you. Though you be angry speak few words and never in passion; for unless one is careful, he may utter words in wrath that he would later give gold to have unspoken. On the whole, I know of no revenge, though many employ it, that profits a man less than to bandy heated words with another, even though he has a quarrel to settle with him. You shall know of a truth that no virtue is higher or stronger than the power to keep one's tongue from foul or profane speech, tattling, or slanderous talk in any form. If children be given to you, let them not grow up without learning a trade; for we may expect a man to keep closer to knowledge and business when he comes of age, if he is trained in youth while under control.

And further, there are certain things which you must beware of and shun like the devil himself: these are drinking, chess, harlots, quarreling, and throwing dice for stakes. For upon such foundations the greatest calamities are built; and unless they strive to avoid these things, few only are able to live long without blame or sin.

Observe carefully how the sky is lighted, the course of the heavenly bodies, the grouping of the hours, and the points of the horizon. Learn also how to mark the movements of the ocean and to discern how its turmoil ebbs and swells; for that is knowledge which all must possess who wish to trade abroad. Learn arithmetic thoroughly, for merchants have great need of that.

If you come to a place where the king or some other chief who is in authority has his officials, seek to win their friendship; and if they demand any necessary fees on the ruler's behalf, be prompt to render all such payments, lest by holding too tightly to little things you lose the greater. . . . If you can dispose of your wares at suitable prices, do not hold them long; for it is the wont of merchants to buy constantly and to sell rapidly. . . .

. . . If you attend carefully to all these

things, with God's mercy you may hope for success. This, too, you must keep constantly in mind, if you wish to be counted a wise man, that you ought never to let a day pass without learning something that will profit you. Be not like those who think it beneath their dignity to hear or learn from others such things even as might avail them much if they knew them. For a man must regard it as great an honor to learn as to teach, if he wishes to be considered thoroughly informed. . . .

. . . Always buy good clothes and eat good fare if your means permit; and never keep unruly or quarrelsome men as attendants or messmates. Keep your temper calm though not to the point of suffering abuse or bringing upon yourself the reproach of cowardice. Though necessity may force you into strife, be not in a hurry to take revenge; first make sure that your effort will succeed and strike where it ought. Never display a heated temper when you see that you are likely to fail, but be sure to maintain your honor at some later time, unless your opponent should offer a satisfactory atonement.

If your wealth takes on rapid growth, divide it and invest it in a partnership trade in fields where you do not yourself travel; but be cautious in selecting partners. Always let Almighty God, the holy Virgin Mary, and the saint whom you have most frequently called upon to intercede for you be counted among your partners. Watch with care over the property which the saints are to share with you and always bring it faithfully to the place to which it was originally promised.

William Fitz-Stephen
DESCRIPTION OF THE MOST NOBLE CITY OF LONDON

Renewed local and international commerce in the eleventh and twelfth centuries spurred urban growth. In addition to the revival of older towns like Milan, Paris, Cologne, and London, which traced their origins back to Roman times, many new towns sprang up around the gates of castles and monasteries, and at ports and important road junctions. The next reading by William Fitz-Stephen, an English churchman of the late twelfth century, reveals the vitality of medieval London.

Among the noble and celebrated cities of the world that of London, the capital of the kingdom of the English, is one which extends its glory farther than all the others and sends its wealth and merchandise more widely into distant lands. Higher than all the rest does it lift its head. It is happy in the healthiness of its air; in its observance of Christian practice; in the strength of its fortifications; in its natural situation; in the honour of its citizens; and in the modesty of its matrons. It is cheerful in its sports, and the fruitful mother of noble men. . . .

It has on the east the Palatine castle,* very great and strong: [tower] and walls rise from very deep foundations and are fixed with a mortar tempered by the blood of animals. On the west there are two castles very strongly fortified, and from these there runs a high and massive wall with seven double gates and with towers along the north at regular intervals. London was once also walled and turreted on the south, but the mighty Thames, so full of fish, has with the sea's ebb and flow washed against,

*The Tower of London.

loosened, and thrown down those walls in the course of time. Upstream to the west there is the royal palace† which is conspicuous above the river, a building incomparable in its ramparts and bulwarks. It is about two miles from the city and joined thereto by a populous suburb.

Everywhere outside the houses of those living in the suburbs, and adjacent to them, are the spacious and beautiful gardens of the citizens, and these are planted with trees. Also there are on the north side pastures and pleasant meadow lands through which flow streams wherein the turning of mill-wheels makes a cheerful sound. Very near lies a great forest with woodland pastures in which there are the lairs of wild animals: stags, fallow deer, wild boars and bulls. The tilled lands of the city are not of barren gravel, but fat Asian plains that yield luxuriant crops and fill the tillers' barns with the sheaves of Ceres [Roman goddess of agriculture].

There are also outside London on the north side excellent suburban wells with sweet, wholesome and clear water that flows rippling over the bright stones. . . . These are frequented by great numbers and much visited by the students from the schools and by the young men of the city, when they go out for fresh air on summer evenings. Those engaged in business of various kinds, sellers of merchandise, hirers of labour, are distributed every morning into their several localities according to their trade. Besides, there is in London on the river bank among the wines for sale in ships and in the cellars of the vintners a public cookshop. There daily you may find food according to the season, dishes of meat, roast, fried and boiled, large and small fish, coarser meats for the poor and more delicate for the rich, such as venison and big and small birds. . . .

Immediately outside one of the gates there is a field. . . . On every sixth day of the week, unless it be a major feast-day, there takes place there a famous exhibition of fine horses for sale. Earls, barons and knights, who are in the town, and many citizens come out to see or to buy. . . . When a race is about to begin [and] . . . [w]hen the signal is given [the horses] stretch their limbs to the uttermost, and dash down the course with courageous speed. The riders, covetous of applause and ardent for victory, plunge their spurs into the loose-reined horses, and urge them forward with their shouts and their whips. . . .

By themselves in another part of the field stand the goods of the countryfolk: implements of husbandry [farming], swine with long flanks, cows with full udders, oxen of immense size, and woolly sheep. There also stand the mares fit for plough, some big with foal, and others with brisk young colts closely following them.

To this city from every nation under heaven merchants delight to bring their trade by sea. The Arabian sends gold; the Sabaean [south of Arabia] spice and incense. The Scythian [from Central Asia] brings arms, and from the rich, fat lands of Babylon comes oil of palms. The Nile sends precious stones; the men of Norway and Russia, furs and sables; nor is China absent with purple silk. The Gauls [French] come with their wines.

We now come to speak of the sports of the city, for it is not fitting that a city should be merely useful and serious-minded, unless it be also pleasant and cheerful. . . . Instead of shows in the theatre and stageplays, London provides plays of a more sacred character, wherein are presented the miracles worked by saintly confessors or the sufferings which made illustrious the constancy of martyrs. Furthermore, every year on the day called Carnival [Mardi Gras, the day before Ash Wednesday] — to begin with the sports of boys (for we were all boys once) — scholars from the different schools bring fighting-cocks to their masters, and the whole morning is set apart to watch their cocks do battle in the schools, for the boys are given a holiday that day. After dinner all the young men of the town go out into the fields in the suburbs to play ball. The scholars

---

†The Palace of Westminster [now the site of the Houses of Parliament].

of the various schools have their own ball, and almost all the followers of each occupation have theirs also. The seniors and the fathers and the wealthy magnates of the city come on horseback to watch the contests of the younger generation, and in their turn recover their lost youth: the motions of their natural heat seem to be stirred in them at the mere sight of such strenuous activity and by their participation in the joys of unbridled youth.

Every Sunday in Lent after dinner a fresh swarm of young men goes forth into the fields on war-horses, steeds foremost in the contest, each of which is skilled and schooled to run in circles. From the gates there sallies forth a host of laymen, sons of the citizens, equipped with lances and shields, the younger ones with spears forked at the top, but with the steel point removed. They make a pretence at war, carry out field-exercises and indulge in mimic combats. . . .

On feast-days throughout the summer the young men indulge in the sports of archery, running, jumping, wrestling, slinging the stone, hurling the javelin beyond a mark and fighting with sword and buckler. Cytherea [a name for Aphrodite, goddess of love] leads the dance of maidens, and until the moon rises, the earth is shaken with flying feet.

In winter on almost every feast-day before dinner either foaming boars, armed with lightning tusks, fight for their lives "to save their bacon," or stout bulls with butting horns, or huge bears do battle with the hounds let loose upon them. When the great marsh that washes the north wall of the city is frozen over, swarms of young men issue forth to play games on the ice. Some, gaining speed in their run, with feet set well apart, slide sideways over a vast expanse of ice. Others make seats out of a large lump of ice, and whilst one sits thereon, others with linked hands run before and drag him along behind them. So swift is their sliding motion that sometimes their feet slip, and they all fall on their faces. Others, more skilled at winter sports, put on their feet the shin-bones of animals, binding them firmly round their ankles, and, holding poles shod with iron in their hands, which they strike from time to time against the ice, they are propelled swift as a bird in flight or a bolt shot from an engine of war. Sometimes, by mutual consent, two of them run against each other in this way from a great distance, and, lifting their poles, each tilts against the other. Either one or both fall, not without some bodily injury, for, as they fall, they are carried along a great way beyond each other by the impetus of their run, and wherever the ice comes in contact with their heads, it scrapes off the skin utterly. Often a leg or an arm is broken, if the victim falls with it underneath him; but theirs is an age greedy of glory, youth yearns for victory, and exercises itself in mock combats in order to carry itself more bravely in real battles.

Many of the citizens take pleasure in sporting with birds of air, with hawks, falcons and suchlike, and with hounds that hunt their prey in the woods.

ORDINANCES OF THE GUILD MERCHANT OF SOUTHAMPTON

Along with revived trade and burgeoning towns in the High Middle Ages came the formation of businessmen's associations, called guilds. Merchant guilds encompassed all townspeople engaged in commerce. Carpenters, bakers, shoemakers, and other skilled craftsmen formed guilds that specialized in each occupation. Though women were employed in many trades, working under male guild masters, they were rarely admitted to full membership. Guilds composed

exclusively of women existed in only a few places like Paris and Cologne. Guilds tried to eliminate competition by barring outsiders from doing business in the town, by limiting membership, by fixing the price of their goods, and by setting quality standards. Guilds provided for the social needs of their members, too, as the following selection of guild regulations for the seaport of Southampton, England, show. The document itself belongs to the fourteenth century, but several of the regulations had been framed earlier.

6. . . . And if a guildsman be ill and in town, one shall send to him two loaves and a gallon of wine, and one dish of cooked food; and two of the approved men of the guild shall go to visit him and look to his condition.

7. And when a guildsman dies, all those who are of the guild and in the town shall be at the service of the dead, and guildsmen shall carry the body, and bring it to the place of sepulture [burial]. And he who will not do this shall pay, on his oath, twopence to be given to the poor. And those of the ward where the dead man shall be, shall find a man to watch with the body the night that the dead person shall lie in his house. . . .

9. And when a guildsman dies, his eldest-born son or his next heir shall have the seat of his father, or of his uncle, if his father was not a guildsman, but of no one else. Nor can any husband, by reason of his wife, either have a seat in the guild or demand it by any right of his wife's ancestors. . . .

10. And no one ought nor can lawfully sell or give his seat in the guild to any man. And the son of a guildsman, other than his eldest, shall be admitted to the guild on payment of ten shillings [120 pence], and shall take the oath.

11. And if any guildsman be imprisoned in England in time of peace, the alderman, with the seneschal[1]. . . shall go at the cost of the guild to procure the release of him that is in prison.

12. And if any guildsman strike another with his fist, and be thereof attainted [found guilty], he shall lose his guildship until he has purchased it again for ten shillings, and shall take the oath like a new member. And if a guildsman strike another with a stick or a knife, or any other weapon, whatever it may be, he shall lose his guildship and his franchise,[2] and shall be held a stranger, until he be reconciled to good people of the guild, and have made satisfaction to the person whom he has injured, and be fined to the guild twenty shillings, which shall not be remitted. . . .

19. And no one shall buy anything in the town of Southampton to sell it again in the same town, unless he be of the guild merchant or of the franchise. And if any one do so and be attainted (thereof), all that he has so bought shall be forfeited to the king. And no one shall be quit of custom unless he has done so as to be of the guild or of the franchise, and this from year to year.

20. And no one shall buy honey, seim [lard], salt herring, or any kind of oil, or millstones, or fresh hides, or any kind of fresh skins, except a guildsman; nor keep a tavern for wine, or sell cloth by retail, except on a market day or fair day; nor keep above five quarters of corn in his granary to sell by retail, if he is not a guildsman; and whoever shall do this, and be attainted (thereof), shall forfeit all to the king.

21. No one of the guild shall be partner or joint dealer in any of the foresaid merchandises with any person who is (not?) of the guild, by any manner of coverture [concealment], art, contrivance, collusion, or any other manner. And whosoever shall do this, and be attainted (thereof), the goods so bought shall be fore-

[1]An alderman was the chief of the guild, and a seneschal acted as its treasurer and vice-president.

[2]A person's franchise was the privilege of citizenship in the town.

feited to the king, and the guildsman shall lose his guildship.

22. And if any guildsman fall into poverty and have not wherewith to live, and cannot work, he shall be provided for: when the guild shall be held he shall have one mark from the guild to relieve his condition. No one of the guild or franchise shall avow another's goods for his own, by which the custom of the town may be defrauded. And if any one so do, and be attainted (thereof), he shall lose the guildship and the franchise, and the merchandise so avowed shall be forfeited to the king. . . .

41. No butcher or cook shall sell to any man other than wholesome and clean provisions, and well cooked; and if any do, and he be thereof attainted, he shall be put in the pillory an hour of the day, or give two shillings to the town for the offence.

42. And that no butcher or cook throw into the street any filth or other matter whereby the town or the street become more dirty, filthy, or corrupt; and if any one do this, and be attainted, he shall pay a fine of twelve pence, as often as he shall offend in the manner aforesaid.

43. No man shall have any pigs going about in the street, or have before his door, or in the street, muck or dung beyond two nights; and if any one has, let whoever will take it away; and he who shall have acted contrary to this statute shall be grievously fined.

REVIEW QUESTIONS

1. What were some hazards that a merchant faced in doing business?
2. What attitudes did the writer recommend that a merchant cultivate when dealing with customers and fellow merchants?
3. What kind of learning was of value to a merchant?
4. What business practices were recommended to merchants?
5. How does William Fitz-Stephen's description of London illustrate medieval economic vitality?
6. What sports did Londoners favor?
7. What artistic entertainments were available to Londoners?
8. What fraternal support did the guild offer its members who suffered illness, death, or business failure?
9. What monopolistic privileges did a guildsman of Southampton enjoy?
10. What legal assistance and personal protection did a guild offer its members?

---

2 ▾ Theological Basis for Papal Power

The authority of the papacy was weakened by lords who dominated churches and monasteries by appointing bishops and abbots and by collecting the income from church taxes. These bishops and abbots, appointed for political reasons, lacked the spiritual devotion to maintain high standards of discipline among priests and monks. Church reformers were determined to end this subordination of the church to lay authority.

The practice of lay investiture led to a conflict between the papacy and the German monarchy. It began when the German king and future Holy Roman Emperor Henry IV (1056–1108) invested the new archbishop of Milan with his pastoral staff and ring, symbols of the episcopal office. Henry was immediately

challenged and threatened with excommunication by Pope Gregory VII (1073–1085), a most ardent champion of reform. Gregory's action sparked a struggle between the papacy and the Holy Roman Empire that lasted for half a century. Later, after he was actually excommunicated for a second time, Henry invaded Italy, and Pope Gregory fled from Rome to the monastery of Monte Cassino and died in 1085. Civil war broke out in the imperial territories between partisans of the pope and those of the empire, and widespread death and destruction ensued. Although a compromise was effected at a synod at Worms, Germany, in 1122, the ideological principles raised in the dispute were never wholly resolved.

Pope Gregory VII
THE SECOND LETTER TO BISHOP HERMAN OF METZ AND THE « DICTATUS PAPAE »

Like no other pope before him, Gregory VII had asserted the preeminence of the papacy over secular rulers. He declared that princes should "not seek to subdue or subject holy Church to themselves as a handmaiden; but indeed let them fittingly strive to honor her eyes, namely the priests of the Lord, by acknowledging them as masters and fathers." His exaltation of the spiritual authority of the church encouraged future popes to challenge the state whenever it threatened the supremacy of Christian moral teachings or the church's freedom to carry out its mission. The first reading is a letter written by Pope Gregory VII to a German bishop, Herman of Metz, at the height of the lay investiture struggle. The pope outlined the theological basis for the authority and powers he claimed. The exalted conception of the papacy as the central authority in the Christian church was expressed in its most extreme and detailed form in a series of propositions called the *Dictatus papae* (Rules of the Pope), which appear as numbered paragraphs in the second excerpt.

You ask us to fortify you against the madness of those who babble with accursed tongues about the authority of the Holy Apostolic See [the bishopric of Rome] not being able to excommunicate King Henry as one who despises the law of Christ, a destroyer of churches and of the empire, a promoter and partner of heresies, nor to release anyone from his oath of fidelity to him; but it has not seemed necessary to reply to this request, seeing that so many and such convincing proofs are to be found in Holy Scripture. . . .

To cite but a few out of the multitude of proofs: Who does not remember the words of our Lord and Savior Jesus Christ: "Thou art Peter and on this rock I will build my Church, and the gates of hell shall not prevail against it. And I will give thee the keys of the kingdom of heaven and whatsoever thou shalt bind on earth shall be bound in heaven and whatsoever thou shalt loose on earth shall be loosed in heaven." Are kings excepted here? Or are they not of the sheep which the Son of God committed to St. Peter? Who, I ask, thinks himself excluded from this universal grant of the power of binding and loosing to St. Peter unless, perchance, that unhappy man who, being unwilling to bear the yoke of the Lord, subjects himself to the burden of the Devil and refuses to be numbered in the flock of Christ? His wretched liberty shall profit him nothing; for if he shakes off from his proud neck the power divinely granted to Peter, so much the heavier shall it be for him in the day of judgment.

This institution of the divine will, this foundation of the rule of the Church, this privilege granted and sealed especially by a heavenly decree to St. Peter, chief of the Apostles, has been accepted and maintained with great reverence by the holy fathers, and they have given to the Holy Roman Church, as well in general councils as in their other acts and writings, the name of "universal mother." They have not only accepted her expositions of doctrine and her instructions in (our) holy religion, but they have also recognized her judicial decisions. They have agreed as with one spirit and one voice that all major cases, all especially important affairs and the judgments of all churches ought to be referred to her as to their head and mother, that from her there shall be no appeal, that her judgments may not and cannot be reviewed or reversed by anyone.

Thus Pope Gelasius [492–496], writing to the [Byzantine] emperor Anastasius, gave him these instructions as to the right theory of the principate of the Holy and Apostolic See, based upon divine authority:

> Although it is fitting that all the faithful should submit themselves to all priests who perform their sacred functions properly, how much the more should they accept the judgment of that prelate who has been appointed by the supreme divine ruler to be superior to all priests and whom the loyalty of the whole later Church has recognized as such. Your Wisdom sees plainly that no human capacity *(concilium)* whatsoever can equal that of him [Saint Peter] whom the word of Christ raised above all others and whom the reverend Church has always confessed and still devotedly holds as its Head.

▷ Pope Gregory then comments on the origins of the authority of civil rulers and their motives when they seek to govern the clergy. Gregory argues that church and state are separate spheres of governing authority and that the responsibility of clergymen is greater than that of civil rulers.

Who does not know that kings and princes derive their origin from men ignorant of God who raised themselves above their fellows by pride, plunder, treachery, murder — in short, by every kind of crime — at the instigation of the Devil, the prince of this world, men blind with greed and intolerable in their audacity? If, then, they strive to bend the priests of God to their will, to whom may they more properly be compared than to him who is chief over all the sons of pride? For he, tempting our High Priest [Jesus], head of all priests, son of the Most High, offering him all the kingdoms of this world, said: "All these will I give thee if thou wilt fall down and worship me."

Does anyone doubt that the priests of Christ are to be considered as fathers and masters of kings and princes and of all believers? Would it not be regarded as pitiable madness if a son should try to rule his father or a pupil his master and to bind with unjust obligations the one through whom he expects to be bound or loosed, not only on earth but also in heaven? Evidently recognizing this the emperor Constantine the Great, lord over all kings and princes throughout almost the entire earth, as St. Gregory [pope, 590–604] relates in his letter to the emperor Mauritius [Maurice, Byzantine ruler, 582–602], at the holy synod of 'Nicaea'[1] took his place below all the bishops and did not venture to pass any judgment upon them but, even addressing them as gods, felt that they ought not to be subject to his

[1]The synod (council of bishops) of Nicaea in Asia Minor mentioned here took place in 325; it was the first ecumenical council of the church — all bishops were invited to participate.

judgment but that he ought to be bound by their decisions.

Pope Gelasius, urging upon the emperor Anastasius not to feel himself wronged by the truth that was called to his attention said: "There are two powers, O august Emperor, by which the world is governed, the sacred authority of the priesthood and the power of kings. Of these the priestly is by so much the greater as they will have to answer for kings themselves in the day of divine judgment;" and a little further: "Know that you are subject to their judgment, not that they are to be subjected to your will."

In reliance upon such declarations and such authorities, many prelates [popes or other powerful church officials] have excommunicated kings or emperors.

▷ Drawn up by the papal government during the pontificate of Gregory VII, the *Dictatus papae* represents claims and ambitions that would inspire many popes and theologians throughout the Middle Ages.

RULES OF THE POPE

1. That the Roman church was established by God alone.

2. That the Roman pontiff [bishop] alone is rightly called universal.

3. That he alone has the power to depose and reinstate bishops.

4. That his legate [emissary], even if he be of lower ecclesiastical rank, presides over bishops in council, and has the power to give sentence of deposition against them.

5. That the pope has the power to depose those who are absent (*i.e.*, without giving them a hearing).

6. That, among other things, we ought not to remain in the same house with those whom he has excommunicated.

7. That he alone has the right, according to the necessity of the occasion, to make new laws, to create new bishoprics, to make a monastery of a chapter of canons,[2] and *vice versa,* and either to divide a rich bishopric or to unite several poor ones.

8. That he alone may use the imperial insignia.

9. That all princes shall kiss the foot of the pope alone.

10. That his name alone is to be recited in the churches.

11. That the name applied to him belongs to him alone.

12. That he has the power to depose emperors.

13. That he has the right to transfer bishops from one see to another when it becomes necessary.

14. That he has the right to ordain as a cleric anyone from any part of the church whatsoever.

15. That anyone ordained by him may rule (as bishop) over another church, but cannot serve (as priest) in it, and that such a cleric may not receive a higher rank from any other bishop.

16. That no general synod may be called without his order.

17. That no action of a synod and no book shall be regarded as canonical [official] without his authority.

18. That his decree can be annulled by no one, and that he can annul the decrees of anyone.

19. That he can be judged by no one.

20. That no one shall dare to condemn a person who has appealed to the apostolic seat.

21. That the important cases of any church whatsoever shall be referred to the Roman church (that is, to the pope).

22. That the Roman church has never erred and will never err to all eternity, according to the testimony of the holy scriptures.

23. That the Roman pontiff who has been canonically ordained is made holy by the merits

---

[2]A chapter of canons is a corporate ecclesiastical body composed of priests who administer cathedrals or monastic communities.

of St. Peter, according to the testimony of St. Ennodius, bishop of Pavia, which is confirmed by many of the holy fathers, as is shown by the decrees of the blessed pope Symmachus [498–513].

24. That by his command or permission subjects may accuse their rulers.

25. That he can depose and reinstate bishops without the calling of a synod.

26. That no one can be regarded as catholic who does not agree with the Roman church.

27. That he has the power to absolve subjects from their oath of fidelity to wicked rulers.

REVIEW QUESTIONS

1. What scriptural basis did Pope Gregory VII claim for his authority as head of the Christian church?
2. What historical precepts did Gregory cite to justify his demand that King Henry IV submit to papal authority?
3. What was Gregory's view on the origin of royal authority?
4. What did Pope Gelasius see as the proper relationship between church and state?
5. What powers did the papacy claim over kings and emperors? Over other bishops of the church?
6. What specific judicial powers within the universal church did the pope claim to have?
7. What special ceremonial powers did the pope claim to have?
8. In what sense had the papacy itself become a kind of monarchy by the late eleventh century?

---

3 ▾ The First Crusade

In the eleventh century the Seljuk Turks, recent converts to Islam, conquered vast regions of the Near East including most of Asia Minor, the heartland of the Byzantine Empire. When the Seljuk empire crumbled, Byzantine emperor Alexius I Comnenus (1081–1118), seeing an opportunity to regain lost lands, appealed to Latin princes and the pope for assistance, an appeal answered by Urban II (1088–1099).

In 1095 at the Council of Clermont, Pope Urban II in a dramatic speech urged Frankish lords to take up the sword against the Muslims, an event that marked the beginning of the Crusades — the struggle to regain the Holy Land from Islam. A Christian army mobilized by the papacy to defend the Christian faith accorded with the papal concept of a just war. Moreover, Urban hoped that such a venture might bring the Byzantine church under papal authority. Nobles viewed Urban's appeal as a great adventure that held the promise of glory, wealth, and new lands; they were also motivated by religious reasons: recovery of Christian holy places and a church-approved way of doing penance for their sins.

The Crusades also demonstrated the growing strength and confidence of Latin Christendom, which previously had been on the defensive against Islam, and thus represented part of a wider movement of expansion on the part of Latin

Christians. In the eleventh century, Italians had already driven the Muslims from Sardinia; Normans had taken Sicily from the Muslims and southern Italy from Byzantium; and Christian knights, supported by the papacy, were engaged in a long struggle to expel the Muslim Moors from Spain.

The First Crusade demonstrated Christian fanaticism as well as idealism and growing power, as contingents of crusaders robbed and massacred thousands of Jews in the Rhineland (see pages 259–260). The First Crusade was climaxed by the storming of Jerusalem in June 1099 and the slaughter of the city's inhabitants.

Robert the Monk
APPEAL OF URBAN II TO THE FRANKS

Pope Urban's speech, as reported by Robert the Monk, shows how skillfully the pope appealed to the Frankish lords.

"O race of the Franks, O people who live beyond the mountains, O people loved and chosen of God, as is clear from your many deeds, distinguished over all other nations by the situation of your land, your catholic faith, and your regard for the holy church, we have a special message and exhortation for you. For we wish you to know what a grave matter has brought us to your country. The sad news has come from Jerusalem and Constantinople that the people of Persia, an accursed and foreign race [the Turks], enemies of God, 'a generation that set not their heart aright, and whose spirit was not steadfast with God' (Ps. 78:8), have invaded the lands of those Christians and devastated them with the sword, rapine, and fire. Some of the Christians they have carried away as slaves, others they have put to death. The churches they have either destroyed or turned into mosques. They desecrate and overthrow the altars. . . . They have taken from the Greek empire a tract of land so large that it takes more than two months to walk through it. Whose duty is it to avenge this and recover that land, if not yours? For to you more than to other nations the Lord has given the military spirit, courage, agile bodies, and the bravery to strike down those who resist you. Let your minds be stirred to bravery by the deeds of your forefathers, and by the efficiency and greatness of . . . [Charlemagne], and of . . . his son [Louis the Pious], and of the other kings who have destroyed [Muslim] kingdoms, and established Christianity in their lands. You should be moved especially by the holy grave of our Lord and Saviour which is now held by unclean peoples, and by the holy places which are treated with dishonor and irreverently befouled with their uncleanness.

"O bravest of knights, descendants of unconquered ancestors, do not be weaker than they, but remember their courage. . . . Let no possessions keep you back, no solicitude for your property. Your land [France] is shut in on all sides by the sea and mountains, and is too thickly populated. There is not much wealth here, and the soil scarcely yields enough to support you. On this account you kill and devour each other, and carry on war and mutually destroy each other. Let your hatred and quarrels cease, your civil wars come to an end, and all your dissensions stop. Set out on the road to the holy sepulchre [site of Jesus' burial], take the land from that wicked people, and make it your own. That land which, as the Scripture says, is flowing with milk and honey, God gave to the children of Israel. Jerusalem is the best of all lands, more fruitful than all others, as it were a second Paradise of delights. This land our Saviour [Jesus] made illustrious by his birth, beautiful with his life, and sacred with his suffering; he redeemed it with his death and glorified it with his tomb. This royal city is now held captive by her enemies, and made pagan by those who know not God. She asks and longs to be liberated and does not cease to beg you to come to her aid. She asks aid especially from you because, as I have said, God has given more of the military spirit to you than to other nations. Set out on this journey and you will obtain the remission of your sins and be sure of the incorruptible glory of the kingdom of heaven."

When Pope Urban had said this and much more of the same sort, all who were present were moved to cry out with one accord, "It is the will of God, it is the will of God." When the pope heard this he raised his eyes to heaven and gave thanks to God, and, commanding silence with a gesture of his hand, he said: "My dear brethren. . . . [L]et these words be your battle cry, because God caused you to speak them. Whenever you meet the enemy in battle, you shall all cry out, 'It is the will of God, it is the will of God.' . . . Whoever therefore shall determine to make this journey and shall make a vow to God and shall offer himself as a living sacrifice, holy, acceptable to God (Rom. 12:1), shall wear a cross on his brow or on his breast. And when he returns after having fulfilled his vow he shall wear the cross on his back. In this way he will obey the command of the Lord, 'Whosoever doth not bear his cross and come after me is not worthy of me'" (Luke 14:27).

REVIEW QUESTIONS

1. What news from the East caused Pope Urban to call the First Crusade?
2. What arguments did the pope use to appeal to the Frankish soldiers?
3. What motives may have influenced the enthusiastic response of the Frankish warriors?
4. Modern political propaganda frequently uses popular fears, bigotry, patriotism, and moral idealism to influence public opinion. Which statements of Urban II express such propaganda techniques?

---

4 ▾ Religious Dissent

Like all groups held together by common ideology, the medieval church wanted to protect its doctrines from novel, dissident, or erroneous interpretations. To ensure orthodoxy and competency, therefore, all preachers were licensed by the bishop; unlicensed preaching, especially by unschooled laymen, was forbidden. In the western church, heresy had not been a serious problem in the post-Roman period. But in the twelfth century, two heretical movements attracted significant numbers of supporters among both the clergy and laity and cut across frontiers and social classes. The first group was the Waldensians, or Poor Men of Lyons, founded about 1173 by Peter Waldo (d. 1217), a rich merchant of Lyons, France, who gave away his wealth to the poor and began to preach in villages in southeastern France.

The second major heretical movement was that of the Cathari, more commonly called the Albigensians. The Albigensian heresy apparently entered western Europe from the Balkans, where similar religious ideas could be traced back to non-Christian sects of the early Roman Empire. The Albigensians were not

Christians in any orthodox sense: they rejected the Old Testament and claimed the God of Israel to be the Evil One, who created the material world in which souls were trapped, separating them from the Good God. Although the Albigensians accepted the New Testament with their own emendations, they rejected the Christian doctrine of Jesus as both God and Man; they believed that Jesus was a disembodied spirit, and that all flesh was evil, marriage was evil, and the begetting of children was evil. They rejected the medieval Christian church and constituted an alternative religion in the midst of Christian southern France and Italy.

Bernard Gui
THE WALDENSIAN TEACHINGS

Neither a priest nor a theologian, Waldo had the Bible translated from Latin into the common language of the people and preached the gospel message without the consent of church authorities. Small groups of Waldo's converts soon were found in towns and villages throughout southeastern France, northern Italy, and Switzerland. Within less than a decade, the Waldensians had aroused the clergy's hostility and were condemned as heretics by Pope Lucius III at a council in Verona in 1184. Gradually, influenced by other heretical groups, the Waldensians adopted a more radical stance toward the medieval church. In the following reading from *Manual of an Inquisitor,* a fourteenth-century Dominican friar, Bernard Gui, describes the origin and the teachings of the Waldensians. The Waldensian criticisms of the church would be echoed in the writings of the great Protestant reformers of the sixteenth century.

The sect and heresy of the Waldenses or Poor of Lyons began about the year of our Lord 1170. Its moving spirit and founder was a certain citizen of Lyons named Waldes, or Waldens, from whom his followers received their name. He was a rich man who, having given up all his property, resolved to devote himself to poverty and to evangelical perfection, just as the apostles had done. He had procured for himself translations of the Gospels and some other books of the Bible in vernacular French, also some texts from St. Augustine, St. Jerome, St. Ambrose, and St. Gregory, arranged topically, which he and his adherents called "sentences." On frequently reading these over among themselves, although very seldom understanding them aright, they were carried away by their emotions and, although they had but little learning, they usurped the function of the apostles by daring to preach "in the streets and the broad ways."

This man Waldes, or Waldens, won over to a like presumption many people of both sexes, made men and women his accomplices, and sent them out to preach as his disciples. They, men and women alike, although they were stupid and uneducated, wandered through villages, entered homes, preached in the squares and even in churches, the men especially, and spread many errors everywhere. Moreover, when they were summoned by the archbishop of Lyons, John of the Fair Hands, and by him forbidden such audacity, they were not at all willing to obey, alleging as excuse for their madness that "we ought to obey God rather than men," Who had commanded His apostles to "preach the gospel to every creature." By virtue of a false profession of poverty and a feigned appearance of sanctity, they arrogated to themselves what had been said to the apostles. Boldly declaring that they were imitators and successors of these apostles, they cast aspersions upon prelates and clergy for abundant wealth and lives of luxury.

Thus, through presumptuously usurping the office of preaching, they became teachers of error. After they had been warned to desist, they rendered themselves disobedient and contumacious, for which they were excommunicated and driven from that city and their native land. Finally, indeed, because they remained obdurate, they were pronounced schismatics [rebels] at a certain council which was held at Rome . . . and were then condemned as heretics. And so, as they had grown in number on the earth, they scattered throughout that province and neighboring areas and into the region of Lombardy [northern Italy]. Separated and cut off from the Church, when they mingled with other heretics and imbibed their errors, they combined with their own fantasies the errors and heresies of heretics of earlier days. . . .

. . . Now, the principal heresy of the aforesaid Waldenses was and still continues to be contempt of ecclesiastical authority. Then, having been excommunicated for this and given over to Satan, they were plunged by him into countless errors, and they combined with their own fantasies the errors of heretics of an earlier day.

The foolish followers and impious teachers of this sect hold and teach that they are not subject to our lord pope, the Roman pontiff, or to other prelates of the Roman Church, for they declare that the Roman Church persecutes and censures them unjustly and unduly. Also, they declare positively that they cannot be excommunicated by the said Roman pontiff and prelates, to none of whom ought obedience be given should he enjoin or command the members and teachers of this sect to desert and abjure it — this despite the fact that it has been condemned as heretical by the Roman Church.

Also, they hold and teach that every oath, in or out of court, without exception or qualification, has been forbidden by God as unlawful and sinful. . . .

Also, out of the same font of error, the aforesaid sect and heresy declares that any judicial process is forbidden by God and is, consequently, a sin and that it is contrary to God's command for any judge, in any case or for any reason, to sentence a man to corporal punishment involving bloodshed, or to death. They seize on the words of the Holy Gospels — "Judge not that ye be not judged"; "Thou shalt not kill"; and other similar passages — without the proper explanation essential to their interpretation. This they do without understanding the sense or accepting the signification or explanation which the Holy Roman Church wisely perceives and transmits to the faithful in accordance with the teaching of the Fathers [early Christian theologians], the doctors, and the canonical decrees.

Also, as it strays from the way and the right path, this sect does not accept or consider valid, but despises, rejects, and damns the canonical decrees, the decretals [judgments] of the supreme pontiffs, the rules concerning observance of fasts and holy days, and the precepts of the Fathers.

Also, in a more pernicious error in respect of the sacrament of penance and the keys [papal powers to legislate] of the Church, these [Waldensians] hold, and teach that, just as the apostles had it from Christ, they have from God alone and from no other the power to hear confessions from men and women who wish to confess to them, to give absolution, and to impose penance. And they do hear the confessions of such persons, they do give absolution [forgiveness] and impose penance, although they are not priests or clerics ordained by any bishop of the Roman Church but are laymen and nothing more. They do not claim to have any such power from the Roman Church, but rather disclaim it. . . .

Also, this sect and heresy ridicules the indulgences [remissions of canonical punishments due to sin] which are published and granted by prelates of the Church, asserting that they are of no value whatever.

In regard to the sacrament of the Eucharist [communion, celebration of the Last Supper] they err, saying, not publicly but in private among themselves, that if the priest who celebrates or consecrates the Mass is a sinner, the bread and wine do not change into the body and blood of Christ in the sacrament of the altar; and in their view anyone is a sinner who is not a member of their sect. Also, they say that any righteous person, even though he be a layman and not a cleric ordained by a Catholic bishop, can perform the consecration of the body and blood of Christ, provided only that he be a member of their sect. This they apply even to women, with the same proviso that they belong to their sect. Thus they teach that every holy person is a priest.

Emperor Frederick II
THE CONSTITUTIONS OF MELFI

The new religious movements threatened to undermine the existing religious, social, and political order. Pope Gregory IX in 1231 decided to create special courts of inquisition to seek out the dissenters, or heretics. Those who repented could be sent to prison for life; those who remained unrepentant were excommunicated from the church and turned over to the secular authorities, who executed them. The ordinary procedural standards of European penal law were abandoned in the courts of inquisition. The inquiry was secret, witnesses were not identified to the accused, guilt was presumed, legal counsel was denied, and torture was applied to verify statements given under oath. Those found guilty lost not only their freedom, but often their lives. Their property was confiscated and divided equally among the local bishop, the inquisitors, and the local civil ruler.

The papal inquisitors were not permitted to function everywhere. The rulers of the northern and eastern European kingdoms forbade them entry, as did England, Portugal, and Castile. In the next reading, from the first section of the Constitutions of Melfi, promulgated for the kingdom of Sicily by the Emperor Frederick II (1220–1250) in 1231, the typical attitude of medieval Christians toward heretics (or those who gave them aid or comfort) and the savage penalties imposed are graphically depicted. Ironically, in 1245, Frederick II himself was accused of heresy and deposed by Pope Innocent IV (1243–1254).

Heretics try to tear the seamless robe of our God. As slaves to the vice of a word that means division [sect], they strive to introduce division into the unity of the indivisible faith and to separate the flock from the care of Peter [the Pope], the shepherd to whom the Good Shepherd [Christ] entrusted it. Inside they are violent wolves, but they pretend the tameness of sheep until they can get inside the sheepfold of the Lord. They are the most evil angels. They are sons of depravity from the father of wickedness and the author of evil, who are resolved to deceive simple souls. They are snakes who deceive doves. They are serpents who seem to creep in secretly and, under the sweetness of honey, spew out poison. While they pretend to administer the food of life, they strike from their tails. They mix up a potion of death as a certain very deadly poison.

. . . Indeed, these miserable Patarines [Patarenes, one group of heretics], who do not possess the holy faith of the Eternal Trinity,[1] offend at the same time three persons under one cover of wickedness: God, their neighbors, and themselves. They offend God because they do not know the faith of God, and they do not know his son. They deceive their neighbors insofar as they administer the delights of heretical wickedness to them under the guise of spiritual nourishment. They rage against themselves even more cruelly insofar as, besides risking their souls, these sectaries, lavish of life and improvident with death, also expose their bodies to the enticements of cruel death which they could avoid by true knowledge and the steadfastness of true faith. What is even worse, the survivors are not frightened by the example. We cannot contain our emotions against such men so hostile to God, to themselves, and to mankind. Therefore, we draw the sword of righteous vengeance against them, and we pursue them more urgently insofar as they are known to practice the crimes of their superstition within the Roman Church herself, which is considered the head of all the other churches, to the more evident injury of the Christian faith. . . . Because we consider this so repulsive, we have decided in the first place that the crime of heresy and these condemned sects should be numbered among the public crimes as it was promulgated in the ancient laws. . . .

[1]The central Christian doctrine that teaches that there are three divine persons in one God: Father, Son, and Holy Spirit, who are coequal, coeternal, and consubstantial.

In order to expose the wickedness of those who, because they do not follow God, walk in darkness, even if no one reports it, we desire that the perpetrators of these crimes should be investigated diligently and should be sought after by our officials like other criminals. We order that those who become known by an inquisition [trial], even if they are touched by the evidence of a slight suspicion, should be examined by ecclesiastics and prelates. If they should be found by them to deviate from the Catholic faith in the least wise, and if, after they have been admonished by them in a pastoral way, they should be unwilling to relinquish the insidious darkness of the Devil and to recognize the God of Light, but they persist in the constancy of conceived error, we order by the promulgation of our present law that these Patarines should be condemned to suffer the death for which they strive. Committed to the judgment of the flames, they should be burned alive in the sight of the people. We do not grieve that in this we satisfy their desire, from which they obtain punishment alone and no other fruit of their error. No one should presume to intervene with us in behalf of such persons. But if anyone does, we shall turn against him the deserved stings of our indignation. . . .

. . . We order that the shelterers, believers, accomplices of Patarines, and those who support them in any way at all, who give no heed to fear for themselves so that they can protect others from punishment, should be sent into perpetual exile and all their goods confiscated.

REVIEW QUESTIONS

1. What was the Waldensian attitude toward the wealth and the temporal powers exercised by the medieval church?
2. How did the Waldensians differ from the orthodox church on the role of the clergy and the administration of the sacraments?
3. What motivated Emperor Frederick II to pursue heretics with the state's full power?
4. How were heretics to be discovered, questioned, and disposed of?
5. What was done to those individuals who offered heretics aid or sympathy?

5 ▾ Orthodox Spiritual Renewal

The efforts of the Gregorian reformers to protect the church from corrupting secular influences had not fully succeeded. The church's landed estates, tax exemptions, and exercise of many feudal offices caused the clergy to profit greatly in the expanding economy of the twelfth and thirteenth centuries. The corrupting influence of wealth on the church's spiritual health became a pressing concern to many devout Christians. In the twelfth century, many Benedictine monks, seeking a stricter, more austere way of life, created the Cistercian order, which grew rapidly as its spiritual fervor attracted both men and women to its ideals. The desire for orthodox spiritual renewal became more acute in the wake of the outbreak of heretical movements.

The most significant of the thirteenth-century orthodox spiritual reformers was Francis of Assisi (Francesco di Pietro di Bernardone, 1181–1226). Son of a wealthy merchant, Francis was a dashing young soldier who underwent a spiritual crisis following an illness in 1205. After experiencing a vision of Christ, he dedicated himself to personal poverty and service to the poor and sick; his ideal was to imitate the life of Jesus as reported in the Gospels. Francis attracted a band of followers, and in 1210 he won the support of Pope Innocent III. The new order, the Friars Minor (Little Brothers), were not monks but laymen who lived in communities with some priests. Due to Francis's magnetic personality and the pope's patronage, the Friars Minor grew rapidly. Its members wandered the roads of Europe, preaching the gospel, caring for the poor and sick, and exemplifying a life of poverty by earning their livelihood by work and begging.

Saint Francis of Assisi
≪ THE TESTAMENT ≫

Francis's vision for a spiritual reform within the orthodox structures of the church can be seen in *The Testament,* written to his fellow friars just before his death. In it he told of his faith and devotion to the church. Stressing the importance of working for a living rather than seeking incomes from properties as the clergy did, he forbade his followers to seek any church office, privilege, or income. Finally, he insisted on strict obedience to the rule (the constitution) of the Franciscan community. Within a decade of his death, the friars were bitterly divided over how strictly to interpret the founder's insistence on poverty. But the spiritual ideals of Francis have been handed down in the Franciscan order to the present day.

The Lord gave to me, Brother Francis, thus to begin to do penance; for when I was in sin it seemed to me very bitter to see lepers, and the Lord Himself led me amongst them and I showed mercy to them. And when I left them, that which had seemed to me bitter was changed for me into sweetness of body and soul. And afterwards I remained a little and I left the world. And the Lord gave me so much faith in churches that I would simply pray and say thus: "We adore Thee Lord Jesus Christ here and in all Thy churches which are in the whole world, and we bless Thee because by Thy holy cross Thou hast redeemed the world."

After that the Lord gave me, and gives me, so much faith in priests who live according to the form of the holy Roman Church, on account of their order, that if they should persecute me, I would have recourse to them. And if I had as much wisdom as Solomon [Hebrew king] had, and if I should find poor priests of this world, I would not preach against their will in the parishes in which they live. And I desire to fear, love, and honor them and all others as my masters; and I do not wish to consider sin in them, for in them I see the Son of God and they are my masters. And I do this because in this world, I see nothing corporally of the most high Son of God Himself except His most holy Body and Blood, which they receive and they alone administer to others [in the sacrament of the Eucharist]. And I will that these most holy mysteries be honored and revered above all things and that they be placed in precious places. Wheresoever I find His most holy Names and written words in unseemly places, I wish to collect them, and I ask that they may be collected and put in a becoming place. And we ought to honor and venerate all theologians and those who minister to us the most holy Divine Words as those who minister to us spirit and life.

And when the Lord gave me some brothers [followers], no one showed me what I ought to do, but the Most High Himself revealed to me that I should live according to the form of the holy Gospel. And I caused it to be written in few words and simply, and the Lord Pope confirmed it for me. And those who came to take this life upon themselves gave to the poor all that they might have and they were content with one tunic, patched within and without, by those who wished, with a cord and breeches, and we wished for no more. . . .

. . . And we were simple and subject to all. And I worked with my hands and I wish to work and I wish firmly that all the other brothers should work at some labor which is compatible with honesty. Let those who know not (how to work) learn, not through desire to receive the price of labor but for the sake of example and to repel idleness. And when the price of labor is not given to us, let us have recourse to the table of the Lord, begging alms from door to door.

The Lord revealed to me this salutation, that we should say: "The Lord give thee peace." Let the brothers take care not to receive on any account churches, poor dwelling-places, and all other things that are constructed for them, unless they are as is becoming the holy poverty which we have promised in the Rule, always dwelling there as strangers and pilgrims. . . .

And let not the brothers say: This is another Rule; for this is a remembrance, a warning, and an exhortation and my Testament which I, little Brother Francis, make for you, my blessed brothers, in order that we may observe in a more Catholic way the Rule which we have promised to the Lord. And let the minister general [elected head of the order] and all the other ministers and custodes [guardians] be bound by obedience not to add to these words or to take from them. And let them always have this writing with them beside the Rule. And in all the Chapters they hold, when they read the Rule let them read these words also. And I strictly enjoin on all my brothers, clerics and laics [laymen], by obedience, not to put glosses [explanatory additions] on the Rule or on these words saying: Thus they ought to be understood; but as the Lord has given me to speak and to write the Rule and these words simply and purely, so shall you understand them simply and purely and with holy operation observe them until the end.

REVIEW QUESTIONS

1. Why was the experience with lepers of such importance to Francis?
2. Why did Francis stress his loyalty to priests, theologians, and other ministers of the church?
3. What was the source of Francis's inspiration to pattern his life on that of Christ as depicted in the New Testament?
4. What were some characteristic features of the Franciscan way of life?
5. Why did Francis forbid glosses of his Rule?
6. In what ways did the Franciscan spiritual ideals reflect a criticism of the moral condition of the church in the thirteenth century?

---

6 ▾ Medieval Learning: Synthesis of Reason and Christian Faith

The twelfth century witnessed a revived interest in classical learning and the founding of universities. Traditional theology was broadened by the application of a new system of critical analysis, called scholasticism. Scholastic thinkers assumed that some teachings of Christianity, which they accepted as true by faith, could also be demonstrated to be true by reason. They sought to explain and clarify theological doctrines by subjecting them to logical analysis.

Adelard of Bath
A QUESTIONING SPIRIT

In the High and Late Middle Ages, ancient scientific texts, particularly the works of Aristotle, were translated from Greek and Arabic into Latin. Influenced by Aristotle's naturalistic and empirical approach, several medieval scholars devoted greater attention to investigating the natural world. An early exponent of this emerging scientific outlook was Adelard of Bath (c. 1080–c. 1145). Born in England, Adelard studied in France and traveled in Muslim lands, becoming an advocate of Arabic science.

Adelard's *Natural Questions* was written before the major Greek works were translated into Latin and made available to western European scholars. But it does show a growing curiosity and a questioning spirit, attitudes that are crucial to scientific thinking. *Natural Questions* is a dialogue between Adelard and his nephew; reproduced below are some of Adelard's responses to his nephew's queries.

ADELARD I take nothing away from God, for whatever exists is from Him and because of Him. But the natural order does not exist confusedly and without rational arrangement, and human reason should be listened to concerning those things it treats of. But when it completely fails, then the matter should be referred to God. Therefore, since we have not yet completely lost the use of our minds, let us return to reason. . . .

. . . It is difficult for me to talk with you about animals, for I have learned one thing, under the guidance of reason, from Arabic teachers; but you, captivated by a show of authority, are led around by a halter. For what should we call authority but a halter? Indeed, just as brute animals are led about by a halter wherever you please, and are not told where or why, but see the rope by which they are held and follow it alone, thus the authority of writers leads many of you, caught and bound by animal-like credulity, into danger. Whence some men, usurping the name of authority for themselves, have employed great license in writing, to such an extent that they do not hesitate to present the false as true to such animal-like men. For why not fill up sheets of paper, and why not write on the back too, when you usually have such readers today who require no rational explanation and put their trust only in the ancient name of a title? For they do not understand that reason has been given to each person so that he might discern the true from the false, using reason as the chief judge. For if reason were not the universal judge, it would have been given to each of us in vain. It would be sufficient that it were given to one (or a few at most), and the rest would be content with their authority and decisions. Further, those very people who are called authorities only secured the trust of their successors because they followed reason; and whoever is ignorant of reason or ignores it is deservedly considered to be blind. I will cut short this discussion of the fact that in my judgment authority should be avoided. But I do assert this, that first we ought to seek the reason for anything, and then if we find an authority it may be added. Authority alone cannot make a philosopher believe anything, nor should it be adduced for this purpose. . . .

NEPHEW One should listen to what you say but not believe it. But I shall gird myself for higher things, so that, as far as my little knowledge permits, light might come forth from the smoke. For although I am ignorant of the Greeks' boasts, and I have not seen Vulcan's cave (i.e., Mt. Aetna), nevertheless I have learned both to know what is true and to disprove what is false, and I have considerable skill in this. So continue! I want to find out what you think about human nature. For although you may consider what you have already said to be very important, nevertheless, if you do not know yourself, I think that your remarks have little value. For men ought most properly to investigate man. . . .

ADELARD I believe that man is dearer to the Creator than all the other animals. Nevertheless it does not happen that he is born with natural weapons or is suited for swift flight. But he has something which is much better and more worthy, reason I mean, by which he so far excels the brutes that by means of it he can tame them, put bits in their mouths, and train them to perform various tasks. You see, therefore, by how much the gift of reason excels bodily defenses. . . .

NEPHEW Since we have been discussing things having to do with the brain, explain, if you can, how the philosophers determined the physical location of imagination, reason and memory. For both Aristotle in the *Physics* (an erroneous reference) and other philosophers in other works, have been able to determine that the operations of imagination are carried on in the front part of the brain, reason in the middle, and memory in the back, and so they have given these three areas the names imaginative, rational and memorial. But by what skill were they able to determine the site of each operation of the mind and to assign to each small area of the brain its proper function, since these operations cannot be perceived by any sense?

ADELARD To one who does not understand, everything seems impossible: but when things are understood, everything becomes clear. I would guess that whoever first undertook this task learned something about it from sense experience. Probably, someone who had formerly had a very active imagination suffered an injury to the front of his head and afterwards no longer possessed the imaginative faculty, although his reason and memory remained unaffected. And when this happened it was noticed by the philosopher. And similarly injuries to other parts of the head impeded other functions of the mind so that it could be established with certainty which areas of the brain controlled which mental functions, especially since in some men these areas are marked by very fine lines. Therefore, from evidence of this sort, which could be perceived by the senses, an insensible and intellectual operation of the mind has been made clear.

Peter Abelard
INQUIRY INTO DIVERGENT VIEWS OF CHURCH FATHERS

Dialectics, a method of logical analysis, applied to the Bible and the writings of early Christian thinkers, was brilliantly taught by Peter Abelard (1079–1142) in the cathedral school at Paris. In his book *Sic et Non (Yes and No),* Abelard listed some hundred and fifty questions on which the early church authorities had taken differing positions over the centuries. He suggested that these issues could be resolved by the careful application of the dialectical method to the language of the texts.

Although he never intended to challenge the Christian faith, Abelard raised, with his critical scrutiny, fears that the dialectical approach would undermine faith and foster heresy. Saint Bernard of Clairvaux, a Cistercian monk and mystic, challenged the new methods of the Parisian professor and sought to silence him. In 1141, Abelard was forced to quit his teaching post, and he retired to a monastery, where he died the following year. Despite Bernard's apparent victory, the new scholastic rationalistic approach swept the schools of Europe. In the following reading, the critical use of rational methods in textual analysis is described by Abelard.

We must be careful not to be led astray by attributing views to the [Church] Fathers which they did not hold. This may happen if a wrong author's name is given to a book or if a text is corrupt. For many works are falsely attributed to one of the Fathers to give them authority, and some passages, even in the Bible, are corrupt through the errors of copyists. . . . We must be equally careful to make sure that an opinion quoted from a Father was not withdrawn or corrected by him in the light of later and better knowledge. . . . Again the passage in question may not give the Father's own opinion, but that of some other writer whom he is quoting. . . .

We must also make a thorough inquiry when different decisions are given on the same matter under canon [church] law. We must discover the underlying purpose of the opinion, whether it is meant to grant an indulgence or exhort to some perfection. In this way we may clear up the apparent contradiction. . . . If the opinion is a definitive judgment, we must determine whether it is of general application or directed to a particular case. . . . The when and why of the order must also be considered because what is allowed at one time is often forbidden at another, and what is often laid down as the strict letter of the law may be sometimes moderated by a dispensation. . . .

Furthermore we customarily talk of things as they appear to our bodily senses and not as they are in actual fact. So judging by what we see we say it is a starry sky or it is not, and that the sun is hot or has no heat at all, when these things though variable in appearance are ever constant. Can we be surprised, then, that some matters have been stated by the Fathers as opinions rather than the truth? Then again many controversies would be quickly settled if we could be on our guard against a particular word used in different senses by different authors. . . .

A careful reader will employ all these ways of reconciling contradictions in the writings of the Fathers. But if the contradictions are so glaring that they cannot be reconciled, then the rival authorities must be compared and the view that has the heaviest backing be adopted. . . .

By collecting contrasting divergent opinions I hope to provoke young readers to push themselves to the limit in the search for truth, so that their wits may be sharpened by their investigation. It is by doubting that we come to investigate, and by investigating that we recognise the truth.

Saint Thomas Aquinas ≪ SUMMA THEOLOGICA ≫ AND ≪ SUMMA CONTRA GENTILES ≫

For most of the Middle Ages, religious thought was dominated by the influence of Saint Augustine (d. 430), the greatest of the church fathers (see pages 191–194). Augustine placed little value on the study of nature; for him, the City of Man (the world) was a sinful place from which people tried to escape in order to enter the City of God (heaven). Regarding God as the source of knowing, he held that reason by itself was an inadequate guide to knowledge: without faith in revealed truth, there could be no understanding. An alternative approach to that of Augustine was provided by Thomas Aquinas (1225–1274), a friar of the Order of Preachers (Dominicans), who taught theology at Paris and later in Italy. Both Augustine and Aquinas believed that God was the source of all truth, that human nature was corrupted by the imprint of the original sin of Adam and Eve, and that God revealed himself through the Bible and in the person of Jesus Christ. But, in contrast to Augustine, Aquinas expressed great confidence in the power of reason and favored applying it to investigate the natural world.

Aquinas held that as both faith and reason came from God, they were not in opposition to each other; properly understood, they supported each other. Because reason was no enemy of faith, it should not be feared. In addition to showing renewed respect for reason, Aquinas — influenced by Aristotelian empiricism (the acquisition of knowledge of nature through experience) — valued knowledge of the natural world. He saw the natural and supernatural worlds not as irreconcilable and hostile to each other, but as a continuous ascending hierarchy of divinely created orders of being moving progressively toward the Supreme Being. In constructing a synthesis of Christianity and Aristotelianism, Aquinas gave renewed importance to the natural world, human reason, and the creative human spirit. Nevertheless, by holding that reason was subordinate to faith, he remained a typically medieval thinker. In the following reading from his most ambitious work, the *Summa Theologica,* Thomas Aquinas uses the categories of Aristotelian philosophy to demonstrate through natural reason God's existence. Also included is a selection from another work, *Summa Contra Gentiles,* a theological defense of Christian doctrines that relies extensively on natural reason.

SUMMA THEOLOGICA

Third Article: Whether God Exists?

I answer that, The existence of God can be proved in five ways.

The first and more manifest way is the argument from motion. It is certain, and evident to our senses, that in the world some things are in motion. Now whatever is moved is moved by another, for nothing can be moved except it is in potentiality to that towards which it is moved; whereas a thing moves inasmuch as it is in act. For motion is nothing else than the reduction of something from potentiality to actuality. But nothing can be reduced from potentiality to actuality, except by something in a state of actuality. Thus that which is actually hot, as fire, makes wood, which is potentially hot, to be actually hot, and thereby moves and changes it. Now it is not possible that the same thing should be at once in actuality and potentiality in the same respect, but only in different respects. For what is actually hot cannot simultaneously be potentially hot; but it is simultaneously potentially cold. It is therefore impossible that in the same respect and in the same way a thing should be both mover and moved, *i.e.,* that it should move itself. Therefore, whatever is moved must be moved by another. If that by which it is moved be itself moved, then this also must needs be moved by another, and that by another again. But this cannot go on to infinity, because then there would be no first mover, and, consequently, no other mover, seeing that subsequent movers move only inasmuch as they are moved by the first mover; as the staff moves only because it is moved by the hand. Therefore it is necessary to arrive at a first mover, moved by no other; and this everyone understands to be God.

The second way is from the nature of efficient cause. In the world of sensible things we find there is an order of efficient causes. There is no case known (neither is it, indeed, possible) in which a thing is found to be the efficient cause of itelf; for so it would be prior to itself, which is impossible. Now in efficient causes it is not possible to go on to infinity, because in all efficient causes following in order, the first is the cause of the intermediate cause, and the intermediate is the cause of the ultimate cause, whether the intermediate cause be several, or one only. Now to take away the cause is to take away the effect. Therefore, if there be no first cause among efficient causes, there will be no ultimate, nor any intermediate, cause. But if in efficient causes it is possible to go on to infinity, there will be no first efficient cause, neither will there be an ultimate effect, nor any intermediate efficient causes; all of which is plainly false. Therefore it is necessary to admit a first efficient cause, to which everyone gives the name of God.

The third way is taken from possibility and necessity, and runs thus. We find in nature things that are possible to be and not to be, since they are found to be generated, and to be corrupted, and consequently, it is possible for them to be and not to be. But it is impossible for these always to exist, for that which can not-be at some time is not. Therefore, if everything can not-be, then at one time there was nothing in existence. Now if this were true, even now there would be nothing in existence, because that which does not exist begins to exist only through something already existing. Therefore, if at one time nothing was in existence, it would have been impossible for anything to have begun to exist; and thus even now nothing would be in existence — which is absurd. Therefore, not all beings are merely possible, but there must exist something the existence of which is necessary. But every necessary thing either has its necessity caused by another, or not. Now it is impossible to go on to infinity in necessary things which have their necessity caused by another, as has been already proved in regard to efficient causes. Therefore we cannot but admit the existence of some being having of itself its own necessity, and not receiving it from another, but rather causing in others their necessity. This all men speak of as God.

The fourth way is taken from the graduation to be found in things. Among beings there are some more and some less good, true, noble, and the like. But *more* and *less* are predicated of different things according as they resemble in their different ways something which is the maximum, as a thing is said to be hotter according as it more nearly resembles that which is hottest; so that there is something which is truest, something best, something noblest, and, consequently, something which is most being, for those things that are greatest in truth are greatest in being. . . . Now the maximum in any genus is the cause of all in that genus, as fire, which is the maximum of heat, is the cause of all hot things. . . . Therefore there must also be something which is to all beings the cause of their being, goodness, and every other perfection; and this we call God.

The fifth way is taken from the governance of the world. We see that things which lack knowledge, such as natural bodies, act for an end, and this is evident from their acting always, or nearly always, in the same way, so as to obtain the best result. Hence it is plain that they achieve their end, not fortuitously, but designedly. Now whatever lacks knowledge cannot move towards an end, unless it be directed by some being endowed with knowledge and intelligence; as the arrow is directed by the archer. Therefore some intelligent being exists by whom all natural things are directed to their end; and this being we call God.

▷ The next reading shows Aquinas' great respect for reason. He defines a human being by the capacity to regulate actions through reason and will.

Sixth Article: Does Man Choose with Necessity or Freely?

I answer that, Man does not choose of necessity. . . . For man can will and not will, act and not act . . . can will this or that, and do this or that. The reason for this is to be found in the very power of the reason. For the will can tend to whatever the reason can apprehend as good. Now the reason can apprehend as good not only this, viz., *to will* or *to act,* but also this, viz., *not to will* and *not to act.* Again, in all particular goods, the reason can consider the nature of some good, and the lack of some good, which has the nature of an evil; and in this way, it can apprehend any single one of such goods as to be chosen or to be avoided. . . . Therefore, man chooses, not of necessity, but freely.

▷ In the following selection Aquinas stresses the necessity of assenting to the truths of faith even if they are beyond the grasp of reason.

SUMMA CONTRA GENTILES

Another benefit that comes from the revelation to men of truths that exceed the reason is the curbing of presumption, which is the mother of error. For there are some who have such a presumptuous opinion of their own ability that they deem themselves able to measure the nature of everything; I mean to say that, in their estimation, everything is true that seems to them so, and everything is false that does not. So that the human mind, therefore, might be freed from this presumption and come to a humble inquiry after truth, it was necessary that some things should be proposed to man by God that would completely surpass his intellect.

A still further benefit may also be seen in what Aristotle says in the *Ethics.* There was a certain Simonides who exhorted people to put aside the knowledge of divine things and to apply their talents to human occupations. He said that "he who is a man should know human things, and he who is mortal, things that are mortal." Against Simonides Aristotle says that "man should draw himself towards what is immortal and divine as much as he can." And so he says in the *De animalibus* that, although what we know of the higher substances is very little, yet that little is loved and desired more than all the knowledge that we have about less noble substances. He also says in the *De caelo et mundo* that when questions about the heavenly bodies can be given even a modest and merely plausible solution, he who hears this experiences intense joy. From all these considerations it is clear that even the most imperfect knowledge about the most noble realities brings the greatest perfection to the soul. Therefore, although the human reason cannot grasp fully the truths that are above it, yet, if it somehow holds these truths at least by faith, it acquires great perfection for itself.

Therefore it is written: "For many things are shown to thee above the understanding of men" (Ecclus. 3:25). . . .

Those who place their faith in this truth, however, "for which the human reason offers no experimental evidence," do not believe foolishly, as though "following artificial fables" (II Peter 1:16). For these "secrets of divine Wisdom" (Job 11:6) the divine Wisdom itself, which knows all things to the full, has deigned to reveal to men. It reveals its own presence, as well as the truth of its teaching and inspiration, by fitting arguments; and in order to confirm those truths that exceed natural knowledge, it gives visible manifestation to works that surpass the ability of all nature. Thus, there are the wonderful cures of illnesses, there is the raising of the dead. . . . [A]nd what is more wonderful, there is the inspiration given to human minds, so that simple and untutored persons, filled with the gift of the Holy Spirit, come to possess instantaneously the highest wisdom and the readiest eloquence. When these arguments were examined [in Roman times], . . . in the midst of the tyranny of the persecutors, an innumerable throng of people, both simple and most learned, flocked to the Christian faith. In this faith there are truths preached that surpass every human intellect, the pleasures of the flesh are curbed; it is taught that the things of the world should be spurned. Now, for the minds of mortal men to assent to these things is the greatest of miracles, just as it is a manifest work of divine inspiration that, spurning visible things, men should seek only what is invisible. Now, that this has happened . . . as a result of the disposition of God, is clear from the fact that through many pronouncements of the ancient prophets God had foretold that He would do this. The books of these prophets are held in veneration among us Christians, since they give witness to our faith.

REVIEW QUESTIONS

1. According to Adelard of Bath, are there limits to a human being's ability to know truth or reality?
2. Why did Adelard of Bath have to stress the importance of using reason rather than authority in studying the natural world?
3. According to Adelard, how might Aristotle have known the specific locations of the faculties of imagination, memory, and reason in the brain?
4. What problems did medieval scholars face in using the hand-copied texts of the Bible or writings of the church fathers?
5. What problems arose when medieval scholars consulted the collections of canon laws reflecting church beliefs and customs from previous centuries?
6. What was Peter Abelard's method of coping with textual problems? What did Abelard recommend doing if it was impossible to reconcile rival authoritative texts?
7. Why did Abelard's method of textual analysis cause controversy?
8. In what ways did Thomas Aquinas use empirical evidence of the senses to sustain his arguments for the existence of God?
9. How did Aquinas use logic to argue that there must be a first mover?
10. Explain why Aquinas concluded that God is the first efficient cause, the uncaused cause of all other efficient causes.

11. How did Aquinas's study of the natural world lead him to conclude that God existed?
12. On what grounds did Aquinas argue that man is free to choose and is not determined or compelled by necessity to act?
13. Would the arguments of Aquinas on the unity of truth encourage or discourage philosophical and scientific research?
14. Do you agree or disagree with Aquinas on the need to seek truth with a spirit of humility? Why?

---

7 ▾ Medieval Universities

The twelfth century witnessed a renaissance of classical learning and cultural creativity. New inventions in engineering and technology produced the first Gothic-style cathedrals; new styles of classical inspiration began to influence sculpture, painting, and literature; new Latin translations of Greek philosophical and scientific texts stimulated scholars; the reintroduction of the study of Roman law began to influence political institutions. These were some of the major changes that would leave a permanent mark on subsequent Western culture.

A significant achievement of this age was the emergence of universities. Arising spontaneously among teachers of the liberal arts and students of the higher studies of law, theology, and medicine, the universities gave more formal and lasting institutional structure to the more advanced levels of schooling. The medieval universities were largely dedicated to educating young men for clerical and secular careers as lawyers, judges, teachers, diplomats, and administrators of both church and state. The educational foundation for such professional careers was the study of the liberal arts.

John of Salisbury
ON THE LIBERAL ARTS

The standard curriculum of medieval schools was based on intensive study of the seven liberal arts divided into two programs: the *trivium,* consisting of Latin grammar, rhetoric, and dialectic (or logic), and the *quadrivium,* consisting of arithmetic, geometry, astronomy, and music. The brilliant, twelfth-century scholar and churchman John of Salisbury (c. 1115–1180) wrote the *Metalogicon,* a defense of the liberal arts curriculum, which was under attack from conservative theologians.

WHY SOME ARTS ARE CALLED "LIBERAL"

While there are many sorts of arts, the first to proffer their services to the natural abilities of those who philosophize are the liberal arts. All of the latter are included in the courses of the Trivium and Quadrivium. The liberal arts are said to have become so efficacious among our ancestors, who studied them diligently, that they enabled them to comprehend everything they read, elevated their understanding to all things, and empowered them to cut through the knots of all problems possible of solution. Those to whom the system of the Trivium has disclosed the significance of all words, or the rules of the Quadrivium have unveiled the secrets of all nature, do not need the help of a teacher in order to understand the meaning of books and to find the solutions of questions. They (the branches of learning included in the Trivium and Quadrivium) are called "arts" because they . . . strengthen minds to apprehend the ways of wisdom. . . . They are called "liberal," either because the ancients took care to have their children instructed in them; or because their object is to effect man's liberation, so that, freed from cares, he may devote himself to wisdom. More often than not, they liberate us from cares incompatible with wisdom. They often even free us from worry about (material) necessities, so that the mind may have still greater liberty to apply itself to philosophy.

Among all the liberal arts, the first is logic, and specifically that part of logic which gives initial instruction about words. . . . [T]he word "logic" has a broad meaning, and is not restricted exclusively to the science of argumentative reasoning. (It includes) Grammar (which) is "the science of speaking and writing correctly — the starting point of all liberal studies." Grammar is the cradle of all philosophy, and in a manner of speaking, the first nurse of the whole study of letters. It takes all of us as tender babes, newly born from nature's bosom. It nurses us in our infancy, and guides our every forward step in philosophy. With motherly care, it fosters and protects the philosopher from the start to the finish (of his pursuits). It is called "grammar" from the basic elements of writing and speaking. *Grama* means a letter or line. . . .

THE IMPORTANCE OF STUDYING GRAMMAR

[It] is clear that (the function of) grammar is not narrowly confined to one subject. Rather, grammar prepares the mind to understand everything that can be taught in words. Consequently, everyone can appreciate how much all other studies depend on grammar. . . . Gaius [Julius] Caesar [100–44 B.C.] wrote books *On Analogy,* conscious that, without grammar, one cannot master philosophy (with which he was thoroughly familiar) or eloquence (in which he was most proficient). Quintilian [A.D. 35–c. 100] also praises this art to the point of declaring that we should continue the use of grammar and the love of reading "not merely during our school days, but to the very end of our life." For grammar equips us both to receive and to impart knowledge. It modulates our accent, and regulates our very voice so that it is suited to all persons and matters. Poetry should be recited in one way; prose in another. . . . [Grammar] is . . . the key to everything written as well as the mother and arbiter of all speech. . . .

WHAT IS A SCHOLAR?

In the next selection, the vocation of the medieval scholar and his duties are summarized in a dialogue that was used in medieval schools.

— Are you a scholar?
— Yes.
— What is a scholar?
— Somebody who earnestly and diligently applies himself to the virtues.
— Where are you a scholar?
— Here, everywhere and in every seemly place.
— How many seemly places are there?
— Four: the church, the

school, at home with my parents and in the company of orderly men.

— How many unseemly places are there?
— They too are four in number: the dance-floor, the brothel, public roads and inns not frequented by orderly men. More places could be added to this list.

— Are you a scholar?
— Yes.
— What kind of Scholar are you?
— As God has created me.
— How many duties does a scholar have?
— Six.
— What are they?
— To get up early, dress immediately, comb my hair, wash my hands, pray to God and go willingly to school.

— Are you a scholar?
— Yes.
— What is the substance of a scholar?
— An animated physical substance susceptible of knowledge and virtue.

— Are you a human being?
— Yes.
— What is a human being?
— A corporal, physical, rational and mortal substance created by God to attain immortal life.

— What is God?
— The best and highest conceivable being who endows everything with its existence and life.

Geoffrey Chaucer
AN OXFORD CLERIC

In his masterpiece, *The Canterbury Tales,* English poet and diplomat Geoffrey Chaucer (c. 1340–1400) describes a typical student on pilgrimage to the shrine of Saint Thomas Becket in Canterbury.

An *Oxford Cleric,* still a student though,
One who had taken logic long ago,
Was there; his horse was thinner than a rake,
And he was not too fat, I undertake,
But had a hollow look, a sober stare.
The thread upon his overcoat was bare;
He had found no preferment [employment] in the church
And he was too unworldly to make search
For secular employment. By his bed
He preferred having twenty books, in red
And black, of Aristotle's philosophy,
To having fine clothes, fiddle, or psaltery [a book of Psalms used for daily prayer].
Though a philosopher, as I have told,
He had not found the stone for making gold.
Whatever money from his friends he took
He spent on learning or another book
And prayed for them most earnestly, returning
Thanks to them thus for paying for his learning.
His only care was study, and indeed
He never spoke a word more than was need,
Formal at that, respectful in the extreme,
Short, to the point, and lofty in this theme.
The thought of moral virtue filled his speech
And he would gladly learn, and gladly teach.

STUDENT LETTERS

The relationship between fathers and their sons enrolled at universities has not changed all that much since the Middle Ages, as the letters that follow demonstrate.

FATHERS TO SONS

I

I have recently discovered that you live dissolutely and slothfully, preferring license to restraint and play to work and strumming a guitar while the others are at their studies, whence it happens that you have read but one volume of law while your more industrious companions have read several. Wherefore I have decided to exhort you herewith to repent utterly of your dissolute and careless ways, that you may no longer be called a waster and your shame may be turned to good repute.

II

I have learned — not from your master, although he ought not to hide such things from me, but from a certain trustworthy source — that you do not study in your room or act in the schools as a good student should, but play and wander about, disobedient to your master and indulging in sport and in certain other dishonorable practices which I do not now care to explain by letter.

SONS TO FATHERS

I

"Well-beloved father, I have not a penny, nor can I get any save through you, for all things at the University are so dear: nor can I study in my Code or my Digest, for they are all tattered. Moreover, I owe ten crowns in dues to the Provost, and can find no man to lend them to me; I send you word of greetings and of money.

The Student hath need of many things if he will profit here; his father and his kin must needs supply him freely, that he be not compelled to pawn his books, but have ready money in his purse, with gowns and furs and decent clothing, or he will be damned for a beggar; wherefore, that men may not take me for a beast, I send you word of greetings and of money.

Wines are dear, and hostels, and other good things; I owe in every street, and am hard bested to free myself from such snares. Dear father, deign to help me! I fear to be excommunicated; already have I been cited, and there is not even a dry bone in my larder. If I find not the money before this feast of Easter, the church door will be shut in my face: wherefore grant my supplication, for I send you word of greetings and of money.

L'ENVOY

Well-beloved father, to ease my debts contracted at the tavern, at the baker's, with the doctor and the bedells [a minor college official], and to pay my subscriptions to the laundress and the barber, I send you word of greetings and of money."

II

Sing unto the Lord a new song, praise him with stringed instruments and organs, rejoice upon the high-sounding cymbals, for your son has held a glorious disputation, which was attended by a great number of teachers and scholars. He answered all questions without a mistake, and no one could get the better of him or prevail against his arguments. Moreover he celebrated a famous banquet, at which both rich and poor were honoured as never before, and he has duly begun to give lectures which are already so popular that others' classrooms are deserted and his own are filled.

REVIEW QUESTIONS

1. What were the liberal arts in the twelfth-century schools?
2. What significance did John of Salisbury give to the word *liberal?* Would a modern writer argue differently?
3. According to John of Salisbury, what was the significance of grammar as an object of study? Do you agree or disagree?
4. Is there any connection between modern learning and the fostering of virtuous citizens? Explain.
5. The medieval scholar was clear about who he was and what was expected of him. Does he resemble his modern counterpart in any specific ways? How does he differ from a modern university student?

---

8 ▾ The Jews in the Middle Ages

Toward the end of the eleventh century, small communities of Jews were living in many of the larger towns of Christian Europe. Most of these Jews were descended from Jewish inhabitants of the Roman Empire. Under the protection of the Roman law or of individual Germanic kings, they had managed to survive amid a sometimes hostile Christian population. But religious fanaticism unleashed by the call for the First Crusade undermined Christian–Jewish relations gravely. Bands of Crusaders began systematically to attack and massacre the Jewish inhabitants of Rhineland towns. Thousands were killed — many because they refused to become converts to Christianity; their houses were looted and burned. Efforts by the bishops and civil authorities to protect their Jewish subjects were largely ineffective. Anti-Semitism became endemic in Latin Christendom.

Albert of Aix-la-Chapelle
MASSACRE OF THE JEWS OF MAINZ

In the next reading, Albert, a twelfth-century priest of the city of Aix-la-Chapelle, describes the massacre of Jews (1096) at the beginning of the First Crusade.

At the beginning of summer in the same year in which Peter [the Hermit] and Gottschalk,[1] after collecting an army, had set out, there assembled in like fashion a large and innumerable host of Christians from diverse kingdoms and lands; namely, from the realms of France, England, Flanders, and Lorraine. . . . I know not whether by a judgment of the Lord, or by some error of mind, they rose in a spirit of cruelty against the Jewish people scattered throughout these cities and slaughtered them without mercy, especially in the Kingdom of

[1]A brilliant propagandist, Peter the Hermit raised a large army of poor and sparsely armed Frenchmen, who marched to Cologne to begin a Crusade to the Holy Land. Most of them were killed by Turkish forces after crossing into Asia Minor. Gottschalk was a German priest who gathered a band of undisciplined soldiers to join the First Crusade. His forces were killed by Hungarians defending their families and property from these Crusaders.

Lorraine,[2] asserting it to be the beginning of their expedition and their duty against the enemies of the Christian faith. This slaughter of Jews was done first by citizens of Cologne.[3] These suddenly fell upon a small band of Jews and severely wounded and killed many; they destroyed the houses and synagogues of the Jews and divided among themselves a very large amount of money. When the Jews saw this cruelty, about two hundred in the silence of the night began flight by boat to Neuss. The pilgrims and crusaders discovered them, and after taking away all their possessions, inflicted on them similar slaughter, leaving not even one alive.

Not long after this, they started upon their journey, as they had vowed, and arrived in a great multitude at the city of Mainz. There Count Emico, a nobleman, a very mighty man in this region, was awaiting, with a large band of Teutons [German soldiers], the arrival of the pilgrims who were coming thither from diverse lands by the King's highway.

The Jews of this city, knowing of the slaughter of their brethren, and that they themselves could not escape the hands of so many, fled in hope of safety to Bishop Rothard. They put an infinite treasure in his guard and trust, having much faith in his protection, because he was Bishop of the city. Then that excellent Bishop of the city cautiously set aside the incredible amount of money received from them. He placed the Jews in the very spacious hall of his own house, away from the sight of Count Emico and his followers, that they might remain safe and sound in a very secure and strong place.

But Emico and the rest of his band held a council and, after sunrise, attacked the Jews in the hall with arrows and lances. Breaking the bolts and doors, they killed the Jews, about seven hundred in number, who in vain resisted the force and attack of so many thousands. They killed the women, also, and with their swords pierced tender children of whatever age and sex. The Jews, seeing that their Christian enemies were attacking them and their children, and that they were sparing no age, likewise fell upon one another, brother, children, wives, and sisters, and thus they perished at each other's hands. Horrible to say, mothers cut the throats of nursing children with knives and stabbed others, preferring them to perish thus by their own hands rather than to be killed by the weapons of the uncircumcised.

From this cruel slaughter of the Jews a few escaped; and a few because of fear, rather than because of love of the Christian faith, were baptized. With very great spoils taken from these people, Count Emico, Clarebold, Thomas, and all that intolerable company of men and women then continued on their way to Jerusalem.

[2]Lorraine, a duchy in the western part of the Holy Roman Empire, is now part of France.

[3]Cologne (Köln), founded by the Romans in the first century A.D., was the largest city in the Rhine Valley, a center of commerce, industry, and learning. Its politically powerful archbishop was a prince of the Holy Roman Empire.

A DECREE BY POPE INNOCENT III

Regarding the Jews as wicked because they refused to accept Christ, the church wanted them to live in humiliation. However, the church did at times seek to protect them from violence.

The Fourth Lateran Council, which was organized by Innocent III (1198–1216), the most powerful of medieval popes, barred Jews from public office and required them to wear a distinguishing badge on their clothing, a sign of their degradation. Yet Innocent, as the following passage indicates, also cautioned against harming Jews. The passage, however, reveals some of the torments faced by Jews.

. . . We decree that no Christian shall use violence to compel the Jews to accept baptism. But if a Jew, of his own accord, because of a change in his faith, shall have taken refuge with Christians, after his wish has been made known, he may be made a Christian without any opposition. For anyone who has not of his own will sought Christian baptism cannot have the true Christian faith. No Christian shall do the Jews any personal injury, except in executing the judgments of a judge, or deprive them of their possessions, or change the rights and privileges which they have been accustomed to have. During the celebration of their festivals, no one shall disturb them by beating them with clubs or by throwing stones at them. No one shall compel them to render any services except those which they have been accustomed to render. And to prevent the baseness and avarice of wicked men we forbid anyone to deface or damage their cemeteries or to extort money from them by threatening to exhume the bodies of their dead. . . .

THE LIBEL OF RITUAL MURDER

Despite efforts by some popes to protect Jews, outbreaks of violence toward them persisted and bizarre myths about them emerged. Jews were seen as agents of Satan conspiring to destroy Christendom and as sorcerers employing black magic against Christians. Perhaps the most absurd (and dangerous) charge against the Jewish people was the accusation of ritual murder — that the Jews, requiring Christian blood for the Passover service, sacrificed a Christian child. Despite the denials of Jews and enlightened Christian leaders, hundreds of such accusations were made, resulting in the torture, murder, and expulsion of many Jews. In the next passage, an English chronicler reports on the death of one young Harold, in Gloucester, England, in 1168.

. . . [The eight-year-old] boy Harold, who is buried in the Church of St. Peter the Apostle, at Gloucester . . . , is said to have been carried away secretly by Jews, in the opinion of many,* on Feb. 21, and by them hidden till March 16. On that night, on the sixth of the preceding feast, the Jews of all England coming together as if to circumcise a certain boy, pretend deceitfully that they are about to celebrate the feast [Passover] appointed by law in such case, and deceiving the citizens of Gloucester with that fraud, they tortured the lad placed before them with immense tortures. It is true no Christian was present, or saw or heard the deed, nor have we found that anything was betrayed by any Jew. But a little while after when the whole convent of monks of Gloucester and almost all the citizens of that city, and innumerable persons coming to the spectacle, saw the wounds of the dead body, scars of fire, the thorns fixed on his head, and liquid wax poured into the eyes and face, and touched it with the diligent examination of their hands, those tortures were believed or guessed to have been inflicted on him in that manner. It was clear that they had made him a glorious martyr to Christ, being slain without sin, and having bound his feet with his own girdle, threw him into the river Severn. (The body is taken to St. Peter's Church, and there performs miracles.)

*Even the chronicler puts it doubly doubtfully.

Maimonides
JEWISH LEARNING

Medieval Jews, despite frequent persecution, carried on a rich cultural and intellectual life based on their ancestral religion. The foremost Jewish scholar of the Middle Ages was Moses ben Maimon, also called by the Greek name Maimonides (1135–1204), who was born in Córdoba, Spain, then under Muslim rule. After his family emigrated from Spain, Maimonides went to Egypt, where he became physician to the sultan. During his lifetime, Maimonides achieved fame as a philosopher, theologian, mathematician, and physician; he was recognized as the leading Jewish sage of his day, and his writings were respected by Christian and Muslim thinkers as well. Like Christian scholastics and Muslim philosophers, Maimonides tried to harmonize faith with reason, to reconcile the Hebrew Scriptures and the Talmud (Jewish biblical commentary) with Greek philosophy. In his writings on ethical themes, Maimonides demonstrated piety, wisdom, and humanity. In the following passages, he discusses education and charity.

[EDUCATION]

Every man in Israel [every Jew] is obliged to study the Torah,[1] whether he be poor or rich, whether he be physically healthy or ailing, whether he be in full vigor of youth or of great age and weakened vitality; even if he be dependent upon alms for his livelihood, or going around from door to door begging his daily bread, yea, even he who has a wife and children to support is obliged to have an appointed time for the study of the Torah, both during the day and at night, for it is said: "But thou shalt meditate therein day and night" (Joshua, I.8).

Some of the great scholars in Israel were hewers of wood, some of them drawers of water, and some of them blind: nevertheless they engaged themselves in the study of the Torah by day and by night. Moreover, they are included among those who translated the tradition as it was transmitted from mouth of man to mouth of man, even from the mouth of Moses our Master [the biblical Moses].

Until what age in life is one obliged to study the Torah? Even until the day of one's demise; for it is said: "And lest they depart from thy heart all the days of thy life" (Deut. 4.9). Forsooth, as long as one will not occupy himself with study he forgets what he did study.

One is obligated to divide his time of study by three; one third for the study of Holy Writ, one third for the study of the Oral Torah [the interpretations of the Torah], and one third for thinking and reflecting so that he may understand the end of a thing from its beginning, and deduct one matter from another, and compare one matter to another. . . .

When a master gave a lesson which the disciples did not understand, he should not get angry at them and be moody, but go over it again and repeat it even many times, until they will understand the depth of the treatise. Likewise, a disciple shall not say, I understood, and he did not understand; but he should repeat and ask even many times. If the master angers at him and becomes moody, he may say to him:

[1]The Torah refers to the first five books of the Hebrew Scriptures, which the Jews believed were written by Moses. In time, *Torah* also acquired a broader meaning that encompassed the entire Hebrew Scriptures and the various commentaries.

"Master, it is Torah, and I need instruction, but my mind is short of understanding!"

A disciple shall not feel ashamed before his fellows who mastered the subject the first or the second time, whereas he did not grasp it until after hearing it many times, for if he will be ashamed of such a thing, he will find himself coming in and going out of the . . . [school] without any instructions at all. The sages, therefore, said: "he who is bashful cannot be instructed and he who is in an angry mood cannot instruct.". . .

Even as a man is under command to honor his father and fear him, so is he obliged to honor his master, but fear him yet more than his father; his father brought him to life upon this world but his master who taught him wisdom, brings him to life in the world to come. . . .

▷ Care for the poor is ingrained in the Jewish tradition. Rabbis gave the highest value to assistance, given in secret, that helps a poor person to become self-supporting. Maimonides drew upon this rabbinical tradition in his discussion of charity.

[CHARITY]

The law of the Torah commanded us to practise *tsedakah,*[1] support the needy and help them financially. The command in connection with this duty occurs in various expressions; e.g., "Thou shalt surely open thy hand unto him" (Deut. xv. 8), "Thou shalt uphold him; as a stranger and a settler shall he live with thee" (Lev. xxv. 35). The intention in these passages is identical, viz., that we should console the poor man and support him to the extent of sufficiency. . . .

There are eight degrees in alms-giving, one higher than the other: Supreme above all is to give assistance to a co-religionist who has fallen on evil times by presenting him with a gift or loan, or entering into a partnership with him, or procuring him work, thereby helping him to become self-supporting.

Inferior to this is giving charity to the poor in such a way that the giver and recipient are unknown to each other. This is, indeed, the performance of a commandment from disinterested motives; and it is exemplified by the Institution of the Chamber of the Silent which existed in the Temple,[2] where the righteous secretly deposited their alms and the respectable poor were secretly assisted.*

Next in order is the donation of money to the charitable fund of the Community, to which no contribution should be made without the donors feeling confident that the administration is honest, prudent and capable of proper management.

Below this degree is the instance where the donor is aware to whom he is giving the alms but the recipient is unaware from whom he received them; as, e.g., the great Sages who used to go about secretly throwing money through the doors of the poor. This is quite a proper course to adopt and a great virtue where the administrators of a charitable fund are not acting fairly.

Inferior to this degree is the case where the recipient knows the identity of the donor, but not *vice versa;* as, e.g., the great Sages who used to tie sums of money in linen bundles and throw them behind their backs for poor men to pick up, so that they should not feel shame.

The next four degrees in their order are: the man who gives money to the poor before he is asked; the man who gives money to the poor after he is asked; the man who gives less than he should, but does it with good grace; and lastly, he who gives grudgingly.

[1]The term *tsedakah* is derived from *tsédek* (righteousness); it denotes showing kindness to others.

[2]The Temple to which Maimonides refers was the Temple in Jerusalem, destroyed by the Romans in A.D. 70.

*This system of charity was adopted by Jews in several Palestinian and Babylonian cities.

REVIEW QUESTIONS

1. What were the apparent motives of those who attacked the Jews in Cologne and elsewhere? Why were the local authorities unable to protect the Jews?
2. Why did the First Crusade spark such violence and religious hatred in some parts of Europe?
3. What harassments and abuses were Jews likely to suffer in medieval society?
4. According to Maimonides, what role should the study of the Hebrew Scriptures play in the life of a medieval Jew?
5. What did Maimonides say that a student's attitude should be as he studied the Hebrew Scriptures?
6. Why did Maimonides believe the highest form of charity to be that which helps a neighbor to maintain his independence?
7. What did Maimonides think of publicizing one's acts of charity?

---

9 ▾ The Status of Women in Medieval Society

The precise status of a woman in medieval society differed immensely depending on the time, the place, and her class. The majority of women managed families and households, often taking part in farmwork or other crafts connected with the family livelihood. However, their legal rights, social standing, and power were inferior to those of adult males in their own families. During the High Middle Ages, the Christian church increasingly supported a patriarchal structure of authority in church and civil society that left women effectively under the domination of males, clerical and lay. Although the teachings of Aristotle about women tended to demean their status among intellectuals, several of the church's teachings recognized the inherent dignity of a woman. The church regarded marriage as a sacrament, considered adultery a sin, and subjected men and women to the same moral standards. Neither sex had any special advantage in attaining salvation.

Despite legal, social, and economic handicaps imposed upon them by males, some women successfully assumed positions of power and achievement. A few ruled kingdoms and principalities or headed convents and religious orders. Others organized guilds; founded nunneries; practiced various crafts; served as teachers, physicians, and midwives; and operated small businesses. Some showed talent as poets, dramatists, and artists.

In the late twelfth century, new kinds of poetry with a distinctive set of themes began to be created at the castles and courts in France, Italy, Spain, and Germany. The poets were themselves knights or noblewomen who composed their poems to be sung or read aloud for the entertainment of fellow feudal nobles. The subject was always that of the love between man and woman.

Cercamon
TROUBADOUR LOVE SONG

The original inspiration for the new troubadour poetry was probably the Arab poetry of Spain and Sicily, where the theme of courtly love was developed earlier. What was revolutionary in later European poetry was its treatment of the relationship between men and women. The troubadours reversed the traditional view of men as superior and women inferior and dependent in their relationships. They introduced what is called "courtly love," a love relationship in which the woman is the superior and dominant figure, the man inferior and dependent. The male courts the lady, paying homage to her beauty and virtue. He suffers humiliation and frustration at her will. Their love remains chaste, and may not be consummated, yet the poet expresses the erotic tensions openly. In the following reading, Cercamon, a twelfth-century troubadour from Gascony, France, tells of a lover's failure to win the attention of his beloved.

Now that the air is fresher
and the world turned green,
I shall sing once more
of the one I love and desire,
but we are so far apart
that I cannot go and witness
how my words might please her.

And nothing can console me
but death, for evil tongues
(may God curse them)
have made us part.
And alas, I so desired her
that now I moan and cry
half mad with grief.

I sing of her, yet her beauty
is greater than I can tell,
with her fresh color, lovely eyes,
and white skin, untanned
and untainted by rouge.
She is so pure and noble
that no one can speak ill of her.

But above all, one must praise,
it seems to me, her truthfulness,
her manners and her gracious speech,
for she never would betray a friend;
and I was mad to believe
what I heard tell of her
and thus cause her to be angry.

I never intended to complain;
and even now, if she so desires,
she could bring me happiness
by granting what I seek.
I cannot go on like this much longer,
for since she's been so far away
I've scarcely slept or eaten.

Love is sweet to look upon
but bitter upon parting;
one day it makes you weep
and another skip and dance,
for now I know that the more
one enters love's service,
the more fickle it becomes.

Messenger, go with Godspeed
and bring this to my lady,
for I cannot stay here much longer
and live, or be cured elsewhere,
unless I have her next to me,
naked, to kiss and embrace
within a curtained room.

Jakob Sprenger and Heinrich Kramer ANTIFEMALE PREJUDICES

The ambivalence in the male attitude (particularly of the intellectuals) toward women arose from several sources. First, medieval and Renaissance authors, who highly esteemed the classical works of the ancient Greco-Roman civilization, were influenced by the hostility evident in the writings of that era toward women who did not accept their position as subordinate and inferior to men. Second, the Christian view of men and women as equals in the sight of God was obscured by certain scriptural texts, such as Saint Paul's "Let your women keep silence in the churches: for it is not permitted unto them to speak" (1 Corinthians 14:34); and "Wives, submit yourselves unto your own husbands, as unto the Lord" (Ephesians 5:22). This ambivalent view of women was symbolized by the Old Testament portrait of Eve as the archetypal temptress, who led Adam to sin, and the New Testament picture of the Virgin Mary, whose acceptance of her role as the mother of Jesus made salvation possible for all people. Third, the clerical insistence that celibacy was superior to marriage (because the former avoided the distractions of the flesh and family life and allowed concentration on spiritual matters) encouraged prejudice against women. In the following passages from *The Hammer of Witches* (1486), the classic textbook on sorcery and witchcraft, the German clergymen Jakob Sprenger and Heinrich Kramer give vent to anti-female prejudices that were not uncommon then.

Now the wickedness of women is spoken of in *Ecclesiasticus xxv* [Old Testament book]: There is no head above the head of a serpent: and there is no wrath above the wrath of a woman. I had rather dwell with a lion and a dragon than to keep house with a wicked woman. And among much which in that place precedes and follows about a wicked woman, he concludes: All wickedness is but little to the wickedness of a woman. Wherefore [Saint] John Chrysostom [fourth-century bishop] says on the text, It is not good to marry *(S. Matthew* xix): What else is woman but a foe to friendship, an unescapable punishment, a necessary evil, a natural temptation, a desirable calamity, a domestic danger, a delectable detriment, an evil of nature, painted with fair colours! Therefore if it be a sin to divorce her when she ought to be kept, it is indeed a necessary torture; for either we commit adultery by divorcing her, or we must endure daily strife. Cicero [Roman statesman and philosopher] in his second book of *The Rhetorics* says: The many lusts of men lead them into one sin, but the one lust of women leads them into all sins; for the root of all woman's vices is avarice. And Seneca [Roman dramatist] says in his *Tragedies:* A woman either loves or hates; there is no third grade. And the tears of a woman are a deception, for they may spring from true grief, or they may be a snare. When a woman thinks alone, she thinks evil. . . .

Others again have propounded other reasons why there are more superstitious women found than men. And the first is, that they are more credulous; and since the chief aim of the devil is to corrupt faith, therefore he rather attacks them. See *Ecclesiasticus* xix: He that is quick to believe is light-minded, and shall be diminished. The second reason is, that women are naturally more impressionable, and more ready to receive the influence of a disembodied spirit; and that when they use this quality well they are very good, but when they use it ill they are very evil.

The third reason is that they have slippery tongues, and are unable to conceal from their fellow-women those things which by evil arts they know; and, since they are weak, they find an easy and secret manner of vindicating themselves by witchcraft. . . .

. . . [S]ince they are feebler both in mind and body, it is not surprising that they should come more under the spell of witchcraft.

For as regards intellect, or the understanding of spiritual things, they seem to be of a different nature from men; a fact which is vouched for by the logic of the authorities, backed by various examples from the Scriptures. Terence [Roman dramatist] says: Women are intellectually like children. And Lactantius [fourth-century Christian writer] *(Institutiones,* III): No woman understood philosophy except Temeste. . . .

But the natural reason is that she is more carnal than a man, as is clear from her many carnal abominations. And it should be noted that there was a defect in the formation of the first woman, since she was formed from a bent rib, that is, a rib of the breast, which is bent as it were in a contrary direction to a man. And since through this defect she is an imperfect animal, she always deceives. For Cato [Roman statesman] says: When a woman weeps she weaves snares. And again: When a woman weeps, she labours to deceive a man. And this is shown by Samson's wife [Delilah], who coaxed him to tell her the riddle he had propounded to the Philistines, and told them the answer, and so deceived him. And it is clear in the case of the first woman [Eve] that she had little faith; for when the serpent asked why they did not eat of every tree in Paradise, she answered: Of every tree, etc. — lest perchance we die. Thereby she showed that she doubted, and had little faith in the word of God. And all this is indicated by the etymology of the word; for *Femina* [woman] comes from *Fe* [to produce] and *Minus* [less], since she is ever weaker to hold and preserve the faith. And this as regards faith is of her very nature; although both by grace and nature faith never failed in the Blessed Virgin [Mary], even at the time of Christ's Passion, when it failed in all men.

Therefore a wicked woman is by her nature quicker to waver in her faith, and consequently quicker to abjure the faith, which is the root of witchcraft.

And as to her other mental quality, that is, her natural will; when she hates someone whom she formerly loved, then she seethes with anger and impatience in her whole soul, just as the tides of the sea are always heaving and boiling. Many authorities allude to this cause. *Ecclesiasticus* xxv: There is no wrath above the wrath of a woman. And Seneca (*Tragedies,* VIII): No might of the flames or of the swollen winds, no deadly weapon is so much to be feared as the lust and hatred of a woman who has been divorced from the marriage bed.

And indeed, just as through the first defect in their intelligence they are more prone to abjure the faith; so through their second defect of inordinate affections and passions they search for, brood over, and inflict various vengeances, either by witchcraft, or by some other means. Wherefore it is no wonder that so great a number of witches exist in this sex.

Women also have weak memories; and it is a natural vice in them not to be disciplined, but to follow their own impulses without any sense of what is due. . . .

To conclude. All witchcraft comes from carnal lust, which is in women insatiable. See *Proverbs* xxx [Old Testament book]: There are three things that are never satisfied, yea, a fourth thing . . . the mouth of the womb. Wherefore for the sake of fulfilling their lusts they consort even with devils. More such reasons could be brought forward, but to the understanding it is sufficiently clear that it is no matter for wonder that there are more women than men found infected with the heresy of witchcraft. And in consequence of this, it is better called the heresy of witches than of wizards, since the name is taken from the more powerful party. And blessed be the Highest Who has so far preserved the male sex from so great a crime. . . .

Christine de Pisan
≪ THE CITY OF LADIES ≫

Toward the end of the Middle Ages, a remarkable woman took up the task of defending women from their many male detractors. Christine de Pisan (1364–1429?) was born in Venice but moved with her parents to Paris, where her father was court physician and astrologer. She married a court notary when she was fifteen, had three children, and was left a widow and penniless ten years later. She decided to use her unusually good education to become a professional writer, an unheard-of occupation for a woman at that time. She won the patronage and friendship of noble ladies at the French royal court and produced many poems and books, including a biography of King Charles V and several polemical attacks upon the poets who slandered womankind. The most famous of these is *The City of Ladies,* written in 1405. In it Christine de Pisan questioned three allegorical figures — Reason, Rectitude, and Justice — about the lies and slanders of males concerning the virtues and achievements of women. The book is really a history of famous women and their accomplishments in many fields of endeavour. In the following passages, she questioned Lady Reason about the alleged inferiority of women to men; de Pisan cleverly changed the subject to that of virtue, proclaiming the equality of the sexes in attaining it.

"My lady [Lady Reason], according to what I understand from you, woman is a most noble creature. But even so, Cicero [Roman statesman] says that a man should never serve any woman and that he who does so debases himself, for no man should ever serve anyone lower than him."

She replied, "The man or the woman in whom resides greater virtue is the higher; neither the loftiness nor the lowliness of a person lies in the body according to the sex, but in the perfection of conduct and virtues. And surely he is happy who serves the Virgin [Mary, the mother of Jesus], who is above all the angels."

"My lady, one of the Catos[1] — who was such a great orator — said, nevertheless, that if this world were without women, we would converse with the gods."

She replied, "You can now see the foolishness of the man who is considered wise, because, thanks to a woman, man reigns with God. And if anyone would say that man was banished because of Lady Eve, I tell you that he gained more through [the Virgin] Mary than he lost through Eve when humanity was conjoined to the Godhead,[2] which would never have taken place if Eve's misdeed [eating the forbidden fruit] had not occurred. Thus man and woman should be glad for this sin, through which such an honor has come about. For as low as human nature fell through this creature woman, was human nature lifted higher by this same creature. And as for conversing with the gods, as this Cato has said, if there had been no woman, he spoke truer than he knew, for he was a pagan, and among those of this belief, gods were thought to reside in Hell as well as in Heaven, that is, the devils whom they called the gods of Hell — so that it is no lie that these gods would have conversed with men, if Mary had not lived."

[1]Several Roman statesmen bore the name Cato. Cato the Censor (234–149 B.C.) was a vigorous critic of women.

[2]This clause refers to the Christian belief that God became a human being in the person of Jesus Christ.

▷ In this next passage, de Pisan discusses the slander that women are not as intelligent as men.

". . . But please enlighten me again, whether it has ever pleased this God, who has bestowed so many favors on women, to honor the feminine sex with the privilege of the virtue of high understanding and great learning, and whether women ever have a clever enough mind for this. I wish very much to know this because men maintain that the mind of women can learn only a little."

She [Lady Reason] answered, "My daughter, since I told you before, you know quite well that the opposite of their opinion is true, and to show you this even more clearly, I will give you proof through examples. I tell you again — and don't doubt the contrary — if it were customary to send daughters to school like sons, and if they were then taught the natural sciences, they would learn as thoroughly and understand the subtleties of all the arts and sciences as well as sons. And by chance there happen to be such women, for, as I touched on before, just as women have more delicate bodies than men, weaker and less able to perform many tasks, so do they have minds that are freer and sharper whenever they apply themselves."

"My lady, what are you saying? With all due respect, could you dwell longer on this point, please. Certainly men would never admit this answer is true, unless it is explained more plainly, for they believe that one normally sees that men know more than women do."

She answered, "Do you know why women know less?"

"Not unless you tell me, my lady."

"Without the slightest doubt, it is because they are not involved in many different things, but stay at home, where it is enough for them to run the household, and there is nothing which so instructs a reasonable creature as the exercise and experience of many different things."

"My lady, since they have minds skilled in conceptualizing and learning, just like men, why don't women learn more?"

She replied, "Because, my daughter, the public does not require them to get involved in the affairs which men are commissioned to execute, just as I told you before. It is enough for women to perform the usual duties to which they are ordained. As for judging from experience, since one sees that women usually know less than men, that therefore their capacity for understanding is less, look at men who farm the flatlands or who live in the mountains. You will find that in many countries they seem completely savage because they are so simple-minded. All the same, there is no doubt that Nature provided them with the qualities of body and mind found in the wisest and most learned men. . . ."

▷ Next, Christine de Pisan argues in favor of giving young women the same opportunities for learning as men.

Following these remarks, I, Christine, spoke, "My lady, I realize that women have accomplished many good things and that even if evil women have done evil, it seems to me, nevertheless, that the benefits accrued and still accruing because of good women — particularly the wise and literary ones and those educated in the natural sciences whom I mentioned above — outweigh the evil. Therefore, I am amazed by the opinion of some men who claim that they do not want their daughters, wives, or kinswomen to be educated because their mores would be ruined as a result."

She responded, "Here you can clearly see that not all opinions of men are based on reason and that these men are wrong. For it must not be presumed that mores necessarily grow worse from knowing the moral sciences, which teach the virtues, indeed, there is not the slightest doubt that moral education amends and ennobles them. How could anyone think or believe that whoever follows good teaching or doctrine is the worse for it? Such an opinion cannot be expressed or maintained. I do not mean that it would be good for a man or a woman to study the art of divination or those fields of learning which are forbidden — for the holy Church did not remove them from common use without good reason — but it should not be believed that women are the worse for knowing what is good. . . .

". . . To speak of more recent times, without searching for examples in ancient history, Giovanni Andrea, a solemn law professor in Bologna [Italy] not quite sixty years ago, was not of the opinion that it was bad for women to be educated. He had a fair and good daughter, named Novella, who was educated in the law to such an advanced degree that when he was occupied by some task and not at leisure to present his lectures to his students, he would send Novella, his daughter, in his place to lecture to the students from his chair. And to prevent her beauty from distracting the concentration of her audience, she had a little curtain drawn in front of her. In this manner she could on occasion supplement and lighten her father's occupation. . . ."

REVIEW QUESTIONS

1. What are the characteristic features that identify the troubadour poem as a "courtly love" poem?
2. Does the time of year seem appropriate to the poet's plight?
3. What caused the breakup of the romance?
4. What ancient authorities do Jakob Sprenger and Heinrich Kramer use to strengthen their arguments against the wiles of females?
5. Evaluate the arguments set forth by Sprenger and Kramer. How would Christine de Pisan have responded to such charges?
6. According to de Pisan, what was the Roman attitude toward women?
7. What standard for judging the superiority of any person did de Pisan recommend?
8. How did Lady Reason reply to those who might argue that man fell into sin through the influence of Eve?
9. What did Lady Reason claim was needed in order for women to demonstrate that they were as intelligent as men?
10. What explanation did Lady Reason give in support of the belief that women's morals would be improved if women were better educated?

---

10 ▾ Medieval Contributions to the Tradition of Liberty

In several ways the Middle Ages contributed to the development of liberty in the Western world. Townsmen organized themselves into revolutionary associations called communes to demand freedom from the domination of feudal lords. They successfully won personal liberties, the end of feudal labor services and arbitrary tax levies, and a system of municipal self-government. Another development crucial to the tradition of liberty was the resistance of lords to kings who attempted to interfere with the lords' customary rights. These actions helped to establish the tradition that kings were not above the law and could

not rule arbitrarily or absolutely. There is a direct link between modern parliaments and medieval representative institutions, particularly in the case of the English Parliament.

Medieval theologians made a significant contribution to the growth of liberty. They held that a monarch's powers were limited by God's laws and by what was for the common good of Christian people. Some argued that a monarch who ignored or violated the laws and liberties of the people or the church became a tyrant and forfeited his right to be ruler. Such rulers could be, and some in fact were, deposed.

John of Salisbury ≪ *POLICRATICUS* ≫ *A DEFENSE OF TYRANNICIDE*

One prelate who opposed the rule of tyrants was an Englishman, John of Salisbury (see Section 7), who became bishop of Chartres, France, in 1176. He composed a statesman's handbook, *Policraticus,* explicitly defending the assassination of tyrants. Paraphrasing the Roman statesman Cicero, John held that it was right, lawful, and just to slay a tyrant.

. . . A tyrant, then, as the philosophers have described him, is one who oppresses the people by the rulership based upon force, while he who rules in accordance with the laws is a prince. Law is the gift of God, the model of equity, a standard of justice, a likeness of the divine will, the guardian of well-being, a bond of union and solidarity between peoples, a rule defining duties, a barrier against the vices and the destroyer thereof, a punishment of violence and all wrong-doing. The law is assailed by force or by fraud, and, as it were, either wrecked by the fury of the lion or undermined by the wiles of the serpent. In whatever way this comes to pass, it is plain that it is the grace of God which is being assailed and that it is God himself who in a sense is challenged to battle. The prince fights for the laws and the liberty of the people; the tyrant thinks nothing done unless he brings the laws to nought and reduces the people to slavery. Hence the prince is a kind of likeness of divinity; and the tyrant, on the contrary, a likeness of the boldness of the Adversary [the devil], even of the wickedness of Lucifer. . . . The prince, as the likeness of the Deity, is to be loved, worshipped and cherished; the tyrant, the likeness of wickedness, is generally to be even killed. The origin of tyranny is iniquity, and springing from a poisonous root, it is a tree which grows and sprouts into a baleful pestilent growth, and to which the axe must by all means be laid.

≪ *MAGNA CARTA* ≫

The feudal nobles sought freedom by limiting the arbitrary powers of the kings, compelling them to issue written charters of liberties. These earliest constitutions spelled out the rights of subjects and the obligations of rulers. In 1215 King John of England (1199–1216) was compelled to recognize the liberties of his vassals, the clergy, and the towns in the Great Charter *(Magna Carta).* The

king and his agents were forbidden to act arbitrarily, and the king swore to govern by due process of law. Similar written constitutions checking the powers of kings and princes were achieved throughout Europe.

The Magna Carta asserted the feudal rights of the subjects of a monarch who allegedly tried to rule by personal will rather than by law. Though many of its detailed clauses subsequently lost their significance, three notions embedded in the Magna Carta became rooted in English constitutional tradition: that the king cannot levy a tax without the consent of his common council (later Parliament); that no one may be imprisoned or otherwise damaged except through due process of law and trial by jury of his (or her) peers; and that the king himself is subject to the law and, if he violates the rights of his subjects, he may be legally disobeyed and deposed. Significant portions of the document follow.

1. In the first place [I, John,] have granted to God and by this our present Charter have confirmed, for us and our heirs in perpetuity, that the English church shall be free, and shall have its rights undiminished and its liberties unimpaired. . . . We have also granted to all the free men of our realm for ourselves and our heirs for ever, all the liberties written below, to have and hold, them and their heirs from us and our heirs. . . .

12. No scutage[1] or aid[2] is to be levied in our realm except by the common counsel of our realm, unless it is for the ransom of our person, the knighting of our eldest son or the first marriage of our eldest daughter; and for these only a reasonable aid is to be levied. Aids from the city of London are to be treated likewise.

13. And the city of London is to have all its ancient liberties and free customs both by land and water. Furthermore, we will and grant that all other cities, boroughs, towns and ports shall have all their liberties and free customs.

14. And to obtain the common counsel of the realm for the assessment of an aid (except in the three cases aforesaid) or a scutage, we will have archbishops, bishops, abbots, earls and greater barons[3] summoned individually by our letters; and we shall also have summoned generally through our sheriffs and bailiffs[4] all those who hold of us in chief for a fixed date, with at least forty days' notice, and at a fixed place; and in all letters of summons we will state the reason for the summons. And when the summons has thus been made, the business shall go forward on the day arranged according to the counsel of those present, even if not all those summoned have come. . . .

20. A free man shall not be amerced [fined] for a trivial offence, except in accordance with the degree of the offence; and for a serious offence he shall be amerced according to its gravity, saving his livelihood; and a merchant likewise, saving his merchandise; in the same way a villein [serf] shall be amerced saving his wainage;[5] if they fall into our mercy. And none of the aforesaid amercements shall be imposed except by the testimony of reputable men of the neighbourhood.

21. Earls and barons shall not be amerced except by their peers and only in accordance with the nature of the offence. . . .

38. Henceforth no bailiff shall put anyone

---

[1]Scutage was a tax paid by knights to the king of England, their feudal overlord, in place of performing actual military service. In the absence of danger of war, the levying of scutage was considered an abuse of the king's authority.

[2]Aid, in this sense, was any obligation, usually financial, due from a vassal to his lord. The word was later used to indicate a tax on income or property paid by his subjects to the English king.

[3]Barons were vassals holding fiefs directly from the king; earls ("counts" in other lands) were nobles who managed counties or shires.

[4]The sheriff was a royal official responsible for the carrying out of laws in a shire or county; bailiffs were his assistants.

[5]*Wainage* (or *gainage*) is a collective term meaning farming tools and implements, including such things as wagons (wains).

on trial by his own unsupported allegation, without bringing credible witnesses to the charge.

39. No free man shall be taken or imprisoned or disseised [dispossessed] or outlawed or exiled or in any way ruined, nor will we go or send against him, except by the lawful judgement of his peers or by the law of the land.

40. To no one will we sell, to no one will we deny or delay right or justice.

41. All merchants are to be safe and secure in leaving and entering England, and in staying and travelling in England, both by land and by water, to buy and sell free from all maletotes [unjust taxes] by the ancient and rightful customs, except, in time of war, such as come from an enemy country. And if such are found in our land at the outbreak of war they shall be detained without damage to their persons or goods, until we or our chief justiciar [legal official] know how the merchants of our land are treated in the enemy country; and if ours are safe there, the others shall be safe in our land.

42. Henceforth anyone, saving his allegiance due to us, may leave our realm and return safe and secure by land and water, save for a short period in time of war on account of the general interest of the realm and excepting those imprisoned and outlawed according to the law of the land, and natives of an enemy country, and merchants, who shall be treated as aforesaid. . . .

Edward I of England
WRITS OF SUMMONS TO PARLIAMENT

The emergence of constitutional government was a major achievement of medieval civilization. The law came to be viewed as a reflection of the moral consent of the whole society rather than the arbitrary will of a despot. The rulers, in principle, governed by consent of the ruled. From the thirteenth century on, that consent was obtained through formal institutions called parliaments or assemblies. In these bodies, members of the different social classes, particularly the clergy, the nobles, small landholders, and townsmen, were present either in person or through their elected representatives. Through the latter, at least some of the populace participated in making new laws, levying taxes, and forming the general policies of the government.

A central principle in calling together assemblies or parliaments was found in Roman law and the canon law of the church: "what affects all should be approved by all" *(Quod omnes tangit ab omnibus approbetur).* Frequently appearing in medieval documents relating to administration of both church and government, the principle is cited in one of the following three summonses issued in 1295 by King Edward I (1272–1307), calling on his subjects to attend his parliament at Westminster Palace near London to deal with the threat of war with France.

The King to the venerable father in Christ, Robert, by the same grace Archbishop of Canterbury, primate [presiding bishop] of all England, greeting. As a most just law, established by the careful providence of sacred princes, exhorts and decrees that what affects all, should be approved by all, so also, very evidently should common danger be met by means provided in common. You know sufficiently well, and it is now, as we believe, known through all regions of the world, how the King of France fraudulently and craftily deprived us of our land of Gascony,[1] by withholding it unjustly from us. Now, however, not satisfied with the aforesaid fraud and injustice, having gathered together for the conquest of our kingdom a very great fleet, and a very large force of warriors, with which he has made a hostile attack on our kingdom and the inhabitants of the kingdom, he now proposes to stamp out the English language altogether from the earth if his power should be equal to the detestable task of the proposed iniquity, which God forbid. Because, therefore, darts seen beforehand do less injury, and your interest especially, as that of other fellow citizens of the same realm, is concerned in this affair, we command you, strictly enjoining you in the fidelity and love in which you are bound to us, that on the Lord's day [Sunday] next after the feast of St. Martin [November 11], in the approaching winter, you be present in person at Westminster; citing beforehand the dean [elected head] and chapter [corporate body of clergy] of your church, the archdeacons and all the clergy of your diocese, causing the same dean and archdeacons in their own persons, and the said chapter by one suitable proctor,[2] and the said clergy by two, to be present along with you, having full and sufficient power of themselves from the chapter and clergy, for considering, ordaining and providing along with us and with the rest of the prelates and principal men and other inhabitants of our kingdom how the dangers and threatened evils of this kind are to be met. Witness, the King at Wengham, the thirtieth day of September.

The King to his beloved and faithful kinsman, Edmund, Earl of Cornwall, greeting. Because we wish to have a conference and meeting with you and with the rest of the principal men of our kingdom, to provide remedies for the dangers which in these days threaten our whole kingdom; we command you, strictly enjoining you by the fidelity and love in which you are bound to us, that on the Lord's day next after the feast of St. Martin, in the approaching winter, you be present in person at Westminster, for considering, ordaining and doing with us, and with the prelates, and the rest of the magnates[3] and other inhabitants of our kingdom, as may be necessary to meet dangers of this kind. Witness, the King at Canterbury, on the first day of October.

The King to the sheriff of Northamptonshire [a county in central England]. Since we purpose to have a conference and meeting, with the earls, barons, and other principal men of our kingdom to provide remedies for the dangers which in these days threaten the same kingdom; and on that account, have commanded them to be with us, on the Lord's day next after the feast of St. Martin, in the approaching winter, at Westminster, to consider, ordain, and do, as may be necessary for the avoidance of these dangers; we strictly require you to cause two knights from the aforesaid county, two citizens from each city in the same county, and two burgesses from each borough, of the more discreet and capable, to be elected without delay, and to cause them to come to us, at the aforesaid time and place.

Moreover, the said knights are to have full and sufficient power, for themselves and for the commonalty of the aforesaid county, and the said citizens and burgesses for themselves and for the commonalty of the aforesaid cities and boroughs separately, then and there to do what shall be ordained by the common advice in the premises; so that the aforesaid business shall not remain unfinished in any way for defect of this power. And you shall have there the names of the knights, citizens and burgesses, and this writ.

Witness, the King at Canterbury, on the third day of October.

---

[1]Gascony was a duchy (dukedom) in the south of France; at this time it was a fief held from the king of France by the king of England, his most powerful vassal.

[2]A proctor in this sense is someone empowered to act for someone else, a proxy.

[3]Magnates were any powerful feudal lords whose wealth and military power gave them exceptional political and social importance.

REVIEW QUESTIONS

1. How did John of Salisbury justify resistance to tyranny, even the assassination of the tyrant?
2. In the selected passages from the Magna Carta, what specific liberties were guaranteed by the king to his subjects?
3. What restraints were placed on the king's power over his subjects?
4. How did the Magna Carta contribute to the development of English parliamentary government?
5. Why did King Edward I summon his parliament in 1295?
6. What constitutional principle did the king invoke in his summons to the Archbishop of Canterbury?

---

11 ▾ Late Medieval Political Theory

The fourteenth century brought a new crisis in church-state relations. King Philip the Fair (1285–1314) tried to raise revenues for the French government by taxing the property and income of the clergy without papal consent, efforts that were resisted by Pope Boniface VIII (1294–1303). When Boniface threatened to excommunicate all who cooperated in such tax collection, the king cut off all papal revenue from France. The struggle continued throughout Boniface's pontificate, ending in an attack in 1303 by French agents on the papal residence in Anagni, Italy, during which the aged pope was physically assaulted. The bitter struggle called forth a series of responses from both sides describing their respective positions on the proper relationship between state and church. Papal theorists, of course, emphasized the superiority of the spiritual power of the church over the temporal power of the state and insisted that it was the duty of earthly authority to aid the church in the performance of its spiritual duties.

John of Paris
≪ ON KINGLY AND PAPAL POWER ≫

In his treatise *On Kingly and Papal Power,* John of Paris (1241–1306), a Dominican theologian at the University of Paris, sought to defend the rights of the French king. In this reading, John distinguished the powers of church and state as parallel and autonomous, rather than hierarchical with the secular subordinate to the spiritual in all matters.

. . . For what is later in time is usually prior in dignity, what is perfect is prior to what is imperfect, and the end is prior to what relates to the end. Therefore, we say that priestly power is greater than kingly power, and excels it in dignity; for we always find that that to which the ultimate end pertains is more perfect, and directs that to which a lesser end pertains. Kingship, however, is ordered to the end that a community be brought together and live together according to virtue, as has been said. . . . And this in turn is further ordered to a higher end, the enjoyment of God, the direction of which was entrusted to Christ, of Whom priests are the vicars and ministers. Therefore, priestly power is of greater dignity than secular power. . . .

However, if the priest is greater than the prince in dignity and absolutely, it is not necessary for him to be superior in all things; for the latter secular power does not relate to the higher spiritual power in such a way that it arises or derives from it. This is how the power of the proconsul relates to the power of the emperor; and the latter is greater in all things because the proconsul's power is derived from the emperor. The relationship, rather, is like that between the power of the head of a family and that of a master of soldiers; one is not derived from the other, but both are derived from some superior power. Therefore, secular power is greater than spiritual power in some things, namely, temporal things; and it is not subject to the spiritual power with reference to them in any way, because secular power does not arise from spiritual power. The two arise directly from a single supreme power: the divine power. Wherefore the inferior is not subject to the superior in all things, but only in those things in respect of which the supreme power made it subordinate to the superior. For who would say that, because a teacher of literature or an instructor in morals orders everyone in a household to a more noble end, namely, to the knowledge of truth, a physician who is concerned with a lesser end, the health of the body, is therefore subject to either of these in the preparation of his medicines? This simply does not follow, since the head of the household, who appointed both to his household, would not for that reason subordinate the physician to one who has a higher purpose. Hence, the priest is superior principally in spiritual matters; and, conversely, the prince is superior in temporal matters, although the priest is superior absolutely insofar as the spiritual is superior to the temporal.

Marsilius of Padua
≪ THE DEFENDER OF THE PEACE ≫

In *The Defender of the Peace,* Marsilius of Padua (c. 1275–1342) made a radical break with traditional medieval political thought. Marsilius argued that Christ never intended that his Apostles or their successors, the bishops, should exercise temporal power; nor did he intend that the clergy should be exempt from civil laws. Marsilius held that political life operated according to its own principles and required no guidance from a higher authority; therefore, he said that the state should not be made to conform to standards formulated by the church. For Marsilius, the church was solely a spiritual institution; it possessed no temporal power, and the clergy were not above the laws of the state. Pope John XXII branded him a heretic for publishing this work, and Marsilius was forced to seek the protection of the German prince, Louis of Bavaria.

. . . I shall first show, that Christ himself came into the world not to dominate men, nor to judge them by [temporal] judgment . . . nor to wield temporal rule, but rather to be subject as regards the status of the present life; and moreover, that he wanted to and did exclude himself, his apostles and disciples, and their successors, the bishops or priests, from all such coercive authority or worldly rule, both by his example and by his words of counsel or command. I shall also show that the leading apostles, as Christ's true imitators, did this same thing and taught their successors to do likewise; and moreover, that both Christ and the apostles wanted to be and were continuously subject in property and in person to the coercive jurisdiction of secular rulers, and that they taught and commanded all others, to whom they preached or wrote the law of truth, to do likewise, under pain of eternal damnation. Then I shall write a chapter on the power or authority of the keys which Christ gave to the apostles and their successors in office, bishops and priests, so that it may be clear what is the nature, quality, and extent of such power, both of the Roman bishop and of the others. For ignorance on this point has hitherto been and still is the source of many questions and damnable controversies among the Christian faithful, as was mentioned in the first chapter of this discourse.

And so in pursuit of these aims we wish to show that Christ, in his purposes or intentions, words, and deeds, wished to exclude and did exclude himself and the apostles from every office of rulership, contentious jurisdiction, government, or coercive judgment in this world. This is first shown clearly beyond any doubt by the passage in the eighteenth chapter of the gospel of John. For when Christ was brought before Pontius Pilate, vicar of the Roman ruler in Judaea, and accused of having called himself king of the Jews, Pontius asked him whether he had said this, or whether he did call himself a king, and Christ's reply included these words, among others: "My kingdom is not of this world," that is, I have not come to reign by temporal rule or dominion, in the way in which worldly kings reign. And proof of this was given by Christ himself through an evident sign when he said: "If my kingdom were of this world, my servants would certainly fight, that I should not be delivered to the Jews," as if to argue as follows: If I had come into this world to reign by worldly or coercive rule, I would have ministers for this rule, namely, men to fight and to coerce transgressors, as the other kings have; but I do not have such ministers, as you can clearly see. . . .

. . . It now remains to show that not only did Christ himself refuse rulership or coercive judgment in this world, whereby he furnished an example for his apostles and disciples and their successors to do likewise, but also he taught by words and showed by example that all men, both priests and non-priests, should be subject in property and in person to the coercive judgment of the rulers of this world. By his word and example, then, Christ showed this first with respect to property, by what is written in the twenty-second chapter of Matthew. For when the Jews asked him: "Tell us therefore, what dost thou think? Is it lawful to give tribute to Caesar, or not?" Christ, after looking at the coin and its inscription, replied: "Render therefore to Caesar the things that are Caesar's, and to God the things that are God's." . . . So, then, we ought to be subject to Caesar in all things, so long only as they are not contrary to piety, that is, to divine worship or commandment. Therefore, Christ wanted us to be subject in property to the secular ruler. . . .

Like Christ and the apostles, then, the Roman bishops and priests and the whole clergy of Rome and the other provinces used to live under the coercive governance of those who were the rulers by authority of the human legislator. But later on, certain Roman bishops succumbed to the persuasion and incitation of that ruler of this world, that first parent of arrogance and presumption, that inculcator of all vices, the devil; and they were led, or rather misled, to a path foreign to that of Christ and the apostles. For cupidity and avarice, invading their minds, expelled therefrom that supreme meritorious poverty which Christ had introduced and established in the church. . . . And again, pride and ambition for secular rule, invading their minds, expelled therefrom that supreme humility which Christ had enjoined and commanded the church or whole priesthood to maintain.

This, then, as we have said, is and was the primary source of the present strife and discord between the emperors and the Roman pontiffs, since the controversies over divine law and over the heresies of certain rulers have died out entirely. For the Roman bishops wrongly wish to possess excessive temporal goods, and refuse to be subject to the laws and edicts of the rulers or the human legislator, thereby opposing the example and teaching of Christ and the apostles. . . .

REVIEW QUESTIONS

1. Compare the views of John of Paris with those of Pope Gelasius and Pope Gregory VII on the proper relationship of church and state (pages 195–196).
2. Compare the views of Marsilius of Padua and John of Paris on the proper relationship between church and state.
3. What arguments did Marsilius use to strip the church of its practice of holding or claiming temporal political authority?
4. In Marsilius's opinion, who and what was to blame for the church's claim to the exercise of temporal political authority?

12 ▾ Fourteenth-Century Pestilence

Until the fourteenth century, the population of Europe had increased steadily from its low point in the centuries immediately following the fall of the Roman Empire in the West. Particularly from the eleventh century on, landlords tried to raise their income by bringing new land into cultivation. By improving farming technology, building dikes, draining marshland, and clearing forests, European peasants produced much more food, which permitted more people to survive and multiply. That advance in population tapered off by the early fourteenth century due to many crop failures and wars, which wasted the countryside and led to economic stagnation. But the greatest catastrophe began in the fall of 1347, when sailors returning to Sicily from eastern Mediterranean ports brought with them a new disease, bubonic plague. Within the next three years, from one quarter to one third of the population of Europe died from what became known, because of some of its symptoms, as the Black Death. Most who caught the plague died, though some survived. No one knew its cause or cure. We now know that the bacteria were transmitted by fleas from infected rats. The unsanitary living conditions of medieval towns and low standards of personal cleanliness helped to spread the disease. The people were so terrified by the incomprehensible pattern of the disease's progress that superstition, hysteria, and breakdown of civility were common.

Jean de Venette
THE BLACK DEATH

The progress of the plague as it made its way through Europe and speculation on its causes, the terrible toll of victims, and various moral responses to the crisis are described in the following reading from the chronicle of Jean de Venette, a fourteenth-century French friar who lived through the events described.

In A.D. 1348, the people of France and of almost the whole world were struck by a blow other than war. For in addition to the famine which I described in the beginning and to the wars which I described in the course of this narrative, pestilence and its attendant tribulations appeared again in various parts of the world. . . . All this year and the next, the mortality of men and women, of the young even more than of the old, in Paris and in the kingdom of France, and also, it is said, in other parts of the world, was so great that it was almost impossible to bury the dead. People lay ill little more than two or three days and died suddenly, as it were in full health. He who was well one day was dead the next and being carried to his grave. Swellings appeared suddenly in the armpit or in the groin — in many cases both — and they were infallible signs of death. This sickness or pestilence was called an epidemic by the doctors. Nothing like the great numbers who died in the years 1348 and 1349 has been heard of or seen or read of in times past. This plague and disease came from *ymaginatione* or association and contagion, for if a well man visited the sick he only rarely evaded the risk of death. Wherefore in many towns timid priests withdrew, leaving the exercise of their ministry to such of the religious as were more daring. In many places not two out of twenty remained alive. So high was the mortality at the Hôtel-Dieu [an early hospital] in Paris that for a long time, more than five hundred dead were carried daily with great devotion in carts to the cemetery of the Holy Innocents in Paris for burial. A very great number of the saintly sisters of the Hôtel-Dieu who, not fearing to die, nursed the sick in all sweetness and humility, with no thought of honor, a number too often renewed by death, rest in peace with Christ, as we may piously believe.

This plague, it is said, began among the unbelievers [Muslims], came to Italy, and then crossing the Alps reached Avignon [site of the papacy in that period], where it attacked several cardinals and took from them their whole household. Then it spread, unforeseen, to France, through Gascony [now part of the south of France] and Spain, little by little, from town to town, from village to village, from house to house, and finally from person to person. It even crossed over to Germany, though it was not so bad there as with us. During the epidemic, God of His accustomed goodness deigned to grant this grace, that however suddenly men died, almost all awaited death joyfully. Nor was there anyone who died without confessing his sins and receiving the holy viaticum [the Eucharistic bread given to the sick or dying]. . . .

Some said that this pestilence was caused by infection of the air and waters, since there was at this time no famine nor lack of food supplies, but on the contrary great abundance. As a result of this theory of infected water and air as the source of the plague the Jews were suddenly and violently charged with infecting wells and water and corrupting the air. The whole world rose up against them cruelly on this account. In Germany and other parts of the world where Jews lived, they were massacred and slaughtered by Christians, and many thousands were burned everywhere, indiscriminately. The unshaken, if fatuous, constancy of the [Jewish] men and their wives was remarkable. For mothers hurled their children first into the fire that they might not be baptized and then leaped in after them to burn with their husbands and children. It is said that many bad Christians were found who in a like manner put poison into wells. But in truth, such poisonings, granted that they actually were perpetrated, could not have caused so great a plague nor have infected so many people. There were other causes; for example, the will of God and the corrupt humors and evil inherent in air and earth. Perhaps the poisonings, if they actually took place in some localities, reenforced these causes. The plague lasted in France for the greater part of the years 1348 and 1349 and then ceased. Many country villages and many houses in good towns remained empty and deserted. Many houses, including some splendid dwellings, very soon fell into ruins. Even in Paris several houses were thus ruined, though fewer here than elsewhere.

After the cessation of the epidemic, pestilence, or plague, the men and women who survived married each other. There was no sterility among the women, but on the contrary fertility beyond the ordinary. Pregnant women were seen on every side. . . . But woe is me! the world was not changed for the better but for the worse by this renewal of population. For men were more avaricious and grasping than before, even though they had far greater possessions. They were more covetous and disturbed each other more frequently with suits, brawls, disputes, and pleas. Nor by the mortality resulting from this terrible plague inflicted by God was peace between kings and lords established. On the contrary, the enemies of the king of France and of the Church were stronger and wickeder than before and stirred up wars on sea and on land. Greater evils than before [swarmed] everywhere in the world. And this fact was very remarkable. Although there was an abundance of all goods, yet everything was twice as dear, whether it were utensils, victuals, or merchandise, hired helpers or peasants and serfs, except for some hereditary domains which remained abundantly stocked with everything. Charity began to cool, and iniquity with ignorance and sin to abound, for few could be found in the good towns and castles who knew how or were willing to instruct children in the rudiments of grammar.

▷ Jean de Venette vividly describes one of the more bizarre reactions to the terrible plague, the sudden appearance of the Flagellants. Marching like pilgrims across the countryside, the Flagellants were a group of laymen and laywomen who sought divine pardon for their sins by preaching repentance to others and scourging themselves in a quasi-liturgical ceremony in local churches or marketplaces. The movement foreshadowed events in which moral, social, and economic discontent would increasingly manifest itself in the form of religiously justified popular uprisings against civil and clerical authorities.

In the year 1349, while the plague was still active and spreading from town to town, men in Germany, Flanders, Hainaut [east of Flanders], and Lorraine uprose and began a new sect on their own authority. Stripped to the waist, they gathered in large groups and bands and marched in procession through the crossroads and squares of cities and good towns. There they formed circles and beat upon their backs with weighted scourges, rejoicing as they did so in loud voices and singing hymns suitable to their rite and newly composed for it. Thus for thirty-three days they marched through many towns doing their penance and affording a great spectacle to the wondering people. They flogged their shoulders and arms with scourges tipped with iron points so zealously as to draw blood. But they did not come to Paris nor to any part of France, for they were forbidden to do so by the king of France, who did not want them. He acted on the advice of the masters of theology of the University of Paris, who said that this new sect had been formed contrary to the will of God, to the rites of Holy Mother Church, and to the salvation of all their souls. That indeed this was and is true appeared shortly. For Pope Clement VI was fully informed concerning this fatuous new rite by the masters of Paris through emissaries reverently sent to him and, on the grounds that it had been damnably formed, contrary to law, he forbade the Flagellants under threat of anathema [excommunication] to practise in the future the public penance which they had so presumptuously undertaken. His prohibition was just, for the Flagellants, supported by certain fatuous priests and monks, were enunciating doctrines and opinions which were beyond measure evil, erroneous, and fallacious. For example, they said that their blood thus drawn by the scourge and poured out was mingled with the blood of Christ. Their many errors showed how little they knew of the Catholic faith. Wherefore, as they had begun fatuously of themselves and not of God, so in a short time they were reduced to nothing. On being warned, they desisted and humbly received absolution and penance at the hands of their prelates as the pope's representatives. Many honorable women and devout matrons, it must be added, had done this penance with scourges, marching and singing through towns and churches like the men, but after a little like the others they desisted.

REVIEW QUESTIONS

1. What was particularly frightening about the outbreak of the plague?
2. Why were the casualties so high among the clergy and religious sisters?
3. In the absence of scientific knowledge about the nature of the disease, what did people believe caused the deadly plague?
4. Why were the Jews singled out for blame?
5. In the chronicler's opinion, what were some of the long-term moral consequences of the Black Death?
6. Why did the authorities quickly act to suppress the Flagellant movement?

---

13 ▾ Lower-Class Rebellions

At times the discontent of European lower classes in town and countryside erupted into rebellions against the ruling authorities. One reason for the discontent of urban laborers and artisans was their exclusion from town affairs by the wealthy merchants and bankers who controlled municipal government. Peasants wanted to end their heavy obligations to lords who exploited their labor and dominated their personal lives. Over the centuries, peasants gained greater personal liberty by purchasing the lords' rights over them, by escaping to towns, or by moving to new lands where ties to lords were less burdensome. At times, peasants resorted to violence in order to gain concessions from lords.

Sir John Froissart
THE PEASANT REVOLT OF 1381

In 1381, a rebellion of peasants and poor artisans in England threatened the political power of the ruling class. The rebellion, which was crushed and whose leaders were betrayed and executed, revealed the massive discontent of the lower classes and the specter of social upheaval that hovered over late medieval society. The following account of the rebellion is by Sir John Froissart (c. 1337–c. 1410), a French historian and poet who chronicled the Hundred Years' War between France and England, which wreaked havoc in the countries concerned. The war began in 1337 when King Edward III of England laid claim to the throne of France. Despite significant military successes in the fourteenth century, by 1453 the English had lost their French possessions except for the port of Calais.

While these conferences [of English nobles] were going forward there happened great commotions among the lower orders in England, by which that country was nearly ruined. In order that this disastrous rebellion may serve as an example to mankind, I will speak of all that was done from the information I had at the time. It is customary in England, as well as in several other countries, for the nobility to have great privileges over the commonality; that is to say, the lower orders are bound by law to plough the lands of the gentry, to harvest their grain, to carry it home to the barn, to thrash and winnow it; they are also bound to harvest and carry home the hay. All these services the prelates and gentlemen exact of their inferiors; and in the counties of Kent, Essex, Sussex, and Bedford, these services are more oppressive than in other parts of the kingdom. In consequence of this the evil[ly] disposed in these districts began to murmur, saying, that in the beginning of the world there were no slaves, and that no one ought to be treated as such, unless he had committed treason against his lord, as Lucifer had done against God; but they had done no such thing, for they were neither angels nor spirits, but men formed after the same likeness as these lords who treated them as beasts. This they would bear no longer; they were determined to be free, and if they laboured or did any work, they would be paid for it. A crazy priest in the county of Kent, called John Ball, who for his absurd preaching had thrice been confined in prison by the Archbishop of Canterbury, was greatly instrumental in exciting these rebellious ideas. Every Sunday after mass, as the people were coming out of church, this John Ball was accustomed to assemble a crowd around him in the marketplace and preach to them. On such occasions he would say, "My good friends, matters cannot go on well in England until all things shall be in common; when there shall be neither vassals nor lords; when the lords shall be no more masters than ourselves. How ill they behave to us! for what reason do they thus hold us in bondage? Are we not all descended from the same parents, Adam and Eve? And what can they show, or what reason can they give, why they should be more masters than ourselves? They are clothed in velvet and rich stuffs, ornamented with ermine and other furs, while we are forced to wear poor clothing. They have wines, spices, and fine bread, while we have only rye and the refuse of the straw; and when we drink, it must be water. They have handsome seats and manors, while we must brave the wind and rain in our labours in the field; and it is by our labour they have wherewith to support their pomp. We are called slaves, and if we do not perform our service we are beaten, and we have no sovereign to whom we can complain or who would be willing to hear us. Let us go to the king and remonstrate with him; he is young, and from him we may obtain a favourable answer, and if not we must ourselves seek to amend our condition." With such language as this did John Ball harangue the people of his village every Sunday after mass. The archbishop, on being informed of it, had him arrested and imprisoned for two or three months by way of punishment; but the moment he was out of prison, he returned to his former course. Many in the city of London envious of the rich and noble, having heard of John Ball's preaching, said among themselves that the country was badly governed, and that the nobility had seized upon all the gold and silver. These wicked Londoners, therefore, began to assemble in parties, and to show signs of rebellion; they also invited all those who held like opinions in the adjoining counties to come to London; telling them that they would find the town open to them and the commonalty of the same way of thinking as themselves, and that they would so press the king, that there should no longer be a slave in England.

By this means the men of Kent, Essex, Sussex, Bedford, and the adjoining counties, in number about 60,000, were brought to London, under command of Wat Tyler, Jack Straw, and John Ball. This Wat Tyler, who was chief of the three, had been a tiler of houses — a bad man and a great enemy to the nobility. . . .

With regard to the common people of London, numbers entertained these rebellious opinions, and on assembling at the bridge asked of the guards, "Why will you refuse admittance to these honest men? they are our friends, and what they are doing is for our good." So urgent were they, that it was found necessary to open the gates, when crowds rushed in and took possession of those shops which seemed best stocked with provisions; indeed, wherever they went, meat and drink were placed before them, and nothing was refused in the hope of appeasing them. Their leaders, John Ball, Jack Straw, and Wat Tyler, then marched through London, attended by more than 20,000 men, to the palace of the Savoy, which is a handsome building belonging to the Duke of Lancaster [the king's uncle], situated on the banks of the Thames on the road to Westminster: here they immediately killed the porters, pushed into the house, and set it on fire. Not content with this outrage, they went to the house of the Knight-hospitalers of Rhodes, dedicated to St. John of Mount Carmel, which they burnt together with their church and hospital.

After this they paraded the streets, and killed every Fleming [citizen of Flanders] they could find, whether in house, church, or hospital: they broke open several houses of the Lombards [Italian bankers], taking whatever money they could lay their hands upon. They murdered a rich citizen, by name Richard Lyon, to whom Wat Tyler had formerly been servant in France, but having once beaten him, the [scoundrel] had never forgotten it; and when he had carried his men to his house, he ordered his head to be cut off, placed upon a pike, and carried through the streets of London. Thus did these wicked people act, and on this Thursday they did much damage to the city of London. Towards evening they fixed their quarters in a square, called St. Catherine's, before the Tower, declaring that they would not depart until they had obtained from the king every thing they wanted — until the Chancellor [chief financial officer] of England had accounted to them, and shown how the great sums which were raised had been expended. Considering the mischief which the mob had already done, you may easily imagine how miserable, at this time, was the situation of the king and those who were with him. . . .

. . . Now observe how fortunately matters turned out, for had these scoundrels succeeded in their intentions, all the nobility of England would have been destroyed; and after such success as this the people of other nations would have rebelled also, taking example from those of Ghent and Flanders, who at the time were in actual rebellion against their lord; the Parisians indeed the same year acted in a somewhat similar manner; upwards of 20,000 of them armed themselves with leaden maces and caused a rebellion. . . .

REVIEW QUESTIONS

1. What were the grievances of the English peasants?
2. What were the political principles expressed by the priest John Ball?
3. The Flemings, Lombards and Knights Hospitalers functioned as bankers and moneylenders in late medieval society. What was the attitude of the rebellious crowds toward them?

---

14 ▾ The Medieval Outlook

The modern world is linked in many ways to the Middle Ages. European cities, the middle class, the state system, English common law, representative institutions, universities — all had their origins in the Middle Ages. Despite these elements of continuity, the characteristic outlook of medieval people is markedly different from that of people today. Whereas science and secularism shape the

modern point of view, religion was the foundation of the Middle Ages. Christian beliefs as formulated by the church made life and death purposeful and intelligible.

Medieval thinkers drew a sharp distinction between a higher, spiritual world and a lower, material world. God, the creator of the universe and the source of moral values, dwelled in the higher celestial world, an abode of perfection. The universe was organized as a hierarchy with God at the summit and hell at the other extremity. Earth, composed of base matter, stood just above hell. By believing in Christ and adhering to God's commandments as taught by the church, people could overcome their sinful nature and ascend to God's world. Sinners, on the other hand, would descend to hell, a fearful place the existence of which medieval people never doubted.

Scholastic philosophy, which sought to demonstrate through reason the truth of Christian doctrines, and the Gothic cathedral, which seemed to soar from the material world to heaven, were two great expressions of the medieval mind. A third was *The Divine Comedy* of Dante Alighieri, the greatest literary figure of the Middle Ages.

Lothario dei Segni (Pope Innocent III) ≪ ON THE MISERY OF THE HUMAN CONDITION ≫

At the center of medieval belief was the image of a perfect God and a wretched and sinful human being. God had given Adam and Eve freedom to choose; rebellious and presumptuous, they had used their freedom to disobey God. In doing so, they made evil an intrinsic part of the human personality. But God, who had not stopped loving human beings, showed them the way out of sin. God became man and died so that human beings might be saved. Men and women were weak, egocentric, and sinful. With God's grace they could overcome their sinful nature and gain salvation; without grace they were utterly helpless. A classic expression of this pessimistic view of human nature was written in the late twelfth century by an Italian canon lawyer, Lothario dei Segni (c. 1160–1216), who was later elected pope in 1198, taking the name Innocent III. *On the Misery of the Human Condition* was enormously popular and inspired numerous rhetorical writings on the same theme as late as the seventeenth century. Scattered excerpts follow.

• For sure man was formed out of earth, conceived in guilt, born to punishment. What he does is depraved and illicit, is shameful and improper, vain and unprofitable. He will become fuel for the eternal fires, food for worms, a mass of rottenness.

I shall try to make my explanation clearer and my treatment fuller. Man was formed of dust, slime, and ashes; what is even more vile, of the filthiest seed. He was conceived from the itch of the flesh, in the heat of passion and the stench of lust, and worse yet, with the stain of sin. He was born to toil, dread, and trouble; and more wretched still, was born only to die. He commits depraved acts by which he offends God, his neighbor, and himself; shameful acts by which he defiles his name, his person, and his conscience; and vain acts by which he ignores all things important, useful, and necessary. He will become fuel for those fires which are forever hot and burn forever bright; food for the worm which forever nibbles and digests; a mass of rottenness which will forever stink and reek. . . .

• A bird is born to fly; man is born to toil. All his days are full of toil and hardship, and at night his mind has no rest. . . .

• How much anxiety tortures mortals! They suffer all kinds of cares, are burdened with worry, tremble and shrink with fears and terrors, are weighted down with sorrow. Their nervousness makes them depressed, and their depression makes them nervous. Rich or poor, master or slave, married or single, good and bad alike — all suffer worldly torments and are tormented by worldly vexations. . . .

• For sudden sorrow always follows worldly joy: what begins in gaiety ends in grief. Worldly happiness is besprinkled indeed with much bitterness. . . .

• Then, suddenly, when least expected, misfortune strikes, a calamity befalls us, disease attacks; or death, which no one can escape, carries us off. . . .

• Men strive especially for three things: riches, pleasures, and honors. Riches lead to immorality, pleasures to shame, and honors to vanity. . . .

• But suppose a man is lifted up high, suppose he is raised to the very peak. At once his cares grow heavy, his worries mount up, he eats less and cannot sleep. And so nature is corrupted, his spirit weakened, his sleep disturbed, his appetite lost; his strength is diminished, he loses weight. Exhausting himself, he scarcely lives half a lifetime and ends his wretched days with a more wretched death. . . .

• Almost the whole life of mortals is full of mortal sin, so that one can scarcely find anyone who does not go astray, does not return to his own vomit and rot in his own dung. Instead they "are glad when they have done evil and rejoice in most wicked things." "Being filled with all iniquity, malice, fornication, avarice, wickedness, full of envy, murders, contention, deceit, evil, being whisperers, detractors, hateful to God, irreverent, proud, haughty, plotters of evil, disobedient to parents, foolish, dissolute, without affection, without fidelity, without mercy." This world is full of such and worse; it abounds in heretics and schismatics [Christians who reject the authority of the pope], traitors and tyrants, simonists [buyers or sellers of spiritual offices or sacred items] and hypocrites; the ambitious and the covetous, robbers and brigands, violent men, extortionists, usurers, forgers; the impious and sacrilegious, the betrayers and liars, the flatterers and deceivers; gossips, tricksters, gluttons, drunkards; adulterers, incestuous men, deviates, and the dirty-minded; the lazy, the careless, the vain, the prodigal, the impetuous, the irascible, the impatient and inconstant; poisoners, fortune tellers, perjurers, cursers; men who are presumptuous and arrogant, unbelieving and desperate; and finally those ensnared in all vices together.

Dante Alighieri
≪ THE DIVINE COMEDY ≫

Dante Alighieri was a poet, political philosopher, soldier, and politician. Born in 1265 in Florence, Italy, he died in exile in 1321. His greatest work, *The Divine Comedy,* was composed of one hundred cantos (individual poems) and written not in Latin, the language of learning, but in the Tuscan Italian dialect of the common people. The poem is an elaborate allegory in which each character and

event can be understood on two or more levels — for example, a literal description of the levels of hell and Dante's (and every Christian's) struggle to overcome a flawed human nature and to ward off worldly sin. Dante, representing all human beings, is guided through the afterworlds: hell (inferno), purgatory, and heaven (paradise). The Roman poet Virgil conducts him through hell and purgatory; Beatrice, his long-dead beloved, leads him through heaven to the point where he sees God in all his glory.

In the descent through the nine concentric circles of hell, Virgil describes the nature and significance of each region through which they pass. In each section of hell, sinners are punished in proportion to their earthly sins. Over the entrance gate to hell, Dante reads these words:

THROUGH ME YOU GO INTO THE CITY OF GRIEF,
THROUGH ME YOU GO INTO THE PAIN THAT IS ETERNAL,
THROUGH ME YOU GO AMONG PEOPLE LOST.

JUSTICE MOVED MY EXALTED CREATOR;
THE DIVINE POWER MADE ME,
THE SUPREME WISDOM, AND THE PRIMAL LOVE.

BEFORE ME ALL CREATED THINGS WERE ETERNAL,
AND ETERNAL I WILL LAST.
ABANDON EVERY HOPE, YOU WHO ENTER HERE.

▷ Dante descends from the first circle to the second circle, where he finds the souls of those who had been guilty of sins of the flesh.

Now I begin to hear the sad notes of pain,
now I have come to where
loud cries beat upon my ears.

I have reached a place mute of all light
which roars like the sea in a tempest
when beaten by conflicting winds.

The infernal storm which never stops
drives the spirit in its blast;
whirling and beating, it torments them.

When they come in front of the landslide,
they utter laments, moans, and shrieks;
there they curse the Divine Power.

I learned that to such a torment
carnal sinners are condemned
who subject their reason to desire.

And, as starlings are borne by their wings
in the cold season, in a broad and dense flock,
so that blast carries the evil spirits.

Here, there, up, and down, it blows them;
no hope ever comforts them
of rest or even of less pain.

And as cranes go chanting their lays,
making a long line of themselves in the air,
so I saw coming, uttering laments,

shades borne by that strife of winds.

▷ Finally the two poets reach the ninth and lowest circle, a frozen wasteland reserved for Satan and traitors.

". . . look ahead,"
my master [Virgil] said, "and try to discern him."

As, when a thick mist covers the land
or when night darkens our hemisphere,
a windmill, turning, appears from afar,

so now I seemed to see such a structure;
then because of the wind, I drew back
behind my guide, for there was no other protection.

Already — and with fear I put it into verse —
I was where the shades are covered in the ice
and show through like bits of straw in glass.

Some were lying, some standing erect,
some on their heads, others on their feet,
still others like a bow bent face to toes.

When we had gone so far ahead
that my master was pleased to show me
the creature (Lucifer)[1] that once had been so fair,

he stood from in front of me, and made me stop,
saying, "Behold, Dis![2] Here is the place
where you must arm yourself with courage."

How faint and frozen I then became,
do not ask, Reader, for I do not write it down,
since all words would be inadequate.

I did not die and did not stay alive:
think now for yourself, if you have the wit,
how I became, without life or death.

The emperor of the dolorous realm
from mid-breast protruded from the ice,
and I compare better in size

with the giants than they do with his arms.
Consider how big the whole must be,
proportioned as it is to such a part.

If he were once as handsome as he is ugly now,
and still presumed to lift his hand against his Maker,
all affliction must indeed come from him.

Oh, how great a marvel appeared to me
when I saw three faces on his head!
The one in front (hatred) was fiery red;

the two others which were joined to it
over the middle of each shoulder
were fused together at the top.

The right one (impotence) seemed between white and yellow;
the left (ignorance) was in color like those
who come from where the Nile rises.

Under each two great wings spread
of a size fitting to such a bird;
I have never seen such sails on the sea.

They had no feathers, and seemed
like those of a bat, and they flapped,
so that three blasts came from them.

Thence all Cocytus[3] was frozen.
With six eyes he wept, and over his three chins
he let tears drip and bloody foam.

In each mouth he chewed a sinner with his teeth
in the manner of a hemp brake,[4]
so that he kept three in pain.

To the one in front the biting was nothing
compared to the scratching, for at times,
his back was stripped of skin.

"The soul up there with the greatest punishment,"
said my master, "is Judas Iscariot.[5] His head
is inside the mouth, and he kicks with his legs.

Of the other two whose heads are down,
the one hanging from the black face is Brutus;[6]
see how he twists and says nothing.

---

[1]Lucifer (light-bringer) was an archangel who led a rebellion against God and was cast into hell for punishment. He was identified with Satan.

[2]Dis was another name for Pluto or Hades, the god of the dead and ruler of the underworld.

[3]The Cocytus, a river in western Greece, was alleged to lead to the underworld.

[4]A hemp brake was a tool used to break up hemp fibers so that they could be made into rope.

[5]Judas Iscariot was the disciple who betrayed Jesus to the authorities.

[6]Brutus, a first-century Roman statesman, conspired to murder Julius Caesar.

The other who seems so heavy set is Cassius.[7]
But night is rising again now,
and it is time to leave, for we have seen all."

▷ Dante and Beatrice make the ascent to the highest heaven, the Empyrean, which is located beyond Saturn, the last of the seven planets, beyond the circle of stars that encloses the planets and above the Primum Mobile — the outermost sphere revolving around the earth. Here at the summit of the universe is a realm of pure light that radiates truth, goodness, and happiness where God is found. Dante is permitted to look at God, but words cannot describe "the glory of Him who moves us all."

For my sight, growing pure, penetrated
ever deeper into the rays
of the Light [God] which is true in Itself.

From then on my vision was greater
than our speech which fails at such a sight,
just as memory is overcome by the excess.

As one who in a dream sees clearly,
and the feeling impressed remains afterward,
although nothing else comes back to mind,

so am I; for my vision disappears
almost wholly, and yet the sweetness
caused by it is still distilled within my heart.

Thus, in sunlight, the snow melts away;
thus the sayings of the Sibyl [a Roman
  oracle], written
on light leaves, were lost in the wind.

O Supreme Light that risest so high
above mortal concepts, give back to my mind
a little of what Thou didst appear,

and make my tongue strong,
so that it may leave to future peoples
at least a spark of Thy glory!

For, by returning to my memory
and by sounding a little in these verses
more of Thy victory will be conceived.

By the keenness of the living ray I endured
I believe I would have been dazed
if my eyes had turned away from it;

and I remember that I was bolder
because of that to sustain the view
until my sight *attained* the Infinite Worth
  [God].

O abundant grace through which I presumed
to fix my eyes on the Eternal Light
so long that I consumed my vision on it!

In its depths I saw contained, bound with love
in one volume, what is scattered
on leaves throughout the world —

substances (things) and accidents (qualities)
  and their modes
as if fused together in such a way
that what I speak of is a single light.

The universal form (principle) of this unity
I believe I saw, because more abundantly
in saying this I feel that I rejoice.

One moment obscures more for me than
  twenty-five centuries
have clouded since the adventure which made
  Neptune [the sea god]
wonder at the shadow of the Argo (the first
  ship).[8]

Thus my mind with rapt attention
gazed fixedly, motionless and attentive,
continually enflamed by its very gazing.

In that light we become such
that we can never consent
to turn from it for another sight,

inasmuch as the good which is the object
of the will is all in it, and outside of it
whatever is perfect there is defective.

---

[7]Cassius, another Roman statesman, was a co-conspirator with Brutus.

[8]The *Argo,* in Greek legends, was the ship in which the hero Jason and his companions sailed in search of the Golden Fleece. A Greek poet, Apollonius of Rhodes, wrote an epic poem, the *Argonautica,* about it in the mid-third century B.C.

Now my speech, even for what I remember,
will be shorter than that of an infant
who still bathes his tongue at the breast.

Not that more than a single semblance
was in the living light I gazed upon
(for it is always as it was before),

but in my vision which gained strength
as I looked the single appearance,
through a change in me, was transformed.

Within the deep and clear subsistence
of the great light three circles of three colors
and of one dimension (the Trinity) appeared to me,

and one (the Son) seemed reflected from the other (the Father)
as Iris by Iris,[9] and the third (the Holy Spirit)
seemed fire emanating equally from both.

O how poor our speech is and how feeble
for my conception! Compared to what I saw
to say its power is "little" is to say too much.

O Eternal Light (Father), abiding in Thyself alone,
Thou (Son) alone understanding Thyself, and Thou (Holy Spirit)
understood only by Thee, Thou dost love and smile!

The circle which appeared in Thee
as a reflected light (the Son)
when contemplated a while

seemed depicted with our image within itself
and of its own (the Circle's) color,
so that my eyes were wholly fixed on it.

Like the geometer who strives
to square the circle and cannot find
by thinking the principle he needs

I was at that new sight. I wanted to see
how the (human) image was conformed
to the (divine) circle and has a place in it,

but my own wings were not enough for that —
except that my mind was illuminated by a flash
(of Grace) through which its wish was realized.

For the great imagination here power failed;
but already my desire and will (in harmony)
were turning like a wheel moved evenly

by the Love which turns the sun and the other stars.

---

[9]Iris, goddess of the rainbow, was the messenger of the gods.

REVIEW QUESTIONS

1. List several reasons that Pope Innocent III gave to prove his point that the human condition is essentially wretched.
2. Compare the outlook of Innocent III with that of ancient Greek humanism.
3. What did Dante Alighieri tell the reader about the character of hell and its inhabitants as he entered its gate?
4. According to Dante, what was the nature of the evil in carnal sin?
5. According to Dante, what was the worst sin?
6. Describe Dante's vision of the bottom circle of hell.
7. What problems did Dante encounter in trying to describe his mystical vision of God?
8. How did Dante finally express his vision of God?
9. What was Dante's goal in seeking the vision of God?
10. How did *The Divine Comedy* exemplify the medieval outlook?

Part Three

Early Modern Europe

The Renaissance

For many historians, the Renaissance, which originated in the city-states of Italy, marks the starting point of the modern era. The Renaissance was characterized by a rebirth of interest in the humanist culture and outlook of ancient Greece and Rome. Although Renaissance individuals did not repudiate Christianity, they valued worldly activities and interests to a much greater degree than did the people of the Middle Ages, whose outlook was dominated by Christian otherworldliness. Renaissance individuals were fascinated by *this* world and by life's possibilities; they aspired to live a rich and creative life on earth and to fulfill themselves through artistic and literary activity.

Individualism was a hallmark of the Renaissance. The urban elite sought to demonstrate their unique talents, to assert their own personalities, and to gain recognition for their accomplishments. The most admired person during the Renaissance was the multitalented individual, the "universal man," who distinguished himself as a writer, artist, linguist, athlete. Disdaining Christian humility, Renaissance individuals took pride in their talents and worldly accomplishments — "I can work miracles," said the great Leonardo da Vinci.

During the High Middle Ages there had been a revival of Greek and Roman learning. Yet there were two important differences between that period called the Twelfth-Century Awakening and the Renaissance. First, many more ancient works were restored to circulation during the Renaissance than during the cultural revival of the Middle Ages. Second, medieval scholastics had tried to fit the ideas of the ancients into a Christian framework; they used Greek philosophy to explain Christian teachings. Renaissance scholars, on the other hand, valued ancient works for their own sake, believing that Greek and Roman authors could teach much about the art of living.

A distinguishing feature of the Renaissance period was the humanist movement, an educational and cultural program based on the study of ancient Greek and Latin literature. By studying the humanities — history, literature, rhetoric, moral and political philosophy — humanists aimed to revive the worldly spirit of the ancient Greeks and Romans, which they believed had been lost in the Middle Ages.

COSIMO DE' MEDICI by Benvenuto Cellini (1500–1571). This sixteenth-century bronze bust of the duke of Florence by the famous Italian sculptor Cellini reflects the power and prestige of one of the most influential Renaissance despots. (*Alinari/Art Resource, N.Y.*)

Humanists were thus fascinated by the writings of the ancients. From the works of Thucydides, Plato, Cicero, Seneca, and other ancient authors, humanists sought guidelines for living life well in this world and looked for stylistic models for their own literary efforts. To the humanists, the ancients had written brilliantly, in an incomparable literary style, on friendship, citizenship, love, bravery, statesmanship, beauty, excellence, and every other topic devoted to the enrichment of human life.

Like the humanist movement, Renaissance art also marked a break with medieval culture. The art of the Middle Ages had served a religious function; its purpose was to lift the mind to God. It depicted a spiritual universe in which the supernatural was the supreme reality. The Gothic cathedral, with its flying buttresses, soared toward heaven, rising in ascending tiers; it reflected the medieval conception of a hierarchical universe with God at its apex. Painting also expressed gradations of spiritual values. Traditionally, the left side of a painting portrayed the damned, the right side the saved; dark colors expressed evil, light colors good. Spatial proportion was relative to spirituality — the less spiritually valuable a thing was, the less form it had (or the more deformed it was). Medieval art perfectly expressed the Christian view of the universe and the individual. The Renaissance shattered the dominance of religion over art, shifting attention from heaven to the natural world and to the human being; Renaissance artists often dealt with religious themes but they placed their subjects in a naturalistic setting. Renaissance art also developed a new concept of visual space that was defined from the standpoint of the individual observer. It was a quantitative space in which the artist, employing reason and mathematics, portrayed the essential form of the object as it appeared in three dimensions to the human eye, that is, it depicted the object in perspective.

The Renaissance began in the middle of the fourteenth century in the northern Italian city-states, which had grown prosperous from the revival of trade in the Middle Ages. Italian merchants and bankers had the wealth to acquire libraries and fine works of art and to support art, literature, and scholarship. Surrounded by reminders of ancient Rome — amphitheaters, monuments, and sculpture — the well-to-do took an interest in classical culture and thought. In the late fifteenth and the sixteenth centuries, Renaissance ideas spread to Germany, France, Spain, and England through books available in great numbers due to the invention of the printing press.

1 ▾ The Humanists' Fascination with Antiquity

Humanists believed that a refined person must know the literature of Greece and Rome. They strove to imitate the style of the ancients, to speak and write as eloquently as the Greeks and Romans. Toward these ends, they sought to read, print, and restore to circulation every scrap of ancient literature that could still be found.

Petrarch
THE FATHER OF HUMANISM

During his lifetime, Francesco Petrarca, or Petrarch (1304–1374), had an astounding reputation as a poet and scholar. Often called the "father of humanism," he inspired other humanists through his love for classical learning; his criticism of medieval Latin as barbaric in contrast to the style of Cicero, Seneca, and other Romans; and his literary works based on classical models. Petrarch saw his own age as a restoration of classical brilliance after an interval of medieval darkness.

A distinctly modern element in Petrarch's thought is the subjective and individualistic character of his writing. In talking about himself and probing his own feelings, Petrarch demonstrates a self-consciousness characteristic of the modern outlook.

Like many other humanists, Petrarch remained devoted to Christianity: "When it comes to thinking or speaking of religion, that is, of the highest truth, of true happiness and eternal salvation," he declared, "I certainly am not a Ciceronian or a Platonist but a Christian." Petrarch was a forerunner of the Christian humanism best represented by Erasmus (see page 320). Christian humanists combined an intense devotion to Christianity with a great love for classical literature, which they much preferred to the dull and turgid treatises written by scholastic philosophers and theologians. In the following passage, Petrarch criticizes his contemporaries for their ignorance of ancient writers and shows his commitment to classical learning.

. . . O inglorious age! that scorns antiquity, its mother, to whom it owes every noble art — that dares to declare itself not only equal but superior to the glorious past. I say nothing of the vulgar, the dregs of mankind, whose sayings and opinions may raise a laugh but hardly merit serious censure. . . .

. . . But what can be said in defense of men of education who ought not to be ignorant of antiquity and yet are plunged in the same darkness and delusion?

You see that I cannot speak of these matters without the greatest irritation and indignation. There has arisen of late a set of dialecticians [experts in logical argument], who are not only ignorant but demented. Like a black army of ants from some old rotten oak, they swarm forth from their hiding places and devastate the fields of sound learning. They condemn Plato and Aristotle, and laugh at Socrates and Pythagoras.[1] And, good God! under what silly and incompetent leaders these opinions are put forth. . . . What shall we say of men who scorn Marcus Tullius Cicero,[2] the bright sun of eloquence? Of those who scoff at Varro and Seneca,[3] and are scandalized at what they choose to call the crude, unfinished style of Livy and Sallust [Roman historians]? . . .

Such are the times, my friend, upon which we have fallen; such is the period in which we live and are growing old. Such are the critics of today, as I so often have occasion to lament and complain — men who are innocent of knowledge and virtue, and yet harbour the most exalted opinion of themselves. Not content with losing the words of the ancients, they must attack their genius and their ashes. They rejoice in their ignorance, as if what they did not know were not worth knowing. They give full rein to their license and conceit, and freely introduce among us new authors and outlandish teachings.

[1]The work of Aristotle (384–322 B.C.), a leading Greek philosopher, had an enormous influence among medieval and Renaissance scholars. A student of the philosopher Socrates, Plato (c. 427–347 B.C.) was one of the greatest philosophers of ancient Greece. His work grew to be extremely influential in the West during the Renaissance period, as new texts of his writings were discovered and translated into Latin and more Westerners could read the originals in Greek. Pythagoras (c. 582–c. 507 B.C.) was a Greek philosopher whose work influenced both Socrates and Plato.

[2]Cicero (106–43 B.C.) was a Roman statesman and rhetorician. His Latin style was especially admired and emulated during the Renaissance.

[3]Varro (116–27 B.C.) was a Roman scholar and historian. Seneca (4 B.C.–A.D. 65) was a Roman statesman, dramatist, and Stoic philosopher whose literary style was greatly admired during the Renaissance.

Leonardo Bruni
STUDY OF GREEK LITERATURE AND A HUMANIST EDUCATIONAL PROGRAM

Leonardo Bruni (1374–1444) was a Florentine humanist who extolled both intellectual study and active involvement in public affairs, an outlook called civic humanism. In the first reading from his *History of His Own Times in Italy*, Bruni expressed the humanist's love for ancient Greek literature and language.

In a treatise, *De Studiis et Literis (On Learning and Literature)* addressed to the noble lady Baptista di Montefeltro (1383–1450), daughter of the Count of Urbino, Bruni outlines the basic course of studies that the humanists recommended as the best preparation for a life of wisdom and virtue. In addition to the study of Christian literature, Bruni encourages a wide familiarity with the best minds and stylists of ancient Greek and Latin cultures.

[LOVE FOR GREEK LITERATURE]

Then first came a knowledge of Greek, which had not been in use among us for seven hundred years. Chrysoloras the Byzantine,[1] a man of noble birth and well versed in Greek letters, brought Greek learning to us. When his country was invaded by the Turks, he came by sea, first to Venice. The report of him soon spread, and he was cordially invited and besought and promised a public stipend, to come to Florence

[1]Chrysoloras (c. 1355–1415), a Byzantine writer and teacher, introduced the study of Greek literature to the Italians, opening a new age of Western humanistic learning.

and open his store of riches to the youth. I was then studying Civil Law,[2] but . . . I burned with love of academic studies, and had spent no little pains on dialectic and rhetoric. At the coming of Chrysoloras I was torn in mind, deeming it shameful to desert the law, and yet a crime to lose such a chance of studying Greek literature; and often with youthful impulse I would say to myself: "Thou, when it is permitted thee to gaze on Homer, Plato and Demosthenes,[3] and the other [Greek] poets, philosophers, orators, of whom such glorious things are spread abroad, and speak with them and be instructed in their admirable teaching, wilt thou desert and rob thyself? Wilt thou neglect this opportunity so divinely offered? For seven hundred years, no one in Italy has possessed Greek letters; and yet we confess that all knowledge is derived from them. How great advantage to your knowledge, enhancement of your fame, increase of your pleasure, will come from an understanding of this tongue? There are doctors of civil law everywhere; and the chance of learning will not fail thee. But if this one and only doctor of Greek letters disappears, no one can be found to teach thee." Overcome at length by these reasons, I gave myself to Chrysoloras, with such zeal to learn, that what through the wakeful day I gathered, I followed after in the night, even when asleep.

ON LEARNING AND LITERATURE

. . . The foundations of all true learning must be laid in the sound and thorough knowledge of Latin: which implies study marked by a broad spirit, accurate scholarship, and careful attention to details. Unless this solid basis be secured it is useless to attempt to rear an enduring edifice. Without it the great monuments of literature are unintelligible, and the art of composition impossible. To attain this essential knowledge we must never relax our careful attention to the grammar of the language, but perpetually confirm and extend our acquaintance with it until it is thoroughly our own. . . . To this end we must be supremely careful in our choice of authors, lest an inartistic and debased style infect our own writing and degrade our taste; which danger is best avoided by bringing a keen, critical sense to bear upon select works, observing the sense of each passage, the structure of the sentence, the force of every word down to the least important particle. In this way our reading reacts directly upon our style. . . .

But we must not forget that true distinction is to be gained by a wide and varied range of such studies as conduce to the profitable enjoyment of life, in which, however, we must observe due proportion in the attention and time we devote to them.

First amongst such studies I place History: a subject which must not on any account be neglected by one who aspires to true cultivation. For it is our duty to understand the origins of our own history and its development; and the achievements of Peoples and of Kings.

For the careful study of the past enlarges our foresight in contemporary affairs and affords to citizens and to monarchs lessons of incitement or warning in the ordering of public policy. From History, also, we draw our store of examples of moral precepts.

In the monuments of ancient literature which have come down to us History holds a position of great distinction. We specially prize such [Roman] authors as Livy, Sallust and Curtius;[4] and, perhaps even above these, Julius Caesar, the style of whose Commentaries, so elegant and so limpid, entitles them to our warm admiration. . . .

The great Orators of antiquity must by all means be included. Nowhere do we find the virtues more warmly extolled, the vices so fiercely decried. From them we may learn, also,

[2]Civil Law refers to the Roman law as codified by Emperor Justinian in the early sixth century A.D. and studied in medieval law schools.

[3]Demosthenes (384–322 B.C.) was an Athenian statesman and orator whose oratorical style was much admired by Renaissance humanists.

[4]Q. Curtius Rufus, a Roman historian and rhetorician of the mid-first century A.D., composed a biography of Alexander the Great.

how to express consolation, encouragement, dissuasion or advice. If the principles which orators set forth are portrayed for us by philosophers, it is from the former that we learn how to employ the emotions — such as indignation, or pity — in driving home their application in individual cases. Further, from oratory we derive our store of those elegant or striking turns of expression which are used with so much effect in literary compositions. Lastly, in oratory we find that wealth of vocabulary, that clear easy-flowing style, that verve and force, which are invaluable to us both in writing and in conversation.

I come now to Poetry and the Poets. . . . For we cannot point to any great mind of the past for whom the Poets had not a powerful attraction. Aristotle, in constantly quoting Homer, Hesiod, Pindar, Euripides and other [Greek] poets, proves that he knew their works hardly less intimately than those of the philosophers. Plato, also, frequently appeals to them, and in this way covers them with his approval. If we turn to Cicero, we find him not content with quoting Ennius, Accius,[5] and others of the Latins, but rendering poems from the Greek and employing them habitually. . . . Hence my view that familiarity with the great poets of antiquity is essential to any claim to true education. For in their writings we find deep speculations upon Nature, and upon the Causes and Origins of things, which must carry weight with us both from their antiquity and from their authorship. Besides these, many important truths upon matters of daily life are suggested or illustrated. All this is expressed with such grace and dignity as demands our admiration. . . . To sum up what I have endeavoured to set forth. That high standard of education to which I referred at the outset is only to be reached by one who has seen many things and read much. Poet, Orator, Historian, and the rest, all must be studied, each must contribute a share. Our learning thus becomes full, ready, varied and elegant, available for action or for discourse in all subjects. But to enable us to make effectual use of what we know we must add to our knowledge the power of expression. These two sides of learning, indeed, should not be separated: they afford mutual aid and distinction. Proficiency in literary form, not accompanied by broad acquaintance with facts and truths, is a barren attainment; whilst information, however vast, which lacks all grace of expression, would seem to be put under a bushel or partly thrown away. Indeed, one may fairly ask what advantage it is to possess profound and varied learning if one cannot convey it in language worthy of the subject. Where, however, this double capacity exists — breadth of learning and grace of style — we allow the highest title to distinction and to abiding fame. If we review the great names of ancient [Greek and Roman] literature, Plato, Democritus, Aristotle, Theophrastus, Varro, Cicero, Seneca, Augustine, Jerome, Lactantius, we shall find it hard to say whether we admire more their attainments or their literary power.

[5]Ennius (239–169 B.C.) wrote the first great Latin epic poem, which was based on the legends of Rome's founding and its early history. Accius (c. 170–c. 90 B.C.), also a Roman, authored a history of Greek and Latin literature.

REVIEW QUESTIONS

1. According to Petrarch, what was the great fault of the scholars of his own age?
2. What made Petrarch aware that a renaissance, or rebirth, of classical learning was necessary in his time?
3. Why did Leonardo Bruni abandon his earlier course of studies to pursue the study of Greek literature?
4. Why did Bruni insist on the importance of studying Latin grammar and imitating the best models of Latin style?
5. Why did Bruni consider the study of history of crucial importance?

6. Why did Bruni recommend the study of ancient classical oratory?
7. What benefit did Bruni see in the study of the ancient poets?
8. From Bruni's viewpoint, what two things were needed to acquire a good education?

2 ▾ Human Dignity

In his short lifetime, Giovanni Pico della Mirandola (1463–1494) mastered Greek, Latin, Hebrew, and Arabic and aspired to synthesize the Hebrew, Greek, and Christian traditions. His most renowned work, *Oration on the Dignity of Man,* has been called the humanist manifesto.

Pico della Mirandola
≪ ORATION ON THE DIGNITY OF MAN ≫

In the opening section of the *Oration,* Pico declares that unlike other creatures, human beings have not been assigned a fixed place in the universe. Our destiny is not determined by anything outside us. Rather, God has bestowed upon us a unique distinction: the liberty to determine the form and value our lives shall acquire. The notion that people have the power to shape their own lives is a key element in the emergence of the modern outlook.

I have read in the records of the Arabians, reverend Fathers, that Abdala the Saracen,[1] when questioned as to what on this stage of the world, as it were, could be seen most worthy of wonder, replied: "There is nothing to be seen more wonderful than man." In agreement with this opinion is the saying of Hermes Trismegistus: "A great miracle, Asclepius, is man."[2] But when I weighed the reason for these maxims, the many grounds for the excellence of human nature reported by many men failed to satisfy me — that man is the intermediary between creatures, the intimate of the gods, the king of the lower beings, by the acuteness of his senses, by the discernment of his reason, and by the light of his intelligence the interpreter of nature, the interval between fixed eternity and fleeting time, and (as the Persians say) the bond, nay, rather, the marriage song of the world, on David's [biblical king] testimony but little lower than the angels. Admittedly great though these reasons be, they are not the principal grounds, that is, those which may rightfully claim for themselves the privilege of the highest admiration. For why should we not admire more the angels themselves and the blessed choirs of heaven? At last it seems to me I have come to understand why man is the most fortunate of creatures and consequently worthy of all admiration and what precisely is that rank which is his lot in the universal chain of Being — a rank to be envied not only by brutes but even by the stars and by minds beyond this world. It is a matter past faith and a wondrous one. Why should it not be? For it is on this very account that man is rightly called and judged a great miracle and a wonderful creature indeed. . . .

. . . God the Father, the supreme Architect, had already built this cosmic home we behold,

[1]Abdala the Saracen possibly refers to the eighth century A.D. writer Abd-Allah Ibn al-Muqaffa.

[2]Ancient writings dealing with magic, alchemy, astrology, and occult philosophy were erroneously attributed to an assumed Egyptian priest, Hermes Trismegistus. Asclepius was a Greek god of healing.

the most sacred temple of His godhead, by the laws of His mysterious wisdom. The region above the heavens He had adorned with Intelligences, the heavenly spheres He had quickened with eternal souls, and the excrementary and filthy parts of the lower world He had filled with a multitude of animals of every kind. But, when the work was finished, the Craftsman kept wishing that there were someone to ponder the plan of so great a work, to love its beauty, and to wonder at its vastness. Therefore, when everything was done (as Moses and Timaeus[3] bear witness), He finally took thought concerning the creation of man. But there was not among His archetypes that from which He could fashion a new offspring, nor was there in His treasure-houses anything which He might bestow on His new son as an inheritance, nor was there in the seats of all the world a place where the latter might sit to contemplate the universe. All was now complete; all things had been assigned to the highest, the middle, and the lowest orders. But in its final creation it was not the part of the Father's power to fail as though exhausted. It was not the part of His wisdom to waver in a needful matter through poverty of counsel. It was not the part of His kindly love that he who was to praise God's divine generosity in regard to others should be compelled to condemn it in regard to himself.

At last the best of artisans [God] ordained that that creature to whom He had been able to give nothing proper to himself should have joint possession of whatever had been peculiar to each of the different kinds of being. He therefore took man as a creature of indeterminate nature and, assigning him a place in the middle of the world, addressed him thus: "neither a fixed abode nor a form that is thine alone nor any function peculiar to thyself have we given thee, Adam, to the end that according to thy longing and according to thy judgment thou mayest have and possess what abode, what form, and what functions thou thyself shalt desire. The nature of all other beings is limited and constrained within the bounds of laws prescribed by Us. Thou, constrained by no limits, in accordance with thine own free will, in whose hand We have placed thee, shalt ordain for thyself the limits of thy nature. We have set thee at the world's center that thou mayest from thence more easily observe whatever is in the world. We have made thee neither of heaven nor of earth, neither mortal nor immortal, so that with freedom of choice and with honor, as though the maker and molder of thyself, thou mayest fashion thyself in whatever shape thou shalt prefer. Thou shalt have the power to degenerate into the lower forms of life, which are brutish. Thou shalt have the power, out of thy soul's judgment, to be reborn into the higher forms, which are divine."

O supreme generosity of God the Father, O highest and most marvelous felicity of man! To him it is granted to have whatever he chooses, to be whatever he wills. Beasts as soon as they are born (so says Lucilius)[4] bring with them from their mother's womb all they will ever possess. Spiritual beings [angels], either from the beginning or soon thereafter, become what they are to be for ever and ever. On man when he came into life the Father conferred the seeds of all kinds and the germs of every way of life. Whatever seeds each man cultivates will grow to maturity and bear in him their own fruit. If they be vegetative, he will be like a plant. If sensitive, he will become brutish. If rational, he will grow into a heavenly being. If intellectual, he will be an angel and the son of God. And if, happy in the lot of no created thing, he withdraws into the center of his own unity, his spirit, made one with God, in the solitary darkness of God, who is set above all things, shall surpass them all.

---

[3]Timaeus, a Greek Pythagorean philosopher, was a central character in Plato's famous dialogue *Timaeus*.

[4]Lucilius, a first century A.D. Roman poet and Stoic philosopher, was a close friend of Seneca — the philosopher-dramatist.

REVIEW QUESTIONS

1. According to Giovanni Pico della Mirandola, what quality did human beings alone possess? What did its possession allow them to do?
2. How does Pico's oration on human dignity exemplify the emergence of the new psychological outlook of the Renaissance?
3. Compare Pico's view of the individual with that of Saint Augustine (page 192).

---

3 ▾ Celebration of the Worldly Life

In the late fifteenth and the sixteenth centuries, the Renaissance spread to Germany, France, England, and Spain. Exemplifying the Renaissance spirit in France was François Rabelais (c. 1495–c. 1553), a Benedictine monk (until he resigned from the order), a physician, and a humanist scholar. *Gargantua and Pantagruel,* Rabelais's significant folk epic, attacked clerical education and monastic orders and expressed an appreciation for secular learning and a confidence in human nature. Like other Renaissance humanists, Rabelais criticized medieval philosophy for its overriding concern with obscure, confused, and irrelevant questions and censured a narrow-minded clergy who deprived people of life's joys. Expressing his aversion to medieval asceticism, he attacked monasticism as life-denying and regarded worldly pleasure as a legitimate need and aim of human nature.

François Rabelais
≪ GARGANTUA AND PANTAGRUEL ≫

The following reading from *Gargantua and Pantagruel* contains a description of life at an imagined monastery, the abbey of Thélème, whose rules differed markedly from those of traditional medieval monasteries. Here Rabelais expressed the Renaissance celebration of the worldly life.

THE RULES ACCORDING TO WHICH THE THÉLÈMITES LIVED

All their life was regulated not by laws, statutes, or rules, but according to their free will and pleasure. They rose from bed when they pleased, and drank, ate, worked, and slept when the fancy seized them. Nobody woke them; nobody compelled them either to eat or to drink, or to do anything else whatever. So it was that Gargantua has established it. In their rules there was only one clause:

DO WHAT YOU WILL

because people who are free, well-born, well-bred, and easy in honest company have a natural spur and instinct which drives them to virtuous deeds and deflects them from vice; and this they called honour. When these same men are depressed and enslaved by vile constraint and subjection, they use this noble quality which once impelled them freely towards virtue, to throw off and break this yoke of slavery. For we always strive after things forbidden and covet what is denied us.

Making use of this liberty, they most laudably rivalled one another in all of them doing what they saw pleased one. If some man or woman said, "Let us drink," they all drank; if he or she said, "Let us play," they all played; if it was "Let us go and amuse ourselves in the fields," everyone went there. If it were for hawking or hunting, the ladies, mounted on fine mares, with their grand palfreys following, each carried on their daintily gloved wrists a sparrow-hawk, a lanneret, or a merlin, the men carrying the other birds.[1]

So nobly were they instructed that there was not a man or woman among them who could not read, write, sing, play musical instruments, speak five or six languages, and compose in them both verse and prose. Never were seen such worthy knights, so valiant, so nimble both on foot and horse; knights more vigorous, more agile, handier with all weapons than they were. Never were seen ladies so good-looking, so dainty, less tiresome, more skilled with the fingers and the needle, and in every free and honest womanly pursuit than they were. . . .

▷ Gargantua writes to his son Pantagruel, studying in Paris; in the letter, he describes a truly liberal education, one befitting a Renaissance humanist.

Now every method of teaching has been restored, and the study of languages has been revived: of Greek, without which it is disgraceful for a man to call himself a scholar, and of Hebrew, [other ancient Semitic languages], and Latin. The elegant and accurate art of printing, which is now in use, was invented in my time, by divine inspiration; as, by contrast, artillery was inspired by diabolical suggestion. The whole world is full of learned men, of very erudite tutors, and of most extensive libraries, and it is my opinion that neither in the time of Plato, of Cicero, nor of Papinian[2] were there such facilities for study as one finds today. No one, in future, will risk appearing in public or in any company, who is not well polished in Minerva's [Roman goddess of wisdom] workshop. I find robbers, hangmen, freebooters, and grooms nowadays more learned than the doctors and preachers were in my time.

Why, the very women and girls aspire to the glory and reach out for the celestial manna[3] of sound learning. So much so that at my present age I have been compelled to learn Greek, which I had not despised like Cato,[4] but which I had not the leisure to learn in my youth. Indeed I find great delight in reading the *Morals* of Plutarch, Plato's magnificent *Dialogues,* the *Monuments* of Pausanias, and the *Antiquities* of Athenaeus,[5] while I wait for the hour when it will please God, my Creator, to call me and bid me leave this earth.

Therefore, my son, I beg you to devote your youth to the firm pursuit of your studies and to the attainment of virtue. You are in Paris. There you will find many praiseworthy examples to follow. You have Epistemon for your tutor, and he can give you living instruction by word of mouth. It is my earnest wish that you shall become a perfect master of languages. First of Greek, as Quintilian [Roman educational theorist] advises; secondly, of Latin; and then of Hebrew, on account of the Holy Scriptures; also of Chaldean and Arabic, for the same reason; and I would have you model your Greek style on Plato's and your Latin on that of Cicero. Keep your memory well stocked with every tale from history, and here you will find

---

[1]*Palfreys* and *lanneret,* archaic terms, refer respectively to a saddle horse usually ridden by women and to a small male falcon native to the Mediterranean area. A merlin is a small black and white European falcon, now also called a pigeon hawk.

[2]Papinian was a Roman jurist of the late second to early third century A.D. whose legal opinions were considered authoritative in late Roman law.

[3]*Manna* refers to a food miraculously provided by God for the Hebrews during their exodus out of Egypt during Moses' time (Exodus 16:14–36).

[4]Cato the Elder (234–149 B.C.), a Roman statesman, was noted for his conservative morals and hostility to Greek influences in Roman society.

[5]Pausanias was a travel writer famous for his guides to the ancient monuments of Greece, and Athenaeus was a compiler of literary and philosophical writings. Both were Greeks of the second century A.D.

help in the Cosmographes[6] of the historians. Of the liberal arts, geometry, arithmetic, and music, I gave you some smattering when you were still small, at the age of five or six. Go on and learn the rest, also the rules of astronomy. But leave divinatory astrology and Lully's[7] art alone, I beg of you, for they are frauds and vanities. Of Civil Law I would have you learn the best texts by heart, and relate them to the art of philosophy. And as for the knowledge of Nature's works, I should like you to give careful attention to that too; so that there may be no sea, river, or spring of which you do not know the fish. All the birds of the air, all the trees, shrubs, and bushes of the forest, all the herbs of the field, all the metals deep in the bowels of the earth, the precious stones of the whole East and the South —let none of them be unknown to you.

Then scrupulously peruse the books of the Greek, Arabian, and Latin doctors once more, not omitting the Talmudists and Cabalists,[8] and by frequent dissections gain a perfect knowledge of that other world which is man. At some hours of the day also, begin to examine the Holy Scriptures. First the New Testament and the Epistles of the Apostles in Greek; and then the Old Testament, in Hebrew. In short, let me find you a veritable abyss of knowledge. For, later, when you have grown into a man, you will have to leave this quiet and repose of study, to learn chivalry and warfare, to defend my house, and to help our friends in every emergency against the attacks of evildoers.

[6]Cosmographes are books on geography, geology, and astronomy.

[7]Lully alludes to Ramon Lull (c. 1236–1315), a Franciscan friar, a mystic, and a philosopher, who was falsely reputed to have authored various books on magic and alchemy.

[8]Talmudists are students of the collection of writings on Jewish civil and religious laws, and Cabalists refers to students of a medieval Jewish occult tradition based on a mystical interpretation of the Hebrew Scriptures.

REVIEW QUESTIONS

1. How did the rules of the abbey of Thélème differ from those of a Benedictine abbey? (See page 194, Rule of Saint Benedict.)
2. How did François Rabelais's description of life at the abbey of Thélème represent Renaissance ideals?
3. What ancient writers did Rabelais consider to be ideal models for acquiring a good literary style?
4. What subjects did Rabelais recommend for study? Which were to be avoided?
5. What connection, if any, is there between the unrestrained life of the abbey of Thélème and a life formed by a humanistic curriculum?
6. In what ways does the humanist educational program continue to influence the curriculum of modern educational institutions?

---

4 ▾ Break with Medieval Political Theory

Turning away from the religious orientation of the Middle Ages, Renaissance thinkers discussed the human condition in secular terms and opened up possibilities for thinking about moral and political problems in new ways. Thus, Niccolò Machiavelli (1469–1527), a Florentine statesman and political theorist, broke with medieval political theory. Medieval political thinkers held that the ruler derived power from God and had a religious obligation to rule in

accordance with God's precepts. Machiavelli, though, ascribed no divine origin to kingship, nor did he attribute events to the mysterious will of God; and he explicitly rejected the principle that kings should adhere to Christian moral teachings. For Machiavelli, the state was a purely human creation. Successful kings or princes, he asserted, should be concerned only with preserving and strengthening the state's power and must ignore questions of good and evil, morality and immorality. Machiavelli did not assert that religion was supernatural in origin and rejected prevailing belief that Christian morality should guide political life. For him, religion's value derived from other factors: a ruler could utilize religion to unite his subjects and to foster obedience to law.

Niccolò Machiavelli
≪ THE PRINCE ≫

In contrast to medieval thinkers, Machiavelli did not seek to construct an ideal Christian community but to discover how politics was *really* conducted. He studied politics in the cold light of reason, as the following passage from *The Prince* illustrates.

It now remains to be seen what are the methods and rules for a prince as regards his subjects and friends. And as I know that many have written of this, I fear that my writing about it may be deemed presumptuous, differing as I do, especially in this matter, from the opinions of others. But my intention being to write something of use to those who understand, it appears to me more proper to go to the real truth of the matter than to its imagination; and many have imagined republics and principalities which have never been seen or known to exist in reality; for how we live is so far removed from how we ought to live, that he who abandons what is done for what ought to be done, will rather learn to bring about his own ruin than his preservation.

▷ Machiavelli removed ethics from political thinking. A successful ruler, he contended, is indifferent to moral and religious considerations. But will not the prince be punished on the Day of Judgment for violating Christian teachings? In startling contrast to medieval theorists, Machiavelli simply ignored the question. The action of a prince, he said, should be governed solely by necessity.

A man who wishes to make a profession of goodness in everything must necessarily come to grief among so many who are not good. Therefore it is necessary for a prince, who wishes to maintain himself, to learn how not to be good, and to use this knowledge and not use it, according to the necessity of the case.

Leaving on one side, then, those things which concern only an imaginary prince, and speaking of those that are real, I state that all men, and especially princes, who are placed at a greater height, are reputed for certain qualities which bring them either praise or blame. Thus one is considered liberal, another . . . miserly; . . . one a free giver, another rapacious; one cruel, another merciful; one a breaker of his word, another trustworthy; one effeminate and pusillanimous, another fierce and high-spirited; one humane, another haughty; one lascivious, another chaste; one frank, another astute; one hard, another easy; one serious, another frivolous; one religious, another an unbeliever, and so on. I know that every one will admit that it would be highly praiseworthy in a prince to possess all the above-named qualities that are reputed good, but as they cannot all be possessed or observed, human conditions not permitting of it, it is necessary that he should be prudent enough to avoid the scandal of those vices which would lose him the state, and guard himself if possible against those which will not lose it [for] him, but if not able to, he can indulge them with less scruple. And yet he must not mind incurring the scandal of those vices, without which it would be difficult to save the state, for if one considers well, it will be found that some things which seem virtues would, if followed, lead to one's ruin, and some others which appear vices result in one's greater security and wellbeing. . . .

. . . I say that every prince must desire to be considered merciful and not cruel. He must, however, take care not to misuse this mercifulness. Cesare Borgia was considered cruel, but his cruelty had brought order to the Romagna,[1] united it, and reduced it to peace and fealty. If this is considered well, it will be seen that he was really much more merciful than the Florentine people, who, to avoid the name of cruelty, allowed Pistoia[2] to be destroyed. A prince, therefore, must not mind incurring the charge of cruelty for the purpose of keeping his subjects united and faithful; for, with a very few examples, he will be more merciful than those who, from excess of tenderness, allow disorders to arise, from whence spring bloodshed and rapine; for these as a rule injure the whole community, while the executions carried out by the prince injure only individuals. . . .

▷ Machiavelli's rigorous investigation of politics led him to view human nature from the standpoint of its limitations and imperfections. The astute prince, he said, recognizes that human beings are by nature selfish, cowardly, and dishonest, and regulates his political strategy accordingly.

From this arises the question whether it is better to be loved more than feared, or feared more than loved. The reply is, that one ought to be both feared and loved, but as it is difficult for the two to go together, it is much safer to be feared than loved, if one of the two has to be wanting. For it may be said of men in general that they are ungrateful, voluble, dissemblers, anxious to avoid danger, and covetous of gain; as long as you benefit them, they are entirely yours; they offer you their blood, their goods, their life, and their children, as I have before said, when the necessity is remote; but when it approaches, they revolt. And the prince who has relied solely on their words, without making other preparations, is ruined; for the friendship which is gained by purchase and not through grandeur and nobility of spirit is bought but not secured, and at a pinch is not to be expended in your service. And men have less scruple in offending one who makes himself loved than one who makes himself feared; for love is held by a chain of obligation which, men being selfish, is broken whenever it serves their purpose; but fear is maintained by a dread of punishment which never fails.

Still, a prince should make himself feared in such a way that if he does not gain love, he at any rate avoids hatred; for fear and the absence of hatred may well go together, and will be always attained by one who abstains from interfering with the property of his citizens and subjects or with their women. And when he is obliged to take the life of any one, let him do so when there is a proper justification and manifest reason for it; but above all he must abstain from taking the property of others, for men forget more easily the death of their father than the loss of their patrimony. Then also pretexts for seizing property are never wanting, and one who begins to live by rapine will always find some reason for taking the goods of others, whereas causes for taking life are rarer and more fleeting.

---

[1]Cesare Borgia (c. 1476–1507) was the bastard son of Rodrigo Borgia, then a Spanish cardinal and later Pope Alexander VI (1492–1503). With his father's aid he attempted to carve out for himself an independent duchy in north-central Italy, with Romagna as its heart. Through cruelty, violence, and treachery, he succeeded at first in his ambition, but ultimately his principality collapsed. Romagna was eventually incorporated into the Papal State under Pope Julius II (1503–1513). Machiavelli uses Borgia as a role model of his ideal of a modern ruler — with little justification.

[2]Pistoia, a small Italian city in Tuscany, came under the control of Florence in the fourteenth century.

But when the prince is with his army and has a large number of soldiers under his control, then it is extremely necessary that he should not mind being thought cruel; for without this reputation he could not keep an army united or disposed to any duty. Among the noteworthy actions of Hannibal[3] is numbered this, that although he had an enormous army, composed of men of all nations and fighting in foreign countries, there never arose any dissension either among them or against the prince, either in good fortune or in bad. This could not be due to anything but his inhuman cruelty, which together with his infinite other virtues, made him always venerated and terrible in the sight of his soldiers, and without it his other virtues would not have sufficed to produce that effect. Thoughtless writers admire on the one hand his actions, and on the other blame the principal cause of them. . . .

▷ Again in marked contrast to the teachings of Christian (and ancient) moralists, Machiavelli said that the successful prince will use any means to achieve and sustain political power. If the end is desirable, all means are justified.

How laudable it is for a prince to keep good faith and live with integrity, and not with astuteness, every one knows. Still the experience of our times shows those princes to have done great things who have had little regard for good faith, and have been able by astuteness to confuse men's brains, and who have ultimately overcome those who have made loyalty their foundation.

You must know, then, that there are two methods of fighting, the one by law, the other by force: the first method is that of men, the second of beasts; but as the first method is often insufficient, one must have recourse to the second. It is therefore necessary for a prince to know well how to use both the beast and the man. . . .

A prince being thus obliged to know well how to act as a beast must imitate the fox and the lion, for the lion cannot protect himself from traps, and the fox cannot defend himself from wolves. One must therefore be a fox to recognise traps, and a lion to frighten wolves. Those that wish to be only lions do not understand this. Therefore, a prudent ruler ought not to keep faith when by so doing it would be against his interest, and when the reasons which made him bind himself no longer exist. If men were all good, this precept would not be a good one; but as they are bad, and would not observe their faith with you, so you are not bound to keep faith with them. Nor have legitimate grounds ever failed a prince who wished to show [plausible] excuse for the nonfulfilment of his promise. Of this one could furnish an infinite number of modern examples, and show how many times peace has been broken, and how many promises rendered worthless, by the faithlessness of princes, and those that have been best able to imitate the fox have succeeded best. But it is necessary to be able to disguise this character well, and to be a great feigner and dissembler; and men are so simple and so ready to obey present necessities, that one who deceives will always find those who allow themselves to be deceived. . . .

. . . Thus it is well to seem merciful, faithful, humane, sincere, religious, and also to be so; but you must have the mind so disposed that when it is needful to be otherwise you may be able to change to the opposite qualities. And it must be understood that a prince, and especially a new prince, cannot observe all those things which are considered good in men, being often obliged, in order to maintain the state, to act against faith, against charity, against humanity, and against religion. And, therefore, he must have a mind disposed to adapt itself according to the wind, and as the variations of fortune dictate, and, as I said before, not deviate from what is good, if possible, but be able to do evil if constrained.

---

[3]Hannibal (247–182 B.C.) was a brilliant Carthaginian general whose military victories almost destroyed Roman power. He was finally defeated at the battle of Zama in 202 B.C. by the Roman general Scipio Africanus.

A prince must take great care that nothing goes out of his mouth which is not full of the above-named five qualities, and, to see and hear him, he should seem to be all mercy, faith, integrity, humanity, and religion. And nothing is more necessary than to seem to have this last quality, for men in general judge more by the eyes than by the hands, for every one can see, but very few have to feel. Everybody sees what you appear to be, few feel what you are, and those few will not dare to oppose themselves to the many, who have the majesty of the state to defend them; and in the actions of men, and especially of princes, from which there is no appeal, the end justifies the means. Let a prince therefore aim at conquering and maintaining the state, and the means will always be judged honourable and praised by every one, for the vulgar is always taken by appearances and the issue of the event; and the world consists only of the vulgar, and the few who are not vulgar are isolated when the many have a rallying point in the prince. A certain prince of the present time, whom it is well not to name, never does anything but preach peace and good faith, but he is really a great enemy to both, and either of them, had he observed them, would have lost him state or repuation on many occasions.

REVIEW QUESTIONS

1. In what respect did Niccolò Machiavelli claim to be breaking new ground in his study of statecraft?
2. What was Machiavelli's view of human nature?
3. In what ways was Machiavelli's advice to princes a break with the teachings of medieval political and moral philosophers?
4. Compare Machiavelli's view of the political man with the picture of human beings outlined by Pico, Rabelais, and Bruni earlier in this chapter.
5. What ethical standard did Machiavelli seem to endorse for politicians who wish to succeed?

---

5 ▾ Art and Science

Renaissance artists were inspired by the art of classical antiquity, which was representational and aspired to show nature as it truly appeared to the eye. But Renaissance artists also went beyond ancient classical art. In his work *Della pittura,* Leon Battista Alberti (1404–1472), the first modern art theoretician, formulated the mathematical theory of artistic perspective, which became commonly used by the artists of the time. His purpose was to enable artists to depict objects as if they were seen through a glass window, creating the illusion of depth, of three dimensions on a two-dimensional surface. This illusion involved establishing a precise mathematical relationship between the object and the observer. By defining visual space and the relationship between the object and the observer in mathematical terms, Renaissance art and artistic theory helped pave the way for the development of the modern scientific approach to nature, which later found expression in the astronomy of Copernicus and the physics of Galileo (see Chapter 12).

Leonardo da Vinci
≪ THE NOTEBOOKS ≫

The works of Leonardo da Vinci (1452–1519) — his drawings, paintings, sculpture, innumerable inventions, and copious writings — exemplify the Renaissance spirit. They announced a new way of looking at nature and the individual. Leonardo examined objects in all their diversity and represented them realistically. For Leonardo, visual art was a means of arriving at nature's truths. Truth was attained when the artist brought both human reason and human creative capacity to bear on the direct experiences of the senses. Leonardo visually delineated the natural world with unprecedented scientific precision and simultaneously asserted his spiritual and intellectual freedom to do so. Through his art, Leonardo helped lay the foundations for modern science.

In his notebooks, Leonardo sketched an infinite variety of objects — inorganic, organic, human — and recorded fragmentary thoughts about them. Everywhere, he demonstrated a concern for the concrete specificity of things, which he depicted in minute detail. In the following excerpts, Leonardo affirms the rigorous and direct observation of nature as a source of truth.

How painting surpasses all human works by reason of the subtle possibilities which it contains:

The eye, which is called the window of the soul, is the chief means whereby the understanding may most fully and abundantly appreciate the infinite works of nature; and the ear is the second, inasmuch as it acquires its importance from the fact that it hears the things which the eye has seen. If you historians, or poets, or mathematicians had never seen things with your eyes you would be ill able to describe them in your writings. And if you, O poet, represent a story by depicting it with your pen, the painter with his brush will so render it as to be more easily satisfying and less tedious to understand. . . .

OF THE ORDER TO BE OBSERVED IN STUDY

I say that one ought first to learn about the limbs and how they are worked, and after having completed this knowledge one ought to study their actions in the different conditions in which men are placed, and thirdly to devise figure compositions, the study for these being taken from natural actions made on occasion as opportunities offered; and one should be on the watch in the streets and squares and fields and there make sketches with rapid strokes to represent features, that is for a head one may make an *o,* and for an arm a straight or curved line, and so in like manner for the legs and trunk, afterwards when back at home working up these notes in a completed form.

My opponent says that in order to gain experience and to learn how to work readily, it is better that the first period of study should be spent in copying various compositions made by different masters either on sheets of paper or on walls, since from these one acquires rapidity in execution and a good method. But to this it may be replied that the ensuing method would be good if it was founded upon works that were excellent in composition and by diligent masters; and since such masters are so rare that few are to be found, it is safer to go direct to the works of nature than to those which have been imitated from her originals with great deterioration and thereby to acquire a bad method, for he who has access to the fountain does not go to the water-pot. . . .

▷ Equally important to Leonardo was the innate ability of the rational mind to use mathematics and to give order, form, and clarity to the individual's experiences of the world. Here he explains using mathematical perspective in art.

THE LIFE OF THE PAINTER IN THE COUNTRY

The painter requires such knowledge of mathematics as belongs to painting, and severance from companions who are not in sympathy with his studies, and his brain should have the power of adapting itself to the tenor of the objects which present themselves before it, and he should be freed from all other cares.

And if while considering and examining one subject a second should intervene, as happens when an object occupies the mind, he ought to decide which of these subjects presents greater difficulties in investigation, and follow that until it becomes entirely clear, and afterwards pursue the investigation of the other. And above all he should keep his mind as clear as the surface of a mirror, which becomes changed to as many different colours as are those of the objects within it, and his companions should resemble him in a taste for these studies, and if he fail to find any such he should accustom himself to be alone in his investigations, for in the end he will find no more profitable companionship. . . .

OF THE REQUISITES OF PAINTING

The first requisite of painting is that the bodies which it represents should appear in relief, and that the scenes which surround them with effects of distance should seem to enter into the plane in which the picture is produced by means of the three parts of perspective, namely the diminution in the distinctness of the form of bodies, the diminution in their size, and the diminution in their colour. Of these three divisions of perspective, the first has its origin in the eye, the two others are derived from the atmosphere that is interposed between the eye and the objects which the eye beholds. . . .

WALL OF GLASS

Perspective is nothing else than the seeing of an object behind a sheet of glass, smooth and quite transparent, on the surface of which all the things may be marked that are behind this glass; these things approach the point of the eye in pyramids, and these pyramids are cut by the said glass.

OF THE DIMINUTION OF OBJECTS AT VARIOUS DISTANCES

A second object as far removed from the first as the first is from the eye will appear half the size of the first, although they are of the same size.

A small object near at hand and a large one at a distance, when seen between equal angles will appear the same size. . . .

Perspective is a rational demonstration whereby experience confirms how all things transmit their images to the eye by pyramidal lines. By pyramidal lines I mean those which start from the extremities of the surface of bodies, and by gradually converging from a distance arrive at the same point; the said point being . . . in this particular case located in the eye, which is the universal judge of all objects. . . .

▷ Leonardo was always engaged in a quest for the essential living form of a thing, the relationship of its parts to its whole, the numerical ratios subsisting among the parts, and the laws operative in the ratios. He found such ratios and laws everywhere in both animate and inanimate objects. In the following excerpt he tries to define the ratio of parts to the whole of the male human body. His written observations are accompanied by a marvelous sketch of the body, conceived and framed with realism and mathematical proportion.

If you set your legs so far apart as to take a fourteenth part from your height, and you open

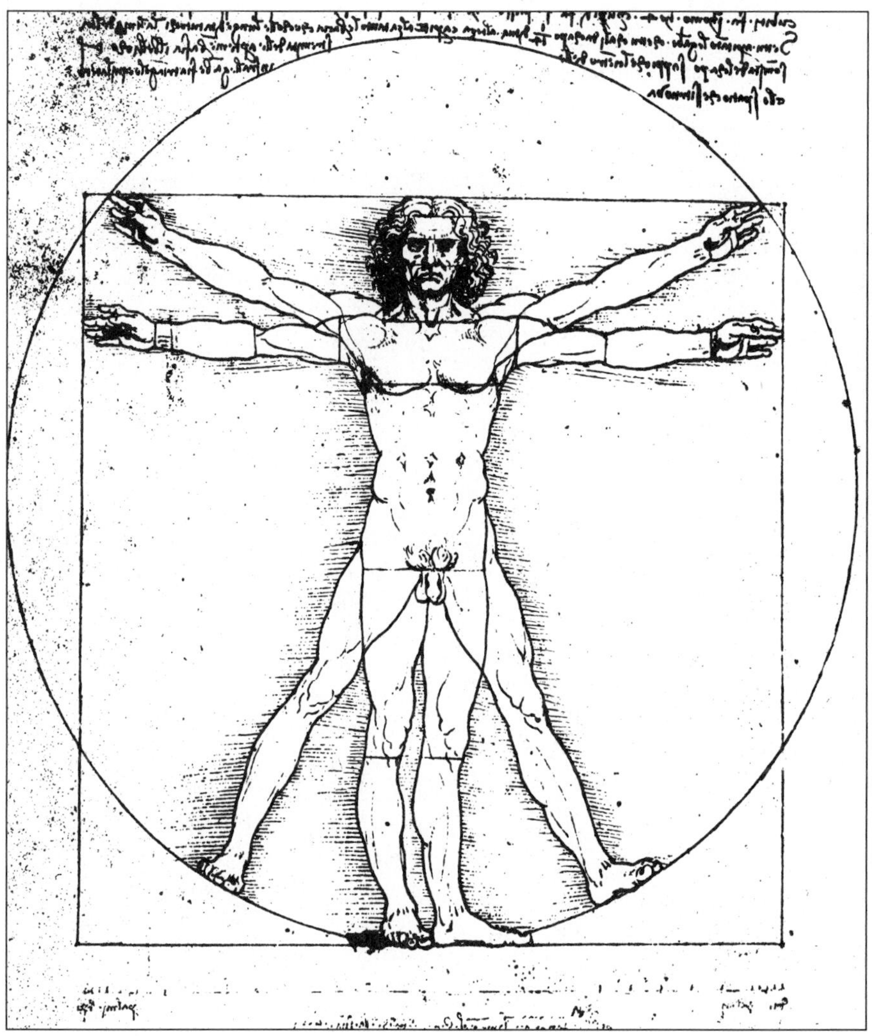

THE PROPORTIONS OF MAN by Leonardo da Vinci, from his Notebooks. See the reading below in which Leonardo described the proportions that this drawing illustrates. (Historical Pictures Service, Chicago)

and raise your arms until you touch the line of the crown of the head with your middle fingers, you must know that the centre of the circle formed by the extremities of the outstretched limbs will be the navel, and the space between the legs will form an equilateral triangle.

The span of a man's outstretched arms is equal to his height.

From the beginning of the hair to the end of the bottom of the chin is the tenth part of a man's height; from the bottom of the chin to the crown of the head is the eighth of the man's height; from the top of the breast to the crown of the head is the sixth of the man; from the top of the breast to where the hair commences is the seventh part of the whole man; from the nipples to the crown of the head is a fourth part of the man. The maximum width of the shoulders is in itself the fourth part of a man; from the elbow to the tip of the middle finger is the fifth part; from this elbow to the end of the shoulder is the eighth part. The complete hand will be the tenth part. The penis begins at the centre of the man. The foot is the seventh part of the man. From the sole of the foot to just below the knee is the fourth part of the man. From below the knee to where the penis begins is the fourth part of the man.

The parts that find themselves between the chin and the nose and between the places where the hair and the eyebrows start each of itself compares with that of the ear, and is a third of the face.

REVIEW QUESTIONS

1. According to Leonardo da Vinci, how did painting surpass all other human arts?
2. How did Leonardo propose to use art to understand nature?
3. What did Leonardo hope to achieve by using mathematics to depict objects?
4. How did Leonardo's approach to painting objects differ from that of medieval artists, as described in the introduction to this chapter?

---

6 ▾ Renaissance Florence

Florence was the city of the Renaissance par excellence. Many Florentines were distinguished humanist scholars, painters, sculptors, architects, and artisans; humanists were appointed to the post of chancellor; the aristocracy funded professional humanists and artists; and many leading families produced humanist scholars. The state sponsored grand architectural projects and gave public recognition to distinguished artists and writers. Because of its reputation, leading scholars and artists from other cities sought to live in Florence.

Francesco Guicciardini
THE GREATNESS OF LORENZO DE MEDICI

For much of the fifteenth century, the Medici family, which had made its fortune in banking, dominated Florentine politics and patronized the arts. In the following reading from his *History of Florence,* Francesco Guicciardini (1483–1540), a Florentine historian and student of politics, described the contribution of Lorenzo de Medici (1449–1492) to Florentine cultural life.

He desired glory and excellence more than any man, but he can be criticized for having carried this desire even into unimportant matters. In versifying, in games, and in other pursuits he got very angry with anyone who equalled or imitated him. The desire was too strong in important matters too. He wanted to equal and compete with all the princes of Italy in everything. . . . On the whole, though, his ambition was praiseworthy and brought him glory and fame everywhere, even outside Italy, for it caused him to strive to make the Florence of his time stand out above all other Italian cities in all arts and skills. He had a university founded in Pisa, principally for the study of letters. When people adduced many reasons to show that it could not have as many students as Padua or Pavia, he said he would be satisfied to have more faculty members than the others. In this time, all the most excellent and most famous men in Italy taught there and received very high salaries, for he avoided neither expense nor labor to get them. In Florence, the study of the humanities flourished under messer Agnolo Poliziano, Greek under messer Demetrio {Chalcondylas} and then under {Constantine} Lascaris, philosophy and art under Marsilio Ficino, Giorgio Benigno, Count Pico della Mirandola, and other excellent men. Lorenzo showed the same favor to poetry in the vernacular, to music, architecture, painting, sculpture, and to all the arts of mind and hand, so that the city overflowed with all these exquisite things. And these arts flourished all the more because Lorenzo, a universal man, could pass judgment and distinguish among men, so that they competed with one another to please him. Furthermore, there was his infinite liberality, which provided all talented men with livelihoods and with all the instruments necessary for their work. To give an example: when he decided to establish a Greek library, he sent the very learned Lascaris all the way to Greece to look for good ancient books.

The same liberality preserved his fame and his friendship with princes in Italy and abroad; for he omitted no form of magnificence — no matter how costly — that might enable him to keep the favor of the powerful. The result was that at Lyons, Milan, Bruges, and other places where he had business interests, his magnificence and his gifts caused his expenses to multiply, whereas his profits diminished because his affairs were governed by men of little ability, such as Lionetto de'Rossi and Tommaso Portinari. Moreover, his accounts were not well rendered, for he knew little and cared less about business. On several occasions his affairs were in such disorder that he was on the verge of bankruptcy, and was forced to avail himself of his friends' money or of public funds.

Benedetto Dei
FLORENCE, 1472

In the following letter written to a Venetian in 1472, Benedetto Dei (*fl.* late fifteenth century), a Florentine merchant, describes the economy of his native city under the domination of Lorenzo de Medici, comparing it favorably to that of Venice and other leading Italian city-states.

Florence is more beautiful and five hundred forty years older than your Venice. We spring from triply noble blood. We are one-third Roman, one-third Frankish, and one-third Fiesolan.[1] . . . We have round about us thirty thousand estates, owned by noblemen and merchants, citizens and craftsmen, yielding us yearly bread and meat, wine and oil, vegetables and cheese, hay and wood, to the value of nine hundred thousand ducats in cash, as you Venetians, Genoese, Chians, and Rhodians who come to buy them know well enough. We have two trades greater than any four of yours in Venice put together — the trades of wool and silk. Witness the Roman court and that of the King of Naples, the Marches and Sicily, Constantinople and Pera, Broussa and Adrianople, Salonika and Gallipoli, Chios and Rhodes {cities and areas in Italy and the eastern Mediterranean}, where, to your envy and disgust, in all of those places there are Florentine consuls and merchants, churches and houses, banks and offices, and whither go more Florentine wares of all kinds, especially silken stuffs and gold and silver brocades, than from Venice, Genoa, and Lucca put together. Ask your merchants who visit Marseilles, Avignon, and the whole of Provence, Bruges, Antwerp, London, and other cities where there are great banks and royal warehouses, fine dwellings, and stately churches; ask

---

[1]Fiesole is an ancient Etruscan hill town three miles northeast of Florence.

those who should know, as they go to fairs every year, whether they have seen the [Florentine] banks of the Medici, the Pazzi, the Capponi, the Buondelmonti, the Corsini, the Falconieri, the Portinari and the Ghini,* and a hundred of others which I will not name, because to do so I should need at least a ream of paper. You say we are bankrupt since Cosimo's [de Medici, 1389–1464] death. If we have had losses, it is owing to your dishonesty and the wickedness of your Levantine merchants, who have made us lose thousands of florins [gold coins]; it is the fault of those with well-known names who have filled Constantinople and Pera with failures, whereof our great houses could tell many a tale. But though Cosimo is dead and buried, he did not take his gold florins and the rest of his money and bonds with him into the other world, nor his banks and storehouses, nor his woolen and silken cloths, nor his plate and jewelry; but he left them all to his worthy sons and grandsons, who take pains to keep them and to add to them, to the everlasting vexation of the Venetians and other envious foes whose tongues are more malicious and slanderous than if they were Sienese. . . . Our beautiful Florence contains within the city in this present year two hundred seventy shops belonging to the wool merchants' guild, from whence their wares are sent to Rome and the Marches, Naples and Sicily, Constantinople and Pera, Adrianople, Broussa and the whole of Turkey. It contains also eighty-three rich and splendid warehouses of the silk merchants' guild, and furnishes gold and silver stuffs, velvet, brocade, damask, taffeta, and satin to Rome, Naples, Catalonia, and the whole of Spain, especially Seville, and to Turkey and Barbary. The principal fairs to which these wares go are those of Genoa, the Marches, Ferrara, Mantua, and the whole of Italy; Lyons, Avignon, Montpellier, Antwerp, and London. The number of banks amounts to thirty-three; the shops of the cabinetmakers, whose business is carving and inlaid work, to eighty-four; and the workshops of the stonecutters and marble workers in the city and its immediate neighborhood, to fifty-four. There are forty-four goldsmiths' and jewelers' shops, thirty gold-beaters, silver wire-drawers, and a wax-figure maker.† . . . Go through all the cities of the world, nowhere will you ever be able to find artists in wax equal to those we now have in Florence, and to whom the figures in the Nunziata‡ can bear witness. Another flourishing industry is the making of light and elegant gold and silver wreaths and garlands, which are worn by young maidens of high degree, and which have given their names to the artist family of Ghirlandaio. Sixty-six is the number of the apothecaries' and grocer shops; seventy that of the butchers, besides eight large shops in which are sold fowls of all kinds, as well as game and also the native wine called Trebbiano, from San Giovanni in the upper Arno Valley; it would awaken the dead in its praise.

*The bank of the Medici and their partners at Milan.

†This was at that time a profitable industry, as such images were used in all churches.

‡SS [Sanctissima] Annuziata [Chuch of the Most Holy Annunciation].

REVIEW QUESTIONS

1. What character traits of Lorenzo de Medici did Francesco Guicciardini admire? Why?
2. What failings in Lorenzo's character did Guicciardini observe?
3. What were the principal sources of Florentine economic wealth and power?

The Reformation

The reformation of the church in the sixteenth century was rooted in demands for spiritual renewal and institutional change. These pressures began as early as the late fourteenth century and came from many sources.

The papacy and orthodox Catholic theology were challenged by English theologian John Wycliffe (c. 1320–1384) and Czech theologian John Huss (c. 1369–1415). Both attacked the bishops' involvement in temporal politics and urged a return to the simple practices of the early apostolic church; and both, claiming that the Bible alone — not the church hierarchy — was the highest authority for Christians, emphasized study of the Holy Scriptures by the laity and sermons in the common language of the people. Wycliffe, though not Huss, also undermined the clergy's authority by denying the priests' power to change the bread and wine into Christ's body and blood during the Mass. Despite severe persecution by church and state, followers of Wycliffe's and Huss's beliefs continued to exist and participated in the sixteenth-century Protestant movement.

Institutional reform from within was attempted through the Conciliar movement, which endeavored to restrict the pope's power through regular meetings of general councils of bishops. The Council of Constance (1414–1418) declared that a general council, not the papacy, was the supreme authority within the church and called for regular assemblies of bishops to consider the church's problems and initiate necessary reforms.

By the mid-fifteenth century, the Conciliar movement had collapsed, and the papacy, unreformed, freely exercised its supremacy. Fearful of losing its autonomy and power, the papacy resisted calling a new council from 1437 until 1512, when the Fifth Lateran Council met in Rome under close papal supervision. The council issued decrees aimed at improving education of the clergy, eliminating many abuses in church administration, and summoning a church council every five years. But the council's decrees were not implemented after the last session ended in 1517, the same year Martin Luther first challenged the papacy, thus starting the Protestant reform movement.

The principal source of the reform spirit was a widespread popular yearning for a more intense spirituality. It took many forms: the rise of new pious practices; greater interest in mystical experiences and in the study of the

MARTIN LUTHER AND THE WITTENBERG REFORMERS (c. 1530), by Lucas Cranach, the Elder. With Luther (left) are Frederick of Saxony, Luther's protector, who dominates the painting, and the Swiss reformer Huldreich Zwingli (to the right of Frederick). (*The Toledo Museum of Art; Gift of Edward Drummond Libbey*)

Bible; the development of communal ways for lay people to live and work following the apostles' example; and a heightened search for ways within secular society to imitate more perfectly the life of Christ — called the New Devotion movement.

Several secular factors contributed to this enhanced level of spiritual feeling. The many wars, famines, and plagues of the late fourteenth and the fifteenth centuries had traumatized Europe. The increasing educational level of the urban middle class and skilled laborers and the invention of the printing press allowed the rapid and relatively inexpensive spread of new ideas. Finally, there was the influence of the humanist movement, particularly in northern Europe and Spain. Many humanists dedicated themselves to promoting higher levels of religious education. They stimulated public interest in biblical study by publishing new editions of the Holy Scriptures and the writings of the church fathers, along with new devotional literature. Nearly all the religious reformers of the sixteenth century were deeply influenced by the ideals and methods of the Christian humanist movement.

In Germany, a spirit of discontent with social and economic conditions coincided with the demand for reform of the church and religious life. For several decades before Luther's revolt against the papacy, the economic conditions of the knights, the peasants, and the lower-class urban workers had deteriorated. The knights' grievances included loss of their political power to the centralizing governments of the German princes and increasing restrictions on their customary feudal privileges. Peasants protested that lords had steadily withdrawn certain of their customary rights and had added burdens, increasing the lords' income and control over their estates. The knights and peasants were squeezed into an ever-worsening social and economic niche. In the cities, the lower-class artisans and laborers were similarly oppressed. Those in the urban upper classes, who controlled town governments, enhanced their own economic privileges at the expense of lower-class citizens. The church, which was a major landowner and active in commercial enterprises in the towns, played an important role in these conflicts. All these grievances formed the explosive background to Martin Luther's challenge to the authority of the church and the imperial government.

The success of the reformers, both Protestant and Catholic, depended on support from the ruling political forces in the various kingdoms, principalities, and city-states of Europe. Usually, the rulers' religious preference determined whether the church remained Catholic or became Lutheran, Calvinist, or some combination of all three, as in England. The rulers of large parts of Germany, especially the imperial city-states, and of the Scandinavian kingdoms adopted the Lutheran reform. The Austrian and Spanish Hapsburg emperors and the French kings remained Catholic, although Calvinism had many adherents in France. In eastern Europe, Protestantism was successful at first but, under the influence of the Catholic reform movement, Catholicism later recovered its dominance. In Switzerland, allegiance was divided among Catholics and the followers of John Calvin, reformer of the church in Geneva, and of Huldreich Zwingli, reformer of the church in Zurich. Calvinism took root in Scotland, and its influence also grew in England where it inspired the Puritan movement.

These divisions in the Christian church marked a turning point in European history and culture, ending forever the coherent world-view of medieval Christendom. The Reformation split the peoples of Europe into two broad political, intellectual, and spiritual camps: Protestant and Catholic. With the moral, political, and ideological power of the church significantly diminished, post-Reformation society was open to increasing secularization on all fronts. The stage was set for a new age in the development of Western civilization.

I ▾ Late Medieval Attempts to Reform the Church

One of the most powerful forces for spiritual reform was the so-called New Devotion *(devotio moderna),* which had its roots in the preaching of Dutch priest Gerard Groote (1340–1384). Groote's disciples founded several reformed religious orders and inspired lay people to adopt his spiritual teaching in their daily lives. These followers were especially active in creating schools; children were taught religion from the Bible itself, often in translations from the Latin into vernacular languages. Groote's ideal of all Christians living in perfect imitation of Christ as depicted in the New Testament became the heart of the New Devotion, which spread throughout the Netherlands, Germany, and Spain in the fifteenth century. Desiderius Erasmus, Martin Luther, and Saint Ignatius Loyola (see pages 320, 323, and 339) were among the many religious reformers of the sixteenth century whose piety was shaped by this orthodox spiritual reform movement.

Thomas à Kempis
≪ *THE IMITATION OF CHRIST* ≫

The character of the New Devotion is best revealed in the following passages from *The Imitation of Christ* by Thomas à Kempis (1380–1471). An Augustinian priest, he was educated by the disciples of Gerard Groote. This work has never gone out of print and is considered one of the great works of practical Christian spirituality.

BOOK 1, CHAPTER 1
On the Imitation of Christ

"He who follows Me shall not walk in darkness," says Our Lord.*

In these words Christ counsels us to follow His life and way if we desire true enlightenment and freedom from all blindness of heart. Let the life of Jesus Christ, then, be our first consideration.

The teaching of Jesus far transcends all the teachings of the Saints, and whosoever has His spirit will discover concealed in it heavenly manna.[1] But many people, although they often hear the Gospel, feel little desire to follow it, because they lack the spirit of Christ. Whoever desires to understand and take delight in the words of Christ must strive to conform his whole life to Him.

Of what use is it to discourse learnedly on the Trinity [God the Father, Son, and Holy Spirit] if you lack humility and therefore displease the Trinity? Lofty words do not make a man just or holy; but a good life makes him dear to God. I would far rather feel contrition [remorse for one's sins] than be able to define it. If you knew the whole Bible by heart, and all the teachings of the philosophers, how would this help you without the grace and love of God?† "Vanity of vanities, and all is vanity," except to love God and serve Him alone. And this is supreme wisdom — to despise the world, and draw daily nearer the kingdom of heaven.

It is vanity to solicit honours, or to raise oneself to high station. It is vanity to be a salve to bodily desires and to crave for things which bring certain retribution. It is vanity to wish for long life, if you care little for a good life. It is vanity to give thought only to this present life, and to care nothing for the life to come. It is vanity to love things that so swiftly pass away, and not to hasten onwards to that place where everlasting joy abides.

Keep constantly in mind the saying, "The eye is not satisfied with seeing, nor the ear filled with hearing."‡ Strive to withdraw your heart from the love of visible things, and direct your affections to things invisible. For those who follow only their natural inclinations defile their conscience, and lose the grace of God.

BOOK 1, CHAPTER 11
On Peace and Spiritual Progress

If only we were completely dead to self, and free from inner conflict, we could savour spiritual things, and win experience of heavenly contemplation. But the greatest, and indeed the whole obstacle to our advance is that we are not free from passions and lusts, nor do we strive to follow the perfect way of the Saints. But when we encounter even a little trouble, we are quickly discouraged, and turn to human comfort.

If we strove to stand firm in the struggle like

---

*John 8:12.

[1]Manna was the food provided by God for the Hebrews during their wanderings in the Sinai Desert.

†Eccles. 1:2.

‡Eccles. 1:8.

men of valour, we should not fail to experience the help of our Lord from heaven. For He is ever ready to help all who fight, trusting in His grace; He also affords us occasions to fight that we may conquer. If we rely only on the outward observances of religion, our devotion will rapidly wane. But let us lay the axe to the root — that, being cleansed from our passions, we may possess our souls in peace.

If each year we would root out one fault, we should soon become perfect. . . .

BOOK 1, CHAPTER 23

A Meditation on Death

Each morning remember that you may not live until evening; and in the evening, do not presume to promise yourself another day. Be ready at all times, and so live that death may never find you unprepared. Many die suddenly and unexpectedly; for at an hour that we do not know the Son of Man [Jesus Christ] will come. When your last hour strikes, you will begin to think very differently of your past life, and grieve deeply that you have been so careless and remiss.

Happy and wise is he who endeavours to be during his life as he wishes to be found at his death. For these things will afford us sure hope of a happy death; perfect contempt of the world; fervent desire to grow in holiness; love of discipline; the practice of penance; ready obedience; self-denial; the bearing of every trial for the love of Christ. While you enjoy health, you can do much good; but when sickness comes, little can be done. Few are made better by sickness, and those who make frequent pilgrimages seldom acquire holiness by so doing. . . .

BOOK 4, CHAPTER 18

How We Should Approach Christ's Sacrament Humbly, Submitting Reason to Holy Faith

. . . Beware of curious and unprofitable inquiry into the Mysteries of this most holy Sacrament [the Eucharist], if you would avoid being plunged into the depths of doubt; for those who attempt to search into the majesty of God will be overwhelmed with its glory. God can do more than man is able to comprehend; yet we may humbly and reverently search for truth, so long as the seeker is always willing to be taught, and to follow the sound teachings of the Fathers.

Blessed is that simplicity which rejects obscure inquiry and advances along the sure and open road of God's Commandments. Many have lost their devotion by attempting to pry into matters too high for them. It is faith and a holy life that are required of you, not a lofty intellect or knowledge of the profound mysteries of God. For if you cannot understand or grasp things that are beneath you, how will you comprehend those that are above you? Therefore submit yourself to God, and humble your reason to faith, and the light of knowledge shall be granted you in so far as it be profitable and necessary. . . .

Go forward, then, with simple, undoubting faith, and come to this Sacrament with humble reverence, confidently committing to almighty God whatever you are not able to understand. God never deceives; but man is deceived whenever he puts too much trust in himself. God walks with the simple, reveals Himself to the humble, gives understanding to little ones, discloses His secrets to pure minds and conceals His grace from the curious and conceited. . . .

REVIEW QUESTIONS

1. According to Thomas à Kempis, where did a person find the true model for living a Christian life?
2. In Thomas à Kempis's view, what was the relationship between piety, learning, and intellectual curiosity?

3. What did Thomas à Kempis believe was a key obstacle to spiritual progress?
4. What attitudes did Thomas à Kempis urge his readers to cultivate?
5. Why did Thomas à Kempis advise his readers to meditate on death daily?
6. Why was Thomas à Kempis concerned about rationalistic inquiry into religious beliefs?

---

2 ▾ A Catholic Critic of the Church

The greatest scholar and most popular humanist author of the early sixteenth century was the Dutch priest Desiderius Erasmus (1466–1536). Educated under the influence of the New Devotion and well trained in the new humanistic studies, Erasmus dedicated his life to purifying the Latin and Greek texts of the Bible and those of the early fathers of the church. He used his wit and humanistic learning in his preaching to advocate a simpler yet more intense Christian life modeled on Christ. Erasmus castigated those who pandered to the superstitions of people by encouraging magical beliefs about relics, the cults of the saints, indulgences (see the next selection) and other abuses of pious practices. He also was hostile to the excessive influence of scholastic philosophers on the church's theology, believing that in their quibbling over obscure philosophical-theological issues, they mocked the Christian faith as revealed in the New Testament. An Augustinian monk who preferred to live outside his own monastery, Erasmus severely criticized the lax practices of monks and clergy. He argued, too, that salvation was not based on ascetic and ceremonial acts, but on deeds of love.

Although Erasmus at first welcomed Martin Luther's call for reform, he quickly discerned that Luther was going far beyond what he, Erasmus, felt was wise or necessary. He urged, instead, reform within the church's framework. Although scandalized by a pope leading armies and engaging in international war against other Christians, Erasmus clung loyally to the hierarchical church. He urged peace and civility on all parties, condemned extremist positions, and tried to work for peaceful reconciliation and reform. In 1524, Erasmus wrote a reasoned defense of the role of free will in the process of salvation, taking a Catholic position on this difficult theological problem. Luther was furious with Erasmus for not supporting him, and Erasmus found himself abused by zealots from both camps. To the end, he remained a devout, loyal, but critical Catholic reformer. His preaching, piety, and literary scholarship exemplified the ideals of Christian humanism.

Desiderius Erasmus
≪ IN PRAISE OF FOLLY ≫

Erasmus's most famous work was ***In Praise of Folly,*** written in 1509, before Luther's first challenge to the church. Speaking through the voice of Folly, in the following passages, Erasmus castigates monks, theologians, and other Chris-

tians for failing to discern the true purpose of the Christian life: the imitation of Christ. It was said of Erasmus that he laid the egg Luther hatched — a judgment Erasmus did not acknowledge.

As for the theologians, perhaps it would be better to pass them over in silence, *"not stirring up the hornets' nest"* and "not laying a finger on the stinkweed," since this race of men is incredibly arrogant and touchy. For they might rise up en masse and march in ranks against me with six hundred conclusions and force me to recant. And if I should refuse, they would immediately shout "heretic." For this is the thunderbolt they always keep ready at a moment's notice to terrify anyone to whom they are not very favorably inclined. . . .

. . . They are so blessed by their Selflove as to be fully persuaded that they themselves dwell in the third heaven, looking down from high above on all other mortals as if they were earth-creeping vermin almost worthy of their pity. They are so closely hedged in by rows of magistral definitions, conclusions, corollaries, explicit and implicit propositions, they have so many *"holes they can run to,"* that Vulcan [Roman god of fire] himself couldn't net them tightly enough to keep them from escaping by means of distinctions, with which they cut all knots as cleanly as the fine-honed edge of "the headsman's axe" — so many new terms have they thought up and such monstrous jargon have they coined. . . .

In all of these there is so much erudition, so much difficulty, that I think the apostles themselves would need to be inspired by a different spirit if they were forced to match wits on such points with this new breed of theologians. Paul could provide a living example of faith, but when he said "Faith is the substance of things to be hoped for and the evidence of things not seen," his definition was not sufficiently magisterial. So too, he lived a life of perfect charity, but he neither distinguished it nor defined it with sufficient dialectical precision in the first epistle to the Corinthians, chapter 13. . . .

. . . But Christ, interrupting their boasts (which would otherwise never come to an end), will say, "Where did this new race of Jews [quibbling theologians] come from? The only law I recognize as truly mine is the only one I hear nothing about. Long ago, not speaking obliquely in parables but quite openly, I promised my Father's inheritance not to hoods [worn by monks], or trifling prayers, or fasts, but rather deeds of faith and charity. Nor do I acknowledge those who too readily acknowledge their own deeds: those who want to appear even holier than I am can go dwell in the heavens of the Abraxasians[1] if they like, or they can order that a new heaven be built for them by the men whose petty traditions they have placed before my precepts." When they hear this and see sailors and teamsters chosen in preference to them, how do you suppose their faces will look as they stare at each other? . . .

Almost as happy as the theologians are those men who are commonly called "religious" and "monks" — though both names are quite incorrect, since a good part of them are very far removed from religion and no one is encountered more frequently everywhere you go. I cannot imagine how anything could be more wretched than these men. . . . For even though everyone despises this breed of men so thoroughly that even a chance meeting with one of them is considered unlucky, still they maintain a splendid opinion of themselves. First of all, they consider it the very height of piety to have so little to do with literature as not even to be able to read. Moreover, when they roar out their psalms in church like braying asses (counting their prayers indeed, but understanding them not at all), then (of all things!) they imagine that the listening saints are soothed and caressed with manifold delight. Among them are some who make a great thing out of their squalor and beggary, who stand at the door bawling out their demands for bread — (indeed there is

[1]A heretical sect that believed there were 365 "heavens."

no inn or coach or ship where they do not make a disturbance,) depriving other beggars of no small share of their income. And in this manner these most agreeable fellows, with their filth, ignorance, coarseness, impudence, recreate for us, as they say, an image of the apostles. . . .

Closely related to such men are those who have adopted the very foolish (but nevertheless quite agreeable) belief that if they look at a painting or statue of that huge . . . Christopher, they will not die on that day; or, if they address a statue of Barbara with the prescribed words, they will return from battle unharmed, or, if they accost Erasmus on certain days, with certain wax tapers, and in certain little formulas of prayer, they will soon become rich.[2] Moreover, in George they have discovered a new Hercules. . . .[3] They all but worship George's horse, most religiously decked out in breastplates and bosses [ornaments], and from time to time oblige him with some little gift. To swear by his bronze helmet is thought to be an oath fit for a king.

Now what shall I [Folly] say about those who find great comfort in soothing self-delusions about fictitious pardons for their sins, measuring out the times in purgatory down to the droplets of a waterclock, parceling out centuries, years, months, days, hours, as if they were using mathematical tables. Or what about those who rely on certain little magical tokens and prayers thought up by some pious impostor for his own amusement or profit? They promise themselves anything and everything: wealth, honor, pleasure, an abundance of everything, perpetual health, a long life, flourishing old age, and finally a seat next to Christ among the saints, though this last they don't want for quite a while yet — that is, when the pleasures of this life, to which they cling with all their might, have finally slipped through their fingers, then it will be soon enough to enter into the joys of the saints. Imagine here, if you please, some businessman or soldier or judge who thinks that if he throws into the collection basket one coin from all his plunder, the whole cesspool of his sinful life will be immediately wiped out. He thinks all his acts of perjury, lust, drunkenness, quarreling, murder, deception, dishonesty, betrayal are paid off like a mortgage, and paid off in such a way that he can start off once more on a whole new round of sinful pleasures.

Now who could be more foolish — rather, who could be happier — than those who assure themselves they will have the very ultimate felicity because they have recited daily those seven little verses from the holy psalms? A certain devil — certainly a merry one, but too loose-lipped to be very clever — is believed to have mentioned them to St. Bernard,[4] but the poor devil was cheated by a clever trick. Such absurdities are so foolish that even I am almost ashamed of them, but still they are approved not only by the common people but even by learned teachers of religion. . . .

But why have I embarked on this vast sea of superstitions?

Not if I had a hundred tongues, a
  hundred mouths,
A voice of iron, could I survey all kinds
Of fools, or run through all the forms of
  folly.[5]

So rife, so teeming with such delusions is the entire life of all Christians everywhere. And yet priests are not unwilling to allow and even foster such delusions because they are not unaware of how many emoluments accumulate from this

[2]Christopher refers to Saint Christopher, a popular legendary giant and the patron saint of travelers. Barbara was a widely venerated but legendary early Christian martyr and saint. Erasmus, an Italian bishop and also a saint, was martyred in about A.D. 303.

[3]George, the patron saint of England and of the Crusaders, was believed to have been martyred in about A.D. 300. Saint George's battle with a dragon was a popular legend. Hercules, a Greek hero, performed twelve difficult tasks that won him immortality as a gift of the gods. He was himself worshiped as a god by later Greeks and Romans.

[4]Saint Bernard (1091–1153) was a leading theologian, Cistercian monk, and preacher.

[5]Virgil's *Aeneid* 6.625–627.

source. In the midst of all this, if some odious wiseman should stand up and sing out the true state of affairs: "You will not die badly if you live well. You redeem your sins if to the coin you add a hatred of evil deeds, then tears, vigils, prayers, fasts, and if you change your whole way of life. This saint will help you if you imitate his life" — if that wiseman were to growl out such assertions and more like them, look how much happiness he would immediately take away from the minds of mortals, look at the confusion he would throw them into!

REVIEW QUESTIONS

1. What superstitious practices of some Christians did Erasmus mock?
2. Why were such abuses allowed to continue?
3. What charges did Erasmus make against the scholastic theologians?
4. What charges did Erasmus make against the monks and the "religious"?
5. What did Erasmus see as the essential principle of a Christian life?

---

3 ▾ The Lutheran Reformation

The reformation of the Western Christian church in the sixteenth century was precipitated by Martin Luther (1483–1546). A pious German Augustinian monk and theologian, Luther had no intention of founding a new church or overthrowing the political and ecclesiastical order of late medieval Europe. He was educated in the tradition of the New Devotion, and as a theology professor at the university in Wittenberg, Germany, he opposed rationalistic, scholastic theology. Sympathetic at first to the ideas of Christian humanists like Erasmus, Luther too sought a reform of morals and an end to abusive practices within the church. But a visit to the papal court in Rome in 1510 left him profoundly shocked at its worldliness and disillusioned with the papacy's role in the church's governance.

Martin Luther
ON PAPAL POWER, JUSTIFICATION BY FAITH, AND THE INTERPRETATION OF THE BIBLE

To finance the rebuilding of the church of St. Peter in Rome, the papacy in 1515 offered indulgences to those who gave alms for this pious work. An indulgence was a mitigation or remission of the austere penance imposed by a priest in absolving a penitent who confessed a sin and indicated remorse. Indulgences were granted by papal decrees for those who agreed to perform some act of charity, alms-giving, prayer, pilgrimage, or other pious work. Some preachers of this particular papal indulgence deceived people into believing that a "purchase" of this indulgence would win them, or even the dead, a secure place in heaven.

In 1517, Luther denounced the abuses connected with the preaching of papal

indulgences. The quarrel led quickly to other and more profound theological issues. His opponents defended the use of indulgences on the basis of papal authority, shifting the debate to questions about the nature of papal power within the church. Luther responded with a vigorous attack on the whole system of papal governance. The principal points of his criticism were set out in his *Address to the Christian Nobility of the German Nation Concerning the Reform of the Christian Estate,* published in August 1520. In the first excerpt that follows, Luther argued that the papacy was blocking any reform of the church and appealed to the nobility of Germany to intervene by summoning a "free council" to reform the church.

A central point of contention between Luther and Catholic critics was his theological teaching on justification (salvation) by faith and on the role of good works in the scheme of salvation. Luther had suffered anguish about his unworthiness before God. Then, during a mystical experience, Luther suddenly perceived that his salvation came not because of his good works but as a free gift from God due to Luther's faith in Jesus Christ.

Thus, while never denying that a Christian was obliged to perform good works, Luther argued that such pious acts were not helpful in achieving salvation. His claim that salvation or justification was attained through faith in Jesus Christ as Lord and Savior, and through that act of faith alone, became the rallying point of the Protestant reformers.

The Catholic position, not authoritatively clarified until the Council of Trent (1545–1563), argued that justification came not only through faith, but through hope and love as well, obeying God's commandments and doing good works. In *The Freedom of a Christian,* published in 1520, Luther outlined his teaching on justification by faith and on the inefficacy of good works; the second excerpt is from this work.

Another dispute between Luther and papal theologians was the question of interpretation of the Bible. In the medieval church, the final authority in any dispute over the meaning of Scriptural texts or church doctrine was ordinarily the pope alone, speaking as supreme head of the church or in concert with the bishops in an ecumenical council. The doctrine of papal infallibility (that the pope could not err in teaching matters of faith and morals) was already well known, but belief in this doctrine had not been formally required. Luther argued that the literal text of Scripture was alone the foundation of Christian truth, not the teaching of popes or councils. Moreover, Luther denied any special ordination of the clergy to power or authority in the church. He said that all believers were priests, and the clergy did not hold any power beyond that of the laity; therefore the special privileges of the clergy were unjustified. The third excerpt contains Luther's views on the interpretation of Scripture and the nature of priestly offices.

[ON PAPAL POWER]

The Romanists [traditional Catholics loyal to the papacy] have very cleverly built three walls around themselves. Hitherto they have protected themselves by these walls in such a way that no one has been able to reform them. As a result, the whole of Christendom has fallen abominably.

In the first place, when pressed by the temporal power they have made decrees and declared that the temporal power had no jurisdiction over them, but that, on the contrary, the spiritual power is above the temporal. In the second place, when the attempt is made to reprove them with the Scriptures, they raise the objection that only the pope may interpret the Scriptures. In the third place, if threatened with a council, their story is that no one may summon a council but the pope.

In this way they have cunningly stolen our three rods from us, that they may go unpunished. They have [settled] themselves within the safe stronghold of these three walls so that they can practice all the knavery and wickedness which we see today. Even when they have been compelled to hold a council they have weakened its power in advance by putting the princes under oath to let them remain as they were. In addition, they have given the pope full authority over all decisions of a council, so that it is all the same whether there are many councils or no councils. They only deceive us with puppet shows and sham fights. They fear terribly for their skin in a really free council! They have so intimidated kings and princes with this technique that they believe it would be an offense against God not to be obedient to the Romanists in all their knavish and ghoulish deceits. . . .

The Romanists have no basis in Scripture for their claim that the pope alone has the right to call or confirm a council. This is just their own ruling, and it is only valid as long as it is not harmful to Christendom or contrary to the laws of God. Now when the pope deserves punishment, this ruling no longer obtains, for not to punish him by authority of a council is harmful to Christendom. . . .

Therefore, when necessity demands it, and the pope is an offense to Christendom, the first man who is able should, as a true member of the whole body, do what he can to bring about a truly free council. No one can do this so well as the temporal authorities, especially since they are also fellow-Christians, fellow-priests, fellow-members of the spiritual estate, fellow-lords over all things. Whenever it is necessary or profitable they ought to exercise the office and work which they have received from God over everyone.

[JUSTIFICATION BY FAITH]

You may ask, "What then is the Word of God, and how shall it be used, since there are so many words of God?" I answer: The Apostle explains this in Romans 1. The Word is the gospel of God concerning his Son, who was made flesh, suffered, rose from the dead, and was glorified through the Spirit who sanctifies. To preach Christ means to feed the soul, make it righteous, set it free, and save it, provided it believes the preaching. Faith alone is the saving and efficacious use of the Word of God, according to Rom. 10(:9): "If you confess with your lips that Jesus is Lord and believe in your heart that God raised him from the dead, you will be saved." Furthermore, "Christ is the end of the law, that every one who has faith may be justified" (Rom. 10:4). Again, in Rom. 1 (:17), "He who through faith is righteous shall live." The Word of God cannot be received and cherished by any works whatever but only by faith. Therefore it is clear that, as the soul needs only the Word of God for its life and righteousness, so it is justified by faith alone and not any works; for if it could be justified by anything else, it would not need the Word, and consequently it would not need faith.

This faith cannot exist in connection with works — that is to say, if you at the same time claim to be justified by works, whatever their character —for that would be the same as "limping with two different opinions" (I Kings 18:21), as worshiping Baal and kissing one's own hand (Job 31:27–28), which, as Job says, is a very great iniquity. Therefore the moment you begin to have faith you learn that all things in you are altogether blameworthy, sinful, and damnable, as the Apostle says in Rom. 3(:23), "Since all have sinned and fall short of the glory of God," and, "None is righteous, no, not one:

. . . all have turned aside, together they have gone wrong" (Rom.3:10–12). When you have learned this you will know that you need Christ, who suffered and rose again for you so that, if you believe in him, you may through this faith become a new man in so far as your sins are forgiven and you are justified by the merits of another, namely, of Christ alone.

Since, therefore, this faith can rule only in the inner man, as Rom. 10(:10) says, "For man believes with his heart and so is justified," and since faith alone justifies, it is clear that the inner man cannot be justified, freed, or saved by any outer work or action at all, and that these works, whatever their character, have nothing to do with this inner man. On the other hand, only ungodliness and unbelief of heart, and no outer work, make him guilty and a damnable servant of sin. Wherefore it ought to be the first concern of every Christian to lay aside all confidence in works and increasingly to strengthen faith alone and through faith to grow in the knowledge, not of works, but of Christ Jesus, who suffered and rose for him, as Peter teaches in the last chapter of his first Epistle (1 Pet. 5:10). No other work makes a Christian. . . .

Our faith in Christ does not free us from works but from false opinions concerning works, that is, from the foolish presumption that justification is acquired by works. Faith redeems, corrects, and preserves our consciences so that we know that righteousness does not consist in works, although works neither can nor ought to be wanting; just as we cannot be without food and drink and all the works of this mortal body, yet our righteousness is not in them, but in faith; and yet those works of the body are not to be despised or neglected on that account. In this world we are bound by the needs of our bodily life, but we are not righteous because of them. "My kingship is not of this world" (John 18:36), says Christ. He does not, however, say, "My kingship is not here, that is, in this world." And Paul says, "Though we live in the world we are not carrying on a worldly war" (II Cor. 10:3), and in Gal. 2(:20), "The life I now live in the flesh I live by faith in the Son of God." Thus what we do, live, and are in works and ceremonies, we do because of the necessities of this life and of the effort to rule our body. Nevertheless we are righteous, not in these, but in the faith of the Son of God.

[THE INTERPRETATION OF THE BIBLE AND THE NATURE OF THE PRIESTHOOD]

They (the Roman Catholic Popes) want to be the only masters of Scriptures. . . . They assume sole authority for themselves and would persuade us with insolent juggling of words that the Pope, whether he be bad or good, cannot err in matters of faith. . . .

. . . They cannot produce a letter to prove that the interpretation of Scripture . . . belongs to the Pope alone. They themselves have usurped this power . . . and though they allege that this power was conferred on Peter when the keys were given to him, it is plain enough that the keys were not given to Peter alone but to the entire body of Christians (Matt. 16:19; 18:18). . . .

. . . Every baptized Christian is a priest already, not by appointment or ordination from the Pope or any other man, but because Christ Himself has begotten him as a priest . . . in baptism. . . .

The Pope has usurped the term "priest" for his anointed and tonsured hordes [clergy and monks]. By this means they have separated themselves from the ordinary Christians and have called themselves uniquely the "clergy of God," God's heritage and chosen people who must help other Christians by their sacrifice and worship. . . . Therefore the Pope argues that he alone has the right and power to ordain and do what he will. . . .

[But] the preaching office is no more than a public service which happens to be conferred on someone by the entire congregation all the members of which are priests. . . .

. . . The fact that a pope or bishop anoints,

makes tonsures, ordains, consecrates (makes holy), and prescribes garb different from those of the laity . . . nevermore makes a Christian and a spiritual man. Accordingly, through baptism all of us are consecrated to the priesthood, as St. Peter says . . . (I Peter 2:9).

To make it still clearer, if a small group of pious Christian laymen were taken captive and settled in a wilderness and had among them no priest consecrated by a bishop, if they were to agree to choose one from their midst, married or unmarried, and were to charge him with the office of baptizing, saying Mass, absolving (forgiving of sins), and preaching, such a man would be as truly a priest as he would if all bishops and popes had consecrated him.

REVIEW QUESTIONS

1. Why did Martin Luther believe it unlikely that the papacy would reform the church?
2. How did Luther hope to break papal control over summoning a church council to undertake needed reforms?
3. In what ways did Luther's teachings attack the hierarchical character of the church's government?
4. How was Luther's doctrine of justification by faith alone linked to his rejection of indulgences?
5. What was Luther's teaching on the interpretation of the Holy Scriptures? How did it conflict with the practice of the medieval church?
6. How did Luther's teachings on the common priesthood of all baptized Christians undermine the traditional view of the clerical ministry?

---

4 ▾ The German Peasants' Revolt

After Luther was outlawed as a heretic by the Imperial Diet (parliament) at Worms in 1521, economic and political grievances among the knights, peasants, and lower-class urban workers fostered a series of rebellions. The uprisings were largely local affairs, mostly in southwestern Gemany. When the knights revolted against their lords in 1523, they were quickly crushed. A more widespread peasant revolt followed in 1525, accompanied in some places by sympathetic rebellions among the lower-class artisans and laborers of nearby towns. Driven to a frenzy by their grievances and religious enthusiasm, the German peasants seized lords' estates and pillaged churches and monasteries in a rebellion covering a third of the country. Lacking effective training and leaders, however, they were soon crushed by the lords' vengeful armies.

Although Luther was not primarily responsible for the peasants' revolt, his attacks on the abuses of the ruling nobles and the clergy coincided with the growing anger and resentment among knights, peasants, and lower-class townspeople. The peasants had hoped that Luther, who had denounced the lords' cruelty and oppression, would endorse if not lead their revolt. They were completely mistaken. Luther was preoccupied with the individual's relationship with God and with attaining salvation through faith. He did not intend to initiate social revolution and regarded rebellion against the constituted authority

of the state as contrary to the Gospel's spirit. To Luther, subjects had the duty to obey state authority, since it was ordained by God.

THE TWELVE ARTICLES

A manifesto was drawn up in 1524 by the leaders of the peasants of Swabia, a large duchy in southwestern Germany. The following passages from the Twelve Articles show the intermingling of Lutheran reform ideas with the peasants' demands for relief from their landlords' domination. In a pamphlet published just prior to the peasants' uprising, Martin Luther criticized the Twelve Articles, opposing what he feared was an egalitarian social revolution that threatened the hierarchical order of society and the legitimate property rights of the lords and clergy. He urged peaceful resolution of the crisis, pointing out the just grievances of the peasants.

Peace to the Christian reader and the grace of God through Christ:

There are many evil writings put forth of late which take occasion, on account of the assembling of the peasants, to cast scorn upon the Gospel, saying: "Is this the fruit of the new teaching, that no one should obey but all should everywhere rise in revolt, and rush together to reform, or perhaps destroy entirely, the authorities, both ecclesiastical and lay?" The articles below shall answer these godless and criminal fault-finders, and serve, in the first place, to remove the reproach from the word of God and, in the second place, to give a Christian excuse for the disobedience or even the revolt of the entire Peasantry. . . .

The Second Article According as the just tithe [a tax paid in grain] is established by the Old Testament and fulfilled in the New, we are ready and willing to pay the fair tithe of grain. The word of God plainly provides that in giving . . . to God and distributing to his people the services of a pastor are required. We will that for the future our church provost [manager of a feudal estate], whomsoever the community may appoint, shall gather and receive this tithe. From this he shall give to the pastor, elected by the whole community, a decent and sufficient maintenance for him and his, as shall seem right to the whole community. . . . The small tithes,* whether ecclesiastical or lay, we will not pay at all, for the Lord God created cattle for the free use of man. We will not, therefore, pay farther an unseemly tithe which is of man's invention.

The Third Article It has been the custom hitherto for men to hold us as their own property, which is pitiable enough, considering that Christ has delivered and redeemed us all, without exception, by the shedding of his precious blood, the lowly as well as the great. Accordingly it is consistent with Scripture that we should be free and should wish to be so. Not that we would wish to be absolutely free and under no authority. God does not teach us that we should lead a disorderly life in the lusts of the flesh, but that we should love the Lord our God and our neighbor. We would gladly observe all this as God has commanded us in the celebration of the communion. He has not commanded us not to obey the authorities, but rather that we should be humble, not only towards those in authority, but towards every one. We are thus ready to yield obedience according to God's law to our elected and regular authorities in all proper things becoming to a

*That is, tithes of other products than the staple crops, — for example, tithes of pigs or lambs.

Christian. We therefore take it for granted that you will release us from serfdom as true Christians, unless it should be shown us from the gospel that we are serfs. . . .

The Tenth Article In the tenth place, we are aggrieved by the appropriation by individuals of meadows and fields which at one time belonged to a community. These we will take again into our own hands. It may, however, happen that the land was rightfully purchased, but when the land has unfortunately been purchased in this way, some brotherly arrangement should be made according to circumstances.

The Eleventh Article In the eleventh place, we will entirely abolish the due called [heriot, a death tax], and will no longer endure it, nor allow widows and orphans to be thus shamefully robbed against God's will. . . .

Martin Luther
AGAINST THE PEASANTS

When in the spring of 1525 the peasants finally took up arms against their manorial lords, they were joined by the lower-class artisans and workers in many towns. In a pamphlet entitled *Against the Thievish, Murderous Hordes of Peasants,* Luther reacted sternly, urging the princes to repress the rebels with every power at their command.

. . . They are starting a rebellion, and are violently robbing and plundering monasteries and castles which are not theirs; by this they have doubly deserved death in body and soul as highwaymen and murderers. Furthermore, anyone who can be proved to be a seditious person is an outlaw before God and the emperor; and whoever is the first to put him to death does right and well. For if a man is in open rebellion, everyone is both his judge and his executioner; just as when a fire starts, the first man who can put it out is the best man to do the job. For rebellion is not just simple murder; it is like a great fire, which attacks and devastates a whole land. Thus rebellion brings with it a land filled with murder and bloodshed; it makes widows and orphans, and turns everything upside down, like the worst disaster. Therefore let everyone who can, smite, slay, and stab, secretly or openly, remembering that nothing can be more poisonous, hurtful, or devilish than a rebel. It is just as when one must kill a mad dog; if you do not strike him, he will strike you, and a whole land with you.

It does not help the peasants when they pretend that according to Genesis 1 and 2 all things were created free and common, and that all of us alike have been baptized. For under the New Testament, Moses does not count; for there stands our Master, Christ, and subjects us, along with our bodies and our property, to the emperor and the law of this world, when he says, "Render to Caesar the things that are Caesar's" (Luke 20:25). Paul, too, speaking in Romans 12 (13:1) to all baptized Christians, says, "Let every person be subject to the governing authorities." And Peter says, "Be subject to every ordinance of man" (I Pet. 2:13). We are bound to live according to this teaching of Christ, as the Father commands from heaven, saying, "This is my beloved Son, listen to him" (Matt. 17:5).

For baptism does not make men free in body and property, but in soul; and the gospel does not make goods common, except in the case of those who, of their own free will, do what the apostles and disciples did in Acts 4 (:32–37). They did not demand, as do our insane peasants in their raging, that the goods of others — of Pilate and Herod — should be common, but only their own goods. Our peasants, however, want to make the goods of other men common, and keep their own for themselves. Fine Christians they are! I think there is not a devil left in hell; they have all gone into the peasants. Their raving has gone beyond all measure. . . .

. . . I will not oppose a ruler who, even though he does not tolerate the gospel, will smite and punish these peasants without first offering to submit the case to judgment. He is within his rights, since the peasants are not contending any longer for the gospel, but have become faithless, perjured, disobedient, rebellious murderers, robbers, and blasphemers, whom even a heathen ruler has the right and authority to punish. Indeed, it is his duty to punish such scoundrels, for this is why he bears the sword and is "the servant of God to execute his wrath on the wrongdoer," Romans 13 (:4).

REVIEW QUESTIONS

1. Why did the leaders of the peasants of Swabia believe it necessary to publish their grievances in the Twelve Articles?
2. On what basis did the peasants agree to pay a tithe on grain, but not on cattle, pigs, or lambs?
3. On what basis did the peasants claim to be free men?
4. What principles seemed to guide Luther in his response to the peasants' demands?
5. What was Luther's view on the proper relationship between rulers and their subjects?

---

5 ▾ Luther and the Jews

Initially, Luther hoped to attract Jews to his vision of reformed Christianity. In *That Jesus Was Born a Jew* (1523), the young Luther expressed sympathy for Jewish sufferings and denounced persecution as a barrier to conversion. He declared, "I hope that if one deals in a kindly way with the Jews and instructs them carefully from the Holy Scripture, many of them will become genuine Christians . . . We {Christians} are aliens and in-laws; they are blood relatives, cousins, and brothers of our Lord." When the Jews did not abandon their faith, however, Luther launched a diatribe against them.

Martin Luther
≪ ON THE JEWS AND THEIR LIES ≫

In *On the Jews and Their Lies* (1543), Martin Luther accepted at face value medieval prejudices against the Jews: that they engaged in sorcery and magic, poisoned the wells of Christians, desecrated the Eucharistic host, and ritually murdered Christian children. In the concluding section, excerpted here, Luther advises civil and clerical authorities to treat the Jews harshly. The authorities did not heed Luther's proposals to raze synagogues and homes, but some anti-Jewish measures were introduced, and Luther's anti-Jewish outbursts influenced German anti-Semitic prejudices in more modern times.

First, to set fire to their synagogues or schools and to bury and cover with dirt whatever will not burn, so that no man will ever again see a stone or cinder of them. This is to be done in honor of our Lord and of Christendom, so that God might see that we are Christians, and do not condone or knowingly tolerate such public lying, cursing, and blaspheming of his Son and his Christians. . . .

Second, I advise that their houses also be razed and destroyed. For they pursue in them the same aims as in their synagogues. Instead they might be lodged under a roof or in a barn, like the gypsies. This will bring home to them the fact that they are not masters in our country, as they boast, but that they are living in exile and in captivity, as they incessantly wail and lament about us before God.

Third, I advise that all their prayer books and Talmudic writings, in which such idolatry, lies, cursing, and blasphemy are taught, be taken from them.

Fourth, I advise that their rabbis be forbidden to teach henceforth on pain of loss of life and limb. . . .

Sixth, I advise that usury be prohibited to them, and that all cash and treasure of silver and gold be taken from them and put aside for safekeeping. The reason for such a measure is that, as said above, they have no other means of earning a livelihood than usury, and by it they have stolen and robbed from us all they possess. . . .

Seventh, I recommend putting a flail, an ax, a hoe, a spade, a distaff, or a spindle into the hands of young, strong Jews and Jewesses and letting them earn their bread in the sweat of their brow, as was imposed on the children of Adam (Gen. 3 [:19]). For it is not fitting that they should let us accursed Goyim [non-Jews] toil in the sweat of our faces while they, the holy people, idle away their time behind the stove, feasting and farting, and on top of all, boasting blasphemously of their lordship over the Christians by means of our sweat. No, one should toss out these lazy rogues by the seat of their pants.

REVIEW QUESTIONS

1. What factors seemed to motivate Luther's attack against the Jews?
2. What steps did Luther advocate to reduce the role of the Jews in German society?

---

6 ▾ The Anabaptists and the Case for Religious Liberty

The break with the Roman church and the rapid growth of a reformed church party in Germany under Luther's leadership was soon complicated by the appearance of other anti-Roman Protestants who differed with both the papacy and Luther on questions of theology and church discipline. In the Swiss city of Zurich, enthusiastic reformers like Ulrich Zwingli (1484–1531) and Conrad Grebel (c. 1500–1526) overthrew the local Catholic authorities but failed to agree fully with Luther or with each other on several theological matters. Grebel and his supporters, called Anabaptists, held that admission to membership in the church must be a voluntary act by adults, and condemned the practice of baptizing infants. When Zwingli insisted that no reforms in ecclesiastical practices

should be undertaken without permission of the public authorities, the Zurich Anabaptists refused to comply, declaring the complete freedom of the church from state control. Condemned by Zwingli and forced into exile, the Zurich Anabaptists soon spread their ideas throughout the German-speaking lands.

Although the majority of Anabaptists renounced the use of force to impose any religious practice, the Anabaptist reformers in Münster, a city in northwestern Germany, did not. After winning control of the city council, they expelled all citizens who refused to become Anabaptists. Under the influence of "prophets," some Münster Anabaptists adopted practicing polygamy, communal ownership of property, and violence in anticipation of the imminent end of the world. In 1535, the forces of neighboring German princes captured Münster, slaughtering the Anabaptists.

The excesses of the Münster sect caused both Protestant and Catholic authorities to persecute more peaceful and orthodox Anabaptists wherever they were discovered. The movement remained small, fervent, but oppressed, and was confined to an underground existence. Modern Christian churches that acknowledge the sixteenth-century Anabaptists as their spiritual forebears are the Mennonites and Amish, the Plymouth Separatists (Pilgrims), and the English and American Baptists.

Menno Simons
A REJECTION OF THE USE OF FORCE

Menno Simons (c. 1496–1561), a Dutch priest who converted to Anabaptism in 1536, is considered the founder of the Mennonite church. In the following passages, Simons offered a biblical justification for the Anabaptist rejection of using force or state power to impose religious beliefs or practices.

Say, my dear people, where do the holy Scriptures teach that in Christ's kingdom and church we shall proceed with the magistrate, with the sword, and with physical force and tyranny over a man's conscience and faith, things subject to the judgment of God alone? Where have Christ and the apostles acted thus, advised thus, commanded thus? Ah, Christ says merely, Beware of false prophets; and Paul ordains that we shall avoid a heretical person after he has been admonished once or twice. John teaches that we shall not greet nor receive into the house the man who goes onward and does not bring the doctrine of Christ. But they do not write, Away with those heretics, Report them to the authorities, Lock them up, Expel them out of the city and the country, Throw them into the fire, the water, as the Catholics have done for many years, and as is still found to a great extent with you — you who make yourselves believe that you teach the Word of God! . . . . . .

Peter was commanded to sheathe his sword. All Christians are commanded to love their enemies; to do good unto those who abuse and persecute them; to give the mantle when the cloak is taken, the other cheek when one is struck. Tell me, how can a Christian defend Scripturally retaliation, rebellion, war, striking, slaying, torturing, stealing, robbing and plundering and burning cities, and conquering countries?

The great Lord who has created you and us, who has placed our hearts within us knows, and He only knows that our hearts and hands are clear of all sedition and murderous mutiny. By His grace we will ever remain clear. For we truly confess that all rebellion is of the flesh and of the devil.

O beloved reader, our weapons are not swords and spears, but patience, silence, and hope, and the Word of God. With these we must maintain our heavy warfare and fight our battle. Paul says, The weapons of our warfare are not carnal; but mighty through God. With these we intend and desire to storm the kingdom of the devil; and not with sword, spears, cannon, and coats of mail. For He esteemeth iron as straw, and brass as rotten wood. Thus may we with our Prince, Teacher, and Example Christ Jesus, raise the father against the son, and the son against the father, and may we cast down imagination and every high thing that exalteth itself against the knowledge of God, and bring into captivity every thought in obedience to Christ.

True Christians do not know vengeance, no matter how they are mistreated. In patience they possess their souls. Luke 21:18. And they do not break their peace, even if they should be tempted by bondage, torture, poverty, and besides, by the sword and fire. They do not cry, Vengeance, vengeance, as does the world; but with Christ they supplicate and pray: Father, forgive them; for they know not what they do. Luke 23:34; Acts 7:60.

According to the declaration of the prophets they have beaten their swords into plowshares and their spears into pruning hooks. They shall sit every man under his vine and under his figtree, Christ; neither shall they learn war any more. Isa[iah] 2:4; Mic[ah] 4:3. . . .

Behold, beloved rulers and judges, if you take to heart these Scriptures and diligently ponder them, then you will observe, first, that your office is not your own but God's, so that you may bend your knees before His majesty; fear His great and adorable name, and rightly and reasonably execute your ordained office. Then you will not so freely with your perishable earthly power invade and transgress against Christ, the Lord of lords in His kingdom, power, and jurisdiction, and with your iron sword adjudicate in that which belongs exclusively to the eternal judgment of the Most High God, such as in faith and matters pertaining to faith. In the same vein Luther and others wrote in the beginning, but after they came to greater and higher estate they forgot it all. . . .

. . . If [anyone] is a preacher called by the Spirit of God, then let him show a single letter in all the New Testament that Christ or the apostles have ever called on the magistrates to defend and protect the true church against the attack of the wicked, as, alas, he calls us. No, no, Christ Jesus and His powerful Word and the Holy Spirit are the protectors and defenders of the church, and not, eternally not, the emperor, king, or any worldly potentate! The kingdom of the Spirit must be protected and defended by the sword of the Spirit, and not by the sword of the world. This, in the light of the doctrine and example of Christ and His apostles, is too plain to be denied.

I would say further, If the magistracy rightly understood Christ and His kingdom, they would in my opinion rather choose death than to meddle with their worldly power and sword in spiritual matters which are reserved not to the judgment of man but to the judgment of the great and Almighty God alone. But they are taught by those who have the care of their souls that they may proscribe, imprison, torture, and slay those who are not obedient to their doctrine, as may, alas, be seen in many different cities and countries.

REVIEW QUESTIONS

1. What were Menno Simons's reasons for rejecting the use of state power to impose religious belief or practices?
2. What did Simons think of Luther's support of state authority in behalf of the Church?

3. Why were Anabaptists like Simons considered dangerous by both Catholic and Protestant authorities?

---

7 ▾ The Calvinist Reformation

In the first decade of the Lutheran movement, Protestant reform had not spread significantly outside Germany due to suppression by the royal governments in France, Spain, and England. But in 1534 a French clergyman, John Calvin (1509–1564), resigned his church offices and fled to Basel, a Swiss city that had accepted Protestant reforms. There he composed a summary of the new Protestant theology, *The Institutes of the Christian Religion,* which was to be revised four times before his death. Written in the elegant Latin style favored by humanists, the work was translated into French and soon became the principal theological text for French, Scottish, Dutch, and English Protestant reformers. Calvin himself settled in Geneva, Switzerland, where his influence dominated the civil and religious life of the townspeople. From Geneva, Calvin carried on an active mission, spreading his reformed faith throughout his native France and elsewhere.

In 1536, the newly Protestant-controlled government of Geneva asked Calvin to draw up a public confession of the reformed faith, a catechism, and rules for liturgical worship. But the Council of Geneva's demand that all citizens be forced to subscribe to the new confession resulted in a change of government at the elections in 1538. Calvin withdrew to Basel. By 1541, the political situation had changed again; Calvin was recalled, and his recommendations for a new government for the church were put into law. He remained the spiritual leader of Geneva and of many reformed Protestants elsewhere until his death. Calvinism was especially influential in England and Scotland, giving rise to the Puritan movement in seventeenth-century England and the Presbyterian churches in Scotland and Ireland. Both of these religious traditions exercised great influence on the settlers of the English colonies in North America.

John Calvin
≪ THE INSTITUTES ≫ ECCLESIASTICAL ORDINANCES, AND THE OBEDIENCE OWED RULERS

One doctrine that assumed greater and greater importance in the four separate revised editions of Calvin's *Institutes* was predestination: the belief that each person's salvation or damnation was already decided before birth. This doctrine raised a question about whether Christ offered salvation for all human beings or only for the elect — a chosen few who were predestined to be saved by God's sovereign will. Some argued that the latter interpretation, one strongly articulated by Saint Augustine, implied that God was a tyrant who created human beings to be damned and that they were not free to acquire salvation by faith. In effect, salvation and damnation were foreordained. To many Christians, this doctrine diminished the justice and mercy of God, made meaningless the idea of freedom of choice in the process of salvation, and stripped good works of any role in gaining salvation. In the first excerpt (from *The Institutes of the Christian Religion*), Calvin offered his definition of predestination and cited Saint Augustine as an authority.

Calvin's ecclesiastical ordinances became a model for Calvinist churches throughout Europe and America. Each local church was governed by four types of officers: ministers, teachers, elders, and deacons. The ministers preached the Word of God and administered the two sacraments: baptism and the Eucharist. The teachers taught children and candidate members. The elders closely supervised the morals of the congregation. The deacons cared for the poor and the sick. An especially important innovation was the consistory, composed of the ministers and elders, who met weekly to hear accusations against and to discipline individuals whose conduct was contrary to the church's moral teachings. Persistent offenders were turned over to the city authorities for punishment.

Like Luther, Calvin had a horror of disobedience of the civil authorities. Although he tended to be skeptical about any good coming from kings, Calvin believed that all authority comes from God and that bad kings or tyrants were to be accepted as an expression of God's wrath and as just punishment for the people's sins.

Yet by 1561 Calvin was forced by circumstance (the severe persecution of his followers in France and elsewhere) to moderate his position. In his *Commentaries on the Book of the Prophet Daniel,* Calvin justified disobeying rulers who deny the rights of God (as understood by the Protestant reformers); an excerpt from this work concludes this selection of Calvin's writings. This teaching would lay the groundwork for Calvinists of France, England, the Netherlands, and Scotland to resist the legitimate kings of those realms to the point of resorting to revolution.

[THE INSTITUTES]
Predestination

Predestination, by which God adopts some to the hope of life, and adjudges others to eternal death, no one, desirous of the credit of piety, dares absolutely to deny. But it is involved in many [disputes], especially by those who make foreknowledge the cause of [predestination]. We maintain, that both belong to God; but it is preposterous to represent one as dependent on the other. When we attribute foreknowledge to God, we mean that all things have ever been, and perpetually remain, before his eyes, so that to his knowledge nothing is future or past, but all things are present; and present in such a manner, that he does not merely conceive of them from ideas formed in his mind, as things remembered by us appear present to our minds, but really beholds and sees them as if actually placed before him. And this foreknowledge extends to the whole world, and to all the creatures. Predestination we call the eternal decree of God, by which he has determined in himself, what he would have to become of every individual of mankind. For they are not all created with a similar destiny; but eternal life is foreordained for some, and eternal damnation for others. Every man, therefore, being created for one or the other of these ends, we say, he is predestinated either to life or to death.[1] This God has not only testified [to this destiny] in particular persons, but has given a specimen of it in the whole posterity of Abraham, which should evidently show the future condition of every nation to depend upon his decision. "When the Most High divided the nations, when he separated the sons of Adam, the Lord's portion was his people; Jacob was the lot of his inheritance" [Deut. 32:8–9]. The separation is before the eyes of all: in the person of Abraham, as in the dry trunk of a tree, one people is peculiarly chosen to the rejection of others: no reason for this appears, except that Moses, to deprive their posterity of all occasion of glorying, teaches them that their exaltation is wholly from God's gratuitous love. . . .

This doctrine [predestination] is maliciously and impudently calumniated by others, as subversive of all exhortations to piety of life. This formerly brought great odium upon Augustine, which he removed by his Treatise on Correction and Grace. . . . A slight acquaintance with [Saint] Paul will enable any one to understand, without tedious arguments, how easily he reconciles things which they pretend to be repugnant to each other. Christ commands men to believe in him. Yet his limitation is neither false nor contrary to his command, when he says, "No man can come unto me, except it were given unto him of my Father" [John 6:65]. Let preaching therefore have its course to bring men to faith, and by a continual progress to promote their perseverance. Nor let the knowledge of predestination be prevented, that the obedient may not be proud as of any thing of their own, but may glory in the Lord. Christ had some particular meaning in saying, "Who hath ears to hear, let him hear" [Matt. 13:9]. . . . "But why (says Augustine) should some have ears, and others not? 'Who hath known the mind of the Lord?' [Rom. 11:34] Must that which is evident be denied, because that which is concealed cannot be comprehended?" These observations I have faithfully borrowed from Augustine; but as his words will perhaps have more authority than mine, I will proceed to an exact quotation of them. "If, on hearing this, some persons become torpid and slothful, and exchanging labour for lawless desire, pursue the various objects of concupiscence [lust], must what is declared concerning the foreknowledge of God be therefore accounted false? If God foreknew that they would be good, will they not be so, in whatever wickedness they now live? and if he foreknew that they would be wicked, will they not be so, in whatever goodness they now appear? Are these, then, sufficient causes why the truths which are declared concerning the foreknowledge of God should be either denied or passed over in silence? especially when the consequence of silence respecting these would be the adoption of other errors. The reason of concealing the truth (he says) is one thing, and the necessity of declaring it is another."

[1]The phrase "predestinated . . . death" means predestined to be saved (life) or to be damned (death).

▷ The Genevan ecclesiastical ordinances illuminate the character of the Calvinist system of public regulation of morals through community pressure and state power.

[ECCLESIASTICAL ORDINANCES]
The Duties of Elders, or Presbyters

The office of the elders is to watch over the conduct of every individual, to admonish lovingly those whom they see doing wrong or leading an irregular life. When there is need, they should lay the matter before the body deputed to inflict paternal discipline (i.e. the consistory), of which they are members. . . .

The Consistory, or Session The elders, who have been described, shall assemble once a week with the ministers, namely Thursday morning, to see if there be any disorders in the Church and discuss together such remedies as shall be necessary. . . . If any one shall in contempt refuse to appear before them, it shall be their duty to inform the [town] council, so that it may supply a remedy. . . .

Extracts from Calvin's Regulations for the Villages About Geneva

The whole household shall attend the sermons on Sunday, except when some one shall be left at home to tend the children or cattle.

If there is preaching on week days, all who can must come, — unless there be some good excuse, — so that at least one from each household shall be present. Those who have men-servants or maid-servants shall bring them when it is possible, so that they shall not live like beasts without instruction. . . . Should any one come after the sermon has begun, let him be warned. If he does not amend, let him pay a fine of three sous [coins]. Let the churches be closed except during service, so that no one may enter them at other hours from superstitious motives. If any one be discovered engaged in some superstition within or near the church, let him be admonished. If he will not give up his superstition, let him be punished.

Persecution of Catholics Those who are found to have rosaries or idols to adore, let them be sent before the consistory, and in addition to the reproof they receive there, let them be sent before the council. Let the same be done with those who go on a pilgrimage. Those who observe feasts or papistical fasts shall only be admonished. Those who go to mass shall, besides being admonished, be sent before the council, and it shall consider the propriety of punishing the offenders by imprisonment or special fines, as it judges best.

He who blasphemes, swearing by the body or blood of our Lord, or in like manner, shall kiss the earth for the first offense, pay five sous for the second and ten for the third. He who contradicts the word of God shall be sent before the consistory for reproof, or before the council for punishment, as the case may require. If any one sings indecent, licentious songs, or dances . . . he shall be kept in prison three days and then sent to the council.*

▷ Commenting on the story of the Hebrew prophet Daniel (who clearly refused to obey the Persian king's order that he not worship the god of Israel) and denying that Daniel had committed any offense against the king, Calvin explains this apparent contradiction. He affirms the traditional Christian view that obedience to divine law takes precedence over obligations to obey the laws of earthly rulers. This view is the Christian basis for civil disobedience and even revolutionary action against a ruler perceived to be an enemy of God. The following passage starts with a biblical quote in which Daniel addresses the Persian king.

[OBEDIENCE TO SECULAR RULERS]

. . . *And even before thee, O king, I have committed nothing wrong.* It is clear that the Prophet had violated the king's edict. Why, then, does he not ingenuously confess this? Nay, why does he contend that he has not transgressed against the king? Because he conducted himself with fidelity in all his duties, he could free himself from every [false charge] by which he knew himself oppressed, as if he had despised the king's sovereignty. But Daniel was not so bound to the king of the Persians when [the king] claimed for himself as a god what ought not to be offered to him. We know how earthly empires are constituted by God, only on the condition that [God] deprives himself of nothing, but shines forth alone, and all magistrates must be set in regular order, and every authority in existence must be subject to his glory. Since, therefore, Daniel could not obey the king's edict without denying God, as we have previously seen, he did not transgress against the king by constantly persevering in that exercise of piety to which he had been accustomed, and by calling

*There are similar provisions for drunkness, gambling, quarreling, taking more than five per cent interest, etc.

on his God three times a-day. To make this the more evident, we must remember that passage of [the Apostle] Peter, "Fear God, honour the king" (1 Pet. 2:17). The two commands are connected together, and cannot be separated from one another. The fear of God ought to precede, that kings may obtain their authority. For if any one begins his reverence of an earthly prince by rejecting that of God, he will act preposterously, since this is a complete perversion of the order of nature. Then let God be feared in the first place, and earthly princes will obtain their authority, if only God shines forth, as I have already said. Daniel, therefore, here defends himself with justice, since *he had not committed any crime against the king;* for he was compelled to obey the command of God, and he neglected what the king had ordered in opposition to it. For earthly princes lay aside all their power when they rise up against God, and are unworthy of being reckoned in the number of mankind. We ought rather utterly to defy than to obey them whenever they are so restive and wish to spoil God of his rights, and, as it were, to seize upon his throne and draw him down from heaven.

REVIEW QUESTIONS

1. Why was the doctrine of predestination so troublesome to many Christian theologians and moralists?
2. What was Saint Augustine's argument against those who feared that the doctrine of predestination endangered good personal morals?
3. How was the Hebrew notion of a "chosen people" interpreted by John Calvin?
4. Compare the views of Menno Simons with those of Calvin on the use of state power to impose religious beliefs or practices.
5. Explain Calvin's views on the proper relationship between Christians and the state.

---

8 ▾ Catholic Spiritual Renewal

Even before the Council of Trent had been called to respond to the challenge of Protestant teachings, the Basque nobleman Saint Ignatius Loyola (1491–1556) founded a new religious order, the Society of Jesus, popularly called the Jesuits. A former soldier, Ignatius underwent a spiritual conversion in 1521–1522 and, after seeking guidance about his vocation, decided to become a priest. Later, while studying at the University of Paris, Ignatius and several companions decided to found their order and received papal recognition in 1540.

The new Jesuit order was characterized by three unusual features. First, the members took a special oath of obedience to the pope, which bound them to support the papacy and its programs with special devotion. Second, they rejected the traditional monastic ideal of a life of contemplation and instead espoused a life of active service in the world. Third, they were especially committed to the Christian education of youth and to missionary work among pagans and heretics.

Saint Ignatius Loyola
≪ THE SPIRITUAL EXERCISES ≫

The Jesuits soon became the vanguard of the Roman Catholic church's effort to resist what it believed to be Protestant errors and to hasten the restoration of Catholicism in those lands where it no longer was the dominant religion. Ignatius himself thought it vital for his followers, and for the Catholic laity as well, to "think with the mind of the Church." To help Catholics achieve a higher spiritual life, Ignatius composed a book during 1521–1535 called *The Spiritual Exercises.* It became a guide for Jesuit confessors or counselors in leading penitents to a greater spiritual maturity. It was a summary of practical ways to order one's life through the imitation of Christ.

In the last section of *The Spiritual Exercises* written during the early 1530s, Ignatius gives final instructions to his followers: a set of rules for "thinking with the Church." These guidelines reflect the response of reformed Catholicism to the great theological issues raised by Luther, Calvin, and other Protestants.

RULES FOR THINKING WITH THE CHURCH

In order to have the proper attitude of mind in the Church Militant [all active, living Christians] we should observe the following rules:

1. Putting aside all private judgment, we should keep our minds prepared and ready to obey promptly and in all things the true spouse of Christ our Lord, our Holy Mother, the hierarchical Church.

2. To praise sacramental confession and the reception of the Most Holy Sacrament [the Eucharist] once a year, and much better once a month, and better still every week, with the requisite and proper dispositions.

3. To praise the frequent hearing of Mass, singing of hymns and psalms, and the recitation of long prayers, both in and out of church; also the hours arranged for fixed times for the whole Divine Office, for prayers of all kinds and for the canonical hours.

4. To praise highly religious life, virginity, and continence; and also matrimony, but not as highly, as any of the foregoing.

5. To praise the vows of religion, obedience, poverty, chastity, and other works of perfection and supererogation.[1] It must be remembered that a vow is made in matters that lead to evangelical perfection. It is therefore improper to make a vow in matters that depart from this perfection; as, for example, to enter business, to get married, and so forth.

6. To praise the relics of the saints by venerating them and by praying to these saints. Also to praise the stations, pilgrimages, indulgences, jubilees,[2] Crusade indulgences, and the lighting of candles in the churches.

7. To praise the precepts concerning fasts and abstinences, such as those of Lent, Ember Days,[3] Vigils, Fridays, and Saturdays; likewise to praise acts of penance, both interior and exterior.

---

[1]The performance of good works beyond what God requires.

[2]*Stations* refers to a set of prayers recited while meditating on certain moments in the passion and death of Christ. Jubilees were certain years set aside by the papacy during which special indulgences were offered to pilgrims attending certain shrines, particularly that of Saint Peter in Rome.

[3]Three Ember Days were set aside by the church each season for special prayers and fasting.

8. To praise the adornments and buildings of churches as well as sacred images, and to venerate them according to what they represent.

9. Finally, to praise all the precepts of the church, holding ourselves ready at all times to find reasons for their defense, and never offending against them.

10. We should be more inclined to approve and praise the directions and recommendations of our superiors as well as their personal behavior. Although sometimes these may not be or may not have been praiseworthy, to speak against them when preaching in public or in conversation with people would give rise to murmuring and scandal rather than to edification. As a result, the people would be angry with their superiors, whether temporal or spiritual. Still, while it does harm to our superiors in their absence to speak ill of them in the presence of the people, it might be useful to speak of their bad conduct to those who can apply a remedy.

11. To praise both positive and scholastic theology, for as it is more characteristic of the [early church] doctors, such as St. Augustine, St. Jerome, St. Gregory, and others, to encourage the affections to greater love and service of God our Lord in all things, so it also is more characteristic of the [medieval] scholastic doctors, such as St. Thomas, St. Bonaventure, and the Master of the Sentences,[4] etc., to define and explain for our times the things necessary for eternal salvation, and to refute and expose all errors and fallacies. Also, the scholastic doctors, being of more recent date, not only have a clearer understanding of the Holy Scripture and of the teachings of the [early church] doctors, but also, being enlightened and inspired by the Divine Power, they are helped by the Councils, Canons, and Constitutions of our Holy Mother Church. . . .

13. If we wish to be sure that we are right in all things, we should always be ready to accept this principle: I will believe that the white that I see is black, if the hierarchical Church so defines it. For, I believe that between the Bridegroom, Christ our Lord, and the Bride, His Church, there is but one spirit, which governs and directs us for the salvation of our souls, for the same Spirit and Lord, who gave us the Ten Commandments, guides and governs our Holy Mother Church.

14. Although it be true that no one can be saved unless it be predestined and unless he have faith and grace, still we must be very careful of our manner of discussing and speaking of these matters. [See Calvin's *Institutes,* page 335.]

15. We should not make predestination an habitual subject of conversation. If it is sometimes mentioned we must speak in such a way that no person will fall into error, as happens on occasion when one will say, "It has already been determined whether I will be saved or lost, and in spite of all the good or evil that I do, this will not be changed." As a result, they become apathetic and neglect the works that are conducive to their salvation and to the spiritual growth of their souls.

16. In like manner, we must be careful lest by speaking too much and with too great emphasis on faith, without any distinction or explanation, we give occasion to the people to become indolent and lazy in the performance of good works, whether it be before or after their faith is founded in charity.

17. Also in our discourse we ought not to emphasize the doctrine that would destroy free will. We may therefore speak of faith and grace to the extent that God enables us to do so, for the greater praise of His Divine Majesty. But, in these dangerous times of ours, it must not be done in such a way that good works or free will suffer any detriment or be considered worthless.

[4]*Master of the Sentences* is a reference to Peter Lombard (c. 1100–c. 1160), an Italian theologian whose book *Sentences* was the most widely used theology textbook in the medieval universities.

REVIEW QUESTIONS

1. How did the "Rules for Thinking with the Church" set forth by Saint Ignatius attempt to respond to Protestant beliefs and attitudes?
2. What medieval Catholic pious devotions did the Jesuits propose to defend?
3. What was the Jesuit attitude toward the hierarchical authority of the pope, bishops, and councils?
4. What were Saint Ignatius Loyola's views on the doctrines of free will and predestination? How did they differ from Calvin's?
5. Why did the Jesuits remain supportive of the scholastic theologians and their contribution to Christian theological doctrine?

---

9 ▾ The Catholic Response to Protestant Reforms

The criticisms of Catholic beliefs and practices by Luther, Calvin, and other Protestant reformers generated a host of theological defenses of traditional Catholicism. However, there was a general admission that grave abuses in Catholic clerical morals and discipline had been allowed to go uncorrected. Almost everyone agreed that a new general council of the church was necessary to clarify and affirm Catholic doctrine and institute reforms in clerical discipline and practices. Despite many promises to summon such a council, the popes delayed. Political conditions never seemed right, and the papacy, remembering the reforms attempted by councils in the fifteenth century, feared that prematurely summoning a council could be a disaster for papal authority.

The council was finally convoked in 1545 at the Alpine city of Trent, on the borders between the German lands and Italy. The papacy was firmly in control and no Protestant theologians participated in the conciliar sessions. The council was suspended several times, the longest hiatus lasting for ten years (1552–1562), and concluded its work in 1563.

The council fathers confessed their responsibility for the evils that had grown up in the church and committed themselves to institutional reforms that would raise the standards of morality and learning among future bishops and clergy. The most significant pastoral reforms included creating an official catechism outlining the orthodox beliefs of the Roman church, establishing seminaries to direct the education of future clergy, and reforming the bishop's office by increasing his responsibilities for the pastoral life of his diocese.

CANONS AND DECREES OF THE COUNCIL OF TRENT

On doctrinal matters, the council gave an authoritative Catholic response to Protestant teachings on a host of issues. In the following excerpt from the

decrees of the Council of Trent (1545–1563), the council condemned the Protestant view that faith alone was necessary for salvation and insisted on the integration of both faith and good works in the process of salvation. This position allowed the council to defend such traditional Catholic practices as monasticism, indulgences, masses for the dead, alms giving, pilgrimages, veneration of saints, and other pious works.

THE NECESSITY OF PREPARATION FOR JUSTIFICATION [SALVATION] IN ADULTS, AND WHENCE IT PROCEEDS

It is furthermore declared that in adults the beginning of that justification must proceed from the predisposing grace of God through Jesus Christ, that is, from His vocation, whereby, without any merits on their part, they are called; that they who by sin had been cut off from God, may be disposed through His quickening and helping grace to convert themselves to their own justification by freely assenting to and cooperating with that grace; so that, while God touches the heart of man through the illumination of the Holy Ghost, man himself neither does absolutely nothing while receiving that inspiration, since he can also reject it, nor yet is he able by his own free will and without the grace of God to move himself to justice in His sight. Hence, when it is said in the sacred writings: *Turn ye to me, and I will turn to you* [Zach. 1:3], we are reminded of our liberty; and when we reply: *Convert us, O Lord, to thee, and we shall be converted* [Lam. 5:21], we confess that we need the grace of God. . . .

HOW THE GRATUITOUS JUSTIFICATION OF THE SINNER BY FAITH IS TO BE UNDERSTOOD

But when the Apostle [Paul] says that man is justified by faith and freely, these words are to be understood in that sense in which the uninterrupted unanimity of the Catholic Church has held and expressed them, namely, that we are therefore said to be justified by faith, because faith is the beginning of human salvation, the foundation and root of all justification, *without which it is impossible to please God* [Heb. 11:6] and to come to the fellowship of His sons; and we are therefore said to be justified gratuitously [unearned, as a freely given gift], because none of those things that precede justification, whether faith or works, merit the grace of justification. For, *if by grace, it is not now by works, otherwise,* as the Apostle says, *grace is no more grace* [Rom. 11:6]. . . .

IN WHAT THE JUSTIFICATION OF THE SINNER CONSISTS, AND WHAT ARE ITS CAUSES

. . . For though no one can be just except he to whom the merits of the passion of our Lord Jesus Christ are communicated, yet this takes place in that justification of the sinner, when by the merit of the most holy passion, *the charity of God is poured forth by the Holy Ghost in the hearts* [Rom. 5:5] of those who are justified and inheres in them; whence man through Jesus Christ, [with] whom he is [now one], receives in that justification, together with the remission of sins, all these infused at the same time, namely, faith, hope and charity. For faith, unless hope and charity be added to it, neither unites man perfectly with Christ nor makes him a living member of His body. For which reason it is most truly said that *faith without works is dead* [James 2:17, 20] and of no profit, and *in Christ Jesus neither circumcision availeth anything nor uncircumcision, but faith that worketh by charity* [Gal. 5:6, 6:15]. This faith, conformably to

Apostolic tradition, catechumens [candidates for baptism] ask of the Church before the sacrament of baptism, when they ask for the faith that gives eternal life, which without hope and charity faith cannot give. Whence also they hear immediately the word of Christ: *If thou wilt enter into life, keep the commandments* [Matt. 19:17]. . . .

▷ The council also condemned individual interpretation of the Bible and set up controls over the publication and sale of unauthorized religious books. It approved the cult of the saints and the use of images, practices condemned by Calvin and the Anabaptists.

Furthermore, to check unbridled spirits, it [the council] decrees that no one relying on his own judgment shall, in matters of faith and morals pertaining to the edification of Christian doctrine, distorting the Holy Scriptures in accordance with his own conceptions, presume to interpret them contrary to that sense which holy mother Church, to whom it belongs to judge of their true sense and interpretation, has held and holds, or even contrary to the unanimous teaching of the [church] Fathers, even though such interpretations should never at any time be published. Those who act contrary to this shall be made known by the ordinaries [bishops] and punished in accordance with the penalities prescribed by the law.

And wishing, as is proper, to impose a restraint in this matter on printers also, who, now without restraint, thinking what pleases them is permitted them, print without the permission of ecclesiastical superiors the books of the Holy Scriptures and the notes and commentaries thereon of all persons indiscriminately, often with the name of the press omitted, often also under a fictitious press-name, and what is worse, without the name of the author, and also indiscreetly have for sale such books printed elsewhere, (this council) decrees and ordains that in the future the Holy Scriptures, especially the old Vulgate [Latin] Edition, be printed in the most correct manner possible, and that it shall not be lawful for anyone to print or to have printed any books whatsoever dealing with sacred doctrinal matters without the name of the author, or in the future to sell them, or even to have them in possession, unless they have first been examined and approved by the ordinary [the local bishop], under penalty of anathema [condemnation and excommunication] and fine. . . .

ON THE INVOCATION, VENERATION, AND RELICS OF SAINTS, AND ON SACRED IMAGES

The holy council commands all bishops and others who hold the office of teaching and have charge of the *cura animarum* [care of souls], that in accordance with the usage of the Catholic and Apostolic Church, received from the primitive times of the Christian religion, and with the unanimous teaching of the holy Fathers and the decrees of sacred councils, they above all instruct the faithful diligently in matters relating to intercession and invocation of the saints, the veneration of relics, and the legitimate use of images, teaching them that the saints who reign together with Christ offer up their prayers to God for men, that it is good and beneficial suppliantly to invoke them and to have recourse to their prayers, assistance and support in order to obtain favors from God through His Son, Jesus Christ our Lord, who alone is our redeemer and savior. . . . Also, that the holy bodies of the holy martyrs and of others living with Christ, which were the living members of Christ and the temple of the Holy Ghost, to be awakened by Him to eternal life and to be glorified, are to be venerated by the faithful, through which many benefits are bestowed by God on men. . . . Moreover, that the images of Christ, of the Virgin Mother of God, and of the other saints are to be placed and retained especially in the churches, and that due honor and veneration is to be given them. . . .

▷ The Council of Trent condemned the Protestant view that clergy were no different than lay people and reaffirmed the Catholic belief that the clergy, for their administration of the church's sacraments, are specially ordained intermediaries between God and human beings. Whereas Luther admitted only three sacraments — baptism, the Eucharist, and penance or confession — and Calvin only two — baptism and the Eucharist — the Council of Trent decreed that there were seven sacraments in the Catholic Church, including ordination of the clergy.

CANONS ON THE SACRAMENTS IN GENERAL

Canon 1. If anyone says that the sacraments of the New Law were not all instituted by our Lord Jesus Christ, or that there are more or less than seven, namely, baptism, confirmation, Eucharist, penance, extreme unction, order and matrimony, or that any one of these seven is not truly and intrinsically a sacrament, let him be anathema [cursed]. . . .

Can. 10. If anyone says that all Christians have the power to administer the word and all the sacraments, let him be anathema. . . .

CANONS ON THE SACRAMENT OF ORDER

Canon 1. If anyone says that there is not in the New Testament a visible and external priesthood, or that there is no power of consecrating and offering the true body and blood of the Lord and of forgiving . . . sins, but only the office and bare ministry of preaching the Gospel; or that those who do not preach are not priests at all, let him be anathema. . . .

Can. 4. If anyone says that by sacred ordination the Holy [Spirit] is not imparted and that therefore the bishops say in vain: *Receive ye the Holy* [*Spirit*], or that by it a character is not imprinted, or that he who has once been a priest can again become a layman, let him be anathema.

Can. 5. If anyone says that the holy unction which the Church uses in ordination is not only not required but is detestable and pernicious, as also are the other ceremonies of order, let him be anathema.

Can. 6. If anyone says that in the Catholic Church there is not instituted a hierarchy by divine ordinance, which consists of bishops, priests and ministers, let him be anathema.

Can. 7. If anyone says that bishops are not superior to priests, or that they have not the power to confirm and ordain, or that the power which they have is common to them and to priests, or that orders conferred by them without the consent or call of the people or of the secular power are invalid, or that those who have been neither rightly ordained nor sent by ecclesiastical and canonical authority, but come from elsewhere, are lawful ministers of the word and of the sacraments, let him be anathema.

REVIEW QUESTIONS

1. How did the Council of Trent interpret the belief that human beings are justified by faith in Christ?
2. How did the council interpret the role of good works in the process of salvation?
3. What was the council's teaching on individual interpretation of the Holy Scriptures?

4. How did the council intend to control unauthorized writings on biblical or other religious subjects?
5. What was the council's teaching on the cult of the saints and the use of images in the churches?
6. How did the council respond to attacks by some Protestants on the hierarchical structure of the clerical ministry in the church?

Early Modern Society and Politics

From the fifteenth through the seventeenth centuries, medieval outlooks and institutions broke down, and distinctly modern economic, political, and cultural forms emerged. The Renaissance produced a more secular attitude and expressed confidence in human capacities. Shortly afterward, the Protestant Reformation ended the religious unity of medieval Latin Christendom and weakened the political power of the church. At the same time the discovery of new trade routes to East Asia and of new lands across the Atlantic widened the imagination and ambitions of Christian Europeans and precipitated a commercial revolution. This great expansion of economic activity produced two developments associated with the modern world: mercantile capitalism and a global economy.

In the late fifteenth century, many Europeans encountered peoples whose cultures markedly differed from their own. The Portuguese, trying to break the Muslim monopoly over trade between Europe and eastern Asia, explored along the Atlantic coast of Africa, establishing their first links with the peoples and kingdoms of the sub-Saharan regions of modern Guinea, Ghana, Dahomey, and the Congo. Setting up fortified trading posts along the way, they eventually sailed around the Cape of Good Hope at the tip of Africa and reached India in 1498. By 1516, Portuguese merchants had reached the port of Canton in southern China. The Portuguese established fortified trading posts in India and Southeast Asia, some of which (Goa, Timor, Macao) they continued to hold into the late twentieth century.

In India, China, and Japan, the Portuguese found highly advanced civilizations that were able to resist European political and cultural domination fairly effectively. In contrast, the Spanish, with the discovery of the Caribbean islands by Christopher Columbus in 1492, encountered a local population living in a Stone Age culture. There were no cities, no state structures, no significant architecture or art; technology was primitive, and contacts with other peoples limited. However, after 1518 when the Spanish landed on the American mainland, they found in Mexico, Yucatán, and Peru advanced civilizations with great cities, well-developed governments, monumental architecture, and extensive

Merchant George Gisze (1532) by Hans Holbein, the Younger. A prominent German trader, Gisze is surrounded by objects, such as a scale and a money box, that clearly identify his occupation and status. (*Staatliche Museen zu Berlin*)

commercial networks. The vast regions and diverse peoples of the Americas were gradually linked to Europe's Christian culture and expanding economy during the sixteenth and seventeenth centuries.

Exploration and commercial expansion created the foundations of a global economy in which the European economy was tied to Asian spices, African slaves, and American silver. A wide variety of goods circulated all over the globe. From the West Indies and East Asia, sugar, rice, tea, cacao, and tobacco flowed into Europe. From the Americas, potatoes, corn, sweet potatoes, and manioc (from which tapioca is made) spread to the rest of the world. Europeans paid for Asian silks and spices with American silver.

The increasing demand for goods and a rise in prices produced more opportunities for the accumulation and investment of capital by private individuals, which is the essence of capitalism. State policies designed to increase national wealth and power also stimulated the growth of capitalism. Governments subsidized new industries, chartered joint-stock companies to engage in overseas trade, and struck at internal tariffs and guild regulations that hampered domestic economic growth. Improvements in banking, shipbuilding, mining, and manufacturing further stimulated economic growth.

In the sixteenth and seventeenth centuries the old medieval political order dissolved, and the modern state began to emerge. The modern state has a strong central government that issues laws that apply throughout the land and a permanent army of professional soldiers paid by the state. Trained bureaucrats, responsible to the central government, collect taxes, enforce laws, and administer justice. The modern state has a secular character; promotion of religion is not the state's concern, and churches do not determine state policy. These features of the modern state were not prevalent in the Middle Ages, when the privileges of nobles, church, and towns had impeded central authority, and kings were expected to rule in accordance with Christian principles. In the sixteenth and seventeenth centuries, monarchs were exercising central authority with ever-greater effectiveness at the expense of nobles and clergy. The secularization of the state became firmly established after the Thirty Years' War (1618–1648); with their states worn out by Catholic-Protestant conflicts, kings came to act less for religious motives than for reasons of national security and power.

Historically, the modern state has been characterized by a devotion to the nation and by feelings of national pride.

There is a national language that is used throughout the land, and the people have a sense of sharing a common culture and history, of being distinct from other peoples. There were some signs of growing national feeling during the sixteenth and seventeenth centuries, but this feature of the modern state did not become a major part of European political life until the nineteenth century. During the early modern period, loyalty was largely given to a town, to a province, to a noble, or to the person of the king rather than to the nation, the people as a whole.

I ▾ The Age of Exploration and Conquest

In 1498, a Portuguese explorer, Vasco da Gama (c. 1460–1524) sailed a fleet of four ships around Africa into the Indian Ocean and landed at the Indian port of Calicut. His voyage marked the first step in the creation of a Portuguese commercial empire in East Asia. For centuries afterward, Europeans competed by fair means and foul for access to and control of the Asian trade. The Dutch, English, and French eventually established trading posts and colonies along the same routes pioneered by the Portuguese. Meanwhile, the Spaniards, following the initial discovery of the Caribbean islands by Columbus in 1492, proceeded to explore, conquer, and settle the mainland of Central, South, and North America.

Bernal Díaz del Castillo
THE DISCOVERY AND CONQUEST OF MEXICO

In 1518, Spanish ships explored the mainland coast along the Gulf of Mexico near the Yucatán Peninsula. The following year an expedition under the leadership of Hernando Cortés (1485–1547) landed at the site of modern Veracruz to explore the newly discovered country. There the Spaniards were unexpectedly confronted with ambassadors from Montezuma (c. 1502–1520), the ruler of an extensive Aztec empire; the Aztecs presented Cortés with gifts made of jade, gold, and silver and with rich textiles, and urged that the Spaniards depart — Montezuma feared Cortés was the Aztec god Quetzalcoatl who had come to reclaim his kingdom. Having 555 troops together with 16 horses and some cannons, Cortés refused and announced that he was sent by his king to speak directly with Montezuma. Sinking his ships to prevent his troops from deserting, Cortés marched inland to the Aztec capital, Tenochtitlán, the site of today's Mexico City; the Spaniards found a civilization with a high level of social and political organization and advanced techniques of engineering, architecture, writing, astronomy, painting, and ceramics. Located on islands in the midst of a lake, Tenochtitlán was approached by three stone causeways that converged

in a great central square, dominated by a high pyramidal temple. Other magnificent stone temples and palaces, paved marketplaces, canals with boats carrying products needed by the busy inhabitants, and cultivated gardens with aviaries presented impressive urban scenes. Thousands of priests, soldiers, civil servants, artisans, and laborers filled the streets and houses.

The following excerpts are from *The Discovery and Conquest of Mexico,* the personal memoir of Bernal Díaz del Castillo (c. 1492–1581). Díaz accompanied Cortés and wrote an eyewitness account of this first confrontation between Christian and Aztec civilizations. In the following passage Díaz described Montezuma and his courtiers. Although generally favorable in his account of Montezuma, Díaz reported a rumor that the Aztec emperor ate human flesh for dinner. Whether the Aztecs were cannibals is still disputed among scholars.

The Great Montezuma was about forty years old, of good height and well proportioned, slender and spare of flesh, not very swarthy, but of the natural colour and shade of an Indian. He did not wear his hair long, but so as just to cover his ears, his scanty black beard was well shaped and thin. His face was somewhat long, but cheerful, and he had good eyes and showed in his appearance and manner both tenderness and, when necessary, gravity. He was very neat and clean and bathed once every day in the afternoon. He had many women as mistresses, daughters of Chieftains, and he had two great Cacicas [noblewomen] as his legitimate wives. He was free from unnatural offences. The clothes that he wore one day, he did not put on again until four days later. He had over two hundred Chieftains in his guard, in other rooms close to his own, not that all were meant to converse with him, but only one or another, and when they went to speak to him they were obliged to take off their rich mantles [cloaks] and put on others of little worth, but they had to be clean, and they had to enter barefoot with their eyes lowered to the ground, and not to look up in his face. And they made him three obeisances [bows], and said: "Lord, my Lord, my Great Lord," before they came up to him, and then they made their report and with few words he dismissed them, and on taking leave they did not turn their backs, but kept their faces towards him with their eyes to the ground, and they did not turn their backs until they left the room. I noticed another thing, that when other great chiefs came from distant lands about disputes or business, when they reached the apartments of the Great Montezuma, they had to come barefoot and with poor mantles, and they might not enter directly into the Palace, but had to loiter about a little on one side of the Palace door, for to enter hurriedly was considered to be disrespectful. . . .

I have heard it said that they were wont to cook for him the flesh of young boys, but as he had such a variety of dishes, made of so many things, we could not succeed in seeing if they were of human flesh or of other things, for they daily cooked fowls, turkeys, pheasants, native partridges, quail, tame and wild ducks, venison, wild boar, reed birds, pigeons, hares and rabbits, and many sorts of birds and other things which are bred in this country, and they are so numerous that I cannot finish naming them in a hurry; so we had no insight into it; but I know for certain that after our Captain [Cortés] censured the sacrifice of human beings, and the eating of their flesh, he ordered that such food should not be prepared for him thenceforth. . . .

. . . While Montezuma was at table eating, as I have described, there were waiting on him two other graceful women to bring him tortillas, kneaded with eggs and other sustaining ingredients, and these tortillas were very white, and they were brought on plates covered with clean napkins, and they also brought him another kind of bread, like long balls kneaded with other kinds of sustaining food, and *pan pachol,* for so they call it in this country, which is a sort of wafer. There were also placed on the table three tubes much painted and gilded, which held *liquidambar* [a sort of sweet gum] mixed with certain herbs which they call *tabaco,* and when he had finished eating, after they had danced before him and sung and the table was removed, he inhaled the smoke from one of those tubes, but he took very little of it and with that he fell asleep. . . .

Let us leave this and go on to another great house, where they keep many Idols, and they say that they are their fierce gods, and with them many kinds of carnivorous beasts of prey, tigers and two kinds of lions, and animals something like wolves and foxes, and other smaller carnivorous animals, and all these carnivores they feed with flesh, and the greater number of them breed in the house. They give them as food deer and fowls, dogs and other things which they are used to hunt, and I have heard it said that they feed them on the bodies of the Indians who have been sacrificed. It is in this way; you have already heard me say that when they sacrifice a wretched Indian they saw open the chest with stone knives and hasten to tear out the palpitating heart and blood, and offer it to their Idols, in whose name the sacrifice is made. Then they cut off the thighs, arms and head and eat the former at feasts and banquets, and the head they hang up on some beams, and the body of the man sacrificed is not eaten but given to these fierce animals. They also have in that cursed house many vipers and poisonous snakes which carry on their tails things that sound like bells. These are the worst vipers of all, and they keep them in jars and great pottery vessels with many feathers, and there they lay their eggs and rear their young, and they give them to eat the bodies of the Indians who have been sacrificed, and the flesh of dogs which they are in the habit of breeding.

Let me speak now of the infernal noise when the lions and tigers roared and the jackals and foxes howled and the serpents hissed, it was horrible to listen to and it seemed like a hell. Let us go on and speak of the skilled workmen Montezuma employed in every craft that was practised among them. We will begin with lapidaries [gem cutters] and workers in gold and silver and all the hollow work, which even the great goldsmiths in Spain were forced to admire. . . . Let us go on to the great craftsmen in feather work, and painters and sculptors who were most refined; then to the Indian women who did the weaving and the washing, who made such an immense quantity of fine fabrics with wonderful featherwork designs; the greater part of it was brought daily from some towns of the province on the north coast near Vera Cruz called Cotaxtla.

▷ Díaz records with amazement the great central marketplace with its merchants and myriad products.

. . . When we arrived at the great market place, called Tlaltelolco, we were astounded at the number of people and the quantity of merchandise that it contained, and at the good order and control that was maintained, for we had never seen such a thing before. The chieftains who accompanied us acted as guides. Each kind of merchandise was kept by itself and had its fixed place marked out. Let us begin with the dealers in gold, silver, and precious stones, feathers, mantles, and embroidered goods. Then there were other wares consisting of Indian slaves both men and women; and I say that they bring as many of them to that great market for sale as the Portuguese bring negroes from Guinea; and they brought them along tied to long poles, with collars round their necks so that they could not escape, and others they left free. Next there were other traders who sold great pieces of cloth and cotton, and articles of twisted thread, and there were *cacahuateros* who sold cacao. In this way one could see every sort of merchandise that is to be found in the whole of New Spain [Spain's name for Mexico]. . . .

. . . And we saw the fresh water that comes from Chapultepec [a wooded area near Tenochtitlán] which supplies the city, and we saw the bridges on the three causeways which were built at certain distances apart through which the water of the lake flowed in and out from one side to the other, and we beheld on that great lake a great multitude of canoes, some coming with supplies of food and others returning loaded with cargoes of merchandise; and we saw that from every house of that great city and of all the other cities that were built in the water it was impossible to pass from house to house, except by drawbridges which were made of wood or in canoes; and we saw in those cities Cues [pyramidal temples] and oratories like towers and fortresses and all gleaming white, and it was a wonderful thing to behold; then the houses with flat roofs, and on the causeways other small towers and oratories which were like fortresses.

After having examined and considered all that we had seen we turned to look at the great market place and the crowds of people that were in it, some buying and others selling, so that the murmur and hum of their voices and words that they used could be heard more than a league off. Some of the soldiers among us who had been in many parts of the world, in Constantinople, and all over Italy, and in Rome, said that so large a market place and so full of people, and so well regulated and arranged, they had never beheld before. . . .

▷ When Cortés mocks the Aztec ruler's religious devotion to his gods and proposes setting up the Christian cross and image of the Virgin Mary, Montezuma reproaches him.

. . . Our Captain said to Montezuma through our interpreter, half laughing: "Señor Montezuma, I do not understand how such a great Prince and wise man as you are has not come to the conclusion, in your mind, that these idols of yours are not gods, but evil things that are called devils, and so that you may know it and all your priests may see it clearly, do me the favour to approve of my placing a cross here on the top of this tower, and that in one part of these oratories where your Huichilobos and Tezcatepuca [Aztec gods] stand we may divide off a space where we can set up an image of Our Lady (an image which Montezuma had already seen) and you will see by the fear in which these Idols hold it that they are deceiving you."

Montezuma replied half angrily (and the two priests who were with him showed great annoyance), and said: "Señor Malinche [Aztec name for Cortés], if I had known that you would have said such defamatory things I would not have shown you my gods, we consider them to be very good, for they give us health and rains and good seed times and seasons and as many victories as we desire, and we are obliged to worship them and make sacrifices, and I pray you not to say another word to their dishonour.". . .

▷ The Spaniards decide to build a Christian chapel within the walls of the huge Aztec palace in which they are quartered, hoping to convert the Aztecs by the example of their own Christian religious devotions. By chance, they discover a secret door to a room filled with treasure.

. . . Now as there was a rumour and we had heard the story that Montezuma kept the treasure of his father Axayaca in that building, it was suspected that it might be in this chamber which had been closed up and cemented only a few days before. Yañes spoke about it to Juan Valásquez de Leon and Francisco de Lugo, and those Captains told the story to Cortés, and the door was secretly opened. When it was opened Cortés and some of his Captains went in first, and they saw such a number of jewels and slabs and plates of gold and chalchihuites [figures of goddesses] and other great riches, that they were quite carried away and did not know what to say about such wealth. The news soon spread among all the other Captains and soldiers, and very secretly we went in to see it. When I saw it I marvelled, and as at that time I was a youth and had never seen such riches as those in my life before, I took it for certain that there could not be another such store of wealth in the whole world. It was decided by all our captains and soldiers, that we should not dream of touching a particle of it, but that the stones should immediately be put back in the doorway and it should be sealed up and cemented just as we found it, and that it should not be spoken about, lest it should reach Montezuma's ears, until times should alter.

REVIEW QUESTIONS

1. What astonished the Spaniards about Montezuma and his royal court?
2. What Aztec religious practices did the Spaniards find strange and contrary to Christian moral beliefs?
3. What amazed the Spaniards as they toured the Aztec capital?
4. Why did the Spaniards keep their discovery of the Aztec treasure secret?
5. What evidence did Bernal Díaz del Castillo offer to show the Aztecs as a highly civilized people?

---

2 ▾ Toward the Modern Economy: The Example of Holland

The Spanish and Portuguese monopoly of trade was challenged in the late sixteenth century, first by English privateers who preyed on the Spanish fleets crossing the Atlantic and then by the Dutch who were in revolt against their sovereign, the Spanish King Philip II (1556–1598). Earlier, the Dutch had traded with both Spanish and Portuguese ports, but were not allowed to seek markets directly with the Americas or the East Indies. When Philip II, who was also king of Portugal from 1580, excluded the rebellious Dutch from trading in his ports — a policy that was renewed by his son, Philip III (1598–1621) — Dutch merchants decided to break the Portuguese monopoly over trade with the East Indies. In doing so, they launched the first of many commercial wars designed to win unhindered control over world trade markets.

Pieter Van Dam
THE CHARTERING OF THE DUTCH EAST INDIA COMPANY

In the following excerpt from his *A Description of the East India Company,* Pieter Van Dam (1621–1706), an officer of the East India Company, describes how the Dutch government encouraged trade with the East Indies. It established a private limited stockholding company, the East India Company, and granted it a monopoly over trade and colonization anywhere east of the Cape of Good Hope or beyond the Straits of Magellan at the southern tip of South America. The company was granted the right to build fortresses, to raise armies, to establish laws and courts in territories it captured from the Spanish or the Portuguese,

and to enter into diplomatic alliances with other princes. The East India Company was the foundation on which the Dutch built their colonial empire. Other European states established similar corporations to further trade and colonization.

After various private merchants joined with others in the 1590s and after the turn of the century to form companies, first in Amsterdam and then in other cities of Holland and Zeeland, to open up and undertake travel and trade with the East Indies, and from time to time equipped and sent out many ships, which returned, on the average, with no small success, the States General came to the conclusion that it would be more useful and profitable not only for the country as a whole but also for its inhabitants individually, especially all those who had undertaken and shared in navigation and trade, that these companies should be combined and this navigation and trade be placed and maintained on a firm footing, with order and political guidance. After much argument and persuasion, this union was worked out by Their High Mightinesses [the government of the United Provinces], in their own words, to advance the prosperity of the United Netherlands, to conserve and increase its industry and to bring profit to the Company and to the people of the country.*

Their High Mightinesses later, by an edict of September 19, 1606, acceded to vigorous requests of the Company and granted to it a charter for a period of twenty-one years, permitting it to voyage east of the Cape of Good Hope or through the Straits of Magellan and excluding all others, under penalty not only of confiscation of ships and cargo but also of fines and imprisonment.

By another edict, Their High Mightinesses declared that terms, franchises, and advantages already accorded were to be maintained and continued, without any direct or indirect infringement within this country or abroad in any matter, personally or through intermediaries, under penalty of imprisonment and fines and with the distribution of said fines.

Furthermore, the Company's charter authorized it to make alliances with princes and potentates east of the Cape of Good Hope and beyond the Straits of Magellan, to make contracts, build fortresses and strongholds, name governors, raise troops, appoint officers of justice, and perform other necessary services for the advancement of trade; to dismiss the said governors and officers of justice if their conduct was found to be harmful and disloyal, provided that these governors or officers could not be prevented from returning here to present such grievances or complaints as they think they might have to Their High Mightinesses. This was further confirmed by the eighth article of the instructions of the year 1617, approved and ratified by Their High Mightinesses, which established and regulated the government in the Indies in such a way that, as is easily seen, the Company after the date of this charter has made great progress in the Indies. It has captured a number of fortresses from the Spaniards and the Portuguese, its enemies, and has established trading posts at several places. It was decided as a consequence that it was desirable to establish a formal government in the Indies, with a Governor General and a Council, and to provide it with proper instructions, and this was done by the assembly of the XVII [the Dutch parliament] and by Their High Mightinesses. . . .

The inhabitants of this country were permitted to invest as much or as little as they pleased in shares of the Company.

The subscription had to be made before September 1, 1602. . . .

. . . When the time for this investment or subscription had expired, various competent persons in different places presented requests in person or by sealed letter to the assembly of the

*The words, that is, of the charter of the United East India Company of 1602.

XVII, asking that they be permitted to join the Company with the investment of certain sums of money; it was decided that no one else should be permitted to join in violation of the charter and to the detriment of the shareholders who had paid in their subscriptions before the expiration of the date fixed, and that the subscribed capital should be neither increased nor reduced.

John Keymer
DUTCH TRADE AND COMMERCE AS A MODEL

The rapid growth of Holland's wealth and the general prosperity of the Dutch people in the early seventeenth century drew the attention of many Europeans to what seemed an economic wonder. Despite the absence of notable natural resources, such as forests, minerals, or climate favorable for growing grain, the Dutch had become the dominant economic power in northern Europe.

In the early seventeenth century, an Englishman named John Keymer published a series of tracts urging major reforms in English economic policies to permit more rapid development of English industry and commerce. Like many other economists of the period, he looked at the Dutch economy as a model to be adopted by other nations. Although Keymer shared the prevalent view that national wealth was measured by stores of precious metals in bullion or coin, his description of the Dutch economy revealed a more complicated reality. In his tract *Observations Touching Trade and Commerce with the Hollanders, and Other Nations* — falsely attributed to Sir Walter Raleigh (c. 1552–1618) who was noted for his interest in promoting English overseas trade and colonization — Keymer described the unusual character of the Dutch economy and the factors leading to its great success.

May it please your most Excellent Majesty,

I have diligently, in my travels, observed how the countries herein mentioned [mainly Holland] do grow potent with abundance of all things to serve themselves and other nations, where nothing groweth; and that their never dryed fountains of wealth, by which they raise their estate to such an admirable height, [so] that they are . . . [now] a wonder to the world, [come] from your Majesty's seas and lands.

I thus moved, began to dive into the depth of their policies and circumventing practices, whereby they drain, and still covet to exhaust, the wealth and coin of this kingdom, and so with our own commodities to weaken us, and finally beat us quite out of trading in other countries. I found that they more fully obtained these their purposes by their convenient privileges, and settled constitutions, than *England* with all the laws, and superabundance of home-bred commodities which God hath [bestowed on] your sea and land. . . .

To bring this to pass they have many advantages of us; the one is, by their fashioned ships called boyers, hoy-barks, hoys, and others that are made to hold great bulk of merchandise, and to sail with a few men for profit. For example, . . . [Dutch ships] do serve the merchant better cheap by one hundred pounds [English money] in his freight than we can, by reason he hath but nine or ten mariners, and we near thirty; thus he saveth twenty men's meat and wages in a voyage; and so in all other their ships according to their burden, by which means they are freighted wheresoever they come, to great profit, whilst our ships lie still and decay. . . .

Of this their smallness of custom [duty] inwards and outwards, we have daily experience; for if two *English* ships, or two of any other nations be at *Bourdeaux* [a French port, exporting mainly wine], both laden with wine of three hundred tons apiece, the one bound for *Holland,* or any other petty [small] states, the other for *England,* the merchant shall pay about nine hundred pounds custom here, and other duties, when the other in *Holland,* or any other petty states, shall be cleared for less than fifty pounds, and so in all other wares and merchandizes accordingly, which draws all nations to traffick with them; and although it seems but small duties which they receive, yet the multitudes of all kind of commodities and coin that is brought in by themselves and others, and carried out by themselves and others, is so great, that they receive more custom and duties to the state, by the greatness of their commerce in one year, than *England* doth in two years. . . .

And if it happen that a trade be stopped by any foreign nation, which they heretofore usually had, or hear of any good trading which they never had, they will hinder others, and seek either by favour, money, or force, to open the gap of traffick for advancement of trade amongst themselves, and employment of their people.

And when there is a new course or trade erected, they give free custom inwards and outwards, for the better maintenance of navigation, and encouragement of the people to that business.

Thus they and others glean the wealth and strength from us to themselves; and these reasons following procure them this advantage of us.

1. The merchant[s] . . . which maketh all things in abundance, by reason of their store-houses continually replenished with all kind of commodities.
2. The liberty of free traffick for strangers to buy and sell in *Holland,* and other countries and states, as if they were free-born, maketh great intercourse.
3. The small duties levied upon merchants, draws all nations to trade with them.
4. Their fashioned ships continually freighted before ours, by reason of their few mariners and great bulk, serving the merchant cheap.
5. Their forwardness to further all manner of trading.
6. Their wonderful employment of their busses [herring boats] for fishing, and the great returns they make.
7. Their giving free custom inwards and outwards, for any new-erected trade, by means whereof they have gotten already almost the sole trade into their hands. . . .

The merchandises of *France, Portugal, Spain, Italy, Turkey, East* and *West-Indies,* are transported most by the *Hollanders,* and other petty states, into the east and northeast kingdoms of [Europe] . . . and the merchandises brought from the last-mentioned. . . , being wonderful many, are likewise by the *Hollanders* and other petty states most transported into the southern and western dominions, and yet the situation of *England* lieth far better for a storehouse to serve the south-east and north-east regions than theirs doth, and hath far better means to do it, if we will bend our course for it.

No sooner a dearth of fish, wine, or corn here, and other merchandise, but forthwith the *Emdeners, Hamburghers* [from the German ports of Emden and Hamburg], and *Hollanders,* out of their store-houses, [load] fifty or one hundred ships, or more, dispersing themselves round about this kingdom, and carry away great store of coin and wealth for little commodity, in those times of dearth; by which means they suck our commonwealth of her riches, cut down our merchants, and decay our navigation; not with their natural commodities, which grow in their own countries, but the merchandises of other countries and kingdoms.

Therefore it is far more easy to serve ourselves, hold up our merchants, and increase our ships and mariners, and strengthen the kingdom; and not only keep our money in our own realm, which other nations still rob us of, but bring in theirs who carry ours away, and make the bank or coin a store-house to serve other nations as well, and far better cheap than they. . . .

The abundance of corn groweth in the east kingdoms [of Europe], but the great store-houses for grain to serve Christendom, and heathen countries in the time of dearth, is in the *Low-Countries* [Holland and modern-day Belgium], wherewith, upon every occasion of scarcity and dearth they do inrich themselves seven years after, employ their people, and get great freights for their ships in other countries, and we not one in that course.

The mighty vineyards and store of salt is in *France* and *Spain;* but the great vintage and staple of salt is in the *Low-Countries,* and they send near one thousand sail of ships with salt and wine only into the east kingdoms yearly, besides other places, and we not one in that course.

The exceeding groves of wood are in the east kingdoms, but the huge piles of [lumber] . . . and timber, is in the *Low-Countries,* where none grow, wherewith they serve themselves and other parts, and this kingdom with those commodities; they have five or six hundred great long ships continually using that trade, and we none in that course.

The wool, cloth, lead, tin, and divers other commodities, are in *England;* but by means of our wool and cloth going out rough, undress'd, and undy'd, there is an exceeding manufactory and drapery in the *Low-Countries,* wherewith they serve themselves and other nations, and advance greatly the employment of their people at home, and traffick abroad, and put down ours in foreign parts, where our merchants trade unto, with our own commodities. . . .

The *Low-Countries* send into the east kingdoms yearly, about three thousand ships, trading into every city and port-town, taking the advantage, and vending their commodities to exceeding profit, and buying and lading their ships with plenty of those commodities, which they have from every of those towns 20 *per cent.* cheaper than we, by reason of the difference of the coin, and their fish yields ready money, which greatly advanceth their traffick, and decayeth ours.

William Carr
CAPITALISM IN AMSTERDAM

In 1693, William Carr, the English consul at Amsterdam, wrote a travelers' guide to the leading cities of Holland, Flanders, northern Germany, and Scandinavia. Of these, the largest and wealthiest was Amsterdam in Holland. In less than a century, this once-small medieval city had grown to become the most important commercial port in the West and the center of European financial capitalism. In the following selections, Carr describes the products and items of trade that flowed through the hands of the Amsterdam merchants; the excerpts have been adapted, using modern language and spelling.

I now come to speak of Amsterdam, my home for several years, which I shall describe in more detail than I do other places. It is considered by intelligent men to be the second city in the world in the matters of trade and not inferior in wealth to any city. Certainly, Amsterdam is one of the most beautiful cities in the world; its buildings are large, and its streets for the most part are pleasantly planted with trees and neatly paved. And although, as I have already said,

Amsterdam may justly be taken for the second or third city in the world after London and Paris, it has neither court nor university as they have.

Amsterdam, for the wise statesmen it has produced, is said to be a second Athens; others regard it as the storehouse of Europe, for it has such great stores of grain that it is able to supply many other nations. And second, it is known for the great stores of spices that are distributed all over Europe and the Indies by the East India Company. Third, it has an inconceivably great supply of war provisions, so that England and other countries purchase military supplies in Amsterdam. There are several shopkeepers in Amsterdam who can deliver arms for four thousand or five thousand men at a cheaper rate than can be obtained anywhere else; they can do this because of their great industry in controlling the market of products from iron works on the Rhine and other rivers that run into Holland. Fourth, Amsterdam has more stores of lumber for shipbuilding than can be found in any nation in the world; this is the reason why its neighboring town Sardam can build ships 20 per cent more cheaply than can be done in England or France. For this reason both France and Spain buy ships in Holland. . . . Fifth, Amsterdam . . . supplies Europe and many places in the Indies with vermillion [a bright red dye]. . . . Sixth, Amsterdam is the market from which the king of France [Louis XIV] bought marble for Versailles, the Louvre, and other palaces in France. There are such vast storehouses of marble in Amsterdam that one would think that there were marble quarries near the city gates. Seventh, Amsterdam has the most active bank in the world. . . . There are many other points I could list to demonstrate the great riches and trade of Amsterdam, including the vast quantities of wines and brandy-wines that its merchants sell in northern Europe, from which they import hemp, pitch, and tar to sell to France, Italy, and Spain. They also control much of the marketing of Sweden's copper and iron.

▷ Carr then describes the commercial trading system of the famous Dutch East India Company, which established trading posts in South Africa, the Persian Gulf area, India, Ceylon, Bangladesh, Indonesia, China, and Japan. (Although not mentioned by Carr, the Dutch West India Company conducted similar operations in the Caribbean and North America. The Dutch trading post of New Amsterdam at the mouth of the Hudson River would become the city of New York, the world center of finance capitalism in the twentieth century.)

. . . The East India Company of the Netherlands is said to be a commonwealth within a commonwealth, and this is true when you consider the sovereign power and privileges the company has been granted by the States General [the ruling council of the Dutch Republic] and also consider its riches and vast number of subjects, and the many territories and colonies it possesses in the East Indies. The company is said to have 30,000 men in its constant employ and more than 200 capital ships, in addition to its sloops, ketches, and yachts. The company possesses many colonies formerly belonging to Spain, Portugal, and various Indian princes, and as good Christians company members have spread the Gospel of Christ in these lands, printing the Bible, prayer books, and catechisms in Indian languages and maintaining ministers and teachers to instruct those that are converted to the faith. Having said that this company is so extensive — as it were a commonwealth apart — I will demonstrate that it is a commonwealth first by its power, riches, and strength in the East Indies, and second, by its position in Europe. . . . But I will begin at the Cape of Good Hope [Africa] where the company has built a fort where it maintains a garrison to defend its ships when they stop there for fresh water. From there let us view the company on the island of Java, where it has built a fair city called Batavia and fortified it with bastions like those in Amsterdam. This city is the residence of the company's grand minister of state, called the General of the Indies. He has six privy counsellors (ordinary) and two extraordinary; they oversee the concerns of the company throughout the Indies, including matters of war and peace. . . . The General of the Indies has horse and foot soldiers, officers, and servants — as if he were a sovereign prince — all paid for by the company. . . . So formidable is the company in the East Indies that it looks as though it aims to rule the South Seas. It also has a great trade with China and Japan. . . . With Persia also it has great commerce and is so confident that it wages war with the Persian monarch if he wrongs it in trade. It also has several colonies on the coast of Malabar and Coromandel [west coast of India] and in the country of the Great Mogul. . . . But especially let us examine the company on the rich island of Ceylon [Sri Lanka] where it controls the plains, so the king of the island is forced to live in the mountains while the company possesses the city of Colombo. . . . I will say no more of the company's power in the Indies, but let us examine its position in Europe. To begin with, in Amsterdam the company has two large stately palaces, one being in the old part of the city, and the other in the new; in the old part it keeps its court — where the Resident Committee of the company sits — and sells the company's goods.

▷ The most important institutional support for the growth of capitalism in Amsterdam was the merchants' exchange bank. Founded in 1609 under municipal supervision, it provided a safe, convenient depository for the coined money and bullion of its several thousand depositors, who included both foreign and Dutch merchants, kings, princely nobles, and governments. The bank allowed merchants to pay debts and receive payments from debtors by a system of bills of exchange or paper notes; for a fee, it provided customers with a daily statement of their accounts. Carr's description of the bank follows.

. . . [T]he Merchants' Bank . . . is governed by divers commissioners, clerks and bookkeepers, and an assay-master who judges [the quality and value of] the gold and silver that at any time is brought into the bank uncoined. The security given for the bank's preservation are the States [the Dutch parliament] and Magistrates of Amsterdam. Now, if you have a mind to put money into the bank, perhaps 1,000 pounds sterling, more or less, you must go to the clerks and ask for a folio for your name, and then pay in your money at 3 or 4 percent [discount for the payee], according to whether the rate of the bank money is high or low. Or you may buy it of those called cashiers or brokers; then get the clerks to set down in the folio what you bring in. Having done so, you may draw this sum or sell it in what parcels you please, but then if you let your money lie seven years in the bank, you receive no interest for it. If you should ask me where the advantage is for the merchant? I would answer: first, you have your money ready at all times for answering bills of exchange and making other payments; you have no charge for bags [storage for coins] or portage [the cost of shipping coins or bullion], no loss by false tale or bad money [counterfeit or badly clipped], no danger from thieves or unfaithful servants or fire; and above all, you have the accounts of your cash most punctually and justly kept without any trouble and without running the risk of goldsmith or cashiers [going broke] in your debt. For such is [the commissioners'] care that twice a year, or sometimes oftener, they shut up the bank for fourteen days and all that have concerns there must bring in their accounts to the clerks, who a few days after, having viewed their books, acquaint any who have brought in wrong accounts about their mistakes, requesting them to return to their books and to rectify their errors. . . . Besides the clerks' care in keeping and stating the accounts, the bank is obliged for five pounds a year to send to every merchant who desires it, their accounts every morning before Exchange-time, of the moneys written by them in the bank the day before upon any merchant's account, and what sums are written by others upon their accounts, so that the merchants may compare the bank's notes with their books and so save much of the charges of bookkeeping. . . .

[Also], . . . the Magistrates of the city take out of the Merchants' Bank a sufficient amount of money to supply the Lumbert, a bank that lends out money and is governed by four commissioners . . . [who have] officers who lend money [secured by any kind of collateral], from a pair of shoes to the richest jewel. This is a great convenience for poor people, yes, for merchants also, . . . and prevents the extraordinary extortion used by pawnbrokers in England, France, and other countries.

REVIEW QUESTIONS

1. Why did the Dutch government create a monopolistic corporation to control all Dutch trade with the East Indies?
2. What fiscal policies did the Dutch adopt to increase their share of foreign commerce?
3. What technical advantages did the Dutch enjoy in shipping?
4. What policy recommendations did John Keymer make to the English king?
5. What were the economic advantages for the Dutch people in having their country become an international marketplace and storehouse?
6. What factors made Amsterdam the first successful modern capitalist economy?
7. Describe the services offered merchants by the Amsterdam banks, and explain how those services stimulated the growth of capitalism.

---

3 ▾ Mercantilism: State-directed Capitalism

According to the principles of mercantilist theory, a state's wealth and power depended on the accumulation of gold and silver, with which the ruler could build and maintain a large army and navy and support a luxurious royal court. To increase their state's supply of precious bullion, rulers encouraged the manufacture of goods for export and discouraged imports. Trade and manufacturing monopolies were encouraged, and subsidies were provided to stimulate the domestic production of certain desired goods and services. Overseas colonies played a crucial role in mercantilist theory: they provided the state with precious metals or other valuable commodities and offered a protected market for the manufactured goods produced in the parent country.

RESTRICTING COLONIAL TRADE: THE HAT ACT

The following text of the Hat Act, passed by the British Parliament in 1732, is an example of mercantilist theory at work. The British government expected its colonies to sell Britain raw materials and to buy British manufactured goods in return. But occasionally the colonists preferred to manufacture their own products or to buy from and sell to non-British traders. Britain decided on the Hat Act because American colonists were manufacturing and selling hats that com-

peted directly with British hats. The mercantilist solution was to forbid Americans to export hats. Similar acts designed to subordinate American economic development to the needs of English industry and trade became a major cause of the American Revolution in 1776.

Whereas the art and mystery of making hats in Great Britain hath arrived to a great perfection and considerable quantities of hats manufactured in this kingdom have heretofore been exported to His Majesty's plantations or colonies in America, who have been wholly supplied with hats from Great Britain; and whereas great quantities of hats have of late years been made, and the said manufacture is daily increasing in the British plantations in America, and is from thence exported to foreign markets, which were heretofore supplied from Great Britain; . . . wherefore for preventing the said ill practices for the future, and for promoting and encouraging the trade of making hats in Great Britain, be it enacted by the King's most excellent majesty, by and with the advice and consent of the Lords spiritual and temporal and commons in this present Parliament assembled, and by the authority of the same: That from and after the twenty-ninth day of September in the year of our Lord one thousand seven hundred and thirty-two, no hats or felts whatsoever, dyed or undyed, finished or unfinished, shall be shipped, loaded, or put on board any ship or vessel in any place or parts within any of the British plantations, upon any pretense whatsoever, by any person or persons whatsoever, and also that no hats or felts, either dyed or undyed, finished or unfinished, shall be loaded upon any horse, cart, or other carriage, to the intent or purpose to be exported, transported, shipped off, carried, or conveyed out of any of the said British plantations to any other of the British plantations, or to any other place whatsoever, by any person or persons whatsoever.

And be it further enacted by the authority aforesaid: That (each) and every . . . offender and offenders, offense and offenses against this act, shall be subject and liable to the penalties and forfeitures hereinafter mentioned, that is to say: The said hats or felts, dyed or undyed, finished or unfinished, so exported, transported, shipped off, carried, conveyed, or loaded contrary to the true intent and meaning of this act, shall be forfeited, and that every (one) of the offender and offenders therein shall likewise forfeit and pay the sum of five hundred pounds for every such offense committed; and every master, mariner, porter, carter, waggoner, boatman, or other person whatsoever knowing (of) such (an) offense, and wittingly aiding and assisting therein, shall forfeit and pay the sum of forty pounds. . . .

Jean Baptiste Colbert
TO THE MAGISTRATES AND INHABITANTS OF MARSEILLES

Jean Baptiste Colbert (1619–1683), leading minister in Louis XIV's reign (1643–1715), sought to increase France's power by using all the state's resources to promote manufacturing and domestic and foreign commerce. These policies are described in the following letter addressed to the people of Marseilles, France's chief Mediterranean port. The letter, written by Colbert, was issued under Louis XIV's name. The establishment of a special council to advise the king on commercial matters was an innovation that would be imitated by other European governments. Policies promised to the French people included

elimination of internal tariffs, subsidies to new industries, repair of highways, and other state efforts to encourage progress in industry and commerce.

26 August 1664

Very dear and well beloved:

Having considered how useful it would be to this kingdom to revive its domestic and foreign commerce . . . we have resolved to establish for this purpose a council, concerned particularly with commerce, that would meet every fifteen days in our presence and would consider all the interests of the merchants and the means of reviving commerce as well as everything that concerns manufactures. We also inform you that we are reserving, in the expenses of our State, a million *livres* [French unit of money] each year, for the renewal of manufacturing and the augmentation of navigation, without even mentioning the considerable sums that we raise to supply the companies of the East and West Indies;

That we are working incessantly to abolish all the tolls that are collected on the navigable rivers;

That more than a million livres have already been expended for the repair of public roads, to which we shall also devote our continuous attention;

That we shall assist with funds from the royal treasury all those who strive to reestablish old manufactures or wish to set up new ones;

That we are ordering all our ambassadors, or residents at the courts of our allies, to take in our name all appropriate measures in order to resolve justly all the grievances of our merchants and to preserve for them the total freedom of trade;

That we will comfortably lodge at our court all the merchants who have business there, during the time that they shall be obliged to remain there, having ordered the grand marshall of our palace to designate a proper place for their stay which will appropriately be called the House of Commerce; . . .

That all the merchants and traders by sea who buy vessels or who construct new ones for their trading activities, shall receive subsidies from us for the purchase or for the construction of said vessels;

And that all those who undertake long voyages, and supply the proper certification in the form prescribed by us, will receive subsidies from us for each ton of merchandise that they export or import on said voyages.

In this letter we desire not only to inform you of these things, but also to require you, as soon as you have received it, to assemble the merchants and traders of Marseilles, and explain to them in particular our intentions regarding all those issues mentioned above, for being informed of the favorable treatment that we desire to extend to them they may be more persuaded to apply themselves to commerce. Let them understand that for everything that concerns the welfare and the advantage of the said commerce they should address themselves to Monsieur Colbert. . . .

REVIEW QUESTIONS

1. Who profited from the mercantilist policies of the English Parliament? Who suffered from them?
2. What measures did Jean Baptiste Colbert believe would increase the foreign and domestic trade of France?
3. Why did Colbert wish to stimulate shipbuilding and the use of French-owned ships for foreign trade?

4 ▾ The Atlantic Slave Trade

As the first Portuguese merchants began to penetrate southward along the coast of western Africa, they found that the local African societies engaged in an extensive trade in slave laborers. Like slaves in the Mediterranean region, African slaves were prisoners of war, criminals, or victims of violence and kidnapping. The Portuguese ships began carrying slaves from one local market to another along the African coast. Some slaves were taken back to Europe, but after 1500 the trade shifted largely to the Portuguese colony in Brazil and the Spanish colonies in the West Indies. In addition, Arabs and Portuguese competed in conveying slaves from East Africa to the markets of the Middle East. The widespread use of African slaves marked a new stage in the history of slavery. In the western world slavery was now identified with race; the myth emerged that blacks were slaves by nature.

In the seventeenth century, the Dutch and English entered the West African slave trade, ousting the Portuguese as the principal slave traders to the West Indies and North America. The supply of laborers from Africa was essential to the New World's successful economic development. The Africans proved themselves to be skilled farmers and artisans who could endure the heavy labor of plantation life without the high rate of sickness and death that afflicted the local Indian populations. The Atlantic slave trade continued for more than three hundred years until finally suppressed by European governments in the nineteenth century. During that period, it is estimated that between 9.5 and 12 million African men, women, and children were shipped to the New World as slaves.

Olaudah Equiano
MEMOIRS OF A FORMER SLAVE

One eighteenth-century African, Olaudah Equiano, an Ibo from what is now Nigeria, wrote about his kidnapping and enslavement in Africa, his subsequent sale to English slave merchants, and his voyage to and first impressions of the West Indian port of Bridgetown, Barbados. Equiano's subsequent life diverged from the pattern of most slaves. He educated himself, engaged in petty trade, purchased his freedom, and traveled to England, Nicaragua, Syria, and New England. In 1786, he was involved in planning the first free black colony, at Freetown, Sierra Leone, in Africa and took an active part in the antislavery movement in England. In the following excerpts from his memoir, *The Interesting Narrative of Olaudah Equiano or Gustavus Vasa the African,* published in two volumes in London in 1789, he records his reactions at the age of eleven when he was placed aboard an English slave ship for the voyage to the West Indies.

The first object which saluted my eyes when I arrived on the coast was the sea, and a slave-ship, which was then riding at anchor, and waiting for its cargo. These filled me with astonishment, which was soon converted into terror, which I am yet at a loss to describe, nor the then feelings of my mind. When I was carried on board I was immediately handled, and tossed up, to see if I were sound, by some of the crew; and I was now persuaded that I had got into a world of bad spirits, and that they were going to kill me. Their complexions too differing so much from ours, their long hair, and the language they spoke, which was very different from any I had ever heard, united to confirm me in this belief. Indeed, such were the horrors of my views and fears at the moment, that, if ten thousand worlds had been my own, I would have freely parted with them all to have exchanged my condition with that of the meanest slave in my own country. When I looked round the ship too, and saw a large furnace or copper boiling, and a multitude of black people of every description chained together, every one of their countenances expressing dejection and sorrow, I no longer doubted of my fate; and, quite overpowered with horror and anguish, I fell motionless on the deck and fainted. When I recovered a little, I found some black people about me, who I believed were some of those who brought me on board, and had been receiving their pay; they talked to me in order to cheer me, but all in vain. I asked them if we were not to be eaten by those white men with horrible looks, red faces, and long hair. They told me I was not. . . .

. . . Soon after this, the blacks who brought me on board went off, and left me abandoned to despair. I now saw myself deprived of all chance of returning to my native country, or even the least glimpse of hope of gaining the shore, which I now considered as friendly; and I even wished for my former slavery, in preference to my present situation, which was filled with horror of every kind, still heightened by my ignorance of what I was to undergo. I was not long suffered to indulge my grief; I was soon put down under the decks, and there I received such a salutation in my nostrils as I had never experienced in my life; so that, with the loathsomeness of the stench, and crying together, I became so sick and low that I was not able to eat, nor had I the least desire to taste any thing. I now wished for the last friend, death, to relieve me; but soon, to my grief, two of the white men offered me eatables; and, on my refusing to eat, one of them held me fast by the hands, and laid me across, I think, the windlass, and tied my feet while the other flogged me severely. I had never experienced any thing of this kind before; and, although not being used to the water, I naturally feared that element the first time I saw it; yet, nevertheless, could I have got over the nettings, I would have jumped over the side; but I could not; and, besides, the crew used to watch us very closely who were not chained down to the decks, lest we should leap into the water: and I have seen some of these poor African prisoners most severely cut for attempting to do so, and hourly whipped for not eating. This indeed was often the case with myself. . . .

. . . At last, when the ship we were in had got in all her cargo . . . we were all put under deck. . . . The closeness of the place, and the heat of the climate, added to the number in the ship, which was so crowded that each had scarcely room to turn himself, almost suffocated us. This produced copious perspirations, so that the air soon became unfit for respiration, from a variety of loathsome smells, and brought on a sickness amongst the slaves, of which many died, thus falling victims to the improvident avarice, as I may call it, of their purchasers. This wretched situation was again aggravated by the galling of the chains, now become insupportable; and filth of the necessary tubs, into which the children often fell, and were almost suffocated. The shrieks of the women, and the groans of the dying, rendered the whole a scene of horror almost inconceivable. Happily perhaps for myself I was soon reduced so low here that it was thought necessary to keep me almost always on deck; and from my extreme youth I was not put in fetters. In this situation I expected every hour to share the fate of my companions, some of whom were almost daily brought upon deck at the point of death, which I began to hope would soon put an end to my miseries. Often did I think many of the inhabitants of the deep much more happy than myself; I envied them the freedom they enjoyed, and as often wished I could change my condition for theirs. Every circumstance I met with served only to render my state more painful, and heighten my apprehensions and my opinion of the cruelty of the whites. . . .

. . . In a little time after, amongst the poor chained men, I found some of my own nation, which in a small degree gave ease to my mind. I inquired of them what was to be done with us? They gave me to understand we were to be carried to these white people's country to work for them. I then was a little revived, and thought, if it were no worse than working, my situation was not so desperate: but still I feared I should be put to death, the white people looked and acted, as I thought, in so savage a manner; for I had never seen among any people such instances of brutal cruelty; and this not only shown towards us blacks, but also to some of the whites themselves. One white man in particular I saw, when we were permitted to be on deck, flogged so unmercifully with a large rope near the foremast, that he died in consequence of it; and they tossed him over the side as they would have done a brute. This made me fear these people the more; and I expected nothing less than to be treated in the same manner. I could not help expressing my fears and apprehensions to some of my countrymen.

▷ The voyage from the African coast to the West Indies covered some 5,500 miles and normally took more than two months. (The mortality rate among the slaves sailing from the Niger Delta in the late eighteenth century averaged 9.7 percent.) Equiano's ship finally reaches Bridgetown, Barbados, where the slaves are to be sold.

. . . The white people got some old slaves from the land to pacify us. They told us we were not to be eaten, but to work, and were soon to go on land where we should see many of our country people. This report eased us much; and sure enough, soon after we landed, there came to us Africans of all languages. We were conducted immediately to the merchant's yard, where we were all pent up together like so many sheep in a fold, without regard to sex or age. As every object was new to me, everything I saw filled me with surprise. What struck me first was, that the houses were built with bricks, in stories, and in every other respect different from those I have seen in Africa: but I was still more astonished on seeing people on horseback. I did not know what this could mean; and indeed I thought these people were full of nothing but magical arts. While I was in this astonishment, one of my fellow prisoners spoke to a countryman of his about the horses, who said they were the same kind they had in their country. . . . We were not many days in the merchant's custody, before we were sold after their usual manner, which is this: on a signal given (as the beat of a drum), the buyers rush at once into the yard where the slaves are confined, and make choice of that parcel they like best. The noise and clamour with which this is attended, and the eagerness visible in the countenances of the buyers, serve not a little to increase the apprehension of the terrified Africans, who may well be supposed to consider them as the ministers of that destruction to which they think themselves devoted. In this manner, without scruple, are relations and friends separated, most of them never to see each other again. I remember in the vessel in which I was brought over, in the men's apartment, there were several brothers who, in the sale, were sold in different lots; and it was very moving on this occasion to see and hear their cries at parting. O, ye nominal Christians! might not an African ask you, learned you this from your God? who says unto you, Do unto all men as you would men should do unto you. Is it not enough that we are torn from our country and friends to toil for your luxury and lust of gain? Must every tender feeling be likewise sacrificed to your avarice? Are the dearest friends and relations, now rendered more dear by their separation from their kindred, still to be parted from each other, and thus preventing from cheering the gloom of slavery with the small comfort of being together, and mingling their sufferings and sorrows? Why are parents to love their children, brothers their sisters, or husbands their wives? Surely this is a new refinement in cruelty, which, while it has no advantage to atone for it, thus aggravates distress, and adds fresh horrors even to the wretchedness of slavery.

REVIEW QUESTIONS

1. What fears did young Olaudah Equiano experience when he was put on the slave ship?
2. What were the living conditions of slaves aboard the trading ship?
3. What did Equiano believe was the worst evil of the slave system?
4. Why did Equiano address his readers as "nominal Christians"?

---

5 ▾ The Witch Craze

In both ancient and medieval times, it was widely believed that certain persons, called sorcerers or witches, had supernatural powers over both nature and human beings and that these powers enabled witches to harm people through magical practices. Those suspected of sorcery were greatly feared and were subject to execution. In the late Middle Ages, Europeans began to view suspected witches as having entered into a pact with the devil. The church began to treat them as devil worshippers, heretics, rebels against the church, and threats to society.

During the sixteenth and seventeenth centuries, both Roman Catholics and Protestants intensified the struggle to destroy alleged witches; thousands were questioned under torture, and if convicted of witchcraft, were put to death, a sentence justified by both the Old Testament and Roman law. Belief in witches was not limited to superstitious peasants and fanatics. Prominent intellectuals, theologians, philosophers, and scientists either supported the prosecution of witches or remained silent. Few doubted the existence of witches, and forced confessions were accepted as proof of sorcery; the idea of witchcraft offered credible explanations for otherwise inexplicable human experiences. Although the number of females accused of witchcraft outnumbered the males, during these times persons of all ages, social classes, education, and occupations found themselves facing the charge of witchcraft. The regular use of torture during interrogation of suspects probably accounted for most confessions, and the alleged bizarre and sometimes lurid practices of suspects seem to have been the products of mental disorders and popular beliefs in occult powers.

Johannes Junius
A CONFESSION OF WITCHCRAFT EXPLAINED

In 1628 Johannes Junius, lord mayor of Bamberg, a city in Bavaria, Germany, was accused of practicing witchcraft. Junius denied the charge and he was tortured. He then confessed to having become a witch and was burned at the stake. The reasons for his confession are revealed in a letter he secretly sent to his daughter.

Many hundred thousand good-nights, dearly beloved daughter Veronica. Innocent have I come into prison, innocent have I been tortured, innocent must I die. For whoever comes into the witch prison must become a witch or be tortured until he invents something out of his head and — God pity him — bethinks him of something. I will tell you how it has gone with me. When I was the first time put to the torture, Dr. Braun, Dr. Kötzendörffer, and two strange doctors were there. Then Dr. Braun asks me, "Kinsman, how come you here?" I answer, "Through falsehood, through misfortune." "Hear, you," he says, "you are a witch; will you confess it voluntarily? If not, we'll bring in witnesses and the executioner for you." I said "I am no witch, I have a pure conscience in the matter; if there are a thousand witnesses, I am not anxious, but I'll gladly hear the witnesses." Now the chancellor's son was set before me . . . and afterward Hoppfen Elss. She had seen me dance on Haupts-moor. . . . I answered: "I have never renounced God, and will never do it — God graciously keep me from it. I'll rather bear whatever I must." And then came also — God in highest Heaven have mercy — the executioner, and put the thumbscrews on me, both hands bound together, so that the blood ran out at the nails and everywhere, so that for four weeks I could not use my hands, as you can see from the writing. . . . Thereafter they first stripped me, bound my hands behind me, and drew me up in the torture. Then I thought heaven and earth were at an end; eight times did they draw me up and let me fall again, so that I suffered terrible agony. . . .*

. . . When at last the executioner led me back into the prison, he said to me: "Sir, I beg you, for God's sake confess something, whether it be true or not. Invent something, for you cannot endure the torture which you will be put to; and, even if you bear it all, yet you will not escape, not even if you were an earl [high nobleman], but one torture will follow after another until you say you are a witch. Not before that," he said, "will they let you go, as you may see by all their trials, for one is just like another.". . .

And so I begged, since I was in wretched plight, to be given one day for thought and a priest. The priest was refused me, but the time for thought was given. Now, my dear child, see in what hazard I stood and still stand. I must say that I am a witch, though I am not, — must now renounce God, though I have never done it before. Day and night I was deeply troubled, but at last there came to me a new idea. I would not be anxious, but, since I had been given no priest with whom I could take counsel, I would myself think of something and say it. It were surely better that I just say it with mouth and words, even though I had not really done it; and afterwards I would confess it to the priest, and let those answer for it who

---

*This torture of the strappado, which was that in most common use by the courts, consisted of a rope, attached to the hands of the prisoner (bound behind his back) and carried over a pulley at the ceiling. By this he was drawn up and left hanging. To increase the pain, weights were attached to his feet or he was suddenly jerked up and let drop.

compel me to do it. . . . And so I made my confession, . . . but it was all a lie.

Now follows, dear child, what I confessed in order to escape that great anguish and bitter torture, which it was impossible for me longer to bear. . . .

Now, dear child, here you have all my confession, for which I must die. And they are sheer lies and made-up things, so help me God. For all this I was forced to say through fear of the torture which was threatened beyond what I had already endured. For they never leave off with the torture till one confesses something; be he ever so good, he must be a witch. Nobody escapes, though he were an earl. . . .

Dear child, keep this letter secret so that people do not find it, else I shall be tortured most piteously and the jailers will be beheaded. So strictly is it forbidden. . . . Dear child, pay this man a dollar. . . . I have taken several days to write this: my hands are both lame. I am in a sad plight. . . .

Good night, for your father Johannes Junius will never see you more. July 24, 1628.

(And on the margin of the letter he adds:)

Dear child, six have confessed against me at once: the Chancellor, his son, Neudecker, Zaner, Hoffmaisters Ursel, and Hoppfen Elss — all false, through compulsion, as they have all told me, and begged my forgiveness in God's name before they were executed. . . . They know nothing but good of me. They were forced to say it, just as I myself was. . . .

Friedrich Spee
THE JUDICIAL TRIALS OF WITCHES

This selection from the *Cautio Criminalis* (*Advice to Prosecutors,* written by a German Catholic priest, Friedrich Spee, and published anonymously in 1631) outlines the ignorance, hysteria, and systemic injustices that led thousands of unfortunate victims to torture and death. For the most part, the witch craze died out during the late seventeenth and early eighteenth centuries.

What, now, is the outline and method of the trials against witches to-day in general use? — a thing worthy [of] Germany's consideration.

I answer:. . .

1. Incredible among us Germans and especially (I blush to say it) among Catholics are the popular superstition, envy, calumnies, backbitings, insinuations, and the like, which, being neither punished by the magistrates nor refuted by the pulpit, first stir up suspicion of witchcraft. All the divine judgments which God has threatened in Holy Writ are now ascribed to witches. No longer do God or nature do aught, but witches [do] everything.

2. Hence it comes that all at once everybody is clamoring that the magistrates proceed against the witches — those witches whom only their own clamor has made seem so many.

3. Princes, therefore, bid their judges and counselors to begin proceedings against the witches.

4. These at first do not know where to begin, since they have no testimony or proofs, and since their conscience clearly tells them that they ought not to proceed in this rashly.

5. Meanwhile they are a second time and a third admonished to proceed. The multitude clamors that there is something suspicious in this delay; and the same suspicion is, by one busybody or another, instilled into the ear of the princes.

6. To offend these, however, and not to defer at once to their wishes, is in Germany a serious matter: most men, and even clergymen, approve with zeal whatever is but pleasing to the princes. . . .

7. At last, therefore, the judges yield to their wishes, and in some way contrive at length a starting-point for the trials.

8. Or, if they still hold out and dread to touch the ticklish matter, there is sent to them a commissioner [an inquisitor] specially deputed for this. And, even if he brings to his task something of inexperience or of haste, as is wont to happen in things human, this takes on in this field another color and name, and is counted only zeal for justice. This zeal for justice is no whit diminished by the prospect of gain, especially in the case of a commissioner of slender means and avaricious, with a large family, when there is granted him as salary so many dollars per head for each witch burned, besides the fees and assessments which he is allowed to extort at will from the peasants.

9. If now some utterance of a demoniac or some malign and idle rumor then current (for proof of the scandal is never asked) points especially to some poor and helpless Gaia [old woman], she is the first to suffer.

10. And yet, lest it appear that she is indicted on the basis of rumor alone, without other proofs, as the phrase goes, lo a certain presumption is at once obtained against her by posing the following dilemma: Either Gaia has led a bad and improper life, or she has led a good proper one. If a bad one, then, say they, the proof is cogent against her; for from malice to malice the presumption is strong. If, however, she has led a good one, this also is none the less a proof; for thus, they say, are witches wont to cloak themselves and try to seem especially proper.

11. Therefore it is ordered that Gaia be haled away to prison. And lo now a new proof is gained against her by this other dilemma: Either she then shows fear or she does not show it. If she does show it (hearing forsooth of the grievous tortures wont to be used in this matter), this is of itself a proof; for conscience, they say, accuses her. If she does not show it (trusting forsooth in her innocence), this too is a proof; for it is most characteristic of witches, they say, to pretend themselves peculiarly innocent and wear a bold front.

12. Lest, however, further proofs against her should be lacking, the Commissioner has his own creatures, often depraved and notorious, who question into all her past life. This, of course, cannot be done without coming upon some saying or doing of hers which evil-minded men can easily twist or distort into ground for suspicion of witchcraft.

13. If, too, there are any who have borne her ill will, these, having now a fine opportunity to do her harm, bring against her such charges as it may please them to devise; and on every side there is a clamor that the evidence is heavy against her.

14. And so, as soon as possible, she is hurried to the torture, if indeed she be not subjected to it on the very day of her arrest, as often happens.

15. For in these trials there is granted to nobody an advocate or any means of fair defense, for the cry is that the crime is an excepted one,* and whoever ventures to defend the prisoner is brought into suspicion of the crime — as are all those who dare to utter a protest in these cases and to urge the judges to caution; for they are forthwith dubbed patrons of the witches. Thus all mouths are closed and all pens blunted, lest they speak or write.

16. In general, however, that it may not seem that no opportunity of defense has been given to Gaia, she is brought out and the proofs are first read before her and examined — if examine it can be called.

17. But, even though she then denies these and satisfactorily makes answer to each, this is neither paid attention to nor even noted down: all the proofs retain their force and value, how-

***Crimina excepta* were those in which, by reason of their enormity, all restraints upon procedure were suspended. Such were treason, and, by analogy, treason against heaven — heresy, that is, and especially witchcraft. In dealing with the latter an added ground for severity was found in the belief that the Devil might aid supernaturally his allies.

ever perfect her answer to them. She is only ordered back into prison, there to bethink herself more carefully whether she will persist in her obstinacy — for, since she has denied her guilt, she is obstinate.

18. When she has bethought herself, she is next day brought out again, and there is read to her the sentence of torture — just as if she had before answered nothing to the charges, and refuted nothing. . . .

21. Then, when Gaia has thus been searched and shaved, she is tortured that she may confess the truth, that is to say, that she may simply declare herself guilty; for whatever else she may say will not be the truth and cannot be. . . .

25. So, whether she confesses [under torture] or does not confess, the result is the same. If she confesses, the thing is clear, for, as I have said and as is self-evident, she is executed: all recantation is in vain, as I have shown above. If she does not confess, the torture is repeated — twice, thrice, four times: anything one pleases is permissible, for in an excepted crime there is no limit of duration or severity or repetition of the tortures. . . .

26. If now Gaia, no matter how many times tortured, has not yet broken silence — if she contorts her features under the pain, if she loses consciousness, or the like, then they cry that she is laughing or has bewitched herself into [silence], and hence deserves to be burned alive, as lately has been done to some who though several times tortured would not confess.

27. And then they say — even clergymen and confessors — that she died obstinate and impenitent, that she would not be converted or desert her paramour [i.e., Satan] but kept rather her faith with him. . . .

30. But if, on the other hand, Gaia does not die and some exceptionally scrupulous judge hesitates to torture her further without fresh proofs or to burn her without a confession, she is kept in prison and more harshly fettered, and there lies for perhaps an entire year to rot until she is subdued.

31. For it is never possible to clear herself by withstanding and thus to wash away the aspersion of crime, as is the intention of the laws. It would be a disgrace to her examiners if when once arrested she should thus go free. Guilty must she be, by fair means or foul, whom they have once but thrown into bonds.

32. Meanwhile, both then and earlier, they send to her ignorant and headstrong priests, more [troublesome] than the executioners themselves. It is the business of these to harass in every wise the wretched creature to such a degree that, whether truly or not, she will at last confess herself guilty; unless she does so, they declare, she simply cannot be saved, nor share in the sacraments.

33. The greatest care is taken lest there be admitted to her priests more thoughtful and learned, who have aught of insight or kindliness; as also that nobody visits her prison who might give her counsel or inform the ruling princes. For there is nothing so much dreaded by any of them as that in some way the innocence of any of the accused should be brought to light. . . .

36. If, now, any under stress of pain has once falsely declared herself guilty, her wretched plight beggars description. For not only is there in general no door for her escape, but she is also compelled to accuse others, of whom she knows no ill, and whose names are not seldom suggested to her by her examiners or by the executioner, or of whom she has heard as suspected or accused or already once arrested and released. These in their turn are forced to accuse others, and these still others, and so it goes on: who can help seeing that it must go on without end?. . .

46. From all which there follows this corollary, worthy to be noted in red ink: that, if only the trials be steadily pushed on with, there is nobody in our day, of whatsoever sex, fortune, rank, or dignity, who is safe, if he have but an enemy and slanderer to bring him into suspicion of witchcraft. . . .

REVIEW QUESTIONS

1. How were apparently innocent people successfully prosecuted for practicing witchcraft?
2. Can you think of reasons why persons might be accused?
3. What legal reforms would have prevented the judicial murder of alleged witches?
4. Did Friedrich Spee offer any clue as to why the witchcraft trials eventually died out?

---

6 ▾ Justification of Absolute Monarchy by Divine Right

Effectively blocking royal absolutism in the Middle Ages were the dispersion of power between kings and feudal vassals, the vigorous sense of personal freedom and urban autonomy of the townspeople, and the limitations on royal power imposed by the church. However, by the late sixteenth century, monarchs were asserting their authority over competing groups with ever-greater effectiveness. In this new balance of political forces, European kings acted out their claim to absolute power as monarchs chosen by and responsible to God alone. This theory, called the divine right of kings, became the dominant political ideology of seventeenth- and eighteenth-century Europe.

James I
≪ TRUE LAW OF FREE MONARCHIES ≫ AND A SPEECH TO PARLIAMENT

One of the most articulate defenders of the divine right of monarchy was James VI, who was king of Scotland (1567–1625) and as James I (1603–1625) also was king of England. A scholar as well as a king, James in 1598 anonymously published a widely read book called the *True Law of Free Monarchies.* He claimed that the king alone was the true legislator. James's notions of the royal prerogative and of the role of Parliament are detailed in the following passages from the *True Law* and a speech to Parliament.

TRUE LAW
Prerogative and Parliament

According to these fundamental laws already alleged, we daily see that in the parliament (which is nothing else but the head court of the king and his vassals) the laws are but craved by his subjects, and only made by him at their [proposal] and with their advice: for albeit the king make daily statutes and ordinances, [imposing] such pains thereto as he thinks [fit], without any advice of parliament or estates, yet it lies in the power of no parliament to make any kind of law or statute, without his sceptre [that is, authority] be to it, for giving it the force of a law. . . . And as ye see it manifest that the king is over-lord of the whole land, so is he master over every person that inhabiteth the same, having power over the life and death of every one of them: for although a just prince will not take the life of any of his subjects without a clear law, yet the same laws whereby he taketh them are made by himself or his predecessors; and so the power flows always from himself. . . . Where he sees the law doubtsome or rigorous, he may interpret or mitigate the same, lest otherwise *summum jus* be *summa injuria* [the greatest right be the greatest wrong]: and therefore general laws made publicly in parliament may upon . . . [the king's] authority be mitigated and suspended upon causes only known to him.

As likewise, although I have said a good king will frame all his actions to be according to the law, yet is he not bound thereto but of his good will, and for good example-giving to his subjects. . . . So as I have already said, a good king, though he be above the law, will subject and frame his actions thereto, for example's sake to his subjects, and of his own free will, but not as subject or bound thereto. . . .

▷ In a speech before the English Parliament in March 1610, James elaborated on his exalted theory of the monarch's absolute power.

A SPEECH BEFORE PARLIAMENT

. . . The state of monarchy is the supremest thing upon earth: for kings are not only God's lieutenants upon earth and sit upon God's throne, but even by God himself they are called gods. There be three principal [comparisons] that illustrate the state of monarchy: one taken out of the word of God, and the two other out of the grounds of policy and philosophy. In the Scriptures kings are called gods, and so their power after a certain relation compared to the Divine power. Kings are also compared to fathers of families: for a king is truly *parens patriae* [parent of the country], the politic father of his people. And lastly, kings are compared to the head of this microcosm of the body of man. . . .

I conclude then this point touching the power of kings with this axiom of divinity, That as to dispute what God may do is blasphemy, . . . so is it sedition in subjects to dispute what a king may do in the height of his power. But just kings will ever be willing to declare what they will do, if they will not incur the curse of God. I will not be content that my power be disputed upon; but I shall ever be willing to make the reason appear of all my doings, and rule my actions according to my laws. . . .

Now the second general ground whereof I am to speak concerns the matter of grievances. . . . First then, I am not to find fault that you inform yourselves of the particular just grievances of the people; nay I must tell you, ye can neither be just nor faithful to me or to your countries that trust and employ you, if you do it not. . . . But I would wish you to be careful to avoid [these] things in the matter of grievances.

First, that you do not meddle with the main points of government: that is my craft . . . to meddle with that, were to lessen me. I am now an old king . . .;

I must not be taught my office.

Secondly, I would not have you meddle with such ancient rights of mine as I have received from my predecessors, possessing them *more majorum* [as ancestral customs]: such things I would be sorry should be accounted for grievances. All novelties are dangerous as well in a politic as in a natural body: and therefore I would be loath to be quarrelled in my ancient rights and possessions: for that were to judge me unworthy of that which my predecessors had and left me.

REVIEW QUESTIONS

1. According to James I, what was the role of the king within his kingdom?
2. What did James concede might limit the king's exercise of power?
3. How did James justify his claim to mitigate or suspend the law in individual cases as he saw fit?
4. What did James believe was the source of kingly supreme authority?
5. What did James see as the function of Parliament?
6. About what did James warn Parliament as being particularly objectionable to him?

---

7 ▾ Constitutional Resistance to Royal Absolutism

Despite severe persecution of suspected Protestants by the French royal authorities, Calvinism in the sixteenth century had won a sizable minority of followers among all social ranks. In 1559, a Protestant national synod met in Paris to organize a national federation of congregations modeled on Calvin's church in Geneva. Within two years, more than two thousand congregations were gathered into a national church, governed by representative assemblies (called synods) organized on a district, provincial, and national level.

The French monarchy faltered when Henry II (1547–1559) and his son Francis II (1559–1560) died within a year and a half of each other. The country was left under the rule of a ten-year-old child, Charles IX (1560–1574), whose mother, Queen Catherine de Médicis, supervised the government. The Calvinists (or Huguenots, as they were called) began openly to attack Roman Catholic churches, and a plot was uncovered to kidnap the child-king and legalize the Protestant religious reform. By spring 1562, France was engulfed in a civil war between Huguenots and Catholics that lasted on and off for some thirty years. When Henry IV (1589–1610), a Protestant, inherited the French throne, the Catholic majority resisted him until he decided to become a Catholic. In 1598, he issued the Edict of Nantes, granting limited religious toleration to the Huguenots.

Philippe du Plessis-Mornay
≪ DEFENSE OF LIBERTY AGAINST TYRANTS ≫

The Huguenots felt obliged to justify their rebellion against their rulers. Calvin had emphasized the obligation of Christians to obey the civil authorities even if persecuted, but this view became increasingly difficult to maintain in the circumstances the Huguenots faced. Out of this crisis, a number of Huguenot political writers sought to make a case for rebellion against or opposition to a king perceived to be their enemy.

Vindiciae contra tyrannos (The Defense of Liberty Against Tyrants) **was published in 1579 anonymously by Philippe du Plessis-Mornay, a Huguenot noble and councilor to Henry of Navarre, later King Henry IV. The arguments of Mornay and other Huguenot political propagandists permanently affected the development of political thought and would provide a moral basis for the English Puritans in their struggle against English kings. Mornay began his work — excerpts from which follow — by asking a question crucial in his religious age: Are subjects bound to obey princes if their orders contradict the laws of God?**

. . . The question here is whether it is permissible to resist a prince who is a violator of God's Law and is trying either to destroy His church or to obstruct its propagation. Holy Scripture, if only we accept its verdict, will provide us with an answer. For if, as may readily be shown, the Jewish people taken as a whole were not only so permitted but enjoined, none, I believe, will deny that the same must surely apply to the whole people of a Christian kingdom.

The prime consideration here is that God, in choosing the Jews from all the other nations as His chosen people, made a covenant with them that they would be God's people, which is documented throughout the Book of Deuteronomy. . . . Hence, we see that the whole people was obligated to maintain God's Law, to defend His Church, and thus to drive the idols of the gentiles [non-Jews] from the Land of Canaan, which stipulation cannot apply to individuals, but only to the people as a whole. And it is significant, in this respect, that all the tribes encamped around the Ark of the Lord,[1] so that what was entrusted to the care of all all were obliged to protect. . . .

▷ Mornay saw the relationship between ruler and ruled as based on a kind of social contract, or as he called it, a compact or covenant.

. . . We have already shown that it is God who makes kings, gives kingdoms, and selects rulers. And now we say that it is the people that establishes kings, gives them kingdoms, and approves their selection by its vote. For God willed that every bit of authority held by kings should come from the people, after Him, so that kings would concentrate all their care, energy, and thought upon the people's interests. And kings are not to think that they are of a higher nature than the rest of men and rule as men rule over cattle. Born the same as all the rest of men, they are always to remember that they were raised up from below to their estates, upon all others' shoulders, as it were, so that thereafter the burdens of the commonwealth should fall, for the most part, upon theirs. . . .

Thus, at the beginning all kings were elected. And even those who seem today to come to the throne by succession must first be inaugurated by the people. Furthermore, even if a people has customarily chosen its kings from a particular family because of its outstanding merits, that decision is not so unconditional that if the established line degenerates, the people may not select another. Indeed, even the nearest kin of the selected family are not born kings but are made such. At their birth they are considered not kings but rather candidates for kingship. . . .

THE PEOPLE IS GREATER THAN THE KING

Since kings, then, are created by the people, it seems to follow that the people as a whole is greater than the king. This is an implication of the term itself, since one who is created by another is considered his inferior. . . . And the

[1]The laws of God, given to Moses on Mount Sinai and engraved on stone tablets, were preserved in a sacred ark, or chest, also called the Ark of the Covenant.

people sets up a king as a kind of minister to the commonwealth. . . .

Let kings obey the law, then, and acknowledge law to be their queen. "I command as I will. Reason is anything I wish" is how Juvenal[2] describes not the strength, but the weakness of a woman, and it should be taken as a form of madness. And let kings not feel that subjection to the law diminishes their dignity as rulers. Law is like an instrument, divinely given, through which human societies are ordered for the best and directed to a blessed end. A king who finds obedience to the law demeaning is therefore as ridiculous as a surveyor who considers the rule and compass and other instruments of skilled geometers to be disgraceful and absurd. . . .

. . . In all properly constituted kingdoms, the king receives laws from the people, which laws he is obligated to protect and observe. If he violates or evades them, he is judged unjust.

We have already said that the creation of a king involved a double compact. The first, between God, the king, and the people. . . . The second, between the king and the people, we shall now take up.

When Saul is made king, he accepts a *lex regia*[3] as the condition of his rule. David[4] at Hebron, in the presence of God — with God, that is, as witness — enters into a covenant with all the elders of Israel, who represented the people as a whole. . . . And Josiah[5] also promises that he will observe the precepts, testimonies, and commandments included in the Book of the Covenant, and he is thus referring to the precepts of religion and justice.

In all the relevant passages, the compact is said to be made with the whole people, or the entire multitude, or all the elders, or all the men of Judah — so that we may understand, even if it were not expressly stated, that not only did the chiefs of the tribes attend, but also the lesser military chiefs and lower magistrates acting in the name of the towns, each of which covenanted of its own right with the king.

This compact created the king. For the people made the king, not the king the people. Therefore, there is no doubt that the people was the stipulator and the king the promiser. And the position of the stipulator is considered stronger under civil law. The people asked, by way of stipulation, whether the king would rule justly and according to the law. He then promised to do so. And the people, finally, replied that they would faithfully obey, as long as his commands were just. Hence, the promise of the king was absolute, that of the people was conditional; and if he does not perform, the people, by the same principle of civil law, are released from any obligation.

By the first covenant, or compact, religious piety becomes an obligation; by the second, justice. In the first the king promises to obey God religiously, in the second, to rule the people justly; in the former, to maintain God's glory, in the latter, to preserve the people's welfare. The condition in the first is: "If you will observe My Law"; the condition in the second is: "If you will render each his own." If the king does not perform the conditions of the first, God is properly the avenger, while the whole people may lawfully punish non-performance of the second.

In all legitimate governments a compact is always to be found. . . .

▷ But what if the compact between the ruler and ruled is violated by the ruler? He thus becomes a tyrant, said Mornay, a criminal who forfeits his right to the obedience of his subjects who may now exercise their right to rebel and form a new compact.

---

[2]Juvenal was a Roman satiric poet of the late first to early second century A.D.

[3]Saul, the first Hebrew king, reigned in the last part of the eleventh century B.C. *Lex regia* means the fundamental law of a kingdom.

[4]David (c. 1012–c. 972 B.C.) was the second Hebrew king. He was considered a religious model for kingship in medieval society.

[5]Josiah was a Hebrew king of Judah during the seventh century B.C. He reformed the Hebrew religion by basing his rule on the laws set down in the book of Deuteronomy.

Tyranny is like a raging fever. At the beginning it is easy to cure but difficult to detect; afterwards, it is easy to recognize but very difficult to cure. The leading men, therefore, will oppose its beginnings and overlook nothing, no matter how trivial it seems. But if the prince persists, pays no heed to repeated remonstrations, and seems only to be aiming at a situation in which he can do anything he pleases with impunity, then the fact of tyranny is proven, and anything that may be done against a tyrant may now be done to him. . . .

We have shown, moreover, that kings receive their royal status from the people; that the whole people is greater than the king and is above him; that the king in his kingdom, the emperor in his empire, are supreme only as ministers and agents, while the people is the true proprietor. It follows, therefore, that a tyrant commits felony against the people who is, as it were, the owner of his fief; that he commits *lèse majesté* [treason] against the kingdom or the empire; and that he is no better than any other rebel since he violates the same laws, although as king he merits even graver punishments. And so, says Bartolus,[6] he may be either deposed by his superior or punished under the *lex Julia*[7] for acts against the public majesty. But the superior here is the whole people or those who represent it. . . . And if things have gone so far that the tyrant cannot be expelled without resort to force, they may call the people to arms, recruit an army, and use force, strategy, and all the engines of war against him who is the declared enemy of the country and the commonwealth. . . .

The obligation between prince and people is ever reciprocal and mutual. He promises to be a just prince; they, to obey him if he is one. The people, therefore, is obligated to the prince conditionally, he to the people absolutely. If the condition is not fulfilled, the people are released, the compact voided, and the obligation nullified. The king is perjured if he rules unjustly; the people, if they fail to obey him when his rule is just. The people, however, is absolved from any charge of perjury if it publicly renounces a ruler who would rule unjustly or if it attempts, by force of arms, to evict a ruler who seeks to retain possession of the kingdom in contravention of the law.

---

[6]Bartolus of Saxoferrato (1314–1357) was a leading Italian jurist. He helped revolutionize the study of Roman law and contributed to the Italian city-states' efforts to legally defend their liberties against the Holy Roman Emperors' claims of sovereignty.

[7]*Lex Julia* was the basic Roman law on treason.

REVIEW QUESTIONS

1. According to Philippe du Plessis-Mornay, what are the sources of legitimate political authority?
2. In Mornay's view, what justified a people's disobedience of a ruler?
3. How did Mornay see Hebrew history as relevant to his political theory?
4. According to Mornay, what was the relationship between kingship and law?
5. What was Mornay's view of the origin, status, and obligations of kings?
6. How did Mornay's views on kingship compare with those of James I?

8 ▾ Radical Attack on Monarchy

The struggle against absolute monarchy in England during the early seventeenth century reached a climax during the reign of Charles I (1625–1649). The king's

failure to support the Protestant cause during the Thirty Years' War (1618–1648) on the Continent and his fervent support of the Anglican Episcopal Church earned him many enemies. Among them were the Puritans, Presbyterians, and Independents (Congregationalists), who composed an influential minority in his early Parliaments. Faced with rising costs of government, the king tried to obtain more revenues by vote of Parliament, but the parliamentarians refused to consent to new taxes unless the king followed policies they supported. After four bitter years of controversy, the king dismissed Parliament in 1629. He ruled in an increasingly absolutist manner without calling a new Parliament for the next eleven years and levied many taxes without the consent of the people's representatives.

Charles's policies collapsed in 1640 when he was compelled to summon Parliament to raise money for an army to put down a rebellion of Scottish Presbyterians. The new Parliament set forth demands for reforms of church and state, which the king refused. He claimed monarchical power and policies to be unlimited by parliamentary controls or consent.

Parliament raised its own army as civil war broke out between its supporters and those of the king. The parties were divided not only on constitutional issues but also by religious differences. Most of the Puritans, Presbyterians, and Independents supported the parliamentary cause; Anglicans and Catholics were overwhelmingly royalist. Captured by the Scottish Presbyterian rebels in 1646 and turned over to the English parliamentary army in 1647, Charles was held prisoner for two years until the Puritan parliamentary general Oliver Cromwell decided to put him on trial for treason. The king was found guilty and executed in 1649.

The Levellers
≪ AN AGREEMENT OF THE PEOPLE ≫

While Charles was still in prison, the victorious parliamentarians and their generals sought to devise a new government for England. Many Puritans and the Presbyterians hoped to retain the monarchy but to reform it suitably to assure the rights of Parliament and to establish a Presbyterian or Calvinist form of church government. But a small, radical party of Independents, called Levellers, demanded a far more radical change. In a vigorous propaganda campaign against the majority Presbyterian and Puritan factions, the Levellers demanded the abolition of both the monarchy and the House of Lords, arguing that the people should exercise their right to self-government through a parliament elected every two years by universal manhood suffrage. The Levellers also demanded complete religious freedom for all except Roman Catholics and an amnesty for all who had participated in the recent civil wars. They also asserted that Parliament itself was limited in its powers over the people, who retained all natural rights and freedoms not otherwise granted explicitly or by implication to Parliament.

The following reading comes from *An Agreement of the People,* a manifesto

drawn up by Leveller army officers in late October 1647. This document summarized their basic political beliefs about the best future constitutional system for England. In the next two years, the Levellers further refined and expanded their conception of democracy and personal freedom, but this first *Agreement* contains the core of their political ideology. Their concept of the people as the supreme source of political authority anticipated the premise of the United States Constitution.

AN AGREEMENT OF THE PEOPLE, FOR A FIRME AND PRESENT PEACE, UPON GROUNDS OF COMMON-RIGHT.

Having by our late labours and hazards made it appeare to the world at how high a rate wee value our just freedome, and God having so far owned our cause, as to deliver the Enemies thereof into our hands: We do now hold our selves bound in mutual duty to each other, to take the best care we can for the future, to avoid both the danger of returning into a slavish condition, and the chargable remedy of another war: . . . since therefore our former oppressions, and scarce yet ended troubles have beene occasioned, either by want of frequent Nationall meetings in Councell [Parliament], or by rendring those meetings ineffectuall; We are fully agreed and resolved, to provide that hereafter our Representatives be neither left to an uncertainty for the time, nor made uselesse to the ends for which they are intended: In order whereunto we declare,

I.

That the People of England being at this day very unequally distributed by Counties, Cities, & Burroughs, for the election of their Deputies in Parliament, ought to be more [fairly] proportioned, according to the number of the Inhabitants: the circumstances whereof, for number, place, and manner, are to be set down before the end of this present Parliament.

II.

That to prevent the many inconveniences apparently arising from the long continuance of the same persons in authority, this present Parliament be dissolved upon the last day of September, which shall be in the year of our Lord, 1648.

III.

That the People do of course chuse themselves a Parliament once in two yeares, viz. upon the first Thursday in every 2d. March, after the manner as shall be prescribed before the end of this Parliament, to begin to sit upon the first Thursday in Aprill following at Westminster, or such other place as shall bee appointed from time to time by the preceding Representatives; and to continue till the last day of September, then next ensuing, and no longer.

IV.

That the power of this, and all future Representatives of this Nation, is inferiour only to theirs who chuse them, and doth extend, without the consent or concurrence of any other person or persons; to the enacting, altering, and repealing of Lawes; to the erecting and abolishing of Offices and Courts; to the appointing, removing, and calling to account Magistrates, and Officers of all degrees; to the making War and peace, to the treating with forraign States: And generally, to whatsoever is not expresly, or impliedly reserved by the represented to themselves.

Which are as followeth,

1. That matters of Religion, and the wayes of Gods Worship, are not at all intrusted by us to any humane power, because therein wee cannot remit or exceed a title of what our Consciences dictate to be the mind of God, without wilfull sinne: neverthelesse the publike way of instructing the Nation (so it be not compulsive) is referred to their discretion.

2. That the matter of [compelling] and constraining any of us to serve in the warres, is against our freedome; and therefore we do not allow it in our Representatives; the rather, because money (the sinews of war) being alwayes at their disposall, they can never want numbers of men, apt enough to engage in any just cause.

3. That after the dissolution of this present Parliament, no person be at any time questioned for anything said or done, in reference to the late publike differences, otherwise then in execution of the Judgments of the present Representatives, or House of Commons.

4. That in all Laws made, or to be made, every person may be bound alike, and that no Tenure, Estate, Charter, Degree, Birth, or place, do confer any exemption from the ordinary Course of Legall proceedings, whereunto others are subjected.

5. That as the Laws ought to be equall, so they must be good, and not evidently destructive to the safety and well-being of the people.

These things we declare to be our native Rights, *and therefore are agreed and resolved to maintain them with our utmost possibilities, against all opposition whatsoever, being compelled thereunto, not only by the examples of our Ancestors, whose bloud* [blood] *was often spent in vain for the recovery of their Freedomes, suffering themselves,* through fradulent accommodations, *to be still deluded of the fruit of their Victories, but also by our own wofull experience, who having long expected, & dearly earned the establishment of these certain rules of Government are yet made to depend for the settlement of our Peace and Freedome, upon him that intended our bondage, and brought a cruell Warre upon us.*

REVIEW QUESTIONS

1. Why did the Levellers believe a radical alternative to the traditional government of England was necessary?
2. What rules did they recommend for holding future parliamentary elections?
3. What limitations did the Levellers seek to impose on the powers of future Parliaments?
4. What policy did the Levellers adopt on the relationship between church and state?
5. What was the Leveller attitude toward military conscription?
6. In what ways did the Levellers want the principle of equality to govern English society?
7. Why were the Levellers determined to abolish monarchy?

---

9 ▾ A Secular Defense of Absolutism

Thomas Hobbes (1588–1679), a British philosopher and political theorist, witnessed the agonies of the English civil war, including the execution of Charles I in 1649. These developments fortified Hobbes's conviction that absolutism was the most desirable and logical form of government. Only the unlimited power of a sovereign, said Hobbes, could contain human passions that disrupt the

social order and threaten civilized life; only absolute rule could provide an environment secure enough for people to pursue their individual interests.

Leviathan (1651), Hobbes's principal work of political thought, broke with medieval political theory. Medieval thinkers assigned each group of people — clergy, lords, serfs, guildsmen — a place in a fixed social order; an individual's social duties were set by ancient traditions believed to have been ordained by God. During early modern times, the great expansion of commerce and capitalism spurred the new individualism already pronounced in Renaissance culture; group ties were shattered by competition and accelerating social mobility. Hobbes gave expression to a society where people confronted each other as competing individuals.

Thomas Hobbes
≪ LEVIATHAN ≫

Hobbes was influenced by the new scientific thought that saw mathematical knowledge as the avenue to truth. Using geometry as a model, Hobbes began with what he believed were self-evident axioms regarding human nature, from which he deduced other truths. He aimed at constructing political philosophy on a scientific foundation and rejected the authority of tradition and religion as inconsistent with a science of politics. Thus, although Hobbes supported absolutism, he dismissed the idea advanced by other theorists of absolutism that the monarch's power derived from God. He also rejected the idea that the state should not be obeyed when it violated God's law. *Leviathan* is a rational and secular political statement. In this modern approach, rather than in Hobbes's justification of absolutism, lies the work's significance.

Hobbes had a pessimistic view of human nature. Believing that people are innately selfish and grasping, he maintained that competition and dissension, rather than cooperation, characterize human relations. Even when reason teaches that cooperation is more advantageous than competition, Hobbes observed that people are reluctant to alter their ways, because passion, not reason, governs their behavior. In the following passages from *Leviathan,* Hobbes described the causes of human conflicts.

Nature hath made men so equall, in the faculties of body, and mind; as that though there bee found one man sometimes manifestly stronger in body, or of quicker mind than another; yet when all is reckoned together, the difference between man, and man, is not so considerable, as that one man can thereupon claim to himselfe any benefit, to which another may not pretend, as well as he. For as to the strength of body, the weakest has strength enough to kill the strongest, either by secret machination, or by confederacy with others, that are in the same danger with himselfe. . . .

And as to the faculties of the mind . . . men are . . . [more] equall than unequall. . . .

From this equality of ability, ariseth equality of hope in the attaining of our Ends. And therefore if any two men desire the same thing, which neverthelesse they cannot both enjoy, they become enemies; and in the way to their End, . . . endeavour to destroy, or subdue one another. . . . If one plant, sow, build, or possesse a convenient Seat, others may probably be expected to come prepared with forces united, to dispossesse, and deprive him, not only of the fruit of his labour, but also of his life, or liberty. . . .

So that in the nature of man, we find three principall causes of quarrell. First, Competition; Secondly, Diffidence; Thirdly, Glory.

The first, maketh men invade for Gain; the second, for Safety; and the third, for Reputation. The first use Violence, to make themselves Masters of other men's persons, wives, children, and cattell; the second, to defend them; the third, for trifles, as a word, a smile, a different opinion, and any other signe of undervalue, either direct in their Persons, or by reflexion in their Kindred, their Friends, their Nation, their Profession, or their Name.

Hereby it is manifest, that during the time men live without a common Power to keep them all in awe, they are in that condition which is called Warre; and such a warre, as is of every man, against every man. . . .

▷ Hobbes then described a state of nature — the hypothetical condition of humanity prior to the formation of the state — as a war of all against all. For Hobbes, the state of nature is a logical abstraction, a device employed to make his point. Only a strong ruling entity — the state — will end the perpetual strife and provide security. For Hobbes, the state is merely a useful arrangement that permits individuals to exchange goods and services in a secure environment. The ruling authority in the state, the sovereign, must have supreme power, or society will collapse and the anarchy of the state of nature will return.

Whatsoever therefore is consequent to a time of Warre, where every man is Enemy to every man; the same is consequent to the time, wherein men live without other security, than what their own strength, and their own invention shall furnish them withall. In such condition, there is no place for Industry; because the fruit thereof is uncertain: and consequently no Culture of the Earth; no Navigation, nor use of the commodities that may be imported by Sea; no commodious Building; no Instruments of moving, and removing such things as require much force; no Knowledge of the face of the Earth; no account of Time; no Arts; no Letters; no Society; and which is worst of all, continuall feare, and danger of violent death; And the life of man, solitary, poore, nasty, brutish, and short. . . .

The Passions that encline men to Peace, are Feare of Death; Desire of such things as are necessary to commodious living; and a Hope by their Industry to obtain them. And Reason suggesteth convenient Articles of Peace, upon which men may be drawn to agreement. . . .

And because the condition of Man, (as hath been declared in the precedent Chapter) is a condition of Warre of every one against every one; in which case every one is governed by his own Reason; and there is nothing he can make use of, that may not be a help unto him, in preserving his life against his enemyes; It followeth, that in such a condition, every man has a Right to every thing; even to one another's body. And therefore, as long as this naturall Right of every man to every thing endureth, there can be no security to any man, (how strong or wise soever he be,) of living out the time, which Nature ordinarily alloweth men to live. . . .

. . . If there be no Power erected, or not great enough for our security; every man will and may lawfully rely on his own strength and art, for caution against all other men. . . .

The only way to erect . . . a Common Power, as may be able to defend them from the invasion of [foreigners] and the injuries of one another, and thereby to secure them in such sort, as that by their owne industrie, and by the fruites of the Earth, they may nourish themselves and live contentedly; is, to conferre all their power and strength upon one Man, or upon one Assembly of men, that may reduce all their Wills, by plurality of voices, unto one Will . . . and therein to submit their Wills, every one to his Will, and their Judgements, to his Judgment. This is more than Consent, or Concord; it is a reall Unitie of them all, in one and the same Person, made by Covenant of every man with every man, in such manner, as if every man should say to every man, *I Authorise and give up my Right of Governing my selfe, to this Man, or to this Assembly of men, on this condition, that thou give up thy Right to him, and Authorise all his Actions in like manner.* This done, the Multitude so united in one Person, is called a COMMON-WEALTH. . . . For by this Authorite, given him by every particular man in the Common-wealth, he hath the use of so much Power and Strength . . . conferred on him, that by terror thereof, he is inabled to forme the wills of them all, to Peace at home, and mutuall [aid] against their enemies abroad. And in him consisteth the Essence of the Commonwealth; which (to define it,) is *One Person, of whose Acts a great Multitude, by mutuall Covenants one with another, have made themselves every one the Author, to the end he may use the strength and means of them all, as he shall think expedient, for their Peace and Common Defence.*

And he that carryeth this Person, is called SOVERAIGNE, and said to have *Soveraigne Power;* and every one besides, his SUBJECT. . . .

. . . They that have already Instituted a Common-wealth, being thereby bound by Covenant . . . cannot lawfully make a new Covenant, amongst themselves, to be obedient to any other, in any thing whatsoever, without his permission. And therefore, they that are subjects to a Monarch, cannot without his leave cast off Monarchy, and return to the confusion of a disunited Multitude; nor transferre their Person from him that beareth it, to another Man, or other Assembly of men: for they . . . are bound, every man to every man, to [acknowledge] . . . that he that already is their Soveraigne, shall do, and judge fit to be done; so that [those who do not obey] break their Covenant made to that man, which is injustice: and they have also every man given the Soveraignty to him that beareth their Person; and therefore if they depose him, they take from him that which is his own, and so again it is injustice. . . . And whereas some men have pretended for their disobedience to their Soveraign, a new Covenant, made, not with men, but with God; this also is unjust: for there is no Covenant with God, but by mediation of some body that representeth God's Person; which none doth but God's Lieutenant, who hath the Soveraignty under God. But this pretence of Covenant with God, is so evident a [lie], even in the pretenders own consciences, that it is not onely an act of an unjust, but also of a vile, and unmanly disposition. . . .

. . . Consequently none of [the sovereign's] Subjects, by any pretence of forfeiture, can be freed from his Subjection.

REVIEW QUESTIONS

1. What was Thomas Hobbes's view of human nature?
2. What did Hobbes believe was the state of human society when man lived according to his nature?
3. What conclusion did Hobbes draw about the best form of government?
4. According to Hobbes, what was the essential nature of the state or commonwealth?
5. What was Hobbes's reasoning in condemning any act of rebellion against the sovereign state?
6. How did Hobbes answer those who offered religious reasons for disobeying the sovereign?
7. Why is Hobbes considered a decisive thinker for the emergence of modern political thought?

10 ▾ The Triumph of Constitutional Monarchy in England: The Glorious Revolution

The revolutionary parliamentary regime evolved not into the popular democracy envisioned by the Levellers, but into a military dictatorship headed by General Oliver Cromwell (1599–1658). After Cromwell's death, Parliament in 1660 restored the monarchy and invited the late king's heir to end his exile and take the throne. Charles II (1660–1685), by discretion and skillful statesmanship, managed to evade many difficulties caused by the hostility of those who opposed his policies. He attempted to ease religious discrimination by ending the laws that penalized dissenters who rejected the official Church of England. But the religious prejudices of Parliament forced the king to desist, and the laws penalizing both Protestant dissenters and Roman Catholics remained in force. The king's motives for establishing religious toleration were suspect, since he himself was married to a French Catholic and his brother and heir James, Duke of York, was also a staunch Catholic.

When James II (1685–1688) succeeded to the throne, he tried unsuccessfully to get Parliament to repeal the Test Act, a law that forbade anyone to hold a civil or military office or to enter a university unless he was a member in good standing of the Church of England. This law effectively barred both Catholics and Protestant dissenters from serving in the king's government. When Parliament refused to act, James got the legal Court of the King's Bench to approve his decree suspending the Test Act. The court affirmed that the king, based on his sovereign authority, had absolute power to suspend any law at his sole discretion. The prerogatives claimed by the king were seen by many as an attempt to impose absolute monarchy on the English people.

King James further roused enemies by appointing many Catholics to high government posts and by issuing his Declaration of Indulgence for Liberty of Conscience on April 4, 1687. This declaration established complete freedom of worship for all Englishmen, ending all civil penalties and discriminations based on religious dissent. Instead of hailing the declaration as a step forward in solving the religious quarrels within the kingdom, many persons viewed this suspension of the laws as a further act of absolutism because James acted unilaterally without consulting Parliament. This act united the king's enemies and alienated his former supporters.

When the king's wife gave birth to a son, making the heir to the throne another Catholic, almost all factions (except the Catholics) abandoned James II and invited the Dutch Protestant Prince William of Orange and his wife Mary, James II's Protestant daughter, to come to England. James and his Catholic family and friends fled to France. Parliament declared the throne vacant and offered it to William and Mary as joint sovereigns. As a result of the "Glorious Revolution," the English monarchy became clearly limited by the will of Parliament.

THE ENGLISH DECLARATION OF RIGHTS

In depriving James II of the throne, Parliament had destroyed forever in Britain the theory of divine right as an operating principle of government and had firmly established a limited constitutional monarchy. The appointment of William and Mary was accompanied by a declaration of rights (later enacted as the Bill of Rights), which enumerated and declared illegal James II's arbitrary acts. The Declaration of Rights, excerpted below, compelled William and Mary and future monarchs to recognize the right of the people's representatives to dispose of the royal office and to set limits on its powers. These rights were subsequently formulated into laws passed by Parliament. Prior to the American Revolution, colonists protested that British actions in the American colonies violated certain rights guaranteed in the English Bill of Rights. Several of these rights were later included in the Constitution of the United States.

And whereas the said late king James the Second having abdicated the government and the throne being thereby vacant, His Highness the prince of Orange (whom it hath pleased Almighty God to make the glorious instrument of delivering this kingdom from popery and arbitrary power) did (by the advice of the lords spiritual and temporal and divers principal persons of the commons)[1] cause letters to be written to the lords spiritual and temporal, being Protestants; and other letters to the several counties, cities, universities, boroughs and Cinque ports[2] for the choosing of such persons to represent them, as were of right to be sent to parliament, to meet and sit at Westminster upon the two and twentieth day of January in this year one thousand six hundred eighty and eight,[3] in order to [guarantee] . . . that their religion, laws and liberties might not again be in danger of being subverted; upon which letters elections having been accordingly made,

And thereupon the said lords spiritual and temporal and commons pursuant to their respective letters and elections being now assembled in a full and free representative of this nation, taking into their most serious consideration the best means for attaining the ends aforesaid, do in the first place (as their ancestors in like case have usually done) for the vindicating and asserting their ancient rights and liberties, declare:

That the pretended power of suspending of laws or the execution of laws by regal authority without consent of parliament is illegal.

That the pretended power of dispensing with laws or the execution of laws by regal authority as it hath been assumed and exercised of late is illegal.

That the commission for erecting the late court of commissioners for ecclesiastical causes and all other commissions and courts of like nature are illegal and pernicious.

That the levying money for or to the use of the crown by pretence of prerogative without grant of parliament for a longer time or in other manner than the same is or shall be granted is illegal.

That it is the right of the subjects to petition the king and all commitments and prosecutions for such petitioning are illegal.

That the raising or keeping a standing army within the kingdom in time of peace unless it be with consent of parliament is against law.

That the subjects which are Protestants may

---

[1]The lords spiritual refers to the bishops of the Church of England who sat in the House of Lords, and the lords temporal refers to the nobility entitled to sit in the House of Lords. The commons refers to the elected representatives in the House of Commons.

[2]The Cinque ports along England's southeastern coast (originally five in number) enjoyed special privileges because of their military duties in providing for coastal defense.

[3]The year was in fact 1689 because until 1752, the English used March 25 as the beginning of the new year.

have arms for their defence suitable to their conditions and as allowed by law.

That election of members of parliament ought to be free.

That the freedom of speech and debates or proceedings in parliament ought not to be impeached or questioned in any court or place out of parliament.

That excessive bail ought not to be required nor excessive fines imposed nor cruel and unusual punishments inflicted.

That jurors ought to be duly impanelled and returned and jurors which pass upon men in trials for high treason ought to be freeholders.

That all grants and promises of fines and forfeitures of particular persons before conviction are illegal and void.

And that for redress of all grievances and for the amending, strengthening and preserving of the laws parliaments ought to be held frequently.

And they do claim, demand and insist upon all and singular the premises as their undoubted rights and liberties and that no declarations, judgments, doings or proceedings to the prejudice of the people in any of the said premises ought in any wise to be drawn hereafter into consequence or example.

REVIEW QUESTIONS

1. Why did Prince William of Orange summon the Parliament to meet in January 1689?
2. What ancient rights and liberties did the Parliament assert?
3. In what ways did the Declaration of Rights repudiate specific theories of monarchy held by James I?

DIALOGO
di
GALILEO GALILEI LINCEO
AL SER.mo FERD. II. GRAN. DUCA DI
TOSCANA

The Scientific Revolution

The Scientific Revolution of the sixteenth and seventeenth centuries replaced the medieval view of the universe with a new cosmology and produced a new way of investigating nature. It overthrew the medieval conception of nature as a hierarchical order ascending toward a realm of perfection. Rejecting reliance on authority, the thinkers of the Scientific Revolution affirmed the individual's ability to know the natural world through the method of mathematical reasoning, the direct observation of nature, and carefully controlled experiments.

The medieval view of the universe had blended the theories of Aristotle and Ptolemy, two ancient Greek thinkers, with Christian teachings. In that view, a stationary earth stood in the center of the universe just above hell. Revolving around the earth were seven planets: the moon, Mercury, Venus, the sun, Mars, Jupiter, and Saturn. Because people believed that earth did not move, it was not considered a planet. Each planet was attached to a transparent sphere that turned around the earth. Encompassing the universe was a sphere of fixed stars; beyond the stars lay three heavenly spheres, the outermost of which was the abode of God. An earth-centered universe accorded with the Christian idea that God had created the universe for men and women and that salvation was the aim of life.

Also agreeable to the medieval Christian view was Aristotle's division of the universe into a lower, earthly realm and a higher realm beyond the moon. Two sets of laws operated in the universe, one on earth and the other in the celestial realm. Earthly objects were composed of four elements: earth, water, fire, and air; celestial objects were composed of the divine ether — a substance too pure, too clear, too fine, too spiritual to be found on earth. Celestial objects naturally moved in perfectly circular orbits around the earth; earthly objects, composed mainly of the heavy elements of earth and water, naturally fell downward, whereas objects made of the lighter elements of air and fire naturally flew upward toward the sky.

The destruction of the medieval world picture began with the publication in 1543 of *On the Revolutions of the Heavenly Spheres,* by Nicolaus Copernicus, a Polish mathematician,

THE FRONTISPIECE from Galileo Galilei's 1632 *Dialogue Concerning the Two Chief World Systems* depicts Aristotle, Ptolemy, and Copernicus engaged in scientific debate. (*Fotomas Index/John Freeman, London*)

astronomer, and clergyman. In Copernicus's system, the sun was in the center of the universe, and the earth was another planet that moved around the sun. Most thinkers of the time, committed to the Aristotelian-Ptolemaic system and to the biblical statements that seemed to support it, rejected Copernicus's conclusions.

The work of Galileo Galilei, an Italian mathematician, astronomer, and physicist, was decisive in the shattering of the medieval cosmos and the shaping of the modern scientific outlook. Galileo advanced the modern view that knowledge of nature derives from direct observation and from mathematics. For Galileo, the universe was a "grand book which . . . is written in the language of mathematics, and its characters are triangles, circles, and other geometric figures without which it is humanly impossible to understand a single word of it." Galileo also pioneered experimental physics, advanced the modern idea that nature is uniform throughout the universe, and attacked reliance on scholastic authority rather than on experimentation in resolving scientific controversies.

Johannes Kepler (1571–1630), a contemporary of Galileo, discovered three laws of planetary motion that greatly advanced astronomical knowledge. Kepler showed that the path of a planet was an ellipse, not a circle as Ptolemy (and Copernicus) had believed, and that planets do not move at uniform speed but accelerate as they near the sun. He devised formulas to calculate accurately both a planet's speed at each point in its orbit around the sun and a planet's location at a particular time. Kepler's laws provided further evidence that Copernicus had been right, for they made sense only in a sun-centered universe, but Kepler could not explain why planets stayed in their orbits rather than flying off into space or crashing into the sun. The resolution of that question was left to Sir Isaac Newton.

Newton's great achievement was integrating the findings of Copernicus, Galileo, and Kepler into a single theoretical system. Newton formulated the mechanical laws of motion and attraction that govern celestial and terrestrial objects.

The creation of a new model of the universe was one great achievement of the Scientific Revolution; another accomplishment was the formulation of the scientific method. The scientific method encompasses two approaches to knowledge, which usually complement each other: the empirical (inductive) and the rational (deductive). Although all sciences use both approaches, the inductive method is generally stressed more in such descriptive sciences as biology, anatomy, and geology, which rely on the accumulation of data. In the inductive approach, general principles are derived from analyzing external experiences — observations and the results of experiments. In the deductive approach, used in mathematics and theoretical physics, truths are derived in successive steps from indubitable axioms. Whereas the inductive method builds its concepts from an analysis of sense experience, the deductive approach constructs its ideas from self-evident principles that are conceived by the mind itself without external experience. The deductive and inductive approaches to knowledge, and their interplay, have been a constantly recurring feature in Western intellectual history since the rationalism of Plato and the empiricism of Aristotle. The success of the scientific method in modern times arose from the skillful synchronization of induction and deduction by such giants as Leonardo, Copernicus, Kepler, Galileo, and Newton.

The Scientific Revolution was instrumental in shaping the modern outlook. It destroyed the medieval conception of the universe and established the scientific method as the means for investigating nature and acquiring knowledge, even in areas having little to do with the study of the physical world. By demonstrating the powers of the human mind, the Scientific Revolution gave thinkers great confidence in reason and led eventually to a rejection of traditional beliefs in magic, astrology, and witches. In the eighteenth century, this growing skepticism led thinkers to question miracles and other Christian beliefs that seemed contrary to reason.

▼▼▼

1 ▼ The Copernican Revolution

In proclaiming that the earth was not stationary but revolved around the sun, Nicolaus Copernicus (1473–1543) revolutionized the science of astronomy. Fearing controversy and scorn, Copernicus long refused to publish his great work, ***On the Revolutions of the Heavenly Spheres.*** However, persuaded by friends, he finally relented and permitted publication; a copy of his book reached him on his deathbed. As Copernicus anticipated, his ideas aroused the ire of many thinkers.

Both Catholic and Protestant philosophers and theologians (including Martin Luther and John Calvin) attacked Copernicus for contradicting the Bible and Aristotle and Ptolemy, and they raised several specific objections. First, certain passages in the Bible imply a stationary earth and a sun that moves (for example, Psalm 93 says, "Yea, the world is established; it shall never be moved"; and in attacking Copernicus, Luther pointed out that "sacred Scripture tells us that Joshua commanded the sun to stand still, and not the earth"). Second, a body as heavy as the earth cannot move through space at such speed as Copernicus

suggested. Third, if the earth spins on its axis, why does a stone dropped from a height land directly below instead of at a point behind where it was dropped? Fourth, if the earth moved, objects would fly off it. And finally, the moon cannot orbit both the earth and the sun at the same time.

Nicolaus Copernicus
≪ ON THE REVOLUTIONS OF THE HEAVENLY SPHERES ≫

***On the Revolutions of the Heavenly Spheres* was dedicated to Pope Paul III, whom Copernicus asked to protect him from vilification. In the dedication, Copernicus explains his reason for delaying publication of *Revolutions*.**

To His Holiness, Pope Paul III,
Nicholas Copernicus' Preface
to His Books on the Revolutions

I can readily imagine, Holy Father, that as soon as some people hear that in this volume, which I have written about the revolutions of the spheres of the universe, I ascribe certain motions to the terrestrial globe, they will shout that I must be immediately repudiated together with this belief. For I am not so enamored of my own opinions that I disregard what others may think of them. I am aware that a philosopher's ideas are not subject to the judgement of ordinary persons, because it is his endeavor to seek the truth in all things, to the extent permitted to human reason by God. Yet I hold that completely erroneous views should be shunned. Those who know that the consensus of many centuries has sanctioned the conception that the earth remains at rest in the middle of the heaven as its center would, I reflected, regard it as an insane pronouncement if I made the opposite assertion that the earth moves. Therefore I debated with myself for a long time whether to publish the volume which I wrote to prove the earth's motion or rather to follow the example of the Pythagoreans[1] and certain others, who used to transmit philosophy's secrets only to kinsmen and friends, not in writing but by word of mouth. . . . And they did so, it seems to me, not, as some suppose, because they were in some way jealous about their teachings, which would be spread around; on the contrary, they wanted the very beautiful thoughts attained by great men of deep devotion not to be ridiculed by those who are reluctant to exert themselves vigorously in any literary pursuit unless it is lucrative; or if they are stimulated to the nonacquisitive study of philosophy by the exhortation and example of others, yet because of their dullness of mind they play the same part among philosophers as drones among bees. When I weighed these considerations, the scorn which I had reason to fear on account of the novelty and unconventionality of my opinion almost induced me to abandon completely the work which I had undertaken.

But while I hesitated for a long time and even resisted, my friends [encouraged me]. . . . Foremost among them was the cardinal of Capua [a city in southern Italy], Nicholas Schönberg, renowned in every field of learning. Next to him was a man who loves me dearly, Tiedemann Giese, bishop of Chelmno [a city in northern Poland], a close student of sacred letters as well as of all good literature. For he repeatedly encouraged me and, sometimes adding reproaches, urgently requested me to publish this volume and finally permit it to appear after being buried among my papers and lying concealed not merely until the ninth year but by now the fourth period of nine years. The same

[1]Pythagoreans were followers of Pythagoras, a Greek mathematician and philosopher of the sixth century B.C.; they were particularly interested in cosmology.

conduct was recommended to me by not a few other very eminent scholars. They exhorted me no longer to refuse, on account of the fear which I felt, to make my work available for the general use of students of astronomy. The crazier my doctrine of the earth's motion now appeared to most people, the argument ran, so much the more admiration and thanks would it gain after they saw the publication of my writings dispel the fog of absurdity by most luminous proofs. Influenced therefore by these persuasive men and by this hope, in the end I allowed my friends to bring out an edition of the volume, as they had long besought me to do. . . .

But you [your Holiness] are rather waiting to hear from me how it occurred to me to venture to conceive any motion of the earth, against the traditional opinion of astronomers and almost against common sense. . . . [Copernicus then describes some of the problems connected with the Ptolemaic system.]

For a long time, then, I reflected on this confusion in the astronomical traditions concerning the derivation of the motions of the universe's spheres. I began to be annoyed that the movements of the world machine, created for our sake by the best and most systematic Artisan of all [God], were not understood with greater certainty by the philosophers, who otherwise examined so precisely the most insignificant trifles of this world. For this reason I undertook the task of rereading the works of all the philosophers which I could obtain to learn whether anyone had ever proposed other motions of the universe's spheres than those expounded by the teachers of astronomy in the schools. And in fact first I found in Cicero that Hicetas supposed the earth to move. Later I also discovered in Plutarch[2] that certain others were of this opinion. . . .

Therefore, having obtained the opportunity from these sources, I too began to consider the mobility of the earth. . . . I thought that I too would be readily permitted to ascertain whether explanations sounder than those of my predecessors could be found for the revolution of the celestial spheres on the assumption of some motion of the earth.

Having thus assumed the motions which I ascribe to the earth later on in the volume, by long and intense study I finally found that if the motions of the other planets are correlated with the orbiting of the earth, and are computed for the revolution of each planet, not only do their phenomena follow therefrom but also the order and size of all the planets and spheres, and heaven itself is so linked together that in no portion of it can anything be shifted without disrupting the remaining parts and the universe as a whole. Accordingly in the arrangement of the volume too I have adopted the following order. In the first book I set forth the entire distribution of the spheres together with the motions which I attribute to the earth, so that this book contains, as it were, the general structure of the universe. Then in the remaining books I correlate the motions of the other planets and of all the spheres with the movement of the earth so that I may thereby determine to what extent the motions and appearances of the other planets and spheres can be saved if they are correlated with the earth's motions. I have no doubt that acute and learned astronomers will agree with me if, as this discipline especially requires, they are willing to examine and consider, not superficially but thoroughly, what I adduce in this volume in proof of these matters. However, in order that the educated and uneducated alike may see that I do not run away from the judgement of anybody at all, I have preferred dedicating my studies to Your Holiness rather than to anyone else. For even in this very remote corner of the earth where I live you are considered the highest authority by virtue of the loftiness of your office and your love for all literature and astronomy too. Hence by your prestige and

---

[2]Hicetas, a Pythagorean philosopher of the fourth century B.C., taught that the earth rotated on its axis while the other heavenly bodies were at rest. Cicero was a Roman statesman of the first century B.C. Plutarch (A.D. c. 50–c. 120) was a Greek moral philosopher and biographer whose works were especially popular among Renaissance humanists.

judgement you can easily suppress calumnious attacks although, as the proverb has it, there is no remedy for a backbite.

Perhaps there will be babblers who claim to be judges of astronomy although completely ignorant of the subject and, badly distorting some passage of Scripture to their purpose, will dare to find fault with my undertaking and censure it. I disregard them even to the extent of despising their criticism as unfounded. For it is not unknown that Lactantius,[3] otherwise an illustrious writer but hardly an astronomer, speaks quite childishly about the earth's shape, when he mocks those who declared that the earth has the form of a globe. Hence scholars need not be surprised if any such persons will likewise ridicule me. Astronomy is written for astronomers. To them my work too will seem, unless I am mistaken, to make some contribution.

[3]Renaissance humanists admired Lactantius (c. 240–c. 320), a Latin rhetorician and Christian apologist, for his classical, Ciceronian literary style.

Cardinal Bellarmine
ATTACK ON THE COPERNICAN THEORY

In 1615, Cardinal Bellarmine, who in the name of the Inquisition warned Galileo (see page 393) not to defend the Copernican theory, expressed his displeasure with heliocentrism in a letter to Paolo Antonio Foscarini. Foscarini, head of the Carmelites, an order of mendicant friars, in Calabria and professor of theology, tried to show that the earth's motion was not incompatible with biblical statements.

Cardinal Bellarmine to Foscarini (12 April 1615)

My Very Reverend Father,

I have read with interest the letter in Italian and the essay in Latin which Your [Reverence] sent me; I thank you for the one and for the other and confess that they are full of intelligence and erudition. You ask for my opinion, and so I shall give it to you, but very briefly, since now you have little time for reading and I for writing.

First, . . . to want to affirm that in reality the sun is at the center of the world and only turns on itself without moving from east to west, and the earth . . . revolves with great speed around the sun . . . is a very dangerous thing, likely not only to irritate all scholastic philosophers and theologians, but also to harm the Holy Faith by rendering Holy Scripture false. For your [Reverence] has well shown many ways of interpreting Holy Scripture, but has not applied them to particular cases; without a doubt you would have encountered very great difficulties if you had wanted to interpret all those passages you yourself cited.

Second, I say that, as you know, the Council [of Trent] prohibits interpreting Scripture against the common consensus of the Holy Fathers; and if Your [Reverence] wants to read not only the Holy Fathers, but also the modern commentaries on Genesis, the Psalms, Ecclesiastes, and Joshua, you will find all agreeing in the literal interpretation that the sun is in heaven and turns around the earth with great speed, and that the earth is very far from heaven and sits motionless at the center of the world. Consider now, with your sense of prudence, whether the Church can tolerate giving Scripture a meaning contrary to the Holy Fathers and to all the Greek and Latin commentators. Nor can one answer that this is not a matter of faith, since if it is not a matter of faith "as regards the topic," it is a matter of faith "as regards the speaker"; and so it would be heretical to say that Abraham did not have two children and Jacob twelve, as well as to say that Christ was not born of a virgin, because both are said by the Holy Spirit through the mouth of the prophets and the apostles.

Third, I say that if there were a true demonstration that the sun is at the center of the world and the earth in the third heaven, and that the sun does not circle the earth but the earth circles the sun, then one would have to proceed with great care in explaining the Scriptures that appear contrary, and say rather that we do not understand them than that what is demonstrated is false. But I will not believe that there is such a demonstration, until it is shown to me. . . . and in case of doubt one must not abandon the Holy Scripture as interpreted by the Holy Fathers. I add that the one who wrote, "The sun also ariseth, and the sun goeth down, and hasteth to his place where he arose," was Solomon [King of ancient Israel], who not only spoke inspired by God, but was a man above all others wise and learned in the human sciences and in the knowledge of created things; he received all this wisdom from God; therefore it is not likely that he was affirming something that was contrary to truth already demonstrated or capable of being demonstrated.

REVIEW QUESTIONS

1. Why did Nicolaus Copernicus fear to publish his theory about the earth's motion?
2. Why did Copernicus dedicate his work to Pope Paul III?
3. What facts encouraged Copernicus to investigate the motions of the universe's spheres?
4. What methods did Copernicus employ in investigating the earth's motion?
5. On what grounds did Cardinal Bellarmine reject the Copernican theory?

---

2 ▾ Expanding the New Astronomy

The brilliant Italian scientist Galileo Galilei (1564–1642) rejected the medieval division of the universe into higher and lower realms and proclaimed the modern idea of nature's uniformity. Learning that a telescope had been invented in Holland, Galileo built one for himself and used it to investigate the heavens. Through his telescope, Galileo saw craters and mountains on the moon; he concluded that celestial bodies were not pure, perfect, and immutable, as had been believed. There was no difference in quality between heavenly and earthly bodies; nature was the same throughout.

Galileo Galilei
≪ THE STARRY MESSENGER ≫

In the following reading from *The Starry Messenger* (1610), Galileo reported the findings observed through his telescope, which led him to proclaim the uniformity of nature.

About ten months ago a report reached my ears that a certain Fleming [a native of Flanders]* had constructed a spyglass by means of which visible objects, though very distant from the eye of the observer, were distinctly seen as if nearby. Of this truly remarkable effect several experiences were related, to which some persons gave credence while others denied them. A few days later the report was confirmed to me in a letter from a noble Frenchman at Paris, Jacques Badovere,† which caused me to apply myself wholeheartedly to inquire into the means by which I might arrive at the invention of a similar instrument. This I did shortly afterwards, my basis being the theory of refraction. First I prepared a tube of lead, at the ends of which I fitted two glass lenses, both plane on one side while on the other side one was spherically convex and the other concave. Then placing my eye near the concave lens I perceived objects satisfactorily large and near, for they appeared three times closer and nine times larger than when seen with the naked eye alone. Next I constructed another one, more accurate, which represented objects as enlarged more than sixty times. Finally, sparing neither labor nor expense, I succeeded in constructing for myself so excellent an instrument that objects seen by means of it appeared nearly one thousand times larger and over thirty times closer than when regarded with our natural vision.

It would be superfluous to enumerate the number and importance of the advantages of such an instrument at sea as well as on land. But forsaking terrestrial observations, I turned to celestial ones, and first I saw the moon from as near at hand as if it were scarcely two terrestrial radii [a measure of distance, obscure today] away. After that I observed often with wondering delight both the planets and the fixed stars, and since I saw these latter to be very crowded, I began to seek (and eventually found) a method by which I might measure their distances apart. . . .

Now let us review the observations made during the past two months, once more inviting the attention of all who are eager for true philosophy to the first steps of such important contemplations. Let us speak first of that surface of the moon which faces us. For greater clarity I distinguish two parts of this surface, a lighter and a darker; the lighter part seems to surround and to pervade the whole hemisphere, while the darker part discolors the moon's surface like a kind of cloud, and makes it appear covered with spots. Now those spots which are fairly dark and rather large are plain to everyone and have been seen throughout the ages; these I shall call the "large" or "ancient" spots, distinguishing them from others that are smaller in size but so numerous as to occur all over the lunar surface, and especially the lighter part. The latter spots had never been seen by anyone before me. From observations of these spots repeated many times I have been led to the opinion and conviction that the surface of the moon is not smooth, uniform, and precisely spherical as a great number of philosophers believe it (and the other heavenly bodies) to be, but is uneven, rough, and full of cavities and prominences, being not unlike the face of the earth, relieved by chains of mountains and deep valleys. . . .

▷ With his telescope, Galileo discovered four moons orbiting Jupiter, an observation that overcame a principal objection to the Copernican system. Galileo showed that a celestial body could indeed move around a center other than the earth; that earth was not the common center for all celestial bodies; that a celestial body (earth's moon or Jupiter's moons) could orbit a planet at the same time that the planet revolved around another body (namely, the sun).

*Credit for the original invention is generally assigned to Hans Lipperhey, a lens grinder in Holland who chanced upon this property of combined lenses and applied for a patent on it in 1608.

†Badovere studied in Italy toward the close of the sixteenth century and is said to have been a pupil of Galileo's about 1598. When he wrote concerning the new instrument in 1609, he was in the French diplomatic service at Paris, where he died in 1620.

On the seventh day of January in this present year 1610, at the first hour of night, when I was viewing the heavenly bodies with a telescope, Jupiter presented itself to me; and because I had prepared a very excellent instrument for myself, I perceived (as I had not before, on account of the weakness of my previous instrument) that beside the planet there were three starlets, small indeed, but very bright. Though I believed them to be among the host of fixed stars, they aroused my curiosity somewhat by appearing to lie in an exact straight line parallel to the ecliptic, and by their being more splendid than others of their size. Their arrangement with respect to Jupiter and each other was the following:

East * * O * *West*

that is, there were two stars on the eastern side and one to the west. The most easterly star and the western one appeared larger than the other. I paid no attention to the distances between them and Jupiter, for at the outset I thought them to be fixed stars, as I have said.‡ But returning to the same investigation on January eighth — led by what, I do not know — I found a very different arrangement. The three starlets were now all to the west of Jupiter, closer together, and at equal intervals from one another as shown in the following sketch:

East O * * * *West*

‡The reader should remember that the telescope was nightly revealing to Galileo hundreds of fixed stars never previously observed. His unusual gifts for astronomical observation are illustrated by his having noticed and remembered these three merely by reason of their alignment, and recalling them so well that when by chance he happened to see them the following night he was certain that they had changed their positions.

On the tenth of January, however, the stars appeared in this position with respect to Jupiter:

East * * O *West*

that is, there were but two of them, both easterly, the third (as I supposed) being hidden behind Jupiter. . . . There was no way in which such alterations could be attributed to Jupiter's motion, yet being certain that these were still the same stars I had observed . . . my perplexity was now transformed into amazement. I was sure that the apparent changes belonged not to Jupiter but to the observed stars, and I resolved to pursue this investigation with greater care and attention. . . .

I had now decided beyond all question that there existed in the heavens three stars wandering about Jupiter as do Venus and Mercury about the sun, and this became plainer than daylight from observations on similar occasions which followed. Nor were there just three such stars; four wanderers complete their revolutions about Jupiter. . . .

Here we have a fine and elegant argument for quieting the doubts of those who, while accepting with tranquil mind the revolutions of the planets about the sun in the Copernican system, are mightily disturbed to have the moon alone revolve about the earth and accompany it in an annual rotation about the sun. Some have believed that this structure of the universe should be rejected as impossible. But now we have not just one planet rotating about another while both run through a great orbit around the sun; our own eyes show us four stars which wander around Jupiter as does the moon around the earth, while all together trace out a grand revolution about the sun in the space of twelve years.

REVIEW QUESTIONS

1. What role did technological innovation play in advancing the possibility of new scientific knowledge?

2. What was the implication for modern astronomy of Galileo Galilei's observation of the surface of the moon? Of the moons of Jupiter?
3. What methods did Galileo use in his scientific investigations?

---

3 ▾ Critique of Authority

Galileo appealed to the Roman Catholic authorities asking them to halt their actions against the theories of Copernicus, but was unsuccessful. His support of Copernicus aroused the ire of both clergy and scholastic philosophers. In 1616, the church placed Copernicus's book on the index of forbidden books, and Galileo was ordered to cease his defense of the Copernican theory. In 1632, Galileo published *Dialogue Concerning the Two Chief World Systems* in which he upheld the Copernican view. Widely distributed and acclaimed, the book antagonized Galileo's enemies, who succeeded in halting further printing. Summoned to Rome, the aging and infirm scientist was put on trial by the Inquisition and ordered to abjure the Copernican theory. Galileo bowed to the Inquisition, which condemned the *Dialogue* and sentenced him to life imprisonment — largely house arrest at his own villa near Florence, where he was treated humanely.

Galileo Galilei
LETTER TO THE GRAND DUCHESS CHRISTINA AND ≪ DIALOGUE CONCERNING THE TWO CHIEF WORLD SYSTEMS — PTOLEMAIC AND COPERNICAN ≫

The first reading illustrates Galileo's active involvement in a struggle for freedom of inquiry many years before the *Dialogue* was published. In 1615, in a letter addressed to Grand Duchess Christina of Tuscany, Galileo argued that passages from the Bible had no authority in scientific disputes.

The second reading (from the *Dialogue*) reveals Galileo's views on Aristotle. Medieval scholastics regarded Aristotle as the supreme authority on questions concerning nature, an attitude that was perpetuated by early modern scholastics. Galileo insisted that such reliance on authority was a hindrance to scientific investigation, that it is through observation, experiment, and reason that one arrives at physical truth.

[BIBLICAL AUTHORITY]

Some years ago, as Your Serene Highness well knows, I discovered in the heavens many things that had not been seen before our own age. The novelty of these things, as well as some consequences which followed from them in contradiction to the physical notions commonly held among academic philosophers, stirred up against me no small number of professors — as if I had placed these things in the sky with my own hands in order to upset nature and overturn the sciences. They seemed to forget that the increase of known truths stimulates the investigation, establishment, and growth of the arts; not their diminution or destruction.

Showing a greater fondness for their own opinions than for truth, they sought to deny and disprove the new things which, if they had cared to look for themselves, their own senses would have demonstrated to them. To this end they hurled various charges and published numerous writings filled with vain arguments, and they made the grave mistake of sprinkling these with passages taken from places in the Bible which they had failed to understand properly, and which were ill suited to their purposes. . . .

. . . Men who were well grounded in astronomical and physical science were persuaded as soon as they received my first message. There were others who denied them or remained in doubt only because of their novel and unexpected character, and because they had not yet had the opportunity to see for themselves. These men have by degrees come to be satisfied. But some, besides allegiance to their original error, possess I know not what fanciful interest in remaining hostile not so much toward the things in question as toward their discoverer. No longer being able to deny them, these men now take refuge in obstinate silence, but being more than ever exasperated by that which has pacified and quieted other men, they divert their thoughts to other fancies and seek new ways to damage me. . . .

. . . Possibly because they are disturbed by the known truth of other propositions of mine which differ from those commonly held, and therefore mistrusting their defense so long as they confine themselves to the field of philosophy, these men have resolved to fabricate a shield for their fallacies out of the mantle of pretended religion and the authority of the Bible. These they apply, with little judgment, to the refutation of arguments that they do not understand and have not even listened to.

First they have endeavored to spread the opinion that such propositions in general are contrary to the Bible and are consequently damnable and heretical. . . . Hence they have had no trouble in finding men who would preach the damnability and heresy of the new doctrine from their very pulpits with unwonted confidence, thus doing impious and inconsiderate injury not only to that doctrine and its followers but to all mathematics and mathematicians in general. . . .

. . . They go about invoking the Bible, which they would have minister to their deceitful purposes. Contrary to the sense of the Bible and the intention of the holy [Church] Fathers, if I am not mistaken, they would extend such authorities until even in purely physical matters — where faith is not involved — they would have us altogether abandon reason and the evidence of our senses in favor of some biblical passage, though under the surface meaning of its words this passage may contain a different sense.

I hope to show that I proceed with much greater piety than they do, when I argue not against condemning [Copernicus'] book, but against condemning it in the way they suggest — that is, without understanding it, weighing it, or so much as reading it. For Copernicus never discusses matters of religion or faith, nor does he use arguments that depend in any way upon the authority of sacred writings which he might have interpreted erroneously. He stands always upon physical conclusions pertaining to the celestial motions, and deals with them by astronomical and geometrical demonstrations, founded primarily upon sense experiences and very exact observations. He did not ignore the Bible, but he knew very well that if his doctrine were proved, then it could not contradict the Scriptures when they were rightly understood. . . .

The reason produced for condemning the opinion that the earth moves and the sun stands still is that in many places in the Bible one may read that the sun moves and the earth stands still. Since the Bible cannot err, it follows as a necessary consequence that anyone takes an erroneous and heretical position who maintains that the sun is inherently motionless and the earth movable.

With regard to this argument, I think in the first place that it is very pious to say and prudent to affirm that the holy Bible can never speak untruth — whenever its true meaning is understood. But I believe nobody will deny that it is often very abstruse, and may say things which are quite different from what its bare words signify. Hence in expounding the Bible if one were always to confine oneself to the unadorned grammatical meaning, one might fall into error. . . .

. . . Now the Bible, merely to condescend to popular capacity, has not hesitated to obscure some very important pronouncements, attributing to God himself some qualities extremely remote from (and even contrary to) His essence. Who, then, would positively declare that this principle has been set aside, and the Bible has confined itself rigorously to the bare and restricted sense of its words, when speaking but casually of the earth, of water, of the sun, or of any other created thing? Especially in view of the fact that these things in no way concern the primary purpose of the sacred writings, which is the service of God and the salvation of souls — matters infinitely beyond the comprehension of the common people.

This being granted, I think that in discussions of physical problems we ought to begin not from the authority of scriptural passages, but from sense-experiences and necessary demonstrations. . . . Nothing physical which sense-experience sets before our eyes, or which necessary demonstrations prove to us, ought to be called in question (much less condemned) upon the testimony of biblical passages which may have some different meaning beneath their words. . . .

. . . I do not feel obliged to believe that that same God who has endowed us with senses, reason, and intellect has intended to forgo their use and by some other means to give us knowledge which we can attain by them. He would not require us to deny sense and reason in physical matters which are set before our eyes and minds by direct experience or necessary demonstrations. . . .

It is obvious that such [anti-Copernican] authors, not having penetrated the true senses of Scripture, would impose upon others an obligation to subscribe to conclusions that are repugnant to manifest reason and sense, if they had any authority to do so. God forbid that this sort of abuse should gain countenance and authority, for then in a short time it would be necessary to proscribe all the contemplative sciences. People who are unable to understand perfectly both the Bible and the sciences far outnumber those who do understand. The former, glancing superficially through the Bible, would arrogate to themselves the authority to decree upon every question of physics on the strength of some word which they have misunderstood, and which was employed by the sacred authors for some different purpose. And the smaller number of understanding men could not dam up the furious torrent of such people, who would gain the majority of followers simply because it is much more pleasant to gain a reputation for wisdom without effort or study than to consume oneself tirelessly in the most laborious disciplines.

▷ Galileo attacked the unquestioning acceptance of Aristotle's teachings in his *Dialogue Concerning the Two Chief World Systems — Ptolemaic and Copernican.* In the *Dialogue*, Simplicio is an Aristotelian and Salviati is a spokesman for Galileo; Sagredo, a third participant, introduces the problem of relying on the authority of Aristotle.

[ARISTOTELIAN AUTHORITY]

SAGREDO One day I was at the home of a very famous doctor in Venice, where many persons came on account of their studies, and others occasionally came out of curiosity to see some anatomical dissection performed by a man who was truly no less learned than he was a careful and expert anatomist. It happened on this day that he was investigating the source and origin of the nerves, about which there exists a notorious controversy between the Galenist and Peripatetic doctors.[1] The anatomist showed that the great trunk of nerves, leaving the brain and passing through the nape, extended on down the spine and then branched out through the whole body, and that only a single strand as fine as a thread arrived at the heart. Turning to a gentleman whom we knew to be a Peripatetic philosopher, and on whose account he had been exhibiting and demonstrating everything with unusual care, he asked this man whether he was at last satisfied and convinced that the nerves originated in the brain and not in the heart. The philosopher, after considering for awhile, answered: "You have made me see this matter so plainly and palpably that if Aristotle's text were not contrary to it, stating clearly that the nerves originate in the heart, I should be forced to admit it to be true." . . .

SIMPLICIO But if Aristotle is to be abandoned, whom shall we have for a guide in philosophy? Suppose you name some author.

SALVIATI We need guides in forests and in unknown lands, but on plains and in open places only the blind need guides. It is better for such people to stay at home, but anyone with eyes in his head and his wits about him could serve as a guide for them. In saying this, I do not mean that a person should not listen to Aristotle; indeed, I applaud the reading and careful study of his works, and I reproach only those who give themselves up as slaves to him in such a way as to subscribe blindly to everything he says and take it as an inviolable decree without looking for any other reasons. This abuse carries with it another profound disorder, that other people do not try harder to comprehend the strength of his demonstrations. And what is more revolting in a public dispute, when someone is dealing with demonstrable conclusions, than to hear him interrupted by a text (often written to some quite different purpose) thrown into his teeth by an opponent? If, indeed, you wish to continue in this method of studying, then put aside the name of philosophers and call yourselves historians, or memory experts; for it is not proper that those who never philosophize should usurp the honorable title of philosopher.

[1]Galenist doctors followed the medical theories of Galen (A.D. 129–c. 199), a Greek anatomist and physician whose writings had great authority among medieval and early modern physicians. Peripatetic doctors followed Aristotle's teachings.

REVIEW QUESTIONS

1. What was Galileo Galilei's objection to using the Bible as a source of knowledge of physical things? According to him, how did one acquire knowledge of nature?
2. What point was Galileo making in telling the story of the anatomical dissection?
3. What was Galileo's view on the use of Aristotle's works as a basis for scientific endeavors?

---

4 ▾ Prophet of Modern Science

Sir Francis Bacon (1561–1626), an English statesman and philosopher, vigorously supported the advancement of science and the scientific method. He believed that increased comprehension and mastery of nature would improve living conditions for people and therefore wanted science to encompass systematic research; he urged the state to fund scientific institutions. Bacon denounced

universities for merely repeating Aristotelian concepts and discussing problems — Is matter formless? Are all natural substances composed of matter? — that did not increase understanding of nature or contribute to human betterment. The webs spun by these scholastics, he said, were ingenious but valueless. Bacon wanted an educational program that stressed direct contact with nature and fostered new discoveries.

Bacon was among the first to appreciate the new science's value and to explain its method clearly. Like Leonardo da Vinci, Bacon gave supreme value to the direct observation of nature; for this reason he is one of the founders of the empirical tradition in modern philosophy. Bacon upheld the inductive approach — careful investigation of nature, accumulation of data, and experimentation — as the way to truth and useful knowledge. Because he wanted science to serve a practical function, Bacon praised artisans and technicians who improved technology.

Francis Bacon
ATTACK ON AUTHORITY AND ADVOCACY OF EXPERIMENTAL SCIENCE

Bacon was not himself a scientist; he made no discoveries and had no laboratory. Nevertheless, for his advocacy of the scientific method, Bacon is deservedly regarded as a prophet of modern science. In the first passage from *Redargutio Philosophiarum* (The Refutation of Philosophies), a treatise on the "idols of the theater" — fallacious ways of thinking based on given systems of philosophy — Bacon attacks the slavish reliance on Aristotle.

But even though Aristotle were the man he is thought to be I should still warn you against receiving as oracles the thoughts and opinions of one man. What justification can there be for this self-imposed servitude [that] . . . you are content to repeat Aristotle's after two thousand [years]? . . . But if you will be guided by me you will deny, not only to this man but to any mortal now living or who shall live hereafter, the right to dictate your opinions. . . . You will never be sorry for trusting your own strength, if you but once make trial of it. You may be inferior to Aristotle on the whole, but not in everything. Finally, and this is the head and front of the whole matter, there is at least one thing in which you are far ahead of him — in precedents, in experience, in the lessons of time. Aristotle, it is said, wrote a book in which he gathered together the laws and institutions of two hundred and fifty-five cities; yet I have no doubt that the customs of Rome are worth more than all of them combined so far as military and political science are concerned. The position is the same in natural philosophy. Are you of a mind to cast aside not only your own endowments but the gifts of time? Assert yourselves before it is too late. Apply yourselves to the study of things themselves. Be not for ever the property of one man.

▷ In these scattered excerpts from *The New Organon* (1620, new system of logic), Bacon criticized contemporary methods used to inquire into nature. He expressed his ideas in the form of aphorisms — concise statements of principles or general truths.

I. Man, being the servant and interpreter of Nature, can do and understand so much and so much only as he has observed in fact or in thought of the course of nature: beyond this he neither knows anything nor can do anything.

VIII. . . . The sciences we now possess are merely systems for the nice ordering and setting forth of things already invented; not methods of invention or directions for new works.

XII. The logic now in use serves rather to fix and give stability to the errors which have their foundation in commonly received notions than to help the search after truth. So it does more harm than good.

XIX. There are and can be only two ways of searching into and discovering truth. The one flies from the senses and particulars to the most general axioms, and from these principles, the truth of which it takes for settled and immoveable, proceeds to judgment and to the discovery of middle axioms. And this way is now in fashion. The other derives axioms from the senses and particulars, rising by a gradual and unbroken ascent, so that it arrives at the most general axioms last of all. This is the true way, but as yet untried.

XXIII. There is a great difference between . . . certain empty dogmas, and the true signatures and marks set upon the works of creation as they are found in nature.

XXIV. It cannot be that axioms established by argumentation should avail for the discovery of new works; since the subtlety of nature is greater many times over than the subtlety of argument. But axioms duly and orderly formed from particulars easily discover the way to new particulars, and thus render sciences active.

XXXI. It is idle to expect any great advancement in science from the superinducing [adding] and engrafting of new things upon old. We must begin anew from the very foundations, unless we would revolve for ever in a circle with mean and contemptible progress.

CIX. There is therefore much ground for hoping that there are still laid up in the womb of nature many secrets of excellent use, having no affinity or parallelism with any thing that is now known, but lying entirely out of the beat of the imagination, which have not yet been found out. They too no doubt will some time or other, in the course and revolution of many ages, come to light of themselves, just as the others did; only by the method of which we are now treating they can be speedily and suddenly and simultaneously presented and anticipated.

▷ Bacon describes those "idols" or false notions that hamper human understanding.

XXXVIII. The idols and false notions which are now in possession of the human understanding, and have taken deep root therein, not only so beset men's minds that truth can hardly find entrance, but even after entrance obtained, they will again in the very instauration [renewal] of the sciences meet and trouble us, unless men being forewarned of the danger fortify themselves as far as may be against their assaults.

XXXIX. There are four classes of Idols which beset men's minds. To these for distinction's sake I have assigned names, — calling the first class *Idols of the Tribe*; the second, *Idols of the Cave*; the third, *Idols of the Market-place*; the fourth, *Idols of the Theatre.*

XLI. The Idols of the Tribe have their foundation in human nature itself, and in the tribe or race of men. For it is a false assertion that the sense of man is the measure of things. On the contrary, all perceptions as well of the sense as of the mind are according to the measure of the universe. And the human understanding is like a false mirror, which, receiving rays irregularly, distorts and discolours the nature of things by mingling its own nature with it.

XLII. The Idols of the Cave are the idols of the individual man. For every one (besides the errors common to human nature in general) has a cave or den of his own, which refracts and discolours the light of nature; owing either to his own proper and peculiar nature; or to his education and conversation with others; or to the reading of books, and the authority of those whom he esteems and admires; or to the differences of impressions, accordingly as they take place in a mind preoccupied and predisposed or in a mind indifferent and settled; or the like. . . .

XLIII. There are also Idols formed by the intercourse and association of men with each other, which I call Idols of the Market-place, on account of the commerce and consort of men there. For it is by discourse that men associate; and words are imposed according to the apprehension of the vulgar. And therefore the ill and unfit choice of words wonderfully obstructs the understanding. Nor do the definitions or explanations wherewith in some things learned men are wont to guard and defend themselves, by any means set the matter right. But words plainly force and overrule the understanding, and throw all into confusion, and lead men away into numberless empty controversies and idle fancies.

XLIV. Lastly, there are Idols which have immigrated into men's minds from the various dogmas of philosophies, and also from wrong laws of demonstration. These I call Idols of the Theatre; because in my judgment all the received systems are but so many stage-plays, representing worlds of their own creation after an unreal and scenic fashion. Nor is it only of the systems now in vogue, or only of the ancient sects and philosophies, that I speak; for many more plays of the same kind may yet be composed and in like artificial manner set forth; seeing that errors the most widely different have nevertheless causes for the most part alike. Neither again do I mean this only of entire systems, but also of many principles and axioms in science, which by tradition, credulity, and negligence have come to be received.

But of these several kinds of Idols I must speak more largely and exactly, that the understanding may be duly cautioned.

REVIEW QUESTIONS

1. What was Francis Bacon's attitude toward the wisdom of Aristotle?
2. What intellectual attitude did Bacon believe hampered new scientific discoveries in his time?
3. What method of scientific inquiry did Bacon advocate?
4. What did Bacon assume would follow from the adoption of his new method of scientific inquiry?
5. Explain how each one of Bacon's idols hamper human understanding.

---

5 ▾ The Autonomy of the Mind

René Descartes (1596–1650), a French mathematician and philosopher, united the new currents of thought initiated during the Renaissance and the Scientific Revolution. Descartes said that the universe was a mechanical system whose inner laws could be discovered through mathematical thinking and formulated in mathematical terms. With Descartes' assertions on the power of thought, human beings became fully aware of their capacity to comprehend the world through their mental powers. For this reason he is regarded as the founder of modern philosophy.

The deductive approach stressed by Descartes presumes that inherent in the mind are mathematical principles, logical relationships, the principle of cause and effect, concepts of size and motion, and so on — ideas that exist indepen-

dently of human experience with the external world. Descartes, for example, would say that the properties of a right-angle triangle ($a^2 + b^2 = c^2$) are implicit in human consciousness prior to any experience one might have with a triangle. These innate ideas, said Descartes, permit the mind to give order and coherence to the physical world. Descartes held that the mind arrives at truth when it "intuits" or comprehends the logical necessity of its own ideas and expresses these ideas with clarity, certainty, and precision.

René Descartes
≪ DISCOURSE ON METHOD ≫

In the *Discourse on Method* (1637), Descartes proclaimed the mind's autonomy and importance, and its ability and right to comprehend truth. In this work he offered a method whereby one could achieve certainty and thereby produce a comprehensive understanding of nature and human culture. In the following passage from the *Discourse on Method,* he explained the purpose of his inquiry. How he did so is almost as revolutionary as the ideas he wished to express. He spoke in the first person, autobiographically, as an individual employing his own reason, and he addressed himself to other individuals, inviting them to use their reason. He brought to his narrative an unprecedented confidence in the power of his own judgment and a deep disenchantment with the learning of his times.

PART ONE

From my childhood I lived in a world of books, and since I was taught that by their help I could gain a clear and assured knowledge of everything useful in life, I was eager to learn from them. But as soon as I had finished the course of studies which usually admits one to the ranks of the learned, I changed my opinion completely. For I found myself saddled with so many doubts and errors that I seemed to have gained nothing in trying to educate myself unless it was to discover more and more fully how ignorant I was.

Nevertheless I had been in one of the most celebrated schools in Europe, where I thought there should be wise men if wise men existed anywhere on earth. I had learned there everything that others learned, and, not satisfied with merely the knowledge that was taught, I had perused as many books as I could find which contained more unusual and recondite knowledge. . . . And finally, it did not seem to me that our times were less flourishing and fertile than were any of the earlier periods. All this led me to conclude that I could judge others by myself, and to decide that there was no such wisdom in the world as I had previously hoped to find. . . .

I revered our theology, and hoped as much as anyone else to get to heaven, but having learned on great authority that the road was just as open to the most ignorant as to the most learned, and that the truths of revelation which lead thereto are beyond our understanding, I would not have dared to submit them to the weakness of my reasonings. I thought that to succeed in their examination it would be necessary to have some extraordinary assistance from heaven, and to be more than a man.

I will say nothing of philosophy except that it has been studied for many centuries by the most outstanding minds without having produced anything which is not in dispute and consequently doubtful. I did not have enough presumption to hope to succeed better than the others; and when I noticed how many different opinions learned men may hold on the same subject, despite the fact that no more than one of them can ever be right, I resolved to consider almost as false any opinion which was merely plausible. . . .

This is why I gave up my studies entirely as soon as I reached the age when I was no longer under the control of my teachers. I resolved to seek no other knowledge than that which I might find within myself, or perhaps in the great book of nature. I spent a few years of my adolescence traveling, seeing courts and armies, living with people of diverse types and stations of life, acquiring varied experience, testing myself in the episodes which fortune sent me, and, above all, thinking about the things around me so that I could derive some profit from them. For it seemed to me that I might find much more of the truth in the cogitations [reflections] which each man made on things which were important to him, and where he would be the loser if he judged badly, than in the cogitations of a man of letters in his study, concerned with speculations which produce no effect, and which have no consequences to him. . . .

. . . After spending several years in thus studying the book of nature and acquiring experience, I eventually reached the decision to study my own self, and to employ all my abilities to try to choose the right path. This produced much better results in my case, I think, than would have been produced if I had never left my books and my country. . . .

PART TWO

. . . As far as the opinions which I had been receiving since my birth were concerned, I could not do better than to reject them completely for once in my lifetime, and to resume them afterwards, or perhaps accept better ones in their place, when I had determined how they fitted into a rational scheme. And I firmly believed that by this means I would succeed in conducting my life much better than if I built only upon the old foundations and gave credence to the principles which I had acquired in my childhood without ever having examined them to see whether they were true or not. . . .

. . . Never has my intention been more than to try to reform my own ideas, and rebuild them on foundations that would be wholly mine. . . . The decision to abandon all one's preconceived notions is not an example for all to follow. . . .

As for myself, I should no doubt have . . . [never attempted it] if I had had but a single teacher or if I had not known the differences which have always existed among the most learned. I had discovered in college that one cannot imagine anything so strange and unbelievable but that it has been upheld by some philosopher; and in my travels I had found that those who held opinions contrary to ours were neither barbarians nor savages, but that many of them were at least as reasonable as ourselves. I had considered how the same man, with the same capacity for reason, becomes different as a result of being brought up among Frenchmen or Germans than he would be if he had been brought up among Chinese or cannibals; and how, in our fashions, the thing which pleased us ten years ago and perhaps will please us again ten years in the future, now seems extravagant and ridiculous; and I felt that in all these ways we are much more greatly influenced by custom and example than by any certain knowledge. Faced with this divergence of opinion, I could not accept the testimony of the majority, for I thought it worthless as a proof of anything somewhat difficult to discover, since it is much more likely that a single man will have discovered it than a whole people. Nor, on the other hand, could I select anyone whose opinions seemed to me to be preferable to those of others, and I was thus constrained to embark on the investigation for myself.

Nevertheless, like a man who walks alone in the darkness, I resolved to go so slowly and circumspectly that if I did not get ahead very rapidly I was at least safe from falling. Also, I did not want to reject all the opinions which had slipped irrationally into my consciousness since birth, until I had first spent enough time planning how to accomplish the task which I was then undertaking, and seeking the true method of obtaining knowledge of everything which my mind was capable of understanding. . . .

▷ Descartes' method consists of four principles that place the capacity to arrive at truth entirely within the province of the human mind. First one finds a self-evident principle, such as a geometric axiom. From this general principle, other truths are deduced through logical reasoning. This is accomplished by breaking a problem down into its elementary components and then, step by step, moving toward more complex knowledge.

. . . I thought that some other method [beside that of logic, algebra, and geometry] must be found to combine the advantages of these three and to escape their faults. Finally, just as the multitude of laws frequently furnishes an excuse for vice, and a state is much better governed with a few laws which are strictly adhered to, so I thought that instead of the great number of precepts of which logic is composed, I would have enough with the four following ones, provided that I made a firm and unalterable resolution not to violate them even in a single instance.

The first rule was never to accept anything as true unless I recognized it to be evidently such: that is, carefully to avoid precipitation and prejudgment, and to include nothing in my conclusions unless it presented itself so clearly and distinctly to my mind that there was no occasion to doubt it.

The second was to divide each of the difficulties which I encountered into as many parts as possible, and as might be required for an easier solution.

The third was to think in an orderly fashion, beginning with the things which were simplest and easiest to understand, and gradually and by degrees reaching toward more complex knowledge, even treating as though ordered materials which were not necessarily so.

The last was always to make enumerations so complete, and reviews so general, that I would be certain that nothing was omitted. . . .

What pleased me most about this method was that it enabled me to reason in all things, if not perfectly, at least as well as was in my power. In addition, I felt that in practicing it my mind was gradually becoming accustomed to conceive its objects more clearly and distinctly. . . .

▷ Descartes was searching for an incontrovertible truth that could serve as the first principle of philosophy. His arrival at the famous dictum "I think, therefore I am" marks the beginning of modern philosophy.

PART FOUR

. . . As I desired to devote myself wholly to the search for truth, I thought that I should . . . reject as absolutely false anything of which I could have the least doubt, in order to see whether anything would be left after this procedure which could be called wholly certain. Thus, as our senses deceive us at times, I was ready to suppose that nothing was at all the way our senses represented them to be. As there are men who make mistakes in reasoning even on the simplest topics in geometry, I judged that I was as liable to error as any other, and rejected as false all the reasoning which I had previously accepted as valid demonstration. Finally, as the same precepts which we have when awake may come to us when asleep without their being true, I decided to suppose that nothing that had ever entered my mind was more real than the illusions of my dreams. But I soon noticed that while I thus wished to think everything false, it was necessarily true that I who thought so was something. Since this truth, *I think, therefore I am,* was so firm and assured that all the most extravagant suppositions of the sceptics[1] were unable to shake it, I judged that I could safely accept it as the first principle of the philosophy I was seeking.

---

[1]The skeptics belonged to the ancient Greek philosophic school that held true knowledge to be beyond human grasp and treated all knowledge as uncertain.

REVIEW QUESTIONS

1. Why did René Descartes conclude that the teachings of his contemporaries did not conform to true reality?
2. Why did Descartes exclude religious truths from his rational analysis?
3. Why was Descartes skeptical about truth being found among the philosophers?
4. What eventually became Descartes' sole object of investigation?
5. What did Descartes discover about the basis of commonly held opinions?
6. What method for rational inquiry did Descartes finally choose? Why did he choose it?
7. What convinced Descartes that the skeptic philosophers were wrong?
8. Compare the methods of Descartes with those advocated by Bacon and Galileo.

---

6 ▾ The Mechanical Universe

By demonstrating that all bodies in the universe — earthly objects as well as moons, planets, and stars — obey the same laws of motion and gravitation, Sir Isaac Newton (1646–1723) completed the destruction of the medieval view of the universe. The idea that the same laws governed the movement of earthly and heavenly bodies was completely foreign to medieval thinkers, who drew a sharp division between a higher celestial world and a lower terrestrial one. In the *Principia Mathematica* (1687), Newton showed that the same forces that hold celestial bodies in their orbits around the sun make apples fall to the ground. For Newton, the universe was like a giant clock, all of whose parts obeyed strict mechanical principles and worked together in perfect precision. To Newton's contemporaries, it seemed as if mystery had been banished from the universe.

Isaac Newton
PRINCIPIA MATHEMATICA

In the first of the following passages from *Principia Mathematica,* Newton stated the principle of universal law and lauded the experimental method as the means of acquiring knowledge.

RULES OF REASONING IN PHILOSOPHY

Rule I. We are to admit no more causes of natural things than such as are both true and sufficient to explain their appearances.

To this purpose the philosophers say that Nature does nothing in vain, and more is in vain when less will serve; for Nature is pleased with simplicity, and affects not the pomp of superfluous causes.

Rule II. Therefore to the same natural effects we must, as far as possible, assign the same causes.

As to respiration in a man and in a beast; the

descent of stones [meteorites] in *Europe* and in *America*; the light of our culinary fire and of the sun; the reflection of light in the earth, and in the planets.

Rule III. The qualities of bodies, which admit neither [intensification] *nor remission of degrees, and which are found to belong to all bodies within the reach of our experiments, are to be esteemed the universal qualities of all bodies whatsoever.*

For since the qualities of bodies are only known to us by experiments, we are to hold for universal all such as universally agree with experiments; and such as are not liable to diminution can never be quite taken away. We are certainly not to relinquish the evidence of experiments for the sake of dreams and vain fictions of our own devising; nor are we to recede from the analogy of Nature, which [is] . . . simple, and always consonant to itself. We no other way know the extension of bodies than by our senses, nor do these reach it in all bodies; but because we perceive extension in all that are sensible, therefore, we ascribe it universally to all others also. That abundance of bodies are hard, we learn by experience; and because the hardness of the whole arises from the hardness of the parts, we, therefore, justly infer the hardness of the undivided particles not only of the bodies we feel but of all others. That all bodies are impenetrable, we gather not from reason, but from sensation. The bodies which we handle we find impenetrable, and thence, conclude impenetrability to be an universal property of all bodies whatsoever. That all bodies are moveable, and endowed with certain powers (which we call . . . *[inertia]*) of persevering in their motion, or in their rest, we only infer from the like properties observed in the bodies which we have seen. The extension, hardness, impenetrability, mobility, . . . of the whole, result from the extension, hardness, impenetrability, mobility, . . . of the parts; and thence we conclude the least particles of all bodies to be also all extended, and hard and impenetrable, and moveable, . . . And this is the foundation of all philosophy. . . .

Lastly, if it universally appears, by experiments and astronomical observations, that all bodies about the earth gravitate towards the earth, and that in proportion to the quantity of matter which they severally contain; that the moon likewise, according to the quantity of its matter, gravitates towards the earth; that, on the other hand, our sea gravitates towards the moon; and all the planets mutually one towards another; and the comets in like manner towards the sun; we must, in consequence of this rule, universally allow that all bodies whatsoever are endowed with a principle of mutual gravitation. . . .

Rule IV. In experimental philosophy we are to look upon propositions collected by general induction from phenomena as accurately or very nearly true, notwithstanding any contrary hypotheses that may be imagined, till such time as other phenomena occur, by which they may either be made more accurate, or liable to exceptions.

This rule we must follow, that the argument of induction may not be evaded by hypotheses.

▷ Newton describes further his concepts of gravity and scientific methodology.

[GRAVITY]

Hitherto, we have explained the phenomena of the heavens and of our sea by the power of gravity, but have not yet assigned the cause of this power. This is certain, that it must proceed from a cause that penetrates to the very centres of the sun and planets, without suffering the least diminution of its force; that operates not according to the quantity of the surfaces of the particles upon which it acts (as mechanical causes used to do) but according to the quantity of the solid matter which they contain, and propagates its virtue on all sides to immense distances, decreasing always in the duplicate portion of the distances. . . .

Hitherto I have not been able to discover the

cause of those properties of gravity from the phenomena, and I frame no hypothesis; for whatever is not deduced from the phenomena is to be called an hypothesis; and hypotheses, whether metaphysical or physical, whether of occult qualities or mechanical, have no place in experimental philosophy. In this philosophy particular propositions are inferred from the phenomena, and afterward rendered general by induction. Thus it was the impenetrability, the mobility, and the impulsive forces of bodies, and the laws of motion and of gravitation were discovered. And to us it is enough that gravity does really exist, and acts according to the laws which we have explained, and abundantly serves to account for all the motions of the celestial bodies, and of our sea.

▷ A devoted Anglican, Newton believed that God had created this superbly organized universe. The following selection is also from the *Principia.*

[GOD AND THE UNIVERSE]

This most beautiful system of the sun, planets, and comets could only proceed from the counsel and dominion of an intelligent and powerful Being. And if the fixed stars are the centers of other like systems, these, being formed by the like wise counsel, must be all subject to the dominion of One, especially since the light of the fixed stars is of the same nature with the light of the sun and from every system light passes into all the other systems; and lest the systems of the fixed stars should, by their gravity, fall on each other mutually, he hath placed those systems at immense distances from one another.

This Being governs all things not as the soul of the world, but as Lord over all; and on account of his dominion he is wont to be called "Lord God" . . . or "Universal Ruler." . . . It is the dominion of a spiritual being which constitutes a God. . . . And from his true dominion it follows that the true God is a living, intelligent and powerful Being. . . . he governs all things, and knows all things that are or can be done. . . . He endures for ever, and is every where present; and by existing always and every where, he constitutes duration and space. . . . In him are all things contained and moved; yet neither affects the other: God suffers nothing from the motion of bodies; bodies find no resistance from the omnipresence of God. . . . As a blind man has no idea of colors so we have no idea of the manner by which the all-wise God preserves and understands all things. He is utterly void of all body and bodily figure, and can therefore neither be seen, nor heard, nor touched; nor ought to be worshipped under the representation of any corporeal thing. We have ideas of his attributes, but what the real substance of any thing is we know not. . . . Much less, then, have we any idea of the substance of God. We know him only by his most wise and excellent contrivances of things. . . . [W]e reverence and adore him as his servants; and a god without dominion, providence, and final causes, is nothing else but Fate and Nature. Blind metaphysical necessity, which is certainly the same always and everywhere, could produce no variety of things. All that diversity of natural things which we find suited to different times and places could arise from nothing but the ideas and will of a Being necessarily existing. . . . And thus much concerning God; to discourse of whom from the appearances of things does certainly belong to Natural Philosophy.

REVIEW QUESTIONS

1. What method did Isaac Newton use to guide his scientific investigations?
2. What would cause Newton to reject a previously held scientific truth?

3. How did Newton's method fulfill the demands set forth both by Bacon and by Descartes?
4. What kind of universe did Newton's rules of reasoning assume?
5. Summarize Newton's argument for God's existence.
6. Is Newton's idea of God compatible with his conception of the universe? What kind of God does Newton envisage?

ENCICLO
PEDIE

The Enlightenment

The Enlightenment of the eighteenth century culminated the movement toward modernity that started in the Renaissance era. The thinkers of the Enlightenment, called *philosophes,* attacked medieval otherworldliness, dethroned theology from its once-proud position as queen of the sciences, and based their understanding of nature and society on reason alone, unaided by revelation or priestly authority.

From the broad spectrum of Western history, several traditions flowed into the Enlightenment: the rational spirit born in classical Greece, the Stoic emphasis on natural law that applies to all human beings, and the Christian belief that all individuals are equal in God's eyes. A more immediate influence on the Enlightenment was Renaissance humanism, which focused on the individual and worldly human accomplishments and which criticized medieval theology-philosophy for its preoccupation with questions that seemed unrelated to the human condition. In many ways, the Enlightenment grew directly out of the Scientific Revolution. The philosophes praised both Newton's discovery of the mechanical laws that govern the universe and the scientific method that made this discovery possible. They wanted to transfer the scientific method — the reliance on experience and the critical use of the intellect — to the realm of society. They maintained that independent of clerical authority, human beings through reason — just as Newton had uncovered the laws of nature that operate in the physical world — could grasp the natural laws that govern the social world. The philosophes said that those institutions and traditions that could not meet the test of reason, because they were based on authority, ignorance, or superstition, had to be reformed or dispensed with.

For medieval philosophers, reason had been subordinate to revelation; the Christian outlook determined the medieval concept of nature, morality, government, law, and life's purpose. During the Renaissance and Scientific Revolution, reason increasingly asserted its autonomy. For example, Machiavelli rejected the principle that politics should be based on Christian teachings; he recognized no higher world as the source of a higher truth. Galileo held that on questions regarding nature, one should trust to observation, experimentation, and mathematical reasoning and should not rely on Scripture. Descartes had rejected reliance on past

MARQUISE DE POMPADOUR, mistress of the French king Louis XV, by Maurice Quentin de La Tour (1704–1788). Intellectually curious, she was interested in the philosophes' thought and encouraged the *Encyclopedia*'s writers — a volume of the work is by her side. (*Giraudon/Art Resource, N.Y.*)

authority and maintained that through thought alone one could attain knowledge that has absolute certainty. Agreeing with Descartes that the mind is self-sufficient, the philosophes rejected the guidance of revelation and its priestly interpreters. They believed that through the use of reason, individuals could comprehend and reform society.

Eighteenth-century thinkers were particularly influenced by John Locke's advocacy of religious toleration, his reliance on experience as the source of knowledge, and his concern for individual liberty. In his first *Letter Concerning Toleration,* Locke declared that Christians who persecute others in the name of their religion violate Christ's teachings. In his *Essay Concerning Human Understanding,* a work of immense significance in the history of philosophy, Locke argued that human beings are not born with innate ideas (the idea of God and principles of good and evil, for example) divinely implanted in their minds. Rather, said Locke, the human mind at birth is a blank slate upon which are imprinted sensations derived from contact with the world. These sensations, combined with the mind's reflections on them, are the source of ideas. In effect, knowledge is derived from experience. In the tradition of Francis Bacon, Locke's epistemology (theory of knowledge) implied that people should not dwell on insoluble questions, particularly sterile theological issues, but should seek practical knowledge that promotes human happiness and enlightens human beings and gives them control over their environment. Locke's empiricism, which aspired to useful knowledge and stimulated an interest in political and ethical questions that focused on human concerns, helped to mold the utilitarian and reformist spirit of the Enlightenment. If there are no innate ideas, said the philosophes, then human beings are not born with original sin, contrary to what Christians believed. All that individuals are derive from their particular experiences. If people are provided with a proper environment and education, they will become intelligent and productive citizens. This was how the reform-minded philosophes interpreted Locke. They preferred to believe that evil stemmed from faulty institutions and poor education, both of which could be remedied, rather than from a defective human nature. Locke himself favored this outlook. In his treatise on education, he wrote, "Of all the men we meet with, nine . . . of ten are what they are, good or evil, useful or not, by their education."

The Enlightenment philosophes articulated basic principles of the modern outlook: confidence in the self-sufficiency of the human mind, belief that individuals possess natural rights that governments should not violate, and the desire to reform society in accordance with rational principles. Their views influenced the reformers of the French Revolution and the Founding Fathers of the United States.

I ▾ The Enlightenment Outlook

The critical use of the intellect was the central principle of the Enlightenment. The philosophes rejected beliefs and traditions that seemed to conflict with reason and attacked clerical and political authorities for interfering with the free use of the intellect.

Immanuel Kant
≪ WHAT IS ENLIGHTENMENT? ≫

The German philosopher Immanuel Kant (1724–1804) is a giant in the history of modern philosophy. Several twentieth-century philosophic movements have their origins in Kantian thought, and many issues raised by Kant still retain their importance. For example, in *Metaphysical Foundations of Morals* (1785), Kant set forth the categorical imperative that remains a crucial principle in moral philosophy. Kant asserted that when confronted with a moral choice, people should ask themselves: "Canst thou also will that thy maxim should be a universal law?" By this, Kant meant that people should ponder whether they would want the moral principle underlying their action to be elevated to a universal law that would govern others in similar circumstances. If they concluded that it should not, then the maxim should be rejected and the action avoided.

Kant valued the essential ideals of the Enlightenment and viewed the French Revolution, which put these ideals into law, as the triumph of liberty over despotism. In an essay entitled "What Is Enlightenment?" (1784), he contended that the Enlightenment marked a new way of thinking and eloquently affirmed the Enlightenment's confidence in and commitment to reason.

Enlightenment is man's leaving his self-caused immaturity. Immaturity is the incapacity to use one's intelligence without the guidance of another. Such immaturity is self-caused if it is not caused by lack of intelligence, but by lack of determination and courage to use one's intelligence without being guided by another. *Sapere Aude!* [Dare to know!] Have the courage to use your own intelligence! is therefore the motto of the enlightenment.

Through laziness and cowardice a large part of mankind, even after nature has freed them from alien guidance, gladly remain immature. It is because of laziness and cowardice that it is so easy for others to usurp the role of guardians. It is so comfortable to be a minor! If I have a book which provides meaning for me, a pastor who has conscience for me, a doctor who will judge my diet for me and so on, then I do not need to exert myself. I do not have any need to think; if I can pay, others will take over the tedious job for me. The guardians who have kindly undertaken the supervision will see to it that by far the largest part of mankind, including the entire "beautiful sex," should consider the step into maturity, not only as difficult but as very dangerous.

After having made their domestic animals dumb and having carefully prevented these quiet creatures from daring to take any step beyond the lead-strings to which they have fastened them, these guardians then show them the danger which threatens them, should they attempt to walk alone. Now this danger is not really so very great; for they would presumably learn to walk after some stumbling. However, an example of this kind intimidates and frightens people out of all further attempts.

It is difficult for the isolated individual to work himself out of the immaturity which has become almost natural for him. He has even become fond of it and for the time being is incapable of employing his own intelligence, because he has never been allowed to make the attempt. Statutes and formulas, these mechanical tools of a serviceable use, or rather misuse, of his natural faculties, are the ankle-chains of a continuous immaturity. Whoever threw it off would make an uncertain jump over the smallest trench because he is not accustomed to such free movement. Therefore there are only a few who have pursued a firm path and have succeeded in escaping from immaturity by their own cultivation of the mind.

But it is more nearly possible for a public to enlighten itself: this is even inescapable if only the public is given its freedom. For there will always be some people who think for themselves, even among the self-appointed guardians of the great mass who, after having thrown off the yoke of immaturity themselves, will spread about them the spirit of a reasonable estimate of their own value and of the need for every man to think for himself. . . . [A] public can only arrive at enlightenment slowly. Through revolution, the abandonment of personal despotism may be engendered and the end of profit-seeking and domineering oppression may occur, but never a true reform of the state of mind. Instead, new prejudices, just like the old ones, will serve as the guiding reins of the great, unthinking mass. . . .

All that is required for this enlightenment is *freedom*; and particularly the least harmful of all that may be called freedom, namely, the freedom for man to make *public use* of his reason in all matters. But I hear people clamor on all sides: Don't argue! The officer says: Don't argue, drill! The tax collector: Don't argue, pay! The pastor: Don't argue, believe! . . . Here we have restrictions on freedom everywhere. Which restriction is hampering enlightenment, and which does not, or even promotes it? I answer: The *public use* of a man's reason must be free at all times, and this alone can bring enlightenment among men. . . .

I mean by the public use of one's reason, the use which a scholar makes of it before the entire reading public. . . .

The question may now be put: Do we live at present in an enlightened age? The answer is: No, but in an age of enlightenment. Much still prevents men from being placed in a position or even being placed into position to use their own minds securely and well in matters of religion. But we do have very definite indications that this field of endeavor is being opened up for men to work freely and reduce gradually the hindrances preventing a general enlightenment and an escape from self-caused immaturity.

REVIEW QUESTIONS

1. Why did Immanuel Kant believe most persons never reached maturity?
2. What did Kant mean by the term *enlightenment*? By *freedom*?
3. What was Kant's explanation for the existence of the "guardians" in Western society?
4. What did Kant think to be the function of statutes and customs?

5. How did Kant propose to increase the maturity of individuals?
6. For Kant, what role did public liberties play in the progress of enlightenment?
7. What are the political implications of Kant's views?

2 ▾ Political Liberty

John Locke (1632–1704), a British statesman, philosopher, and political theorist, was a principal source of the Enlightenment. Locke's political philosophy as formulated in the *Two Treatises on Government* (1690) complements his theory of knowledge, described in the introduction to this chapter; both were rational and secular attempts to understand and improve the human condition. The Lockean spirit pervades the American Declaration of Independence, the Constitution, and the Bill of Rights and is the basis of the liberal tradition that aims to protect individual liberty from despotic state authority.

Viewing human beings as brutish and selfish, Thomas Hobbes (see Chapter 1) had prescribed a state with unlimited power; only in this way, he said, could people be protected from each other and civilized life preserved. Locke, regarding people as essentially good and humane, developed a conception of the state differing fundamentally from Hobbes's. Locke held that human beings are born with natural rights of life, liberty, and property; they establish the state to protect these rights. Consequently, neither executive nor legislature, neither king nor assembly has the authority to deprive individuals of their natural rights. Whereas Hobbes justified absolute monarchy, Locke explicitly endorsed constitutional government in which the power to govern derives from the consent of the governed and the state's authority is limited by agreement.

John Locke
≪ SECOND TREATISE ON GOVERNMENT ≫

Locke said that originally, in establishing a government, human beings had never agreed to surrender their natural rights to any state authority. The state's founders intended the new polity to preserve these natural rights and to implement the people's will. Therefore, as the following passage from Locke's *Second Treatise on Government* illustrates, the power exercised by magistrates cannot be absolute or arbitrary.

. . . *Political power* is that power, which every man having in the state of nature, has given up into the hands of the society, and therein to the governors, whom the society hath set over itself, with this express or tacit trust, that it shall be employed for their good, and the preservation of their property: now this *power,* which every man has *in the state of nature,* and which he parts with to the society in all such cases where the society can secure him, is to use such means, for the preserving of his own property, as he thinks good, and nature allows him; and to punish the breach of the law of nature in others, so as (according to the best of his reason) may most conduce to the preservation of himself, and the rest of mankind. So that the *end and measure of this power,* when in every man's hands in the state of nature, being the preservation of all of his society, that is, all mankind in general, it can have no other *end or measure,* when in the hands of the magistrate, but to preserve the members of that society in their lives, liberties, and possessions; and so cannot be an absolute, arbitrary power over their lives and fortunes, which are as much as possible to be preserved; but a *power to make laws,* and annex such *penalties* to them, as may tend to the preservation of the whole, by cutting off those parts, and those only, which are so corrupt, that they threaten the sound and healthy, without which no severity is lawful. And this *power has its original only from compact,* and agreement, and the mutual consent of those who make up the community. . . .

These are the *bounds,* which the trust, that is put in them by the society, and the law of God and nature, have *set to the legislative* power of every common-wealth, in all forms of government.

First, They are to govern by *promulgated established laws,* not to be varied in particular cases, but to have one rule for rich and poor, for the favourite at court, and the country man at plough.

Secondly, These *laws* also ought to be designed *for* no other end ultimately, but *the good of the people.*

Thirdly, They must *not raise taxes* on the *property of the people, without the consent of the people,* given by themselves, or their deputies. And this properly concerns only such governments, where the *legislative* is always in being, or at least where the people have not reserved any part of the legislative to deputies, to be from time to time chosen by themselves.

Fourthly, The *legislative* neither must *nor can transfer the power of making laws* to any body else, or place it any where, but where the people have. . . .

▷ If government fails to fulfill the end for which it was established — the preservation of the individual's right to life, liberty, and property — the people have a right to dissolve that government.

. . . The *legislative acts against the trust* reposed in them, when they endeavour to invade the property of the subject, and to make themselves, or any part of the community, masters, or arbitrary disposers of the lives, liberties, or fortunes of the people.

The reason why men enter into society, is the preservation of their property; and the end why they chuse and authorize a legislative, is, that there may be laws made, and rules set, as guards and fences to the properties of all the members of the society, to limit the power, and moderate the dominion of every part and member of the society: for since it can never be supposed to be the will of the society, that the legislative should have a power to destroy that which every one designs to secure, by entering into society, and for which the people submitted themselves to legislators of their own making; whenever the *legislators endeavour to take away, and destroy the property of the people,* or to reduce them to slavery under arbitrary power, they put themselves into a state of war with the people, who are thereupon absolved from any farther obedience, and are left to the common refuge, which God hath provided for all men, against force and violence. Whensoever therefore the *legislative* shall transgress this fundamental rule of society; and either by ambition, fear, folly or corruption, *endeavour to grasp* themselves, *or put into the hands of any other, an absolute power* over the lives, liberties, and estates of the people; by this breach of trust they *forfeit the power* the people had put into their hands for quite contrary ends, and it devolves to the people, who have a right to resume their original liberty, and, by the establishment of a new legislative, (such as they shall think fit) provide for their own safety and security, which is the end for which they are in society. What I have said here, concerning the legislative in general, holds true also concerning the supreme executor, who having a double trust put in him, both to have a part in the legislative, and the supreme execution of the law, acts against both, when he goes about to set up his own arbitrary will as the law of the society. He *acts* also *contrary to his trust,* when he either employs the force, treasure, and offices of the society, to corrupt the *representatives,* and gain them to his purposes; or openly pre-engages the *electors,* and prescribes to their choice, such, whom he has, by sollicitations, threats, promises, or otherwise, won to his designs; and employs them to bring in such, who have promised beforehand what to vote, and what to enact. . . .

▷ Locke responds to the charge that his theory will produce "frequent rebellion." Indeed, says Locke, the true rebels are the magistrates who, acting contrary to the trust granted them, violate the people's rights.

. . . Such *revolutions happen* not upon every little mismanagement in public affairs. *Great mistakes* in the ruling part, many wrong and inconvenient laws, and all the *slips* of human frailty, will be *borne by the people* without mutiny or murmur. But if a long train of abuses, prevarications and artifices, all tending the same way, make the design visible to the people, and they cannot but feel what they lie under, and see whither they are going; it is not to be wondered at, that they should then rouze themselves, and endeavour to put the rule into such hands which may secure to them the ends for which government was at first erected. . . .

. . . I answer, that *this doctrine* of a power in the people of providing for their safety a-new, by a new legislative, when their legislators have acted contrary to their trust, by invading their property, is *the best {de}fence against rebellion,* and the probablest means to hinder it: for *rebellion* being an opposition, not to persons, but authority, which is founded only in the constitutions and laws of the government; those, whoever they be, who by force break through, and by force justify their violation of them, are truly and properly *rebels*: for when men, by entering into society and civil government, have excluded force, and introduced laws for the preservation of property, peace, and unity amongst themselves, those who set up force again in opposition to the laws, do *rebellare,* that is, bring back again the state of war, and are properly rebels: which they who are in power, (by the pretence they have to authority, the temptation of force they have in their hands, and the flattery of those about them) being likeliest to do; the properest way to prevent the evil, is to shew them the danger and injustice of it, who are under the greatest temptation to run into it.

The end of government is the good of mankind; and which is *best for mankind,* that the people should always be exposed to the boundless will of tyranny, or that the rulers should be sometimes liable to be opposed, when they grow exorbitant in the use of their power, and employ it for the destruction, and not the preservation of the properties of their people?

Thomas Jefferson
DECLARATION OF INDEPENDENCE

Written by Thomas Jefferson (1743–1826) to justify the American colonists' break with Britain, the Declaration of Independence enumerated principles that were quite familiar to English statesmen and intellectuals. The preamble to the Declaration, excerpted below, articulated clearly Locke's philosophy of natural rights. Locke had viewed life, liberty, and property as the individual's essential natural rights; Jefferson substituted the "pursuit of happiness" for property.

A DECLARATION BY THE REPRESENTATIVES OF THE UNITED STATES OF AMERICA, IN GENERAL CONGRESS ASSEMBLED.

When in the Course of human Events, it becomes necessary for one People to dissolve the Political Bands which have connected them with another, and to assume among the Powers of the Earth, the separate and equal Station to which the Laws of Nature and of Nature's God entitle them, a decent Respect to the Opinions of Mankind requires that they should declare the causes which impel them to the Separation.

We hold these Truths to be self-evident, that all Men are created equal, that they are endowed by their Creator with certain unalienable Rights, that among these are Life, Liberty, and the Pursuit of Happiness — That to secure these Rights, Governments are instituted among Men, deriving their just Powers from the Consent of the Governed, That whenever any Form of Government becomes destructive of these Ends, it is the Right of the People to alter or to abolish it, and to institute new Government, laying its Foundation on such Principles, and organizing its Powers in such Form, as to them shall seem most likely to effect their Safety and Happiness. Prudence, indeed, will dictate that Governments long established should not be changed for light and transient Causes; and accordingly all Experience hath shewn, that Mankind are more disposed to suffer, while Evils are sufferable, than to right themselves by abolishing the Forms to which they are accustomed. But when a long Train of Abuses and Usurpations, pursuing invariably the same Object, evinces a Design to reduce them under absolute Despotism, it is their right, it is their duty, to throw off such Government, and to provide new Guards for their future Security. Such has been the patient Sufferance of these Colonies; and such is now the Necessity which constrains them to alter their former Systems of Government. The History of the present King of Great-Britain is a History of repeated Injuries and Usurpations, all having in direct Object the Establishment of an absolute Tyranny over these States. . . .

REVIEW QUESTIONS

1. According to John Locke, what were the purposes for which governments might legitimately be formed?
2. According to Locke's theory, where did sovereignty rest in the state of nature? Where did it reside after governments were formed?
3. According to Locke, what limits bound legislators in any government?
4. What did Locke believe were the rights of the people faced with a government that failed to protect their lives, liberties, and possessions?
5. Compare the views of Locke with those of Thomas Hobbes (in the section introduction) regarding human nature, political authority, and rebellion.
6. Compare Locke's theory of natural rights with the principles stated in the American Declaration of Independence.

---

3 ▾ Attack on the Old Regime

François Marie Arouet (1694–1778), known to the world as Voltaire, was the recognized leader of the French Enlightenment. Few of the philosophes had a better mind, and none had a sharper wit. A relentless critic of the Old Regime

(the social structure in prerevolutionary France), Voltaire attacked superstition, religious fanaticism and persecution, censorship, and other abuses of eighteenth-century French society. Spending more than two years in Great Britain, Voltaire acquired a great admiration for English liberty, toleration, commerce, and science. In *Letters Concerning the English Nation* (1733), he drew unfavorable comparisons between a progressive Britain and a reactionary France.

Voltaire's angriest words were directed against established Christianity, to which he attributed many of the ills of modern society. Voltaire regarded Christianity as "the Christ-worshiping superstition" that someday would be destroyed "by the weapons of reason." He rejected revelation and the church hierarchy and was repulsed by Christian intolerance, but he accepted Christian morality and believed in God as the prime mover who set the universe in motion.

Voltaire
A PLEA FOR TOLERANCE AND REASON

The following passages compiled from Voltaire's works — grouped according to topic — provide insight into the outlook of the philosophes. The excerpts come from sources that include his *Candide* (1759), *Treatise on Tolerance* (1763), and *The Philosophical Dictionary* (1764).

TOLERANCE

It does not require any great art or studied elocution to prove that Christians ought to tolerate one another. I will go even further and say that we ought to look upon all men as our brothers. What! call a Turk, a Jew, and a Siamese, my brother? Yes, of course; for are we not all children of the same father, and the creatures of the same God?

———

What is tolerance? . . . We are all full of weakness and errors; let us mutually pardon our follies. This is the last law of nature. . . .

It is clear that every private individual who persecutes a man, his brother, because he is not of the same opinion, is a monster. . . .

Of all religions, the Christian ought doubtless to inspire the most tolerance, although hitherto the Christians have been the most intolerant of all men.

———

. . . Tolerance has never brought civil war; intolerance has covered the earth with carnage. . . .

What! Is each citizen to be permitted to believe and to think that which his reason rightly or wrongly dictates? He should indeed, provided that he does not disturb the public order; for it is not contingent on man to believe or not to believe; but it is contingent on him to respect the usages of his country; and if you say that it is a crime not to believe in the dominant religion, you accuse then yourself the first Christians, your ancestors, and you justify those whom you accuse of having martyred them.

You reply that there is a great difference, that all religions are the work of men, and that the Apostolic Roman Catholic Church is alone the work of God. But in good faith, ought our religion because it is divine reign through hate, violence, exiles, usurpation of property, prisons, tortures, murders, and thanksgivings to God for these murders? The more the Christian religion is divine, the less it pertains to man to require it; if God made it, God will sustain it without you. You know that intolerance produces only hypocrites or rebels; what distressing alternatives! In short, do you want to sustain through executioners the religion of a God whom executioners have put to death and who taught only gentleness and patience?

I shall never cease, my dear sir, to preach tolerance from the housetops, despite the complaints of your priests and the outcries of ours, until persecution is no more. The progress of reason is slow, the roots of prejudice lie deep. Doubtless, I shall never see the fruits of my efforts, but they are seeds which may one day germinate.

DOGMA

. . . Is Jesus the Word? If He be the Word, did He emanate from God in time or before time? If He emanated from God, is He co-eternal and consubstantial with Him, or is He of a similar substance? Is He distinct from Him, or is He not? Is He made or begotten? Can He beget in His turn? Has He paternity? or productive virtue without paternity? Is the Holy Ghost made? or begotten? or produced? or proceeding from the Father? or proceeding from the Son? or proceeding from both? Can He beget? can He produce? is His hypostasis consubstantial with the hypostasis of the Father and the Son? and how is it that, having the same nature — the same essence as the Father and the Son, He cannot do the same things done by these persons who are Himself?

Assuredly, I understand nothing of this; no one has ever understood any of it, and that is why we have slaughtered one another.

The Christians tricked, cavilled, hated, and excommunicated one another, for some of these dogmas inaccessible to human intellect.

FANATICISM

Fanaticism is to superstition what delirium is to fever, what rage is to anger. He who has ecstasies and visions, who takes dreams for realities, and his own imaginations for prophecies is an enthusiast; he who reinforces his madness by murder is a fanatic. . . .

The most detestable example of fanaticism is that exhibited on the night of St. Bartholomew,[1] when the people of Paris rushed from house to house to stab, slaughter, throw out of the window, and tear in pieces their fellow citizens who did not go to mass.

There are some cold-blooded fanatics; such as those judges who sentence men to death for no other crime than that of thinking differently from themselves. . . .

Once fanaticism has infected a brain, the disease is almost incurable. I have seen convulsionaries who, while speaking of the miracles of Saint Paris [a fourth-century Italian bishop], gradually grew heated in spite of themselves. Their eyes became inflamed, their limbs shook, fury disfigured their face, and they would have killed anyone who contradicted them.

There is no other remedy for this epidemic malady than that philosophical spirit which, extending itself from one to another, at length softens the manners of men and prevents the access of the disease. For when the disorder has made any progress, we should, without loss of time, flee from it, and wait till the air has become purified.

PERSECUTION

What is a persecutor? He whose wounded pride and furious fanaticism arouse princes and magistrates against innocent men, whose only crime is that of being of a different opinion. "Impudent man! you have worshipped God; you have preached and practiced virtue; you have served man; you have protected the orphan, have helped the poor; you have changed deserts, in which slaves dragged on a miserable existence, into fertile lands peopled by happy families; but I have discovered that you despise me, and have

[1]St. Bartholomew refers to the day when the populace of Paris, instigated by King Charles IX at his mother's urging, began a week-long slaughter of Protestants that began on August 24, 1572.

never read my controversial work. You know that I am a rogue; that I have forged G[od]'s signature, that I have stolen. You might tell these things; I must anticipate you. I will, therefore, go to the confessor [spiritual counselor] of the prime minister, or the magistrate; I will show them, with outstretched neck and twisted mouth, that you hold an erroneous opinion in relation to the cells in which the Septuagint was studied; that you have even spoken disrespectfully ten years ago of Tobit's dog,[2] which you asserted to have been a spaniel, while I proved that it was a greyhound. I will denounce you as the enemy of God and man!" Such is the language of the persecutor; and if precisely these words do not issue from his lips, they are engraven on his heart with the pointed steel of fanaticism steeped in the bitterness of envy. . . .

O God of mercy! If any man can resemble that evil being who is described as ceaselessly employed in the destruction of your works, is it not the persecutor?

SUPERSTITION

In 1749 a woman was burned in the Bishopric of Würzburg [a city in central Germany], convicted of being a witch. This is an extraordinary phenomenon in the age in which we live. Is it possible that people who boast of their reformation and of trampling superstition under foot, who indeed supposed that they had reached the perfection of reason, could nevertheless believe in witchcraft, and this more than a hundred years after the so-called reformation of their reason?

In 1652 a peasant woman named Michelle Chaudron, living in the little territory of Geneva [a major city in Switzerland], met the devil going out of the city. The devil gave her a kiss, received her homage, and imprinted on her upper lip and right breast the mark that he customarily bestows on all whom he recognizes as his favorites. This seal of the devil is a little mark which makes the skin insensitsive, as all the demonographical jurists of those times affirm.

The devil ordered Michelle Chaudron to bewitch two girls. She obeyed her master punctually. The girls' parents accused her of witchcraft before the law. The girls were questioned and confronted with the accused. They declared that they felt a continual pricking in certain parts of their bodies and that they were possessed. Doctors were called, or at least, those who passed for doctors at that time. They examined the girls. They looked for the devil's seal on Michelle's body — what the statement of the case called *satanic marks*. Into them they drove a long needle, already a painful torture. Blood flowed out, and Michelle made it known, by her cries, that satanic marks certainly do not make one insensitive. The judges, seeing no definite proof that Michelle Chaudron was a witch, proceeded to torture her, a method that infallibly produces the necessary proofs: this wretched woman, yielding to the violence of torture, at last confessed every thing they desired.

The doctors again looked for the satanic mark. They found a little black spot on one of her thighs. They drove in the needle. The torment of the torture had been so horrible that the poor creature hardly felt the needle; thus the crime was established. But as customs were becoming somewhat mild at that time, she was burned only after being hanged and strangled.

In those days every tribunal of Christian Europe resounded with similar arrests. The faggots were lit everywhere for witches, as for heretics. People reproached the Turks most for having neither witches nor demons among them. This absence of demons was considered an infallible proof of the falseness of a religion.

A zealous friend of public welfare, of humanity, of true religion, has stated in one of his writings on behalf of innocence, that Christian

[2]The Septuagint, the version of the Hebrew Scriptures used by Saint Paul and other early Christians, was a Greek translation done by Hellenized Jews in Alexandria sometime in the late third or the second century B.C. *Tobit's dog* appears in the Book of Tobit, a Hebrew book contained in the Catholic version of the Bible.

tribunals have condemned to death over a hundred thousand accused witches. If to these judicial murders are added the infinitely superior number of massacred heretics, that part of the world will seem to be nothing but a vast scaffold covered with torturers and victims, surrounded by judges, guards and spectators.

▷ The following passage is from *Candide,* Voltaire's most famous work of fiction. The king of the Bulgarians goes to war with the king of the Abares, and Candide is caught in the middle of the conflict.

WAR

Nothing could be smarter, more splendid, more brilliant, better drawn up than the two armies. Trumpets, fifes, hautboys [oboes], drums, cannons, formed a harmony such as has never been heard even in hell. The cannons first of all laid flat about six thousand men on each side; then the musketry removed from the best of worlds some nine or ten thousand blackguards who infested its surface. The bayonet also was the sufficient reason for the death of some thousands of men. The whole might amount to thirty thousand souls. Candide, who trembled like a philosopher, hid himself as well as he could during this heroic butchery. At last, while the two Kings each commanded a Te Deum[3] in his camp, Candide decided to go elsewhere to reason about effects and causes. He clambered over heaps of dead and dying men and reached a neighboring village, which was in ashes; it was an Abare village which the Bulgarians had burned in accordance with international law. Here, old men dazed with blows watched the dying agonies of their murdered wives who clutched their children to their bleeding breasts; there, disemboweled girls who had been made to satisfy the natural appetites of heroes gasped their last sighs; others, half-burned, begged to be put to death. Brains were scattered on the ground among dismembered arms and legs. Candide fled to another village as fast as he could; it belonged to the Bulgarians, and Abarian heroes had treated it in the same way. Candide, stumbling over quivering limbs or across ruins, at last escaped from the theater of war. . . .

[3]A Te Deum is a special liturgical hymn praising and thanking God for granting some special favor, like a military victory or the end of a war.

REVIEW QUESTIONS

1. What argument did Voltaire offer in favor of a policy of religious toleration?
2. Why was religious toleration of such central importance to enlightened philosophes like Voltaire?
3. Why did Voltaire ridicule Christian theological disputation?
4. What did Voltaire mean by the term *fanaticism?* How was it to be cured?
5. According to Voltaire, what moral evils arose from persecuting people for having differing opinions?
6. According to Voltaire, how did religion, science, and law contribute to the evil of persecuting ideological dissenters in society?
7. What did Voltaire imply about the rationality and morality of war?

▼▼▼

4 ▾ Attack on Religion

Christianity came under severe attack during the eighteenth century. The philosophes rejected Christian doctrines that seemed contrary to reason. Deism,

the dominant religious outlook of the philosophes, taught that religion should accord with reason and natural law. To deists, it seemed reasonable to believe in God, for this superbly constructed universe required a creator in the same manner that a watch required a watchmaker. But, said the deists, after God had constructed the universe, he did not interfere in its operations; the universe was governed by mechanical laws. Deists denied that the Bible was God's work, rejected clerical authority, and dismissed miracles — like Jesus walking on water — as incompatible with natural law. To them, Jesus was not divine but an inspiring teacher of morality. Many deists still considered themselves Christians; the clergy, however, viewed the deists' religious views with horror.

Thomas Paine
≪ THE AGE OF REASON ≫

Exemplifying the deist outlook was Thomas Paine (1737–1809), an Englishman who moved to America in 1774. Paine's *Common Sense* (1776) was an eloquent appeal for American independence. Paine is also famous for *The Rights of Man* (1791–1792), included in the next chapter, in which he defended the French Revolution. In *The Age of Reason* (1794–1795), he denounced Christian mysteries, miracles, and prophecies as superstition and called for a natural religion that accorded with reason and science.

I believe in one God, and no more; and I hope for happiness beyond this life.

I believe in the equality of man; and I believe that religious duties consist in doing justice, loving mercy, and endeavoring to make our fellow-creatures happy.

But, lest it should be supposed that I believe many other things in addition to these, I shall, in the progress of this work, declare the things I do not believe, and my reasons for not believing them.

I do not believe in the creed professed by the Jewish church, by the Roman church, by the Greek church, by the Turkish church, by the Protestant church, nor by any church that I know of. My own mind is my own church. . . .

When Moses told the children of Israel that he received the two tables of the [Ten] commandments from the hands of God, they were not obliged to believe him, because they had no other authority for it than his telling them so; and I have no other authority for it than some historian telling me so. The commandments carry no internal evidence of divinity with them; they contain some good moral precepts, such as any man qualified to be a lawgiver, or a legislator, could produce himself, without having recourse to supernatural intervention. . . .

When also I am told that a woman called the Virgin Mary, said, or gave out, that she was with child without any cohabitation with a man, and that her betrothed husband, Joseph, said that an angel told him so, I have a right to believe them or not; such a circumstance required a much stronger evidence than their bare word for it; but we have not even this — for neither Joseph nor Mary wrote any such matter themselves; it is only reported by others that *they said so* — it is hearsay upon hearsay, and I do not choose to rest my belief upon such evidence.

It is, however, not difficult to account for the credit that was given to the story of Jesus Christ being the son of God. He was born when the heathen mythology had still some fashion and repute in the world, and that mythology had prepared the people for the belief of such a story. Almost all the extraordinary men that lived under the heathen mythology were reputed to be the sons of some of their gods. It was not a new thing, at that time, to believe a man to have been celestially begotten; the intercourse of gods with women was then a matter of familiar opinion. Their Jupiter [chief Roman god], according to their accounts, had cohabited with hundreds: the story, therefore, had nothing in it either new, wonderful, or obscene; it was conformable to the opinions that then prevailed among the people called Gentiles, or Mythologists, and it was those people only that believed it. The Jews who had kept strictly to the belief of one God, and no more, and who had always rejected the heathen mythology, never credited the story. . . .

Nothing that is here said can apply, even with the most distant disrespect, to the real character of Jesus Christ. He was a virtuous and an amiable man. The morality that he preached and practised was of the most benevolent kind; and though similar systems of morality had been preached by Confucius [Chinese philosopher], and by some of the Greek philosophers, many years before; by the Quakers [members of the Society of Friends] since; and by many good men in all ages, it has not been exceeded by any. . . .

. . . The resurrection and ascension [of Jesus Christ], supposing them to have taken place, admitted of public and ocular demonstration, like that of the ascension of a balloon, or the sun at noon-day, to all Jerusalem at least. A thing which everybody is required to believe, requires that the proof and evidence of it should be equal to all, and universal; and as the public visibility of this last related act was the only evidence that could give sanction to the former part, the whole of it falls to the ground, because that evidence never was given. Instead of this, a small number of persons, not more than eight or nine, are introduced as proxies for the whole world, to say they saw it, and all the rest of the world are called upon to believe it. But it appears that Thomas [one of Jesus' disciples] did not believe the resurrection, and, as they say, would not believe without having ocular and manual demonstration himself. *So neither will I,* and the reason is equally as good for me, and for every other person, as for Thomas.

It is in vain to attempt to palliate or disguise this matter. The story, so far as relates to the supernatural part, has every mark of fraud and imposition stamped upon the face of it. Who were the authors of it is as impossible for us now to know, as it is for us to be assured that the books in which the account is related were written by the persons whose names they bear; the best surviving evidence we now have respecting this affair is the Jews. They are regularly descended from the people who lived in the times this resurrection and ascension is said to have happened, and they say, *it is not true.*

Baron d'Holbach
≪ GOOD SENSE ≫

More extreme than the deists were the atheists, who denied God's existence altogether. The foremost exponent of atheism was Paul-Henri Thiry, Baron d'Holbach (1723–1789), a prominent contributor to the *Encyclopedia* (see selection 5). Holbach hosted many leading intellectuals, including Diderot, Rousseau, and Condorcet (all represented later in this chapter), at his country estate outside of Paris. He regarded the idea of God as a product of ignorance, fear,

and superstition and said that terrified by natural phenomena — storms, fire, floods — humanity's primitive ancestors attributed these occurrences to unseen spirits, whom they tried to appease through rituals. In denouncing religion, Holbach was also affirming core Enlightenment ideals — reason and freedom — as the following passage from *Good Sense* reveals.

In a word, whoever will deign to consult common sense upon religious opinions, and will bestow on this inquiry the attention that is commonly given to any objects we presume interesting, will easily perceive that those opinions have no foundation; that Religion is a mere castle in the air. Theology is but the ignorance of natural causes reduced to a system; a long tissue of fallacies and contradictions. In every country, it presents us with romances void of probability. . . .

Savage and furious nations, perpetually at war, adore, under divers names, some God, conformable to their ideas, that is to say, cruel, carnivorous, selfish, bloodthirsty. We find, in all the religions of the earth, "a God of armies," a "jealous God," an "avenging God," a "destroying God," a "God," who is pleased with carnage, and whom his worshippers consider it as a duty to serve to his taste. Lambs, bulls, children, men, heretics, infidels, kings, whole nations, are sacrificed to him. Do not the zealous servants of this barbarous God think themselves obliged even to offer up themselves as a sacrifice to him? Madmen may every where be seen who, after meditating upon their terrible God, imagine that to please him they must do themselves all possible injury, and inflict on themselves, for this honour, the most exquisite torments. The gloomy ideas more usefully formed of the Deity, far from consoling them under the evils of life, have every where disquieted their minds, and produced follies destructive to their happiness.

How could the human mind make any considerable progress, while tormented with frightful phantoms, and guided by men, interested in perpetuating its ignorance and fears? Man has been forced to vegetate in his primitive stupidity: he has been taught nothing but stories about invisible powers upon whom his happiness was supposed to depend. Occupied solely by his fears, and by unintelligible reveries, he has always been at the mercy of his priests, who have reserved to themselves the right of thinking for him, and directing his actions.

Thus man has remained a child without experience, a slave without courage, fearing to reason, and unable to extricate himself from the labyrinth, in which he has so long been wandering. He believes himself forced to bend under the yoke of his gods, known to him only by the fabulous accounts given by his ministers, who, after binding each unhappy mortal in the chains of his prejudice, remain his masters, or else abandon him defenceless to the absolute power of tyrants, no less terrible than the gods, of whom they are the representatives upon earth.

Oppressed by the double yoke of spiritual and temporal power, it has been impossible for the people to know and pursue their happiness. As Religion, so Politics and Morality became sacred things, which the profane were not permitted to handle. Men have had no other Morality, than what their legislators and priests brought down from the unknown regions of heaven. The human mind, confused by its theological opinions ceased to know its own powers, mistrusted experience, feared truth and disdained reason, in order to follow authority. Man has been a mere machine in the hands of tyrants and priests, who alone have had the right of directing his actions. Always treated as a slave, he has contracted the vices of a slave.

Such are the true causes of the corruption of morals, to which Religion opposes only ideal and ineffectual barriers. Ignorance and servitude are calculated to make men wicked and unhappy. Knowledge, Reason, and Liberty, can alone reform them, and make them happier. But every thing conspires to blind them and to confirm them in their errors. Priests cheat them, tyrants corrupt, the better to enslave them. Tyranny ever was, and ever will be, the true cause of man's depravity, and also of his habitual calamities. Almost always fascinated by religious fiction, poor mortals turn not their eyes to the natural and obvious causes of their misery; but attribute their vices to the imperfection of their natures, and their unhappiness to the anger of the gods. They offer up to heaven vows, sacrifices, and presents, to obtain the end of their sufferings, which in reality, are attributable only to the negligence, ignorance, and perversity of their guides, to the folly of their customs, to the unreasonableness of their laws, and above all, to the general want of knowledge. Let men's minds be filled with true ideas; let their reason be cultivated; let justice govern them; and there will be no need of opposing to the passions, such a feeble barrier, as the fear of the gods. Men will be good, when they are well instructed, well governed, and when they are punished or despised for the evil, and justly rewarded for the good, which they do to their fellow citizens.

To discover the true principles of Morality, men have no need of theology, of revelation, or of gods: They have need only of common sense. They have only to commune with themselves, to reflect upon their own nature, to consult their visible interests, to consider the objects of society, and of the individuals who compose it; and they will easily perceive, that virtue is advantageous, and vice disadvantageous to such beings as themselves. Let us persuade men to be just, beneficent, moderate, sociable; not because such conduct is demanded by the gods, but, because it is pleasure to men. Let us advise them to abstain from vice and crime; not because they will be punished in the other world, but because they will suffer for it in this. — *There are,* says a great man [Montesquieu], *means to prevent crimes, and these means are punishments; there are means to reform manners, and these means are good examples. . . .*

. . . Men are unhappy, only because they are ignorant; they are ignorant, only because every thing conspires to prevent their being enlightened; they are wicked, only because their reason is not sufficiently developed.

REVIEW QUESTIONS

1. What positive religious beliefs were held by a deist like Thomas Paine?
2. What Christian beliefs did Paine reject?
3. How did Paine use the new rules of scientific methodology to attack Christian beliefs?
4. What was Baron d'Holbach's view of religion?
5. Compare the views of Holbach with those of Kant (at the beginning of this chapter) on most human beings' intellectual and psychological development.
6. How did Holbach propose to change people's views on religion, politics, and morals?

---

5 ▾ Compendium of Knowledge

A 38-volume *Encyclopedia,* whose 150 or more contributors included leading Enlightenment thinkers, was undertaken in Paris during the 1740s as a monu-

mental effort to bring together all human knowledge and to propagate Enlightenment ideas. The *Encyclopedia*'s numerous articles on science and technology and its limited coverage of theological questions attest to the new interests of eighteenth-century intellectuals. Serving as principal editor, Denis Diderot (1713–1784) steered the project through difficult periods, including the suspension of publication by French authorities. After the first two volumes were published, the authorities denounced the work for containing "maxims that would tend to destroy royal authority, foment a spirit of independence and revolt, . . . and lay the foundations for the corruption of morals and religion." In 1759, Pope Clement XIII condemned the *Encyclopedia* for having "scandalous doctrines [and] inducing scorn for religion." It required careful diplomacy and clever ruses to finish the project and still incorporate ideas considered dangerous by religious and governmental authorities. With the project's completion in 1772, Diderot and Enlightenment opinion triumphed over clerical censors and powerful elements at the French court.

Denis Diderot
≪ ENCYCLOPEDIA ≫

The *Encyclopedia* was a monument to the Enlightenment, as Diderot himself recognized. "This work will surely produce in time a revolution in the minds of man, and I hope that tyrants, oppressors, fanatics, and the intolerant will not gain thereby. We shall have served humanity." Some articles from the *Encyclopedia* follow.

Encyclopedia . . . In truth, the aim of an *encyclopedia* is to collect all the knowledge scattered over the face of the earth, to present its general outlines and structure to the men with whom we live, and to transmit this to those who will come after us, so that the work of past centuries may be useful to the following centuries, that our children, by becoming more educated, may at the same time become more virtuous and happier, and that we may not die without having deserved well of the human race. . . .

. . . We have seen that our *Encyclopedia* could only have been the endeavor of a philosophical century. . . .

I have said that it could only belong to a philosophical age to attempt an *encyclopedia*; and I have said this because such a work constantly demands more intellectual daring than is commonly found in [less courageous periods]. All things must be examined, debated, investigated without exception and without regard for anyone's feelings. . . . We must ride roughshod over all these ancient puerilities, overturn the barriers that reason never erected, give back to the arts and sciences the liberty that is so precious to them. . . . We have for quite some time needed a reasoning age when men would no longer seek the rules in classical authors but in nature. . . .

Fanaticism . . . is blind and passionate zeal born of superstitious opinions, causing people to commit ridiculous, unjust, and cruel actions, not only without any shame or remorse, but even with a kind of joy and comfort. *Fanaticism,* therefore, is only superstition put into practice. . . .

Fanaticism has done much more harm to the world than impiety. What do impious people claim? To free themselves of a yoke, while *fanatics* want to extend their chains over all the earth. Infernal zealomania! . . .

Government . . . The good of the people must be the great purpose of the *government*. The governors are appointed to fulfill it; and the civil constitution that invests them with this power is bound therein by the laws of nature and by the law of reason, which has determined that purpose in any form of *government* as the cause of its welfare. The greatest good of the people is its liberty. Liberty is to the body of the state what health is to each individual; without health man cannot enjoy pleasure; without liberty the state of welfare is excluded from nations. A patriotic governor will therefore see that the right to defend and to maintain liberty is the most sacred of his duties. . . .

If it happens that those who hold the reins of *government* find some resistance when they use their power for the destruction and not the conservation of things that rightfully belong to the people, they must blame themselves, because the public good and the advantage of society are the purposes of establishing a *government*. Hence it necessarily follows that power cannot be arbitrary and that it must be exercised according to the established laws so that the people may know its duty and be secure within the shelter of laws, and so that governors at the same time should be held within just limits and not be tempted to employ the power they have in hand to do harmful things to the body politic. . . .

History . . . *On the usefullness of history*. The advantage consists of the comparison that a statesman or a citizen can make of foreign laws, morals, and customs with those of his country. This is what stimulates modern nations to surpass one another in the arts, in commerce, and in agriculture. The great mistakes of the past are useful in all areas. We cannot describe too often the crimes and misfortunes caused by absurd quarrels. It is certain that by refreshing our memory of these quarrels, we prevent a repetition of them. . . .

Humanity . . . is a benevolent feeling for all men, which hardly inflames anyone without a great and sensitive soul. This sublime and noble enthusiasm is troubled by the pains of other people and by the necessity to alleviate them. With these sentiments an individual would wish to cover the entire universe in order to abolish slavery, superstition, vice, and misfortune. . . .

Intolerance . . . Any method that would tend to stir up men, to arm nations, and to soak the earth with blood is impious.

It is impious to want to impose laws upon man's conscience: this is a universal rule of conduct. People must be enlightened and not constrained. . . .

What did Christ recommend to his disciples when he sent them among the Gentiles? Was it to kill or to die? Was it to persecute or to suffer? . . .

Which is the true voice of humanity, the persecutor who strikes or the persecuted who moans?

Peace . . . War is the fruit of man's depravity; it is a convulsive and violent sickness of the body politic. . . .

If reason governed men and had the influence over the heads of nations that it deserves, we would never see them inconsiderately surrender themselves to the fury of war; they would not show that ferocity that characterizes wild beasts. . . .

Political Authority No man has received from nature the right to command others. Liberty is a gift from heaven, and each individual of the same species has the right to enjoy it as soon as he enjoys the use of reason. . . .

The prince owes to his very subjects the *authority* that he has over them; and this *authority* is limited by the laws of nature and the state. The laws of nature and the state are the conditions under which they have submitted or are supposed to have submitted to its government. . . .

Moreover the government, although hereditary in a family and placed in the hands of one person, is not private property, but public property that consequently can never be taken from the people, to whom it belongs exclusively, fundamentally, and as a freehold. Consequently it is always the people who make the lease or the agreement: they always intervene in the contract that adjudges its exercise. It is not the state that belongs to the prince, it is the prince who belongs to the state: but it does rest with the prince to govern in the state, because the state has chosen him for that purpose: he has bound himself to the people and the administration of affairs, and they in their turn are bound to obey him according to the laws. . . .

The Press [*press* includes newspapers, magazines, books, and so forth] . . . People ask if freedom of the *press* is advantageous or prejudicial to a state. The answer is not difficult. It is of the greatest importance to conserve this practice in all states founded on liberty. I would even say that the disadvantages of this liberty are so inconsiderable compared to its advantages that this ought to be the common right of the universe, and it is certainly advisable to authorize its practice in all governments. . . .

The Slave Trade [This trade] is the buying of unfortunate Negroes by Europeans on the coast of Africa to use as slaves in their colonies. This buying of Negroes, to reduce them to slavery, is one business that violates religion, morality, natural laws, and all the rights of human nature.

Negroes, says a modern Englishman full of enlightenment and humanity, have not become slaves by the right of war; neither do they deliver themselves voluntarily into bondage, and consequently their children are not born slaves. Nobody is unaware that they are bought from their own princes, who claim to have the right to dispose of their liberty, and that traders have them transported in the same way as their other goods, either in their colonies or in America, where they are displayed for sale.

If commerce of this kind can be justified by a moral principle, there is no crime, however atrocious it may be, that cannot be made legitimate. Kings, princes, and magistrates are not the proprietors of their subjects: they do not, therefore, have the right to dispose of their liberty and to sell them as slaves.

On the other hand, no man has the right to buy them or to make himself their master. Men and their liberty are not objects of commerce; they can be neither sold nor bought nor paid for at any price. We must conclude from this that a man whose slave has run away should only blame himself, since he had acquired for money illicit goods whose acquisition is prohibited by all the laws of humanity and equity.

There is not, therefore, a single one of these unfortunate people regarded only as slaves who does not have the right to be declared free, since he has never lost his freedom, which he could not lose and which his prince, his father, and any person whatsoever in the world had not the power to dispose of. Consequently the sale that has been completed is invalid in itself. This Negro does not divest himself and can never divest himself of his natural right; he carries it everywhere with him, and he can demand everywhere that he be allowed to enjoy it. It is, therefore, patent inhumanity on the part of judges in free countries where he is transported, not to emancipate him immediately by declaring him free, since he is their fellow man, having a soul like them.

REVIEW QUESTIONS

1. Why was the publication of the *Encyclopedia* a vital step in the philosophes' hopes for reform?

2. What was the *Encyclopedia*'s view on the nature of liberty?
3. To what extent were John Locke's political ideals reflected in the *Encyclopedia*?
4. Why did the *Encyclopedia* recommend the study of history for the "enlightened" mind?
5. What moral ideals did the authors of the *Encyclopedia* promote for "great and sensitive" souls?
6. Why was freedom of the press of such significance to the enlightened philosophes?
7. Why did the philosophes condemn slavery?

---

6 ▾ Critique of Christian Sex Mores

Diderot reviewed Louis Antoine de Bougainville's *Voyage Around the World* (1771) and later wrote *The Supplement to the Voyage of Bougainville*. In this work, Diderot explored some ideas, particularly the sex habits of Tahitians, treated by the French explorer. Diderot also denounced European imperialism and the exploitation of non-Europeans and questioned traditional Christian sexual standards.

Denis Diderot
≪ THE SUPPLEMENT TO THE VOYAGE OF BOUGAINVILLE ≫

In *Supplement*, Diderot constructed a dialogue between a Tahitian (Orou), who possesses the wisdom of a French philosophe, and a chaplain, whose defense of Christian sexual mores reveals Diderot's critique of the Christian view of human nature. Diderot thus used a representative of an alien culture to attack those European customs and beliefs that the philosophes detested. In the opening passage, before Orou's dialogue, a Tahitian elder rebukes Bougainville and his companions for bringing the evils of European civilization to his island.

"We [Tahitians] are free — but see where you [Europeans] have driven into our earth the symbol of our future servitude. You are neither a god nor a devil — by what right, then, do you enslave people? Orou! You who understand the speech of these men, tell every one of us, as you have told me, what they have written on that strip of metal — 'This land belongs to us.' This land belongs to you! And why? Because you set foot in it? If some day a Tahitian should land on your shores, and if he should engrave on one of your stones or on the bark of one of your trees: 'This land belongs to the people of Tahiti,' what would you think? You are stronger than we are! And what does that signify? When one of our lads carried off some of the miserable trinkets with which your ship is loaded, what an uproar you made, and what revenge you took! And at that very moment you were plotting, in the depths of your hearts, to steal a whole country! You are not slaves; you would suffer death rather than be enslaved, yet you want to make slaves of us! Do you believe, then, that the Tahitian does not know how to die in defense of his liberty? This Tahitian, whom you want to treat as a chattel, as a dumb animal — this Tahitian is your brother. You are both children of Nature — what right do you have over him that he does not have over you?

"You came; did we attack you? Did we plunder your vessel? Did we seize you and expose you to the arrows of our enemies? Did we force you to work in the fields alongside our beasts of burden? We respected our own image in you. Leave us our own customs, which are wiser and more decent than yours. We have no wish to barter what you call our ignorance for your useless knowledge. We possess already all that is good or necessary for our existence. Do we merit your scorn because we have not been able to create superfluous wants for ourselves? When we are hungry, we have something to eat; when we are cold, we have clothing to put on. You have been in our huts — what is lacking there, in your opinion? You are welcome to drive yourselves as hard as you please in pursuit of what you call the comforts of life, but allow sensible people to stop when they see they have nothing to gain but imaginary benefits from the continuation of their painful labors. If you persuade us to go beyond the bounds of strict necessity, when shall we come to the end of our labor? When shall we have time for enjoyment? We have reduced our daily and yearly labors to the least possible amount, because to us nothing seemed more desirable than leisure. Go and bestir yourselves in your own country; there you may torment yourselves as much as you like; but leave us in peace, and do not fill our heads with a hankering after your false needs and imaginary virtues. Look at these men — see how healthy, straight and strong they are. See these women — how straight, healthy, fresh and lovely they are. Take this bow in your hands — it is my own — and call one, two, three, four of your comrades to help you try to bend it. I can bend it myself. I work the soil, I climb mountains, I make my way through the dense forest, and I can run four leagues [about 12 miles] on the plain in less than an hour. Your young comrades have been hard put to it to keep up with me, and yet I have passed my ninetieth year. . . .

"Woe to this island! Woe to all the Tahitians now living, and to all those yet to be born, woe from the day of your arrival! We used to know but one disease — the one to which all men, all animals and all plants are subject — old age. But you have brought us a new one [venereal disease]: you have infected our blood. We shall perhaps be compelled to exterminate with our own hands some of our young girls, some of our women, some of our children, those who have lain with your women, those who have lain with your men. Our fields will be spattered with the foul blood that has passed from your veins into ours. Or else our children, condemned to die, will nourish and perpetuate the evil disease that you have given their fathers and mothers, transmitting it forever to their descendants. . . .

▷ Before the arrival of Christian Europeans, lovemaking was natural and enjoyable. Europeans introduced an alien element, guilt.

But a while ago, the young Tahitian girl blissfully abandoned herself to the embraces of a Tahitian youth and awaited impatiently the day when her mother, authorized to do so by her having reached the age of puberty, would remove her veil and uncover her breasts. She was proud of her ability to excite men's desires, to attract the amorous looks of strangers, of her own relatives, of her own brothers. In our presence, without shame, in the center of a throng of innocent Tahitians who danced and played the flute, she accepted the caresses of the young man whom her young heart and the secret promptings of her senses had marked out for her. The notion of crime and the fear of disease have come among us only with your coming. Now our enjoyments, formerly so sweet, are attended with guilt and terror. That man in black [a priest], who stands near to you and listens to me, has spoken to our young men, and I know not what he has said to our young girls, but our youths are hesitant and our girls blush. Creep away into the dark forest, if you wish, with the perverse companion of your pleasures, but allow the good, simple Tahitians to reproduce themselves without shame under the open sky and in broad daylight.

▷ In the following conversation between Orou and the chaplain, Christian sexual mores and the concept of God are questioned. Orou addresses the chaplain.

[OROU] "You are young and healthy and you have just had a good supper. He who sleeps alone, sleeps badly; at night a man needs a woman at his side. Here is my wife and here are my daughters. Choose whichever one pleases you most, but if you would like to do me a favor, you will give your preference to my youngest girl, who has not yet had any children."

The mother said: "Poor girl! I don't hold it against her. It's no fault of hers."

The chaplain replied that his religion, his holy orders, his moral standards and his sense of decency all prevented him from accepting Orou's invitation.

Orou answered: "I don't know what this thing is that you call 'religion,' but I can only have a low opinion of it because it forbids you to partake of an innocent pleasure to which Nature, the sovereign mistress of us all, invites everybody. It seems to prevent you from bringing one of your fellow creatures into the world, from doing a favor asked of you by a father, a mother and their children, from repaying the kindness of a host, and from enriching a nation by giving it an additional citizen. I don't know what it is that you call 'holy orders,' but your chief duty is to be a man and to show gratitude. . . . I hope that you will not persist in disappointing us. Look at the distress you have caused to appear on the faces of these four women — they are afraid you have noticed some defect in them that arouses your distaste. But even if that were so, would it not be possible for you to do a good deed and have the pleasure of honoring one of my daughters in the sight of her sisters and friends? Come, be generous!"

THE CHAPLAIN You don't understand — it's not that. They are all four of them equally beautiful. But there is my religion! My holy orders! . . .

. . . [God] spoke to our ancestors and gave them laws; he prescribed to them the way in which he wishes to be honored; he ordained that certain actions are good and others he forbade them to do as being evil.

OROU I see. And one of these evil actions which he has forbidden is that of a man who goes to bed with a woman or girl. But in that case, why did he make two sexes?

THE CHAPLAIN In order that they might come together — but only when certain conditions are satisfied and only after certain initial ceremonies have been performed. By virtue of these ceremonies one man belongs to one woman and only to her; one woman belongs to one man and only to him.

OROU For their whole lives?

THE CHAPLAIN For their whole lives.

OROU So that if it should happen that a woman should go to bed with some man who was not her husband, or some man should go to bed with a woman that was not his wife . . . but that could never happen because the workman [God] would know what was going on, and since he doesn't like that sort of thing, he wouldn't let it occur.

THE CHAPLAIN No. He lets them do as they will, and they sin against the law of God (for that is the name by which we call the great workman) and against the law of the country; they commit a crime.

OROU I should be sorry to give offense by anything I might say, but if you don't mind, I'll tell you what I think.

THE CHAPLAIN Go ahead.

OROU I find these strange precepts contrary to nature, and contrary to reason. . . . Furthermore, your laws seem to me to be contrary to the general order of things. For in truth is there anything so senseless as a precept that forbids us to heed the changing impulses that are inherent in our being, or commands that require a degree of constancy which is not possible, that violate the liberty of both male and female by chaining them perpetually to one another? Is there anything more unreasonable than this perfect fidelity that would restrict us, for the enjoyment of pleasures so capricious, to a single partner — than an oath of immutability taken by two individuals made of flesh and blood under a sky that is not the same for a moment, in a cavern that threatens to collapse upon them, at the foot of a cliff that is crumbling into dust, under a tree that is withering, on a bench of stone that is being worn away? Take my word for it, you have reduced human beings to a worse condition than that of the animals. I don't know what your great workman is, but I am very happy that he never spoke to our forefathers, and I hope that he never speaks to our children, for if he does, he may tell them the same foolishness, and they may be foolish enough to believe it. . . .

OROU Are monks faithful to their vows of sterility?

THE CHAPLAIN No.

OROU I was sure of it. Do you also have female monks?

THE CHAPLAIN Yes.

OROU As well behaved as the male monks?

THE CHAPLAIN They are kept more strictly in seclusion, they dry up from unhappiness and die of boredom.

OROU So nature is avenged for the injury done to her! Ugh! What a country! If everything is managed the way you say, you are more barbarous than we are.

REVIEW QUESTIONS

1. According to Denis Diderot, why did European imperialism violate natural law?
2. How did Europeans influence the health and sexual mores of the Tahitians?
3. How did Diderot attempt to use the Tahitians to criticize the sexual mores of Europeans?
4. How did Diderot use the concept of the law of nature to undermine Christian sexual morality?

---

7 ▾ Rousseau: Political and Educational Reform

To the philosophes, advances in the arts were hallmarks of progress. The French philosopher Jean Jacques Rousseau (1712–1778) argued that the accumulation of knowledge improved human understanding but corrupted the morals of human beings. In *A Discourse on the Arts and Sciences* (1750) and *A Discourse on the Origin of Inequality* (1755), Rousseau diagnosed the illnesses of modern civilization. He said that human nature, which was originally good, had been corrupted by society. As a result, he stated at the beginning of *The Social Contract* (1762), "Man is born free; and everywhere he is in chains." How can humanity be made moral and free again? In *The Social Contract,* Rousseau suggested one

cure: reforming the political system. He argued that in the existing civil society the rich and powerful who controlled the state oppressed the majority. Rousseau admired the small, ancient Greek city-state (polis), where citizens participated actively and directly in public affairs. A small state modeled after the ancient Greek polis, said Rousseau, would be best able to resolve the tensions between individual freedom and the requirements of the collective community. In *Émile* (1762), Rousseau sought to improve the individual through educational reforms.

Jean Jacques Rousseau *≪ THE SOCIAL CONTRACT ≫ AND ≪ ÉMILE ≫*

In the opening chapters of *The Social Contract,* Rousseau rejected the principle that one person has a natural authority over others. All legitimate authority, he said, stemmed from human traditions, not from nature. Rousseau had only contempt for absolute monarchy and in *The Social Contract* sought to provide a theoretical foundation for political liberty. In *Émile,* he suggested another cure for the ills of modern society: educational reforms that would instill in children self-confidence, self-reliance, and emotional security.

THE SOCIAL CONTRACT

[To rulers who argued that they provided security for their subjects, Rousseau responded as follows:]

It will be said that the despot assures his subjects civil tranquillity. Granted; but what do they gain, if the wars his ambition brings down upon them, his insatiable avidity, and the vexatious conduct of his ministers press harder on them than their own dissensions would have done? What do they gain, if the very tranquillity they enjoy is one of their miseries? Tranquillity is found also in dungeons; but is that enough to make them desirable places to live in? The Greeks imprisoned in the cave of the Cyclops lived there very tranquilly, while they were awaiting their turn to be devoured. . . .

Even if each man could alienate himself, he could not alienate his children: they are born men and free; their liberty belongs to them, and no one but they has the right to dispose of it. Before they come to years of discretion, the father can, in their name, lay down conditions for their preservation and well-being, but he cannot give them irrevocably and without conditions: such a gift is contrary to the ends of nature, and exceeds the rights of paternity. It would therefore be necessary, in order to legitimize an arbitrary government, that in every generation the people should be in a position to accept or reject it; but, were this so, the government would be no longer arbitrary.

To renounce liberty is to renounce being a man, to surrender the rights of humanity and even its duties. For him who renounces everything no indemnity is possible. Such a renunciation is incompatible with man's nature; to remove all liberty from his will is to remove all morality from his acts.

▷ Like Hobbes and Locke, Rousseau refers to an original social contract that terminates the state of nature and establishes the civil state. The clash of particular interests in the state of nature necessitates the creation of civil authority.

I suppose men to have reached the point at which the obstacles in the way of their preservation in the state of nature show their power of resistance to be greater than the resources at the disposal of each individual for his maintenance in that state. That primitive condition can then subsist no longer; and the human race would perish unless it changed its manner of existence. . . .

This sum of forces can arise only where several persons come together: but, as the force and liberty of each man are the chief instruments of his self-preservation, how can he pledge them without harming his own interests, and neglecting the care he owes to himself? This difficulty, in its bearing on my present subject, may be stated in the following terms:

"The problem is to find a form of association which will defend and protect with the whole common force the person and goods of each associate, and in which each, while uniting himself with all, may still obey himself alone, and remain as free as before." This is the fundamental problem of which the *Social Contract* provides the solution.

▷ In entering into the social contract, the individual surrenders his rights to the community as a whole, which governs in accordance with the general will — an underlying principle that expresses what is best for the community. The general will is a plainly visible truth that is easily discerned by reason and common sense purged of self-interest and unworthy motives. For Rousseau, the general will by definition is always right and always works to the community's advantage. True freedom consists of obedience to laws that coincide with the general will. Obedience to the general will transforms an individual motivated by self-interest, appetites, and passions into a higher type of person — a citizen committed to the general good. What happens, however, if a person's private will — that is, expressions of particular, selfish interests — clashes with the general will? As private interests could ruin the body politic, says Rousseau, "whoever refuses to obey the general will shall be compelled to do so by the whole body." Thus Rousseau rejects entirely the Lockean principle that citizens possess rights independently of and against the state. Because Rousseau grants the sovereign (the people constituted as a corporate body) virtually unlimited authority over the citizenry, some critics view him as a precursor of modern dictatorship.

The clauses of this contract. . . . properly understood, may be reduced to one — the total alienation of each associate, together with all his rights, to the whole community; for, in the first place, as each gives himself absolutely, the conditions are the same for all; and, this being so, no one has any interest in making them burdensome to others.

Moreover, the alienation being without reserve, the union is as perfect as it can be, and no associate has anything more to demand: for, if the individuals retained certain rights, as there would be no common superior to decide between them and the public, each, being on one point his own judge, would ask to be so on all; the state of nature would thus continue, and the association would necessarily become inoperative or tyrannical.

Finally, each man, in giving himself to all, gives himself to nobody; and as there is no associate over which he does not acquire the same right as he yields others over himself, he gains an equivalent for everything he loses, and an increase of force for the preservation of what he has.

If then we discard from the social compact what is not of its essence, we shall find that it reduces itself to the following terms:

"Each of us puts his person and all his power in common under the supreme direction of the general will, and, in our corporate capacity, we receive each member as an indivisible part of the whole."

At once, in place of the individual personality of each contracting party, this act of association creates a moral and collective body, composed of as many members as the assembly contains voters, and receiving from this act its unity, its common identity, its life, and its will. . . .

In order then that the social compact may not be an empty formula, it tacitly includes the undertaking, which alone can give force to the rest, that whoever refuses to obey the general will shall be compelled to do so by the whole body. This means nothing less than that he will be forced to be free; for this is the condition which, by giving each citizen to his country, secures him against all personal dependence. In this lies the key to the working of the political machine; this alone legitimizes civil undertakings, which, without it, would be absurd, tyrannical, and liable to the most frightful abuses.

The passage from the state of nature to the civil state produces a very remarkable change in man, by substituting justice for instinct in his conduct, and giving his actions the morality they had formerly lacked. Then only, when the voice of duty takes the place of physical impulses and right of appetite, does man, who so far had considered only himself, find that he is forced to act on different principles, and to consult his reason before listening to his inclinations. Although, in this state, he deprives himself of some advantages which he got from nature, he gains in return others so great, his faculties are so stimulated and developed, his ideas so extended, his feelings so ennobled, and his whole soul so uplifted, that, did not the abuses of this new condition often degrade him below that which he left, he would be bound to bless continually the happy moment which took him from it for ever, and, instead of a stupid and unimaginative animal, made him an intelligent being and a man.

Let us draw up the whole account in terms easily commensurable. What man loses by the social contract is his natural liberty and an unlimited right to everything he tries to get and succeeds in getting; what he gains is civil liberty and the proprietorship of all he possesses. If we are to avoid mistake in weighing one against the other, we must clearly distinguish natural liberty, which is bounded only by the strength of the individual, from civil liberty, which is limited by the general will; and possession, which is merely the effect of force or the right of the first occupier, from property, which can be founded only on a positive title.

We might, over and above all this, add, to what man acquires in the civil state, moral liberty, which alone makes him truly master of himself; for the mere impulse of appetite is slavery, while obedience to a law which we prescribe to ourselves is liberty. . . .

The first and most important deduction from the principles we have so far laid down is that the general will alone can direct the State according to the object for which it was instituted, i.e. the common good: for if the clashing of particular interests made the establishment of societies necessary, the agreement of these very interests made it possible. The common element in these different interests is what forms the social tie; and, were there no point of agreement between them all, no society could exist. It is solely on the basis of this common interest that every society should be governed. . . .

It follows from what has gone before that the general will is always right and tends to the public advantage; but it does not follow that the deliberations of the people are always equally correct. Our will is always for our own good, but we do not always see what that is; the people is never corrupted, but it is often deceived, and on such occasions only does it seem to will what is bad.

There is often a great deal of difference between the will of all and the general will; the latter considers only the common interest, while the former takes private interest into account, and is no more than a sum of particular wills: but take away from these same wills the pluses and minuses that cancel one another, and the general will remains as the sum of the differences.

If, when the people, being furnished with

adequate information, held its deliberations, the citizens had no communication one with another, the grand total of the small differences would always give the general will, and the decision would always be good. But when factions arise, and partial associations are formed at the expense of the great association, the will of each of these associations becomes general in relation to its members, while it remains particular in relation to the State: it may then be said that there are no longer as many votes as there are men, but only as many as there are associations. The differences become less numerous and give a less general result. Lastly, when one of these associations is so great as to prevail over all the rest, the result is no longer a sum of small differences, but a single difference; in this case there is no longer a general will, and the opinion which prevails is purely particular.

It is therefore essential, if the general will is to be able to express itself, that there should be no partial society [factions] within the State, and that each citizen should think only his own thoughts. . . . But if there are partial societies, it is best to have as many as possible and to prevent them from being unequal. . . . These precautions are the only ones that can guarantee that the general will shall be always enlightened, and that the people shall in no way deceive itself.

▷ Rousseau understood that children should not be treated like little adults. He railed against chaining young children to desks and filling their heads with rote learning. Instead, he urged that children experience direct contact with the world to develop their ingenuity, resourcefulness, and imagination so that they might become productive and responsible citizens. Excerpts from Rousseau's influential treatise on education follow.

ÉMILE

When I thus get rid of children's lessons, I get rid of the chief cause of their sorrows, namely their books. Reading is the curse of childhood, yet it is almost the only occupation you can find for children. Emile, at twelve years old, will hardly know what a book is. "But," you say, "he must, at least, know how to read." When reading is of use to him, I admit he must learn to read, but till then he will only find it a nuisance.

If children are not to be required to do anything as a matter of obedience, it follows that they will only learn what they perceive to be of real and present value, either for use or enjoyment; what other motive could they have for learning? . . .

People make a great fuss about discovering the best way to teach children to read. They invent "bureaux"* and cards, they turn the nursery into a printer's shop. Locke would have them taught to read by means of dice. What a fine idea! And the pity of it! There is a better way than any of those, and one which is generally overlooked — it consists in the desire to learn. Arouse this desire in your scholar [a student who is taught by a "learned tutor"] and have done with your "bureaux" and your dice — any method will serve.

Present interest, that is the motive power, the only motive power that takes us far and safely. Sometimes Emile receives notes of invitation from his father or mother, his relations or friends; he is invited to a dinner, a walk, a boating expedition, to see some public entertainment. These notes are short, clear, plain, and well written. Some one must read them to him, and he cannot always find anybody when wanted; no more consideration is shown to him than he himself showed to you yesterday. Time passes, the chance is lost. The note is read to him at last, but it is too late. Oh! if only he had known how to read! He receives other

***Translator's note* — The "bureau" was a sort of case containing letters to be put together to form words. It was a favourite device for the teaching of reading and gave its name to a special method, called the bureau-method, of learning to read.

notes, so short, so interesting, he would like to try to read them. Sometimes he gets help, sometimes none. He does his best, and at last he makes out half the note; it is something about going to-morrow to drink cream — Where? With whom? He cannot tell — how hard he tries to make out the rest! I do not think Emile will need a "bureau." Shall I proceed to the teaching of writing? No, I am ashamed to toy with these trifles in a treatise on education. . . .

If, in accordance with the plan I have sketched, you follow rules which are just the opposite of the established practice, if instead of taking your scholar far afield, instead of wandering with him in distant places, in far-off lands, in remote centuries, in the ends of the earth, and in the very heavens themselves, you try to keep him to himself, to his own concerns, you will then find him able to perceive, to remember, and even to reason; this is nature's order. . . . Give his body constant exercise, make it strong and healthy, in order to make him good and wise; let him work, let him do things, let him run and shout, let him be always on the go; make a man of him in strength, and he will soon be a man in reason.

Of course by this method you will make him stupid if you are always giving him directions, always saying come here, go there, stop, do this, don't do that. If your head always guides his hands, his own mind will become useless. . . .

It is a lamentable mistake to imagine that bodily activity hinders the working of the mind, as if these two kinds of activity ought not to advance hand in hand, and as if the one were not intended to act as guide to the other. . . .

. . . Your scholar is subject to a power which is continually giving him instruction; he acts only at the word of command; he dare not eat when he is hungry, nor laugh when he is merry, nor weep when he is sad, nor offer one hand rather than the other, nor stir a foot unless he is told to do it; before long he will not venture to breathe without orders. What would you have him think about, when you do all the thinking for him? . . .

As for my pupil, or rather Nature's pupil, he has been trained from the outset to be as self-reliant as possible, he has not formed the habit of constantly seeking help from others, still less of displaying his stores of learning. On the other hand, he exercises discrimination and forethought, he reasons about everything that concerns himself. He does not chatter, he acts. Not a word does he know of what is going on in the world at large, but he knows very thoroughly what affects himself. As he is always stirring he is compelled to notice many things, to recognise many effects; he soon acquires a good deal of experience. Nature, not man, is his schoolmaster, and he learns all the quicker because he is not aware that he has any lesson to learn. So mind and body work together. He is always carrying out his own ideas, not those of other people, and thus he unites thought and action; as he grows in health and strength he grows in wisdom and discernment.

REVIEW QUESTIONS

1. What did Jean Jacques Rousseau mean by the "general will"? What function did it serve in his political theory?
2. Why do some thinkers view Rousseau as a champion of democracy, whereas others see him as a spiritual precursor of totalitarianism?
3. What was Rousseau's basic approach in educating a child?
4. What was Rousseau's view of human nature, and how did it influence his educational theory?
5. Compare and contrast the type of person produced by Rousseau's educational theory and that produced by his political theory.

8 ▾ On the Progress of Humanity

Marie Jean Antoine Nicolas Caritat, Marquis de Condorcet (1743–1794), was a French mathematician and historian of science. He contributed to the *Encyclopedia* and campaigned actively for religious toleration and the abolition of slavery. During the French Revolution, Condorcet attracted the enmity of the dominant Jacobin party and in 1793 was forced to go into hiding. Secluded in Paris, he wrote *Sketch for a Historical Picture of the Progress of the Human Mind.* Arrested in 1794, Condorcet died during his first night in prison from either exhaustion or self-inflicted poison.

Marquis de Condorcet
PROGRESS OF THE HUMAN MIND

Sharing the philosophes' confidence in human goodness and in reason, Condorcet was optimistic about humanity's future progress. Superstition, prejudice, intolerance, and tyranny — all barriers to progress in the past — would gradually be eliminated, and humanity would enter a golden age. The following excerpts are from Condorcet's *Sketch*.

. . . The aim of the work that I have undertaken, and its result will be to show by appeal to reason and fact that nature has set no term to the perfection of human faculties; that the perfectibility of man is truly indefinite; and that the progress of this perfectibility, from now onwards independent of any power that might wish to halt it, has no other limit than the duration of the globe upon which nature has cast us. This progress will doubtless vary in speed, but it will never be reversed as long as the earth occupies its present place in the system of the universe, and as long as the general laws of this system produce neither a general cataclysm nor such changes as will deprive the human race of its present faculties and its present resources. . . .

. . . It will be necessary to indicate by what stages what must appear to us today a fantastic hope ought in time to become possible, and even likely; to show why, in spite of the transitory successes of prejudice and the support that it receives from the corruption of governments or peoples, truth alone will obtain a lasting victory; we shall demonstrate how nature has joined together indissolubly the progress of knowledge and that of liberty, virtue and respect for the natural rights of man. . . .

After long periods of error, after being led astray by vague or incomplete theories, publicists have at last discovered the true rights of man and how they can all be deduced from the single truth, that *man is a sentient being, capable of reasoning and of acquiring moral ideas*. . . .

At last man could proclaim aloud his right, which for so long had been ignored, to submit all opinions to his own reason and to use in the search for truth the only instrument for its recognition that he has been given. Every man learnt with a sort of pride that nature had not forever condemned him to base his beliefs on the opinions of others; the superstitions of antiquity and the abasement of reason before the [rapture] of supernatural religion disappeared from society as from philosophy.

Thus an understanding of the natural rights of man, the belief that these rights are inalienable and [cannot be forfeited], a strongly expressed desire for liberty of thought and letters, of trade and industry, and for the alleviation of the people's suffering, for the [elimination] of all penal laws against religious dissenters and the abolition of torture and barbarous punishments, the desire for a milder system of criminal legislation and jurisprudence which should give complete security to the innocent, and for a simpler civil code, more in conformance with reason and nature, indifference in all matters of religion which now were relegated to the status of superstitions and political [deception], a hatred of hypocrisy and fanaticism, a contempt for prejudice, zeal for the propagation of enlightenment: all these principles, gradually filtering down from philosophical works to every class of society whose education went beyond the catechism and the alphabet, became the common faith . . . [of enlightened people]. In some countries these principles formed a public opinion sufficiently widespread for even the mass of the people to show a willingness to be guided by it and to obey it. . . .

Force or persuasion on the part of governments, priestly intolerance, and even national prejudices, had all lost their deadly power to smother the voice of truth, and nothing could now protect the enemies of reason or the oppressors of freedom from a sentence to which the whole of Europe would soon subscribe. . . .

Our hopes for the future condition of the human race can be subsumed under three important heads: the abolition of inequality between nations, the progress of equality within each nation, and the true perfection of mankind. Will all nations one day attain that state of civilization which the most enlightened, the freest and the least burdened by prejudices, such as the French and the Anglo-Americans [by virtue of their revolutions], have attained already? Will the vast gulf that separates these peoples from the slavery of nations under the rule of monarchs, from the barbarism of African tribes, from the ignorance of savages, little by little disappear? . . .

Is the human race to better itself, either by discoveries in the sciences and the arts, and so in the means to individual welfare and general prosperity; or by progress in the principles of conduct or practical morality; or by a true perfection of the intellectual, moral, or physical faculties of man, an improvement which may result from a perfection either of the instruments used to heighten the intensity of these faculties and to direct their use or of the natural constitution of man?

In answering these three questions we shall find in the experience of the past, in the observation of the progress that the sciences and civilization have already made, in the analysis of the progress of the human mind and of the development of its faculties, the strongest reasons for believing that nature has set no limit to the realization of our hopes. . . .

The time will therefore come when the sun will shine only on free men who know no other master but their reason; when tyrants and slaves, priests and their stupid or hypocritical instruments will exist only in works of history and on the stage; and when we shall think of them only to pity their victims and their dupes; to maintain ourselves in a state of vigilance by thinking on their excesses; and to learn how to recognize and so to destroy, by force of reason, the first seeds of tyranny and superstition, should they ever dare to reappear amongst us.

REVIEW QUESTIONS

1. What image of human nature underlies the Marquis de Condorcet's theory of human progress?

2. According to Condorcet, what economic, political, and cultural policies were sought by enlightened philosophes?
3. According to Condorcet, what had to occur before other peoples were to achieve the goal of sharing in an enlightened civilization?
4. Was the Enlightenment philosophy an alternative moral order to that of Christianity? Or was it an internal reformation of the Christian moral order?

Credits continued from page iv.

"Guidelines for the Ruler" from Adolph Erman, *The Ancient Egyptians,* pp. 279–290, 57, 72, 74, 76–78. Reprinted by permission of Random House, Inc. P. 13: "Deceased Pharaoh" from Arthur Weigall, *A History of the Pharoahs* (London: T. Butterworth, 1925), Vol. 1, p. 215. ***Section 4*** P. 15: From Howard Carter, *The Tomb of Tut-Ankh-Amen* (Totowa, NJ: Cooper Square Publishers), Vol. 2, pp. 44–47, 51–53, 79–80, 82–83, 113–114, 116, 118; Vol. 3, pp. 56–57, 77–78, 82. Reprinted by permission of Littlefield, Adams & Company. ***Section 5*** P. 19: From "Hymn to Aton" in *Ancient Near Eastern Texts: Relating to the Old Testament,* 3rd Edition with Supplement, ed. James B. Pritchard, p. 370. Copyright © 1969 by Princeton University Press. Reprinted with permission of Princeton University Press. ***Section 6*** P. 20: From R. F. Harper, *Assyrian and Babylonian Literature* (New York: D. Appleton, 1904), pp. 12–14. ***Section 7*** P. 23: "O Salt" and "Scorching Fire" from Henri Frankfort, H. A. Frankfort, John A. Wilson, Thorkild Jacobsen and William A. Irwin, *The Intellectual Adventure of Ancient Man: An Essay on Speculative Thought in the Ancient Near East,* pp. 143, 147. Copyright © 1946, 1977 by The University of Chicago. All rights reserved. Used by permission of The University of Chicago Press. P. 23: From "Enuma elish" in *Ancient Near Eastern Texts: Relating to the Old Testament,* 3rd Edition with Supplement, ed. James B. Pritchard, p. 370. Copyright © 1969 by Princeton University Press. Reprinted with permission of Princeton University Press. P. 24: From Thorkild Jacobsen, *The Treasures of Darkness: A History of Mesopotamian Religion,* pp. 88–90. Reprinted by permission of Yale University Press. Copyright © 1976 Yale University Press.

Chapter 2

Section 1 P. 29: From Lawrence Boadt, *Reading the Old Testament,* pp. 544–551. © 1984 by The Missionary Society of St. Paul the Apostle in the State of New York. Used by permission of the Paulist Press. ***Sections 2–6*** Pps. 33–45: Scripture quotations from the Revised Standard Version of the Bible. Copyright 1946, 1952, 1971 by the Division of Christian Education of the National Council of the Churches of Christ in the USA. Reprinted with permission.

Chapter 3

Section 1 P. 50: From Homer, *The Iliad,* trans. by E. V. Rieu (Penguin Classics, 1950), pp. 128–130, 450–451. Copyright © the Estate of E. V. Rieu, 1950. Reproduced by permission of Penguin Books Ltd. ***Section 2*** P. 52: From "Thales of Miletus," "Anaximander," and "Pythagoras" from G. S. Kirk, J. E. Raven and M. Scholfield, *The Pre-Socratic Philosophers* (1957, 2nd ed. 1984), pp. 89, 107, 125, 131, 137–138, 141, 329, 330. Copyright 1957, 1984 by Cambridge University Press. Reprinted by permission of Cambridge University Press. ***Section 3*** P. 56: Reprinted by permission of the publishers and The Loeb Classical Library from *Hippocrates,* Vol. 2, translated by W. H. S. Jones, Cambridge, Mass.: Harvard University Press, 1923. P. 56: From Thucydides, *History of the Peloponnesian War,* trans. by Rex Warner (Penguin Classics, 1954), pp. 13, 23–25. Translation copyright © Rex Warner, 1954. Reproduced by permission of Penguin Books Ltd. P. 58: Reprinted by permission of the publishers from *Ancilla to the Pre-Socratic Philosophers* by Kathleen Freeman, Cambridge, Mass.: Harvard University Press, 1948. ***Section 4*** P. 59: From H. D. F. Kitto, *The Greeks* (Penguin Classics, 1957), pp. 174–175. Copyright © H. D. F. Kitto, 1951, 1957. Reproduced by permission of Penguin Books Ltd. P. 60: From *Antigone of Sophocles: An English Version* by Dudley Fitts and Robert Fitzgerald; copyright 1939 by Harcourt Brace Jovanovich, Inc., renewed 1967 by Dudley Fitts and Robert Fitzgerald; reprinted by permission of the publisher. ***Section 5*** P. 61: From Herodotus, *The Histories,* trans. Aubrey de Selincourt, revised by A. R. Burn (Penguin Classics, 1954). Copyright © The Estate of Aubrey de Selincourt, 1954. Copyright © A. R. Burn, 1972. Reproduced by permission of Penguin Books Ltd. ***Section 6*** P. 64: From Scenes II and III in *Antigone of Sophocles: An English Version* by Dudley Fitts and Robert Fitzgerald; copyright 1939 by Harcourt Brace Jovanovich, Inc., renewed 1967 by Dudley Fitts and Robert Fitzgerald; reprinted by permission of the publisher. ***Section 7*** P. 70: From Thucydides, *History of the Peloponnesian War,* trans. by Rex Warner (Penguin Classics, 1954), pp. 118–120. Translation copyright © Rex Warner, 1954. Reproduced by permission of Penguin Books Ltd. ***Section 8*** P. 72: Reprinted by permission of the publishers and The Loeb Classical Library from *Xenophon,* Vol. IV, translated by E. C. Marchant, Cambridge, Mass.: Harvard University Press, 1923. P. 74: From *The Lysistrata of Aristophanes,* copyright 1954 by Harcourt Brace Jovanovich, Inc. and renewed 1982 by Cornelia Fitts, Daniel H. Fitts, and Deborah W. Fitts, reprinted by permission of Harcourt Brace Jovanovich, Inc. ***Section 9*** P. 80 and 81: From Thucydides, *History of the Peloponnesian War,* trans. Rex Warner (Penguin Classics, 1954), pp. 57–60, 359–365. Translation copyright © Rex Warner, 1954. Reproduced by permission of Penguin Books Ltd. ***Section 10*** P. 84: From *The Trial and Death of Socrates,* trans. F. J. Church (London: Macmillan, 1880), pp. 37–41, 50–53, 56–57. ***Section 11*** P. 88: From *The Republic of Plato,* trans. F. M. Cornford (Oxford University Press, 1941), pp. 178–179, 181, 190–192, 228–231, 282–283, 286, 288–289. Reprinted by permission of Oxford University Press. ***Section 12*** P. 94: From "Historia Animalium," trans. Arcy Wentworth Thompson from *The Works of Aristotle,* Vol. 4, ed. J. A. Smith and W. D. Ross. Reprinted by permission of Oxford University Press. P. 95: From Aristotle, *The Politics,* trans. T. A. Sinclair, rev. Trevor J. Saunders (Penguin Classics, Revised Edition, 1981), pp. 120–121, 121–123, 171–173. Translation copyright © the Estate of T. A. Sinclair, revised translation copyright © Trevor J. Saunders, 1981. Reproduced by permission of Penguin Books Ltd. ***Section 13*** P. 99: Reprinted by permission of the publishers and The Loeb Classical Library from *Plutarch: Moralia,*

Vol. IV, translated by Frank C. Babbitt, Cambridge, Mass.: Harvard University Press, 1948. ***Section 14*** P. 101: From *Epicurus: The Extant Remains,* trans. Cyril Bailey, pp. 53, 83, 85, 89, 97, 101, 115, 117, 119. Reprinted by permission of Oxford University Press.

Chapter 4

Section 1 P. 106: From Polybius, *The Rise of the Roman Empire,* trans. Ian Scott-Kilvert (Penguin Classics, 1979), Bk. 1, Sec. 1–4, pp. 41–44, Bk. 6, Sec. 37–39, pp. 332–335. Copyright © Ian Scott-Kilvert, 1979. Reproduced by permission of Penguin Books Ltd. ***Section 2*** P. 110: From Cicero, *Selected Works,* trans. Michael Grant (Penguin Classics, Revised Edition, 1971), pp. 38, 41, 42, 51–53. Copyright © Michael Grant, 1960, 1965, 1971. Reproduced by permission of Penguin Books Ltd. ***Section 3*** P. 113: Reprinted by permission of the publishers and The Loeb Classical Library from *The Library of History,* Diodorus of Sicily, translated by C. H. Oldfather, Cambridge, Mass.: Harvard University Press, 1939. Copyright 1939 by the President and Fellows of Harvard College. Reprinted by permission of the publishers and The Loeb Classical Library from *The Library of History,* Diodorus Siculus, translated by Francis R. Walton, Cambridge, Mass.: Harvard University Press, 1967, Copyright 1967 by the President and Fellows of Harvard College. ***Section 4*** P. 116: Reprinted by permission of the publishers and The Loeb Classical Library from Livy, *Ad Urbe Condita,* translated by Evan T. Sage, Cambridge, Mass.: Harvard University Press, 1953. P. 118: From *A Source Book of Roman History,* ed. Dana C. Munro (Boston: D. C. Heath, 1904), pp. 201–204. ***Section 5*** P. 120: Reprinted by permission of the publishers and The Loeb Classical Library from *Plutarch's Lives,* translated by Bernadotte Perrin, Cambridge, Mass.: Harvard University Press, 1921. Copyright 1921 by the President and Fellows of Harvard College. ***Section 6*** P. 123: From Sallust, *The Jugurthine War/The Conspiracy of Catline,* trans. S. A. Handford (Penguin Classics, 1963), pp. 180–182, 203–205, 77–79. Copyright © S. A. Handford, 1963. Reproduced by permission of Penguin Books Ltd. ***Section 7*** P. 126: From Cicero, *Selected Works,* trans. Michael Grant (Penguin Classics, Revised Edition, 1971), pp. 79–81. Copyright © Michael Grant, 1960, 1965, 1971. Reproduced by permission of Penguin Books Ltd. ***Section 8*** P. 128: From Cicero, *De Officiis,* (Cambridge: Harvard University Press, 1913), p. 128. P. 128: Reprinted with permission of the publishers and The Loeb Classical Library from *Roman History,* Dio Cassius, translated by Ernest Cary, Cambridge, Mass.: Harvard University Press, 1916.

Chapter 5

Section 1 P. 133: From Augustus, *Res Gestae Divi Augusti,* edited by P. A. Brunt & J. M. Moore (1967), pp. 19, 21, 25, 27, 31, 35, 37. Reprinted by permission of Oxford University Press. P. 135: From Tacitus, *The Annals of Imperial Rome,* trans. Michael Grant (Penguin Classics, Revised Edition, 1971), pp. 29–31. Copyright © Michael Grant Publications, Ltd., 1956, 1959, 1971. Reproduced by permission of Penguin Books Ltd. ***Section 2*** P. 136: Translation copyright © 1980, 1982, 1983 by Robert Fitzgerald. Reprinted from *The Aeneid,* translated by Robert Fitzgerald, by permission of Random House, Inc. P. 137: Reprinted by permission of the publishers and The Loeb Classical Library from *Quintilian,* translated by H. E. Butler, Cambridge, Mass.: Harvard University Press, 1920. P. 139: Adapted from *The Satires of Juvenal,* translated by Hubert Creekmore (New York: New American Library, 1963), pp. 53–54, 57–61. Copyright © 1963 by Hubert Creekmore. Reprinted by permission of Schaffner Agency, Inc. ***Section 3*** P. 142: Adapted from Seneca, *The Epistles,* trans. Thomas Morell (London: W. Woodfall, 1786), Vol. 1, Epistles 7, 47. P. 143: From Aurelius, *Meditations,* trans. Maxwell Staniforth (Penguin Classics, 1964), pp. 45–47, 58, 63, 65, 77. Copyright © Maxwell Staniforth, 1964. Reproduced by permission of Penguin Books Ltd. ***Section 4*** P. 146: Extracts reprinted by permission of the publishers and The Loeb Classical Library from *Letters and Panegyricus,* Pliny the Younger, translated by Betty Radice, Cambridge, Mass.: Harvard University Press, 1969. Copyright 1969 by the President and Fellows of Harvard College. ***Section 5*** P. 149: From Aelius Aristides, "Oration on the Pax Romana" from Moses Hadas, *A History of Rome,* pp. 142–145. Reprinted by permission of Doubleday, a division of Bantam, Doubleday, Dell Publishing Group, Inc. P. 151: From Tacitus, *On Britain and Germany,* trans. H. Mattingly (Penguin Classics, 1958), pp. 79–83. Copyright © The Estate of H. Mattingly, 1958. Reproduced by permission of Penguin Books Ltd. P. 152: From Josephus, *The Jewish War,* trans. G. A. Williamson (Penguin Classics, Revised Edition, 1970), pp. 145–149. Copyright © G. A. Williamson, 1959, 1969. Reproduced by permission of Penguin Books Ltd. ***Section 6*** P. 155: Reprinted by permission of the publishers and The Loeb Classical Library from *Roman History,* Dio Cassius, Volume IX, translated by Earnest Cary, Cambridge, Mass.: Harvard University Press, 1927. P. 156: From *Roman Civilization,* ed. Naphtali Lewis & Meyer Reinhold (Harper & Row Torchbook edition, 1966), II, 454. Reprinted by permission of Columbia University Press. P. 157: From Herodian, *History of the Roman Empire,* trans. Edward C. Echols, pp. 177–179. University of California Press, 1961. Used by permission. ***Section 7*** P. 159: From Salvian, "The Governance of God" in *The Writings of Salvian, the Presbyter,* trans. J. F. O'Sullivan, pp. 134–138, 141. Catholic University of America Press, 1962. Used by permission. P. 160: From James Harvey Robinson, *Readings in European History* (Boston: Ginn, 1904), pp. 23–24. P. 161: From Gregory the Great, *Homiliarum in Ezechielem* in *Gregory the Great,* trans. F. Homes Dudden (New York: Longmans, Green and Co., 1905), II, 18–20. ***Section 8*** P. 163: From *Corpus Iuris Civilis,* trans. S. P. Scott (1932), Vol. 1, p. 321, Vol. 5, p. 224, Vol. 11, pp. 110, 118, 308, 309, 119, 287, 102, Vol. 14, pp. 332, 333. Reprinted by permission of The Central Trust Company, Cincinnati, Ohio.

Chapter 6

Section 1 P. 173: Mark 12: 28–34, Matthew 5: 1–12, 17–48, 6: 1–4 from the *Holy Bible,* Revised Standard Edition. Reprinted by permission of The National Council of Churches in the USA. ***Section 2*** P. 176: Ephesians 4: 17–32, Cor. 12: 31, 13: 1–13 from the *Holy Bible,* Revised Standard Edition. Reprinted by permission of The National Council of Churches in the USA. ***Section 3*** P. 177: From Athenagoras, "A Plea for Christians" in *The Writings of Justin Martyr and Athenagoras,* ed. Alexander Roberts and James Donaldson in *Ante-Nicene Christian Library* (Edinburgh: T. & T. Clark, 1867), Vol. 2, pp. 416–419. ***Section 4*** P. 180: From Eusebius, *Ecclesiastical History,* Book 5, Chap. 1, in *Translation and Reprints from the Original Sources of European History,* Vol. 4 (1897 series), ed. D. C. Munro and Edith Bramhall (Philadelphia: University of Pennsylvania Press, 1898), pp. 11–19. ***Section 5*** P. 182: From *Early Latin Theology,* trans. and ed. S. L. Greenslade (Volume V: The Library of Christian Classics), 35–36. Published simultaneously in Great Britain by SCM Press, Ltd., London and the USA by The Westminister Press, Philadelphia. Used by permission of Westminister/John Knox Press, Louisville, KY and SCM Press Ltd. P. 183: From Clement of Alexandria, *Stromata (Miscellanies),* trans. William Wilson in A. Roberts and James Donaldson, Ante-Nicene Christian Library in *The Writings of Clement of Alexandria* (Edinburgh: T. & T. Clark, 1867–1872), Vol. 4, pp. 303–305, 307–310, 318. ***Section 6*** P. 184 and 186: "First Apology of Justin Martyr," trans. Edward Roche Hardy and "Letters of St. Ignatius of Antioch," trans. Cyril C. Richardson from *Early Christian Fathers,* trans. and ed. Cyril C. Richardson (Volume I: The Library of Christian Classics), pp. 282, 285–287, 98–101. Published simultaneously in Great Britain by SCM Press, Ltd., London and the USA by The Westminister Press, Philadelphia. Used by permission of Westminister/John Knox Press, Louisville, KY and SCM Press, Ltd. ***Section 7*** P. 188: From Oliver J. Thatcher, *Library of Original Sources* (Milwaukee, WI: University Research Extension Co., 1907), Vol. 4, pp. 130–133, 155, 144, 147–148, 153, 136–139. ***Section 8*** P. 192: From St. Augustine, *The City of God,* pp. 295, 300–301, 308–309, 519–520, 522, 321, 507, 540–541. Reprinted by permission of the Catholic University of America Press. P. 195: From *The Library of Original Sources,* ed. Oliver J. Thatcher (Milwaukee, WI: University Research Extension Co., 1907), pp. 133–134. P. 196: From *The Crisis of Church & State 1050–1300* by Brian Tierney. © 1964. Reprinted by permission of the publisher, Prentice Hall, a division of Simon & Schuster, Englewood Cliffs, NJ 07632.

Chapter 7

Section 1 P. 203: From Bede, *A History of the English Church and People,* trans. Leo Sherley-Price (Penguin Classics, Revised Edition, 1968), pp. 86–87, 124–125. Copyright © Leo Sherley-Price, 1955, 1968. Reproduced by permission of Penguin Books Ltd. P. 206: From Einhard, *Life of Charlemagne,* trans. Samuel B. Turner, pp. 30–32. Reprinted by permission of the University of Michigan Press. ***Section 2*** P. 208: From Cassiodorus Senator, *An Introduction to Divine and Human Readings,* trans. Leslie W. Jones, pp. 133–135. Copyright 1946, renewed 1974 Columbia University Press. Reprinted by permission. ***Section 3*** P. 210: From Einhard, *Life of Charlemagne,* trans. Samuel B. Turner, pp. 53–54. Reprinted by permission of the University of Michigan Press. ***Section 4*** P. 213 and 214: From Galbert, "Commendation and Oath of Fealty" and Fulbert, "Obligations of Lords and Vassals" from *Translations and Reprints from the Original Sources of European History,* ed. E. P. Cheyney (Philadelphia: University of Pennsylvania Press, 1895), Vol. 4, No. 3, pp. 18, 23–24. P. 214: From Dhouda, "The Ideal Relationship" from F. L. Ganshoff, *Feudalism* (Harper & Row Torchbook edition, 1961), pp. 33–34. ***Section 5*** P. 216: From *Troubador Poets* by Barbara Smythe, pp. 92–94. Reprinted by permission of Chatto & Windus. ***Section 6*** P. 217: From *The Ledgerbook of Vale Royal Abbey,* ed. John Brownbill (The Record Society for the Publication of Original Documents Relating to Lancashire and Cheshire, 1914), Vol. 68, pp. 117–120. P. 219: From "Select Pleas in Manorial Courts," ed. F. W. Maitland in *Social Life in Britain from the Conquest to the Reformation,* ed. G. G. Coulton (1918), pp. 306–308. Copyright by Cambridge University Press. Reprinted by permission. ***Section 7*** P. 221: Extract taken from *Medieval Monarchy in Action,* edited by Boyd H. Hill, Jr., reproduced by kind permission of Unwin Hyman Ltd. Copyright 1972. P. 222: From *Translations and Reprints from the Original Sources of European History,* ed. E. P. Cheyney (Philadelphia: University of Pennsylvania Press, 1898), Vol. 4, No. 3, pp. 19–20. P. 223: Alfred the Great, "Blood Feuds" from *The Laws of the Earliest English Kings,* ed. and trans. F. L. Attenborough (1922) pp. 83–85. Reprinted by permission of Cambridge University Press, 1922.

Chapter 8

Section 1 P. 229: From Lawrence M. Larson, *The King's Mirror,* pp. 79–85. Reprinted by permission of The Scandinavian-American Foundation. P. 231: William Fitz-Stephen, "Description of the Most Noble City of London" in *English Historical Documents 1042–1189,* ed. David C. Douglas and George Greenway, pp. 956–961. Reprinted by permission. P. 234: From P. Studer, *The Oak Book of Southampton* in Publications of the Southampton Record Society (Southampton: Cox & Sharland, 1910), Vol. I, no. 10, pp. 29, 21, 25, 37, 51, 53. ***Section 2*** P. 236: From *The Correspondence of Pope Gregory VII,* ed. and trans. Ephraim Emerton, pp. 166–170. Copyright 1932, renewed 1960 Columbia University Press. Reprinted by permission. P. 238: From *A Sourcebook of Medieval History,* ed. Oliver J. Thatcher and Edgar Holmes McNeal (New York: Charles Scribner's Sons, 1905), pp. 136–138. ***Section 3*** P. 240: From *Translations and Reprints from the Original Sources of European History,* ed. D. C. Munro (Philadelphia: University of Pennsylvania, 1897), pp. 5–8. ***Section 4*** P. 242: From

Bernard Gui, "Manual of an Inquisitor" in *Heresies of the High Middle Ages: Selected Sources,* ed. W. L. Wakefield and A. P. Evans, pp. 368–390. Copyright © 1969 Columbia University Press. Reprinted by permission. P. 244: Emperor Frederick II, *The Liber Augustalis or Constitutions of Melfi,* trans. James M. Powell, pp. 7–10. Reprinted by permission of Syracuse University Press. ***Section 5*** P. 246: From *The Writings of St. Francis of Assisi,* trans. Paschal Robinson (Philadelphia: Dolphin, 1906), pp. 81–86. ***Section 6*** P. 248: Adelard of Bath, *The Scientific Achievement of the Middle Ages,* ed. Richard C. Dales (Philadelphia: University of Pennsylvania Press, 1973), pp. 40–45. Reprinted by permission. P. 250: Peter Abelard, *Records of Christianity,* Vol. II, ed. David Ayerst and A. S. T. Fisher (1977), pp. 196–197. Reprinted by permission of Basil Blackwell, Ltd. P. 252: St. Thomas Aquinas, "Summa Theologica" from *The Basic Writings of St. Thomas Aquinas,* ed. and trans. Anton G. Pegis (1945), Vol. 1, pp. 22–23, Vol. 2, p. 285. Reprinted by permission. P. 253: St. Thomas Aquinas, "Summa Contra Gentiles" from *Summa Contra Gentiles,* ed. and trans. Anton Pegis (New York: Doubleday, 1955), Book 1, Chap. 5, 6, pp. 70–72. Reprinted by permission of Doubleday, Bantam, Doubleday, Dell Publishing Group, Inc. ***Section 7*** P. 255: John of Salisbury, *The Metalogican of John of Salisbury,* trans. Daniel D. McGarry (Westport, CT: Greenwood Press, 1982), pp. 36–37, 60–61. Reprinted by permission. P. 256: Anders Piltz, "What Is a Scholar?", *The World of Medieval Learning,* trans. David Jones (Oxford: Basil Blackwell, 1981), pp. 221–222. Reprinted by permission. P. 257: From Geoffrey Chaucer, *The Canterbury Tales,* trans. Neville Coghill (Penguin Classics, Revised Edition, 1977) p. 27. Copyright © Neville Coghill, 1951, 1958, 1960, 1975, 1977. Reproduced by permission of Penguin Books Ltd. P. 258: Charles Homer Haskins, *Studies in Medieval Culture* (Oxford: Clarendon Press, 1929), pp. 15–16. Reprinted by permission Oxford University Press. P. 258: G. G. Coulton, *Life in the Middle Ages* (Cambridge: Cambridge University Press, 1928/29), Vol. 3, p. 113. Reprinted by permission. ***Section 8*** P. 259: From *The First Crusade,* ed. August C. Krey (Princeton: Princeton University Press, 1921), pp. 54–55. Reprinted by permission. P. 261: From *A Source Book for Medieval History,* eds. Oliver J. Thatcher and Edgar H. McNeal (New York: Charles Scribner's Sons, 1905), pp. 212–213. P. 261: From Joseph Jacobs, *The Jews of Angevin England* (London: David Nutt, 1893), p. 45. P. 262: From *The Teachings of Maimonides,* ed. A. Cohen (KTAV Publishing House, Inc., 1968), pp. 289–293, 236–237, 252–253, 262. ***Section 9*** P. 265: Ballad from Anthony Boner, *Songs of the Troubadours,* pp. 42–43. Copyright © 1972 by Schocken Books, Inc. Reprinted by permission. P. 266: J. Sprenger and H. Kramer in *Witchcraft in Europe 1100–1700,* eds. Alan C. Kors and Edward Peters (University of Pennsylvania Press, 1972), pp. 117, 120, 121, 123, 124, 127. Reprinted by permission. P. 268: From Christine de Pizan, *The Book of the City of Ladies,* trans. Earl J. Richards, pp. 24, 63–64, 153–154. Copyright © 1982 Persea Books. Reprinted by permission. ***Section 10*** P. 271: John of Salisbury from *The Statesman's Book of John of Salisbury,* trans. John Dickinson (New York: Russell and Russell, 1963), pp. 335–336. P. 272: J. C. Holt, *Magna Carta* (1965, reprinted and reissued 1976), pp. 317, 321–323, 327–329, 333–335. Reprinted by permission of Cambridge University Press. P. 273: Edward I, "Writs" from *A Sourcebook of English History,* ed. Elizabeth K. Kendall (London: Macmillan, 1900), p. 89–91. ***Section 11*** P. 275: From *John of Paris on Royal and Papal Power,* trans. Arthur P. Monahan, pp. 19–20. Copyright © 1974 Columbia University Press. Reprinted by permission. P. 276: From *Marsilius of Padua: The Defender of the Peace,* trans. Alan Gewirth, Discourse 2, Chp. 4, Sections 3–4, 9, pp. 114–115, 119, Chp. 25, Sections 7, 13, pp. 335, 339–340. Copyright © 1956 Columbia University Press. Reprinted by permission. ***Section 12*** P. 278: From *The Chronicle of Jean de Venette,* ed. Richard A. Newhall, trans. Jean Birdsall, pp. 48–52. Copyright 1953, renewed 1981 Elizabeth H. B. Newhall. Reprinted by permission. ***Section 13*** P. 281: From John Froissart, *The Chronicles of England, France and Spain,* trans. Thomas Johnes, pp. 207–208, 214, 210–211. Reprinted by permission of the publishers, J. M. Dent & Everyman's Library. ***Section 14*** P. 284: Excerpts reprinted with permission of Macmillan Publishing Company from Lothario dei Segni (Pope Innocent III), *On the Misery of the Human Condition,* ed. Donald R. Howard and trans. Margaret Mary Dietz. Copyright © 1969 by The Bobbs-Merrill Co. P. 286: From *The Divine Comedy* by Dante Alighier, trans. Howard R. Huse, Cantos 3, 5, 6, 7, 34, pp. 17, 28, 162–164, Xro 33, pp. 478–481. Copyright © 1954 H. R. Huse. Reprinted by permission of Holt, Rinehart and Winston, Inc.

Chapter 9

Section 1 P. 295: From J. H. Robinson and H. W. Rolfe, *Petrarch the First Modern Scholar and Man of Letters* (New York: G. P. Putnam's Sons, 1909), pp. 208, 210, 213. P. 296: "Love for Greek Literature" from Henry Osborn Taylor, *Thought and Expression in the Sixteenth Century,* 2nd rev. ed. (New York: Frederick Ungar, 1930, repub. 1959), Vol. 1, pp. 36–37, 291. "On Learning and Literature" from *Vittorino de Feltre and Other Humanist Educators,* ed. W. H. Woodward (Cambridge: Cambridge University Press, 1897), pp. 124, 127–129, 132–133. ***Section 2*** P. 299: From Giovanni Pico della Mirandola, "Oration on the Dignity of Man," trans. Elizabeth L. Forbes in *The Renaissance Philosophy of Man,* eds. Ernst Cassirer, Paul Oskar Kristeller and John H. Randall, Jr., pp. 223–225. © 1948 The University of Chicago Press. Reprinted by permission. ***Section 3*** P. 301: François Rabelais, *The Histories of Gargantua and Pantagruel,* trans. J. M. Cohen (Penguin Classics, 1955), pp. 159, 194–195. Copyright © J. M. Cohen, 1955. Reproduced by permission of Penguin Books Ltd. ***Section 4*** P. 304: From Niccolo Machiavelli, *The Prince,* trans. Luigi Ricci, rev. E. R. P. Vincent (1935), pp. 92–93, 97, 98–99, 101–103. Reprinted by permission of Oxford University Press. ***Section 5*** P. 308: From *The Notebooks of Leonardo da Vinci,* ed. and trans. Edward MacCurdy, pp. 852, 904–905, 908, 992, 993, 213,

214. Reprinted by permission of Jonathan Cape. ***Section 6*** P. 311: Excerpts from *The History of Florence* by Francesco Guicciardini, translated Mario Domandi, pp. 72–73, 307. English translation copyright © 1970 by Mario Domandi. Reprinted by permission of HarperCollins Publishers, Inc. P. 312: Reprinted from Gertrude R. B. Richards, ed., *Florentine Merchants in the Age of the Medici* (Cambridge: Harvard University Press, 1932), pp. 44–46. Reprinted by permission.

Chapter 10

Section 1 P. 318: From Thomas à Kempis, *The Imitation of Christ,* trans. Leo Sherley-Price (Penguin Classics, 1952), pp. 27–28, 38–58, 216–217. Translation copyright © Leo Sherley-Price, 1952. Reproduced by permission of Penguin Books Ltd. ***Section 2*** P. 320: From Desiderius Erasmus, *In Praise of Folly,* trans. Clarence H. Miller, pp. 87–88, 90, 100–101, 98–99, 63. Copyright 1979 by Yale University Press. Reprinted by permission. ***Section 3*** P. 323: "On Papal Power" from Martin Luther, *Luther's Works,* Vol. 44, ed. James Atkinson and Helmut Lehmann, pp. 126–127, 136–137, copyright © 1966 Fortress Press. Used by permission of Augsburg Fortress. P. 325: "Justification by Faith" from Martin Luther, *Luther's Works,* Vol. 31, ed. H. J. Grimm and Helmut Lehmann, pp. 346–347, 372–373, copyright © 1957 by Fortress Press. Used by permission of Augsburg Fortress. P. 326: "Interpretation of the Bible" from Martin Luther, *What Luther Says: An Anthology,* ed. Ewald Plass, 1959, Vol. 1, p. 943; Vol. 2, pp. 1062–1063; Vol. 3, pp. 1139–1140. Reprinted by permission of Concordia Publishing House. ***Section 4*** P. 328: From *Translations and Reprints from the Original Sources of European History,* (1895 series) ed. D. C. Munro (Philadelphia: University of Pennsylvania, 1899), Vol. 2, pp. 25–30. P. 329: Reprinted from *Luther's Works,* Vol. 46, copyright © 1967 Fortress Press. Used by permission of Augsburg Fortress. ***Section 5*** P. 331: Reprinted from *Luther's Works,* Vol. 47, copyright © 1971 Fortress Press. Used by permission of Augsburg Fortress. ***Section 6*** P. 332: From *The Complete Works of Menno Simons,* ed. John C. Wagner, trans. Leonard Verduin, pp. 537, 555, 550, 779. Reprinted by permission of Herald Press. ***Section 7*** P. 335: From John Calvin, *The Institutes of the Christian Religion,* trans. John Allen (1928), Vol. II, pp. 175–176, 213–214. Reprinted by permission of Westminister/John Knox Press. P. 336: From *Translations and Reprints from the Original Sources of European History* (Philadelphia: University of Pennsylvania Press, 1896), Vol. 3, No. 3, pp. 10–11. P. 337: From John Calvin, *Commentaries on the Book of the Prophet Daniel,* trans. Thomas Myers (Edinburgh: The Calvin Translation Society, 1852), Vol. 1, pp. 278–279, 281–282. ***Section 8*** P. 339: From *The Spiritual Exercises of St. Ignatius,* trans. Anthony Mottola, pp. 139–141. Copyright © 1964 by Doubleday, a division of Bantam, Doubleday, Dell Publishing Group, Inc. Reprinted by permission. ***Section 9*** P. 341: From *Canons and Decrees of the Council of Trent,* trans. H. J. Schroeder, pp. 31–32, 34, 35, 33–34, 18–19, 215, 51–52, 162–163. Reprinted by permission of TAN Books and Publications.

Chapter 11

Section 1 P. 350: From *The Discovery and Conquest of Mexico* by Bernal Diaz del Castillo. Translation copyright © 1956 by Farrar, Straus and Cudahy. Renewal copyright © 1984 by Farrar, Straus and Giroux. Reprinted by permission of Farrar, Straus and Giroux, Inc. and Routledge. ***Section 2*** P. 354: Excerpts from *The Low Countries in Early Modern Times: A Documentary History,* edited and translated by Herbert H. Rowen, pp. 147–149. Copyright © 1972 by Herbert H. Rowen. Reprinted by permission of HarperCollins Publishers, Inc. P. 355: Reprinted from John Keymer, *Observations Touching Trade and Commerce with the Hollanders, and Other Nations in A Select Collection of Scarce and Valuable Tracts on Commerce,* ed. John R. McCulloch (London: 1859; New York: Augusts M. Kelly Publisher, 1966), pp. 59, 13–14. P. 357: From William Carr, *Travels Through Holland, Germany, Sweden and Danmark by An English Gentleman* (London: Randall Taylor, 1693), pp. 14–18, 33–34, 60–64. ***Section 3*** P. 361: From "5 George II, Chapter 22" in *The Statutes at Large,* ed. Danby Pickering (Cambridge: Joseph Bentham, Printer to the University, 1765), Vol. 16, pp. 304–305. P. 362: From Pierre Clement, *Letters, Instructions et Memoires de Colbert,* (Paris, Imperial Press, 1863), Vol. 2, pp. 426–427, trans. Marvin Perry. ***Section 4*** P. 364: From Philip D. Curtin, *Africa Remembered* (Madison, WI: University of Wisconsin Press, 1967), pp. 92–94, 95–96, 97–98. Reprinted by permission. ***Section 5*** P. 367: From *Translations and Reprints from the Original Sources of European History,* ed. George L. Burr (Philadelphia: University of Pennsylvania, 1907), pp. 26–28. P. 368: From *Witchcraft in Europe 1100–1700,* eds. Alan C. Kors and Edward Peters (Philadelphia: University of Pennsylvania Press, 1972), pp. 351–352, 354–357. Reprinted by permission. ***Section 6*** P. 371: From *Select Statutes and Other Constitutional Documents Illustrative of the Reigns of Elizabeth and James I,* 3rd ed., ed. G. W. Prothero (Oxford: Clarendon Press, 1906), pp. 400–401, 293–294. ***Section 7*** P. 373: Reprinted with permission of Macmillan Publishing Company from *Constitutionalism and Resistance in the Sixteenth Century,* ed. and trans. Julius H. Franklin, pp. 146, 158, 161, 169–170, 180–181, 190–191. Copyright © 1969 by Macmillan Publishing Company. ***Section 8*** P. 378: From *Leveller Manifestoes of the Puritan Revolution,* ed. Don M. Wolfe (New York: Thomas Nelson and Sons, 1944), pp. 226–228. Reprinted by permission. ***Section 9*** P. 380: From *The English Works of Thomas Hobbes of Malmesbury: Leviathan, or the Matter Form and Power of a Commonwealth Ecclesiastical and Civil,* collected and ed. Sir William Molesworth (London: John Bohn, 1839), Vol. 3, pp. 110–113, 116, 117, 154, 157–158, 160–161. ***Section 10*** P. 384: From *Select Documents of English Constitutional History,* eds. George Burton Adams and H. Morse Stephens (New York: Macmillan Company, 1902), pp. 464–465.

Chapter 12

Section 1 P. 390: From Copernicus, *On the Revolutions,* trans. Edward Rosen, ed. Jerry Dobrzycki. Reprinted by permission of Macmillan, London and Basingstoke. P.

392: From *Galileo Affair: A Documentary History,* ed. Maurice A. Finocchiaro, pp. 67–68. Copyright © 1989 The Regents of the University of California. Reprinted by permission of The University of California Press. ***Section 2*** P. 394: Excerpts from *Discoveries and Opinions of Galileo* by Galileo Galilei, translated by Stillman Drake, pp. 28–31, 51–53, 57. Translation copyright © 1957 by Stillman Drake. Used by permission of Doubleday, a division of Bantam, Doubleday, Dell Publishing Group, Inc. ***Section 3*** P. 396: From Galileo Galilei, *Dialogue Concerning The Two Chief World Systems,* trans. Stillman Drake, pp. 107–108, 112–113, 175–177, 179–184, 190. Copyright © 1962 The Regents of the University of California. Reprinted by permission of The University of California Press. ***Section 4*** P. 400: From *The Philosophy of Francis Bacon,* ed. and trans. Benjamin Farrington (Liverpool: Liverpool University Press, 1970), pp. 114–115. P. 45: From *The Works of Francis Bacon,* ed. Spedding, Ellis, and Heath (Boston: Taggard and Thompson, 1863), VIII, 67–69, 71–72, 74, 76–79, 142. ***Section 5*** P. 403: Extracts reprinted with permission of Macmillan Publishing Company from René Descartes, *Discourse on Method,* trans. Laurence J. Lafleur. Copyright 1956 by Macmillan Publishing Company. ***Section 6*** P. 406: From Sir Isaac Newton, *The Mathematical Principles of Natural Philosophy, Book III,* trans. Andrew Motte (London: H. D. Symonds, 1803), II, 160–162, 313–314. P. 408: From Sir Isaac Newton, *The Mathematical Principles of Natural Philosophy, Book III,* trans. Andrew Motte (London: H. D. Symonds, 1803), II, 310–313.

Chapter 13

Section 1 P. 413: From Immanuel Kant, *The Philosophy of Kant,* translated and edited by Carl J. Friedrich, pp. 132–134, 138–139. Copyright 1949 by Random House, Inc. Reprinted by permission of the publisher. ***Section 2*** P. 415: From John Locke, *Two Treatises on Civil Government* (London: 1688, 7th reprinting by J. Whiston et al., 1772), pp. 292, 315–316, 354–355, 358–359, 361–362. P. 418: First printing of the Declaration of Independence, July 4, 1776, Papers of the Continental Congress No. 1, Rough Journal of Congress, III. ***Section 3*** P. 419: From *Candide and Other Writings* by Voltaire, edited by Haskell M. Block, pp. 114, 368, 374, 375, 441, 443–444, 525. Copyright © 1956 & renewed 1984 by Random House, Inc. Reprinted by permission of the publisher. ***Section 4*** P. 423: From Thomas Paine, *Age of Reason being an investigation of True and Fabulous Theology* (New York: Peter Eckler, 1892), pp. 5–11. P. 425: From Paul Heinrich Dietrich Baron d'Holbach, *Good Sense or Natural Ideas opposed to Ideas that are Supernatural* (New York: G. Vale, 1856), pp. vii–xi. ***Section 5*** P. 427: From Denis Diderot, *The Encyclopedia: Selections,* ed. and trans. Stephen J. Gendzier, pp. 92–93, 104, 124–125, 134, 136, 153, 183–187, 199, 229–230. Reprinted by permission of Stephen J. Gendzier. ***Section 6*** P. 430: Extracts reprinted with permission of Macmillan Publishing Company from Denis Diderot, *Rameau's Nephew and Other Works,* trans. Jacques Barzun and Ralph H. Bowen, pp. 188–190, 194–195, 197–199, 213. Copyright © 1956 by Jacques Barzun and Ralph H. Bowen; copyright renewed 1984. ***Section 7*** P. 434: From Jean Jacques Rousseau, *The Social Contract* in *The Social Contract and Discourses,* trans. G. D. H. Cole (New York: E. P. Dutton, 1950), pp. 8–9, 13–15, 18–19, 23, 26–28. Reprinted by permission of J. M. Dent & Everyman's Library as Publishers. P. 437: From Jean Jacques Rousseau, *Émile,* trans. Barbara Foxley, pp. 80–84. Everyman's Library Series, reprinted by permission of J. M. Dent & Everyman's Library as Publishers. ***Section 8*** P. 439: From Antoine-Nicolas de Condorcet, *Sketch for a Historical Picture of the Progress of the Human Mind,* trans. June Barraclough, pp. 4–5, 9–10, 128, 136, 140–142, 173–175, 179. Reprinted by permission of George Weidenfeld & Nicolson Ltd.